NEWGATE NARRATIVES

T0316190

CONTENTS OF THE EDITION

NEWGATE NARRATIVES

Edited by Gary Kelly

Volume 1
Newgate Narratives: General Introduction and Newgate Documents

Routledge
Taylor & Francis Group
LONDON AND NEW YORK

First published 2008 by Pickering & Chatto (Publishers) Limited

2 Park Square, Milton Park, Abingdon, Oxon OX14 4RN
711 Third Avenue, New York, NY 10017, USA

Routledge is an imprint of the Taylor & Francis Group, an informa business

First issued in paperback 2017

Copyright © Taylor & Francis 2008
Copyright © Editorial material Gary Kelly

All rights reserved, including those of translation into foreign languages.
No part of this book may be reprinted or reproduced or utilised in any form or
by any electronic, mechanical, or other means, now known or hereafter
invented, including photocopying and recording, or in any information storage
or retrieval system, without permission in writing from the publishers.

Notice:
Product or corporate names may be trademarks or registered trademarks, and
are used only for identification and explanation without intent to infringe.

BRITISH LIBRARY CATALOGUING IN PUBLICATION DATA

Newgate narratives
1. Newgate (Prison : London, England) – Fiction 2. Newgate (Prison : London, England) – History – Sources 3. Prisons – England – Fiction 4. Prisons
– England – History – 19th century – Sources 5. Crime – England – London
– Fiction 6. English fiction – 19th century
I. Kelly, Gary
823.8'0803556[F]

ISBN-13: 978-1-85196-812-1 (set)
ISBN-13: 978-1-1387-5560-4 (hbk)
ISBN-13: 978-1-138-11164-6 (pbk)

Typeset by Pickering & Chatto (Publishers) Limited

CONTENTS

ACKNOWLEDGEMENTS

I wish to acknowledge my deep gratitude for the advice and support of Kirsten MacLeod, the patience of Mark Pollard and Pickering and Chatto, research funding from the Social Sciences and Humanities Research Council of Canada and the Canada Research Chairs program, help from the staffs of the University of Alberta, British and University of California (Los Angeles) Libraries, and the research assistance of Tram Nguyen, Amy Stafford, Drew Small, Kirsten MacLeod, Rosie Lines, and Sarah Jefferies.

I dedicate these five volumes to the memory of my father, Don Kelly – film-maker, photographer, wood-turner and artisan of the everyday.

Edmonton
March 2008

GENERAL INTRODUCTION

This series of volumes offers a selection of edited texts representing different kinds of narratives centred around or connected with Newgate Prison as a physical reality and as a symbol. *Newgate Narratives* includes but goes beyond the so-called 'Newgate novels' that have received some critical and scholarly attention since the 1960s. *Newgate Narratives* returns to but also goes beyond the mid nineteenth-century moral panic around what was called 'Newgate literature', which included these 'Newgate novels'. *Newgate Narratives* presents, and aims to contextualize for further study, a wide range of documents, from street literature through parliamentary inquiries to melodramas and novels, that drew on, contributed to, challenged, and expressed the complex and interconnected social, cultural, economic and political discourses and practices exemplified and symbolized by London's Newgate Prison.

'Narrative' is taken here in a double sense, as an account, relation or representation that connects a series of events or facts, with an explicit or implicit purpose to account for or explain them, but also understanding that any such account tacitly constitutes the 'facts' or 'events' as such and as having a particular meaning, according to a particular ideology, or set of values and beliefs. To put it another way, rather than re-presenting some pre-existing thing, representation brings that thing into being as such and as having a certain meaning and value. 'Narratives' here can also mean texts not strictly narrative in form, but nevertheless implying a narrative of some kind or other; such texts might include images, street ballads, theoretical or philosophical arguments, scientific experiments, statistical tables and, indeed, architectural designs, management structures, physical spaces. All of these may encapsulate or signify a narrative about 'Newgate' matters, that is, law and order and crime and punishment. Written 'Newgate narratives' in a wide variety of forms aimed to persuade people that Newgate or what it exemplified or symbolized had a certain meaning. These narratives were in turn situated within various specific disciplines or discourses with their own sets of explanatory narratives, including the religious, moral, legal, legislative, architectural, judicial, penal, socio-psychological, economic, imperial, cultural and others. These narratives were in various modes, including the argumentative, didactic, historical, polemical, satirical, comic, sentimental, pathetic, speculative and so on. 'Newgate narratives' were also couched in all sorts of genres and intellectual discourses high and low, including poetry, drama, fiction, historiography, philosophy, essays, memoirs and more. All of these narratives, however, participated in what can be called 'Newgate discourse': a large body of diverse but interconnected texts, practices, values and beliefs in which Newgate prison figured as a setting, an example, a therapy, a metaphor, a symbol, a synecdoche, a system, a scandal, a warning and much else. Newgate was the metropolitan, national, and imperial centre for and symbol of the defence of property by the state's exercise of main force, including death.

There was over centuries, and apparently there still is now, a demand for yet more 'Newgate narratives', partly because Newgate, and with it the entire system of incarceration and punishment, continually failed to effect what it was ostensibly or actually intended for – the defence of property. This failure was crucially and, to contemporaries who dominated state institutions and print culture, scandalously apparent during the period covered by *Newgate Narratives*. That purpose was, as writer after writer insisted, to prevent, deter from and ultimately punish 'crime'. Then and now, the great majority of the actions designated as 'crime' by those who had the power to do so were crimes against property. The systemic failure of prison and punishment continues today, at least in part because, as the historian David Garland has pointed out, 'we have tried to convert a deeply social issue into a technical task for specialist institutions'.[1] The 'deeply social issue' has changed over time and has been defined in different ways by different academic disciplines and public political discourses. In the period covered by this set, 'Newgate narratives' ranged from theories of crime and punishment through architectural proposals and management schemes, parliamentary reports and journalistic reportage, and new 'model' prisons and regimes of punishment and reformation, to street ballads, stage melodramas and 'Newgate novels'. It was, however, the 'literary' group of narratives that represented for the widest range of readers what Garland calls the 'social issue' of crime and punishment, however that issue was and is understood. In fact, treatments of crime and punishment have tended to be divided into, and studied separately as, the literary and social representations on the one hand and the theoretical, statistical, documentary, legislative and similar kinds of representations on the other. Cultural studies and 'new historicist' approaches to crime and punishment in the past few decades have been more inclined to bring these separate disciplinary and discursive spheres closer together. Nevertheless, there remains a need for, and usefulness to, enabling that convergence, as this set aims to do, thereby constituting yet another Newgate narrative, not purporting to reveal the 'truth' of Newgate but aiming to illustrate and make available for further study the diversity of Newgate narratives as representations of Newgate and all it could be made to stand for, for better or worse.

The seedy site and star of these narratives, whether actually present in any particular narrative or not, is of course Newgate prison itself. Newgate prison in one physical shape or another loomed over London, and loomed symbolically over the English-speaking world and beyond, for at least seven centuries. As the satirist and picaresque Newgate novelist Thomas Nashe (*c.* 1567–*c.* 1601) noted over 400 years ago, Newgate was 'a common name for all prisons'[2] and prisons across Britain and its empire were named after Newgate in London. Though Newgate Prison was physically demolished in the early twentieth century, it and Newgate discourse maintain a strong symbolic presence in popular culture even now: in certain kinds of paperback historical romance today a scene in or reference to Newgate seems almost a required part of the appeal. Most of the texts in the present set, however, are taken from the last quarter of the eighteenth century and the first half of the nineteenth. This was the crucial period in the development and transformation of Newgate and its social, cultural, legislative and other meanings. The central interest of this selection of Newgate narratives is the representation of Newgate and the social, cultural, political and economic issues it both symbolized and was made to address during this period of Britain's formation as a modern state and modernized economy, society and culture. In that process and struggle over state formation, Newgate narratives of one kind or another performed important ideological and cultural work, communicating the national debate on Newgate and what it could be made to represent far beyond the small but powerful circles who read reformist polemics, social surveys, and political, moral and social theory. No one of these kinds of narrative was foundational, however, serving as the basis or point of departure or reference for the others. Parliamentary reports on Newgate Prison did not determine the themes and techniques of the so-called 'Newgate novels' any more than did proposals and legislation for administrative, penal, judicial, architectural and other reforms. Rather, each kind of Newgate narrative informed the others in the ever-changing field of struggle that was Newgate discourse. Nevertheless, it can be argued that the cultural-social discourse around Newgate, communicated in media from newspapers and street ballads, through stage melodramas and popular criminal biography, to novels and magazine fiction, had the greatest impact and farthest reach. As the sociologist of crime Vincenzo Ruggiero put it in a recent study on the refraction of ideologies of crime and punishment in literature, 'We are used to seeing the world through the lenses of the law, rather than those of values and imagination.'[3] Accordingly, the texts selected here are predominantly 'literary', as conventionally understood. Novels occupy four of these five volumes, but selections from the range of historical, legislative, polemical, sociological and journalistic texts are included in the series, not merely as context for the 'literary texts', but as part of a complex and continuing dialogue with them.

At the same time there was, as Peter Linebaugh and other historians have shown,[4] a powerful and widely diffused plebian Newgate discourse that was hardly captured in print at all, apart from the pages of the proceedings of the Old Bailey and other courts of law, the popular broadsheet and chapbook 'Last Dying Words and Confession' of numerous hanged convicts, the 'true crime' biographies in such compilations as the *Malefactor's Bloody Register* and the *Newgate Calendar,* and between the lines of street ballads such as 'Newgate Walls' and chapbooks such as the early nineteenth-century version of Defoe's *Moll Flanders*, both included in this volume. The Newgate discourse that is visible in such documents and that circulated in working-class oral culture and social practice, including what the property owning classes called 'crime' and 'riot', had its own ideological bearings, political understandings, 'moral economy' and forms of activism and action. These plebeian Newgate narratives can be pieced together from the documents just mentioned and other, unpublished sources, as Linebaugh has done in *The London Hanged*, and they remain to challenge, contradict and engage with the Newgate narratives collected and edited here, which were admittedly almost entirely by and for the property-owning middle and upper classes in whose interests the dominant Newgate discourses were fashioned and re-fashioned.

The aim of this edition, then, is to provide a core of diversely representing and representative Newgate narratives for the study, consideration and reconsideration of Newgate and Newgate discourse in history and culture, with the warning that these should be read alongside the counter-narratives teased out in such histories as Linebaugh's *The London Hanged.* The place of Newgate and the broad issues of crime and punishment in which it was implicated have been well documented and narrated since the mid-twentieth century, in a wide range of social, legal, penal, architectural, and other kinds of history; these studies are referred to at various points in this introduction, though not summarized in detail. The aim of this general introduction is to give a brief account of Newgate and Newgate narratives in several related perspectives, relying on primary documents for illustration. This introduction opens with a brief account of Newgate Prison as a physical entity. This is followed by an account of Newgate in theory, in relation to a succession of reform documents of various kinds from the early eighteenth to mid-nineteenth century, many of which are also represented by selections in this volume. This introduction then gives a longer account of Newgate in practice, as a perceived and lived experience, from the point of view of various individuals with varying interests, before turning to Newgate culture, or the social and cultural life and values of inmates which so troubled reformists and their opponents during the heyday of Newgate narrative. Part of this culture and representing it was what came to be called 'Newgate literature', largely for the lower classes, and the 'Newgate novel', mainly by and for the middle classes, and these are then surveyed in the next two parts of the introduction. The introduction then closes with a review of Newgate today, in culture high and low. Separate introductions give accounts of, and contexts for, the principal works in the series of volumes that follow.

The Surly Bulk of Newgate

Prisons are, among other things, buildings and like many prisons Newgate began as a town jail adjacent to, and then housed in, a fortified building – in this case, a gate in the town wall.[5] New Gate had been built in the twelfth century on the site of one of the gates of the Roman city of Londinium. The 'new' gate was built to improve access between the eastern and western parts of London after construction of St Paul's cathedral obstructed the previous route. The jail was extended in 1187–8 so as to accommodate prisoners from beyond London and its environs, making Newgate the national jail. Much later, in 1837, the *Penny Magazine*, a middle-class production designed to educate and enlighten the lower classes, described the location of Newgate prison, which had remained unchanged over the centuries:

> The street called the Old Bailey strikes off from Ludgate Hill, and terminates at the intersection of Newgate Street and Skinner Street. The continuation of the Old Bailey is called Giltspur Street, which leads into Smithfield. The city wall ran along here from Lud Gate to New Gate. The New Gate appears to have been made a place of custody, at least as early as the beginning of the thirteenth century; and the name has been applied to every successive structure that has occupied the site.[6]

The first records of committals to the prison date to 1218. This jail, sometimes known as the 'First Newgate', was a royal prison but control steadily passed to the corporation or self-perpetuating governing body of the City of London, a process probably finalized under a charter granted by Edward IV. The prison's reputation was bad from the outset: as Margery Bassett states, 'Mediaeval records are unanimous in their description of the vileness of Newgate'.[7] Newgate gradually deteriorated, and it was rebuilt from 1423 with a bequest from Richard Whittington, semi-legendary philanthropic lord mayor of London, in a program to improve conditions for the prisoners. Regulations of 1431 provided for prisoners to be separated by class of crime and for installation of running water and a fountain and in 1461 a system of annual inspections by officials of the City of London was instituted. This 'Second Newgate' was refronted in 1630–2 and repaired in 1672 after damage from the Great Fire of London, making this the 'Third Newgate'.

The Third Newgate was just over 400 square metres in area and five storeys high. Newgate was administered by the two sheriffs elected annually by and from the corporation of the City of London. In an arrangement characteristic of those times, day-to-day management would be sold to a 'keeper' or governor, who in turn aimed to make a profit from running Newgate, and who lived in quarters that were part of the prison complex. Thus Newgate was characteristic of any other profit-making enterprise of the time, right down to the employer or 'master' living on the business premises. Just as Newgate was 'produced' by the relations of property outside it, and the efforts of the property-owning classes both to protect their property and to make it, and labour, more productive, so Newgate internally was a business generating income and profit for those who held Newgate as property, from the 'keeper' down through the chaplain and warders to selected prisoners. Alterations and extensions continued to be made into the eighteenth century. To maintain this property and its profit-generating processes, additional buildings were acquired in 1732 to house condemned prisoners, and a windmill-driven ventilation system was installed on the roof. Nevertheless, overcrowding continued to be a problem, with accompanying difficulties in separating classes of prisoners, keeping order, ensuring adequate sanitation, controlling disease, and preventing prisoners from exploiting and abusing each other to the detriment of the enterprise. Outbreaks of 'jail fever' were common here and in other prisons throughout the land, sometimes carrying off court officials and visitors along with prisoners. Newgate was now a large prison, mainly housing those awaiting trial or the carrying out of sentences. A physical description is given in the extract from Batty Langley's *An Accurate Description of Newgate* ... (1724), in this volume. The City of London decided in 1755 to rebuild Newgate, but the plan was shelved for lack of financial support from the national government. The Press Yard, so called from being the place where those who refused to plead guilty or not guilty were crushed with weights until they offered a plea or died, was rebuilt in 1762 after a fire, the plan to reconstruct the prison was revived, and the architect George Dance's earlier proposal was modified for the purpose and carried out by his son, also George Dance.

Work began in 1770 and was virtually completed by 1780. The new Newgate was designed according to the neoclassical architectural models fashionable at the time among the well-to-do. It had a massive exterior with no windows and was built around three courtyards with accommodation for debtors, male felons, and female felons. Its external appearance was clearly meant to have a socio-psychological effect: a century later the novelist George Gissing referred to it as 'the surly bulk of Newgate'.[8] Prominent new interior features were a chapel and infirmary, indicating a growing public and official concern for the moral as well as physical health of the prisoners. Even before the new prison was completed, however, it was subjected to criticism. William Smith summarized the criticisms in his *State of the Gaols in London, Westminster, and Borough of Southwark* (1776):

> The New Prison of Newgate is built upon the old principle, of a great number being crouded together into one ward, with a yard for them to assemble in the day, and a tap-room where they may get drunk when they please, and have money to pay. The wards are large, airy, high, and as clean as can well be supposed where such a motley crew are lodged. The cells for the condemned prisoners are dark, unhealthy, and unfit for the purpose. The situation is more unhealthy than where the old prison stood. An immense sum of money has already been laid out, and it will require much more to finish it. Strength is not the only thing necessary to be attended to in the construction of a gaol; the situation should be high and dry, in an open field, and at a distance from a town; the building spacious, to obviate the bad effects of a putrid accumulation of infectious air, and extended in breadth rather than heighth; the wards should have many divisions to keep the prisoners from associating. ...
>
> The numbers, that are ill and die by means of impure and corrupted air are much greater than is imagined; therefore where many are crouded together in one place, there is an absolute necessity for a sufficient quantity of fresh air. The earth was made for us all; why should so small a portion of it be denied to those unhappy creatures, while so many large tracks lay waste and uncultivated?[9]

In June 1780, however, large anti-Catholic 'riots', or popular activism and demonstrations, instigated by George Gordon, broke out and lasted several days, during which the rioters attacked Newgate and other sites associated with the establishment and the legal and penal systems. The attack is described in the extract from George Walker's later political novel, *The Vagabond* (1799), included in this volume; the Gordon Riots also provided the setting for Dickens's novel *Barnaby Rudge* (1841). The attack was also a salient illustration of the moral and political economy of the lower classes, who furnished most of those who ended up imprisoned in Newgate.[10] The damage done to the new prison by the 'rioters' was repaired by 1785, and in the same year public hangings were moved from Tyburn, near present-day Marble Arch, to the street outside Newgate, where they continued until 1868, when they were moved inside the prison.

This, the 'Fourth' or 'Final Newgate' was the prison of life and lore throughout the period covered by this series of *Newgate Narratives*. It is described in the extracts included in this volume from the fourth edition of prison reformer John Howard's pioneering *The State of the Prisons in England and Wales* (1792); James Neild's *State of the Prisons in England, Scotland, and Wales* (1812); Henry Grey Bennet's *Letter to the Common Council and Livery of the City of London, on the Abuses Existing in Newgate* (1818); Edward Gibbon Wakefield's *Facts Relating to the Punishment of Death in the Metropolis* (1831); Thomas Wontner's *Old Bailey Experience* (1833); and the 1836 parliamentary *Reports* of the Inspectors of Prisons. A further selection, from George Chesterton's *Revelations of Prison Life* (2 vols, 1856), gives an account of Coldbath (or Cold Bath) Fields house of correction in London, on the site now occupied by the Mount Pleasant mail-sorting office. To supplement these, extracts from other descriptions over the years are included in this introduction. Here, for example, is a description of the accommodation for debtors, who were held in Newgate up to the early nineteenth century, from a 1793 handbook for debtors and creditors:

> In *Newgate* there are generally about 200 prisoners for debt, who are always in close confinement. There is a place called the common side of the prison, and a part called the master's side. Those prisoners who go on the master's side should pay a weekly rent of one shilling, which however is not enforced; and if provided with beds, two shillings and sixpence. But after the old gaol was pulled down, and the new one built, the common side was not so much separated from the master's side, as it used to be, and they can now go from one side to the other. Those who are able find themselves in beds. The two sides are divided into separate rooms or wards. On the north side of the *quadrangle*, which is part of the common side, there are six wards; on the south side, there are three wards, and the east side is divided into two wards, one for the women, and one for the men.
>
> The master's side, which is the west side of the *quadrangle*, is divided into three wards, and contains 18 rooms, for which no rent is ever paid. The only distinction between the prisoners on the common side and the master's side is, that those who do not chuse to partake of the donations,[11] do not go to the common side. The poorer debtors are confined on the common side, and those of a better condition on the master's side. There are some who have no beds, but they are very few. Here, as well as in the King's Bench, and the Fleet,[12] many support themselves by work. The prisoners, however, in Newgate, generally appear in a state of extreme poverty and distress.
>
> The prisoners are allowed by the City of London, *one pennyworth of bread* per day, and the sheriffs send *eight stone*[13] of *meat* per week to those on the common side, which is divided amongst them; besides this, there are several donations, amounting, in the whole, to £.51 10s. per annum, which are also divided amongst them.
>
> The average number of debtors committed and discharged every year is 450, and since the year 1780, forty-five prisoners for debt have died in Newgate. Of the prisoners, 26 receive their groats,[14] which, with the prison allowance, is reckoned sufficient for them in point of sustenance.[15]

The handbook also advocated reform of the laws on imprisonment for debt, the hardship of which was a familiar topic of sentimental literature throughout this period, and which was an expanding area of humanitarian activism and reform agitation. As was the case with other aspects of Newgate, such agitation often aimed at broader institutional and constitutional reforms.

The overall arrangement of Newgate up to the early decades of the nineteenth century is described in the 1814 parliamentary *Report from the Committee on the State of the Gaols of the City of London, &c*. As already indicated, the prison was divided between those imprisoned for debt and those awaiting or convicted at trial, with some others, notably a few insane persons. The 'Criminal Side' consisted of six yards and men were separated from women. The Press Yard was for prisoners condemned to death and awaiting execution, and had fifteen cells, nine feet by seven feet, and holding two or three prisoners each, partly for 'society' and partly to deter the desperate from attempting suicide. The Middle Yard held prisoners condemned to transportation to the new penal colony of Australia and awaiting removal. Superior accommodation was available on the Master's Side of this part of the prison, on payment of thirteen shillings and sixpence admission fee and two shillings and sixpence per week for a bed. Even better accommodation was available on the State Side, so called from once having held 'state' prisoners or those accused of crimes against the state; here prisoners could obtain a single bed on payment of two guineas for admission and ten shillings and sixpence per week, and a share of a bed for seven shillings each for two. With these prices, it is understandable that the State Side held only twenty prisoners at the time of the Committee's report, when it could accommodate forty. The *Report* concluded, 'Most of the evils and inconveniencies of Newgate have proceeded from its being in extent wholly inadequate to the purposes for which it was intended . . .'.[16]

Overall, the 'surly bulk of Newgate' itself changed little over the period covered by this series, despite periodic tinkerings. The attitude of descriptions of Newgate changed, however. Eighteenth- and early nineteenth-century accounts exhibit attitudes of disgust and outrage on the one hand and of philosophical or religious aims for 'improvement' on the other. Mid-nineteenth-century accounts, especially after the institutional and political reforms of the late 1820s and early 1830s, tended to regard Newgate as a 'Gothic' relic from an earlier, less enlightened and moral age, an incorrigible repeat offender, a tourist attraction, a warning, an occasion for titillation or the arousal of sensations of 'horror', like a Gothic romance or 'sensation' novel. In 1837 the *Penny Magazine* gave a description of Newgate after decades of admittedly futile attempts to improve its layout and facilities so as to make it a more effective instrument in the 'prevention of crime'. The outer appearance of the prison was of course virtually unchanged since 1780:

> About the middle of the Old Bailey Street commences the extensive range of buildings which form the courts of justice and the prison. The prison, a massive and frowning structure, occupies the end of the Old Bailey, and turns up Newgate Street.[17]

The interior and its arrangement for accommodating prisoners were described as follows:

> The plan of Newgate is quadrangular. The untried prisoners are kept separate from the tried, and the young from the old. It was built originally without sleeping cells for separate confinement, except the condemned cells [for those condemned to death]; the number of night rooms is 33, in each of which there are at night from 15 to 30 persons; the number of day rooms, or wards, is 10; 129 sleeping cells might be got by

dividing these large rooms, but 462 additional cells would still be wanting, for which the prison affords no space.[18]

The cells for those condemned to death typically received particular attention from the *Penny Magazine*, for here was where Newgate's power of Gothic 'horror' truly began:

> Fearfully narrow and dark are they, with a small grated aperture in each, receiving light from the court in which the prisoners are permitted to walk during the day. The prisoners against whom sentence of death is recorded sleep on a mat in these cells during the night.[19]

By this time the Gothic 'otherness' of Newgate was widely associated with the otherness of those it imprisoned. The *Penny Magazine* imagined a visit to the prison to see its principal internal features and inhabitants:

> We shall find the officers, from the governor downwards, civil, attentive, and obliging. Ascending a few steps, and expressing a wish to see the boys' ward, we are conducted through a dark labyrinthine passage, and on mounting a stair, the merry shouts that we hear seem to proceed from the play-ground of a school. Here are two rooms—one the school-room by day and sleeping-room by night, the other the day-room. In the latter, about fifteen or sixteen boys are tumbling about at play. A well-known voice calls out 'Stand around!' but the quick eyes of the youngsters tell them that the strangers are not official visiters; and they therefore come forward, bobbing their heads, or rather pulling them down by the front-locks, and boisterously elbowing each other as they fall into line. An almost indistinct murmur, however, lets them know the extent of their discretion, and they stand quiet. 'That boy,' pointing to a child of about ten or eleven years of age, 'is under sentence of death!' In a moment, the little creature feels himself the object of greatest importance in the group, and his look evinces it.[20]

Here the school clearly represents what most commentators now saw Newgate as a whole to be – a 'nursery of crime'. The tour continued:

> Let us pass now from the boys' ward to that of the men's. Here they are lounging about the day-room; but at the command of 'Stand around!' they fall into line for inspection with a quieter promptness than did the boys—one or two with a sullen scowl, some with an easy indifference, others with a half-kind of smile, as if not so much accustomed to the discipline. They are mostly young men, from sixteen years of age to twenty-five. The greater part of these individuals have probably come through the first part of their apprenticeship in crime, and are now rising into life with seared hearts, depraved and almost irreclaimable habits, and their intellectual powers exercised in nothing but the dexterity and meanness of theft.[21]

Here the tourist has encountered the various gradations of the 'apprenticeship in crime' that Newgate was considered to offer or impose on its inmates. The women's section is not described by the *Penny Magazine*; perhaps this was considered indecorous or unnecessary or unlikely to jibe with the *Penny Magazine*'s intent to find Newgate a Gothic relic. Accounts of the women's section by visitors from this period were almost universally celebratory, attributing the apparent discipline, repentance and harmony they found there to the ministrations of Elizabeth Fry and her associates. Inmate accounts from the 1836 report of the Inspectors of Prisons (included in this volume) suggest that the women prisoners were better actors than the men. Though the arrangements described by the *Penny Magazine* were the result of decades of crusading by reformers and intervention by parliament and the City of London, Newgate was still, and would remain, chronically overcrowded and hence, in the eyes of many, ineffective in its official purpose of reforming criminals and so preventing crime, but also a continuing burden on the public purse. Newgate could only remain an unsolvable problem from the past, an unfixable object for administrative and architectural tinkering, in the bureaucratic modern state that Britain was becoming. Its interior was remodeled in 1856 and only prisoners awaiting trial were incarcerated there. Control of Newgate passed from the City of London to the government Prison Commissioners in 1877 and soon it was used only to hold prisoners convicted of capital crimes, and to hang them. Newgate was closed and demolished in 1902; in its place was built the still existing Central Criminal Court.

'The Proper End of Human Punishment Is ... the Prevention of Crimes': Newgate in Theory 1

The narratives just cited constructed Newgate as a physical site for the application by the state of certain techniques of main force on a segment of its population for the purposes of the state. These were mainly the purposes of the propertied defending their property against the depredations of the propertyless, and of the deployers of capital against resistance to exploitation of those they employed. Newgate was also, however, constructed within larger narratives, usually in the form of theoretical discourses known as theology, philosophy, and political economy.[22] In these narratives, Newgate was purposely represented as less or not at all a physical site for exercise of state power in a class struggle, and more a symbol and rhetorical trope in a struggle between factions of the propertied and the capital-owning classes contending for control and direction of the state and its apparatus during the heyday of Newgate narratives.

Perhaps the oldest narrative constructing Newgate as a symbol and rhetorical trope was the religious narrative of humanity's inherent sinfulness. In the Bible narrative, humanity's sinfulness derived from the original act of disobedience against God's law committed by Adam and Eve, resulting in their expulsion from paradise, condemnation to mortality, sentencing to hard labour and, for Eve, the additional sentence of childbirth pangs necessary to reproduce humanity over time and through history. In this narrative, crime and punishment, and hence

Newgate, were but instances of that sentence, necessary on earth to punish sin/ crime and to warn others from it, and a type or anticipation of the punishment for sin/crime in the life hereafter. This form of Newgate narrative had long been more local and pragmatic than theological and philosophical, however, because it was a narrative known and understood by all with any religious instruction, and most frequently made explicit as a topic of sermons preached on the occasion of assizes, or trials, and before executions. The religious Newgate narrative entered more largely into wider public discourse with late eighteenth century clerical writers on crime and punishment, such as the Rev. Martin Madan (1725–90) and Bishop William Paley (1743–1805), included here. Madan, Paley and others like them were not so much developing the long tradition of preaching against sin and crime, however, as responding to a contemporary line of secular, Enlightenment, rationalist, reformist and anti-clerical and anti-ecclesiastical narratives of crime and punishment.

These are represented here by the philosophers Cesare Beccaria (1738–94) and William Godwin (1756–1836) and the philosophical historian William Eden (1744–1814). Beccaria's short treatise *Dei delitti e delle pene* (1764), translated into English in 1767 as *An Essay on Crimes and Punishments*, became a contemporary classic of political theory. Beccaria drew on the ideas of Montesquieu (Charles-Louis de Secondat, baron de La Brède et de Montesquieu, 1689–1755) in his work of political philosophy, *De l'Esprit des lois* (1748), setting aside the historic religious and moral view of crime as a manifestation of humanity's sinful nature. Beccaria typified Enlightenment approaches to social and cultural difference, insisting that the definition and determination of 'crime' changed over the ages, and differed from one society and culture to another, indicating that 'crime' was a relative concept and historically and socially particular, rather than inherent in divine law or human nature. Beccaria argued that laws should not embody merely local human prejudices and passions but aim to achieve 'the greatest happiness of the greatest number'.[23] Accordingly, punishment should only be meted out when absolutely necessary, and should only be severe enough to deter from subsequent crimes. For these reasons, Beccaria argued against the death penalty on grounds of utility: it was not as effective as other punishments in deterring from crime. The young and ambitious William Eden engaged with Beccaria's radical historicism and cultural relativism in his *Principles of Penal Law* (1771). Eden combined Beccaria's rationalism with historical and classical literary research, exhaustively documenting ancient and medieval theory, commentary, and practice to argue that 'The prevention of crimes should be the great object of the Lawgiver'. Eden, whose aristocratic family was associated with reformist politics, was concerned to show from historical examples that cruel or excessive punishments were characteristic of despotic regimes and barbarous societies, and so ought to be rejected by a civilized nation with a constitutional government, such as the political class of Britain maintained themselves to be. Beccaria's arguments and Eden's researches prepared the ground for John Howard's epochal *The State of the Prisons in England and Wales* (1777), a survey of actual prison conditions caused, in Howard's view, by bad laws, bad policy, and bad administration. Howard's approach was part of a gathering movement not so much to reform government, laws, and practice as to improve them in the cause of efficiency and effectiveness.[24] For those like Howard, this cause would serve the interests both of humanity and of the dominant property-owning classes.

It was against this movement for rationalist and secular 'improvement' in the legal and penal systems that Madan and Paley wrote their Newgate narratives in the 1780s. In their theologically based view, humanity was indeed inherently depraved and required strict laws and punishments to deter it from sin and crime and so assist its spiritual salvation. In effect, however, 'humanity' for Madan, Paley and others of their view meant primarily the lower classes. Further, the interests of the dominant property-owning classes who, in their view, were appointed as custodians of the whole of society and government, would be best served not by relaxing laws and lessening punishments but by tightening and enforcing them. The self-interest and the spiritual and social mission of property coincided, or rather, were variations of each other. Madan was a Church of England clergyman who sympathized with the Methodist faction in the Church, or those who emphasized human sinfulness and redemption through conviction of sin and salvation through divine grace. Madan acquired notoriety, however, when he published a book advocating polygamy as a preventative to sexual transgressions and crimes. In his retirement, Madan turned to the larger issues of crime and punishment, and in 1785 published *Thoughts on Executive Justice, with Respect to Our Criminal Laws*. Madan based his arguments on a religious view of the fallen human condition and on the same principle adopted by Beccaria, Eden, Howard and other reformists and improvers, declaring that 'The prevention of crimes, is the great end of all legal severity'. Madan added to his arguments an element of the middle-class and property-owning moral panic that would characterize successive crime and punishment debates, insisting that Britain was in the midst of a crime wave requiring severe laws, strictly enforced.

William Paley was closer to the English scientific and philosophical Enlightenment than Madan, and though a clergyman and bishop, attempted to meet the challenge of the secular rationalists by adopting much of their cool language, methodical organization, and forensic argumentation in his *Principles of Moral and Political Philosophy* (1785). Like Madan and the philosophers he opposed, Paley too assumed that 'The proper end of human punishment is, not the satisfaction of justice, but the prevention of crimes'. Accordingly, Paley defended the practice of attaching capital punishment to many crimes and then placing in the hands of magistrates and the monarch the power to exercise leniency in the individual case. Paley also argued that human sinfulness was seen in the tendency to idleness, which led to crime and had to be punished partly by inducing the criminal to accept the need to labour. With its apparent combination of traditional theology and Enlightenment argumentation, and its simple and direct style, *Principles* was reprinted on average once a year to 1817, on both side of the Atlantic, and translated into German and French. By the late 1810s, however, respect for Paley's book was waning. His arguments had been rebutted by a number of reformist writers, such as Samuel Romilly in his *Observations on the Criminal Law of England, as It Relates to Capital Punishments* (1810), and a different, aggressively crusading Evangelical movement had taken up the religious argument on crime and punishment, addressing the concerns and fears of the property-owning middle classes faced with seemingly more recalcitrant, violent and criminal lower classes.

William Godwin published his comprehensive treatise, *An Enquiry Concerning Political Justice, and Its Influence on General Virtue and Happiness* (2 vols, 1793), the year after the appearance of the fourth, augmented edition of Howard's *State of the Prisons in England and Wales*. Godwin wrote *Political Justice* in the excitement and sense of new possibilities stimulated by the French Revolution. He was surrounded by a circle of English Enlightenment intellectuals who welcomed the early, middle-class dominated phase of the French Revolution and saw it as an example for Britain, and was in contact with Revolutionary figures from France and America. By the time Godwin's book was nearing publication, however, the Revolution was also foundering into spasmodic violence featuring the lower classes and international warfare waged by France's 'citizen armies'. The Revolution debate in Britain seemed to be dividing the nation and possibly setting the stage for violent internal and external conflict like that occurring in France. Godwin's treatise was intended in part to turn away from previous and existing positions and set the debate on a higher, theoretical, trans-historical plane, one that could accommodate the 'enlightened' of both the upper and middle classes. For Godwin, the issue of crime and punishment was related to the nature of society and government, or 'political justice', and it was within this narrative that actual institutions such as Newgate and what it represented should first be constructed. Godwin the republican, philosophical anarchist and atheist swept aside religious writers such as Paley and went much farther than the likes of Montesquieu, Beccaria and Howard, while drawing on their ideas and example. In *Political Justice*, Godwin insisted that humans are naturally virtuous and benevolent rather than sinful and selfish and that 'crime' is only another term for error, which is due to ignorance, which in turn is the consequence of a government and society based on false or erroneous principles. The solution to 'crime' is not punishment but education, not the reform of government, laws and so on but their abolition, so that education and enlightenment may spread freely without restraint or perversion.

The comprehensiveness, meticulous argumentation and plain style of *Political Justice*, as well as its appearance of transcending local differences, animosities and hostilities, gave it a great appeal to young middle-class professionals and intellectuals at the time. But the French Revolution crisis was already leaving such lofty exercises behind. Britain became embroiled in the Revolutionary wars, and the government and loyalist organizations set about intimidating, harassing and even trying for treason people like Godwin. In 1794, one of these people was his intellectual collaborator on *Political Justice*, Thomas Holcroft, who treated similar 'Newgate' issues in his successful plays and novels. Reformists such as William Hodgson found themselves in Newgate simply for expressing sympathy with the French republic and one of Godwin's friends was sentenced to transportation to Australia, where he died, for participating in a reformist meeting. To many others at the time, however, places such as Newgate could seem a reassuring reality and symbol of the state's power to control and suppress dangerous dissidence. The political context of the 1790s gave new persuasiveness to the arguments of the likes of Madan and Paley. The problems represented by Newgate did not vanish in political reaction and counter-revolution, however, and new kinds of theoretical Newgate narrative appeared, proposing and even effecting ways of dealing with them, especially within the discourse known as political economy.

The lawyer and political and economic theorist Jeremy Bentham had already proposed a new kind of prison in *Panopticon; or, The Inspection-House* (1791). In his general philosophy, sometimes called utilitarianism, Bentham worked from principles, also enunciated by Enlightenment philosophers from Beccaria to Godwin, that the aim of government and society was to achieve the greatest happiness of the greatest number, that humans were motivated by desire to avoid pain and seek pleasure, and that the aim of the legal and penal systems should be to diminish crime. In fact, 'the rigorous Benthamite technique of space'[25] in prison design and management had been devised not so much by Jeremy as by his brother Samuel, a business entrepreneur, while he was managing a factory in Russia. Its aim was to achieve maximum productivity from workers by constructing the workplace so as to allow, or give the appearance of allowing, constant inspection or oversight of the labourers, thereby spurring them to work to maximum capacity and, in the factory setting, reducing what workers regarded as customary rights or perquisites and control of working conditions, and what employers increasingly regarded as 'criminal' pilfering, recalcitrance and idleness.[26] Jeremy Bentham fused this economic objective in the late eighteenth-century architectural movement for rebuilding and designing new kinds of prison with the aim of increasing cost effectiveness, that is, reducing crime by well planned punishment while reducing the cost of doing so. As a later writer remarked of Millbank, the prison built for the government to Bentham's plan, 'although a place of penal detention', it had 'more the appearance of a general convict workshop'.[27] As Bentham himself put it in his proposal, the panopticon would unite 'the joint purposes of punishment, reformation, and pecuniary economy'. One kind of economy would be reduction in staff and time required to control and supervise inmates, by means of the panopticon design; as Bentham declared, 'Were Newgate upon this plan, all Newgate might be inspected by a quarter of an hour's visit . . .'. To achieve greatest 'pecuniary economy' in terms of cost effectiveness, Bentham proposed that government assign the prison to a contractor, in a form of what is now called 'public private partnership', who would build and operate the prison, under a set of regulations and targets, and take the profits or losses. In fact, since the 1990s, several prisons have been built in England using the Private Public Partnership, devised by the Conservative government and later renamed the Private Finance Initiative by the Labour government.

The key element in Bentham's proposal was not so much the method of financing construction, however, as the 'means of extracting labour' once the prison was built. This was where Bentham's panopticon joined the emergent discourse of 'political economy', which focused on the 'problem' of inducing greater productivity from the work force. Bentham's method and was based on the pleasure–pain principle developed by Enlightenment materialist philosophers. Bentham wrote:

> If he [the prisoner] will work, his time is occupied, and he has his meat and his beer, or whatever else his earnings may afford him, and not a stroke does he strike but he gets something, which he would not have got otherwise. This encouragement is necessary to his doing his utmost; but more than this is not necessary. It is necessary, every exertion he makes should be sure of its reward: but it is not necessary, that such reward be so great, or any thing near so great, as he might have had, had he worked elsewhere. This confinement, which is his punishment, preventing his carrying the work to another market, subjects him to a monopoly; which the contractor, his master, like any other monopolist, makes of course as much of as he can.

Bentham's proposal reduced the convict to a mechanical element in an industrialized process, and is indicative of the attitude of many in the middle and upper classes, including reformists, toward the lower classes from whom most criminals came. For this reason, as well as for its emphasis on financial economy, the 'panopticon' system had obvious appeal to government and taxpayers, and just after the turn of the century, while his brother Samuel was engaged to reform the naval dockyards, Jeremy Bentham was encouraged to proceed with construction of a new prison on land at Millbank, south-west of London, near the present site of the Tate Britain Gallery. After much effort and expenditure on Bentham's part, the plan was abandoned and he was given compensation. Pressure for a new prison and attacks on the inadequacy of Newgate and other London prisons mounted, however; construction of a prison at Millbank based on Bentham's plan was undertaken in 1812 and after delays and huge cost overruns, the prison was fully opened 1821, though it had already been receiving prisoners.

Millbank was controversial from the outset and was never the success that Bentham projected. It was blamed for causing mental illness among prisoners, and condemned by supporters of the 'separate' system of incarceration that came to prevail in the 1830s. The panopticon and political economy had their effect on Newgate and other prisons, however, in respect to the increasing emphasis on 'extracting labour' from convicts, from purposely humiliating and meaningless kill-times such as oakum picking, crank turning, and walking the treadwheel, to marginally 'useful' work such as toiling at water prison pumps, cleaning public spaces, or serving as indentured labour in the penal colony of Australia. Almost two centuries later, the French philosophical historian Michel Foucault would single out the panopticon plan and 'panopticism', or the extension of the panopticon plan to factories, schools, hospitals, and asylums, as exemplifying a new historical era of surveillance and discipline of the populace, especially in France.[28] In Britain, however, Bentham's panopticon scheme for prisons was imperfectly realized (at Millbank prison), too expensive, widely disparaged, and soon abandoned or drastically modified.

'A Mansion of Woe': Newgate in Theory 2

The French Revolution crisis in Britain had, meanwhile, discredited theory and reform generally, the Napoleonic wars distracted the public and policy-makers for a decade and a half, and later the problems and failure of the panopticon project turned the debate on crime and punishment in different directions. Newgate narratives through the first three decades of the nineteenth century turned from theory to observation, inspection, statistics and proposals for improvement in design and management, along with regularization of the criminal laws and court system. Important legacies of Enlightenment rationalism and humanitarianism, religious moralism and political economy remained, however, in attention to the issues of rationalizing criminal laws, diminishing and deterring from crime, educating and 'enlightening' criminals, providing 'humane' conditions of incarceration and punishment, encouraging repentance and reform of convicts, and habituating or 'breaking' convicts to labour discipline and a 'productive' life in society and the economy. Different Newgate narratives gave different emphasis to these issues, according to the narratives' different ideological and political bearings. In general, extensive theorizing, especially linked to an obvious and broad reformist politics, was rejected, downplayed, or disguised. Nevertheless, for the first three decades of the nineteenth century, the topics and tone of the debate on crime and punishment, both within and outside parliament, were set by writers with reformist backgrounds, sympathies and politics, implicitly invoking the theoretical narratives of earlier writers from Beccaria through Eden and Howard to Godwin.

Sir Richard Phillips (1767–1840) was one of those who downplayed and disguised his reformist politics, using Newgate and the prisons as a legitimate topic of public concern but also as a stalking horse for wider reformist objectives. He significantly raised the temperature of the crime and punishment debate, with specific reference to Newgate, in his *Letter to the Livery of London, Relative to the Views of the Writer in Executing the Office of Sheriff* (1808). Phillips was a political reformist, self-made man, enterprising and successful publisher, and recently one of the two annually elected sheriffs of the City of London, with responsibility for, among other things, the City's prisons and jails. Like many who had been Revolutionary sympathizers in the 1790s, Phillips adjusted his politics to the conservative reaction that followed by clothing them in the language of late eighteenth-century sentimental humanitarianism and Christian charity. He described the mere deprivation of liberty by imprisonment as a 'heartrending punishment', to which, he declared, the maladministration of the prisons added additional punishments of 'the loathsomeness of the place, the immediate contact of kindred miseries; want of food and every other necessary; loss of character; dread of future consequences; wives, children, and frequently aged parents, involved in one common ruin, and plunged in shame and wretchedness; the prisoner suffering at the same instant the complicated tortures of despair, remorse, and unavailing repentance!' These made the prison a 'mansion of woe', and Phillips went on to give details of the abject conditions endured by the prisoners, in the face of the positive reports by inspectors. Phillips assured his readers that 'no man is a more zealous friend than I am to the principles of the English constitution', and he invoked the example of the 'Divine Legislator', but in fact his language and rhetorical posture were those of the political protest literature of the 1790s, as he described the wretchedness of the prisoners in order to denounce the incompetent and callous prison managers, implying that they were part of a corrupt system that required a more comprehensive reform of the criminal laws and the penal system, and perhaps the political system itself. In short, though Phillips avoided theory for evocative and tendentious description, his book implied a theory and narrative of reform in which Newgate, as a 'mansion of woe' exemplifying the unreformed system, had a major role.

Two years later, in *Observations on the Criminal Law of England, as It Relates to Capital Punishments, and on the Mode in Which It Is Administered* (1810), another former Revolutionary sympathizer, Sir Samuel Romilly (1757–1818), assailed capital punishment, the large number of crimes that could incur it and the supposed system of exercising leniency towards those, including many children and females, so convicted. Romilly avoided Phillips's colourful language and rhetoric and adopted a cooler tone; he also avoided theory and amassed numerous instances of the cruelty and unequal application of the death penalty; but his polemic was clearly indebted to the arguments of Beccaria and Eden, and was explicitly directed at William Paley's defence of capital punishment in the still influential *Principles of Moral and Political Philosophy*. Two years after Romilly's book was published, the retired London jeweler and active philanthropist James Neild (1744–1814) published the results of his first-hand observations, thorough collecting of documents, and meticulous marshalling of figures, as *State of the Prisons in England, Scotland, and Wales* (1812). As its title would have indicated, this was clearly a diligent updating and amplification of Howard's groundbreaking *The State of the Prisons in England and Wales*, first published in 1777 and brought up to date by Howard before his death for the fourth edition of 1792. Neild was very understated in his 'remarks', which were inserted only intermittently in the information he amassed, but the whole book implied a humanitarian narrative, and was characteristic of the growing tendency to use such comprehensive and massive documentation to persuade the public and parliament to effect change. A year later, parliament received its own *Report from the Committee on the State of the Gaols of the City of London*. The Committee was chaired by George Eden (1784–1849), son of William Eden, author of the *Principles of Penal Law* (1771) already referred to.

The end of the Napoleonic wars and the discharge of thousands of men from the armed forces, together with economic depression, created a widespread perception of another crime wave, with corresponding re-examination of the criminal laws and penal and policing systems. Policing was receiving greater attention, with support of property owners and resistance from middle-class libertarians, those afraid of increased government cost, and the working classes. Increasingly, official and middle-class public opinion would favour legal and penal change, but with a view to enhancing the deterrent effect of punishments, more than their reformative effect.[29] In 1816 parliament received a massive *Report from the Committee on the State of the Police of the Metropolis*. The committee was chaired by the reform-oriented Henry Grey Bennet (1777–1836), who published a damning critique of prison administration in London, titled *A Letter to the Common Council and Livery of the City of London, on the Abuses Existing in Newgate, Showing the Necessity of an Immediate Reform in the Management of that Prison* (1818). It was published by the 1790s radical reformist, James Ridgway, himself familiar, alongside other reformist publishers, with the interior of Newgate, from having been incarcerated there for his political views. Among the witnesses called to the 1818 parliamentary committee on prisons was Thomas Fowell Buxton (1786–1845), who had married into the prominent Quaker banking family of the Gurneys, one of whom was Elizabeth Fry (1780–1845).

She was at this time active in the female side of Newgate and would become the most famous of women prison reform advocates; she was also a witness before the 1818 committee. In 1818 Buxton published his own intervention in the growing public and parliamentary debate on crime and punishment, *An Inquiry, whether Crime and Misery Are Produced or Prevented, by Our Present System of Prison Discipline*. It adopted some elements of the Benthamite approach along with Quaker humanitarianism to argue that a reformed prison regime incorporating separation of classes of prisoners, provision of work, and improved physical conditions would assist reform of criminals and hence reduce crime. Buxton and Fry represented a large movement of Quaker activism informed by both evangelical protestant theology and utilitarianism. These forms of theory and their associated narratives of humanity's sin and salvation on the one hand and Enlightenment philosophical materialism on the other may seem a paradoxical combination, but they were highly influential through the late 1810s and the 1820s, perhaps because this heterogeneous kind of Newgate narrative could appeal to different factions within the propertied classes.

This coalition of interests increasingly demanded government action in defence of their property and their application of capital. Newgate narrative was prominently inserted into parliamentary business. There was a parliamentary *Report of the Commission of Inquiry into the State of the Colony of New South Wales* in 1822 (selections included herein), which was much concerned with the same questions of convict reformation, living conditions, and the operating cost as recurred in investigations of the prisons and courts in Britain. There was a major Gaol (or Gaols) Act in 1823, enjoining comprehensive reforms in construction and management of prisons, but which remained largely ineffective because of lack of provisions for enforcement of the act, which would have required increased government expenditure. By now parliament required annual returns on convictions and crimes, as a basis for drawing up policy and legislation. In discussions inside and outside parliament, Newgate and what it symbolized were still constructed by implied theories and political ideologies that conflicted, merged, and altered as the wider political debate took new turns and topics, drawing variously on religious, moral, philanthropic, economic, socio-psychological, utilitarian and other discourses. Parliamentary business in a larger sense would also bring about a new turn for Newgate in theory, in the aftermath of the intense debate and, in the opinion of many, near revolution over parliamentary and electoral reform in the late 1820s and early 1830s. As discussed in more detail later, the movement for political reform at this time created the conditions for a coalition of working-class and middle-class elements demanding reform in parliament to give greater influence to cities, towns and regions in which they lived and worked and greater access to the vote for themselves. The strength of this movement precipitated a prolonged and difficult process of negotiation between parliamentary parties and factions and between parliament and the extra-parliamentary forces for reform. In the reformists' narrative, Newgate was but one instance, though a salient one, of the system of 'Old Corruption' standing in the way of reform and progress. More importantly, with the eventual passage of the Great Reform Bill in June 1832, though a crisis and possibly a revolution had been averted, the minimal concessions made to those demanding the ballot meant that the excluded majority remained a 'problem'.

The Reform Act conceded the vote to adult males of the more well-to-do urban middle classes, and partly disarmed the incipient coalition of lower and middle classes. The coalition of upper and middle classes that now dominated the state had to find better ways to control and discipline the excluded majority. This need became more pressing through the decades following the Great Reform Act thanks to increasing working-class resistance to industrialization and mechanization, formation of working-class labour and political organizations, the emergence of the Chartist movements, uprisings and revolutions elsewhere in Europe and so on. The criminal laws and penal system were obvious instruments for the purpose of consolidating political, social and economic control, but even the reforms so far effected under the theories of religious moralism and utilitarian cost effectiveness had not solved the 'problem' of crime, which was, so it seemed to many middle-class observers, rooted mainly in the lower classes and their culture. A revealing document in this new turn to Newgate narratives and Newgate in theory was Edward Gibbon Wakefield's *Facts Relating to the Punishment of Death in the Metropolis*, published in 1832. Wakefield (1796–1862) was born into a prominent Quaker family but had difficulty settling in life, and was imprisoned for abducting a teenaged heiress in an attempt to obtain money for a career in politics. Though his book, written from his experience in Newgate, was directed at the issue of capital punishment, it focused attention on the lower-class and criminal culture that flourished inside and outside Newgate, suggesting that Newgate as constructed and administered could not uproot this culture, and so could not solve the problem of Newgate as one of what Wakefield called 'nurseries of crime'. In the aftermath of the Great Reform Act, this problem became the focus of theory and legislation directed at Newgate and what it had come to represent.

Apparently the answer did not lie in England, or had not yet been discovered there, however, and in 1833 the reformist government sent William Crawford (1788–1847) to the United States to examine the two rival penal systems in operation there – the 'silent' system and the 'separate' system. Crawford returned enchanted with the latter and spent the rest of his life in public service promoting it. The differences between the systems and Crawford's reasons for choosing one rather than the other are less significant than the fact that he saw one of them as the solution to the long-standing 'problem' of Newgate and what it represented for people like him, and he singled Newgate out for particular condemnation in his 1834 *Report* to parliament. The separate system, described in more detail later, was informed by a particular socio-psychological theory of reform and rehabilitation from what were seen as both inherent human (that is, lower-class) attributes and acquired 'errors' and 'bad' habits. This theory and the separate system constructed Newgate inmates as a striking example of such flaws, errors, and habits, and constructed Newgate Prison as irretrievably unsuited to the purpose of reforming them.

From the 1830s, this socio-psychological theory also impelled construction of 'model' prisons across Britain and its empire based on the 'separate' system. Like Millbank, these, too, did not achieve the purposes for which they were built. The working classes had to be granted some participation in the political nation and in 1867 national education was assigned the task of socio-psychological correction and adaptation of the lower classes to the prevailing order. And though Newgate was rearranged internally to approximate to the separate system as much as possible, it had in effect to be abandoned as a meaningful instrument of state power, becoming a holding space and place of execution, eventually to be demolished.

'A Prolific Source of Corruption, a Disgrace to the Metropolis, and A National Reproach': Newgate in Practice

In his 1834 report to parliament on the United States prison systems, William Crawford singled out Newgate Prison in London as a striking contrast to the American separate system, and as 'a prolific source of corruption, a disgrace to the metropolis, and a national reproach'. Though forcefully stated, this view had been advanced in different terms many times over the previous century, referring to Newgate in practice. It is true that Newgate was but part of a larger public anxiety over law and order and legal and penal reform, but it had, or was assigned, a continuing power to exemplify and represent those concerns. Thus, the living, daily reality of Newgate was described often, from various perspectives, in various discourses, and for various purposes, represented in certain of the Newgate narratives presented in this set, including many already referred to, such as the works by Howard, Phillips, Neild, Bennet and Wakefield. In addition to these there is the series of sentimental reflective poems, *Thoughts in Prison* (1777), written by the clergyman William Dodd (1729–77) as he awaited execution on a conviction for forgery, at that time a capital offence. There is *The Case of William Hodgson, Now Confined in Newgate* (1796), written as a protest by the middle-class physician, reformist and later publisher of that name (1745–1851), who was sentenced in 1793 to two years in Newgate for having proposed a toast to the French republic. There is the anonymous street ballad

'Newgate Walls' (*c.* 1820s), relating in just a few stanzas, and from the convict's viewpoint, the increasingly common sentence of transportation to the penal colony of Australia. There is *Old Bailey Experience* (1833) by Thomas Wontner, lawyer, son of a governor of Newgate, and energetic voice in the moral panic over Newgate, its inmate culture and the larger 'problem' of the lower classes and their culture, in the aftermath of passage of the Great Reform Act of 1832. There is the first report of the Inspectors of Prisons to parliament in 1836, which advocated a prison system different from what Newgate could ever accommodate, and which accordingly marked the canonization of Newgate and its inmate culture as example and symbol of the larger 'problem' of the lower classes, indicated a few years earlier by Wontner. There is the 1847 biography of the Quaker social campaigner Elizabeth Fry (1780–1845), after whom societies around the world for assisting female convicts are still named, and whose work in Newgate in the 1810s and 20s brought to prominence the distinctive 'problem' of female crime and criminals. This 'problem', among others, is also described from first-hand experience, though from a different perspective, by the former military officer and governor of Coldbath Fields prison, George Laval Chesterton, in his *Revelations of Prison Life* (1856).

All of these narratives were by outsiders or framed by outsiders' interests. With four exceptions – Dodd, Hodgson, Wakefield, and the prisoners in the 1836 Inspectors' reports – these narrators of Newgate practice had not been incarcerated in Newgate. Dodd, Hodgson and Wakefield considered themselves to be outsiders to the social class and experience of the vast majority of those who passed through Newgate. Prisoners' testimony to government inspectors was bound to be self-censored, conditioned by the inspectors' assumptions and questions and the inspection processes, and so also framed according to what the prisoners considered to be outsiders' interests. With that said, and although Newgate in practice was constantly changing throughout the period, an impression of it as a lived reality can be constructed from these and other documents.

People could find themselves in Newgate or any other jail or prison for a wide range of crimes. In 1811 the reformist Sir Richard Phillips provided a summary list in a handbook of criminal law for the use of juries. Like the lists in Jonathan Swift's satire *Gulliver's Travels*, the one presented here suggests not order but disorder, and even a kind of madness:

> By the English Law as it now stands, the punishment of death is inflicted for treason, murder, forgery, burglary in the night or grand larceny, arson, coining,[30] horse-stealing, sheep-stealing, the second conviction for passing counterfeit money, rape, servants robbing their employers, sodomy,[31] beastiality,[32] passing forged instruments[33] knowing them to be forged, highway robbery or grand larceny, cutting or stabbing in the hazard of murder, rioting, armed persons resisting custom-house officers, bankrupts secreting effects, mutiny, piracy, secreting letters containing property, assaulting

a privy councillor[34] in his duty, disobedience of quarantine, obstructing Magistrates in their duty, wilfully destroying ships, administering poison, attempting to set fire to any place, stealing to the value of 40s.[35] in any house or ship, embezzling stores, plundering wrecks, and about ONE HUNDRED OTHER CAPITAL FEL-ONIES created by statute in regard to the Bank of England, the Customs, Inland Navigation, various larcenies, &c. &c. Death is inflicted by hanging; and in cases of treason, the body is quartered,[36] and of murder, dissected.[37] The property of the parties also is forfeited, and they are considered as having neither ancestry nor heirs.

There are also about ONE HUNDRED and FIFTY FELONIES which have *benefit of Clergy*,[38] or are thereby exempted from DEATH, but which, on conviction, subject the parties to transportation[39] for seven or fourteen years, and to civil forfeitures as above.

Single larcenies, or petty thefts, misdemeanors, conspiracies, assaults, &c. are punishable in the discretion of the Court, according to the nature of the offence, or the character of the offender, by imprisonment for three, six, twelve, eighteen, or twenty-four months, accompanied by hard labour,[40] pillory,[41] fine, whipping,[42] &c., and generally regulated by precedents, and the usage of the Courts for particular species of offences.[43]

Though the criminal laws were constantly being amended, augmented, or weeded throughout this period, and the severity of many laws and punishments decreased, the basic distinctions persisted – crimes against property, the person, the state, or community (in fact, middle-class) moral standards – and the aim of the criminal laws remained the same, at least in official pronouncements and in theory. In the words of the 1818 parliamentary committee on the prisons of the metropolis, 'The whole system of enlightened criminal jurisprudence is devised for the *prevention* of crime, not of abstract punishment.'[44]

Who found themselves in Newgate as a result of these laws, and what happened to them? Earlier in the period, Newgate held a number of people imprisoned for debt, a few insane persons for whom there was no other accommodation and whose relatives refused to take responsibility for them, and those serving brief sentences for minor offences. The bulk of the prisoners, however, were those awaiting trial for various criminal offences and those tried and awaiting the carrying out of their sentences. In 1837, after some years of regularization of the criminal justice system, the *Penny Magazine* gave a brief description of how a person might come to find himself or herself in Newgate:

Let us suppose a person apprehended by the police for a crime alleged to have been committed in London, and carried before the magistrates of one of the metropolitan police-offices. These police magistrates can punish summarily, by inflicting a fine or a short imprisonment; they may remand the prisoner for further inquiry, or they may admit to bail. In our supposed case, the evidence appears to the magistrates sufficient to warrant the sending of the case before a superior tribunal; the prisoner cannot procure bail, or the magistrates refuse to take it; he is committed to Newgate, and the witnesses are bound over to give their testimony on the trial. [45]

The *Penny Magazine*, funded by middle-class social activists and aimed at a working-class readership, clearly represents this process in such a way as to make it seem unproblematic, even-handed and free from bias to vested interests. Throughout this period, then, Newgate was mainly, and later almost entirely, a holding centre for those awaiting trial and those tried and sentenced and awaiting execution or corporal punishment, depending on the crime, or distribution to some other place of punishment – for serious crimes this was principally transportation to the penal colony of Australia for a period of seven or fourteen years or life, and for lesser crimes it would be incarceration in a 'house of correction' for a brief period. The conditions in such a house of correction are delineated in one of the Newgate novels in this set, Edward Bulwer's *Paul Clifford* (1830).

In 1818, a generation before the *Penny Magazine* article, the parliamentary committee on the prisons of the metropolis reported on what happened to the 2,396 persons 'admitted' to Newgate during the year 1817. Of these, 1,141 (almost half) were acquitted and discharged 'for various reasons'. Of the remainder eighteen were executed, 492 were placed on the 'hulks' – dismasted ships stationed at various places on the coast – in preparation for being transported to the penal colony in Australia, 121 were taken to the new and as yet unfinished Millbank prison to serve their sentences, eight were taken to the Refuge for the Destitute, one was delivered to the Philanthropic Society, one was removed to Bethlem Hospital (for the insane), forty-six were taken away to be tried at various assizes, twenty-five were pardoned, nine died in prison and 531 were taken to the London and Middlesex Bridewell or 'House of Correction' to serve brief sentences. Of the 1,375 persons in Newgate who were tried and convicted in the same year at the sessions or trials held at the Old Bailey court, adjacent to Newgate, one was convicted of murder, thirty-seven of burglary, thirteen of housebreaking, forty-four of highway robbery, eight of forgery, one of sheep-stealing, four of horse-stealing, fifty-seven of stealing in a dwelling house, three of stealing on the Thames river, eleven of stealing in a shop, two of stealing goods above forty shillings in value, two of stealing Post Office letters, one of rape, two of maliciously cutting, two of returning from transportation before their sentenced time was up, twenty-five of knowingly having forged notes, five of manslaughter, three of child stealing, fifteen of 'fencing' or receiving stolen goods, 1,119 of grand larceny, or theft and twenty of misdemeanors or petty crimes. By the time of this committee report, there was increasing public and parliamentary concern over a supposed increase in crimes by children and youths. There had always been juvenile crime, but as the historian Peter King puts it, 'What was novel in the 1810s was the way that broader socio-political anxieties, reforming agendas, philanthropic energies and changing attitudes to childhood focused on, and helped to create, a new set of discourses about the "alarming increase" of juvenile offenders in urban areas.'[46] This concern impelled

the parliamentary committee to report specifically on the age of offenders in
Newgate under twenty-one: of those juveniles convicted in 1817, eighty-one
were between age ten and fourteen, 238 between fourteen and eighteen, and
211 between eighteen and twenty-one, for a total of 530, almost forty per cent
of all those convicted. Sick prisoners in the male and female infirmaries of Newgate at any one time varied from about five to about eight per cent of the total
prison population.

As William Smith pointed out in 1776, even before completion the 'new'
Newgate was clearly physically inadequate for its diverse and contradictory purposes, but Smith also stressed that administration and regulation of the prison
and prisoners were faulty and pointed out specific abuses: 'There is no act hung
up;[47] no baths or bathing-tubs', and though a surgeon, or physician, visited the
prison regularly, and the 'extremely humane' keeper tried to keep 'the place as
wholesome as possible', nevertheless, 'This gaol is filled with nasty ragged inhabitants swarming with vermin'.[48] John Howard gave classic and highly influential
reinforcement to such criticisms of Newgate and other prisons in his 1777 report
on the *State of the Prisons in England and Wales*. Many of these abuses were the
effect of neglect and under-funding, but Smith pointed to one abuse that represented the particular nature of the Newgate administrative system as commerce
in human misery. This was the practice of fettering, or putting iron fetters on
a prisoner on admission, even before the prisoner had been tried and convicted:

> Even within this rock of strength the barbarous *trade* of fettering is continued, where
> there is no excuse, or shadow of excuse, for it. The practice should be utterly abol-
> ished, and no gaoler should have a power to put double, heavy or light irons, or any
> at all, according as the prisoner's purse is heavy or light. If the walls and gaoler cannot
> prevent an escape, the one should be demolished for its weakness and insufficiency,
> and the other discharged for his negligence. The infamous trade of chains is a disgrace
> to the nation, humanity and civilization, especially before conviction.

Fettering or being ironed was a classic illustration of the way Newgate was made
to produce profits from crime, or rather punishment, for the benefit of the pun-
ishers. Not surprisingly, fettering was particularly irksome and humiliating to
prisoners who considered themselves of a better class, or who were imprisoned
for debt or crimes they considered minor or perhaps not crimes at all, such as
those that were in effect political crimes. The account of one such person dis-
closes the basis of attitudes to crime and punishment in class experience and
identity, and the connection between middle-class political reformism and certain aspects of Newgate in practice.

In 1809 Richard Andrews, a reformer who may have been subjected to har-
assment by the authorities for his political views, published at his own expense
a bitter complaint of his treatment in Newgate and other London prisons on

apparently being charged falsely with theft of some silverware.[49] He was particularly offended by being fettered, and protested,

> If irons be meant to degrade the wearer it is cruel and unjust they should be resorted
> to, till the party be convicted of the crime alleged, for is it not unjust an innocent man
> should meet the scorn of his fellow subject, because a perjured wretch chuses to swear
> before a Magistrate, a robbery, which a jury of his countrymen finds (as has frequently
> been the case) false and iniquitous; yet so it is, the most honorable acquital cannot
> wash the stain away, and an innocent man is degraded all his life, leaving infamy to
> fall on his unhappy offspring.[50]

Andrews paid to avoid being fettered at this time, but found that fettering or the threat of it was used to extract money from him again when he went for trial and returned to prison. Andrews also pointed to other ways in which fees were exacted from those able to pay: 'To become an inmate on the state side', where conditions were less harsh, 'certain fees are demanded and of course paid, and 7 shillings per week afterwards'. Andrews calculated that this practice produced a revenue of over £665 annually. He paid for a while, but when he could no longer do so he was turned out of his room. Even getting out of Newgate legitimately required payment. Andrews had a friend take out a writ of *habeas corpus*, compelling the authorities to release Andrews or bring him to trial; he was detained in the lodge of the debtor's side until he paid a fee of a few shillings, then put in a room with sixteen others where he had to spend his remaining money. On being taken finally to the judge's chambers, another fee was expected. Andrews described other abuses he had heard of. On the 'Master Felon's side' a man could pay for a bed and pay extra to have his wife stay with him, which Andrews thought turned the prison into a 'bagnio', or brothel. He called for investigation into distribution of the required bread allowance for prisoners, implying that it was unequal and again based on ability to pay. He had also heard that 'Coals sold on the State side for 2s. per bushel' were 'charged an extra 2d.[51] on the Felon's side'. He noted that prisoners who had turned 'King's evidence', or agreed to testify against others, were liable to life-threatening beatings by other prisoners, which were ignored by prison staff. Andrews proposed a number of reforms, and eventually was released: 'I left Newgate, that mansion of the unhappy, where imposition bears down all before it, where every thing that is vicious is sure to meet encouragement, and poverty the most marked oppression.'

At the time Andrews published his protest pamphlet, administration of Newgate and the penal system generally was drawing increased public and parliamentary attention. The Common Council or governing body of the City of London, which was responsible for Newgate, responded to Sir Richard Phillips's critical *Letter to the Livery of London* (1808) by establishing a committee to investigate the metropolis's prisons, and in 1810 they passed a number of resolutions for improvement in Newgate, thereby indicating what conditions were like. First, it was resolved 'That the Prison of Newgate is inadequate to the purposes required for the average number of Prisoners usually confined therein, particularly for the female prisoners'. It was resolved that prisoners awaiting trial should be kept separate from those convicted; that many prisoners were kept too long in Newgate, especially those awaiting transportation; that those imprisoned for debt, who amounted to twice the number that could reasonably be accommodated, should be confined elsewhere; that a 'house of correction should be built to hold those convicted of lesser crimes' and sentenced to brief periods of incarceration; that the insane should be removed to more suitable quarters; that 'ironing' or placing fetters on all admitted to Newgate should be restricted; that gratuities paid by prisoners to prison officers and servants for small 'indulgences' should be eliminated and that likewise all fees paid by prisoners to the keeper and clerks of the prison should be abolished.[52] Characteristically, however, both the national government and the government of the City of London feared incurring increased expense, and these recommendations would take some years to be implemented.

Internally, Newgate's space continued to be organized according to three principles, reflecting both the persistence of old methods of prison administration and reformist desire to make imprisonment less horrific and liable to spread instruction in crime, and hence more reformative. These principles were ability to pay, sex of the prisoner and seriousness of the crime. The 1814 parliamentary *Report* on London's jails outlined this system. Those imprisoned for debt were kept separate from those awaiting or convicted at trial; males were kept separate from females and those convicted of murder and awaiting execution were kept separate from others on the criminal side. Within these categories, prisoners were separated according to their ability to pay for better accommodation, and this remained the grand principle of the Newgate economy. On the debtors' side, the buildings called the Master's Side and the Common Side supposedly had a better 'society', or class of people, as well as facilities, and accordingly cost three shillings for admission. The inferior Cabin Side cost two shillings admission. There was a male yard and a female yard. Debtors were supposed to receive money for subsistence from their creditors while awaiting payment of their debts and discharge, but often this was not done. The debtors had their own internal organization and representatives; they could receive visitors from opening to closing time; debtors who committed 'misconduct' could be removed to a 'Disorderly Ward'. On the 'Criminal Side', too, men were separated from women and had several yards, and prisoners awaiting execution were separated from the rest, in their own cells. They were visited by the Newgate 'Ordinary', or official chaplain, and had access to a clergyman of their own faith if they wished. On the last Sunday before execution they attended a chapel service and were seated in full view, with a coffin placed before them. This was one of the sights of London, and viewing the condemned on this occasion was a popular tourist attraction. Prisoners slept on barracks beds, or an inclined wooden flooring on one side of the room, with a beam at the top which served as a pillow. The floor space allotted per person was eighteen inches wide. There was no bedding but each prisoner had two 'rugs'. All prisoners could buy wine and beer, and receive food from relatives and friends. Various fees were charged by prison and court officers, and prisoners exacted from new arrivals a 'garnish' or fee, consisting of money or drink.

In the midst of a mounting public debate on the criminal justice and penal systems, in 1818 a parliamentary committee was charged with investigating the prisons of the metropolis and making recommendations for their improvement to the prime end of 'prevention of crime'. The committee reported the figures for committals and the various classes of prisoners, detailed above. The committee also deplored the conditions in Newgate. Various categories of prisoners were allowed or forced to mix indiscriminately; though boys were provided with a school, the teacher was a convict; and, while the prison itself was on the whole clean and well kept, there was 'a great neglect of cleanliness amongst the prisoners generally'. The prisoner's bedding allowance 'consists of a hempen mat, worked with a portion of tar, to prevent the lodgment of vermin, and to exclude damp, and two rugs'; as the committee noted, 'This allowance seems sparing and inadequate'. There was no prison uniform provided and inadequate provision for clothing, even though many prisoners were 'committed to prison half naked' and 'others are in the habit of selling their shoes and other parts of their dress' (often to buy drink). Fettering had been banned for those not yet put on trial. Though the infirmary was adequate and the physician diligent, different classes of prisoners were placed there indiscriminately because of insufficient space. The Ordinary was diligent, in the committee's opinion, visiting the prison once a day to offer religious counsel to whoever requested it, and performing religious services on Wednesday and Friday and twice on Sundays; but the chapel could accommodate only 350 persons, less than the prison population. The committee thought that the provision for food was satisfactory:

> Formerly, the provision-allowance was one pound of beef, without bone, delivered twice a week, and cooked by the prisoners themselves at their own time and pleasure, and daily sixteen ounces of brown bread. The filth created by the cooking, and the improvidence of the prisoners, added to a conviction of the propriety of giving an allowance of vegetables, induced the Court of Aldermen to adopt a new system. A kitchen has been provided, a cook appointed, and an alteration of the diet established. The allowance now is a pint of good gruel for breakfast; for dinner, alternately, half a pound of beef, (which when cooked weighs about six ounces) and a quart of soup, in which the meat was boiled the previous day, with barley, and a variety of vegetables.

The committee reported to parliament that 'Many of Your Committee have tasted the bread, and several have tasted the soup and gruel, and are perfectly satisfied that they are good of their kind'.[53] What 'their kind' might be was not specified by the committee.

As always, the cost of running Newgate was a concern to local and national governments; accounts supplied to the 1818 parliamentary committee showed that expenditure on Newgate in 1817 was just over £10,470. It is difficult to calculate modern equivalents for this sum, but standard calculators used today result in figures of about £565,000 in purchasing power, £733,000 according to the retail price index, £8,000,000 using average earnings, and £11,000,000 using average per capita gross domestic product. Of expenditure at Newgate in 1817, just over £1,773 went on repairs and whitewashing the premises; £3,721 to salaries of the keeper, the ordinary, the surgeon (or physician) and servants; just under £3,650 for bread and meat for the prisoners; just under £200 for 'necessaries to sick prisoners'; almost £165 for taxes and water; almost £150 for bedding and clothing for those about to be transported to the penal colony; just over £356 for subsistence and clothing for the insane held in Newgate and £452 for coal. There were no expenditures recorded in 1817 for 'prayer-books and homilies', though just over £219 had been spent on these items in 1815.

In the end, the question of money, which governed the lives of the prisoners as witnessed by Richard Andrews and others, also governed the 1818 committee's recommendations. The committee concluded that the major problem of Newgate prison was inadequate space. This prevented systematic separation of classes of prisoners, leading to what the committee saw as exploitation of the weak by the strong and corruption of the less hardened by the thoroughly vicious. It obstructed any efforts to keep the prisoners clean, free of vermin and disease, properly fed, educated and instructed in religion. Worse, inadequate space thwarted attempts to instill remorse, discipline and reform, and still further, to exact labour from the imprisoned sufficient to meet the costs of their imprisonment – an objective mentioned with increasing frequency by penal reformers. The committee thought that this problem could be solved only by a new prison on the site of Newgate; this, however, would cost too much. Consequently, the best the committee felt they could do was recommend administrative measures, such as timely removal of convicts to their places of sentenced punishment, and improvements in bedding, clothing and so on. In short, the committee saw Newgate as an inherently insoluble problem. It would remain a scandal to the general public and government.

Nevertheless, another parliamentary committee was established in 1822 to address the entire penal system, resulting the following year in the so-called 'Gaols' or 'Gaol Act', or a 'Bill for Consolidating and Amending Laws Relating to Building, Repairing and Regulating of Gaols, Bridewells and Houses of Correction in England and Wales'. The act consolidated or weeded out legislation going back generations and posited twenty-five administrative regulations for penal institutions. These represented the consensus thinking at this moment. The regulations included separation of male and female inmates, separation of tried and untried prisoners, separation of these into classes according to seriousness of offence, regular inspections and record-keeping by the keepers, female warders for female prisoners, work required from all convicts, regular religious service and instruction and daily reading of prayers, mandatory attendance at religious services, instruction in reading and writing for all prisoners, no fettering of prisoners unless they be deemed dangerous, provision of appropriate food and bedding and clothing and none other permitted than that provided, restricted and controlled visiting, medical examination on admission and discharge and medical attendance as required, regular cleaning of the prisons, sale of alcoholic beverages abolished, no gambling permitted, no 'garnish' permitted and others. The act also required that there be a central jail for each administrative district, that magistrates have powers to institute additional regulations, that regulations be displayed in prisons, that regular returns be filed by prison governors to central government, that prisons be regularly inspected by appointed officials or bodies, that prisoners be furnished with a means of earning a living upon their discharge, that there be regular procedures for appointing governors, chaplains and physicians and numerous other provisions. Tellingly, much of the act was concerned with ways of acquiring land for new or expanded prisons while avoiding corruption in the process. The act also ordered that jails and prisons should be constructed, altered, or repaired in such a way 'as shall afford the most effectual means for the security, classification [or appropriate separation of categories of prisoners], health, inspection, and religious, and moral instruction of the prisoners'[54]. This provision clearly indicated the government's, and probably the public's, priorities.

This was the core of the new system of prison design and management that would prevail for generations and the Gaols Act is widely considered to be a landmark in penal history. There was no provision for enforcement of the act, however, and it would take some years for the act's vision to be realized. In 1833 the attorney Thomas Wontner surveyed the landscape of crime in London from his experience in Newgate and the criminal courts, and declared:

> The multiplicity of penal enactments in this country must, in the very nature of things, defeat those ends the attainment of which ought to be the object of all law, namely, *the prevention of crime.* Our criminal code exhibits too much the appearance of a heterogeneous mass, concocted too often on the spur of the occasion, (as Lord Bacon expresses it,) and frequently without that degree of accuracy which is the result of able and minute discussion, or a due attention to the revision of the existing laws, or considering how far their provisions bear upon new and accumulated stat-

utes introduced into parliament, often without either consideration or knowledge, and without those precautions which are always necessary when laws are to be made which may affect the property, the liberty, and perhaps even the lives of thousands.

Wontner also gave a taxonomy of the principal crimes against property, with the names in standard English and in '*vulgus*', or slang:[55]

	Vulgus—	
Housebreakers		Craksman, pannymen.
Highwaymen and footpads.		Grand-tobymen and spicemen.
Coiners.		Bit-makers.
Utterers of base metal		Smashers.
Pickpockets		Buzzmen, clyfakers, conveyancers.
Stealers of goods and money from shops, areas, &c. &c.		Sneaks.
Shoplifters.		Shop-bouncers.
Snatchers of reticules, watches, &c. &c. from the person		Grabbers.
Horse and cattle stealers		Prad-chewers.
Women and men who waylay inebriate persons for the purpose of robbery		Ramps.
Receivers of stolen goods		Fences.
Forgers		Fakers.
Embezzlers		Bilkers.
Swindlers of every description, among which are. .		Macers, duffers, and ring-droppers.
Stealing from carts and carriages of all kinds		Dragsmen.
To which may be added, all kinds of plundering on the river and its banks, on board shipping, barges, &c..		Light-horsemen, heavy horse-men, game watermen, do. lightermen, scuffle-hunters, copemen, &c.

Though regarded by educated people as an abuse of 'proper' language, or at best a sometimes quaint example of the culture of the 'vulgar', such 'slang' constituted both a secret code for its users and a refusal to accept the terminology, along with the rest of the language and culture, of the dominant classes.

Wontner's dissatisfaction with the criminal laws and penal system was widely shared. As noticed earlier, in 1833 the liberal prime minister, Lord Melbourne, sent William Crawford to the United States to examine the prisons systems there and report back. Son of a London wine merchant, Crawford was a religious Evangelical who associated with Quaker philanthropists and social reformers and was a co-founder in 1815 of the Society for the Improvement of Prison Discipline and Reformation of Juvenile Offenders. Crawford went on to become one of the new kind of campaigning civil servants who reconstructed Britain as a modern state during the middle third of the nineteenth century. In America, Crawford was enchanted by the 'Philadelphia' or 'Pennsylvania' system, also called the 'separate' system, which involved confining convicts in individual cells and subjecting them to manual labour, religious instruction, basic education and vocational training. Crawford found the entire system in Britain, shamefully exemplified by Newgate, to be radically deficient by contrast and lambasted it in his 1834 *Report* to parliament. In 1835 parliament established prison inspectors to cover the entire country and report annually. At the same time, parliament received a massive report of over 1300 pages from the select committee of the House of Lords on 'the present state of the several gaols and houses of correction in England and Wales'; their first witness was William Crawford. Newgate was mentioned frequently in the report. So alarmed were the committee by what they were finding that they brought their report to parliament even before they had completed their inquiries. The report recommended a consistent and unified system throughout the country, central control of prison regulations, appoint-ment of prison inspectors reporting to cabinet through the Home Secretary, that the 'separate' system be instituted and prisoners forbidden to communicate with each other before and after trial, and that the insane be removed from prisons. The conclusion of witnesses was that Newgate, while reasonably well managed, could not be reconstructed to meet the committee's recommendations. In 1836 a select committee of the House of Commons 'on the laws relating to prisons' did recommend that Newgate be rebuilt, to house untried prisoners only; a question that remained unresolved in the committee's report was who was to pay for the reconstruction.

In their first report of 1836 the newly appointed inspectors of prisons for England and Wales echoed the testimony of the witnesses at the 1835 select committee. The report is worth referring to in detail because it illustrated the new approach to prisons in general and Newgate in particular; it marked a major turning point in prison policy, with repercussions that continue today; and it marked a significant shift in Newgate narratives of all kinds. The first part of the inspectors' report dealt only with Newgate, but the inspectors averred that, even with only an 'unavoidably imperfect inquiry' they had 'collected much informa-tion which calls for immediate and serious consideration'. They reported that they had found many of the provisions of the 1823 Gaols Act and subsequent enactments and regulations to be widely ignored. They began what they entitled the 'Narrative' of their inspection on the male side of the prison. In the Chapel Yard 'were associated together the convicted and the untried, the felon and the misdemeanant, the sane and the insane, the old and the young offender'. 'In ward No. 10 we found that the wardsman, a convicted prisoner, owned all the bed-ding, the crockery ware, the knives, forks, kettles and saucepans for the use of which each prisoner pays him 2 *s.* 6 *d.* per week.' They found 'a good supply of Bibles and Prayer-books, provided by the prison, together with many religious books, the gift of a Captain Brown'. But, the inspectors had to observe, 'These books, particularly the Bibles, bore little appearance of having been used.' There was worse.

> On examining the cupboards of this ward we discovered a pack of cards, apparently much used, a cribbage-board and pegs, and two draught-boards and men. We also found four tobacco-pipes, in some of which the tobacco still remained; and a box with tobacco in it. These, though forbidden by the prison regulations, were quite exposed on the shelves of the cupboards, and must have been detected, on the most superficial inspection of the ward, by any officer of the prison.
>
> We found also a bundle of newspapers, twelve in all; and, upon inquiring, we were informed that a daily paper is taken in, in this ward. ... One of the principal turnkeys, who accompanied us, said that the daily papers were allowed by the governor, but that no Sunday paper was admitted; such papers [which contained reports of crimes and other entertaining matter], he said, were strictly forbidden. ... But we subsequently ascertained that Sunday papers were as publicly brought into the prison on the Sunday morning, as the other papers were during the rest of the week ... that on Sunday evenings the turnkey above alluded to regularly borrowed the Sunday paper, The Dispatch, from a prisoner, and returned it to him on the Monday.
>
> We found porter in a bottle on the shelf, though none could have been brought into the ward since one o'clock the day before.
>
> The wardsman had a snuff-box and snuff, which he used continually and openly: there was also another snuff-box in the ward; and each prisoner, if he liked, might have had one.
>
> We observed in the cupboard mince pies and cold provisions, any quantity of which may be brought in by the friends of the prisoners ...
>
> We found two boxes, containing two or three strong files, four brad-awls, several large iron spikes, screws, nails and knives; all of them instruments calculated to facilitate attempts at breaking out of prison, and capable of becoming most dangerous weapons in the hands of desperate and determined men.
>
> We also found several books: amongst them Guthrie's Grammar, a song book, the Keepsake Annual for 1836, and the —— by ——, 18 plates, published by Stockdale, 1827. This last is a book of a most disgusting nature, and the plates are obscene and indecent in the extreme.[56]

In fact, the books mentioned here represent those that might be of interest to someone wanting to 'improve' himself, or pass the time. There was William Guthrie's *A New System of Modern Geography; or, A Geographical, Historical, and Commercial Grammar, and Present Sate of the Several Kingdoms of the World,* first published in 1745 and reprinted up to 1809, and the kind of book useful to the self-educated. *The Keepsake* was an up-market literary anthology of short pieces by fashionable authors published annually and designed as a gift book. It would have been of interest to those with an interest in acquiring genteel belletristic culture; perhaps it was planted to catch the eye of the inspectors. The book so 'disgusting' as to remain unidentified by the inspectors was later identified by a committee of the City of London, as noted below. In another ward the inspectors saw a copy of 'Mavor's British Tourist' lying on a table; in this case presumably it was the presence rather than the contents of the book that was objectionable – William Mavor's *The British Tourist; or, Traveller's Pocket Companion* (1809) was a guide book, though it was published by Richard Phillips, a well-known reformist. In the inspector's imagination the owner of the book may have been using it for nefarious purposes such as planning possible places to waylay travelers. The inspectors may also have been alerted to the danger of travel books, and indeed all the forms of print they uncovered in Newgate, by the assertion of Archibald Alison in *Blackwood's Edinburgh Magazine* less than two years earlier that the 'lighter productions which attract and are alone read by the multitude' consisted of 'newspapers, magazines, reviews, novels, [and] superficial travels'.[57]

The inspectors found papers prepared by some prisoners for others, regarding their upcoming trials; it seems that some literate prisoners earned money by providing such services to their illiterate fellow inmates. The inspectors found that visitors were admitted without regard for the established regulations or proper supervision.

> Among the visitors, persons of notoriously bad character, prostitutes, and thieves, find admission. Many of the prostitutes are very young girls, sometimes not more than twelve or thirteen years of age: others have visited different men, yet are admitted under the name of wives and sisters.[58] (p. 6)

The inspectors found that 'Cold provisions, in any quantity, are brought in', often by such women, and including 'whole joints, meat pies, and almost any kind of delicacy'. A 'beer-man' came into the prison daily from noon till one with four three-gallon cans to sell to inmates and when these were empty, he sent for more. Money, too, was brought in by visitors, 'and we have reason to know that individuals have had in their possession several sovereigns at one time' – at this time a sovereign was a gold coin worth a pound. There were other inappropriate practices: 'When we visited the rooms, there was a comfortable fire in each of them, round which the prisoners were seated at their ease; and we noticed scarcely anything in the apartments that indicated the discomfort or privations of a place of penal confinement.'

Similar conditions prevailed in other wards, but in the Middle Ward, holding the poorest prisoners, conditions were 'much worse':

> Here are herded together the very worst class of prisoners; certainly a more wretched combination of human beings can hardly be imagined: we have reason to fear that poverty, ragged clothes, and an inability to pay the ward dues, elsewhere exacted for better accommodations, consign many of the more petty and unpractised offenders to this place, where they inevitably meet with further contamination from the society of the most abandoned and incorrigible inmates of the gaol. On some occasions we

> found the prisoners squalid and filthy in the extreme, with ragged clothing, scarcely any linen [underclothes], and some without shoes or stockings.[59]

Here the inspectors learned that 'Rioting, uproar, and fighting, are frequently going on', and sometimes had to be broken up by prison officers armed with cutlasses. From the statements of the prisoners themselves the inspectors learned 'that many of their more violent fights have taken place on a Sunday afternoon; that the more quiet and inoffensive dare not go to sleep, from an apprehension of being made the subjects of tricks of a very painful nature; that the act of locking-up [at night] becomes, from the consequent removal of all superintendance, a signal for the commencement of obscene talk, revelry, and violence; and that gaming, swearing, singing, narration of adventures, instruction in crime, proceed unchecked, and without ceasing, until a late hour of the night'. Perhaps the inspectors were not surprised to find that 'In the wards of this yard there is not a single Bible or prayer-book; and the reason assigned for this is, that no sooner are they given than they are torn up'.[60]

The inspectors expressed particular concern over sleeping arrangements in Newgate, implying that these gave opportunities for 'unnatural' sexual activities. Prisoners slept in rooms together on the sloping flooring called barracks beds, each on a mat and with two rugs, but these conditions gave less concern to the inspectors than the way the prisoners arranged themselves: 'Those mats may be placed as close together as the prisoners choose; and on our visits at night to the wards, we found them sleeping, some by themselves, others two, three, and even four together, as close as bodies could possibly be placed.' Other forms of association gave even greater concern. In ward 12 'we found a man aged 38, under a sentence of 12 months' imprisonment for an assault on a lad, with an intent to commit an unnatural offence', 'two lads of 17 and 18 years of age', and others; the man convicted of an 'unnatural offence' was allowed to associate freely with another in ward 11 'under a similar atrocious charge' and, the inspectors exclaimed, 'even the other prisoners did not feel indignant at their offences, or avoid associating with them!'[61] In the condemned cells, the inspectors found that 'At night the two men who had been convicted and sentenced to death for sodomy, had each two other prisoners locked up with them; one of those doomed to this detestable association being the boy before mentioned only thirteen years of age'.[62]

The inspectors found the female side of Newgate to be better run, but still in need of more rigorous enforcement of legislated regulations. There were inadequate facilities for bathing and washing clothes, too frequent opportunities for association with male inmates and prison staff, and excessive hardships for those who could not pay fees for better accommodations. The inspectors acknowledged the beneficial efforts of Elizabeth Fry's Ladies' Committee:

It is only due to these Ladies to say, that they have been the means of introducing much order and cleanliness; that they have provided work for those who had before passed their time in total idleness; that they have introduced much better regulations than had been heretofore observed for the government of the women on their passage to New South Wales, furnishing them with many necessaries and with materials for keeping them employed during the voyage. They have also, by the occasional presence and by the disinterested efforts of the virtuous and pure of their own sex, restrained the dissolute manners and vicious language of these unhappy women, constraining them by the silent but powerful influence of their own virtuous example to the adoption of improved principles and conduct; and, above all, they have been the means of conveying both moral and religious instruction by their regular readings of the Holy Scriptures.[63]

But, reflecting a growing criticism of such efforts as too indulgent towards prisoners, the inspectors also felt it their 'duty to point out those parts' of the ladies' 'proceedings which appear to us inexpedient and injudicious, and to interfere materially with the laudable objects which they themselves have in view'. Such proceedings included bringing too many visitors, among whom were a number of men, to observe the ladies' ministrations, leading to amusement and levity among the prisoners; the holding of separate religious services, resulting in inmates being absent from chapel services; and maintaining a shop for sale of tea, coffee, butter, and various other articles, both for male and female prisoners, 'which is productive of much evil'. The inspectors also noted the ladies' concern that a 'young, rosy-cheeked girl' was frequently taken from the prison to the governor's house to perform servant's duties, where she had opportunity to mix with men, partake of wine, and so on;[64] in fact, the inspectors became quite exercised about the young rosy-cheeked girl.

The inspectors included a wide range of detailed information besides their 'Narrative', such as testimony of prison staff, prisoners, and others, and the now familiar if still controversial and disputed kinds of tables, accounts, and statistics.[65] Ultimately, however, it was the social and moral condition of Newgate that was their concern. In this regard they concluded:

It is impossible to close this narrative of the habits which have prevailed for years in Newgate, without pausing to make one short comment on the object of committing a criminal to gaol, and on the very contrary effects which are produced by a committal to this prison. That object, unquestionably, is to deter, not only the criminal himself, but others, from crime, by the endurance of hardship and privation, and to dispose him, by seclusion and meditation, to return to an honest life. But instead of privation and hard fare, he is permitted to purchase whatever his own means or the means of his friends, in or out of prison, can afford, and he can almost invariably procure the luxuries of his class of life, beer and tobacco, in abundance. Instead of seclusion and meditation, his time is passed in the midst of a body of criminals of every class and degree, in riot, and debauchery, and gaming, vaunting his own adventures, or listening to those of others; communicating his own skill and aptitude in crime, or acquiring the lessons of greater adepts. He has access to newspapers, and of course he prefers that description which are expressly prepared for his own class, and which abound in vulgar adventure, in criminal enterprise, and in the histories of the police, the gaol and the scaffold. He is allowed intercourse with prostitutes, who in nine cases out of ten have originally conduced to his ruin; and his connexion with them is confirmed by that devotion and generosity towards their paramours in adversity, for which these otherwise degraded women are remarkable. Having thus passed his time in gaol, he returns a greater adept in crime, with a wider acquaintance among criminals, and what, perhaps, is even more injurious to him, is generally known to the worst men in the country; not only without the inclination, but almost without the ability of returning to an honest life.[66]

Without at all intending to do so, the inspectors here gave a clear picture of the working classes' independence, mutual loyalties, ingenuity, survival skills and determination to enjoy themselves in whatever way possible, even in the most adverse conditions.

The thrust of the *Report* is clear, however – promotion of the 'separate' system so dear to the inspectors, led by the same William Crawford. The other inspectors were William Whitworth Russell (1795–1847) and Francis Bisset Hawkins (1796–1894). Russell was a cousin of the reformist government home secretary and later Prime Minister, Lord John Russell (1792–1878), and was chaplain of Millbank penitentiary. This was built on a cellular plan and potentially well suited to the separate system, architecturally, if not administratively. Russell aimed to correct the latter, and crusaded strenuously for the separate system during his years as a prison inspector; but he suffered financial losses from speculating in railway stock, had to fend off concerns that the separate system was inducing mental illness and suicidal tendencies in many inmates, and was accused in 1847 of ordering excessive corporal punishments at Millbank; in August that year he shot himself to death in the prison board room. Hawkins was a physician, author of *The Elements of Medical Statistics* (1829) and a history of cholera (1831), and professor of *materia medica* at King's College London, from 1830 until appointed prison inspector in 1835; he went on to have a distinguished career in medical public service. Crawford had of course reported only two years earlier to parliament on the separate system as practised in the United States. Newgate could never be fully part of that system, being structurally unfit for it, and could only ever be partially accommodated to it by significant structural modification, rigorous enforcement of regulations, and drastic reduction in the number of prisoners held there. These measures would be adopted in succeeding decades, while the government embarked on an ambitious program of prison building led by Crawford and his associates.

Newgate was under the control of the City of London. The City's officers and government, understandably, disagreed with much in the 1836 Inspectors' report and ordered their own inspection, carried out by a committee of the

Court of Aldermen. Their *Report* responded both to particular points made by the government inspectors and to the inspectors' general criticism of Newgate and its administration.[67] The aldermen's committee found that the instruments for amusement and gaming, such as cards, cribbage boards and draughts, were very old and appeared long disused, were made of paper and so easily concealed from administrative inspection, or had long been incised on tabletops and so were not easily removed. They found that the bundle of newspapers was actually 'several years old' and contained accounts of an inmate's case which he was using for his defence. They found that Sunday papers were in fact prohibited and that those admitted were Saturday afternoon editions. They found that the tools and weapons discovered by the government inspectors, and supposed by them to have been secreted for effecting a prison break or assaulting others, were in fact workman's tools. They found that the book discovered by the government inspectors, published by Stockdale in 1827 with eighteen illustrations 'obscene and indecent in the extreme', was in fact John Robertson's *The Generative System*, with illustrations 'purely anatomical', a scientific book for the study of surgery, which one of the prisoners was pursuing.[68] They found that the system for admitting sale of beer, objected to by the inspectors, was the best that could be effected without compelling purchasers to consume their whole allowance at once and on the spot and they found that smoking, declared by the inspectors to be universally banned, was only expressly forbidden in the wards but permitted in the yards. They found that the system of appointing wardsmen from among the prisoners occasionally led to abuses, such as those the inspectors found, but that these had been promptly dealt with, and that the position of wardsman was also of moral benefit to those convicts so appointed in giving them a sense of responsibility and achievement, and so on. The aldermen's committee agreed with the government inspectors on some points, such as inadequate soap, insufficient washing and bathing facilities, and the ladies' shop, and stated that measures had or would be taken to deal with these matters. More generally, the aldermen's committee pleaded that most of the faults that the government inspectors had found were unavoidable due to the structure of Newgate and the burden it bore of accommodating a large number of very diverse classes of prisoners, which the inspectors themselves had pointed out but that, nevertheless, prisoners had been kept in separate classes insofar as possible.

Reading the *Report* of the aldermen's committee, it is difficult to avoid the impression that, while the aldermen and the inspectors had similar basic attitudes to crime and punishment, the inspectors had a more ideological and inflexible approach and the aldermen a more pragmatic and humanitarian approach to the issue. Many of the Newgate narratives of the period, including the so-called 'Newgate novels', sided with the latter, but to a large extent all would agree with the judgment of the *Penny Magazine*, published in 1837, a year after the first inspectors' report and the aldermen's response:

> Newgate has a wide-spread notoriety ... . It has lain in the heart of this great city like some foul and undrained marsh, into which all the waters of corruption were poured. It has ever been a fertile nursery of crime. From within its walls physical as well as moral contagion has issued, and spread disease in most noxious and aggravated forms. ... Newgate now is a palace to what Newgate was; yet Mr. Crawford, in his official 'Report on Penitentiaries' (1834),[69] says, it is 'a prolific source of corruption,—a disgrace to the metropolis, and a national reproach.'[70]

Here is emphatically deployed the disease metaphor so commonplace and useful in nineteenth-century discourses of social separation and hierarchy, from class and gender through 'race' and ethnicity. Newgate would go on for the rest of the century, disgracing the metropolis, reproaching the nation, afflicting the consciences of humanitarians, trying the charity of religious evangelicals, energizing the activism of moral reformers, challenging the vigilance of government inspectors, obtruding on the attention of legislators, vexing the watchfulness of officials, stimulating the imaginations of novelists, exercising the ingenuity of inmates, and stinking in the noses of passersby.

By the 1840s, the 'separate' system advocated by Crawford and Russell was the basis of government prisons policy, and Newgate had become more important as a cultural and social symbol than as a prison.[71] In December 1842 the 'model' prison at Pentonville north of London was opened, enabling the separate system to be fully implemented. The system was designed to reform the criminal by first secluding him or her from others, forcing reflection that would lead to repentance, reinforced by chaplain's visits and religious instruction, consolidated by practising or learning a manual trade and by daily labour, and confirmed by basic education, thereby fitting the prisoner for eventual return to society adequately equipped spiritually and intellectually for usefulness, according to the prevailing economic system. This separate system at Pentonville was combined with a reorganized convict transportation system, in which the convict would first be subjected to eighteen months of the separate system at Pentonville and then sent to Australia, not as an indentured servant but as free, and presumably self-disciplined, labour. Through the 1840s Crawford and Russell promoted the system throughout the land, assisted by the architect Joshua Jebb, with new local and regional prisons being built on their system. In the process the earlier, panopticon system of Jeremy Bentham, exemplified at Millbank prison, which aimed to make convicts pay for their own imprisonment, punishment, and reform by profitable labour, fell by the wayside.

Newgate, of course, became even more of a scandal. Joseph Adshead, another proponent of the separate system, clearly stated the position. In his 1845 book,

Prisons and Prisoners, Adshead comprehensively condemned the City of London administration of its prisons and jails and exclaimed:

> What masses of the population are continually passing, without a thought, the murky façade of Newgate, the well-known City Prison of detention, which has been from time almost immemorial, or for about 700 years, a felon's Gaol! What dark and deep streams of moral pollution have issued from this pestiferous source, distributing their morally contagious miasma amongst the community![72]

Pursuing the medical-sanitary-disease metaphor that infected the prisons debate for decades, Adshead asked,

> What ought our penal institutions to be but ethical hospitals to correct the moral maladies of the community? What ought the discipline of such institutions to be but as acting in harmony with the great objects of penal infliction (the oft derided ideas) 'to deter and to reform'?[73]

As noted earlier, Adshead also condemned Millbank, observing that, 'although a place of penal detention', it had 'more the appearance of a general convict workshop',[74] with consequent opportunities for contaminative association between prisoners. Bentham designed Millbank to allow constant surveillance of the prisoners in their individual cells as they presumably meditated on their poor life choices and worked at their appointed tasks, thereby paying for their own incarceration and reformation. But, Adshead noted, prisoners were allowed to associate in sleeping rooms and at certain work tasks, and after a certain period they could work together. Apart from criticisms such as Adshead's, it was by this time widely thought that the construction and regime at Millbank undermined the physical and mental health of its inmates, and in 1843 legislation turned it into a depot for prisoners about to be transported to Australia, with internal remodelling of the prison and establishment of the separate system that Adshead supported. Eventually, in the mid-1850s, even Newgate's interior was remodeled to make it as much like one of the 'separate' system prisons as was possible.

A decade after this, in 1865, Thomas Archer described the remodelled Newgate in his book on London's lower-class purlieus and subcultures, *The Pauper, the Thief, and the Convict: Sketches of Some of Their Homes, Haunts, and Habits* – the title clearly indicates the widespread middle-class perception of the lower classes as inherently 'criminal'. Archer could declare that, thanks to architectural and administrative reforms, the Newgate inmate culture described by the outraged 1836 prison inspectors was much diminished. Even so, Archer was clearly prepared to be appalled, or at least titillated, and his account is in effect a 'literary' reading of Newgate, invoking at once the Gothic romances and Newgate novels of an earlier period and the commonplace othering of the lower classes by middle-class social commentary, which represents those others as 'savages' or

'beasts'. Aiming to undergo vicariously, for himself and his readers, the experience of someone entering Newgate as a prisoner, Archer proceeds. 'Having
obtained the necessary credentials, I present myself before the darkly frown-
ing prison entrance and, ascending the high flight of stone steps, peep between
the long iron spikes and look into the lobby, before I ring the bell by the long
iron handle which hangs beside the gate'.[75] Entering, he notes 'that the prison-
like elements of the building are evident even at this early stage'. Proceeding,
he observes that 'many of the corridors and lobbies remain entirely unaltered
in their gloomy strength and dark intricacy' – an aspect that, as critics of Newgate long complained, made observation and supervision, and hence control of
prisoners difficult. Archer passes a room with interior windows, where prisoners
may meet their legal counsel before trial.

> Beyond this, and looking into one of the yards, is a partition of iron bars closely inter-
> twined with a network of twisted wire; at a distance of about three feet from this are
> more upright iron bars, behind which, in the yard, the prisoners stand to talk to their
> friends, who speak to them through the trellis-work in the lobby, so that they are
> separated in such a manner that no other than verbal communications are possible,
> especially as an officer walks up and down in the intermediate space. Very strange and
> melancholy it is to see a place like a doubly secured cage for wild beasts by which it is
> necessary for these unfortunate wretches to be separated from their fellows lest they
> should attempt some further breach of the law.[76]

Following the route that a newly admitted prisoner would typically be taken,
Archer continues to the main building, entering a great hall, with two staircases
leading to the basement and doors to prisoners' cells. Descending to the basement, Archer finds 'two large but not very light rooms, each containing an ample
bath and means for washing'. Here the newly admitted prisoner is cleansed and
his clothes likewise in another room. Here, too, the prisoner has his hair cut
and is shaved, if necessary, and he dons prison garb. 'It is astonishing', Archer
notes, 'how these regulations and the greyish-brown jacket and trousers seem
to obliterate the identity of the prisoners to a casual observer'.[77] The uniform
incorporates the individual prisoner into a mass, to the observer and, perhaps
the intention was, to the prisoner himself or herself. Untried prisoners and those
on remand could remain individuals, for the time being, as they need not wear
the uniform and had other privileges, such as having their own food brought in.
The convict, however, is placed under full regulations.

After being examined by a doctor and having an 'interview' with the chaplain,
the prisoner is taken through a stout door into a cell and put to work 'picking
oakum'.[78] Archer describes the space, which is clearly designed to eradicate physical as well as moral 'contagion':

Perhaps the most terrible thing about the aspect of the cell itself is its intense and hopeless cleanliness. Everything within it is so bare and spotless that no association of ideas can cling to it or serve to break its blank monotony. The flat walls are whitened so that the print of a thumbnail might be discovered on their unbroken surface. The light from the small high window falls upon nothing that will cast a fanciful shadow. The floor is of asphalte, never washed, but dry-rubbed; firm, but almost noiseless to the tread. The furniture consists of a fixed copper basin for washing, over which stands a water tap, supplied from a separate cistern holding as many gallons of water as may suffice for all purposes of cleanliness and for drinking; a small, square flap of white deal, fastened to the wall by hinges, supported by a movable bracket, and used as a table; a three-legged wooden stool; and a nest of three deal shelves. The prisoner sleeps in a hammock suspended from wall to wall by four hasps, and containing a bed and as many blankets as may be found necessary for comfort. Over the table is a gas jet, protected by a white-painted tin shade, but of course without a tap, the gas being turned on from outside. The hammock is slung before eight o'clock at night, at which hour the gas is turned out; and at six o'clock in the morning the prisoner cleans out his cell, the bedding is taken down, folded in regular order, so that it may be inspected at a glance, and packed on the top shelf. The lower shelves contain the tin porringer holding about a quart, a tin plate, a spoon, and a tin knife—sharp iron instruments being forbidden, not so much on account of their being used in any endeavour to escape, but to guard against any momentary temptation to self-injury in that excess of excitement and misery which frequently supervenes immediately after conviction. In one corner of the lower shelf is a Bible, a prayer-book, and some volume for general reading which is supplied from the prison library, and may be changed every day if the prisoner should desire it. It is pleasant to see a volume of a well-known magazine, cheerfully wholesome and amusing in its character, lying there; and indeed this is a merciful—nay, only a just—arrangement, when we count the weary hours in which the evildoer is left to wait sitting at his work for the coming of the gaoler who brings his food. The separation of the prisoners is entire, the lock being turned upon them in their cells for the whole day, except during the two hours' exercise in the yard and the three quarters of an hour spent at chapel.[79]

This is the sublime of unhomeliness, the opposite of the lower-class 'homes, haunts, and habits' that it was the purpose of Archer's book – manifestly not aimed at the lower classes themselves – to describe. Archer implies that in this way, with the thorough institution of the separate system, the old Newgate inmate culture seemed to have been tamed and Newgate 'cleansed' of it at last.

Archer goes on to the chapel, which he finds satisfyingly Gothic: 'as gloomy-looking a place of worship as can be seen anywhere away from the old underground vaults beneath Canterbury Cathedral, and there is the same air of secrecy and suppression pervading it'. One Gothic suppresses another: it is the 'suppression' effected by the prison regime that has eliminated the outmoded 'Gothic' of lower-class culture and 'habits'. While at chapel, the prisoners are overseen by several officers, 'and, of course, all attempts to speak to each other are instantly repressed', and 'the same regulation is observed in the exercise yards'.

This is the addition of an element of the 'silent' system where the 'separate' system might be compromised. Archer learns that 'unruly' prisoners were put on a bread and water diet or, if persistent, confined in 'the dark cell'; here, 'a few hours are frequently enough to bring a stubborn rebel to submission'.[80] Archer finds the exercise yards 'quiet enough, since, as each detachment of prisoners go out for exercise, they walk apart from each other and under constant surveillance'. This scene was mournfully depicted by the French artist Gustave Doré in a well-known illustration published in Blanchard Jerrold's *London: A Pilgrimage* (1872), and later copied by Vincent Van Gogh in 1890. 'In the old time', Archer observes, 'these yards were scenes of profanity, obscenity, and wild riot, which it seemed impossible to check, much more to control.' On the stairs to the main building, Archer observes spy-holes, formerly used by the jailers to look 'into the dark and filthy wards to note the riots of the ruffians who were confined there'. 'Not unfrequently', Archer notes, indulging himself in the kind of sensationalism that Newgate seemed to invite, 'some brutal [inmate] sentinel would, in his turn, watch for the appearance of an eye at one of these holes, which widen into a square aperture on the room-side, and make a dart at it with a burnt stick or some sharp weapon amidst a yell of groans and curses'.[81]

Archer goes on to visit the condemned cells, which, however, he finds have 'little to excite the imagination', apart from the 'awful reflections' with which the cells are associated. On being asked, his guide assures him that capital punishment is indeed a deterrent. Archer also learns that the prisoners have good food, and they can see the governor of the prison whenever they want by pulling a handle to a corridor bell, summoning a jailer, though it has been necessary to add a mechanical device identifying which cell has issued the summons, 'lest some of the unruly might ring this bell for their own amusement'.[82] It seems Newgate culture is not entirely tamed, an appearance confirmed when Archer learns that 'One common trick of the prisoners in Newgate is to save a few spoonfuls of their gruel, and, after diluting it from the water tap, to ring for the governor, in order to complain of the bad quality of the food'. To counteract this 'trick', the jailers keep a portion of the original batch of gruel for comparison. Archer continues on to the 'female side of Newgate', finding that it 'resembles the male side in almost every particular, with the addition of a commodious laundry'.[83]

There is now little for Archer to see but the 'final localities', which 'are full of associations too terrible to dwell upon': these are the passages by which the condemned leave the prison to the gallows in the street outside. Archer is led through a corridor beneath which the executed are buried, their graves marked only by initials carved on the wall above – a final suppression of lower-class individuality and identity. He reaches the 'bread-room', which is where the daily bread ration is cut up but also where a closet contains mementoes of the past, such as what are purported to be Jack Sheppard's fetters, weighing twenty-nine pounds, as well as the straps and belt still used to bind those about to be hanged – the latter a testimony to the inability of prisoners any longer to achievement of Sheppard's famous escape, symbolized by the discarded fetters. Archer reaches the prison kitchen, the door of which, he finds, is the so-called 'debtors' door', by which debtors formerly entered the prison, but which later became the door through which the condemned were taken out to be hanged in the street. Archer pauses briefly in the lodge anteroom to examine the exhibit of plaster casts taken from the faces of the hanged, which he finds to his surprise 'not evidently much distorted'. He turns to go, for 'the air of Newgate clogs and stifles with a strange oppression'. And, perhaps finding he was not as shocked by his visit as he hoped to be, he indulges a last flight of imagination:

> The figure, which, even in spite of an occasionally assumed bravado, is cowed with trembling horror, gasping till the shoulders work in spasms as it is led slowly onward; the wild imploring tenacity of that final grasp of the gaoler's hand, which is held as though it were felt to be the last remaining spar upon which to keep a moment's hold of life before the final hurling into the awful, fathomless sea beyond; the sickening moment, when the sheriffs recoil behind the drapery, holding their fingers in their ears to stop the sound of the sharp click of the bolt and the thud of the falling trap; the swaying crowd rolling and surging in one awful wave of white upturned faces, all pass before me like an unearthly dream, till I find myself waiting at the grim, spiked door to be let out into the glimpse of sunshine and the morning air. [84]

Having in imagination become the mere 'figure' – an 'it' – of the criminal about to be hanged, Archer returns to himself, becoming once again a free and self-possessed 'I'. At the end of his tour, Archer has managed to experience, or induce in himself, the source of Newgate's fascination to those who believed themselves above, or outside it: the thought that there where the condemned went, but for the grace of God, or good fortune, or better circumstances and what are now called 'life choices', he himself might have gone. It is a moment similar to those described by Charles Dickens in 'A Visit to Newgate' and William Makepeace Thackeray in 'Going to See a Man Hanged'.[85] It is a moment, however fleeting, in which the middle-class professional person experiences the moral economy of his social 'other', the crowd.

'Scenes of Profanity, Obscenity, and Wild Riot': Newgate Culture and the Moral Economy of the Crowd

When Archer visited Newgate in the 1860s, the 'scenes of profanity, obscenity, and wild riot' for which it had been notorious seemed relegated by architectural and administrative reform to the past. Yet even in the cleansed, 'separated' and highly regulated Newgate, prisoners found ways, as people will, to assert some independence and seize some pleasure, if only by teasing the jailers and governor with small 'tricks' such as pulling on the summons bell or making spurious complaints about the food or at times going so far as to be 'unruly' – though this meant additional punishment – and even, on occasion, harming themselves. The regulations, precautions, and punishments that Archer observed, was shown and was told about are witness to the continued difficulty, despite separate cells, bars, wire mesh and 'surveillance', of controlling prisoners for the purposes of the state and of the property owners who controlled the state in their own interests. Our knowledge of modern prisons with similar regimes of regulation and surveillance makes it hard to believe that there was not much more that went on in reformed Newgate that Archer did not see and was not told about. In *A Just Measure of Pain: The Penitentiary in the Industrial Revolution 1750–1850* (1978), Michael Ignatieff refers to 'inmate subcultures' in Newgate and other prisons, that were supposed to be eradicated in the new model prisons such as Millbank, based on constant surveillance, and Pentonville, based on separation and isolation. In his essay on the creation of the 'well-ordered prison' between 1780 and 1850, Randall McGowen refers to 'prison culture' as a version of the plebeian culture outside the prison.[86] In these accounts, inmate culture was indicated by several features. There was the extraction of 'garnish', or the payment of a fee, from new inmates by those already imprisoned and other inmate 'rules', sometimes actually written up and posted on the wall. Prisoners held 'trials' of those who broke these rules, and disputes might be settled by more or less formally arranged boxing matches or trial by combat. The prison keeper and jailers, government inspectors found, not only did not suppress such practices, but tacitly condoned them, and even collaborated with them as a way of maintaining some kind of presentable order within the prison. A distinctively female inmate culture is described in the memoirs of G. L. Chesterton, former military officer and supporter of the silent system, recounting what he saw as his success in repressing if not eradicating inmate culture during his time as governor of Coldbath Fields prison from 1828; selections are included in this volume. The extent and persistence of an inmate identity and certain social and cultural practices in Newgate and similar prisons suggest that here was more than a subculture; here was a distinctive culture and moral economy, or set of values, beliefs, and social and economic practices – ones, moreover, that were continuous with those of the world outside Newgate.

There is plenty of evidence of the nature of Newgate inmate culture. Besides the observations and testimony of successive visitors, keepers, jailers, chaplains, parliamentary committees and others, there was the testimony of prisoners themselves. In the mid-1790s these included middle-class reformists and publishers imprisoned in the crackdown on political dissidence and who formed what Iain McCalman has called a 'prison republic' of shared political and cultural values and prison social life.[87] Somewhat later witnesses included the outraged middle-class inmates who dashed off protest pamphlets after release, such as William Hodgson, included in this volume, or Richard Andrews, referred to earlier in this introduction. There were also those unnamed prisoners summoned before the various inquiries, investigations and inspections that marked the heyday of Newgate discourse, or the field of discussion, debate, legislation and speculation on crime and punishment, centred on the reality and the symbol of Newgate prison, in the first third of the nineteenth century. Some of the testimony from these compelled witnesses is also included in this volume. Of course all of these testimonies except those of the middle-class radical reformists and inmate-pamphleteers were filtered through the state apparatus itself, with use of leading questions by the committees and inspectors, self-censorship by the prisoners themselves, and unknown consequences in the 'cleaning up' of witnesses' language and testimony. Nevertheless, these testimonies enable us to form a picture of leading features of Newgate inmate culture. As E. P. Thompson, the historian of working-class identity, culture and politics in this period, urges, such evidence should be looked at 'not with a moralizing eye ... but with an eye for Brechtian values—the fatalism, the irony in the face of Establishment homilies, the tenacity of self-preservation', and bearing in mind 'the "underground" of the ballad-singer and the fair-ground' – and prison, one should add – 'which handed on traditions to the nineteenth century'. It was in such ways, Thompson argues, that 'the "inarticulate" conserved certain values—a spontaneity and capacity for enjoyment and mutual loyalties—despite the inhibiting pressures of magistrates, mill-owners, and Methodists'.[88]

In Newgate culture, then, there was more or less collusion between wardsmen, who were chosen by prison management from the prisoners, and the prisoners themselves as to how laxly official rules could be enforced for the convenience of all. Furthermore, there was a persistent 'spontaneity and capacity for enjoyment'. There was a good deal of drinking and smoking in Newgate and, prison food being poor in quality, extra food was brought in by those who could afford to do so or who had friends and family to supply money for the purpose. There was much playing of games, including cards and board games, often with improvised materials and often involving gambling – the classic expression of lower-class 'fatalism' in the face of the realities of a subsistence economy, from which 'luck' or the lottery offered one of the few escapes. There was probably a certain amount of reading individually and reading aloud by the literate to the illiterate. As ever, these 'undisciplined' readers read what interested them and what interested them was not 'escapism' but narratives that addressed their readers' real material interests. Before 1800 such reading would have included 'street literature' that embodied, in plot, character and mythic form, the historic plebeian lottery mentality; after 1800 such reading would have included the new kind of sensational chapbooks that were drastically shortened versions of middle-class

Sentimental, Gothic and Romantic novels, or novelizations of theatrical forms of such fiction. Another form of this new plebeian literature was in the daily newspapers and especially Sunday newspapers, which were more sensational and included crime news, and these were taken and loaned or rented about to others, including jailers. Some prisoners read such books as could be obtained, probably by chance, and these seem to have been very diverse, but likely included some 'self-improvement' literature.

Much time was spent in the yards and talking to other prisoners, or in such activities as having literate fellow inmates write up statements for trial or other purposes, often for hire. At night, when prisoners were locked in the wards, there was talking, singing, telling stories, playing pranks, especially on inmates who may have broken the prisoners' code of moral economy, and probably in some cases sexual activity. Prisoners seem to have expected to make the best of a bad situation but to be treated more or less fairly, as they understood it, by each other and by the prison administration, and they could individually or collectively take revenge on anyone, jailer, prisoner, or visitor, whom they felt to have crossed the line of fair play. Though often dirty themselves, prisoners had a sense of when someone was too filthy to be tolerated, and had to be attended to or dealt with by themselves or by the prison management. No doubt there was some exploitation of the weak by the strong, and ignoring of the plight of the worse off by the better off, but there also seems to have been a shared understanding of how much of this should be tolerated by the collective body. Prisoners also seem to have had a good sense of when to play along with administration, inspectors, philanthropic and evangelizing visitors, or journalists when it suited their interests to do so. Prisoners also felt able to reject unwanted philanthropy, such as donation of Bibles and prayer-books and would destroy these. There seems to have been a status culture according to seriousness or ingenuity of crime committed. Prisoners could be creative in burlesquing, mocking, and appropriating the social and legal procedures and rituals of the system and society that had incarcerated and condemned them;[89] in this way, prisoners collectively could gain a symbolic ascendancy over that system. Finally and perhaps above all, it is clear that narratives, about themselves and other criminals, reinforced by similar narratives in books and especially newspapers, formed a large part of inmate culture.

There was clearly a 'moral economy' among the prisoners – tolerated, shared in and at times used to some extent by the prison administration for their own convenience and objectives. This moral economy was a largely unspoken collective sense of what was right and wrong, just and unjust, fair and unfair, acceptable and unacceptable, in relation to the prisoners' own experience, reality, expectations and interests.[90] It included a sense of what Thompson calls 'mutual loyalties'. It was the same moral economy that prevailed outside the prison but adapted to prison conditions. Though occasionally imposed on others by force, this moral economy was not imposed by all on all or at all times and in fact it was enforced only when occasion prompted, opportunity presented and a sufficient number of inmates felt moved to enforce it. It was the moral economy specifically of the lower classes, who made up the majority of the prisoners – even more so after Newgate ceased holding debtors, among whom would have been a high proportion of middle- and lower-middle-class people, that is, the kind of people who could afford or be allowed to incur debt. The plebeian moral economy seemed alien and threatening to middle-class inmates, including imprisoned working- and middle-class political reformists, who lived by a different moral economy, of investment in moral and intellectual capital and 'progress' in life, and even in society and government, though theirs may have accommodated elements of the plebeian one. The plebeian moral economy was based on and shaped by centuries of experience of living in a subsistence economy, sometimes called poverty, at that time a condition in which the individual and entire communities would have a strong sense that their ability to survive, let alone prosper, was not in their control. Prison only presented a more sharply focused instance of that experience.

In a subsistence economy, physical survival depended on a combination of cleverness, ethical flexibility, opportunism, rapid adaptability, the assistance (when available) of family and immediate peer community, a consistent nurturing of such relationships of mutuality, a willingness to act with solidarity in crises and luck. To survive psychologically required moral relativism, an ability to live for and in the moment and a certain fatalism or ability to be resigned to the apparently inevitable, while remaining alert to opportunity. The lower classes' perception that their life was a kind of lottery, or game of chance, was distinct from the perception of most middle-class people that life could or should be based on investment – in knowledge, skills, and self-discipline, as well as in profession or business – or planned progress to prosperity. The plebeian lottery mentality could be manifested in various ways. For most, it meant living for the pleasures of the moment, which the middle classes often perceived as the kind of 'riot and debauchery' found in Newgate by the 1836 prison inspectors and by generations of other observers before and after. 'Riot' here meant 'revelry' but also 'wasteful living', or improvidence – what middle-class social reformers liked to see as the improvidence that, rather than systemic economic exploitation, they blamed for poverty and crime. Inevitably, the lower classes' lottery mentality generated also a strong interest in luck or chance, manifested in such pastimes as gambling, lotteries, fortune telling and narratives in which coincidence or chance played a large part, such as stories of adventure and – increasingly in the nineteenth century – crime. Not surprisingly, middle-class social reformers worked hard to discourage, abolish, or criminalize such pursuits and such stories. For some lower-class people this fatalism did take the form of religious piety or a sustaining hope, against the evidence, that economic justice, clearly unavailable from human agents here and now, would be provided by divine agency if not in this life then in the life hereafter. This was the line worked so hard by successive prison chaplains and evangelical prison visitors. When lower-class people did turn to religion in this period, however, it was increasingly to forms alternative to the established state church and the social hierarchies it served, to millenarian movements led by plebeian prophets such as Joanna Southcott, to Methodism or to other predominantly lower-class 'sects'.

From time to time, however, as during the 'Gordon Riots' of 1780 when Newgate and other public institutions were attacked, the lower-class moral economy, or collective sense of justice and right, could quickly be transformed into what the middle classes perceived as 'riot' of another kind – 'mob' action, tumult and violence.[91] In such events, riot as revelry and riot as protest and tumult could be combined. As the historian V. A. C. Gattrell has recently pointed out, more frequent exhibitions of the way these different kinds of riot come together occurred at public executions, often accompanied by a carnivalesque atmosphere and sometimes breaking out into crowd protest or even violence[92] – eventually inducing the authorities to remove the place of execution from Tyburn to the constricted area outside Newgate and, in 1868, to move executions inside the prison. By the heyday of Newgate discourse in the late eighteenth and early nineteenth century such 'riot' increasingly took the form of overtly political resistance, protest and activism, though rarely amounting to violence. The lower classes always knew that their abjection was at least partly if not predominantly a consequence of their economic exploitation, and they could in certain circumstances mobilize in various kinds of action. A long-established form of such action was what they perceived as their 'right to riot', or the right to engage in short-term protest or punishment, such as the 'bread riot' or the execution of 'rough justice'. In the bread 'riot', members of a community would deal with what they perceived to be exploitatively high food prices by temporarily taking over the food supplier and selling the commodity at what the crowd considered a fair price. 'Rough justice' would involve property destruction or public mocking or physical rough treatment by a crowd, often wearing disguises, as a warning to or punishment of a community member or social superior perceived by the crowd to have transgressed a communal moral or social standard. What the property-owning classes saw as a 'riot', the 'rioting' classes may on certain occasions have seen as an expression and assertion of their sense of economic and social justice. What the property-owning classes saw as the irrational act of a 'mob', the 'mob' may on certain occasions have seen as a necessary and reassuring demonstration of the communal values and collective power of what historians now prefer to call the 'crowd'. By the late eighteenth and early nineteenth century more enduring forms of lower-class economic and political organization and militancy were emerging and Britons of all classes had the inspiring or alarming spectacle across the channel in France of violent and prolonged political revolution, in which the lower classes were at times the prime agents. Henceforth it would be difficult for many in the property-owning classes in Britain not to see any form of lower-class 'riot', even in a prison, as a manifestation of otherwise submerged class grievance and perhaps a prelude to more comprehensive 'unruliness' or revolution. Control of lower-class 'riot', and the moral economy that motivated it, became more pressing; one response to this pressure was Newgate discourse, exemplified in documents in this volume.

For, clearly, the plebeian moral economy was not determined by, and did not necessarily coincide with, the values, beliefs and practices of other classes, or with religiously-based or ecclesiastically promulgated standards of 'virtue' and 'vice', or – for those who fell foul of the police and the courts – with the regime of the criminal laws, state judicial process, or with prison administration. If on occasions the lower classes invoked their moral economy in terms of middle- or upper-class values, church morality or state institutions of legality, it was likely because they momentarily saw it as in their interest to do so and not because they had been indoctrinated by or internalized those others' values and interests. Furthermore, since the accidents of mortality, the vagaries of weather and climate, the hazards of business and trade, and numerous other instances of 'chance' had a prominent role in lives of people in all classes over the centuries, many people in other classes could share, to different degrees, in the moral economy of the lower classes or at least see some validity in it. There was, or had been up to the late eighteenth century, a high degree of collaboration by all classes in 'customs in common' – a recognition of mutual interdependence, reinforced by seasonal festivals, regular social and cultural rituals and 'manners', or shared codes of social conduct.[93] By the time Newgate discourse began to burgeon in the 1770s, however, major transformations in economy and society were altering such attitudes. Inevitably, these transformations had an impact on Newgate discourse, Newgate inmate culture, and Newgate itself; in fact, Newgate discourse was a creation of these transformations and participated in them.

Accelerated by the demands of Britain's imperial wars over nearly a century, the modernization of the economy and state in the eighteenth century involved several factors: the more rigorous application of capitalist methods of production, increased efficiency (or at least effectiveness) in government and administration, from the national to the local level; increased professionalization and the rise of the professional middle class to intellectual and cultural, if not yet political, hegemony; and the rise of a 'fashion system' of commercialized consumption built on class distinction and emulation. In this complex process, it was the lower or labouring classes who felt themselves to be the losers, losing customary 'rights' such as access to common lands, periodic food doles and the 'right to riot', losing hard-won and fiercely-defended historic freedoms such as when and how to work, and being increasingly subjected to a wage economy and controlled work regimes. At the same time, the labouring classes perceived that social distances between ranks and classes were widening; that they themselves were increasingly the objects of suspicion, surveillance and control, including criminalization, incarceration and exile, by the upper and middle classes; that their moral economy was coming increasingly under attack as irrational 'tradition' and 'superstition'; that their festivals, rituals and ceremonies were being suppressed and outlawed; that their culture, pleasures and patterns of consumption were increasingly being reprobated, regulated, discouraged and banned; and that the dominant classes were attempting to replace the plebeians' moral economy with a simplified version of those classes' own ideology and worldview, through such activities as promotion of evangelical religion. In short, modernization could, and to many in the lower classes did, have the appearance of deliberate class conflict or class warfare. It may be understandable, then, that many in the lower classes resisted these campaigns to eradicate and replace their historic moral economy, culture, customary 'rights' and control of working conditions, and saw such campaigns to 'reform' the lower classes, ostensibly for their own good, as serving the economic interests of the upper- and middle-class people conducting it.

Certainly the leaders of this multi-faceted national crusade – since the church and Christianity were often adapted as weapons, the metaphor seems appropriate – were members of the professional, commercial and administrative middle classes. They included people already noted here, such as William Whitworth Russell, colonial judge's son, clergyman, religious evangelical, chaplain of Millbank prison and government inspector of prisons; and William Crawford, wine merchant's son, civil servant, religious evangelical and also government inspector of prisons. They included authors of the numerous Newgate narratives of all kinds that issued from press and parliament during the period covered by the present series of volumes, and aimed at subjecting Newgate and the entire penal system and its predominantly lower-class inmates to the larger process of modernization across a wide range of endeavour. There was the reformer of prison space, Jacob Leroux, professional architect and justice of the peace and author of *Thoughts on the Present State of the Prisons of This Country, Exemplified by a Plan, Adapted to the Objects of Such Consideration* (1780). There was the legal reformer Martin Madan, a judge's grandson, military officer's son and Methodist preacher. There was the moral philosopher William Paley, clergyman's son, Cambridge mathematician and bishop in the state church. There was the political economist and prison-building entrepreneur Jeremy Bentham, son of a London attorney and brother of an innovative factory designer and manager – the source of Bentham's 'panopticon' prison system. There was the humanitarian prison reformer John Howard, the most famous such reformer in the English speaking world, son of a London businessman in the carpet and upholstery trade. There was the former Dissenting clergyman and political theorist and professional writer William Godwin, himself the son of a Dissenting clergyman. There was the law reformer and politician Sir Samuel Romilly, son of a London jeweller and for a time himself a jeweller. There was the private prison investigator James Neild, retired London jeweler. And so on, through the Newgate narrators whose work is excerpted in this volume, with a few exceptions from upper-class backgrounds, such as William Eden and Henry Grey Bennett. To such people, as their writings show, Newgate and its inmate culture were just a particular instance among many others, though a particularly striking and symbolic one – and hence widely publicized – of the larger and crucial task of subjecting the lower classes as a whole to the process of economic and social modernization and the reformation of Britain as a modern state.

'The Low Publications, of which There Are Now so Many Sold': 'Newgate Literature', the Rise of the 'Popular Press', and Middle-class Moral Panic

By the last decades of the eighteenth century, many economic and social modernizers and uprooters of the lower-class moral economy had, quite correctly, begun focusing their attention on lower-class print culture as a sustainer of the plebeian moral economy, a possible source of ideological contamination of middle-class children and youths and a seedbed for a dissident and even revolutionary lower-class politics. By the 1830s, such concerns had blossomed again into a middle-class moral panic, much of it focused on Newgate narratives of kinds widely consumed by the lower classes. Today, such narratives may seem innocuous enough. Alongside the Newgate narratives in this volume written by and for the property-owning classes are a few examples from the street literature produced for and read by the lower classes and lower-middle classes. There is a much reduced and adapted chapbook version from about 1810 of Daniel's Defoe's fictitious criminal autobiography, *The Fortunes and Misfortunes of the Famous Moll Flanders*, originally published 1722. There is a true crime biography of George Foster, hanged in 1803 for domestic murder, from an 1810 edition, originally published in cheap serial parts of the often reprinted *Newgate Calendar*. There is a ballad of the kind hawked about the street and at fairs, 'Newgate Walls', from about 1820, which laments the plight of convicts transported to the penal colony of Australia and celebrates return to England. There is a chapbook true crime biography from about 1820 of the eighteenth-century highwayman Dick Turpin (1706–39), perhaps the most famous highway robber in the English-speaking world after Robin Hood and the inspiration for numerous novels and plays, including such Newgate novels as Edward Bulwer's *Paul Clifford* (1830) and Harrison Ainsworth's bestselling *Rookwood* (1834). And there is a catch-penny account from 1848 of the trial of Annette Myers, a domestic servant, for murdering her unfaithful lover, a soldier. These examples of Newgate narratives from the street, though incorporating some of the moralistic tone of texts by the likes of prison reformers, evangelical crusaders and government prison inspectors, convey nevertheless a sense of the human dimension of crime experienced by its perpetrators, whether it is as a challenge and adventure, an exercise of ingenuity and skill against the odds, an apparently inescapable destiny, an affliction that can be survived or an ultimate act of self-assertion. For these and related characteristics, the lower- and middle-class reading public and theatre audiences avidly consumed Newgate street narratives of all kinds, from reports of the kind read by Newgate inmates in the Sunday newspapers, through the ballads, chapbooks and true crime narratives presented here, to stage melodramas.

For these and related characteristics, too, by the 1830s such Newgate narratives were widely condemned and where possible suppressed and banned by the likes of prison reformers, evangelical crusaders and prison inspectors, among others. They did so because such people were, or professed to be, fearful that these narratives would not only condone Newgate culture, both inside and outside prison, but even contaminate other classes, perhaps their own, with it. 'Newgate literature', as it was called, was viewed with a kind of moral panic by middle-class religious and social reformers and named as one of the principal causes of crime, because it supposedly sentimentalized and glamourized crime and criminals, inspiring imitation, especially among the young. The notion of 'moral panic' was developed by sociologists and cultural theorists in the 1960s and 70s to describe the over-reaction to a 'crisis' in youth and drug culture on the part of media, public institutions, and government – a crisis which these bodies had partly invented and whipped up for their own purposes. The notion of 'moral panic' was then extended to describe particular instances of a dominant order's constant efforts to exercise surveillance, discipline and control over subordinate and potentially or actually dissident social groups.[94] In this, its 'classic' formulation, the notion of moral panic applies well to the response to 'Newgate literature' in the 1830s and 40s, in which professionals, government prison inspectors, members of parliament and others joined to invent a 'crisis' implicating Newgate culture, the moral economy of the lower classes, popular print and crime, eventually bringing in the form of middle-class fiction known as the 'Newgate novel'. The 'classic' model of moral panic also applies well to the history of the wider 'problem' of popular print culture from at least the 1790s; in this panic, cheap political literature and cheap fiction and drama were linked.

During the British debate of the early 1790s over the significance and relevance of the French Revolution for Britain itself, the upper and middle classes were shocked and alarmed by evidence that the lower classes were buying hundreds of thousands of cheap copies of Tom Paine's *Rights of Men*, and some commentators linked the market for cheap political literature to the market for cheap fiction and other kinds of literature. Hannah More, a prominent religious Evangelical[95] and social crusader, identified the historic repertory of street literature as a 'sans-culotte library', alluding to the lower-class revolutionaries or 'sans-culottes' of Paris, and indicating an alternative print culture which, these commentators supposed, fostered the same values among the lower classes that led to social insubordination and that served as a seedbed for dissident lower-class politics.[96] More tried to stop sale of traditional forms of street literature and created her own 'Cheap Repository' of chapbooks and ballads, which promoted 'correct' social, political and religious values, to supplant the traditional forms. When the task proved too large for More, it was taken over by a committee that formed itself as the Religious Tract Society, which carried on the work into the twentieth century. To an extent, More and other middle-class commentators were right to associate lower-class fiction and lower-class politics. From about 1800, enterprising publishers of cheap print, many of whom had reformist political sympathies, refurbished the traditional street literature repertory by printing it in more stylish formats and adding drastically cut-down versions of fashionable middle-class novels and novelizations of popular dramas, adapted to the form of the traditional street literature.[97] Alongside such 'entertaining' literature, these publishers also printed cheap reformist political literature of various kinds, creating in the first two decades of the century, along with cheap newspapers and magazines, a lively and manifestly distinct body of print embodying lower-class and lower-middle-class culture and politics. The response from leaders of the property-owning classes was to reprint More's 'Cheap Repository', to expand the Religious Tract Society's program and similar efforts, to found educational institutes and libraries of 'good' literature for 'mechanics' (that is, artisans or skilled manual labourers), to publish cheap magazines (such as the *Penny Magazine*, quoted earlier) that contained 'solid and useful' reading and that purposely excluded both fiction and politics, and to apply taxes to cheap papers and magazines to drive up the price.

By the early 1820s and the national political crisis of the 'Queen Caroline Affair' (see introduction to Volume 2), it was clear that the lower-class and lower-middle-class culture and politics embodied in cheap print had converged in the issues of and movement for political and institutional reform. As discussed earlier, Newgate was implicated in these issues; so was 'Newgate literature'; but they did not become the focus of a middle-class moral panic until after the eventual passage of the Great Reform Act in 1832. The Act marked a significant turning point in the struggle of the lower and middle classes to gain access to government and state institutions of power, historically dominated and controlled by the landed or upper classes acting together with the crown and royal court and assisted by members of the professional and financial middle classes. By the late 1820s and early 1830s it was clear that some such access to the excluded had to be conceded by the ruling class or there could be a violent revolution, perhaps dominated by a coalition of lower and middle classes, as in the early stages of the French Revolution. In the prolonged agitation preceding passage of the Great Reform Bill, such a coalition had in fact been mobilized and, more importantly, organized, in the Political Unions formed at Birmingham and elsewhere to campaign for parliamentary and electoral reform.[98] The Reform Act of 1832, among other things, made concessions to the better-off middle classes by extending the vote to male owners of property above a certain value, thereby detaching many in those classes from coalition with the lower classes, making them more inclined to coalition (though not to complete political agreement) with the historic ruling class and, as it turned out, staving off the need for further major extension of access until the 1860s. It was clear to many, however, that the lower classes and lower-middle classes could not be excluded from the political nation indefinitely. The growth of working-class organizations and political agitation in the mid and late 1830s increased and confirmed these apprehensions.

It became a matter of pressing concern, then, to consolidate political power and control of the institutions of state by those admitted to the political nation in 1832, and to achieve greater surveillance and physical control and, if possible, ideological influence over those who continued to be excluded.[99] Reform of policing and the judicial and especially the penal systems was an important part of this program, and was already underway; 'education' of the lower classes was, if anything, even more important. 'Education' of the lower classes, or supplanting their moral economy and subjecting them to the values and culture of their 'betters', would largely obviate the need for state apparatuses of surveillance and control, which were, furthermore, costly. For the recalcitrant, there would be 'model' prisons, also called 'penitentiaries' and 'reformatories' – in these applications, the first term came into use early in the nineteenth century and the second in the 1830s. Of course, these kinds of reforms had been gathering ideological and political impetus since the emergence of reformist Newgate discourse in the last third of the eighteenth century, had been given new urgency by the political and economic crisis and class conflicts of the period of the French Revolution and Napoleonic wars, and had been implemented here and there, in an *ad hoc* but increasingly coordinated manner by the second and third decades of the nineteenth century. Increasing numbers of middle-class-led volunteer societies of all kinds, often with religious association, had been organized since the 1790s, engaged in various humanitarian, philanthropic and educational activities among the lower classes, but with the common objective of overseeing, supervising, disciplining, indoctrinating, reforming and controlling them. To say this is not to gainsay the genuineness of the religious and philanthropic motivations of these organizations, but to observe that these motives also had a dimension of self-interest. By the 1820s there were increasing demands from the middle classes that the government second these efforts or take primary responsibility for them, and for their cost. By the 1830s, the middle classes and the government – now, because of the Reform Bill, more closely associated with that public – were increasingly demanding that this should be the case.

Concern over the contents, diffusion and influence of lower-class print was part of this larger concern with surveillance and control of the lower classes. Just over two years after the Great Reform Act received royal assent, Archibald Alison pointed to the 'problem' of popular print in an article on 'The Influence of the Press' published in the conservative *Blackwood's Edinburgh Magazine*:

> Every one gifted with powers of foresight or historical information, is sensible of the influence of the press, and deplores its present pernicious tendency. Every one sees that it has effected a greater change in human affairs, than either gunpowder or the compass. Every wise man trembles at the perilous tendency of democratic ambition which the extension of political reading, with which it is attended, to the lower orders has given, and every good man laments the ruinous vigour with which the depraved principles of our nature have shot up under its fostering influence; but no one thinks of considering how this new and terrible power is to be mastered, and the dissolving principles with which it is invested, again brought under the dominion of virtue and religion.[100]

In recognition of the growing role of elite literature in consolidating upper-middle-class identity and furthering the coalition of this fraction with landed property and the upper class, Alison distinguished between 'the great works which are destined permanently to delight and instruct mankind' and 'those lighter productions which attract and are alone read by the multitude—newspapers, magazines, reviews, novels, superficial travels'. Alison argued that the cheap press sought wide circulation and hence profits in two main but related ways – by stimulating 'the political or the private passions' of its readers, that is, by flattering its readership as to their political rights and ability to govern, and by appealing to their basest natures with sensational literature. In the first case, Alison observed, 'The immense majority of mankind, totally incapable, from their habits, capacity, and acquirements, of taking any useful part in public affairs, like nothing so much as to be told that they are perfectly qualified to take the lead'. Alison went on to make a revealing comparison: 'The less that they are so qualified, the more are they gratified by being told so; just as a woman who has long been accustomed to the sway of beauty, is less liable to intoxication from its praises, than one who, from a homelier appearance, has been less habituated to resist the insinuating poison'. In other words, the 'lower orders', like a 'homelier' woman, are more liable to be seduced by flattery than the frequently flattered and in fact more 'qualified' upper classes and beautiful women. As to the second case, the appeal of the popular press to its readership's baser natures, Alison observed, 'The licentiousness and depraved character of so large a portion, at least of the lower strata, of the press, is the natural consequence of the inherent corruption of our nature; and of the fatal truth, that the human mind, when left to itself, will take to wickedness as the sparks fly upwards'.

Alison acknowledged that those properly qualified to govern by education, experience and independence of mind based on ownership of substantial property were relatively few, and so could not counter-balance the influence of the many on publishers of cheap print. Furthermore, Alison asserted, 'It is vain to talk of coercing the press by fetters, or prosecutions', for such 'brutal remedies, fit only for a savage age, are in the end totally inadequate to coerce' the 'excesses' of the popular press. The problem, then, was this: 'How are the many to be induced to read works or journals which cease to flatter their vanity, and discard those which do?' Alison clearly set this problem in the context of the aftermath of the Great Reform Act and the continued and vociferous claims of the lower-middle and lower classes to participate in power: 'Who', Alison asked, 'is to persuade the multitude, that property should be the moving, and numbers only the restraining power?'

In proposing a solution to the 'problem' of the popular press in Britain after passage of the Reform Bill, Alison implicitly recalled the dangerous days of the Revolutionary 1790s, the Napoleonic crisis, and such later episodes as the 'Peterloo Massacre' and the 'Queen Caroline affair', when mounted middle-class militias had organized, in the early cases ostensibly to resist a French invasion, but in fact to intimidate lower-class 'mobs'. 'The grand point' Alison proposed, 'is to organize a Conservative militia to combat the force of anarchy with its own weapons; to fight the demons of hell, not with the coarse and vulgar instruments of prosecutions and dungeons, but the diamond of genius and the sword of truth'. What was needed, Alison thought, was a Milton, Newton, Walter Scott or Chateaubriand of the popular press, 'some mighty genius', animated as geniuses are, not by motives of gain but by 'inward inspiration' and 'ebullitions of the *feu sacré*', or sacred fire. Such a one, 'measuring the whole extent of the power to be resisted, and the immeasurable perils consequent on its triumph, shall devise the means of organizing the powers of thought in an effective and systematic manner, in defence of justice, order, and truth, and counter-balancing, by the concentrated influence of government and property, the present overwhelming ascendency of numbers'. As Alison should perhaps have known, such a 'Conservative militia' of the press had been in existence since the 1790s at least. These forces included Hannah More and her 'Cheap Repository', the Religious Tract Society and similar organizations, the Society for the Diffusion of Useful Knowledge, the promoters of 'Mechanics' Institutes' and magazines and such promoters and publishers of 'instructive' and 'improving' literature for the 'lower orders' as Charles Knight and his *Penny Magazine*, begun in the year of the Great Reform Bill, and William and Robert Chambers, publishers of the cheap *Chambers's Edinburgh Journal*, also begun in 1832. Perhaps Alison ignored this already existing 'militia' because it was not 'Conservative' enough or because it had not stemmed the growing tide of 'licentious and depraved' popular print. Furthermore, as Alison also must have known, the government had not shown itself averse to using the 'brutal remedies' and 'coarse and vulgar instruments 'of 'fetters', 'prosecutions' and 'dungeons' to intimidate and suppress the popular press, to just as little avail. Nevertheless, Alison stated clearly the issues involved in the 'problem' of the popular press and his tone and language clearly indicated that the 'problem' was creating a moral panic on the part of those middle- and upper-class people who supported the interests of 'property' and who read such periodicals as *Blackwood's Edinburgh Magazine*.

Newgate literature was a particular and particularly alarming instance of the 'licentious and depraved' print causing this moral panic. A year before Alison's article appeared, Thomas Wontner, criminal court lawyer, son of a Newgate governor and a former teacher in the Newgate school, had formulated the problem of and panic over Newgate literature with particular clarity and edge. In his 1833 book, *Old Bailey Experience* (selections from which are included in this volume), Wontner included a chapter 'On Juvenile Offenders' in which he declared that 'if means could be taken to suppress the low publications, of which there are now so many sold, many boys would be saved from destruction who are now lost entirely by the influence these works have on their vitiated tastes, viz. the fictitious lives of robbers, pirates, and loose women'. By 'loose women' here Wontner would include chapbook stories such as the version of *Moll Flanders* included in this volume. Wontner went on to claim that there was not one such book in print 'that these boys have not by rote; their infatuation for them is unbounded, and the consequent perversion of their minds very fatal, in every instance when this passion seizes them'. Despite their ingrained restlessness, the boys would 'sit for six or eight hours together, relating and hearing tales of criminal heroes'. Some boys even became Newgate narrators themselves, sufficiently 'expert at telling these stories' that the other boys would pay them half their food allowance in return.

Wontner blamed another kind of Newgate narrative – dramatized narrative – for contributing to this reproduction of criminality, in his chapter 'On the Effects of Theatrical Exhibitions on Untaught Boys'. Unlike those who saw all theatrical presentations as corrupting, Wontner approved of the two so-called 'legitimate' or licensed theatres (Drury Lane and Covent Garden), which catered mainly to the upper and middle classes and operated by government permit and under a government-appointed censor of plays and which he thought did 'more than the pulpit in promoting virtue, and in repressing the vicious habits of society'. 'Below' the legitimate theatres, the so-called 'minor' theatres were, Wontner thought, merely entertaining, but nevertheless encouraged their largely lower-middle-class patrons to 'waste the meridian of their youth' at low entertainments that vitiated the taste and encouraged further vulgar pastimes. Much worse, however, were the penny theatres that catered to the 'totally ignorant and uneducated' lower classes, especially the young:

> Here the highwayman, the brigand, the pirate, and even the murderer, are shown under circumstances of the most favourable view; their crimes being either wholly excused, or very much palliated, and a taste engendered among youth for every species of adventure connected with desperate undertakings. Ignorant and uneducated children of both sexes, if constitutionally of a temperament above par, immediately on witnessing these representations, take fire, and imaginatively become heroes and heroines; they set up half the night, imitating to the best of their ability the scenes which they have beheld on the stage; and from that moment all moral restraint on their desires are lost.

Wontner further believed that the pleasure created by such dramas was specifically sexual, declaring that he had 'invariably found' their audiences 'to show more signs of interest, and even internal delight, when one or more deaths are annexed to the catastrophe of the plot of a performance. The excitement evinced both by males and females, is extraordinary, and there cannot remain a doubt but that the sensations at the time are of a pleasurable kind.' Wontner claimed that he knew from personal inquiry among criminal youths that audiences at such performances experienced a kind of erotic excitement similar to that they experienced at public executions, which produced in the males what Wontner termed 'priapism', meaning sexual arousal.[101]

Wontner's concern was so commonplace that it could be given a more humorous turn a few years later in the *Penny Satirist: A Cheap Substitute for a Weekly Newspaper*, which burlesqued periodicals such as the *Penny Magazine* that aimed to wean the lower classes from sensationalist publications. A cartoon in the *Penny Satirist* for 14 December 1839 showed five youths leaving a performance of *Jack Sheppard*, with a dialogue in which the Fifth Juvenile declares, 'Blow'd if I shouldn't just like to be another *Jack Sheppard*—it only wants a little pluck to begin with'.[102] In 1840 the *Examiner* newspaper denounced the 'Newgate school of sentiment' in literature, along with Chartist literature, for giving ammunition to the Conservatives in their resistance to reform.[103] In 1845 the same newspaper observed that 'the Newgate school of drama was objectionable, because it exhibited in a heroic light those qualities which any youthful invader of his master's till might possess, and rendered attractive those exploits that any lubberly ruffian might achieve.'[104] In 1849 this view of the relation between reading or viewing certain kinds of Newgate narrative and living out a similar narrative was given the kind of statistical certainty characteristic of modern state formation, in Thomas Beggs's *Inquiry into the Extent and Causes of Juvenile Depravity*, published in London, Dublin, Liverpool, Edinburgh, Glasgow, and Manchester. Referring to the youths arrested for petty crimes, Beggs declared:

> The amusements of these youths are the low theatres, the dancing saloons, and entertainments of a like description. Many of the penny theatres are frequented only by boys and girls who are already thieves and prostitutes. 'Jack Sheppard,' 'Dick Turpin,' 'Claude Duval,'[105] and other exhibitions of dexterous and daring crime attract the attention and the ambition of these boys, and each one endeavours to emulate the conduct of his favourite hero. In fact, what the stage representations of a former period have done to excite the admiration of the vulgar for military and naval glory, these wretched places effect for the unhappy youths brought within the sphere of their influence. In a continual whirl of excitement and intoxication, the boy learns the lessons which finish the candidate for the Penal Settlements, if disease or death does not arrest his career. Few who traverse the gay streets of the Metropolis, have any conception of the number of pitfalls, showily and artfully covered over, but full of misery and wickedness, 'of rottenness and dead men's bones.'[106]

To confirm his assertion, Beggs adduced the following table,[107] taken from a survey in one prison of inmates convicted at trial and by summary conviction by a magistrate. The table was 'intended to show the degree of ignorance in prisoners, on the most ordinary subjects, as compared to their direct or indirect acquaintance with demoralizing literature':

DEGREES OF IGNORANCE, &c.	SESSIONS.			SUMMARY.		
	M.	F.	PER CENT.	M.	F.	PER CENT.
Unable to name the months	156	53	61.8	486	147	60.5
Ignorant of the name of the reigning sovereign	154	46	59.1	489	129	59.1
Ignorant of the words, 'virtue,' 'vice,' &c.	157	51	61.5	479	132	58.4
Unable to count a hundred	8	15	6.8	103	31	12.8
Having read, or heard read, Books about Dick Turpin and Jack Sheppard	146	32	52.6	392	68	44.0

The observation regarding prisoners having 'heard read' books that were 'demoralizing' recognized that many of the prisoners would have been illiterate, but could nevertheless be contaminated by stories of criminal adventure featuring true crime or fictionalized accounts of the highwaymen Dick Turpin and Jack Sheppard. Of course it did not occur to Beggs, or if it did occur to him he suppressed the thought, that the juveniles interviewed were simply pulling the interviewer's leg.

A year after Beggs's book appeared, the London *Morning Chronicle* newspaper noted with alarm:

> We are persuaded that there can be no greater bane to a country in which a certain amount of intelligence and of taste for reading prevails among the poorer classes, than the cheap diffusion of low and corrupting publications. We fear it is but too true that the multiplication of those noxious productions, which belong to the 'JACK SHEPPARD' style of literature, tends most powerfully at the present time to undermine the morals of the young, and to initiate them into a career of profligacy and crime. The reports of our Special Correspondents have borne ample testimony to this fact. In some of our manufacturing towns, it appears that a very extensive demand exists for the low catch-penny tracts and serials in which translations of vile French novels, fictions that outrage sense and decency, and biographies of the Newgate Calendar school, afford the exciting mental aliment for the million. The last-named class of publications in particular, by which ruffians and desperadoes are exalted into heroes of Romance, have been, in many instances, as the same Reports attest, the acknowledged sources of juvenile depravity.[108]

Newspaper reports continued to circulate that young criminals had been inspired to their misdeeds, like the murderer Courvoisier (see below), by reading Newgate literature. In 1851, for example, the London *Morning Chronicle* reported that two youths arrested after an attempted robbery had been found to be 'regularly fitted out with masks and pistols, and all the paraphernalia of highwaymen'. They had apparently been led into crime after being encouraged by their employer to read 'low publications, such as "Jack Sheppard," and "Paul Clifford," and other works illustrating the actions of notorious robbers and highwaymen'.[109]

Others thought, however, that the vogue and influence of Newgate literature had passed. William Makepeace Thackeray declared as early as 1840 that 'The taste for Newgate literature is on the wane',[110] though he was taking the credit for having effected this decline by his parody, *Catherine*. In 1880 a commentator stated that the heyday of 'Newgate' and similar cheap literature had been forty years earlier:

> None but persons who have acquired some knowledge of the trade can possibly know how enormous was the demand 40 years ago for such periodicals and serial publications. They were sold everywhere, and disposed of by the then newsagents and periodical vendors in literal, tens of thousands. The late Mr Abel Heywood, of Manchester, personally assured us that he has scattered over his counters in the course of one week to hawkers and petty dealers a quarter of a million of varied sheets of newspapers and novels. Mr William Love of this city [Glasgow], Mr Guest of Birmingham, and Mr Henry Robinson of Edinburgh used also to dispose of enormous numbers of these London serial publications, some of which are, we believe, still occasionally re-issued.[111]

Nevertheless, the writer thought that 'the sickly sentimentality of such productions as "Ada the Betrayed" and the romances of the Newgate school—at one time so much in fashion—did ... some service in creating a taste for reading, which has never been quenched, and which has led to a demand for serial literature of a higher class'.[112] Whether this was true or not, dire warnings about the effects of 'Newgate literature' on the lower classes and youth continued to be issued for decades and, extended to other genres and other media, are still made.

The 'Newgate Novel', Newgate Discourse, and Formation of the Modern State

Thackeray's reference to Newgate literature in 1840 may have been intended to take in cheap print of the kind that alarmed Wontner, Beggs and various newspaper editorialists, but his attack at this time was in fact on a particular and controversial form of this literature produced for middle-class readers – what later came to be called the 'Newgate novel'. To an extent, Thackeray created the Newgate novel controversy, and paradoxically and unintentionally created an outstanding form of it in *Catherine*, his burlesque of 1839–40 based on the actual *Newgate Calendar* figure of Catherine Hayes. In fact, the particular Newgate novels that Thackeray singled out or alluded to, including Bulwer's *Paul Clifford* and *Eugene Aram*, Dickens's *Oliver Twist* and Ainsworth's *Rookwood* and *Jack Sheppard*, had already drawn criticism from reviewers for glamourizing crime and criminals. Nevertheless, though Thackeray had declared the taste for it to be on the wane, the 'Newgate novel', along with 'Newgate literature', 'Newgate drama' and the entire 'Newgate school', continued to arouse moral indignation and social and political alarm. Early in 1842, for example, the new middle-class satire magazine *Punch* addressed one of 'Punch's Valentines' to 'The Literary Gentleman', who was clearly a writer of 'Newgate novels' and probably meant to be taken as Edward Bulwer, or a combination of Bulwer, Ainsworth, and Dickens:

> Illustrious scribe! whose vivid genius strays
> 'Mid Drury's stews to incubate her lays,
> And in St. Giles's slang conveys her tropes,
> Wreathing the poet's lines with hangmen's ropes.
> You who conceive 'tis poetry to teach
> The sad bravado of a dying speech,
> Or, when possess'd with a sublimer mood,
> Show '*Jack o' Dandies*' dancing upon blood!
> Crush bones—bruise flesh—recount each festering sore—
> Rake up the plague pit—write—and write in gore!
> Or, when inspired to humanize mankind,

Where doth your soaring soul its subjects find?
Not 'mid the scenes that simple Goldsmith sought,
And found a theme to elevate his thought;
But you, great scribe, more greedy of renown,
From Hounslow's gibbet drag a hero down.
Embue his mind with virtue; make him quote
Some moral truth, before he cuts a throat.
Then wash his hands, and—soaring o'er your craft,—
Refresh the hero with the bloody draught;
And, fearing lest the world should miss the act,
With noble zeal *italicize* the fact.
Or would you picture woman meek and pure,
By love and virtue tutor'd to endure,
With cunning skill you take a felon's trull,
Stuff her with sentiment, and scrunch her skull!
Oh! would your crashing, smashing, mashing pen were mine,
That I could 'scorch your eye-balls' with my words,
                    'MY VALENTINE.'[113]

Despite its humour, Punch's 'Valentine', along with Thackeray's burlesque and reviewers' and editorialists' warnings, expressed a concern that Newgate literature was being produced not only for the lower classes but also for readers like themselves. It seems, however, that it was the controversy that created the Newgate novel, and indeed Newgate literature more broadly, for there is a suggestive asynchronicity in the appearance of such literature and especially the 'Newgate novel', and attacks on it.

This is not just another case of a literary form being invented before a term was created to identify, locate and define it. The *New Oxford English Dictionary* defines the Newgate novel as 'a kind of English fiction popular in the second quarter of the 19th century, which took actual criminal cases as the basis for its narrative and was typically picaresque in form'. According to the *Dictionary*, however, the term 'Newgate literature', referring to such novels, is first recorded as used by Thackeray in the post-amble to *Catherine*, published in 1840. And though the novels singled out by Thackeray had been criticized by reviewers in the 1830s for glamourizing crime and criminals, there were very similar novels published in the 1820s. The phrase 'Newgate novel-monger', referring to the publishing firm of Richard Bentley, who published fashionable fiction for an upscale middle-class market, is found in an 1845 article in *Punch* entitled 'Poisoners, Living and Dead—Arsenic Novels'.[114] The phrase 'Newgate novels' itself is first recorded by the *New Oxford English Dictionary* as used by Charles Knight in his 1854 book, *The Old Printer and the Modern Press*. It was not until over a century later that the term 'Newgate novel' was recovered for literary history and criticism, in Keith Hollingsworth's 1963 book, *The Newgate Novel, 1830–1847: Bulwer, Ainsworth, Dickens and Thackeray*, which remains the fullest treatment of the subject. Chris Baldick added 'Newgate novel' to later editions of his *Concise Oxford Dictionary of Literary Terms* (1990; 2nd edn, 2001), stating that it was 'a term applied to certain popular novels of the 1830s that are based on legends of 18th century highwaymen and other notorious criminals as recorded in the *Newgate Calendar*' and giving the 'principal examples' as Bulwer's *Paul Clifford* and *Eugene Aram* and Ainsworth's *Rookwood* and *Jack Sheppard*. Dickens's *Oliver Twist* (1837–8) was also mentioned by Baldick as sharing 'many features of Newgate fiction'. Lynn Pykett, in an essay in the *Cambridge Companion to Crime Fiction* (2003), treated the Newgate novel and the later 'sensation' novel as 'sub-genres of the literature of crime'. In his book, Hollingsworth mentioned a few other novels associated with the form, such as *Richmond; or, Memoirs of a Bow Street Officer* (1827), attributed to Thomas S. Surr or Thomas Gaspey, and Charles Whitehead's *Autobiography of Jack Ketch* (1834, dated 1835).

In fact, it was Hollingsworth's treatment that informed all other current definitions of the Newgate novel', including that in the *New Oxford English Dictionary*, which treat the 'Newgate novel' as a more or less coherent form with certain attributes. Hollingsworth acknowledges, however, that although the various works identified as Newgate novels have certain similar features, the category was less a 'school', movement, body of literature, or subgenre than a rhetorical figure invented by and for a particular literary, political and personal controversy around 1840. It is possible to go further than this and argue that the 'Newgate novel' controversy of the 1830s and 40s was another aspect of the social, cultural and governmental and administrative panic directed at Newgate, at the inmate culture that Newgate permitted, at the plebeian moral economy of which this culture was a part and at Newgate narratives of kinds that were perceived to embody or encourage this culture and moral economy, even among the middle-class reading public. It is possible to see the Newgate novel controversy as a moment in the longer and larger struggle to influence, direct and control print culture in the formation of Britain as a modern state.

It is revealing, for example, that the categories 'Newgate school' and 'Newgate literature' were created somewhat after the fact, applied negatively and applied both to the cheap forms of Newgate narratives consumed by the lower classes and denounced by Thomas Wontner and others, and to the much more expensive 'triple-decker' or three-volume novels by Bulwer, Ainsworth and others, produced for the well-to-do middle-class reading public. This belated response has been explained as the coincidence of an actual sensational murder in which the perpetrator, Benjamin Courvoisier, was reported to have been inspired to commit the crime by reading Ainsworth's *Jack Sheppard*.[115] The murder and publicity over it were probably a precipitating factor in the reaction against representations of Sheppard, Newgate literature and the Newgate novel; but the intensity and longevity of the reaction were sustained by the movement to liquidate Newgate and its culture, emerging in the mid 1830s and clearly stated in William Craw-ford's 1835 report to parliament on the prison system in the United States, and by the 1836 prison inspectors' report to parliament on the prisons of England and Wales. In short, the attack on 'Newgate literature' of any kind for any class of readers was part of a larger attack on the moral economy of the lower classes and on those in other classes perceived as sympathetic to, or willing to tolerate, it and them. This attack may in turn be seen as part of the struggle over the formation or reformation of Britain and its empire as a modern state in the aftermath of passage of the Reform Bill of 1832 and issues associated with it.

This is the larger context of the rise – or rise into controversial notice – of Newgate literature and the Newgate novel in the 1830s and 40s. For of course Newgate literature of various kinds was already centuries old and much of it was still being reprinted and read by all classes.[116] It included sixteenth- and seventeenth-century Spanish, German and English picaresque novels, early eighteenth-century English and French 'rogue' fiction by writers such as Dan-iel Defoe and Alain-René Lesage, seventeenth-century to nineteenth-century street ballads and broadsheets purporting to give the 'last dying words and con-fession' of hanged convicts, true crime chapbooks and collections such as *The Malefactor's Bloody Register* and the *Newgate Calendar*, chapbook story and song collections relating to famous robbers such as Robin Hood, collections of the lives and adventures of pirates and bandits, popular stage plays, novels such as Henry Fielding's often reprinted *Jonathan Wild* and dramatic satires such as John Gay's *Beggar's Opera* and so on. Such earlier forms of the literature of crime were consumed by all classes but embodied to varying degrees the moral economy and lottery mentality of the common people. In the later part of the eighteenth century, however, aspects of this earlier Newgate literature were appropriated by Enlightenment and Sentimental or humanitarian discourses embodying the val-ues of 'progressive' and reformist elements among the upper and middle classes. Writers embodied these values in novels drawing on philosophical and humani-tarian works of the kind referred to earlier in this introduction, and included in this volume, such as Beccaria's *Dei Delitti e delle pene*, Howard's *The State of the Prisons in England and Wales* and Godwin's *An Enquiry Concerning Political Justice*.

In order to diffuse his philosophy and politics more widely, Godwin him-self turned from philosophical treatise to philosophical and political novel of crime and detection, in *Things as They Are; or, The Adventures of Caleb Williams* (1794). This is the first-person narrative of a lower-class intellectual who discov-ers a crime committed by his upper-class employer and is hounded by him into a final confrontation disastrous for both. It was a fable for the mid-1790s and its social-political conflicts.[117] Godwin's novel was widely read and influenced several generations of reformist and Newgate novelists, including Edward Bulwer. Godwin's friend, the successful playwright and novelist Thomas Holcroft, adapted the picaresque form in *The Adventures of Hugh Trevor* (1794–7) and *The Memoirs of Bryan Perdue* (1805). Godwin's wife, Mary Wollstonecraft adapted this form of philosophical picaresque to feminism in *The Wrongs of Woman; or, Maria* (1798), as did their friend Mary Hays in *The Victim of Prejudice* (1799). These reformists and their works were criticized, burlesqued and countered by loyalist writers. They adapted Newgate literature in their own way to pillory the Godwin circle and others like them as criminals and encouragers of crime, if not against the law then against 'morality', 'decency' and religion, in such novels as George Walker's *The Vagabond* (1799) and Elizabeth Hamilton's *Memoirs of Modern Philosophers* (1800). As otherwise contending social and political factions closed ranks in face of the threat from Revolutionary and then Napoleonic France, and from plebeian political mobilization in Britain, overtly reformist Newgate literature for the middle-class reading public was suppressed or marginalized, while cheap Newgate literature in chapbook, broadsheet and *Newgate Calendar* form continued to be published. At the same time, noble bandits, pirates, criminals, outlaws, and rebels were becoming important cultural figures symbolizing a wide variety of dissidence from the established order, drawing on Continental European literature such as Friedrich von Schiller's popular drama *Die Räuber* (*The Robbers*, 1781), and especially in Byron's bestselling narrative poems of the 1810s such as *The Giaour* (1813) and *The Corsair* (1814). At the same time, fashionable Gothic novels and melodramas appropriated elements of the Godwinian crime and detection novel, German rebel and robber dramas, and Byronic verse narratives of criminal anti-heroes, as well as earlier picaresque rogue fiction.

Further, most of the 'Newgate novels' were closely related to, and in fact a branch of, the numerous and widely-read eighteenth- and early nineteenth-century romance-mysteries of social identity. In this form, a 'crime' of concealment or misrepresentation of the protagonist's identity precipitates a romance plot of adventure and character testing. This romance is combined with a plot of investigation, discovery, or revelation of the protagonist's true social identity, along with his or her hitherto concealed, obscured or compromised inner merit or worth. The plot closes with the protagonist's accession or restoration to his or her 'rightful' social status and property, which is often upper-class or aristocratic. In some cases the 'crime' committed against the protagonist is not actually against the law, in others it may involve fraud or deception amounting to a crime in law, or sometimes the crime may be a serious one, such as murder. In many of these novels, too, the protagonist's concealed or falsified identity and/or inner worth may lead or force the character into pretended, perceived or actual crimes. Widely-read examples of such novels can be found from Fielding's *Joseph Andrews* and *Tom Jones*, at least, to Godwinian reformist novels of the 1790s, Gothic and historical romances of the early nineteenth century and other novels by some of the Newgate novelists, such as Thomas Gaspey. In fact, Bulwer's Newgate novel *Paul Clifford* is just such story. The romance-mystery of identity, in many different versions, formed a major part of fiction for the middle classes over this period and its wide diffusion indicates that for this readership the fictional form embodied a myth, in the sense of a story form that powerfully addressed the interests of a large social group or class. The myth in this case can be seen as addressing the middle-class novel-reading public's sense of itself at this time as wrongly and perhaps illegally misidentified, misrepresented and even outlawed by a social, political, legal and property system illegitimately dominated or criminally 'usurped' by the upper classes.

The trajectory of upward social mobility enacted in this myth could have two sides, one more potentially revolutionary than the other. The conservative or less revolutionary form of the myth demonstrates that the idealized middle-class or even lower-class protagonist is actually or rightfully or deservedly a member of the dominant class, whose dominance is not challenged in the story. This is the form practised by the Newgate novelist Thomas Gaspey, who was in fact a reformist conservative. The more reformist or revolutionary form of the myth shows that the protagonist has been deprived of participation in the dominant order by a crime, usually some kind of usurpation and that the criminals should be overthrown, punished and replaced by their victims. This is the form practised by the Newgate novelist Edward Bulwer. It is rare to see the myth extended to envisaging the overthrow of the hierarchical social order itself, and then the revolution is usually displaced in some way, in manifestly utopian prose fiction and narrative poetry. Such an overthrow was, by the end of the eighteenth century, the discourse of minority radical reformist politics; identity mystery-romance could, however, help readers entertain such possibilities. At the same time, many such novels appropriated elements of the picaresque novel or rogue romance, in which the lower-class or deracinated protagonist, rejected by family or patrons, or in search of freedom and fortune, is forced on or takes to the road, where he or (less often) she is often exploited, abused or victimized, and at times engages in deception, fraud, or crime, while on his or her journey to some better future. Early picaresque romance embodied the moral economy and lottery mentality of the lower classes, shared to an extent by other classes at that time. Eighteenth- and early nineteenth-century identity mystery-romances appropriated such elements of the already familiar picaresque and rogue romance and adapted them to the different moral economy and ideology of the middle classes. These classes had historically been the assistants and dependents of the hegemonic upper class, as the middle classes were in the process of consolidating their own identity, as distinct and separate from the hegemonic class, and 'entitled' to greater status and power, if not themselves entitled to assume the position of dominance. This they were in fact about to do at the time when the novels later identified as Newgate novels began to appear.

The ways in which these elements of the predecessors of Newgate novels were adapted in the particular Newgate work are discussed in the introductions to those novels included in this series. What remains here is to point out the relations between such novels and the wider field of Newgate literature with which they were associated in the Newgate panic of the 1830s and 40s. This panic involved, as described earlier, singling out a certain kind of popular literature – 'Newgate literature' – as the co-cause of crime, along with supposedly inadequate and incorrect prison structure and management, education of the lower classes, policing, licensing of theatres and so on – all exemplified and symbolized by Newgate prison. The Newgate novel was a creation of this movement, directed at a certain body of works published for the middle-class reading public. The Newgate novel controversy fashioned by Thackeray was precipitated by serialization of Ainsworth's *Jack Sheppard* in the literary magazine, *Bentley's Miscellany*, in 1839–40. As Keith Hollingsworth has pointed out, all of the Newgate novels named or implicated in the controversy, and others that were not, were based on real criminals of the past – *Paul Clifford* and *Rookwood* partly on the exploits of Dick Turpin, *Eugene Aram* and *Jack Sheppard* on the persons so named, and even Dickens's Fagin in *Oliver Twist* was thought to be based on Isaac (or 'Ikey') Solomon (1785–1850). These figures and others like them were already circulating in various kinds of cheap print, especially chapbooks and the successive editions of the *Newgate Calendar*. Chapbook accounts of Eugene Aram had been reprinted frequently since the first appearance of the *Genuine Account of the Trial of Eugene Aram for the Murder of Daniel Clark*, just after Aram's execution in 1759, and William Godwin intended to novelize the story to illustrate his argument in *Political Justice* that criminals were reformable. Thomas Hood had used the Aram story in his 1829 poem, *The Dream of Eugene Aram*. The figures of Dick Turpin and Jack Sheppard were so widely known as to be proverbial.

There was nothing new in appropriation of figures real or fictitious from cheap lower-class literature by fiction and drama aimed at a middle-class audience and reading public. In fact, such appropriation was a feature of literature and especially fiction, of the Romantic period, such as the Scottish chapbook hero and political 'outlaw' William Wallace in Jane Porter's novel *The Scottish Chiefs* (1810) and Robin Hood in Walter Scott's historical romance *Ivanhoe* (1819). There were dramas and melodramas based on figures from popular literature and there were quasi-learned editions of historic popular literature and street literature of various kinds. In part, these appropriations participated in a larger programme of taming of the popular and plebeian in middle-class Romantic literature. The Newgate novels also appropriated elements of the popular picaresque fiction. In this respect, and in their appropriation of figures from earlier 'Newgate literature', the Newgate novels singled out for condemnation in the 1830s and 40s were typical of the period. But such appropriations could seem like condoning or even promoting the values, or the implicit moral economy, of lower-class literature. Worse, 'Newgate novels', current and recent, glamourized certain crimes and kinds of criminal. Hence such novels could be perceived to be or accused of glamourizing crime and criminals in general, by the time in the mid 1830s when parliament, government, press and much of the property-owning public were creating, for their own purposes, a moral panic over Newgate and what it symbolized. It was perhaps to redeem their reputation as Newgate novel-mongers that the firm of Richard Bentley began publishing a moralistic yet reformist fictionalized account of Newgate criminals by the novelist and clergyman Erskine Neale (1804–83) entitled *The Gaol Chaplain; or, A Dark Page from Life's Volume*, serialized from May 1843 in *Bentley's Miscellany*, which had carried Ainsworth's infamous *Jack Sheppard*, and later republished in 1847 as a three-volume work entitled *Experiences of a Gaol Chaplain*.

Worse again, though probably mainly in the perception of reviewers and upmarket writers such as Thackeray, Newgate novels seemed to attribute to their protagonists the kind of subjective identity, or 'nobility of soul', that had been a central feature in the development of middle-class fiction since the mid- and late eighteenth century. In the fiction of the half century and more preceding the Newgate novels, the lower classes, including the criminal classes, had been portrayed as virtually subjectless, merely social and instinctual beings, however sentimentalized, deferential and docile. By contrast, or in distinction, middle- and upper-class protagonists were generally represented as possessing a complex plenitude of self. This new kind of selfhood was theorized in philosophical works such as Adam Smith's *Theory of Moral Sentiments* (1759). It was represented in a wide range of European and British writers of Sensibility (or Sentimentalism) and Romanticism and was made almost into a cult by such writers as Jean-Jacques Rousseau. Finally, it was politicized in demands for civic, electoral and other 'rights' based on individual self-governing subjectivity – a kind of subjectivity that was widely assumed to be achievable and sustainable only by those with a certain corresponding independence of property. It was the supposed lack of such subjectivity (and such property) that implicitly underlay the general denial of these rights to the lower classes, women and others, culminating in the conservative compromise of the Great Reform Act of 1832. Godwin, Holcroft and other proleptic Newgate novelists had already attempted to depict complex plebeian protagonists during the Revolutionary 1790s and been denounced, vilified and even tried for treason. But their experiments were valued and emulated by Newgate novelists such as Bulwer and Ainsworth, partly for political and partly for commercially opportunistic reasons. The scandal of the Newgate novel was waiting to be created and was perhaps invited. The scandal was triggered by the aftermath of the Great Reform Act in the mid and late 1830s, partly because Bulwer and others such as Ainsworth continued to publish novels that could be read as reformist in sympathies.

Perhaps worst of all as the moral panic over Newgate literature ran on, the 'Newgate novels' quickly and obviously repaid their debt to lower-class literature by inspiring cheap versions of themselves in fiction and drama and by being reprinted in progressively cheaper editions. Bulwer's *Eugene Aram* was immediately turned into a three-act melodrama entitled *Eugene Aram; or, Saint Robert's Cave!* (1832) by the prolific W. T. Moncrieff. Benjamin Webster and Edward Fitzball each produced popular dramatizations of Bulwer's *Paul Clifford*. Later, in the 1850s, Bulwer's novel was re-novelized by Elizabeth Grey as *Paul Clifford; or, Hurrah for the Road: A Romance of Old Times*, a cheap 'Salisbury Square' serial novel – so called from the place of publication in London. There were other spin-offs. Ainsworth's *Rookwood*, featuring Dick Turpin, and *Jack Sheppard* had even more progeny. The latter was dramatized by Matthew Howell as *Harlequin Jack Sheppard; or, The Blossom of Tyburn Tree! A Comic Pantomime* in 1839, by John Thomas Haines as *Jack Sheppard: A Domestic Drama; in Three Acts* and by John Buckstone as *Jack Sheppard: A Drama; in Three Acts* in the same year; immediately, Buckstone's play was adapted for the 'juvenile' or 'toy' theatre – plays with small cutout figures and stage sets for use by children at home. The following year T. L. Greenwood gave fuller dramatic form to Ainsworth's story in *Jack Sheppard; or, The House-breaker of the Last Century: A Romantic Drama in Five Acts*. Different cheap and shorter re-novelizations of Sheppard's story and Ainsworth's novel appeared in 1840 as *The Eventful Life and Unparalleled Exploits of the Notorious Jack Sheppard, the Housebreaker* and *The Life and Adventures of Jack Sheppard* by Obadiah Throttle – a reference to the hangman. A longer re-novelization appeared in the same year and another by 'Lincoln Fortescue' appeared in 1845. Most of these works continued to be reprinted or re-staged over the following decades. Dick Turpin, who is fictionalized in Ainsworth's *Rookwood*, was also quickly dramatized by H. M. Milner in *Turpin's Ride to York; or, Bonnie Black Bess: An Equestrian Drama, in Two Acts* (1836 or earlier). Henry Miles Downes produced a serialized novelization in 1839 as *The Life of Richard Palmer Better Known as Dick Turpin, the Notorious Highwayman and Robber; Including His Numerous Exploits, Adventures, and Hair-breadth Escapes, Trial and Execution; with Notices of Many of his Contemporaries*. In 1845 George Dibdin Pitt dramatized Ainsworth's *Rookwood* itself as a 'Romantic drama'. Other dramatizations followed in the 1840s and 50s, including William Suter's *The Adventures of Dick Turpin and Tom King: A Serio-comic Drama in Two Acts* and Morris Barnett's *Dick Turpin and Tom King: A Farce in*

One Act. Given the ephemeral nature of cheap literature, there are likely other print versions of the exploits of Turpin and Sheppard that remain unknown.

In such popular proliferations of certain Newgate novels, too, there was nothing new, however. Since the beginning of the century, down-market publishers had been turning out new forms of chapbook literature consisting of much-abbreviated thirty-page versions of middle-class three-volume novels and successful stage plays, with sensational engraved frontispieces and brightly coloured paper covers. Such novelties were published alongside traditional chapbook fiction, which were republished in the same attractive but still relatively inexpensive formats. Significantly, and as noticed earlier, in the 1810s and 20s much reformist literature, including racy satires on the upper classes, aristocratic privilege, established church and the monarch, began appearing from the same publishers and using the same formats and frames of social and cultural reference. In the 1820s and 30s the opening of cheaper, unlicensed, 'non-legitimate' theatres of the kind complained about by Thomas Wontner in 1833 greatly expanded the scope of such plebeian appropriations of middle-class literature. Together, this body of cheap literature and drama clearly indicated the existence of an 'other' reading public and theatrical audience, comprised mainly of the lower and lower-middle classes. The Newgate novels were only part of a much larger body of literature appropriated for this other reading public and audience. In short, the double scandal of the 'Newgate novel' was that it brought the contamination of lower-class 'Newgate literature' into literature for the middle classes and then that it seemed to have inspired or contributed to such lower-class literature. The first scandal emerged as some of the better-selling Newgate novels were published, in the mid and late 1830s. The second emerged in the 1840s and 50s when it became apparent that such novels were being transformed back into the kind of Newgate literature that they were supposed to have sprung from and that was believed to help sustain the lower-class moral economy and thus to form new generations of criminals.

Certainly there were other novels of the period, going back to the 1820s, that had some traits of the Newgate fiction of Bulwer and Ainsworth. These included *Richmond; or, Memoirs of a Bow Street Officer* (1827), likely by Thomas Gaspey but also attributed to Thomas S. Surr; Gaspey's *George Godfrey* (1828); Charles Whitehead's *Autobiography of Jack Ketch* (dated 1835); William Mudford's *Stephen Dugard* (1840); Dickens's *Oliver Twist* (1837-39) – though sometimes seen as an anti-Newgate novel – George W. M. Reynolds's *Robert Macaire in England* (1840) and Thomas P. Prest's *Newgate: A Romance* (1847). All of these except the last three, but including Bulwer's *Paul Clifford* and *Eugene Aram*, Ainsworth's *Rookwood* and Whitehead's *Autobiography of Jack Ketch*, were originally published for the genteel middle-class fiction market. This was predominantly in copies sold to commercial circulating libraries for rental to the libraries' subscribers, though there was also a market in elegantly illustrated novels, usually shorter in length, for direct sale to the reading public – Whitehead's novel belongs to this category. *Oliver Twist* and Ainsworth's *Jack Sheppard* were published in instalments in the fashionable *Bentley's Miscellany* magazine. Most were published by the leading firms specializing in fashionable fiction during these decades, such as Henry Colburn and Richard Bentley. In a sense, however, Thackeray was correct in declaring the taste for 'Newgate literature', at least in the form of the three-volume upmarket 'Newgate novel', to be fading in 1840, if by 'fading' Thackeray meant 'going downmarket'. Reynolds's and Prest's 'Newgate novels' were clearly aimed at a lower- and lower-middle-class readership from the outset, being sold in penny parts, Reynolds's by the downmarket publisher Thomas Tegg and later J. Dicks, and Prest's by E. Lloyd, the leading publisher of 'penny dreadfuls', or cheap sensational fiction.

In the end, then, the Newgate novels, whether identified or identifiable as such, were a diverse lot, spanning the fiction formats and fiction markets of the day, aimed at different readerships and with diverse features: set in the past or in the present or recent past; sentimental, 'tragic', comic, or satirical and ironic in mode; in first-person or third-person narration and so on. Nevertheless, all take up in various ways and to a varying extent the tradition of picaresque crime fiction from the sixteenth to the early nineteenth centuries; all engage in different ways and more or less overtly in social criticism; all represent crime and criminals with varying degrees of sympathy and aversion; all engage to a greater or lesser extent with Newgate discourse – the evolving complex of issues, ideas, projects, investigation, activism, controversy, legislation and literature around the reality and the symbol of Newgate.

Newgate Today

Though demolished in 1902 (1904 is also given as the date in some sources), Newgate lived and lives on. Its demolition stimulated interest in Newgate memorabilia, with an auction of 'unique fittings' from the prison in 1903. A string of popular books for the middlebrow or educated reading public appeared over the ensuing decades, down to the present. There were collections of anecdotes from the history of the prison and the Old Bailey court, anticipated by Arthur Griffiths (1838–1908) with *The Chronicles of Newgate* (1884), reprinted into the twentieth century and including Charles Gordon's *The Old Bailey and Newgate* (1902), Reginald Sharpe's *Memorials of Newgate Gaol* (1907) and William Eden Hooper's *The Central Criminal Court of London* (1909) – the last was reprinted several times in the next few decades. In the 1920s there was another revival of interest, marked by publication in 1925 of a compilation from the various eighteenth- and early nineteenth-century collections of criminal biographies known as the 'Newgate Calendar': this was *The Complete Newgate Calendar* (1925) in five volumes by the Navarre Society, which specialized in elegant reprints of fiction and biography that could be made out to have erotic, decadent, risqué, louche or picaresque underworld associations, or, in the publishing argot of the time, books that were 'spicy'. This association of Newgate with the 'spicy' continues still. In 1926, Edwin Valentine Mitchell (1890–1960), an American maker of popular books on earlier times, published a selection from the *Newgate Calendar* with that title and an introduction by Henry Savage, American writer of popular history. In his introduction, Savage declared, 'Imagination is stirred by the thought of Newgate' and went on to exclaim, 'Newgate! What suffering, what cruelty, what dirt and disease and depravity is in the tale with that title!' As an American, Savage saw Newgate as 'essentially an English institution': 'There was a certain freedom about it, some desperate jollity, even' and Savage compared it favourably with the French Bastille, of French Revolutionary notoriety. These associations with Newgate, too, have stuck. Inevitably, Newgate would appear in the 'Regency romances' that became popular in the 1920s, and moved to the increasingly popular mystery genre with John Dickson Carr's oft-reprinted and translated *Bride of Newgate* (1946).

In 1932, B. Laurie published a selection from Knapp and Baldwin's early nineteenth-century version of the *Newgate Calendar*. In 1951 the Folio Society, a subscription publisher for bibliophiles of somewhat modest means, published a selection of trials from 1700 to 1780, taken from a late eighteenth-century version of the *Newgate Calendar*, 'edited and selected' by Sir (William) Norman Birkett (1883–1962). From 1945 to 1949 Birkett had been a British judge at the Nuremberg war crimes trials of prominent Nazis. The purpose of his selection, stated in his introduction, was to correct what he thought was a widespread view of the eighteenth century as an age of civility: 'For let it be said at once that the trials here set out exhibit the criminal law in what we now regard as a barbaric and even savage state'. A further selection was published by the Folio Society in 1960. By then, a more popular interest in true crime, past and present, was met by Howard Culpin's *Newgate Noose: An Account of Some Famous Crimes in the Eighteenth and Early Nineteenth Centuries* (1957). The paperback market received another edition of the *Newgate Calendar* in the swinging 60s, published by Panther in London and Capricorn in New York – two publishers serving the growing popular market for trendy counter-cultural, avant-garde and pseudo-illicit fiction and non-fiction. In 1972 Jane Dorner, author of non-fiction books for schoolchildren on such topics as the Spanish conquest of Mexico, canals, fashions of the past, care of the violin, and markets and fairs, published *Newgate to Tyburn* with the educational publisher Wayland. The profusely illustrated book has an implied 'Whig' narrative of progress, tracing crime and punishment from an origin in poverty through criminal laws, policing, punishments,

Newgate and public execution at Newgate, to humanitarian amelioration and reform, symbolized by Elizabeth Fry. The book closes by asking its young readers, 'Would you have liked to live at the time of Newgate and Tyburn?' In a more literary vein, Rayner Heppenstall (1911–81), English novelist, translator, essayist, and author of several books on crime in France, published in 1975 *Reflections on the Newgate Calendar*, which links certain crimes and criminals with English literary history from the mid-eighteenth to the mid-nineteenth century. Heppenstall's book included a chapter on 'The Newgate Novelists', apparently unaware of Keith Hollingsworth's 1963 book on the subject. Heppenstall later produced another Newgate anthology, *Tales from the Newgate Calendar*, in 1981. For some time, the music critic on the New York *Times*, Harold Schonberg (1915–2003), also reviewed crime fiction under the pen name, Newgate Callendar. In 2006, Stephen Halliday, English writer of history for the general reader, published *Newgate: London's Prototype of Hell*, including a chapter on 'Newgate in Literature', dealing mainly with Dickens.

Such publications indicated the continuing existence of Newgate as a subject of interest, if no longer fascination, with a middle-class reading public. By the aftermath of World War II, however, Newgate and what it represented were being taken up by academic specialists on the one hand and on the other hand by writers serving a market for more sensational treatments. Newgate was carried into three different discourses and kinds of narrative – legal and social history, literary history, and popular literature and culture. In 1948 Leon Radzinowicz, who was a leading figure in formation of the academic discipline of criminology, began publishing his *History of English Criminal Law and Its Administration from 1750* – actually a study of changing social attitudes to crime and punishment – completed with the fifth volume in 1986. Radzinowicz's *History* was accused by some of being a Whig history, or narrative based on an assumption of steady progress in its designated field of study. But it was a richly detailed, useful and influential document and also a sign of a growing if not unproblematic collaboration between academic research and government policy and agencies in respect to the legal and penal systems. Radzinowicz's work would be amplified, extended, questioned, and corrected by many academic social and legal historians in the decades after *A History of English Criminal Law* began to appear, especially after the second and third volumes of 1957. From the rebellious 1960s a sociological and often Marxist historical narrative and analysis of the legal and penal systems developed in academic research, by writers such as Edward P. Thompson and Eric Hobsbawm, using but also maintaining a distance from Radzinowicz, recuperating earlier socialist work, such as Sidney and Beatrice Webb's *English Prisons under Local Government* (1922), and generally relating the development of criminal laws and penal systems to the development of capitalist economic practices.[118] This work continued, producing such later studies as

Peter Linebaugh's *The London Hanged: Crime and Civil Society in the Eighteenth Century* (1992). In the late 1970s a third strand of academic theory and research, or set of narratives on the prison emerged, distinct from both Radzinowicz's liberal approach and that of the Marxist theorists and researchers. Michel Foucault's *Surveiller et punir: naissance de la prison* (1975), translated in 1977 as *Discipline and Punish: The Birth of the Prison*, emphasized the prison as an instrument for the exercise of power created at a moment when the attention of such exercise shifted from the bodily and social to the subjective being of the individual and society at large. In Foucault's narrative, Bentham's 'panopticon' was a major symptom of this shift from one system of power to another. Foucault's approach to the subject appeared to be augmented by Michael Ignatieff's *A Just Measure of Pain: The Penitentiary in the Industrial Revolution 1750–1850* (1978), which focused attention on the 'model' penitentiary at Pentonville and which, as its title suggests, incorporated ideas and research by socialist historians of crime and punishment, and power and resistance, that Foucault's approach seemed to ignore, or implicitly counter. In the 'Conclusion' of his book, however, Ignatieff suggested – though in a section he soon dropped – that he and Foucault were engaged in the same, reformist project in which 'history, as one of the human sciences, has a discrete but important role to play in combating carceral power and the coercive structures of thought that underpin it'.[119]

By 1987, another historian, Clive Emsley, could state that 'in the last ten or fifteen years historians have increasingly turned their attention to crime and how former societies understood it and sought to deal with it'.[120] Emsley's book, designed for history students, proposed to 'synthesise' this work, and effectively did so. Already, however, Foucault's book, with others by him, was being seen as part of a movement, commonly indicated by the term 'post-structuralism', that spread rapidly through academic theory and research in the 1980s. Anti-foundational, such an approach denied the universal validity of any particular theory or body of knowledge and emphasized the radical relativity of discourses and knowledge. Sometimes also referred to simply as 'theory', post-structuralist theory seemed to enjoin a rejection of liberal, Marxist or any methodology making claims to universal explanatory power and pointed out that all narratives are fictions based on forms of myth that embody particular ideologies or worldviews. In academic historiography around crime, policing and punishment emphasis shifted to critical examination of the construction of such categories as 'crime' by systems or languages of representation. Thus, in purporting to describe, define or narrate a certain subject, the often unstated assumptions of the description, definition or narration actually brought its subject into existence as having a certain meaning and value, and not others. Even earlier, however, investigations in what was then called the 'philosophy of history' and in stylistic and formal approaches to historical writing had pointed out that historical narrative was always rhetorical, inevitably based on certain ideological assumptions and shaped to persuade its readers of the 'truth' of its representation of its subject.[121] Earlier still, Karl Marx had, with characteristic irony and self-reflection, suggested something like a post-structuralist view of 'crime' and the 'criminal' as constructions of a particular discourse or narrative rather than 'facts' discovered and described by discourse: 'The criminal produces not only crimes but also criminal law, and with this also the professor who gives lectures on criminal law and in addition to this the inevitable compendium in which this same professor throws his lectures onto the general market as commodities.'[122] Nevertheless, in various ways most historians of crime and punishment found ways to combine the radical scepticism of post-structuralist theory with the emancipationist and reformist project announced by Ignatieff and claimed by him and others for Foucault, perhaps despite him. In this work, the relationship between historical research and theory has been one of ongoing negotiation, challenging and also underwriting differing positions in the academic discipline of penology and the field of penal policy and administration. New approaches have joined the disciplinary field, such as cultural studies and feminism. In all of this literature, Newgate is seldom mentioned for it has been the 'industrial' prisons from Millbank through Pentonville and their successors that have attracted the attention of critical historians and cultural theorists of the past half century.

It seemed otherwise in literary history and criticism, at least beginning with the pioneering studies of Philip Collins in *Dickens and Crime* (1962) and Keith Hollingsworth in *The Newgate Novel* (1963), mentioned earlier. The interest in representations of Newgate in literature did not last, however. Influenced to some extent by the 'new social history' that aimed to present history from 'below' – and 'outside' – much of this literary history and criticism has in fact been devoted to crime fiction in the sense of the fiction of crime and detection of the kinds that became a major element of popular print culture in the twentieth century. Less attention, though more academic in its location, has been devoted to crime in popular literature of the preceding century of the kind denounced by Thomas Wontner and many others. More closely connected to the work of historians and theorists just discussed has been the interest of literary criticism and history in, on the one hand, treatment in literature of social and sexual dissidence and transgression and, on the other hand, largely influenced by Foucault's work, treatment of regimes of power in canonical or 'serious' literature, and the operation of this literature and the 'literary' as one of those regimes. Such work proliferated rapidly in the 1980s and 90s with the diversification of academic literary studies, bringing in feminism, post-colonialism, queer studies, gender studies and so on, and sometimes collaborating with work in legal theory and history. Newgate as reality and symbol hardly appears in this work.

The situation in popular literature and culture has been very different. Here there has seemed to be a continuing and even growing fascination with Newgate and Newgate is more 'popular', in several senses, than ever. Newgate is represented as a site and symbol of cultural and social danger and transgression on the one hand, and on the other of the decadent, erotic, louche and, in a broad sense, romantic. The February 1952 issue of *Sir!* monthly (New York), 'A Magazine for Males', featured an article entitled 'Torture, Lust and Death at Newgate', by Robert J. Galway. In 1973 the weekly true crime magazine *Crimes and Punishment* carried a sensational article on Newgate Prison in its regular feature, 'A-Z of Crime'. A 1986 booklet entitled *London—The Sinister Side*, issued by Wicked Publications to accompany the 'Tragical History Tours' bus tour of London, carried an article entitled 'Newgate—The English Bastille: A Prototype of Hell', along with other pieces on true crime and punishment over the centuries. In 2001 the *True Crime Detective Monthly* (London) serialized a 'History of Newgate' to go along with articles such as 'Murderabilia for Sale' and 'Canada's Worst Serial Killer'. Such articles seem designed for the large popular readership for sensational true crime literature.

Designed to appeal to a somewhat different segment of the popular market have been the increasing number of historical and 'Regency' romances, scores of which seem to consider it a strong selling point to work Newgate into the story. A few examples of many will have to suffice. This, for example, is the blurb to Constance Gluyas's 1972 Restoration historical romance, *The King's Brat*:

> Angel Dawson was a flame-haired beauty sprung from the squalor of the teeming London slums. The streets were her school, whore-masters and thieves were her teachers, and when she was seized by the law, it seemed that the dread confines of Newgate prison would be the terrified 16 year old girl's grave. But this was the tumultuous, lustful era of Charles II, when a lovely young girl could be trained to please the fancy of the king, and no law was stronger than the licentiousness of the age. Angel Dawson's career had just begun ... .

Within the huge market for historical and Regency romances there is another line that combines romance with crime and detection. Here, from almost twenty years later, is the blurb to the bestselling Regency mystery novel, *Gallows Thief* (2001), by Bernard Cornwell, author of the 'Sharpe's Rifles' series of adventure novels set in the Napoleonic wars:

> It is the end of the Napoleonic Wars and England has just fought its last victorious battle against the French. As Rider Sandman and the other heroes of Waterloo begin to make their way back to England, they find a country where corruption, poverty, and social unrest run rampant, and where 'justice' is most often delivered at the end of a hangman's noose. Nowhere in London are the streets as busy as in front of Newgate Prison, its largest penitentiary, where mobs gather regularly to watch the terrible spectacle of the doomed men and women on the gallows' stands. ... In a

race against the clock, Sandman moves from the hellish bowels of Newgate prison to the perfumed drawing rooms of the aristocracy, determined to rescue the innocent man from the rope. As he begins to peel back the layers of an utterly corrupt penal system, he finds himself pitted against some of the wealthiest and most ruthless men in Regency England.

The appeal here seems to be to an interest in, or fascination with, Newgate as a site, instrument and symbol of government and ruling-class corruption, inefficiency, and injustice. This Newgate is perhaps not unlike the contemporary world in certain popular perceptions and representations and yet it is also a site and symbol for confirming what E. P. Thompson referred to as 'the tenacity of self-preservation' and values such as 'a spontaneity and capacity for enjoyment and mutual loyalties—despite the inhibiting pressures' of modernity. Many more examples could be adduced, collectively indicating that in such narratives, which sell in the millions. Newgate continues to be a figure of powerful social and cultural significance, though in new ways as yet difficult to unpack, even by a professor with an 'inevitable compendium' on the subject, to throw on the 'general market' of academic commodities.

Notes

1. D. Garland, *Punishment and Society: A Study in Social Theory* (Chicago, IL: University of Chicago Press, 1990), p. 1.
2. T. Nashe, *Pierce Penniless* (1592), sig. E3, marginal note.
3. V. Ruggiero, *Crime in Literature: Sociology of Deviance and Fiction* (London and New York, NY: Verso, 2003), p. 4.
4. P. Linebaugh, *The London Hanged: Crime and Civil Society in the Eighteenth Century* (Cambridge: Cambridge University Press, 1992); D. Hay, P. Linebaugh, J. G. Rule, E. P. Thompson and C. Winslow, *Albion's Fatal Tree: Crime and Society in Eighteenth-Century England* (London: Allen Lane, 1975); E. P. Thompson, *Whigs and Hunters: The Origin of the Black Act* (London: Allen Lane, 1975).
5. Information on the history of Newgate prison from W. Eden Hooper, *The History of Newgate and the Old Bailey* (London: Underwood Press, 1935); M. Bassett, 'Newgate Prison in the Middle Ages', *Speculum*, 18:2 (April 1943), pp. 233–46; S. McConville, *A History of English Prison Administration*, vol. 1, *1750–1877* (London: Routledge and Kegan Paul, 1981), ch. 2; R. Byrne, *Prisons and Punishments of London* (London: Harrap, 1989); A. Brodie, J. Croom, and J. O. Davies, *English Prisons: An Architectural History* (Swindon: English Heritage, 2002); Stephen Halliday, *Newgate: London's Prototype of Hell* (London: Sutton Publishing, 2006).
6. *Penny Magazine*, 6:312 (11 February 1837), pp. 49–51 (p. 49); subsequent references to this article are indicated in parentheses after the quotation.
7. Bassett, 'Newgate Prison in the Middle Ages', *Speculum*, 18:2 (April 1943), p. 244.
8. G. Gissing, *The Nether World: A Novel*, 3 vols (London: Smith, Elder, and Co., 1889), vol. 3, ch. 4; 3.72.

9. W. Smith, *State of the Gaols in London, Westminster, and Borough of Southwark* (London: J. Bew, 1776), pp. 39–41.

10. See Linebaugh, *The London Hanged*, ch. 10, 'The Delivery of Newgate, 6 June 1780'.

11. There were a number of charities and bequests for imprisoned debtors, some of them centuries old; see the extracts in this volume from James Neild, *State of the Prisons in England, Scotland, and Wales* ... (London: John Nichols and Son, 1812).

12. King's Bench was a notoriously filthy, overcrowded and disease-ridden prison mainly for debtors, located in Southwark, on the south bank of the Thames from the City of London, replacing an earlier prison demolished in 1754. Fleet was an infamous prison mainly for debtors located off what is now Farringdon Street in the City of London and, like King's Bench prison, a profit-making enterprise charging prisoners for their keep.

13. In English measure a 'stone' is 14 pounds or 6.35 kilograms in weight.

14. 'Groats' here means food allowance, literally crushed grain.

15. *The Debtor and Creditors Assistant; or, A Key to the King's Bench and Fleet Prisons; Calculated for the Information and Benefit of The Injured Creditor, as well as The Unfortunate Debtor: Including Newgate, Ludgate, and the three Compters. To which are added, Reflections on Perpetual Imprisonment for Debt; and Outlines of a Bill for Abolishing the Same, &c. &c.* (London: G. Riley, 1793), pp. 58–61.

16. *Report from the Committee on the State of the Gaols of the City of London* (London: House of Commons Parliamentary Papers, 1814), p. 8.

17. *Penny Magazine*, pp. 49–50.

18. Ibid., p. 50

19. Ibid., p. 51

20. Ibid., p. 50

21. Ibid., p. 51

22. For a full survey, see L. Radzinowicz, *A History of English Criminal Law and Its Administration from 1750*, vol. 1, *The Movement for Reform* (New York, NY: Macmillan, 1948), Part 3, 'Leading Currents of Thought on the Principles of Punishment in the Eighteenth Century' and Part 4, 'The Beginnings of the Movement for the Reform of Criminal Law'.

23. Unless otherwise indicated, quotations in this section are to be found in the primary texts included in this volume.

24. P. Harling, 'Parliament, the State, and "Old Corruption": Conceptualizing Reform, *c.* 1790–1832', in *Rethinking the Age of Reform Britain 1780-1850*, ed. Arthur Burns and Joanna Innes (Cambridge, Cambridge University Press, 2003), pp. 98–113.

25. Ruggiero, *Crime in Literature* (2003), p. 2.

26. On S. Bentham's effectiveness in introducing his plan in the naval dockyards, see Linebaugh, *The London Hanged*, ch. 11, 'Ships and Chips: Technological Repression and the Origin of the Wage'.

27. J. Adshead, *Prisons and Prisoners* (London: Longman, Brown, Gree and Longman, 1845), p. 222; on Adshead, see also the discussion below.

28. M. Foucault, *Discipline and Punish: The Birth of the Prison*, trans. A. Sheridan (New York, NY: Pantheon Books, 1977), originally published as *Surveiller et punir: naissance de la prison* (Paris: Gallimard, 1975).

29. On the shift see M. Ignatieff, *A Just Measure of Pain: The Penitentiary in the Industrial Revolution, 1750–1850* (New York, NY: Pantheon, 1978), pp. 174–6; R. McGowen, 'The Well-Ordered Prison: England, 1780–1865', in *The Oxford History of the Prison:*

The Practice of Punishment in Western Society, ed. N. Morris and D. J. Rothman (New York, NY, and Oxford: Oxford University Press, 1998), pp. 71–91 (88–90).

30. 'Coining' in law applied to making counterfeit metal or paper currency.

31. 'Sodomy' in law at this time meant anal or oral sexual intercourse between a man and man, man and woman or man and animal; two witnesses were required for a conviction.

32. 'Beastiality', or bestiality, as a law term meant sexual intercourse between humans and animals.

33. 'Instruments' as a term in law denoted formal documents creating or affirming a right, such as a deed, agreement, charter.

34. A privy councilor was an appointed advisor of the monarch.

35. forty shillings, or about £100 in 2005, using the retail price index.

36. To be quartered was part of a punishment in which the body of the executed person was cut into four parts, considered an additional indignity.

37. 'Dissected' at this time meant that the body of the executed person was to be given over to anatomical dissection for instructional or scientific purpose, considered by most people at the time as an indignity on the body.

38. 'Benefit of Clergy' as a term in law was the right to claim exemption from trial by a secular court for a felony charge; originally an exemption for the clergy, it was later extended to anyone who could read; it was abolished in 1827.

39. Transportation was the punishment of judicial banishment from Britain, at this time to Australia.

40. Hard labour in law was a punishment involving exacting physical work of various kinds such as beating hemp or working manual water pumps, intended to occupy the convict's time and prevent 'corrupting' association with other prisoners, deter the convict from future crime and instill the work discipline that would ensure the convict would enter useful labour on release.

41. The pillory was a wooden frame restraining the convict's head and arms, exposing him or her to the public, who frequently pelted the pilloried the person with refuse, sometimes causing death; to reduce the public disorder caused by such incidents, in 1816 the practice was restricted to convictions for perjury, and was abolished in 1837.

42. There were several forms of punishment by whipping: public flogging 'at the cart's tail', or stripped to the waist and tied to a cart pulled through the streets near the scene of the crime and whipped until the convicted person's back was bloody; public flogging tied to a frame; or 'private' flogging inside a prison or house of correction. Public whipping of women was abolished in 1817, and ended for men in the 1830s; private flogging in prisons continued into the twentieth century.

43. Sir Richard Phillips, *On the Powers and Duties of Juries, and on the Criminal laws of England* (London: Sherwood, Neely, and Jones, 1811), pp. 287–9.

44. *Report from the Committee on the Prisons within the City of London and Borough of Southwark*, part 1, Newgate (London: House of Commons Parliamentary Papers, 1818), p. 4.

45. *Penny Magazine*, p. 49.

46. P. King, 'The Rise of Juvenile Delinquency in England 1780-1840: Changing Patterns of Perception and Prosecution', *Past and Present*, 160 (Aug. 1998), pp. 116–66 (p. 165). See also H. Shore, *Artful Dodgers: Youth and Crime in Early Nineteenth-Century London* (London: Boydell Press, 1999).

47. It was required by law to place in open view a summary of the legislative act or acts governing administration and conditions.

48. W. Smith, *State of the Gaols in London, Westminster, and Borough of Southwark* (London: J. Bew, 1776), pp. 39–41.

49. R. Andrews, *The Goal [sic] of Newgate Unmasked; in a Letter to Joshua Jonathan Smith, Esq., Alderman and Sheriff of the City of London and County of Middlesex* (London: for the Author, 1809).

50. Andrews, *The Goal of Newgate Unmasked*, p. 6.

51. Two pence, about £0.40 in 2005, using the retail price index.

52. *Report from the Committee on the State of the Gaols of the City of London* (London: House of Commons Parliamentary Papers, 1814), p. 93.

53. *Report from the Committee on the Prisons within the City of London and Borough of Southwark*, part 1, Newgate (London: House of Commons Parliamentary Papers, 1818), pp. 6–7.

54. 'Bill for Consolidating and Amending Laws Relating to Building, Repairing and Regulating of Gaols, Bridewells and Houses of Correction in England and Wales', p. 25.

55. T. Wontner, *Old Bailey Experience: Criminal Jurisprudence and the Actual Working of Our Penal Code of Laws; also, An Essay on Prison Discipline, to Which Is Added a History of the Crimes Committed by the Offenders in the Present Day* (London: James Fraser, 1833), pp. 328–29.

56. *Reports of the Inspectors Appointed to Visit the Different Prisons of Great Britain* (1836), pp. 4–5.

57. A. Alison, 'The Influence of the Press', *Blackwood's Edinburgh Magazine*, 36 (Sept. 1834), pp. 373–91, excerpted in *Victorian Print Media: A Reader*, ed. A. King and J. Plunkett (Oxford: Oxford University Press, 2005), p. 25.

58. *Reports of the Inspectors Appointed to Visit the Different Prisons of Great Britain* (1836), p. 6.

59. Ibid., p. 10

60. Ibid.

61. Ibid., p. 7.

62. Ibid., p. 12.

63. Ibid., p. 19.

64. Ibid., p. 20

65. On the development of statistical accounting of crime, see L. Radzinowicz and R. Hood, *A History of English Criminal Law and Its Administration from 1750*, vol. 5, *The Emergence of Penal Policy* (London: Stevens and Sons, 1986), pp. 91–107, 'The Emergence of Criminal Statistics'; also J. J. Tobias, *Crime and Industrial Society in the 19th Century* (New York, NY: Schocken Books, 1967), ch. 2, 'The Statistics of Crime'.

66. Ibid., p. 22

67. *Newgate Gaol: Return to an Order of the Honourable The House of Commons, dated 5 July 1836;—for Copy of a Report Made on 2d July 1836 by a Committee of the Court of Aldermen to that Court, upon the Report of the Inspectors of Prisons in Relation to the Gaol of Newgate* (London: Parliamentary Papers, 1836).

68. Court of Aldermen report, p. 5.

69. W. Crawford, *Report of William Crawford, Esq., on the Penitentiaries of the United States, addressed to His Majesty's Principal Secretary of State for the Home Department* (London: Parliamentary Papers, 1834), p. 30 note.

70. *Penny Magazine*, 6:312 (11 February 1837), p. 50.

71. U. R. Q. Henriques, 'The Rise and Decline of the Separate System of Prison Discipline', *Past and Present*, 54 (Februrary 1972), pp. 61–93.

72. J. Adshead, *Prisons and Prisoners* (London: Longman, Brown, Green, and Longman, 1845), p. 150;

73. Ibid., p. 209.

74. Ibid., p. 222.

75. T. Archer, *The Pauper, the Thief, and the Convict: Sketches of Some of Their Homes, Haunts, and Habits* (London: Groombridge and Sons 1865), p. 174.

76. Ibid., p. 175.

77. Ibid., pp. 176–7.

78. 'Picking oakum' was a monotonous task which involved separating the fibres in old ropes so they could be used in caulking the hulls of ships.

79. Archer, *The Pauper, the Thief, and the Convict*, pp. 178–9

80. Ibid., p. 182.

81. Ibid., p. 183.

82. Ibid., p. 185.

83. Ibid., p. 185.

84. Ibid., p. 188.

85. C. Dickens, 'A Visit to Newgate', in *Sketches by Boz*, first series (1836); W. M. Thackeray, 'On Going to See a Man Hanged', *Fraser's Magazine*, 22 (August 1840), pp. 150–8.

86. Ignatieff, *A Just Measure of Pain*, pp. 39–42; McGowen, 'The Well-Ordered Prison', pp. 71–91.

87. I. McCalman, 'Newgate in Revolution: Radical Enthusiasm and Romantic Counterculture', *Eighteenth-Century Life*, 22:1 (1998), pp. 95–110; see also *Newgate in Revolution: An Anthology of Radical Prison Literature in the Age of Revolution*, ed. M. Davis, I. McCalman, and C. Parolin (London: Continuum, 2005).

88. E. P. Thompson, *The Making of the English Working Class* (Harmondsworth: Penguin Books, 1968), pp. 63–4.

89. On mock trials held by prisoners in Newgate, see V. A. C. Gattrell, *The Hanging Tree: Execution and the English People 1770–1868* (Oxford: Oxford University Press, 1994), pp. 93–4.

90. See E. P. Thompson, *Customs in Common* (New York: The New Press, 1993), especially ch. 4, 'The Moral Economy of the English Crowd in the Eighteenth Century', reprinted from *Past and Present*, 50 (1971), pp. 76–136.

91. See the account by G. Rudé, 'The Gordon Riots: A Study of the Rioters and Their Victims', *Transactions of the Royal Historical Society*, 5th series, 6 (1956), pp. 93–114, which finds 'that behind the slogan of "No Popery" and other outward forms of religious fanaticism' of the predominantly working-class rioters, 'there lay a deeper social purpose: a groping desire to settle accounts with the rich, if only for a day, and to achieve some rough kind of social justice' (p. 111).

92. Gattrell, *The Hanging Tree* (1994), ch. 3, 'Carnival or Consent'.

93. E. P. Thompson, *Customs in Common*, ch. 3, 'Custom, Law and Common Right', pp. 97–184; B. Bushaway, *By Rite: Custom, Ceremony and Community in England 1700–1880* (London: Junction Books, 1982).

94. See A. McRobbie and S. L. Thornton, 'Rethinking "Moral Panic" for Multi-Mediated Social Worlds', *British Journal of Sociology*, 46:4 (December 1995), pp. 559–74.

95. 'Evangelical' is often capitalized by historians to indicate a socially and historically particular form of the wider activity of evangelizing; in this case, 'Evangelical' refers to a person within the established (Anglican) state church who associated with others in a particular set of beliefs and practices, including the importance of an inward experience

of conversion, revival of such practices as hymn singing and use of the catechism, and certain kinds of social activism combined with evangelizing, usually directed at the lower classes, children, and colonized peoples.

96. G. Kelly, 'Revolution, Reaction, and the Expropriation of Popular Culture: Hannah More's Cheap Repository', *Man and Nature/L'Homme et la nature*, 6 (1987), pp. 148–59.

97. See G. Kelly, 'Fiction and the Working Classes', in R. Maxwell and K. Trumpener (eds) *The Cambridge Companion to Fiction in the Romantic Period* (Cambridge: Cambridge University Press, 2008), pp. 207–33.

98. See N. D. LoPatin, *Political Unions, Popular Politics and the Great Reform Act of 1832* (Basingstoke: Macmillan and New York, NY: St Martin's Press, 1999).

99. For a survey of the issues and measures adopted with regard to policing and the criminal and penal systems, see Leon Radzinowicz, *A History of English Criminal Law and Its Administration from 1750*, vol. 4, *Grappling for Control* (London: Stevens and Sons, 1968).

100. A. Alison, 'The Influence of the Press', review of Georges, conte Libri-Bagnano, *De l'Autocratie de la presse et des moyens d'organiser son action périodique et commerciale, dans l'intérêt de la stabilité des états et de la prospérité des peuples* (La Haye: Van Weelden, 1834), in *Blackwood's Edinburgh Magazine*, 36 (September 1834), pp. 373–91; quotations here from the selections in *Victorian Print Media: A Reader*, ed. Andrew King and John Plunkett (Oxford, Oxford University Press, 2005), pp. 25–30.

101. Wontner, *Old Bailey Experience* (1833), pp. 309–11.

102. *Penny Satirist: A Cheap Substitute for a Weekly Newspaper*, 3 (14 December 1839), p. 1, quoted in A. King and J. Plunkett (eds), *Victorian Print Media: A Reader*, (Oxford: Oxford University Press, 2005), pp. 38–9.

103. 'Conservative Yearnings to Chartism', *Examiner* (London), Sunday 19 January 1840, p. 34.

104. 'Theatrical Examiner', *Examiner* (London), Saturday 18 January 1845, p. 37.

105. Sheppard (1702–24), Turpin (1705–39), and Duval (1643–70) were famous highwaymen, whose lives were recounted in the successive editions of the *Newgate Calendar*, a collection of criminal biographies, and in other cheap publications, and fictionalized in such Newgate novels as Edward Bulwer's *Paul Clifford* (1830) and William Harrison Ainsworth's *Rookwood* (1834), as well as in popular stage melodramas.

106. T. Beggs, *An Inquiry into the Extent and Causes of Juvenile Depravity* (London: Charles Gilpin, 1849), p. 97; the quotation is from the Bible, Matthew 23:27, 'Woe unto you, scribes and Pharisees, hypocrites! for ye are like unto whited sepulchres, which indeed appear beautiful outward, but are within full of dead men's bones, and of all uncleanness.'

107. Beggs, *An Inquiry*, p. 35.

108. Article beginning, 'Scholars and philanthropists . . .', reviewing Charles Knight's *Penny Cyclopædia*, *Morning Chronicle* (London), Tuesday 12 February 1850, p. 4.

109. 'Assize Intelligence', in the *Morning Chronicle* (London), Saturday 13 December 1851, p. 7.

110. *Fraser's Magazine*, 21 (February 1840), p. 210.

111. 'Literature', *Glasgow Herald*, Saturday 13 November 1880, p. 3.

112. Ibid.

113. *Punch; or, The London Charivari* (London), 1 (January 1842), p. 68.

114. *Punch* (London), 22 February 1845, p. 68.

115. K. Hollingsworth, *The Newgate Novel 1830–1847: Bulwer, Ainsworth, Dickens, and Thackeray* (Detroit, MI: Wayne State University Press, 1963), p. 143; M. Buckley, 'Sensations of Celebrity: *Jack Sheppard* and the Mass Audience', *Victorian Studies* (Spring 2002), pp. 424–63.

116. On the branch of eighteenth- and nineteenth-century Newgate literature dealing with hanging, see Gattrell, *The Hanging Tree* (1994), ch. 4, 'Scaffold Culture and Flash Ballads', with its Appendix, an anthology of such ballads (pp. 149–55), and ch. 5, 'Broadsides and the Gallows Emblem'.

117. For a fuller treatment, see G. Kelly, *The English Jacobin Novel 1780–1805* (Oxford: Clarendon Press, 1976), ch. 4.

118. See E. Hobsbawm and G. Rudé, *Captain Swing* (London: Lawrence and Wishart, 1969); E. Hobsbawm, *Bandits* (London: Wiedenfeld and Nicolson, 1969); E. P. Thompson, *Whigs and Hunters: The Origin of the Black Act* (London: Allen Lane, 1975); D. Hay, P. Linebaugh, J. G. Rule, E. P. Thompson, and C. Winslow, *Albion's Fatal Tree: Crime and Society in Eighteenth-Century England* (London: Allen Lane, 1975);

119. Ignatieff, *A Just Measure of Pain*, p. 220; the section referred to does not appear in the Penguin Books paperback edition, published the same year as the hardcover edition cited here.

120. C. Emsley, *Crime and Society in England 1750–1900* (London and New York, NY: Longman, 1987), p. 1.

121. See for example, W. H. Dray, *Philosophy of History* (Englewood Cliffs, NJ: Prentice-Hall, 1964), which itself looked back on several decades of discussion of the topic; and H. White, *Metahistory: The Historical Imagination in Nineteenth-Century Europe* (Baltimore, MD: Johns Hopkins University Press, 1973), which, working from Northrop Frye's *Anatomy of Criticism* (Princeton, NJ: Princeton University Press, 1957), argued that major historical narratives were based on one of the myth-forms of romance, comedy, tragedy, or satire.

122. K. Marx, Manuscripts, 'Theories of Surplus Value' (1863), Addenda to Part 1, section 11, 'Apologist Conception of the Productivity of All Professions'.

SELECT BIBLIOGRAPHY

M. Bassett, 'Newgate Prison in the Middle Ages', *Speculum*, 18:2 (April 1943), pp. 233–46.

J. M. Beattie, *Crime and the Courts in England 1660-1800* (Princeton, NJ: Princeton University Press, 1986).

A. Brodie, J. Croom, and J. O. Davies, *English Prisons: An Architectural History* (Swindon: English Heritage, 2002).

M. Buckley, 'Sensations of Celebrity: *Jack Sheppard* and the Mass Audience', *Victorian Studies* (Spring 2002), pp. 424–63.

B. Bushaway, *By Rite: Custom, Ceremony and Community in England 1700–1880* (London: Junction Books, 1982).

C. Emsley, *Crime and Society in England 1750-1900* (London and New York, NY: Longman, 1987).

C. Emsley, *The English Police: A Political and Social History* (Hemel Hempstead: Harvester Wheatsheaf; New York, NY: St Martin's Press, 1991).

M. Foucault, *Discipline and Punish: The Birth of the Prison*, trans. Alan Sheridan (New York, NY: Pantheon, 1977).

D. Garland, *Punishment and Society: A Study in Social Theory* (Chicago, IL: University of Chicago Press, 1990).

V. A. C. Gattrell, *The Hanging Tree: Execution and the English People 1770–1868* (Oxford: Oxford University Press, 1994).

S. Halliday, *Newgate: London's Prototype of Hell* (London: Sutton Publishing, 2006).

P. Harling, 'Parliament, the State, and "Old Corruption": Conceptualizing Reform, *c.*1790–1832', in A. Burns and J. Innes (eds), *Rethinking the Age of Reform Britain 1780–1850*, (Cambridge: Cambridge University Press, 2003), pp. 98–113.

D. Hay, P. Linebaugh, J. G. Rule, E. P. Thompson and C. Winslow, *Albion's Fatal Tree: Crime and Society in Eighteenth-Century England* (London: Allen Lane, 1975).

U. R. Q. Henriques, 'The Rise and Decline of the Separate System of Prison Discipline', *Past and Present*, 54 (February 1972), pp. 61–93.

C. Hibbert, *The Roots of Evil: A Social History of Crime and Punishment* (London: Weidenfeld and Nicolson, 1963).

E. Hobsbawm, *Bandits* (London: Wiedenfeld and Nicolson, 1969).

E. Hobsbawm and G. Rudé, *Captain Swing* (London: Lawrence and Wishart, 1969).

K. Hollingsworth, *The Newgate Novel 1830–1847: Bulwer, Ainsworth, Dickens, and Thackeray* (Detroit, MI: Wayne State University Press, 1963).

W. Eden Hooper, *The History of Newgate and the Old Bailey* (London: Underwood Press, 1935).

A. Howe, *Punish and Critique: Towards a Feminist Analysis of Penality* (London and New York, NY: Routledge, 1994).

R. Hughes, *The Fatal Shore: A History of the Transportation of Convicts to Australia* (New York, NY: Knopf, 1986).

M. Ignatieff, *A Just Measure of Pain: The Penitentiary in the Industrial Revolution, 1750–1850* (New York, NY: Pantheon, 1978).

G. Kelly, *The English Jacobin Novel 1780–1805* (Oxford: Clarendon Press, 1976).

—., 'Fiction and the Working Classes', in R. Maxwell and K. Trumpener (eds) *The Cambridge Companion to Fiction in the Romantic Period*, (Cambridge: Cambridge University Press, 2008), pp. 207–33.

P. King, 'The Rise of Juvenile Delinquency in England 1780–1840: Changing Patterns of Perception and Prosecution', *Past and Present*, 160 (August 1998), pp. 116–66.

P. Linebaugh, *The London Hanged: Crime and Civil Society in the Eighteenth Century* (Cambridge: Cambridge University Press, 1992).

N. D. LoPatin, *Political Unions, Popular Politics and the Great Reform Act of 1832* (Basingstoke, Macmillan; New York, NY: St Martin's Press, 1999).

D. Low, *Thieves' Kitchen: The Regency Underworld* (Gloucester: Alan Sutton, 1982).

I. McCalman, 'Newgate in Revolution: Radical Enthusiasm and Romantic Counterculture', *Eighteenth-Century Life*, 22:1 (1998), pp. 95–110.

S. McConville, *A History of English Prison Administration*, vol. 1, *1750-1877* (London: Routledge and Kegan Paul, 1981).

R. McGowen, 'The Well-Ordered Prison: England, 1780–1865', in N. Morris and D. J. Rothman (eds) *The Oxford History of the Prison: The Practice of Punishment in Western Society*, (New York and Oxford: Oxford University Press, 1998).

Angela McRobbie and Sarah L. Thornton, 'Rethinking "Moral Panic" for Multi-Mediated Social Worlds', *British Journal of Sociology*, 46:4 (December 1995), pp. 559–74.

L. Radzinowicz, *A History of English Criminal Law and Its Administration from 1750*, 5 vols (London: Macmillan; Stevens and Sons, 1948–86).

S. Rees, *The Floating Brothel: The Extraordinary True Story of an Eighteenth-century Ship and Its Cargo of Female Convicts* (London: Headline, 2001).

G. Rudé, 'The Gordon Riots: A Study of the Rioters and Their Victims', *Transactions of the Royal Historical Society*, 5th series, 6 (1956), pp. 93–114.

V. Ruggiero, *Crime in Literature: Sociology of Deviance and Fiction* (London and New York, NY: Verso, 2003).

D. Rumbelow, *The Triple Tree: Newgate, Tyburn and Old Bailey* (London: Harrap, 1982).

H. Shore, *Artful Dodgers: Youth and Crime in Early Nineteenth-Century London* (London: Boydell Press, 1999).

E. P. Thompson, *Customs in Common* (New York, NY: The New Press, 1993).

—., *The Making of the English Working Class* (Harmondsworth: Penguin Books, 1968).

—., *Whigs and Hunters: The Origin of the Black Act* (London: Allen Lane, 1975).

J. J. Tobias, *Crime and Industrial Society in the 19th Century* (New York, NY: Schocken Books, 1967).

S. Webb and B. Webb, *English Prisons under Local Government* (London: Longmans, Green, and Co., 1922).

M. J. Wiener, 'Homicide and "Englishness": Criminal Justice and National identity in Victorian England', *National Identities*, 6:3 (2004), pp. 203–13.

—., *Reconstructing the Criminal: Culture, Law, and Policy in England, 1830–1914* (Cambridge: Cambridge University Press, 1990).

A NEWGATE CHRONOLOGY

1218 First records of Newgate, a gatehouse in the walls of London, being used to house criminals, though the practice probably began earlier.

1556 Bridewell house of correction, London, opened.

1571 Permanent gallows ('triple tree') erected at Tyburn (present day Marble Arch, London) for public hangings.

1699 Establishment of sentence of branding on the cheek for theft; most forms of petty theft made capital offences; county justices empowered to build and repair jails.

1702 Society for Promotion of Christian Knowledge inspects prisons, approves keeping prisoners in separate cells.

1706 Legislation permits judges to sentence felons to up to two years in a house of correction, including hard labour.

1707 Branding for theft restricted to the thumb.

1718 Transportation Act regularizes transportation of convicts to American colonies; 30,000 transported between 1718 and 1775.

1724 Batty Langley, *An Accurate Description of Newgate* published.

1728 Law requires jailers to post schedule of fees charged to prisoners.

1738 Juries required to give verdicts immediately after trial proceedings.

1739 Bow Street Magistrates' Office established; execution of Richard Turpin for horse-stealing.

1749 Henry Fielding appointed salaried chief magistrate for Westminster.

1751 Law forbids sale of liquor in prisons; the practice continues; Henry Fielding, *Inquiry into the Causes of the Late Increase of Robbers*.

1752 Act of Parliament provides for bodies of the hanged to be turned over for dissection for medical or educational purposes.

1755 Beginnings of London detective and security police force later known as Bow Street officers, or 'runners'.

1760	Permanent gallows at Tyburn replaced with portable one.
1764	Publication of Count Cesare Beccaria, *Dei Delitti e delle pene* (*Of Crimes and Punishments*).
1770	Construction of new Newgate Prison begun, completed 1785.
1772	Ending use of *peine forte et dure*, or pressing, in which a person refusing to plead guilty or not guilty to a charge had weights placed on his body until he relented or died.
1773	Law permits magistrates to appoint salaried chaplains to jails.
1774	Law permits magistrates to appoint physician for prisoners.
1775	Model reformed prison built at Horsham, Sussex.
1776	American Revolution closes colonies for transportation of convicts; old ships (hulks) anchored in the Thames used to house convicts, with rigorous discipline and hard labour; William Smith, *State of the Gaols of London, Westminster, and Borough of Southwark*; Jonas Hanway, *Solitude in Imprisonment*, recommends solitary confinement as means to religious conversion and moral reformation of convicts.
1777	John Howard, *The State of the Prisons in England and Wales*; expanded in subsequent editions.
1779	Penitentiary Act proposes two reformed prisons (one for males, one for females), incorporating measures such as solitary confinement, uniforms, work discipline, religious instruction, coarse food, profits from prisoners' labour to meets costs and imposition of a fine in place of branding; implementation of many of the measures delayed into nineteenth century.
1780	Unfinished Newgate Prison damaged by fire during Gordon Riots against Roman Catholics.
1782	Law empowers magistrates to repair prisons.
1783	Introduction of the sharp drop in the gallows to break the victim's neck at hanging, causing swift death rather than slow strangulation, but lack of scientific method often results in strangulation; public executions in London moved from Tyburn to Old Bailey, street outside Newgate prison, to reduce public disorder around executions.
1784	Sir George Onesiphorus Paul, *Considerations on the Defects of Prisons*; law empowers magistrates to order separation of various categories of prisoners.
1785	Josiah Dornford, *Seven Letters ... on the Police*; Martin Madan, *Thoughts on Executive Justice*; William Paley, *Principles of Moral and Political Philosophy*, defends harsh punishments and death penalty.

1787	First fleet carrying convicts to new penal colony near Botany Bay, Australia.
1789	Last woman burned at the stake in England; last Old Bailey sentence to punishment by branding
1790	Punishment by burning at the stake abolished.
1791	Law empowers magistrates to pay jailers salaries.
1792	New model prison opened at Gloucester, designed by prominent prison architect William Blackburn, incorporating reform ideas of George Onesiphorus Paul.
1793	William Godwin, *Enquiry Concerning Political Justice*.
1794	Penitentiary Act; Godwin's novel, *Things As They Are; or, The Adventures of Caleb Williams*, first novel of crime and detection.
1800	Thames River Police Act introduces measures to police shipping and warehouses.
1801	Bedfordshire Prison opened, anticipating later architectural and administrative reforms across the country.
1805	Revival of the Bow Street Horse Patrol to suppress highway robberies within sixty miles of London.
1808	Sir Richard Phillips, *Letter to the Livery of London*, on prisons; Society for the Diffusion of Information on the Death Penalty founded; death penalty for pickpocketing abolished.
1810	Parliamentary committee re-examines issues of 1779 Penitentiary Act; Sir Samuel Romilly, *Observations of the Criminal Law of England*.
1810s	Treadwheel introduced into various prisons to punish, instill discipline, and provide exercise
1811	December: 'Ratcliffe Highway Murders' cause public panic over violent crime.
1813	Quaker Elizabeth Fry begins charitable work with women in Newgate Prison; report of parliamentary committee investigating jails of the City of London, including Newgate.
1815	parliamentary committee into begging and vagrancy in London; law abolishes fees charged to prisoners in jails.
1816	Millbank new model prison, based on 'panopticon' surveillance plan of Jeremy Bentham, receives prisoners, though still under construction; report of parliamentary committee on state of the police of London; Society for the Improvement of Prison Discipline founded.

1817   Public whipping of women abolished.

1818   Henry Grey Bennet, *A Letter ... on the Abuses Existing in Newgate*; report of parliamentary committee on prisons in City of London and borough of Southwark.

1820   Last sentence of hanging, drawing and quartering carried out (the quartering was omitted).

1822   Report of parliamentary commission of inquiry into state of the (penal) colony of New South Wales, Australia.

1823   Gaol Act legislates appointment of prison chaplains and physicians, provision of education, classification of prisoners and ban on alcohol in prisons; Punishment of Death Act gives judges power to commute sentences for capital crimes except murder and treason.

1827   Act raises the threshold for applying death penalty for theft from property worth 40 shillings to property worth 100 shillings; *Richmond; or, Scenes in the Life of a Bow Street Officer*, police detective novel.

1828   publication in France of *Mémoires de Vidocq*, French criminal turned police informer and official; Thomas Gaspey's novel *History of George Godfrey*.

1827–30 Four parliamentary acts consolidate and repeal over three hundred laws relating to crime.

1829   Metropolitan Police Act establishes centralized London police force; last hanging for forgery.

1830   Edward Lytton Bulwer's novel *Paul Clifford*.

1831   Edward Gibbon Wakefield, *Facts Relating to the Punishment of Death in the Metropolis*.

1832   Punishment of Death, etc. Act reduces capital crimes by two-thirds and abolishes dissection of bodies of hanged murderers.

1833   Last hanging of a juvenile, Thomas Knapton, seventeen (for rape).

1834   Report to parliament by Charles Crawford on penal systems in the United States; success of W. H. Ainsworth's novel *Rookwood*, featuring fictionalized Dick Turpin; Charles Whitehead's novel *The Autobiography of Jack Ketch* (dated 1835).

1832–4 Legislation removes many crimes from category of capital offence.

1835   Act of Parliament on administration of jails and appointment of prison inspectors; report of committee of House of Lords on jails and houses of correction in England and Wales.

1836	Last hangings for robbery; first report to parliament of official inspectors of prisons; report to parliament of City of London response to prison inspectors' reports.
1837	Abolition of punishment of being made to stand in the pillory.
1840	Construction of Pentonville Prison, based on system of separating prisoners, begins; opened 1842, and remains in use today; 'Newgate novels' controversy.
1839–40	Serialization of Ainsworth's *Jack Sheppard*.
1849	Construction of Holloway house of correction begun; opened 1852.
1851	Surrey house of correction opened, later to be Wandsworth prison, still in use today.
1853	Penal Servitude Act.
1856	Newgate Prison internally reconstructed.
1861	Criminal Law Consolidation Act reduces capital crimes to four.
1863	House of Lords establishes Carnarvon committee to examine prison discipline.
1865	Prison Act established two systems, of local and convict prisons.
1868	Public executions abolished; henceforth executions to be within prison walls.
1869	Last convict convoy arrives in Australia.
1872	Professional hangman William Marwood introduces 'long drop' at hangings to ensure swift death.
1877	Newgate Prison badly damaged by fire; Prisons Act reduces Newgate to holding prison for those awaiting trial or execution.
1890	Millbank prison demolished.
1902	Newgate Prison closed and demolished.
1903	Holloway Prison, opened in 1852 as a house of correction, refurbished and made a women's prison; it remains in use as such today.
1965	Murder (Abolition of Death Penalty) Act effectively suspends capital punishment, though some crimes remained capital offences.
1999	The United Kingdom signs European convention abolishing capital punishment.

from [Batty Langley], *An Accurate Description of Newgate, with the Rights, Privileges, Allowances, Fees, Dues, and Customs thereof, together with a Parallel between the Master Debtors Side of the said Prison, and the several Sponging-Houses in the County of Middlesex ... written for the Publick Good* (London: T. Warner, 1724), pp. 1–2, 42–56.

Langley's *Accurate Description* is one of the earliest detailed accounts of Newgate, as it had been rebuilt in the seventeenth century after the great fire of London of 1666. Langley (1696–1751) was born and raised at Twickenham, on the river Thames to the west of London, where many titled and wealthy people had villas, usually with extensive gardens. Langley trained for his father's profession of gardener and published garden designs, advocating the irregular style, but in the late 1720s turned to architecture as potentially more remunerative, and moved to London to pursue commissions, at which he was not very successful. A freemason, he criticized the fashionable Palladian style as foreign and promoted the 'Anglo-Saxon', or Gothic style of architecture, as more English, notably in his books *Ancient Masonry* (1733–6) and *Ancient Architecture Restored and Improved* (1741–2), with engravings by his brother Thomas. He also published manuals and pattern-books for builders, opened a design academy, and also manufactured and sold garden and architectural ornaments. At the time he published his *Description of Newgate* his brother was a sub-turnkey in the prison. The book compares conditions for debtors in Newgate and in the various private, for-profit 'sponging houses' or debtors' prisons of London, and condemns the latter with an energy that suggests Langley had personal experience of them. The extracts here describe the exterior and the parts of Newgate appropriated for felons.

PART I.

SECT. I.

NEWGATE the County Gaol of *Middlesex*, is situated in an Elegant Part of the West of the City of *London*, called *Newgate Street*.

This Prison was first built either in the Time of *Henry* I. or that of King *Stephen*,[1] but in which there is no Certainty; And was then (as it has ever since continued to be) a Prison for Debtors, Felons, &c.

About Three hundred Years after the first Founding of this Prison, it became terribly Loathsome: And therefore, was in the Year 1412, rebuilt by the Executors of Sir *Richard Whittington*,[2] in the Reign of *Henry* VI.

The Architecture of this Structure is according to the *Tuscan Order*,[3] magnificently built with Stone, with great Strength and Beauty.

In this magnificent Edifice are Three several Prisons, which are comprized under the following Denominations, *viz.* The *Master's Side*,[4] The *Common Side* and *Press-Yard*. [pp. 1–2]

PART V.

Of the Common Felons Side.

THIS *Common Felons*[5] Side, is a most Terrible Wicked and Dreadful Place. *Solomon* says, *The Curse of the Lord is in the House of the Wicked*, Prov. ii. 33.[6] And this is too much verified amongst these poor unfortunate Wretches: who, instead of Humbling themselves to Almighty God, and beseeching Him to give them His Grace, and to pardon their horrid Sins, continually augment the same, and in the most Sinful and Wicked Manner they possibly can contrive, accelerate their own Destruction.

In this Side there are Five Wards, Two of which are for Women, and Three for Men.

The Names of the Mens Wards are, *The Stone Hold, The Lower Ward*, and *The Middle Ward*.

1. The *Stone Hold*, a most terrible stinking, dark and dismal Place, situated under Ground, in which no Day-light can come, as also in which is a small Room at the Entrance therein, called *The Passage*.

This Hold (as likewise the Passage) is paved with Stone, on which the Prisoners lie without any Beds, and thereby endure great Misery and Hardship.

The Unhappy Persons imprisoned therein, are such as at their unfortunate Entrance, cannot pay the Customary Dues[7] of the Gaol.

2. Adjacent thereunto, is a large Ward, called *The Lower Ward*, wherein are imprisoned such Felons, as are Fined in certain Sums of Money, till such time as those Fines are paid, or they are otherwise discharg'd.

This Ward is the same in all respects whatsoever with the *Stone Hold*.

In this Ward is Imprison'd *William Fuller*, who for imposing upon the Government, upon pretence of proving one Mrs. *Mary Gray*, to be the Mother of the Pretender,[8] was Pillory'd,[9] Imprisoned and Fined; for the last of which he now remains confined, till the same be paid.

3. Over the preceding Ward, is situated the *Middle Ward*, wherein are imprison'd such Felons as have paid their Dues at their coming in.

This Ward is also very Dark, but not so cold as the foregoing, the Floor thereof being Oaken Plank, on which, however, the Felons lie without any sort of Bed.

The *Women Felons Wards* are Two; the first of which is situated over the *Bilbows*[10] (an Account of which I shall give hereafter) called *Waterman's Hall*; And this is also a very terrible dark and stinking Place; the Floor is of Oaken Planks, and is all the Bed allotted for its miserable Inhabitants.

Near to this Ward is a Cistern of Lead, which is plentifully supply'd every Day with fresh Water for the Use of the Prisoners therein.

The Second *Women Felons Ward*, is situated in the highest part of the whole Gaol, in the North part thereof, and is of a large Extent, in which is one Window only, and that very small.

On each side of this Ward are Barracks[11] placed, on which the Prisoners lie, but without any kind of Bed whatsoever.

The Persons imprisoned herein, are generally those that lie for Transportation;[12] and they knowing their Time to be short here, rather than bestow one Minute towards cleaning the same, suffer themselves to live far worse than Swine; and, to speak the Truth, the *Augean* Stable[13] could bear no Comparison to it, for they are almost poisoned with their own Filth, and their Conversation is nothing but one continued Course of Swearing, Cursing and Debauchery, insomuch that it surpasses all Description and Belief.

It is with no small Concern, that I am obliged to observe, That the Women in every Ward of this Prison, are exceedingly worse than the worst of the Men, not only in respect to Nastiness and Indecency of living, but more especially as to their Conversation, which, to their great Shame, is as prophane and wicked, as Hell itself can possibly be.

PART VI.

Of the Press-Room, Bilbows *and* Condemned Holds.

THE *Press-Room* is a close and dark Place, situated near the Place call'd *Waterman's Hall*, in which such Prisoners as will not Plead, are Pressed to Death.[14]

The *Bilbows* (a Room so call'd) adjacent to the *Press-Room*, is also very dark; in which are put such Prisoners, as occasion any Quarrel or Disturbance.

There are Two Condemned Holds, one for each Sex; that for the Men, is situated adjacent to the Lodge, in which is a very good Fire-place, and a Receptacle for necessary Conveniency.[15]

The Entrance therein, is at the Lodge, into which Place the Condemned Prisoners are admitted to come, upon Payment of 18 *d.*[16] and to speak to those they are disposed to see; and this is the nearest Access that the most affectionate and faithful Friends, can have with the unhappy Prisoners confined therein.

This *Hold* (as 'tis called) is a large Room, about 20 Foot in Length, and 15 in Breadth, and at the farthest End thereof, is an Arch of the *Gothick* Order,[17] whose Diameter is equal to the Breadth of the Whole, and makes appear, that anciently the Common Way for Foot Passengers was under the same, as it is now on the opposite Side.

The Floor of this *Hold* is of Plank, on which the Prisoners take their Nightly Rest, and wherein are divers Ring-bolts, to which such Prisoners are lock'd as are disorderly.

There is one Window herein, which is so very small, that little Light comes thereby, so that this Room is very dark.

'Tis Customary when any Felons are brought to the Lodge in *Newgate*, to put them first into this *Condemned Hold*, where they remain till they have paid 2 *s.* 6 *d.* after which they are admitted either to the *Master* or *Common Felons Side*.

The Condemned Prisoners twice every Day are conducted to the Chapel, where they receive such Admonitions as are necessary to prepare them for future Happiness, &c. And at proper times the Blessed Sacrament[18] is Administred to them, and in particular on the Morning before they take their final Farewel of this World.

The Administration of the Holy Sacrament being ended, the Prisoners are led down into the *Stone Hall* of the Debtors (before described) in the midst of which their Irons are knock'd off, and then they are bound with the same fatal Hempen String,[19] which shortly after finally determinates their wicked Days.

After that, they are conveyed down Stairs into the Street, at the bottom of which is provided a Cart, Coach, &c. in which they are conveyed to *Tyburn*;[20] and in the Passage thither, at St. *Sepulchre's* Church, they are stopt some Minutes, till a certain Ceremony*[21] is performed, and then they are carry'd to the

---

*   *N.B.* That in the Reign of King *James* I. *Robert Dows* of *London*, Merchant Taylor, gave a competent Maintenance for ever, unto St. *Sepulchre's* Parish for the Tolling the great Bell, and for finding a Divine, to come to the *Condemned Hold* of *Newgate*, the Midnight before their Execution (which is now performed by a Bellman) and there to ring a Hand Bell, to put the Prisoners in Mind of their approaching Death, with a Christian Remembrance and Exhortation. And the next Morn-

Place of Execution, and by an infamous Death, make some sort of Atonement for the scandalous Misdeeds of their past shameful Lives.

The Womens *Condemned Hold* is situated adjacent to the *Press-Room*, and is a small dismal dark Dungeon, wherein is a Barrack for the Prisoners to lie on, but no Fire place, and is therefore very cold at all times.

The Dues, Customs, &c. herein, are the same with those of the Mens *Condemned Hold* before mentioned.

After the Execution is over, if the Sufferers have not Friends present to see them immediately decently Interred, 'tis customary to dispose of the dead Bodies by way of Sale to Surgeons for Anatomies, at the Price of 5 *s.* and sometimes 10 *s.* and very often 2 *s.* and 6 *d.* each.[22]

Of TRANSPORTATION.

HAVING given a Description of the several Parts of *Newgate*, (the *Press-Yard* excepted, which I shall take Notice of by-and-by) I shall now proceed to speak a Word or two in relation to the Transportation of Criminals.

The limitted Time for Transportation is generally in proportion to the Offence, *viz.*[23] if for Felony, Seven Years; and for those who are under Sentence of Death, or such who buy Stoln Goods (knowing the same to[24] Stoln) Fourteen Years; and for such Criminals whose Actions appear to be very enormously Wicked, and are reprieved[25] after Condemnation, they are generally Transported for Term of Life.

The Commencing of the Time of Transportation, is accounted from the Day the Keeper of *Newgate* delivers the Criminals out of his Gaol, to the Captain who Transports them to the Places assigned.

At the Captain's receiving of them out of *Newgate*, they (being Hand-cuff'd two and two together) are directed to the Transport Ship; between the Decks of which is a Prison or Gaol, wherein they are strongly secured, till such time as they arrive at the intended Port, being allow'd each Day such Subsistance as is requisite for them.

The Person who at present Transports those unhappy Creatures is known by the Name of Captain *Forward*, who twice a Year, or oftner, is imployed in this kind of Traffick, which he disposes of by way of Sale to the Plantations, &c. at *Annapolis, Boston* in *New England, Saffron River* between *Maryland* and *New England*, and *James River* in *Virginia*, in the following Manner.

First, At their coming into the Bay, the Captain sends his Boat ashore, to his Factor or Correspondent, who comes on Board, to whom the Captain delivers the List he received at *Newgate*, of the several Persons delivered to him, and

---

ing to Toll the great Bell, from Six in the Morning till Ten, and then to raise the same, and ring it out; till the Execution is over.

upon View of the same, an Examination is made of what Number (if any) died in their Passage, what are remaining Alive, and in what Condition they are; which Inspection being made (and a Receipt or Discharge being given from the Merchant or Factor to the Captain for the same) Notice is immediately given to all the Planters, and other Inhabitants of the Islands, who thereupon come on Board, and take a View of every Person to be disposed of; and after having chosen such as they think for their Purpose, an Agreement is made for them, and the Money paid, which for each Person, is from 20 *s.* to 10 *l.* the Price being always in proportion to the Health, Age, and Trade of the Person.

And altho' these unhappy Persons are thus Transported from their Native Country, and sold (as Beasts are in *Smithfield*[26]) from one Man to another as Slaves, yet if they live to go through the first Four Years, and behave themselves well, their Slavery is then over, and they are generally rewarded with a Plantation of their own, of Tobacco, Sugar, Ginger, &c.

And provided that they are not inclinable to be the Proprietors of such Plantation, for the Residue of the Time they are Transported for, be it either for Seven, Fourteen Years, or Life, they are at Liberty to spend the same as Servants, or in any other manner they please; but not to depart from thence before their assigned time of Transportation, on the Peril of Death.

'Tis a Custom in every Town in those Western Parts, that before any Person departs from thence to come for *England*, he is obliged publickly to put up his Name and Reason of his Departure, Twenty Days before he goes, at the Publick Market Place or Cross of each Town, and also to have a Certificate from the Justice of Peace, Mayor, or other Officers of the Town he departs from, to the Officer of the next Town he is travelling unto; and for want of such Certificate, is imprisoned till such time as he gives a true and faithful Account of himself, and that he hath not cheated or defrauded any Person in that Town or Place whereunto he last belonged, which being made appear, he is discharged, or otherwise imprisoned at the Discretion of the respective Magistrates of such Town, &c.

For every Person as is delivered to the aforesaid Captain *Forward* to be Transported, the said Captain pays to the Keeper of *Newgate* the Fees, &c. of the same; and for the Transportation of them, is paid by the Government the Sum of 3 *l.* Sterling, for each Person so Transported.

Fœlix quam faciunt, aliena periculi cautum.[27]

Of the CHAPEL.

IN the South-East Angle of this Gaol, in the upper Part thereof, is situated the Chapel of *Newgate*, in which, on the North side thereof, are three large Apartments called Penns, which, are all in general strongly built, wherein are placed every *Sunday*, the Common-Debtors and Felons of both kinds.

Near to the North-West Angle of this Chapel, is placed the Pulpit, against which are the Male Common-Debtors,[28] and adjacent thereunto are the Male and Female Felons; but in separate Apartments (or Penns) through the square Grates of which, they are seen by those who are in the Pews of the Chapel.

On the South-side thereof, opposite to the Felons Penns, are two very handsome Inclosures for the Master-Debtors to sit in during Divine Service, which are better situated than the opposite ones.

Adjoining to the Pulpit is a large Pew, wherein are placed such Prisoners as are under Sentence of Death, in which Place also is Administred the Blessed Sacrament unto them at proper times, and particularly on the Morning before their Execution.

Besides those Apartments before mentioned, there are many very handsome open Pews, in which all Persons who come are free to sit, which are generally well filled on such *Sundays* as the Condemned Sermons are preached to the Prisoners before they Die.

The present Ordinary of this Chapel, is the Reverend Mr. *T. Purney*,[29] who, in proportion to his Age, is not much inferior to any of his Predecessors of that Imploy. His Annual Salary is about 60 *l.* and altho' he hath not the Benefit of any Tythes, *Easter*-Offerings,[30] and other such like Benefits, as are Customary to most Gentlemen of his Cloth;[31] yet once in Six Weeks, he, by giving an Account of the Lives of his Auditors, their Transactions, Dying Speeches, &c. augments his Annual Stipend to about One hundred Pounds *per Annum.*

Of the Press-Yard *and* Castle.

At the Basis of the Stairs, which enter into the *Common Debtors* and *Felons Side* (before describ'd) is the Entrance into that Part of *Newgate*, known by the Name of *The Press-Yard*.

This Part of the Prison is composed of divers large spacious Rooms, which in general have very good Air and Light, free from all Ill Smells, with all necessary Appurtenances thereunto belonging. The Yard or Place for walking to take the Air, is situated between the Door which enters from *Newgate Street*, and the Fabrick itself, the Dimensions whereof, are in Length about 54 Foot, and Breadth 7 Foot, being handsomly paved with Purbeck Stone. The Persons imprison'd here, are generally State Prisoners,[32] Felons, &c. or any Prisoners whatsoever, as are able to pay such a Præmium at their Entrance, as shall be agreed on by the Gaoler thereof, and the Weekly Rent afterwards.

The Præmium is always in proportion to the Quality[33] of the Prisoner, and is from 20 to 500 *l.* The Weekly Rent of each Room (except in Time of Necessity, as when the *Preston* Gentlemen[34] were imprison'd therein) is 11 *s.* and 6 *d.*; 1 *s.* of which is paid to a Woman call'd the Landress, for making the Fires, cleaning the

Rooms, &c. and the Residue to the Gaoler. The Fires and Candles are provided by the Prisoners themselves, as also all other Necessaries, except Beds, which of their kinds are very good, and are provided by the Gaoler, Sheets being always excepted.

Over the *King's Bench* and *Stone Wards*, (before described) are Two Wards called *The Castle*, in which are kept State Prisoners also. These Two Wards are of the same Dimensions, Air, Light, &c. as those underneath the same, in which are divers Partitions for Beds, as in the *King's Bench Ward* before describ'd, for which each Prisoner pays 2 *s.* 6 *d. per* Week.

N.B. That when the Three Wards of the *Master Debtors Side*, have not convenient Room for Prisoners, then, at such Times, such Debtors are imprison'd in the *Castle Wards*, wherein they have the same Government, Allowances, &c. as those of the *Hall*, *King's Bench*, and *Stone Wards*, before described. [pp. 42–56]

from Cesare Beccaria, *An Essay on Crimes and Punishments, Translated from the Italian* ... (London: J. Almon, 1767), Introduction, chapters 1, 2, 3, 4, 6, 7, 8, 28.

Beccaria (1738–94) was an Italian nobleman from Milan, part of a self-consciously enlightened circle of intellectuals with reformist ideas, which they circulated through an essay periodical called *Il Caffè* (1764–6). Beccaria published his widely influential *Dei Delitti e delle pene* (*Of Crimes and Punishments*) in 1764, translated into English in 1767. It approaches the issues from a rationalist and utilitarian point of view, arguing that crimes are caused by social inequality and injustice, that punishments should only be applied for some useful end and that the death penalty was both unjust and ineffective. Appointed professor of law and economy at a college in Milan, he gave lectures and published a short treatise on literary style. Late in life he was appointed to a law reform panel. His grandson was Alessandro Manzoni, author of the major Italian patriotic historical novel, *I Promessi sposi* (*The Betrothed*, 1825–7). Beccaria's work was reprinted several times into the first years of the nineteenth century, and had a great influence on British legal and penal reformers during that period, particularly William Godwin in his *Political Justice* (1793), extracts from which are included here.

Note on the text: present editor's omission indicated by three points of ellipsis in square brackets.

INTRODUCTION.

[...]

IF we look into history we shall find, that laws, which are, or ought to be, conventions between men in a state of freedom, have been, for the most part, the work of the passions of a few, or the consequences of a fortuitous, or temporary necessity; not dictated by a cool examiner of human nature, who knew how to collect in one point, the actions of a multitude, and had this only end in view, *the greatest happiness of the greatest number*. Happy are those few nations, who have not waited, till the slow succession of human vicissitudes, should, from the extremity of evil, produce a transition to good; but, by prudent laws, have facilitated the progress from one to the other! And how great are the obligations due from mankind to that philosopher, who from the obscurity of his closet, had the courage to scatter amongst the multitude, the seeds of useful truths, so long unfruitful!

THE art of printing has diffused the knowledge of those philosophical truths, by which the relations between sovereigns and their subjects, and between nations, are discovered. By this knowledge, commerce is animated, and there has sprung up a spirit of emulation, and industry, worthy of rational beings. These are the produce of this enlightened age; but the cruelty of punishments, and the irregularity of proceedings in criminal cases, so principal a part of the legislation, and so much neglected throughout Europe, has hardly ever been called in question. Errors, accumulated through many centuries, have never yet been exposed by ascending to general principles; nor has the force of acknowledged truths been ever opposed to the unbounded licentiousness of ill-directed power, which has continually produced so many authorized examples of the most unfeeling barbarity. Surely, the groans of the weak, sacrificed to the cruel ignorance, and indolence of the powerful; the barbarous torments lavished, and multiplied with useless severity, for crimes either not proved, or in their nature impossible; the filth, and horrors of a prison, increased by the most cruel tormentor of the miserable, uncertainty, ought to have roused the attention of those, whose business is to direct the opinions of mankind.

THE immortal *Montesquieu*[1] has but slightly touched on this subject. Truth, which is eternally the same, has obliged me to follow the steps of that great man; but the studious part of mankind, for whom I write, will easily distinguish the superstructure from the foundation. I shall be happy, if, with him, I can obtain the secret thanks of the obscure, and peaceful disciples of reason, and philosophy, and excite that tender emotion, in which sensible minds sympathize with him, who pleads the cause of humanity.

CHAP. I.

Of the Origin of Punishments.

LAWS are the conditions, under which men, naturally independent, united themselves in society. Weary of living in a continual state of war, and of enjoying a liberty, which became of little value, from the uncertainty of its duration, they sacrificed one part of it, to enjoy the rest in peace and security. The sum of all these portions of the liberty of each individual constituted the sovereignty of a nation; and was deposited in the hands of the sovereign, as the lawful administrator. But it was not sufficient only to establish this deposite; it was also necessary to defend it from the usurpation of each individual, who will always endeavour to take away from the mass, not only his own portion, but to encroach on that of others. Some motives, therefore, that strike the senses, were necessary, to prevent the despotism of each individual from plunging society into its former chaos. Such motives are the punishments established against the infractors of the laws. I say, that motives of this kind are necessary, because, experience shews, that the multitude adopt no established principle of conduct; and because, society is prevented from approaching to that dissolution, (to which, as well as all other parts of the physical, and moral world, it naturally tends) only by motives, that are the immediate objects of sense, and which being continually presented to the mind, are sufficient to counterbalance the effects of the passions of the individual, which oppose the general good. Neither the power of eloquence, nor the sublimest truths, are sufficient to restrain, for any length of time, those passions, which are excited by the lively impression of present objects.

CHAP. II.

Of the Right to punish.

EVERY punishment, which does not arise from absolute necessity, says the great *Montesquieu*, is tyrannical. A proposition which may be made more general, thus. Every act of authority of one man over another, for which there is not an absolute necessity, is tyrannical. It is upon this then, that the sovereign's right to punish crimes is founded; that is, upon the necessity of defending the public liberty, entrusted to his care, from the usurpation of individuals; and punishments are just in proportion, as the liberty, preserved by the sovereign, is sacred and valuable.

LET us consult the human heart, and there we shall find the foundation of the sovereign's right to punish; for no advantage in moral policy can be lasting, which is not founded on the indelible sentiments of the heart of man. Whatever law deviates from this principle will always meet with a resistance, which will destroy it in the end; for the smallest force, continually applied, will overcome the most violent motion communicated to bodies.

No man ever gave up his liberty, merely for the good of the public. Such a chimera exists only in romances. Every individual wishes, if possible, to be exempt from the compacts, that bind the rest of mankind.

THE multiplication of mankind, though slow, being too great for the means, which the earth, in its natural state, offered to satisfy necessities, which every day became more numerous, obliged men to separate again, and form new societies. These naturally opposed the first, and a state of war was transferred from individuals to nations.

THUS it was necessity, that forced men to give up a part of their liberty; it is certain then, that every individual would chuse to put into the public stock the smallest portion possible; as much only as was sufficient to engage others to defend it. The aggregate of these, the smallest portions possible, forms the right of punishing: all that extends beyond this is abuse, not justice.

OBSERVE, that by *justice* I understand nothing more, than that bond, which is necessary to keep the interest of individuals united; without which, men would return to their original state of barbarity. All punishments, which exceed the necessity of preserving this bond, are in their nature unjust. We should be cautious how we associate with the word *justice*, an idea of any thing real, such as a physical power, or a being that actually exists. I do not, by any means, speak of the justice of God, which is of another kind, and refers immediately to rewards and punishments in a life to come.

CHAP. III.

Consequences of the foregoing Principles.

THE laws only can determine the punishment of crimes; and the authority of making penal laws can only reside with the legislator, who represents the whole society, united by the social compact. No magistrate then, (as he is one of the society) can, with justice, inflict on any other member of the same society, punishment, that is not ordained by the laws. But as a punishment, increased beyond the degree fixed by the law, is the just punishment, with the addition of another; it follows, that no magistrate, even under a pretence of zeal, or the public good, should increase the punishment already determined by the laws.

IF every individual be bound to society, society is equally bound to him, by a contract, which from its nature, equally binds both parties. This obligation, which descends from the throne to the cottage, and equally binds the highest, and lowest of mankind, signifies nothing more, than that it is the interest of all, that conventions, which are useful to the greatest number, should be punctually observed. The violation of this compact by any individual, is an introduction to anarchy.

THE sovereign, who represents the society itself, can only make general laws, to bind the members; but it belongs not to him to judge whether any individual has violated the social compact, or incurred the punishment in consequence. For in this case, there are two parties, one represented by the sovereign, who insists upon the violation of the contract, and the other is the person accused, who denies it. It is necessary then that there should be a third person to decide this contest; that is to say, a judge, or magistrate, from whose determination there should be no appeal; and this determination should consist of a simple affirmation, or negation of fact.

IF it can only be proved, that the severity of punishments, though not immediately contrary to the public good, or to the end for which they were intended, viz. to prevent crimes, be useless; then such severity would be contrary to those beneficent virtues, which are the consequence of enlightened reason, which instructs the sovereign to wish rather to govern men in a state of freedom and happiness, than of slavery. It would also be contrary to justice, and the social compact.

CHAP. IV.

Of the Interpretation of Laws.

JUDGES, in criminal cases, have no right to interpret the penal laws, because they are not legislators. They have not received the laws from our ancestors as a domestic tradition, or as the will of a testator, which his heirs, and executors, are to obey; but they receive them from a society actually existing, or from the sovereign, its representative. Even the authority of the laws is not founded on any pretended obligation, or ancient convention; which must be null, as it cannot bind those who did not exist at the time of its institution; and unjust, as it would reduce men, in the ages following, to a herd of brutes, without any power of judging, or acting. The laws receive their force, and authority from an oath of fidelity, either tacit, or expressed, which living subjects have sworn to their sovereign, in order to restrain the intestine fermentation of the private interests of individuals. From hence springs their true and natural authority. Who then is their lawful interpreter? The sovereign, that is, the representative of society, and not the judge, whose office is only to examine, if a man have, or have not committed an action contrary to the laws.

IN every criminal cause the judge should reason syllogistically. The *major* should be the general law; the *minor*, the conformity of the action, or its opposition to the laws; the *conclusion*, liberty, or punishment. If the judge be obliged by the imperfection of the laws, or chuses, to make any other, or more syllogisms than this, it will be an introduction to uncertainty.

THERE is nothing more dangerous than the common axiom: *the spirit of the laws is to be considered.* To adopt it is to give way to the torrent of opinions. This may seem a paradox to vulgar minds, which are more strongly affected by the smallest disorder before their eyes, than by the most pernicious, though remote, consequences produced by one false principle adopted by a nation.

OUR knowledge is in proportion to the number of our ideas. The more complex these are, the greater is the variety of positions, in which they may be considered. Every man hath his own particular point of view, and at different times, sees the same objects in very different lights. The spirit of the laws will then be the result of the good, or bad logic of the judge; and this will depend on his good or bad digestion; on the violence of his passions; on the rank, and condition of the accused, or on his connections with the judge; and on all those little circumstances, which change the appearance of objects in the fluctuating mind of man. Hence we see the fate of a delinquent changed many times in passing through the different courts of judicature, and his life and liberty, victims to the false ideas, or ill humour of the judge; who mistakes the vague result of his own confused reasoning, for the just interpretation of the laws. We see the same crimes punished in a different manner at different times in the same tribunals; the consequence of not having consulted the constant, and invariable voice of the laws, but the erring instability of arbitrary interpretation.

THE disorders, that may arise from a rigorous observance of the letter of penal laws, are not to be compared with those produced by the interpretation of them. The first are temporary inconveniences which will oblige the legislator to correct the letter of the law, the want of preciseness, and uncertainty of which has occasioned these disorders; and this will put a stop to the fatal liberty of explaining; the source of arbitrary and venal declamations. When the code of laws is once fixed, it should be observed in the literal sense, and nothing more is left to the judge, than to determine, whether an action be, or be not conformable to the written law. When the rule of right which ought to direct the actions of the philosopher, as well as the ignorant, is a matter of controversy, not of fact, the people are slaves to the magistrates. The despotism of this multitude of tyrants is more insupportable, the less the distance is between the oppressor and the oppressed; more fatal than that of one, for the tyranny of many is not to be shaken off, but by having recourse to that of one alone. It is more cruel, as it meets with more opposition, and the cruelty of a tyrant is not in proportion to his strength, but to the obstacles that oppose him.

THESE are the means, by which security of person and property is best obtained; which is just, as it is the purpose of uniting in society; and it is useful, as each person may calculate exactly the inconveniences attending every crime. By these means, subjects will acquire a spirit of independence and liberty; however it may appear to those, who dare to call the weakness of submitting blindly to their capricious and interested opinions, by the sacred name of virtue.

THESE principles will displease those, who have made it a rule, with themselves, to transmit to their inferiors the tyranny they suffer from their superiors. I should have every thing to fear, if tyrants were to read my book; but tyrants never read.

CHAP. VI.

Of the Proportion between Crimes and Punishments.

IT is not only the common interest of mankind, that crimes should not be committed, but that crimes of every kind should be less frequent, in proportion to the evil they produce to society. Therefore, the means made use of by the legislature to prevent crimes, should be more powerful, in proportion as they are definitive of the public safety and happiness, and as the inducements to commit them are stronger. Therefore there ought to be a fixed proportion between crimes and punishments.

IT is impossible to prevent entirely all the disorders which the passions of mankind cause in society. These disorders increase in proportion to the number of people, and the opposition of private interests. If we consult history, we shall find them increasing, in every state, with the extent of dominion. In political arithmetic, it is necessary to substitute a calculation of probabilities, to mathematical exactness. That force, which continually impels us to our own private interest, like gravity, acts incessantly, unless it meets with an obstacle to oppose it. The effects of this force are the confused series of human actions. Punishments, which I would call political obstacles, prevent the fatal effects of private interest, without destroying the impelling cause, which is that sensibility inseparable from man. The legislator acts, in this case, like a skilful architect, who endeavours to counteract the force of gravity by combining the circumstances which may contribute to the strength of his edifice.

THE necessity of uniting in society being granted, together with the conventions, which the opposite interests of individuals must necessarily require, a scale of crimes may be formed, of which the first degree should consist of those, which immediately tend to the dissolution of society, and the last, of the smallest possible injustice done to a private member of that society. Between these extremes will be comprehended, all actions contrary to the public good, which are called criminal, and which descend by insensible degrees, decreasing from the highest to the lowest. If mathematical calculation could be applied to the obscure and infinite combinations of human actions, there might be a corresponding scale of punishments, descending from the greatest to the least: but it will be sufficient that the wise legislator mark the principal divisions, without disturbing the order, lest to crimes of the *first* degree, be assigned punishments of the *last*. If there were an exact and universal scale of crimes and punishments, we should there have a common measure of the degree of liberty and slavery, humanity and cruelty of different nations.

ANY action, which is not comprehended in the above-mentioned scale, will not be called a crime or punished as such, except by those who have an interest in the denomination. The uncertainty of the extreme points of this scale, hath produced a system of morality which contradicts the laws; a multitude of laws that contradict each other; and many, which expose the best men to the severest punishments, rendering the ideas of *vice* and *virtue* vague, and fluctuating, and even their existence doubtful. Hence that fatal lethargy of political bodies, which terminates in their destruction.

WHOEVER reads, with a philosophic eye, the history of nations, and their laws, will generally find, that the ideas of virtue and vice, of a good or a bad citizen, change with the revolution of ages; not in proportion to the alteration of circumstances, and consequently conformable to the common good; but in proportion to the passions and errors by which the different law-givers were successively influenced. He will frequently observe, that the passions and vices of one age, are the foundation of the morality of the following; that violent passion, the offspring of fanatiscism and enthusiasm, being weakened by time, which reduces all the phenomena of the natural and moral world to an equality, become, by degrees, the prudence of the age, and an useful instrument in the hands of the powerful, or artful politician. Hence the uncertainty of our notions of honour and virtue; an uncertainty which will ever remain, because they change with the revolutions of time, and names survive the things they originally signified; they change with the boundaries of states, which are often the same both in physical and moral geography.

PLEASURE and pain are the only springs of action in beings endowed with sensibility.[2] Even amongst the motives which incite men to acts of religion, the invisible legislator has ordained rewards and punishments. From a partial distribution of these, will arise that contradiction, so little observed, because so common; I mean, that of punishing by the laws, the crimes which the laws have occasioned. If an equal punishment be ordained for two crimes that injure society in different degrees, there is nothing to deter men from committing the greater, as often as it is attended with greater advantage.

CHAP. VII.

Of estimating the Degree of Crimes.

THE foregoing reflections authorise me to assert, that crimes are only to be measured by the injury done to society.

THEY err, therefore, who imagine that a crime is greater, or less, according to the intention of the person by whom it is committed; for this will depend on the actual impression of objects on the senses, and on the previous disposition of the mind; both which will vary in different persons, and even in the same person at different times, according to the succession of ideas, passions, and circumstances. Upon that system, it would be necessary to form, not only a particular code for every individual, but a new penal law for every crime. Men, often with the best intention, do the greatest injury to society, and with the worst, do it the most essential services.

OTHERS have estimated crimes rather by the dignity of the person offended, than by their consequences to society. If this were the true standard, the smallest irreverence to the divine Being ought to be punished with infinitely more severity, than the assassination of a monarch.

IN short, others have imagined, that the greatness of the sin should aggravate the crime. But the fallacy of this opinion will appear on the slightest consideration of the relations between man and man, and between God and man. The relations between man and man, are relations of equality. Necessity alone hath produced, from the opposition of private passions and interests, the idea of public utility, which is the foundation of human justice. The other are relations of dependance, between an imperfect creature and his creator, the most perfect of beings, who has reserved to himself the sole right of being both lawgiver, and judge; for he alone can, without injustice, be, at the same time, both one and the other. If he hath decreed eternal punishments for those who disobey his will, shall an insect dare to put himself in the place of divine justice, or pretend to punish for the Almighty, who is himself all-sufficient; who cannot receive impressions of pleasure, or pain, and who alone, of all other beings, acts without being acted upon? The degree of sin depends on the malignity of the heart, which is impenetrable to finite beings. How then can the degree of sin serve as a standard to determine the degree of crimes? If that were admitted, men may punish when God pardons, and pardon when God condemns; and thus act in opposition to the supreme Being.

CHAP. VIII.

Of the division of Crimes.

WE have proved, then, that crimes are to be estimated by *the injury done to society*. This is one of those palpable truths, which, though evident to the meanest capacity, yet, by a combination of circumstances, are only known to a few thinking men in every nation, and in every age. But opinions, worthy only of the despotism of Asia, and passions, armed with power and authority, have, generally by insensible and sometimes by violent impressions on the timid credulity of men, effaced those simple ideas, which perhaps constituted the first philosophy of infant society. Happily the philosophy of the present enlightened age seems again to conduct us to the same principles, and with that degree of certainty, which is obtained by a rational examination, and repeated experience.

A SCRUPULOUS adherence to order would require, that we should now examine, and distinguish the different species of crimes, and the modes of punishment; but they are so variable in their nature, from the different circumstances of ages, and countries, that the detail would be tiresome, and endless. It will be sufficient for my purpose, to point out the most general principles, and the most common and dangerous errors, in order to undeceive, as well those, who, from a mistaken zeal for liberty, would introduce anarchy and confusion, as those, who pretend to reduce society in general to the regularity of a convent.

SOME crimes are immediately destructive of society, or its representative; others attack the private security of the life, property, or honour of individuals; and a third class consists of such actions as are contrary to the laws which relate to the general good of the community.

THE first, which are of the highest degree, as they are most destructive to society, are called crimes of *Leze-majesty*.[3] Tyranny, and ignorance, which have confounded the clearest terms and ideas, have given this appellation to crimes of a different nature, and consequently have established the same punishment for each; and on this occasion, as on a thousand others, men have been sacrificed, victims to a word. Every crime, even of the most private nature, injures society; but every crime does not threaten its immediate destruction. Moral, as well as physical actions, have their sphere of activity differently circumscribed, like all the movements of nature, by time and space; it is therefore a sophistical interpretation, the common philosophy of slaves, that would confound the limits of things, established by eternal truth.

To these succeed crimes which are destructive of the security of individuals. This security being the principal end of all society, and to which every citizen hath an undoubted right, it becomes indispensably necessary, that to these crimes the greatest of punishments should be assigned.

THE opinion, that every member of society has a right to do any thing, that is not contrary to the laws, without fearing any other inconveniences, than those which are the natural consequences of the action itself, is a political dogma, which should be defended by the laws, inculcated by the magistrates, and believed by the people; a sacred dogma, without which there can be no lawful society; a just recompence for our sacrifice of that universal liberty of action, common to all sensible beings, and only limited by our natural powers. By this principle, our minds become free, active, and vigorous; by this alone we are inspired with that virtue which knows no fear, so different from that pliant prudence, worthy of those only who can bear a precarious existence.

ATTEMPTS, therefore, against the life, and liberty of a citizen, are crimes of the highest nature. Under this head we comprehend not only assassinations, and robberies, committed by the populace, but by grandees, and magistrates; whose example acts with more force, and at a greater distance, destroying the ideas of justice and duty among the subjects, and substituting that of the right of the strongest, equally dangerous to those who exercise it, and to those who suffer.

CHAP. XXVIII.

Of the Punishment of Death.

THE useless profusion of punishments, which has never made men better, induces me to enquire, whether the punishment of *death* be really just or useful in a well-governed state? What *right*, I ask, have men to cut the throats of their fellow-creatures? Certainly not that on which the sovereignty and laws are founded. The laws, as I have said before, are only the sum of the smallest portions of the private liberty of each individual, and represent the general will, which is the aggregate of that of each individual. Did any one ever give to others the right of taking away his life? Is it possible, that in the smallest portions of the liberty of each, sacrificed to the good of the public, can be contained the greatest of all good, life? If it were so, how shall it be reconciled to the maxim which tells us, that a man has no right to kill himself? Which he certainly must have, if he could give it away to another.

BUT the punishment of death is not authorised by any right; for I have demonstrated that no such right exists. It is therefore a war of a whole nation against a citizen, whose destruction they consider as necessary, or useful to the general good. But if I can further demonstrate, that it is neither necessary nor useful, I shall have gained the cause of humanity.

THE death of a citizen cannot be necessary, but in one case. When, though deprived of his liberty, he has such power and connexions as may endanger the security of the nation; when his existence may produce a dangerous revolution in the established form of government. But even in this case, it can only be necessary, when a nation is on the verge of recovering or losing its liberty; or in times of absolute anarchy, when the disorders themselves hold the place of laws. But in a reign of tranquility; in a form of government approved by the united wishes of the nation; in a state well fortified from enemies without, and supported by strength within, and opinion, perhaps more efficacious; where all power is lodged in the hands of the true sovereign; where riches can purchase pleasures and not authority, there can be no necessity for taking away the life of a subject.

IF the experience of all ages be not sufficient to prove, that the punishment of death has never prevented determined men from injuring society; if the example of the Romans; if twenty years reign of Elizabeth, empress of Russia, in which she gave the fathers of their country an example more illustrious than many conquests bought with blood; if, I say, all this be not sufficient to persuade mankind, who always suspect the voice of reason, and who chuse rather to be led by authority, let us consult human nature in proof of my assertion.

IT is not the intenseness of the pain that has the greatest effect on the mind, but its continuance; for our sensibility is more easily and more powerfully affected by weak but repeated impressions, than by a violent, but momentary, impulse. The power of habit is universal over every sensible being. As it is by that we learn to speak, to walk, and to satisfy our necessities, so the ideas of morality are stamped on our minds by repeated impressions. The death of a criminal is a terrible but momentary spectacle, and therefore a less efficacious method of deterring others, than the continued example of a man deprived of his liberty, condemned, as a beast of burthen, to repair, by his labour, the injury he has done to society. *If I commit such a crime,* says the spectator to himself, *I shall be reduced to that miserable condition for the rest of my life.* A much more powerful preventive than the fear of death, which men always behold in distant obscurity.

THE terrors of death make so slight an impression, that it has not force enough to withstand the forgetfulness natural to mankind, even in the most essential things; especially when assisted by the passions. Violent impressions surprize us, but their effect is momentary; they are fit to produce those revolutions which instantly transform a common man into a Lacedemonian or a Persian;[4] but in a free and quiet government they ought to be rather frequent than strong.

THE execution of a criminal is, to the multitude, a spectacle, which in some excites compassion mixed with indignation. These sentiments occupy the mind much more than that salutary terror which the laws endeavour to inspire; but in the contemplation of continued suffering, terror is the only, or at least the predominant sensation. The severity of a punishment should be just sufficient to excite compassion in the spectators, as it is intended more for them than for the criminal.

A PUNISHMENT, to be just, should have only that degree of severity which is sufficient to deter others. Now there is no man, who upon the least reflection, would put in competition the total and perpetual loss of his liberty, with the greatest advantages he could possibly obtain in consequence of a crime. Perpetual slavery, then, has in it all that is necessary to deter the most hardened and determined, as much as the punishment of death. I say it has more. There are many who can look upon death with intrepidity and firmness; some through fanaticism, and others through vanity, which attends us even to the grave; others from a desperate resolution, either to get rid of their misery, or cease to live: but fanaticism and vanity forsake the criminal in slavery, in chains and fetters, in an iron cage; and despair seems rather the beginning than the end of their misery. The mind, by collecting itself and uniting all its force, can, for a moment repel assailing grief; but its most vigorous efforts are insufficient to resist perpetual wretchedness.

IN all nations, where death is used as a punishment, every example supposes a new crime committed. Whereas in perpetual slavery, every criminal affords a frequent and lasting example; and if it be necessary that men should often be witnesses of the power of the laws, criminals should often be put to death; but this supposes a frequency of crimes; and from hence this punishment will cease to have its effect, so that it must be useful and useless at the same time.

I SHALL be told, that perpetual slavery is as painful a punishment as death, and therefore as cruel. I answer, that if all the miserable moments in the life of a slave were collected into one point, it would be a more cruel punishment than any other; but these are scattered through his whole life, whilst the pain of death exerts all its force in a moment. There is also another advantage in the punishment of slavery, which is, that it is more terrible to the spectator than to the sufferer himself; for the spectator considers the sum of all his wretched moments, whilst the sufferer, by the misery of the present, is prevented from thinking of the future. All evils are increased by the imagination, and the sufferer finds resources and consolations, of which the spectators are ignorant; who judge by their own sensibility of what passes in a mind, by habit grown callous to misfortune.

LET us, for a moment, attend to the reasoning of a robber or assassin, who is deterred from violating the laws by the gibbet or the wheel. I am sensible, that to develop the sentiments of one's own heart, is an art which education only can teach? but although a villain may not be able to give a clear account of his principles, they nevertheless influence his conduct. He reasons thus. 'What are these laws, that I am bound to respect, which make so great a difference between me and a rich man? He refuses me the farthing I ask of him, and excuses himself by bidding me have recourse to labour, with which he is unacquainted. Who made these laws? The rich and the great, who never deigned to visit the miserable hut of the poor; who have never seen him dividing a piece of mouldy bread, amidst the cries of his famished children and the tears of his wife. Let us break those ties, fatal to the greatest part of mankind, and only useful to a few indolent tyrants. Let us attack injustice at its source. I will return to my natural state of independance. I shall live free and happy on the fruits of my courage and industry. A day of pain and repentance may come, but it will be short; and for an hour of grief I shall enjoy years of pleasure and liberty. King of a small number, as determined as myself, I will correct the mistakes of fortune; and I shall see those tyrants grow pale and tremble at the sight of him, whom, with insulting pride, they would not suffer to rank with their dogs and horses.'

RELIGION then presents itself to the mind of this lawless villain, and promising him almost a certainty of eternal happiness upon the easy terms of repentance, contributes much to lessen the horror of the last scene of the tragedy.

BUT he who foresees, that he must pass a great number of years, even his whole life, in pain and slavery; a slave to those laws by which he was protected; in sight of his fellow citizens, with whom he lives in freedom and society; makes an useful comparison between those evils, the uncertainty of his success, and the shortness of the time in which he shall enjoy the fruits of his transgression. The example of those wretches continually before his eyes, makes a much greater impression on him than a punishment, which, instead of correcting, makes him more obdurate.

THE punishment of death is pernicious to society, from the example of barbarity it affords. If the passions, or the necessity of war, have taught men to shed the blood of their fellow-creatures, the laws, which are intended to moderate the ferocity of mankind, should not increase it by examples of barbarity, the more horrible, as this punishment is usually attended with formal pageantry. Is it not absurd, that the laws, which detest and punish homicide, should, in order to prevent murder, publicly commit murder themselves? What are the true and most useful laws? Those compacts and conditions which all would propose and observe, in these moments when private interest is silent, or combined with that of the public. What are the natural sentiments of every person concerning the punishment of death? We may read them in the contempt and indignation with which every one looks on the executioner, who is nevertheless an innocent executor of the public will; a good citizen, who contributes to the advantage of society; the instrument of the general security within, as good soldiers are without. What then is the origin of this contradiction? Why is this sentiment of mankind indelible, to the scandal of reason? It is, that in a secret corner of the mind, in which the original impressions of nature are still preserved, men discover a sentiment which tells them, that their lives are not lawfully in the power of any one, but of that necessity only, which with its iron scepter rules the universe.

WHAT must men think, when they see wise magistrates and grave ministers of justice, with indifference and tranquility, dragging a criminal to death, and whilst a wretch trembles with agony, expecting the fatal stroke, the judge, who has condemned him, with the coldest insensibility, and perhaps with no small gratification from the exertion of his authority, quits his tribunal to enjoy the comforts and pleasures of life? They will say, 'Ah! those cruel formalities of justice are a cloak to tyranny, they are a secret language, a solemn veil, intended to conceal the sword by which we are sacrificed to the insatiable idol of despotism. Murder, which they would represent to us as an horrible crime, we see practised by them without repugnance, or remorce. Let us follow their example. A violent death appeared terrible in their descriptions, but we see that it is the affair of a moment. It will be still less terrible to him, who not expecting it, escapes almost all the pain.' Such is the fatal, though absurd reasoning of men who are disposed to commit crimes; on whom, the abuse of religion has more influence than religion itself.

IF it be objected, that almost all nations in all ages have punished certain crimes with death, I answer, that the force of these examples vanishes, when opposed to truth, against which prescription is urged in vain. The history of mankind is an immense sea of errors, in which a few obscure truths may here and there be found.

BUT human sacrifices have also been common in almost all nations. That some societies only, either few in number, or for a very short time, abstained from the punishment of death, is rather favourable to my argument, for such is the fate of great truths, that their duration is only as a flash of lightning in the long and dark night of error. The happy time is not yet arrived, when truth, as falshood has been hitherto, shall be the portion of the greatest number.

I AM sensible that the voice of one philosopher is too weak to be heard amidst the clamours of a multitude, blindly influenced by custom; but there is a small number of sages, scattered on the face of the earth, who will echo to me from the bottom of their hearts; and if these truths should haply force their way to the thrones of princes, be it known to them, that they come attended with the secret wishes of all mankind; and tell the sovereign who deigns them a gracious reception, that his fame shall outshine the glory of conquerors, and that equitable posterity will exalt his peaceful trophies above those of a Titus, an Antoninus or a Trajan.[5]

HOW happy were mankind, if laws were now to be first formed; now that we see on the thrones of Europe, benevolent monarchs, friends to the virtues of peace, to the arts and sciences, fathers of their people, though crown'd yet citizens; the increase of whose authority augments the happiness of their subjects, by destroying that intermediate despotism, which intercepts the prayers of the people, to the throne. If these humane princes have suffered the old laws to subsist, it is doubtless, because they are deterred by the numberless obstacles, which oppose the subversion of errors established by the sanction of many ages; and therefore every wise citizen will wish for the increase of their authority.

from William Eden, *Principles of Penal Law*, 2nd edn (London: T. Cadell, 1771), chapters 2, 3, 4, 7, and 9.[1]

Eden (1744–1814) was born into a wealthy and titled family of County Durham, England, and educated at Eton and Oxford. As a younger son, he had to seek a profession, and intended to become a clergyman but was turned to the law by hearing the lectures of Sir William Blackstone (1723–80), author of the main English law manual of the time, *Commentaries on the Laws of England* (1765–9). Eden was called to the bar in 1768 but found law practice less interesting than legal history and philosophy. Influenced by Blackstone and by Beccaria (see extracts included in this volume), Montesquieu's *L'Esprit des lois* (1748), and other Enlightenment writers, Eden published his *Principles of Penal Law*, representing the law as a human and social creation, hence liable to change and reform. The book made Eden's reputation and he was appointed to public office as under-secretary to the secretary of state for home affairs, where he was able to put some of his reform ideas into practice. Elected MP in 1774, he saw a Penitentiary Act through Parliament in 1779, though some of his other measures failed to become law. After this, Eden was appointed to a succession of administrative, trade, and diplomatic offices. In 1789 he was made baron Auckland in the Irish peerage. He held major diplomatic responsibilities in the early years of the French Revolution, and his title was affirmed in the English peerage in 1793. His pamphlet on the possibility of peace with republican France (1795) elicited Edmund Burke's angry reply, *Letters on a Regicide Peace* (1796–7). Eden was close to the Prime Minister, William Pitt, who seems to have briefly considered marrying Eden's daughter, Eleanor. Eden held further government posts, though he broke with Pitt on several issues. One son became governor-general of India, and his daughter Emily became a successful novelist.

Eden's *Principles* remained a major reference and source for legal and penal reformers through the early nineteenth century. The text itself is written in an energetic and forceful style, but it is studded with numerous learned footnotes and citations, typifying the legal discourse of a wealthy, cultivated, and often titled legal and political elite of which Eden would subsequently become a notably successful member. Published while Eden was still in his thirties, *Principles* is an advertisement – effective, as it turned out – for its author's qualifications to be made a man of public affairs and join this elite. By the time Eden wrote, however, their longstanding hegemony was beginning to be challenged by a professional middle class who, while often agreeing with Eden's humanitarian and reformist arguments, would advocate legal and penal reform in a more egalitarian, less theoretical, more investigative and journalistic plain style.

CHAP. II.

Of penal Laws.

§ I. THE prevention of crimes should be the great object of the Lawgiver; whose duty it is, to have a severe eye upon the offence, but a merciful inclination towards the offender. It is from an abuse of language, that we apply the word 'Punishment' to human institutions: Vengeance belongeth not to man.[2] Criminals, said Plato,* are punished, not because they have offended; for what is done can never be undone: but that for the future the criminals themselves, and such as see their punishment, may take warning, and learn to shun the allurements of vice. 'Meti Suffeti, inquit Tullus, si ipse discere posses foedera ac fidem servare, vivo tibi ea disciplina a me adhibita esset: nunc, *quoniam tuum insanabile ingenium est, Tu tuo supplicio doce humanum genus ea sancta credere, quæ a te violata sunt.*'† It is the end then of penal laws to deter, not to punish.

§ 2. But let not for this purpose the severity of the penalty be augmented in proportion to the increase of the temptation; which is a cruel and mistaken policy.

'*Qui vi rapuit, fur improbior videtur.*'‡ Such was the maxim of the Roman law, which punished the open, daring thief with whipping, and the pilferer by fine only. The English law, adopting a less equitable idea, hath made it death§ to take privately from the pocket a hankerchief, or other thing of the value of twelvepence; but any Larceny (below the degree of robbery by putting in fear) committed openly, and avowedly on the person, to any extent, and even in a dwelling-house or out-house, under the value of forty shillings, is within the benefit of clergy.¶

Under the same perversion of distributive justice it is made** only a transportable offence, 'to assault another with an offensive weapon, or by menaces, demanding money, goods or chattels, with a felonious intent to rob:' whereas by another statute†† it is death without benefit of clergy, merely 'to write an anonymous Letter, signed with a fictitious name, demanding money, venison, or other valuable thing.'

§ 3. The punishment should be proportioned to the flagitiousness of the crime; but the flagitiousness of the crime diminishes in proportion to the facil-

---

*   De Legibus, p. 977.[3]
†   Liv. Hist. I. i. c. 28.[4]
‡   ff. 4. 2. 14. 12.[5]
§   8 Eliz. c.4.[6]
¶   I Hawk. P. C. p.97.[7]
**   7 Geo. II. c. 21.
††   9 Geo. I. c. 22.

ity, with which it may be committed:* for that facility in general constitutes the degree of the temptation.

Were I to leave the support of this position to the internal evidence of its own truth, or to the mere unassisted dictates of moral sentiment, it might appear perhaps presumptuous; because contradictory to the most ingenious and elegant writer on the law of England.

'The severity of our law in certain instances (says that writer†) seems to be owing to the ease with which such offences are committed.' Again‡ – 'It is but reasonable, that, among crimes of equal malignity, those should be most severely punished, which a man has the most frequent, and easy opportunities of committing; which cannot be so easily guarded against as others; and which therefore the offender has the strongest inducement to commit: according to what Cicero observes, "*ea sunt animadvertenda peccata maximè, quæ difficillimè præcaventur.*"§ He then proceeds to several Examples, on which it may be sufficient to observe, that when 'it is made capital for a servant to rob his master' in certain cases, which extend not to a stranger committing the same offence against indifferent persons; and, when 'it is a species of treason for a servant to kill his master, or for a wife to kill her husband, which act in others is only murder;' we are not in those cases to suppose the frequent opportunities of perpetrating the offence to have excited the peculiar severity of the law.¶ The malignity of the fact is the true measure of the penalty; and that malignity is in these cases aggravated by the gross breach and flagrant abuse of domestic confidence.** Cicero has certainly said, *quod ea sunt animadvertenda peccata maximè, quæ difficillimè præcaventur*: but the learned Commentator should have cited also the context, which supports the very principle for which I contend; '*ad cujus enim fidem aliquis*

---

*   By the flagitiousness of a crime, I mean its abstract nature and turpitude, in proportion to which the criminal should be considered as more or less dangerous to society. And surely, in the eye of the Lawgiver, who as a Man must make allowances for the imbecillities of mankind, the abstract turpitude of the offence decreases in proportion to the inducements which naturally influence the mind of the offender.

C'est le triomphe de la Liberté, lorsque les loïx criminelles tirent chaque peine de la nature du crime: tout l'arbitraire cesse; la peine ne descend point du caprice du legislateur, mais de la nature de la chose; et ce n'est pas l'homme qui fait violence à l'homme.L'Esprit des Loix, xii. 4.[8]

†   See the Commentaries on the Laws of England, b. iv. p. 241.[9]

‡   Ib. b. iv. p. 16.

§   Orat. pro Sexto Roscio, c. 40.[10]

¶   *Commune est hoc malum, communis metus, commune periculum. Nullæ sunt occultiores insidiæ, quam eæ quæ latent in simulatione officii, aut in aliquo necessitudinis nomine. Nam eum, qui palam est adversarius, facile cavendo vitare possis. Hoc vero occultum, intestinum, ac domesticum malum, non modò non existit, verùm etiam opprimit, antequam prospicere atque explorare potueris.*

Cic. inVerrem, II. l. i. c.15.[11]

**   Upon this principle, by a declaration of Lewis the XVth, A. D. 1724, Le vol domestique sera puni de mort. This was only the renewal of a very ancient Law made by Lewis the IXth, A. D. 1270, which considers this offence as a species of treason. 'Hons, quand il emble a son Saignour, et il est à son pain et à son vin, il est pendable; *car c'est maniere de trahison.*'   Code penal. 103.[12]

confugiet, cum per ejus fidem læditur cui se commiserit? tecti esse ad alienos pos-
sumus; socium cavere qui possumus? quem etiam si metuimus, jus officii lædimus:
– Nam neque mandat quisquam ferè nisi amico: neque credit nisi ei quem fidelem
putat. Perditissimi est igitur hominis, simul et amicitiam dissolvere, et fallere eum,
qui læsus non esset, nisi credidisset.[13]

§ 4. From these positions, 'that the penalty ought to be increased in proportion to the outrage of the crime,' and 'not in proportion to the temptation which
misleads the mind of the criminal;' I would by no means infer, 'that the penal
sanction relative to every particular offence should be mitigated in proportion
to the facility with which that offence may be committed.'

Political wisdom is the result of experience, rather than of theory. And the
history of every state will shew to us, that in some cases the emergencies of
society make it expedient to place great severities in opposition to the strongest temptations; that in others it is necessary to punish the offence without any
research into its motives; and that in every case it is impracticable for Lawgivers
to assume the divine attribute of animadverting on the fact, only according to
the internal malice of the intention.

The safety of the Public is the supreme law of policy: and when Legislature
is thus necessitated in any degree to deviate from the principles of justice and
humanity, we must submit to the deviation merely as to an occasional result from
the imperfections of our nature. But the principles of justice and humanity are
unchangeable: and to those principles I appeal, when I controvert the position,
'that among crimes of equal malignity, those should be most severely punished
which the offender has the strongest inducement to commit.' A position! which,
if generally established, would lead to sanguinary and cruel consequences.

§ 5. 'That Legislature may justify the infliction of whatever degree of severity
is necessary for the prevention of any particular crime;' is also a position, which,
when offered without limitation, I conceive to be both morally and politically
false. It is a pretence, which, if once suffered to hurry us beyond the bounds of
humanity, is subject to no other restraint.

§ 6. When the rights of human nature are not respected, those of the citizen
are gradually disregarded. Those æras are in history found fatal to Liberty, in
which cruel punishments predominate. Lenity should be the guardian of moderate governments: severe penalties, the instruments of despotism, may give a
sudden check to temporary evils; but they have a tendency to extend themselves
to every class of crimes, and their frequency hardens the sentiment of the people. *Une loi rigoureuse produit des crimes.*[14] The excess of the penalty flatters the
imagination with the hope of impunity, and thus becomes an advocate with the
offender for the perpetrating of the offence.

The convicts, who have stolen cloth* from the tenters, fustian from the bleaching ground,† or a lamb from their landlord's pasture, knew the law to have assigned death, without the benefit of clergy, to each of their offences: but, in the depth of ignorance and profligacy, mere instinct informed them, that common humanity would recoil at the idea, and they relied for their security on the ingenuity of mercy to evade the law.

§ 7. Legislators should then remember, that the acerbity of justice deadens its execution; and that the increase of human corruptions proceeds, not from the moderation of punishments, but from the impunity of criminals.

§ 8. In the promulgation of every new offence, let the lawgiver expose himself to feel what wretches feel; and let him not seem to bear hardest on those crimes, which, in his elevated station, he is least likely to commit. 'Si les supplices en usage dans presque tout l'orient font horreur à l'humanité, c'est que le Déspote, qui les ordonne, se sent au dessus des loix. Il n'en est pas ainsi dans les republiques; les loix sont toujours douces, parce que celui qui les établit, s'y soumet.'‡ If this reasoning be founded in truth, it furnishes a mortifying inference, that men are naturally cruel, when they can be so with safety.

§ 9. Penal laws are to check the arm of wickedness; but not to wage war with the natural sentiments of the heart.

Contrary to this principle is the statute,§ which, making the concealment of infamy evidence of murder, compels unhappy women to break through the becoming pride and modesty of their sex, and to be the first officious publish-

---

*   22 Car. II. c. 25. § 3.

†   4 Geo. II. c. 16. and 18 Geo. II. c. 19.

‡   De l'Esprit, t. ii. p. 68.[15]

§   21 James I. c. 27. which recites, 'That women, delivered of bastard children, *to avoid their shame, and to escape punishment*, do secretly bury, and conceal the death of, their children, alledging, if the child or children be afterwards found, that they were born dead; whereas it falleth out sometimes (although hardly it is to be proved) that the said children were murthered by the said women.' For the prevention of this mischief, it is hereby enacted, 'That in every case the said mother so offending shall suffer death as in case of murder, except such mother can make proof by one witness at the least, that the child, whose death was by her so intended to be concealed, was born dead.'

The modern exposition of this statute is a good instance, that *cruel laws have a natural tendency to their own dissolution in the abhorrence of mankind*. It is now the constant practice of the courts to require, that the body of the child shall be found, before any conviction can take place; and, if it should happen, that the mother had any child-bed linen, or other preparatives in her possession, prior to her delivery, it is generally admitted as a proof, that no concealment was intended. Moreover, it is not unusual to require some degree of evidence that the child was actually born alive, before the ungenerous presumption, that the mother was the wilful author of the death of her new-born infant, is permitted to affect her. These humane deviations from the harsh injunction of the statute have nearly amounted to a tacit abrogation of it.

The expressions of the Swedish Law on this subject are very severe – 'Mulier impudica, quæ ex illegitimo concubitu uterum gestat, nec hoc ante partum aperit, latebras quærens quo furtim enitatur partum, et deinde abscondit, percutiatur securi, et in pegmate comburatur, *non attento prætextu mortuum vel ante justum terminum editum fuisse*.'

ers of their own shame. Harsh is the construction of treasons,* which subjects to that sentence full of horrors the son, husband, and father, for the protection given to the wife, parent, and child.

The laws of Japan oblige the person accused to give an answer to the accusation; if his answer be false, he is punished with death. This is a violation of the first principle of self-preservation.

§ 10. It is one of the unavoidable imperfections of legislatures, that they are necessitated to assign the same name and penalty to whole classes of crimes, each of which differs from the other by an infinite variety of unsearchable circumstances. Yet some offences are so intimately, and so undistinguishably classed in their nature, that it is difficult to conceive any possible reason for a diversity in their punishment.

It seems a strange incongruity, that the offence of counterfeiting foreign coin legitimated by proclamation, should work† a corruption of blood; which is saved‡ by special proviso in the offence of counterfeiting the current coin of the kingdom. Again, it is a clergyable[19] felony by our law to destroy or damage the bridges of Brentford or Blackfriars: but it is death to commit the same offence on the bridges of London, Westminster, or Putney. There is a similar unaccountable distinction between prison-breakers convicted of perjury,§ or committed for entering black-lead mines with intent to steal;¶ and such as are convicted of, or committed for any other offence within clergy.[20] God forbid, that I should insinuate a necessity to drag all this variety of discordant instances to the same bloody line of uniformity! Their cruelty appears to me equal to their inconsistency; and it would not perhaps be difficult to prove their folly equal to their cruelty.

There is a law to the same purport in France; which may also be found in the 'Observations on the ancient statutes,' p. 425; and I find that it is strictly enjoined by an ordinance of Henry III. and by a declaration of Lewis XIV. to be published once in every three months in all the parish churches.　　　　Code penal. Paris, 1755, 8vo. titre 29.[16]

* A. D. 1689, Lady Lisle and Mrs. Gaunt were convicted of high treason, and executed: the former for harbouring a dissenting priest, who had been concerned in the Duke of Monmouth's rebellion; the latter for giving refuge to another rebel, on whose evidence, voluntarily offered, the conviction was grounded. The man was pardoned for his treachery; she was burned alive for her charity.

I make no observations on their respective trials; because the proceedings of our criminal courts, at this æra, are so disgraceful, not only to the nation, but to human nature, that, as they cannot be disbelieved, I wish them to be buried in oblivion.　　See Hume's Hist. vi. 385. – Burnet i. 649.[17]

† 　Foster, p. 226.[18]

‡ 　5 Eliz. c. 11. and 8 & 9 W. III. c. 29, &c.

§ 　2 Geo. II. c. 25. § 2.

¶ 　25 Geo. II. c. 10.

§ 11. Laws made on the spur of the occasion, should have a short and limited duration; otherwise in the course of years it will be said, '*magis sæculum suum sapiunt, quam rectam rationem.*'[21]

It is still a Felony to steal a hawk, and death to associate one month with Egyptians,* or to wander, being a soldier or mariner,† without a testimonial under the hand of a Justice.

§ 12. Obsolete and useless statutes should be repealed; for they debilitate the authority of such as still exist and are necessary. Neglect on this point is well compared by Lord Bacon to the cruelty of Mezentius,[23] who left the living to perish in the arms of the dead.

Persons carrying subjects out of the northern counties,‡ or giving black mail for protection, Jailers forcing prisoners to become approvers,§ Masons confederating to prevent the statutes of labourers,¶ Purveyors in certain cases** though purveyance is abolished, are all capital offenders:[25] and none shall bring pollardz and crockardz (which were foreign coins of base metal) into the realm, on pain of forfeiture of life and goods.†† The alterations in our government have rendered these particular provisions totally ineffective; but there are other obsolete statutes, which exist, the possible instruments of mischief in the hand of tyranny.

§ 13. Civil and criminal laws must accumulate, and become complicated, in proportion to the increased riches of the state, and to the security given to the liberties, lives, honours, and properties of the people. Despotic states admit a simplicity of legislation, the forms and principles of which depend on the caprices of a weak and ignorant Monarch, whose breast is the repository of precedents: but it should be the primary object of free governments, to have the outlines of their privileges fixed and determinate. When the laws for this purpose are explicit, it is the duty of the Judge strictly to conform to them; when they are otherwise, it is the immediate duty of the Legislator to ascertain them.

It is not therefore sufficient, that the decision of the fact be guarded from the influence of fear and affection: the adjudication of the law should be a certain consequence of that decision. But, when the penalty prescribed bears an evident and excessive disproportion to the offence, the humanity of the Judges will be interested in the evasion of it, '*et magis valebunt acumina ingeniorum, quam auctoritas legis.*'‡‡ And this is a consideration, which, exclusive of every motive of

---

*   5 Eliz. c. 20. p. 23. See the declaration of Lewis XIV, contre les Bohemiens, et ceux qui leur donnent retraite.   Code penal. p. 114.[22]

†   39 Eliz. c. 17.

‡   43 Eliz. c. 13.

§   14 Ed. III. c. 10.[24]

¶   3 Hen. VI. c. 1.

**   28 Ed. I. Stat; iii. c. 1.

††   27 Ed. I. ex Rot. In Turr.

‡‡   Bac. de Augm. Scient.[26]

humanity, should induce the lawgiver carefully to discuss the different modes of punishment, as applicable to the different degrees of moral and political guilt.

CHAP. III.

Of the Infliction of Death.

§ 1. It is impossible to read the histories of executive justice in different governments without shuddering at the very idea of those miseries, which men, with unrelenting ingenuity, have devised for each other. In some countries it hath been usual to sow up criminals in the warm skins of beasts, and in this condition to expose them to wild dogs; in others the limbs are torn asunder by horses; in others recourse is had to crucifixions, burnings, boilings, flayings, famishings, impalements, and other modes of destruction, equally shocking to decency and humanity.

> 'Merciful heaven!
> Thou rather with thy sharp and sulphurous bolt
> Split'st the unwedgeable and gnarled oak,
> Than the soft myrtle: O but man, proud man,
> Drest in a little brief authority,
> (Most ignorant of what he's most assur'd,
> His glassy essence) like an angry ape,
> Plays such fantastic tricks before high heaven
> As make the angels weep.'*

§ 2. This imputation of tyranny and cruelty hath at different periods been applicable to every government, of which we have any authentic history. Livy, in respect to his countrymen, hath endeavoured to establish a different inference in his account of the punishment of Metius Suffetius;† '*Exinde, duabus admotis quadrigis, in currus earum distentus illigatur Metius; deinde in diversum iter equi concitati, lacerum in utroque curru corpus, quâ inhæserant vinculis membra, portantes. Avertêre omnes a tantâ fœditate spectaculi oculos. Primum, ultimumque illud supplicium apud Romanos exempli parum memoris legum humanarum fuit; in aliis gloriari licet, nulli gentium mitiores placuisse pœnas.*' We know that national benevolence ought to be the concomitant of national liberty, and are therefore inclinable to give credit to this assertion; but it will not be found in any degree reconcileable to the united testimony of many other Historians. The modes of capital punishment, used by the Romans, were at least as numerous, and as exceptionable, as those of other nations. The head of the malefactor was in some cases fastened within the furca,[29] and in this attitude he was whipped to

---

*   Shakespeare, Meas. for Meas.[27]
†   L. i. c. 28.[28]

death;* and this was distinguished by the name of *supplicium more majorum*.† In other cases, as in the execution of Antigonus, the whipping terminated in beheading.‡ Crucifixion, or the *servile supplicium*,[33] was in use during many centuries, and first abrogated by Constantine;[34] the sentence also inflicted whipping, '*verbera intra aut extra pomœrium, arbore infelici suspendito*.'§ The criminal was naked in the execution of these different punishments. Parricides¶ were sewed up in a leathern sack, with an ape, a cock, a serpent and a dog, and so cast into the sea. It was also usual to cover some offenders with a mantle dawbed over with pitch, and then to set fire to it; *Cogita*, inquit Seneca,** *illam tunicam alimentis igneis illatam et intextam*. The Emperors introduced a punishment called '*Serræ-dissectio*'.†† *Damnatio in gladium*, or sentence to the public combats, and *damnatio ad bestias*,‡‡ were also frequent; and the latter appears to have been very fatal to offenders; '*præclara ædilitas!* said Cicero, *unus Leo, ducenti Bestiarii*.'[40]

These cruelties were founded on the twelve tables of the Decemvirs,[41] and were contrary to the republican spirit. Accordingly by the Porcian law, made in the 454th year of Rome, by Porcius Lecca the Tribune, it was ordained, that no Citizen should he put to death. This exemption was in the extreme of lenity, and erroneous in its foundation. Capital executions are in all states necessary.

§ 3. Nothing, however, but the evident result of absolute necessity, can authorize the destruction of mankind by the hand of man.

The infliction of Death is not therefore to be considered, in any instance, as a mode of punishment, but *merely* as our last melancholy resource in the extermination of those from society, whose continuance among their fellow-citizens is become inconsistent with the public safety.

§ 4. We may pronounce it then contrary both to sentiment and morality, to aggravate capital executions by any circumstances of terror or pain beyond the sufferings inseparable from a violent death.

---

　*　　*C. C. Caligula curatorem munerum ac venationum per continuos dies in conspectu suo catomis verberatum, non prius occidit, quam offensus putrefacti cerebri odore.*　　　　Sueton. in vita Calig. c. 27.[30]

　†　　*Codicillos præripuit Nero, legitque se hostem a senatu judicatum, et quæri ut puniatur more majorum: interrogavitque quale esset id genus poenæ. Et cum comperissit, nudi hominis cervicem inseri furcæ, corpus virgis ad necem cædi; conterritus ferrum jugulo adegit.*　　　　Sueton, in vita Neron. c. 49.[31]

　‡　Dion. I. xlix.[32]

　§　Liv. I. i. & Val. Max. I. 5. c. 7.[35]

　¶　*Cujus supplicio non debuit una parari*
　　　Simia, nec serpens unus, nec culeus unus. Juv. I. viii.

See also, Dig. 48. ad Leg. Pomp. & Cic. Orat. pro Sext. Roscio.[36]

　**　Ep. 14.[37]

　††　Sueton. in vitâ Calig. c. 27.[38]

　‡‡　Dig. 48. 19. 11. 3.[39]

The punishment of the murderer after tryal and conviction was by the Athenians left to the relations of the deceased, who might put him to death if they thought proper; but they were not permitted to use any degree of torture, or to extort money;* Excellent restrictions! which taught the prosecutor to seek justice, not revenge; in wrath to remember mercy; and to feel less, what he in his own interests had suffered, than what the Offender was about to suffer.

It was a custom among the Jews to give wine mingled with myrrh to the malefactor at the time of his execution; in order, as it is said, to cause a stupor, and deaden the sensibility of the pain.

I transcribe the following passage from the English State-tryals. 'Hugh Peters, being carried on a sledge to the scaffold, was made to sit thereon within the rails, to behold the execution of Mr. Cook. When Mr. Cook was cut down, and brought to be quartered, Col. Turner ordered the Sheriff's men to bring Mr. Peters near, *that he might see it*; and bye and bye the hangman came to him all besmeared in blood and, rubbing his bloody hands together, he tauntingly asked, "Come how do you like this work, Mr. Peters? how do you like it?" He replied, "Friend, you do not well to trample on a dying Man."'†

Shall we plant thorns in the path of Misery? God forbid! Such refinements of inhumanity are admissible only in governments so abominable in their Constitution, as to make the mere loss of life desirable.

§ 5. Solemnity indeed is requisite, for the sake of example; but let not death be drawn into 'lingering sufferance;'[44] detain not the excruciated soul upon the verge of eternity. It was consistent only with the brutal insanity of Caligula to order the executioner to protract the death of the mangled criminal, *perpetuo, notoque jam præcepto, 'Ita feri, ut se mori sentiat.'*[45]

§ 6. Lawgivers should remember, that they are, mediately, and in effect, the executioners of every fellow-citizen, who suffers death in consequence of any

---

*   Demosthenes hath given a full explanation of this law, which ordered the murderer, if put to death, to be executed in the district, or parish of the deceased; εν τη τε ωεπονϑοτζ ωατριδι: 'sequitur in lege λυμαινεϑαι δε μη, quibus verbis significatur, non licere flagris cædere homicidam, vincire, laniare, lacerare ora, manus, populari tempora raptis auribus, &c.'   Pet. Leg. Att. p. 611.

Demosth. Orat. adv. Aristoc. p. 410.[42]

†   This is not the only instance of ungenerous insults towards the Republican sufferers at the Restoration. 'The Regicides (says Bishop Burnet) had at that time been odious beyond expression, yet *the odiousness of the crime began to be much flattened by the frequent executions.'*

And therefore when Sir Henry Vane was brought to the scaffold; lest his words should leave impressions on the hearers to the disadvantage of the government, drummers were placed under the scaffold, who, as loon as he began to address the people, upon a sign given, struck up with their drums. After being thus repeatedly interrupted, and even when he was taking leave of his friends, 'he gave over and died with so much composedness, that it was generally thought, that the Government had lost more than it had gained by his death.'   Vol. i. p. 164.[43]

penal statute; and there are certain contracted points of view, in which it may be of use to them to consider criminals at the approach of death.

'Master Barnardine, what hoa! your friend the hangman! you must be so good, Sir, to rise, and be put to death: Pray, Master Barnardine, awake, till you are executed, and sleep afterwards.'*

The wretch, to whom this last summons is so ludicrously addressed, is represented to us, 'as a man, that apprehends death no more dreadfully, but as a drunken dream; careless, reckless, and fearless of what's past, present, or to come.'[47]

The crimes of such a man may perhaps have made him unfit to live; but he is certainly unfit to die. The safety of the community, and the preservation of individuals, may call for his execution; but the bosom of humanity will heave in agony at the idea, the eye of religion will turn with horror from the spectacle.

Suppose the sufferer on the contrary to have been a valuable member of society, and to have erred only from some momentary impulse of our imperfect nature; one, who in the recollection of reason hath found repentance; who resigns with chearfulness that life, which is become a forfeiture to the law, and looks up in confidence to heaven for that forgiveness which is not to be found on earth. The last footsteps of such a man, are watered with the tears of his fellow-citizens; and we hear from the mouth of every spectator,

> ' Yes, I do think, that you might pardon him,
> And neither heaven, nor man grieve at the mercy.'

CHAP. IV.

Of Banishment.

§ I. THE Romans permitted an accused *Citizen*, in every case *before* judgement to withdraw himself from the consequences of conviction into voluntary exile.

'*Exilium* (inquit Cicero)† *non supplicium est, sed perfugium, portusque supplicii. Itaque nulla in lege nostra reperietur, ut apud cæteras civitates, maleficium ullum exilio esse multatum. Sed cum homines vincula, neces, ignominiasque vitant, quæ sunt legibus constitutæ; confugiunt, quasi ad aram, in exilium; qui, si in civitate legis vim subire vellent, non prius civitatem, quam vitam amitterent. Quia nolunt, non adimitur his civitas; sed ab his relinquitur atque deponitur.*'

§ 2. Transportation‡ was totally unknown to the common law of England; but the antient practice of abjuration of the realm bore a strong resemblance to

---

*   Shakespeare, Meas. for Meas. Act. iv. Sc. 3.[46]

†   Orat. pro A. Cæcin. c. 34.[48]

‡   We may easily form a probable guess as to its first introduction into our laws; for by stat. 39 Eliz. c. 4. it was enacted, 'that dangerous rogues, and such as will not be reformed of their roguish course of life, may lawfully by the Justices in their Quarter-sessions be banished out of the realm

the Roman institution. 'This was permitted, says Sir E. Coke, when the felon chose rather, *perdere patriam, quam vitam*.'[50] The oath of perpetual banishment was then administered to him by the Coroner in the church, or churchyard, to which he had fled; and a cross was delivered into his hand for his protection on his journey. This custom no longer subsists; for the privileges of sanctuary* being taken away by the act of Ja. I.[52] the abjuration, as at the common law, being founded thereon, was virtually abolished.

§ 3. At present, banishment is in England, as in Russia,† more frequently inflicted as a mode of punishment, than permitted as an act of mercy. But in Russia it is made subservient to political utility; and those, who have by their misconduct lost all claim to the indulgence of their countrymen, are compelled to undergo a separation from all domestic connections, the rigours of a horrid climate, and the unhealthiness of mines, in the place of better citizens, who must otherwise be necessitated to accept so severe a lot.

On the contrary; every effect of banishment, as practised in England; is often beneficial to the criminal; and always injurious to the community. The kingdom is deprived of a subject, and renounces all the emoluments of his future existence. He is merely transferred to a new country; distant indeed, but as fertile, as happy, as civilized, and in general as healthy, as that which he hath offended.

It would not be incredible then, if this punishment should be asserted in some instances to have operated even as a temptation to the offence; in many

---

and all other the dominions thereof, into such parts beyond the seas as shall be for that purpose assgned by the Privy Council: *or otherwise be adjudged perpetually to the Gallies of this Realm*.' And further, every rogue so banished, and returning without licence, was made guilty of felony, but within the benefit of Clergy. And for the better indemnifying of such rogues so returning, it was also enacted that prior to their banishment they should be 'thoroughly burned upon the left shoulder with a hot burning iron of the breadth of an English shilling, with a great Roman R upon the iron, for a perpetual mark upon such rogue during his or her life.'   See Rastall's Statutes p. 429.

But Transportation more nearly as now practised seems to have taken place about the time of the Restoration. For, saith L. C. J. Kelyng, p. 45, 'Copeland (the prisoner) alledged, that he had done nothing but what he ought to do to serve his friend; and this favourable circumstance was allowed to be put into the King's pardon, amongst those prisoners of that nature who were to be sent beyond the sea; *it having been lately used*, that for felonies within clergy, if the prisoner desire it, not to give his book, but procure a conditional pardon from the King, and send him beyond sea to serve five years in some of the King's plantations, and then to have land there assigned to him, according to the use in those plantations for servants after their time expired; with a condition in the pardon to be void if they do not go, or if they return into England during seven years, or after without the King's Licence.'[49]

    * A very particular description of sanctuary and abjuration may be found in 'Le Grand Coustumier,' f. 13. § 81. See also the Mirror, c. 1. § 13.[51]

    † L'exil en Siberie porte avec soi une sorte de reprobation; il rend un homme si malheureux, que quoiqu'il vive au milieu de ses semblables, tout le monde le fuit; personne n'ose avoir avec lui aucune espece de liaison; mais c'est moins à cause du crime qu'on lui suppose, que par la crainte qu'on a du despôte.   Voyages en Sib. t. i. p. 236.[53]

instances hath its insufficiency been a fatal argument for the multiplication of capital penalties.

§ 4. It deserves serious and immediate consideration, how far, and by what means, this defect in our law may be redressed. It might perhaps be practicable to direct the strict employment of a limited number of convicted felons in each of the dock-yards, in the stannaries, saltworks, mines, and public buildings of the kingdom. The more enormous offenders might be sent to Tunis, Algiers, and other Mahometan ports, for the redemption of Christian slaves: others might be compelled to dangerous expeditions; or be sent to establish new colonies, factories, and settlements on the coasts of Africa, and on small islands for the benefit of navigation. It must however be confessed, that it is not easy to deter-mine upon theory the success of political innovations; it is indeed impossible for a speculative writer in his closet to collect the proper materials for this purpose. Practicable schemes on such subjects can only be obtained from merchants and others, who are qualified by experience to point them out, and have the induce-ment of interest to promote their success.

§ 5. I cannot dismiss this subject without expressing a doubt, relative to the propriety of punishing with death a return from transportation; especially where the original offence was not capital. It certainly is not justified by necessity; for it is easy, if requisite, to send the delinquent abroad again, without any consid-erable degree either of expence or trouble. Will it be said, that he deservedly suffers for the breach of a compact, which he is supposed to have made? In many instances the transportation is not in the nature of a conditional pardon, but directed by positive law;* in no instance is such a compact reconcileable to the law of nature.

---

*   In support of this assertion I shall cite some authorities; *previously observing*, that 'exclusion from society is the proper punishment of those only, who are become objects of terror to their fel-low-citizens in consequence of very heinous crimes, either not equivalent to the *ultimum supplicium*, or of which they have been convicted by disputable and unsatisfactory evidence.'

By 6 Geo. I. c. 23. and 4 Geo I. c. II. any persons convicted of larceny either grand or petit, and entitled to clergy, may in the discretion of the court be directed to be transported to America for seven years; and if they return within that time, it shall be felony without benefit of clergy.

By stat. 10 Geo. II. c. 32. the penalty of transportation for seven years is inflicted on the second offence of stealing deer in any uninclosed forest; and for the first offence upon such as come to hunt there, armed with offensive weapons.

By 26 Geo. II. c. 19. § II. persons convicted of assaulting any magistrate or officer, &c. in the salvage of any vessel or goods, are to be transported for seven years.

Ibid. c. 33. § 8. persons convicted of solemnizing matrimony without banns or licence, &c. shall be transported for fourteen years.

Also, by 5 Geo. III. c. 14. persons stealing or taking fish in any water within a park, paddock, orchard or yard, and the receivers, aiders, and abettors shall be transported for seven years.

I have not selected these as the *most* exceptionable instances; there are many others, in which transportation is inflicted upon offences by no means so heinous in their nature, as to require the extirpation of the criminal from the society of his fellow-citizens.

On the whole, is not such severity inconsistent with that leading principle, which forbids penal laws to attack the natural sentiments of the heart? *'Duri est non desiderare patriam. Cari sunt parentes, cari liberi, propinqui, familiares; sed omnes omnium caritates patria una complexa est: pro quâ quis bonus dubitet mortem oppetere?'*[54]

§ 6. By stat. 20 Geo. II. c. 46. it is made a felony, without benefit of clergy, for rebels under sentence of transportation to go into France or Spain; and the same severity is extended to all the friends of such persons, keeping or entertaining any correspondence with them by letters, messages, or otherwise.

In the wording of this clause, there is not any saving of even the most innocent interchanges of friendship. Shall then the lawgiver infringe all the ties and privileges of humanity? Shall he point the sword of justice against the bosom of fidelity? To such a lawgiver I would say, 'Consult your own heart, and inflict not chastisement on actions, which a good mind cannot disapprove!'

CHAP. VII.

Of Corporal Punishments, and of Infamy.

§ I. WE are told, that in Sparta[55] it was thought a very disgraceful sentence to the criminal, to lose the privilege of lending his wife to another man, or to be confined to the society of virgins.

The authenticity of the fact is immaterial, if the inference be admitted; which is, that, *in a moderate and virtuous government, the idea of shame will follow the finger of the law*; and that, whatever species of punishment is pointed out as infamous, will have the effect of infamy. *Existimatio est dignitatis illæsæ status, legibus ac moribus comprobatus, qui ex delicto nostro, auctoritate legum aut minuitur, aut consumitur.** The punishment of strangling is deemed honourable by the Ottoman family, who think it infamous, that their blood should be spilt upon the ground; in England, it is thought a more respectable death to be beheaded.

§ 2. Let legislators then remember, that the stamp of ignominy is intrusted to their disposal; and let them use with œconomy, and discretion, this best instrument for the promotion of morality, and the extirpation of vice.

Shame loses its effect, when it is inflicted without just and cautious distinction; or when, by the wantonness of oppression, it is made familiar to the eye. The sensibility of the people, under so extravagant an exertion of power, degenerates into despondency, baseness, and stupidity: their virtue is of forced extraction, the child of fear, with all the meanness of the parent entailed upon it. The tranquillity of such a state, says Montesquieu, is the mournful silence of a city, which the enemy is about to storm.

---

* Dig. 1. i. t. 13. 5. § I.[56]

The present Empress of Russia[57] is aware, that immoderate efforts are the symptoms of insufficiency, and have always more fury than force; that the security of the prince decreases in proportion to the exorbitance of his despotism; and that the national sensibility is the best spring of national power. But a few years ago, prior to the reign of the late Empress Elizabeth, it was no more disgrace to a Russian nobleman to receive a public flogging from the arm of the hangman, than it is at this moment to a miserable Japonese to pay with his skin the costs of a civil action, thought nugatory by the judge. The Muscovites no longer wed their wives with a whip instead of a wedding ring; and Russia rises into the respect of Europe. The Japonese still submit to the daily discipline of the lash; and Japan continues the contempt of the world. – The cudgel (says du Halde[58]) is the Governor of China; the Chinese (says the writer of Lord Anson's voyage[59]) are eminent for timidity, hypocrisy, and dishonesty.

§ 3. Corporal punishments immediately affecting the body, and publickly inflicted, ought to be infamous in the estimation of the people; so should degradations from titles of honour, civil incapacities, brandings, and public exhibitions of the offender: all which penalties should be applied with great caution, and only to offences infamous in their nature.

§ 4. In any case, to fix a lasting, visible stigma upon the offender, is contrary both to humanity and sound policy. The wretch, finding himself subjected to continual insult, becomes habituated to his disgrace, and loses all sense of shame. It is impossible for him to form any irreproachable connection; for virtue, though of a social nature, will not associate with infamy.* Yet this practice of branding hath prevailed in every known system of laws; as with us at present, in the punishment of many offences; and in all cases, when the offender, not being a clergyman, is admitted to the benefit of clergy. In like manner by the laws of France, '*Ceux & celles, qui après avoir été condamnés pour vol, ou flétris de quelque autre crime que ce soit, seront convaincus de récidive en crime de vol, ne pourront être condamnès a moindre peine que, scavoir lès hommes aux galeres à tems, ou à perpétuité, et lès femmes à être de nouveau flétries d'un W. si c'est pour récidive de vol, ou d'un simple V. si la premiere flétrissure a été encourue pour autre crime.†* Et ceux qui seront condamnés aux galeres à tems ou a perpétuité pour quelque crime que ce puisse être, *serront flétris, avant d'y être conduits, dès trois lettres* G. A. L.

---

*   The Preamble of stat. 5 Ann. c. 6. is a strong instance in support of this position. – 'Whereas by stat. 11 & 12 W. III. § 6. it is enacted that all and every person and persons, who should be convicted of any Theft, and should have the Benefit of Clergy allowed thereupon, or ought to be burnt in the hand for such offence, instead of being burnt in the hand, should be burnt in the most visible part of the left cheek nearest the nose: *and whereas it hath been found by experience, that the said punishment hath not had the desired effect, by deterring such offenders from the further committing such crimes and offences, but on the contrary, such offenders, being rendered thereby unfit to be entrusted in any honest and lawful way, became the more desperate:* Be it therefore enacted, that the aforesaid clause shall be and is hereby repealed.'

†   Code penal. 8vo. A. D. 1755, p. 105. Declaration du Louis XV.

pour, en cas de récidive en crime qui mérite peine afflictive, être punis de mort.'* So also among the Romans, it was usual, but only when the crime was infamous in its nature, to affix some branding, or ignominious letter, on the forehead of the criminals; and persons so branded were afterwards called, *inscripti* or *stigmatici*,[61] or, by a more equivocal term, *literati*.† One might almost say that those literary acquisitions were in some instances voluminous: for Zonaras relates that Theophilus the Emperor caused twelve verses to be inscribed on the foreheads of two monks; and we find in Petronius, '*quod implevit Eumolpus frontem Encolpi & Gytonis ingentibus literis, & nolunt fugitivorum epigramma per totam faciem liberali manu duxit.*'[63]

§ 5. There are two kinds of infamy, the one founded in the opinions of the people respecting the mode of punishment, the other in the construction of law respecting the future credibility of the delinquent: the law of England was erroneous, when it declared the latter a consequence of the punishment, not of the crime.‡ – There still exist some unrepealed statutes, which inflict perpetual infamy on offences of civil institution.§ But in general the rigour of this doctrine is now reduced to reason;¶ and it is holden that, unless a man be put in the pillory, or stigmatized, for *crimen falsi*,[66] as for perjury, forgery, or the like, it infers no blemish on his attestation. It may be highly penal to engross corn, or to publish a pamphlet offensive to government; but mercantile avarice, and political sedition, have no connection with the competence of testimony; the credit of an oath can only be overbalanced by the nature and weight of the precedent iniquity. Such was the reasoning of the Roman law. '*Ictus fustium infamiam non importat, sed causa, propter quam id pati meruit; si ea fuit, quæ infamiam damnato irrogat.*'**

§ 6. I say nothing of bastinadoes, mutilations, and a variety of other modes of corporal punishment, equally inconsistent with decency and humanity: such refinements of cruelty put the whole species, rather than the criminal, to disgrace.

Artaxerxes moderated the severity of the laws of Persia, by enacting,†† that the nobility who debased themselves, instead of being lashed, which had been the practice, should be stripped, and the whipping be given to their vestments;

---

* Ibid. p. 138.[60]
† Cœl. Rod. I. vii. c. 13. *Nulli Samiis literatiores.* Plaut. Cas. II. vi. 49. '*Si hic literatus me sinat.*'
I was mistaken in supposing that this expression had been adopted by stat. 4 H. VII. c. 13. which recites 'that divers persons *lettered* had been more bold to commit mischievous deeds, &c.' That word clearly relates only to scholars and the clergy.[62]
‡ Coke, Litt. 6. b.[64]
§ 2 & 3 Edw. VI.
¶ Gilbert's Law of Evidence, p. 143.[65]
** Dig. 48. t. xix. § 26.[67]
†† Plutarch.[68]

and that, instead of having the hair plucked off, they should only be deprived of their high-crowned Tiaræ.

§ 7. The English constitution, ever anxious to preserve the virtuous pride of the people, hath used this branch of the penal code with a reserve so scrupulous, that it may almost be doubted, whether more attention hath not been shewn to the protection of this principle, than to the preservation of life: for corporal pains might certainly with good effect be substituted, in some cases, in the room of capital judgments.

Yet, without any very strict scrutiny into our statute books, one may point out many provisions still existing, which are disgustful to humanity, and offensive to common sense.

It is easy to conceive, why the hand which gives a blow in a court of justice should be cut off by edict of law; the analogy between the offence and the penalty is evident: though it was at least a condescension to minutenesses in that parliament, which, 'to give more solemnity to the operation,'* ordered the master-cook, and serjeant of the larder to attend with dressing knives; the serjeant of the wood-yard to furnish a chopping-block; the yeoman of the scullery to attend with a pan of coals, and the serjeant-farrier to bring hot irons to sear the stump. But it is not so easy to acquiesce in the propriety of punishing a blow given in a churchyard, with the loss of an ear;† though we are told, that it was intended to obviate the quarrels of Protestants, and Papists, at the first establishment of the Reformation. Under a similar disregard to relative propriety, Henry the First seems to have enacted '*quod falsarii monetæ oculos et genitalia amitterent, absque aliqua redemptione.*'‡ Less absurd was the conduct of Severus,[70] who punished a notary for the exhibition of a forged pleading, by ordering the nerves of his fingers to be cut, that he might never be able to write again; as was also a Law of Edward the First, how unjustifiable soever on account of its cruelty, against the third offence of theft from the lead mines in Derbyshire; 'that a knife should be struck through the hand of the criminal fixed on the table; and that in this agony and attitude he should continue, till he had freed himself by cutting off his hand.'§

The eighth of Eliz. c. 3. punishes with imprisonment, and the loss of the left hand, the sending of live sheep out of the kingdom, or the embarkation of them

---

*   Stat. 33 Hen. VIII. c. 12.

†   5 and 6 Edw. VI. c. 4. or, 'having no Ears, the offender shall be branded with the letter F in his cheek.'

‡   Wilkins, Leg. Anglo-sax. p. 304. Knyghton, p. 2377. and in the Annales de Margan, sub anno 1124. 'Monetarii autem numero xciv jussu Regis in Normanniâ consistentis die Epiphaniæ Genitalibus privati sunt.' And in the Records about the time of the Conquest, it is very frequently said, in regard to other offences, that the convict 'pro felonia suâ fuit occœcatus, et ementulatus, et bona sua eschaet. Regi.'[69]

§   Fuller – and Observ. on the ancient Statutes, p. 380.[71]

on board of any ship; and this too, without any exceptions of the necessary provisions for the ship's crew: the second offence is made only a clergable[72] felony.
– Sir Edward Coke thinks,* that the benefit of clergy might be pleaded, as well
in case of cutting off the hand, as in case of felony; if so, and if the offender were
fortunate enough to have learnt to read, he could never have suffered under this
act.

The 14th of Eliz. c. 5. directed vagabonds to be severely whipped, and burned
through the ear with a hot iron, the compass of an inch; and for the second
offence to suffer death. This was a temporary act, and not continued in force.

It will not easily be credited by those, who do not possess the Statute which I
am about to mention, yet it is certainly true, that by *Stat.* 10 *Geo III.*† *c.* 10. *A. D.*
1770, 'every person whatsoever, taking, killing, or destroying any hare, pheasant,
partridge, moor-game, &c. or using any dog, gun, &c. for that purpose, between
an hour after sun-setting, and one hour before sun-rising, and convicted thereof
before one or more justice or justices, *upon the oath of one* or more witness or
witnesses; shall for the first offence be imprisoned, not less than three months,
for other offences not less than six months; and either for the first, or any other
offence, *be once publicly whipped* in the town, where the jail or house of correction shall be, within three days from the time of his commitment, between the
hours of twelve and one o'clock in the day.' And this is enacted even *without any
reservations, or distinctions, as to the rank, quality, or fortune of the offender.*

The tacit disapprobation of mankind consigns such laws to disregard and
oblivion: but they should be repealed, to prevent every possibility of oppression
on the one hand, and to stifle all hopes of impunity on the other.

---

* 3 Inst. 104. – Staunford 37. b. is referred to by Sir Ed. Coke; but I have not been able to find
any such opinion.[73]

† It is remarkable, that this Statute was made at a time, when 'the Commentaries on the Laws
of England' must be supposed to have been very recently perused by every Member of the Legislature. The writer of that admirable work hath, with peculiar anxiety, shewn 'the necessity of not
deviating any further from our ancient constitution, by ordaining new penalties to be inflicted
upon summary convictions.'

And surely, the corporal punishment of an Englishman, by the suffrage of one person only, is
inconsistent with every idea of English Liberty. Yet this unsatisfactory mode of trial was instituted for the promotion of speedy justice; and as a species of mercy to Delinquents, who, in trivial
misdemeanors, might otherwise be ruined by the expence and delay of frequent prosecutions by
indictment: but it hath been extended in a degree truly formidable. The Courts Leet and Sheriff's
Tourns are fallen into disuse, and the jurisdiction of individuals is aggrandized beyond measure: a
jurisdiction, which, by its burthensome consequences becoming disgustful to men of fortune and
education, too often falls into the hands of the mercenary and the ignorant.[74]

CHAP. IX.

Of the Disposal of the dead Body of the Criminal.

§ I. THE Roman Law permitted the murderer to remain on the gibbet after execution, as a comfortable sight to the friends and relations of the deceased.*

> *Nec furtum feci, nec fugi, si mihi dicat*
> *Servus: Habes pretium; loris non ureris, aio.*
> *Non hominem occidi: Non pasces in cruce corvos.†*

The Mosaical Law directed the body of the criminal to be buried on the day of his death, 'that the land might not be defiled.'‡

It cannot with any propriety be said, that there is inhumanity, but it may be doubted, whether there be wisdom, in the adoption, which the Laws of England have made on this point, of the rescripts of the Emperors, in preference to the command of Moses.

We leave each other to rot, like scarecrows in the hedges; and our gibbets are crowded with human carcases. May it not be doubted, whether a forced familiarity with such objects can have any other effect, than to blunt the sentiments, and destroy the benevolent prejudices, of the people?

§ 2. The ignominious burial of persons guilty of suicide might perhaps, if strictly executed, form some check on the sin of self-murder; but, in this case, Juries are more generally guided by the momentary impulse of compassion, than by a proper attention to the general benefit.

§ 3. To the dissection of criminals it is impossible to offer any solid objection. Modern ages will confine it to the dead, and turn a deaf ear to the anatomist, who laments the Æra of his own existence, '*Ubi, præ iniquitate temporum, vivos homines dissecare non licet.*'§

§ 4. There is a seeming liberality of sentiment in the proposal, to subject certain classes of criminals to medical experiments for the benefit of mankind. England was by these means enabled to extend inoculation through Europe, and consequently to save the lives of millions.

I am apprehensive, that I dissent from a very learned writer,¶ when I assert, that such a plan can never with any propriety receive the legislative sanction.

If the experiments be without hazard, they are unnecessary; because equally practicable on the innocent and on the guilty: if of a nature to maim and disable;

---

*   *Ut et conspectu deterreantur alii, et Solatio sit cognatis interemptorum.* ff. 48. 19. 28. § 15. – A. D. 1741, when the English Regency made an order to hang the murderer of Mr. Penny in chains, they inserted therein 'that it was on the petition of the relations of the deceased.' St. Tr. vol. x. 39.[75]

†   Horat. Epist. l. I. cp. xvi. 46.[76]

‡   Deuteron. xxi. 23.[77]

§   Vide Corn. Cels. in Præfat.[78]

¶   Observations on the ancient Statutes, p. 353.[79]

they are cruel and impolitic: if dangerous to the life; the uncertainty of the event destroys all the solemnity of the example in the eyes of the people. The criminal himself too expects the decision, under all the heated anxiety of a gambling adventurer; and meets the perils of death in a state of mind, very unsuitable to the dictates and temper of Christianity.

The modern advancement of medical knowledge, and the benevolence of its professors, make such aids useless and ineligible.

from William Dodd, *Thoughts in Prison* (London: Edward and Charles Dilly; G. Kearsley, 1777), pp. 1–2, 62–4, 69–73.

The Rev. William Dodd (1729–77) was the son of a Lincolnshire clergyman. Educated at Cambridge university, where he excelled, Dodd went to London in 1749 to make a career as a writer. He had some success, but lived above his means and married a woman with no social status or money. He fell back on the church, was ordained in 1752, became a fashionable preacher able to move his hearers to tears, and tried to cultivate the aristocratic patrons necessary for advancement. He also kept publishing: a frequently reprinted compilation, *The Beauties of Shakespeare* (1752); *The Sisters* (1754), a novel; a translation of the hymns of the Latin writer Callimachus (1755); popularizations of Anglican theology; an account of the Magdalen charity for reclaiming prostitutes; a commentary on Milton (1762); *Reflections on Death* (1763); *Poems* (1767), some sermons, including one attacking capital punishment (1768); and books of religious consolation. He also edited *The Christian's Magazine; or, A Treasury of Divine Knowledge* (1760–7), and the Bible with commentary, in monthly parts (1764). He made gradual progress in his clerical career and in 1765 was appointed tutor to the earl of Chesterfield's son. When his wife won a lottery prize he used the money to open a chapel near the royal palace, hoping to attract noble and even royal patrons, but he continued to live beyond his means, and his stylish dress and bearing earned him the nickname of the 'macaroni' (dandy or fop) parson. An attempt by his wife to obtain a lucrative post for him by a bribe lost him his appointments and patronage, and he was publicly ridiculed. He fled to join his former pupil, now himself the earl of Chesterfield, on the Continent for two years. Back in England, and again in financial difficulties, Dodd forged a bond in Chesterfield's name, but was detected, imprisoned and sentenced to death. Despite the jury's recommendation of mercy, his legal challenge to the validity of evidence against him, sympathetic press coverage, a campaign for a pardon led Samuel Johnson, and public petitions in his behalf, he was hanged at Tyburn on 27 June 1777.

Shortly thereafter his best known book was published, *Thoughts in Prison*, featuring a five-part poem of this title with some other pieces. Characteristic of the fashionable literature of 'Sensibility', or refined feeling, 'Thoughts in Prison' is in blank verse, the form of Milton's *Paradise Lost*, and there are many verbal echoes of Milton's poem. Dodd's poem is structured according to the sequence of his imprisonment: Week I, The Imprisonment; Week II, The Retrospect; Week III, Public Punishment; Week IV, The Trial; Week V, Futurity. 'Thoughts in Prison' surveys from the perspective of a condemned man the issues of crime and punishment as treated by humanitarian reformists such as William Eden (see the selections included in this volume). Dodd connects these issues to his own situation as a flawed 'man of feeling', possessed of a nobility of soul expressed in his poem, both in its main themes and its artistic form. The themes are the social division, misery and crime spawned by the excessive luxury and decadence of the age; the ineffectiveness of harsh laws meant to deter from such crime, as seen in the thieves at work in the shadow of the gallows; the hardening of criminals by the deficiencies of the penal system, such as inconsistent sentences, poor prison conditions and lack of a rehabilitative regime; and the idleness and revel of prison life. Instead, the poem promotes the reformist programme that would prevail for the next half-century, including provision of work and education; religious instruction; adequate accommodation, food and clothing; and solitude for reflection and reformation. Dodd, or the character created to narrate the poem, represents himself as both inside this vortex of human frailty and oppression and outside, observing, describing, and deploring it, and urging the reader (implicitly the social and cultural elite who read poems such as this) to forward the divine program for redeeming humanity, including the narrator. In its blank verse and language the poem is a sustained allusion to Milton's epic of the fall and redemption of humanity, *Paradise Lost* (1664) and *Paradise Regained* (1671). Generically, 'Thoughts in Prison' recalls several prominent meditative poems of the period, such as the Rev. Edward Young's *Nights Thoughts* (1742–5), with its self-representation of the author-narrator as 'man of feeling', reflections on human frailty and mortality, and structure based on progression of time. On several levels, then, 'Thoughts in Prison' is an advertisement for its author, thereby resembling several important contributions to the age's crime and punishment debate, such as Eden's *Principles of Penal Law*, but with life or death consequences for Dodd. Certainly *Thoughts in Prison* long survived its author. It was translated into French (1777, 1780) and Russian (1784, 1789, 1795), and there were numerous editions at London, elsewhere in the British Isles, and in the United States into the middle decades of the nineteenth century.

Dodd's prison complaint may be compared to that of the political reformer William Hodgson (1796), and the street ballad 'Newgate Walls', also included here.

Note on the text: […] indicates the present editor's omission.

THOUGHTS IN PRISON:

Commenced Sunday Evening, Eight o'Clock,*
Feb. 23, 1777.

from WEEK THE FIRST.

THE IMPRISONMENT.

MY Friends are gone! Harsh on its sullen hinge
Grates the dread door: the massy bolts respond
Tremendous to the surly Keeper's touch.
The dire keys clang: with movement dull and slow
While their behest the ponderous locks perform:
And, fastened firm, the object of their care
Is left to Solitude, – to Sorrow left!

But wherefore fastened! Oh still stronger bonds
Than bolts, or locks, or door of molten brass,
To Solitude and Sorrow would consign
His anguish'd Soul, and prison him, tho' free!
For, whither should he fly, or where produce
In open day, and to the golden Sun,
His hapless head! whence every laurel torn,
On his bald brow sits grinning infamy;
And all in sportive triumph twines around
The keen, the stinging Adders of Disgrace!

Yet what's Disgrace with Man? or all the stings
Of pointed scorn? What the tumultuous voice
Of erring Multitudes? Or what the shafts
Of keenest Malice, levell'd from the bow
Of human Inquisition?[1] – if the GOD
Who knows the heart, looks with complacence down
Upon the struggling victim; and beholds
Repentance bursting from the earth-bent eye,
And *Faith's* red cross held closely to the breast! [pp. 1–20]

---

* The hour when they lock up in this dismal place.

from WEEK THE THIRD.

PUBLIC PUNISHMENT.
[...]

Why do we *punish?* Why do penal laws
Coercive, by tremendous sanctions bind
Offending Mortals? – Justice on her throne
Rigid on this hand to EXAMPLE points;
More mild to REFORMATION upon that:
– She balances,[2] and finds no ends but these.

Crowd then, along with yonder revel-rout,
To EXEMPLARY Punishment![3] and mark
The language of the multitude, obscene,
Wild, blasphemous and cruel! Tent[4] their Looks
Of madding,[5] drunken, thoughtless, ruthless gaze,
Or giddy curiosity and vain!
Their Deeds still more emphatic, note; and see,
By the sad spectacle unimpress'd, they dare
Even in the eye of death, what to their doom
Brought their expiring Fellows![6] Learn we hence,
How to EXAMPLE's salutary end
Our Justice sagely ministers! But one, –
Should there be *one* – thrice hapless, – of a mind
By guilt unhardened, and above the throng
Of desperate miscreants, thro' repeated crimes
In stupor lull'd, and lost to every sense; –
Ah me, the sad reverse! – should there be *one*
Of generous feelings; whom remorseless Fate,
Pallid Necessity, or chill Distress,
The Family's urgent call, or just demand
Of honest Creditor, – (solicitudes
To reckless, pamper'd worldlings all unknown)[7]
Should there be *one*, whose trembling, frighted hand
Causes like these in temporary guilt,
Abhorrent to his inmost soul, have plung'd,
And made obnoxious to the rigid Law!
Sentenc'd to pay, – and, wearied with its weight,
Well-pleas'd to pay with *life* that Law's demand!
Aweful Dispensers of strict Justice, say,
Would you have more than one *life?* or, in an Age,
A Country, where Humanity reverts
At Torture's bare idea, would you tear
Worse than on racking wheels a Soul like This;
And make him to the stupid Crowd a gaze
For ling'ring hours? – drag him along to death

An useless spectacle; and more than *slay*
Your living victim? – DEATH is your demand:
DEATH your Law's sentence: Then his *Life* is yours.
Take the just forfeit: you can claim no more! [pp. 62–4]

But equal Laws, on Truth and Reason built,
Look to Humanity with lenient eye,
And temper rigid Justice with the claims
Of heaven-descended Mercy! to condemn
Sorrowing and slow; while studious to correct,
Like Man's all-gracious Parent, with the view
Benign and laudable, of moral good,
And *Reformation* perfect. Hither then,
Ye Sons of Sympathy, of Wisdom; Friends
To order, to Compassion, to the State,
And to your Fellow Beings; hither come,
To this wild Realm of Uproar! hither haste,
And see the *Reformation*, see the good
Wrought by *Confinement* in a Den[8] like this!

View with unblushing front, undaunted heart,
The callous *Harlot* in the open day
Administer her poisons, 'midst a rout
Scarcely less bold or poison'd than herself!
View, and with eyes that will not hold the tear
In gentle pity gushing for such griefs, –
View, the *young Wretch*, as yet unfledg'd in vice,
Just shackled here, and by the *veteran* Throng,
In every infamy and every crime
Grey and insulting, quickly taught to dare,
Harden'd like them in Guilt's opprobrious school!
Each bashful sentiment, incipient grace,
Each yet remorseful thought of Right and Wrong
Murder'd and buried in his darken'd heart!
– Hear how those Veterans clank, – ev'n jovial clank –
Such is obduracy in vice, – their chains!*
Hear, how with Curses hoarse, and Vauntings bold,
Each spirits up, encourages and dares
His desperate Fellow to more desperate Proofs
Of future hardy enterprize; to plans
Of Death and Ruin! Not exulting more
Heroes or Chiefs for noble Acts renown'd,
Holding high converse, mutually relate

* This circumstance is slightly mentioned Page 59; and alludes to a fact singular and disgust-ful: The rattling of their fetters is frequently, and in a wanton manner practised, amongst some of the worst offenders; as if an amusement, or to shew their insensibility to shame. How shocking to see *Human Nature* thus *in Ruins!* Here it is emphatically so; worse than in Bedlam, as Madness *with* Reason, is more dreadful *without* it![9]

Gallant Atchievements worthy; than the Sons
Of Plunder and of Rapine *here* recount
On peaceful life their devastations wild;
Their dangers, hair-breadth 'scapes, atrocious Feats,
Confederate, and confederating still
In schemes of deathful horror! Who, surpris'd,
Can such effects contemplate, upon minds
Estrang'd to good; fermenting on the lees
Of pregnant ill; associate and combin'd
In intercourse infernal, restless, dire;
And goading constant each to other's thoughts
To Deeds of Desperation from the Tale
Of vaunted Infamy oft told: sad fruit
Of the mind's vacancy! – And to that *Mind*
Employment none is offer'd: Not an hour
To secret recollection is assign'd;
No seasonable sound instruction brought,
Food for their thoughts, self-gnawing. Not the Day
To *Rest* and *Duty* dedicate, finds here
Or Rest or Duty; revel'd off, unmark'd;
Or like the others undistinguish'd, save
By Riot's roar, and self-consuming sloth!
For useful occupation none is found,
Benevolent t' employ their listless hands,
With indolence fatigued! Thus every day
Anew they gather Guilt's corrosive rust;
Each wretched day accumulates fresh ills;
And, horribly advanc'd, *flagitious* grown
From *faulty*, they go forth, tenfold of Hell
More the devoted Children: to the State
Tenfold more dangerous and envenom'd Foes
Than first they enter'd this improving School!
So, cag'd and scanty fed, or taught to rage
By taunting insults, more ferocious bursts
On Man the tyger or hyæna race
From fell confinement; and, with hunger urg'd,
Gnash their dire fangs, and drench themselves in blood. [pp. 69–73]

J. Leroux, *Thoughts on the Present State of the Prisons of This Country; Exemplified by a Plan, Adapted to the Objects of Such Consideration* (London: for the Author; and J. Dixwell; M. Babb; and J. Bew, 1780).

On the title page, the author identifies himself as a Justice of the Peace for the counties of Hertford and Middlesex; he was probably Jacob Leroux, architect living in Clerkenwell, London, and a Middlesex magistrate, who designed buildings ranging from town houses to country villas from at least the 1760s. Magistrates were active in building new jails at this time, as the power and complexity of the state grew and local and national governments turned their attention to crime and punishment as part of the broad movement for modernization of society, economy, and the state. The book also illustrates the widespread view of supporters of penal reform that design and organization of space had a key role to play in effective penology. John Howard's *State of the Prisons* (1777), excerpts from the expanded 1792 edition of which are included here, had disclosed the extent of prison mismanagement. It was increasingly felt that improved design and organization could address the issues Howard raised. They could help reduce dirt and disease – jail fever killed not only prisoners but also warders, managers, magistrates, and any sort of persons who had contact with prisons. They could reduce prisoners' fraternizing and hence supposedly corrupting each other and forming new generations of criminals. They could enable better control and surveillance of prisoners and more efficient and economical management. Above all, they could, by enforcing a particular external regime, affect prisoners subjectively so as to achieve a higher incidence of reform in behaviour. The most famous of these reform designs was Jeremy Bentham's Panopticon, selections from which are included in the present volume, but Leroux's proposal represents other, less grandiose visions of the time. At the same time, the book is clearly an advertisement for its author's services as an architect.

In reflecting on the present state of the several prisons of this country, whether for the reception of Felons and others, or for debtors, I am inclined to believe they are productive of those crimes that punishment was intended to reform; and the cause appears in many instances, from too close a connection with each other; from whence the alarming influence of bad example, which, in prisons, is spontaneously exhibited from the most abandoned of all classes.

Being requested by some friends in my professional department, as an architect, to turn my thoughts to the forming a plan to prevent the many evils arising from the present mode of imprisonment, and the buildings constructed for that purpose (and I glory in the opportunity which has humanity and good policy for its basis) many thoughts were naturally incorporated with my architectural ideas, and therefore to communicate my sentiments the more clearly, I was of course led,

First, To consider the general state and management of the several prisons now in being.

Secondly, What effects arise from such constructed buildings and management.

And Thirdly, To propose my plan for reformation; and to point out, at the same time, those observations that occurred independent of what could be exhibited by the plan.

In viewing the state of the prisons, and the common practices therein, the extent of this enquiry, will not permit my considering it in a particular, but a general point of view.

Prisons are comprehended under the titles of county or town gaols, bridewells and houses of correction; and are either applied as temporary places for safe custody, or permanent expedients of reformation.

But in whatever light they are considered, they will be found generally, with very few exceptions, to be improperly built; composed but of few rooms, them large, and intended to crowd therein as many prisoners as they will hold, whether healthy, sick or infirm. The tap rooms[1] are equally large, upon the same idea, and few, very few, have hospitals, or receptacles for the sick; if there are any places of divine worship, they are calculated to receive the crowd promiscuously, and as places of retreat only from the tap; where the clergyman becomes exposed to the insolence and intoxication of the several members of these dreadful regions, and where the effect of his doctrine is frustrated by the situation in which his auditors receive it.

In many prisons there is an absolute want of water, and in almost all, from the size and contracted number of the apertures, a want of air, with bad or scarcely any drains, and few ventilators of either kind; either a total want of warmth, or fire recesses dangerously or improperly placed.

I believe this account not exaggerated in respect to the buildings; nor the following, respecting the common practices therein.

Scanty or improper food, great want of proper bedding, and of rayment to the naked; no provision for work, or if there be, injudiciously enforced, and for useless purposes, neither producing the effect of more comfort in the prisons, or profit to the public; on whom so considerable a burden is lain for their support.

Gaol distemper and small pox engendered by numbers, filth and excess,[2] are extended to the whole prison, destroying the constitution, and impregnating the air with poisonous effects.

Debtors, felons, those only guilty of small crimes, women, and youth, are blended together; listening to, and encouraging each other in every act of wretchedness and vice. Nor can I stop here; the extortion of keepers[3] and servants, under the many cant names made use of, the suffering them to keep the tap, and farm[4] the allowance of food in the prison, only increase the general disorder; and to which if the gaming[5] practiced therein be added, it will readily be perceived, that these receptacles are indeed promoters only of profligacy and disease.

From hence appear to be produced distempers of the most malignant nature, which have often extended, and still oftner may extend their baneful influence to those who are ministers of justice, and others perfectly innocent of their crimes, and who frequently become guiltless victims to such disorders.

Confederacies, insurrections, and escapes are equally to be dreaded, and have often happened (too lately indeed) in many instances for the peace and happiness of individuals.

Nor is the connection that is kept up with artful and designing men, less to be attended to; such as the lowest of attorneys, &c. and which often contribute to wrest from justice, persons, whose crimes call for exemplary punishment, and who, by such assistance, are again let loose to trouble and harass mankind. These harpies[6] live on the unfortunate, and frequently by buoying up their hopes, at a great expence, deprive them and their wretched families of substance; and ultimately disappoint and disregard both their interests and persons.

Those who are committed by the magistrates for smaller crimes, where either no bail[7] can be procured, or where (consistent with law) the crimes do not admit of bail, are equally exposed to every evil produced in prison, and become connected with the greatest villains; and I may truly assert, under all the influence of bad example, come forth worse members of society. There are many among the number, whose crimes originate from trifling causes or who (after they are acquitted by one or other of the juries, are detained only for non payment of fees) become corroded in iniquity, and whose practices destroy every latent principle of good, producing in these nurseries of crimes the very objects the laws meant to lessen.

Nor are the impositions of the inferior officers less to be complained of. Nature retorts at ill usage; and I see no reason why the unfortunate or even the guilty should be loaded with oppression, which the already miserable alone cannot fly from.

How far a plan adapted to prevent all these inconveniences, with the additional advantages resulting from industry in useful and well-applied labour, good air and cleanliness, may deserve the public attention, the author submits with great deference; happy if it only shows the outline of what more enlarged ideas may correct and bring to perfection.

A general DESCRIPTION *of a* BUILDING *proposed*
(see the plan annexed)

To be situated if possible detached from a city or town, near water, and upon an eminence, and elevated above the surface of the walk that environs the same, at least three feet; to be composed of as many stories, and to be of such extent, as the size of the county or district, and the probable number of prisoners may require. This plan, with four stories, will contain in number about 150 persons.

The walls that surround the area or walk to be thick and formed pyramidically, and at least thirty feet high; the said area to be paved, and to have proper conveyances for water, as well as drains underneath (to prevent bad smells) out of the premises into a common sewer.

The several cells and areas in each story to be arched in brickwork, and to be about eight feet high. Water to be lain in to each respective cell with cocks from a reservoir above; also sinks and pipes for the immediate discharge of waste water; and flews in the walls, occasionally to warm the same, from one common furnace below, similar to the manner of heating hot-houses.

The whole building may be of brick or stone, according to the situation, and to be arched under the roof. The middle space, which is proposed to be but one story from bottom to the top, to be amply lighted from Palladian[8] windows, or a dome above, with a ventilator, or ventilators, in the ceiling of the same.

As for the elevation, with the decorations thereof, they must be submitted to the ingenuity of the architect employed; which, it is presumed, he will think necessary to be applicable to the subject.

It might not be amiss on the battlements or parapets of the building, to have small cannon placed for common defence, as well as a conspicuous alarum bell on the roof, with cords to the different parts of the building.

Whatever may be the necessary extent of the prison, it may be enlarged by adding more stories thereto; such a method being in itself cheaper than extending the building, as the roofs and foundations remain the same.

BASEMENT STORY,

Which must be sunk no lower below the surface, than the natural moisture of springs of the ground admit; it may contain hot and cold baths for the use of the prisoners; a tap room, and kitchen, of sufficient size for the extent of the building, which will differ according to circumstances; also cellars for coals, liquors, &c. and places for the punishment of the prisoners, and for sundry inferior purposes, and for making fires to heat the respective apartments.

N.B. The middle space need not make part of this story.

THE FIRST OR GROUND STORY.

A.   A walk of thirty feet to environ the building, divided into four parts, which may be made use of by the sick, and the prisoners, with the consent of the keeper; but so that few be permitted at one time, and them divided into classes.

B.   Watchmen at each angle (with fire arms).

C.   Engine houses.

D.   Water closets,[9] open to the air, with iron grates and ventilators.

E.   Keeper's house, which is to command the avenues and be connected by doors with the prison only.

F.   The hall (being the only entrance), wherein is room for the necessary attendants.

G.   A passage of communication railed off from the vestibule (in each story).

H.   The common vestibule, wherein divine service is to be performed by the chaplain in the center, so elevated that the prisoners may attend the same from their respective cells in each story, without coming out of the same. This vestibule, at times, may be applied to other purposes.

I.   Cells, with iron grates high enough to be above the head.

K.   Open areas adjoining, in which the prisoners may enjoy the benefit of air, by grated openings next the walks; in which open spaces their manual labour may be performed.

L.   Stone staircase for the use of the prison, shut off by iron doors.

M.   Guards at the entrance (the only one).

N.   Wash-houses, brewhouses, and other offices.

O.   An infirmary for the sick to be removed to, (on arches).

P.   Store-houses, or ware-houses, (as many stories as are necessary) for the work executed in the prison.

Q.   Occasional ward on each story either for imprisonment or work.

THE SECOND, THIRD OR FOURTH PRISON STORIES,

Which may be augmented according to the necessary extent of the prison,

To be the same as the several parts already described on the ground story, except over the engine houses are to be apartments for the keeper's servants, and additional cells over the hall.

IN THE UPPER STORY.

The same plan to be observed; but the cells may be made double the size, for those who can afford it, or whose rank entitle them to larger apartments, upon paying for such extra advantage.

In designing such a building, the author conceives more real advantages would result from this size, than if more extended; for should that, in any situation, be necessary, two or more buildings of the like kind would prevent many inconveniences resulting from a larger fabric, and more inhabitants. But as every situation will require some alterations to be attended to, and this work is only intended to convey general ideas, by application to the author, or any other architect, particular objects may be reconciled on these principles, as well as the elevation and estimates be adapted thereto.

To the foregoing observations on the plan, it may be necessary to add, the following political[10] regulations, with such others as local circumstance may require.

That the keepers and other attendants be not permitted directly or indirectly, on pain of removal or pecuniary punishments, to extort, demand, or require from any of the prisoners any kind of fee or gratuity whatever.

That the general regulations, as well as prices of every article within the prison, be painted and fixed up in the public hall.

That the salaries of the several officers be fully sufficient to keep them above the necessity of improper measures, and in particular that they have nothing to do with the sale of the liquor, or farming the food allowed in the prison.

That no visits be paid to the prisoners without the express consent of the head keeper; that such visits be paid only at the grate of each respective apartment; that nothing in any degree be delivered to the prisoners without it has undergone his immediate inspection; that no liquor be supplied, but with his consent both as to quantity and quality.

That every cell be scraped and cleaned effectually upon the departure of the prisoner, before another enter therein.

That the person keeping the tap room in the basement story have no manner of connection with the prisoners, but be paid upon the delivery of his liquor by the keeper's servants.

That the chaplain, in his appointment, be directed to assist and visit separately the several prisoners, as well as perform his public duty.

That committees from among the magistrates be appointed to survey and inspect the safety and regulations of the prisons, the health, rayment, food, &c. of the prisoners; and to hear the complaints against the keepers and attendants.

That their work be of that nature, as not only to be useful to the public, but productive of profit, whereby the expenses of the prison may be lessened.

Upon the whole, in forming such a plan, great respect and attention has been had to keep each prisoner unconnected with each other, not only on different stories, and in separate classes, but even out of the possibility of hearing, speaking or forming such connection; in which attempt, their being secluded from company may produce those sober thoughts so necessary in a work of reformation.[11]

The means of constant and useful employment; and that in good air, and with every convenience for cleanliness, will be considered equally necessary in this state of durance.[12]

Together with opportunities of attending divine service from their separate apartment, without removal; the means by the disposition of the plan of separating the sexes, and classing the prisoners according to the malignity of their crimes, and their rank and situation in life; and in particular separating the youthful offenders from the rest; with occasional opportunities of fresh air and exercise according to certain regulations.

In which plan, the security of the prison and the prisoners is attended to, by a judicious arrangement of the apartments, by engines and fire arms, and by the proper distribution of the houses and apartments of the keepers, and their attendants, with watchmen, and other proper officers.

Nor are the common comforts of life forgot, (if comforts in such situations may be said to exist), by a temporary means of warming the several apartments without the hazard of fire; by fresh water lain in, and by a proper discharge of the foul; by ventilators where necessary; by walks, to be used occasionally according to the discretion of the superintendant, for the invalids and others; a proper supply of liquor and food, by the favour of their friends or their money, without that excess resulting from common tap rooms, or the usual incitements to debauchery in every way; the opportunity of attending divine service, freed from those evils that have been complained of, arising from intoxication.

I trust that this plan will be found consistent with what I proposed, viz.[13] the preventing bodily disorders, confederacies, escapes, insurrections, excesses, quarrels, improper connections and debaucheries of every kind; and upon the whole produce what undoubtedly is the object of imprisonment, reformation and safe custody.*

FINIS.

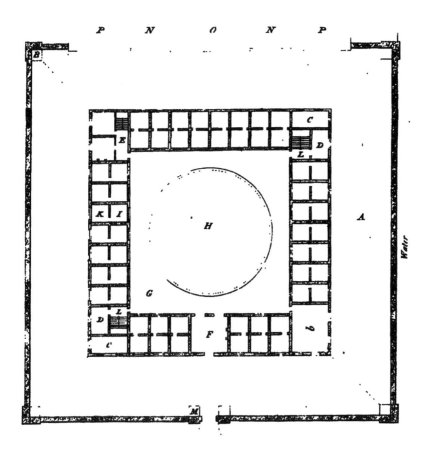

* Since this pamphlet was wrote, and not before, the author has seen a valuable work, published some time since, by John Howard, Esq; F. R. S. had he seen it sooner, he perhaps had not ventured to exhibit this feeble attempt on the same subject to the public; but as some thoughts are contained herein not to be found there, and as the plan materially differs, he flatters himself, the publication will not be ill timed; especially, as the price will put it within the power of many to peruse, who otherwise would remain unacquainted with the subject. He is happy to find his thoughts in many instances to coincide with so respectable an author.[14]

from [Martin Madan], *Thoughts on Executive Justice, with Respect to Our Criminal Laws, Particularly on the Circuits. Dedicated to the Judges of Assize; and Recommended to the Perusal of all Magistrates; and to all Persons Who Are liable to Serve on Crown Juries. By a Sincere Well-wisher to the Public* (London: J. Dodsley, 1785), pp. 1–34; 67–74.[1]

Madan (1725–90) was the London-born son of a judge's daughter and a military officer and Member of Parliament. He went to Oxford and then qualified as a lawyer but, when on a dare he attended a sermon by the Evangelical John Wesley, he experienced a strong religious calling. Under the patronage of the methodist countess of Huntingdon, he took up the ministry, became a popular London preacher, published an often reprinted collection of hymns and worked to reclaim prostitutes. He lost much of his support in the Evangelical and Methodist movement, however, with publication of *Thelyphthora; or, A Treatise on Female Ruin* (1780), advocating the social benefits of polygamy. He retired a year later, and it was during this time that he published an annotated translation of the Roman satirists Juvenal and Persius, and his *Thoughts on Executive Justice*. The latter argues that, especially in the face of what many perceived to be a national crime wave, strict execution of the laws by judges would better ensure security of persons and property and be more merciful to criminals than leniency in prosecution and sentencing. Madan was responding in his own way to the late eighteenth-century philanthropic movement evidenced by, among others, the movement for penal and law reform, indicated by the impact of such works as John Howard's *State of the Prisons* (1777), selections from which are included here. Though Madan argues for energetic enforcement of the laws, his approach yet resembles the emphasis of more obviously humanitarian and reformist writers on the justice system's impact on individual feelings and social psychology, in both offenders and the wider public. In *Thoughts*, Madan stresses the 'aweful', that is, awe-inspiring, and hence emotionally and morally transformative power of the justice system, if conducted as he advocates. In this, Madan participates in the turn away from punishment as infliction of bodily pain to punishment for subjective reformation, a turn taken by many reformers as well as, more famously, by the utilitarian reformer Jeremy Bentham, selections from whose writings on this topic are also included here.

THE honour and welfare of the kingdom in general, as well as the security and happiness of individuals, must depend on a due administration of the laws. Without laws to protect the persons and properties of the people, they must become a prey to each other; the *weak*, oppressed by the *strong*, must be liable to the loss of all enjoyment of liberty and safety; the honest and industrious, plundered by the idle and abandoned, must be reduced to poverty and distress; and even the richest and greatest, must be liable to that sort of dread and disquiet, which must reduce them, in point of comfort, to the standard of the poorest and meanest of their fellow-subjects; perhaps even below this, as those who have most to lose, have most to fear. But though there be laws, and such as are admirably calculated to meet with, oppose, and crush those violences and disorders, which must ever attend a mere state of nature; yet, if these laws are not duly, constantly, and impartially enforced and executed, the condition of the people will be but little, if at all, benefited by them. *Vigilance, faithfulness*, and *activity* in the magistrate, will ever be the parents of security and comfort to the people: where *these* prevail, there will be peace and safety; but where *these* are neglected, there will be disorder, confusion, and every evil work.

I am very unhappy, that I can, with the utmost truth, refer to the present state of this country, for an illustration of what has been said on the disagreeable side of the question. No civilized nation, that I know of, has to lament, as we have, the daily commission of the most dangerous and atrocious crimes, insomuch that we cannot travel the roads, or sleep in our houses,* or turn our cattle into our fields, without the most imminent danger of thieves and robbers. These are increased to such a degree in numbers, as well as audaciousness, that the *day* is now little less dangerous than the *night* to travel in; and we are not without fatal instances of the most wanton cruelty and barbarity, exercised on many of those unfortunate persons, who have fallen into the hands of these plunderers of the public.

As these are, apparently, increasing evils, they call aloud for redress; and we have one comfort yet remaining, which is, that a complete and adequate redress is to be found in our laws, whenever those laws are restored to their vigour and activity, by the several executive powers, or magistrates, whose province it is to declare and administer them, within their several jurisdictions.

I do not at all mean to enter into jurisprudential disquisition, or to carry the reader back to the days of *King Alfred,*[3] who, by the wise institution and adjustment of provincial divisions, into tithings, hundreds, &c. laid such a scheme of responsibility, among the subjects of England, for each other, as made it every

---

* An house in *Paris*, a few years ago, was supposed to have been attempted in the night-time; – the matter ended in the family being disturbed, and whatever occasioned this, soon ceased; but the master of the house said, that he thought his house had been attacked '*par des rossignols Anglois:*' – which droll expression sufficiently shews, that the frequency of *burglaries* in this country, are so far from being unnoticed by our neighbours on the continent, as to have become in a manner *proverbial.*[2]

man's business and interest to prevent disorders of all kinds. – These wise and salutary regulations have long since been obsolete, and, from various causes, retain little more than their names. – My intention is to take things as I find them, and to treat the laws of our country as they stand at present before us. I would be understood to confine myself to the penal or criminal laws; and, however it may be fashionable with many, to find great fault with the number and severity of these, yet I think it our happiness, that, as crimes have arisen, there have been laws made to repress them; nor do I conceive, that any man can reasonably find fault with this, except indeed it be the villain who is the object of them, and who certainly would wish to be free and exempt from all restraint whatsoever. – As to the *severity* of our laws, I know of none but of the most wholesome kind; for it is this alone which can deter the savage minds of those who are the objects of that *severity*, from the commission of those outrages and mischiefs against which the *severity* of our laws is levelled. The regular, sober, and virtuous part of the society has nothing to fear from the *severity* of the laws, but they have much to *hope* for; they may hope by this to be protected in their persons and properties, and in the secure possession of their lawful rights; for, however the profligate and abandoned assailant may have cast off every humane and virtuous inducement to good, and have put on the savageness, fierceness, and cruelty of a wild beast, so as to have forfeited all right and title even to the character of a man – there will be yet some principle of FEAR left, on which the *severity* of our laws is intended to operate, so as to check and prevent the mischiefs he would otherwise commit; or, if he proceeds to the full extent of his wickedness, to fall upon him, as an example to others, who may yet be stopped before it be too late.

It is certainly most of all to be wished, that crimes might be lessened by *prevention*; and this is never so likely to be the case, as when the fears of severe punishment duly operate on the minds of those whom no other consideration can restrain.

Oderunt peccare mali formidine pœnæ,[4]

is an old and true maxim, and is, no doubt, the reasonable foundation on which the *severity* of our laws is built: and indeed, when this once ceases to operate, the sooner the malefactor is removed out of the society the better; for the wretch who can be hardened against the *fear* of what he may himself suffer, leaves the innocent part of the society but too probable reasons to *fear*, that they shall find no end to their sufferings from him.

The prevention of crimes, is the great end of all legal severity: nay, the exerting that severity, by making examples of the *guilty*, has no other intention but to deter others, and thus pursue the great end of *prevention*. If this were not the case, all punishment would be nugatory, and therefore cruel; for the past could not be recalled, nor the least advantage accrue to the injured party, however much the criminal might suffer.

But if, by *severity* exercised on the guilty, those who are following the example of their wickedness and outrage, are deterred by the example of their sufferings, the two grand purposes of all criminal law are answered: the *one*, in the prevention of evil; the *other*, in the security of the public.

Instead of lamenting the multiplicity of our penal laws, we ought rather to lament the occasions of them; which indeed are so frequent, as to make it impossible for society to exist, unless remedies are thought of and prescribed to stop their progress. These remedies, like all others, must be applicable to the diseases which they are to encounter, and be faithfully and duly administered, otherwise they can be of no effect, and consequently of no value whatsoever. I may say, that the legislature has from time to time been assiduous in meeting crimes, as they have arisen, with wholesome laws; but those, whose duty and office it is to administer these laws, have now, for many years, been preferring their own *feelings* as *men*, to the duty which they owe the public as *magistrates*; and have been making so wanton and indiscriminate an use, or rather *abuse*, of certain discretionary powers with which they are invested, that safety and impunity invite forth and harden offenders, while danger and distress are everywhere menacing the innocent.

Highway-robberies threaten the traveller, whether by night or by day – the lurking footpad lies, like a dangerous adder, in our roads and streets – the horrid burglar, like an evil spirit, haunts our dwellings, '*Making night hideous*.'[5] – The farmer loses his sheep from the fold, the ox from his stall, and all sorts of people their horses from their fields, and even from their stables. These are but a part of that dreadful catalogue of offences, with which every *Old-Bailey*, and every *Assize-Calendar*[6] is filled and with which this country is disgraced and insulted: and for which it has become a taunt and a proverb in the mouths of foreigners.

Such is our reproachful and alarming situation: – the cause of this has been already hinted; and, as it is now prevailing more and more, the state of the criminal laws in this land may soon be said to resemble that of the laws of *Vienna*, as represented by *Duke Vincentio*, in *Shakespeare's Measure for Measure*.

> *We have strict statutes, and most biting laws,*
> *The needful bits and curbs for headstrong steeds,*
> *Which for these* MANY *years we have let sleep,*
> *Ev'n like an o'ergrown lion in a cave*
> *That goes not out to prey: now, as fond fathers*
> *Having bound up the threatning twigs of birch,*
> *Only to stick it in their children's sight,*
> *For terror, not for use; in time the rod*
> *Becomes more mock'd than fear'd: so our decrees,*
> *Dead to infliction, to themselves are dead,*

> And liberty plucks justice by the nose;
> The baby beats the nurse, and quite athwart
> Goes all decorum.————[7]

Whoever examines the *common* and *statute* laws,[8] which respect the criminal jurisdiction to be exercised over offenders of all kinds, must surely acknowledge the watchfulness of the legislative powers, both ancient and modern, over the lives, liberties, and properties of the inhabitants of this country: a stranger, who should read over an accurate and well-digested code of our *crown law*,[9] would imagine us to be the happiest, the securest, and best-protected people under the sun, in point of our internal police. He would admire the disposition of the *whole*, as well as the adapting of every *part* for the public good. – No dangerous crime without a prescribed severity of punishment – so contrived, as that the offender has nothing to *hope* – this inducement so precluded, as to leave no encouragement to villainy: – in short, he might be led almost to imagine, that the account we have of our safety from thieves and robbers, must be as perfect as in the days before the *Conquest*,[10] when it was said, that 'a child might go from one end of the kingdom to the other, with a bag of money in his hand, without fear of having it taken from him.'

But when such a reader of our laws is told, that offences against those laws are daily committed – that they are multiplied now beyond the example of former ages – that no country is so infested with the depredations of robbers of all kinds; – he would be at an utter loss to account for this, till he was told, that the dispensers of these laws very rarely put them in execution; and therefore, that they were little more than a *scarecrow*, set in a field to frighten the birds from the corn, which at first might be terrible in apprehension, but in a little time became familiar, and approached without any danger, by even the most timorous of the feathered race.

The wisdom of our constitution has placed the executive power in the hands of the *King*; who is the chief magistrate in all causes, and over all persons: but, forasmuch as he cannot himself administer this power in his own person, he delegates this to others, who, particularly with respect to the *criminal* laws, act in his name, and represent his person: the chief of these delegated magistrates are the *Twelve Judges of England*, whose high and important office it is to try criminals, to pronounce the sentence of the law upon them when found guilty, and thus consign them to that exemplary punishment, which the laws allot to their particular offences. These Judges are sages of the law, chosen from their professional situation at the bar, from among the ablest and most learned lawyers; – they are invested with great dignity, looked up to (as they ought) with very high respect,* and regarded as the great oracles of law and justice: – they are bound by a most solemn oath of office, duly to administer justice, according to the best of their skill and abilities, to all their fellow-subjects, &c.

Besides their attendance by turns at the session of *oyer and terminer*[12] and *gaol-delivery*,[13] at the *Old-Bailey*, for the counties of *London* and *Middlesex*, eight times in a year; they are sent with a like commission, *twice* every year, into all the counties of *England*, that they may administer justice: two Judges are in each commission on the *circuits*, which are divided into *six*; and thus these magistrates set forth to carry terror to the guilty, and protection to the innocent, into every part of England.

Their fellow-subjects, of course, look up to them for security and protection, and depend on their faithful and strict administration of the laws, for the punishment of wrong and robbery, and for the maintenance and protection of their persons and properties from violence and depredation – they must naturally expect that such *examples* will be made as the law intends; and as naturally hope, that, by means of such *examples*, they shall sit down in peace and safety,[14] and have none to make them afraid.[15]

The very appearance of the *Judges* at the assizes, if we include the attendance of the high-sheriff, his under-sheriff, and other officers – the first gentlemen in the county forming that constitutional bulwark, the *grand jury*[16] – that other excellent institution, the *petty jury*, who are to pass between the crown and the prisoners, on the trials of their several lives and deaths: – add to this, the vast concourse of people flocking from every part of the county, and assembling in multitudes to hear the solemn determinations of punitive justice – the sound of the trumpets – the Judge's solemn appearance in his robes, when seated in the place of judgment: – these, and many other circumstances, form one of the most affecting, the most awful scenes, that can be exhibited to the eyes of mortals; and, if duly improved, might be supposed to strike a terror into the minds of the beholders, not easily to be forgotten.

I have described what ought to be, and what the constitution intended by the circuits of the Judges – which was no less than to carry terror and astonishment into the minds of all; or, as it is well said,

Ut pæna ad paucos, metus ad omnes perveniat.[17]

---

* Our *Judges* are not only respectable with regard to their *office*, but are so *incorrupt*, as magistrates, that they *are*, what *Cæsar* said his wife *ought to be* –
    Not only chaste – but unsuspected. –
As *private citizens*, I think it no disparagement to the rest of the kingdom, to say, that there are not *twelve* honester or worthier men in it. But, as they are sharers in the common lot of, what Lord *Chesterfield* so pathetically styles, 'poor human nature,' they are liable to err, even (as *Voltaire* says of a certain *Abbé*) '*par l'excès de leurs bonnes intentions.*'[11]

And at what a vast advantage does the Judge's situation place him, over the feelings, affections, and passions of his auditory!

Methinks I see him, with a countenance of solemn sorrow, adjusting the cap of judgment on his head – while the crier proclaims –

'O yes!* O yes! O yes! – My lords, the king's justices, strictly charge and command all manner of persons to keep silence, while sentence of death is passing on the prisoners at the bar, on pain of imprisonment.'

His lordship then, deeply affected by the melancholy part of his office, which he is now about to fulfil, embraces this golden opportunity to do most exemplary good – He addresses, in the most pathetic terms, the consciences of the trembling criminals – he expatiates on the nature of their several offences – shews them how just and necessary it is, that there should be laws to remove out of society those, who, instead of contributing their honest industry to the public good and welfare, have exerted every art, that the blackest villainy can suggest, to destroy both – he enlarges on the fearful situation which the honest, the industrious, the virtuous part of the community must be in, if such as then stand before him at the bar, are any longer permitted, like savage beasts, to prey upon the public. No person, no property can be secured, no liberty enjoyed. – He then vindicates the *mercy*, as well as the *severity* of the law, in making such examples, as shall not only protect the innocent from outrage and violence, but also deter others from bringing themselves to the same fatal and ignominious end which now awaits the prisoners. – He then, in the most pathetic terms, exhorts the unhappy convicts, to consider well how best to employ the little space that yet remains between that moment and the grave – he acquaints them with the certainty of speedy death, and consequently with the necessity of speedy repentance – and on this theme he may so deliver himself, as not only to melt the wretches at the bar into contrition, but the whole auditory into the deepest concern. – Tears express their feelings – and many of the most thoughtless among them may, for the rest of their lives, be preserved from thinking lightly of the first steps to vice, which they now see will lead them to destruction. The dreadful sentence is now pronounced – every heart shakes with terror. – The almost fainting criminals are taken from the bar – the crowd retires – each to his several home, and carries the mournful story to his friends and neighbours; – the day of execution arrives – the wretches are led forth to suffer and exhibit a spectacle to the beholders, too aweful and solemn for description. They now *see*, that certainty of punishment must await the guilty, and the whole *county feels* a lasting benefit, in the security and protection which such an example of punitive justice has procured them. These impressions will last their time, and carry their salutary effects, perhaps, for years together. Many, many wretches, warned by such examples, turn from

---

*   A corrupt way of pronouncing the French word, *Oyez – hear*.

the evil of their ways, cease to do evil, learn to do well. Thus the law has its effect – thus are the persons, properties, and lives of men most mercifully preserved, the public peace secured, and the most valuable ends of civil government fully answered.

The MAGISTRATE who thus dispenses justice, is a blessing to the community – a protector of the innocent, a terror to the guilty. – He is not only a representative of an earthly KING, but of the KING of KINGS – for he is a *minister* of GOD *for good.*[18] – *He bears not the sword in vain.*[19] And when he is called to give an account of his *ministry,*[20] with what an unspeakable comfort will he be able to reflect, that, through the faithful, upright, impartial, steady, and uniform discharge of his high office, he has contributed to the peace, welfare, and good order of society, as far as the powers with which the constitution invested him could enable him so to do; and that he has left an example to those who shall succeed him, that they may tread in his steps, and thus continue the exercise of justice and truth from generation to generation![21]

Is this the case in our day? are all our dispensers of the laws such as I have been describing? – The natural connection between *cause* and *effect*, must (alas!) lead us to answer in the *negative*.

Holy writ tells us, that, when *Saul* the king of *Israel* had received a positive commission from God to destroy the *Amalekites* utterly, and all that belonged to them; he executed his commission with such partiality, as to save the *Amalekite* king *Agag* alive; and the best of the sheep, oxen, and fatlings, and all that was good, and would not utterly destroy them; but every thing that was vile and refuse, that he destroyed utterly. When *Samuel* afterwards met *Saul*, *Saul* expressed himself thus: – 'Blessed be thou of the Lord, I have performed the commandment of the Lord.' And *Samuel* said, 'What meaneth then this bleating of the sheep in mine ears, and the lowing of the oxen which I hear?'[22]

Now, if our *Judges* of *assize* really execute their commissions as they ought, what meaneth then these numbers of burglaries, highway robberies, these depredations, by day and night, in our roads, streets, houses, fields? – How are our news-papers filled with daily accounts of mischiefs done on the persons and properties of his majesty's subjects, by *felons* of every denomination?

One reason, and only *one*, can be given for these things. The law is not in fault, it is wisely contrived to prevent them, by holding forth *certain* punishment; but that punishment has been rendered so *uncertain*, or rather the suspension of it so *certain*, as to prevent the operation of the laws. [pp. 1–34]

The public have an undoubted right to look up to the Judges of the land for protection and safety; and those laws, which are the birthright of every subject, from the highest to the lowest, ought to be employed in the defence of their persons and properties from violence and outrage of every kind: if this be not the case, every man must stand in dread of perpetual injury; and has a right to complain, in the loudest and strongest terms, of those, who, instead of preventing these disorders, are little better than accessaries* before the fact to the daily commission of them.

This

> —— *Savior ense*
> *Parcendi rabies,*[24]

so far from deserving the sacred name of *mercy*, is in fact the highest *cruelty*.

In the first place, it encourages the daring and profligate to prey on their fellow subjects, insomuch, that no man is safe but the robber himself.

Secondly. It draws forth many, by the hopes of impunity, to commit actions, which in the end bring them to an ignominious death – in all such instances, it is no better than *murder.*

Thirdly. It so destroys the force of the examples that are made, as to take away their *terror*, consequently their *use*; and this is no better than throwing away the lives of those who are executed – and if so, little better than *murder.*

Fourthly. Though the number of the executed are *comparatively few*, with respect to the numbers that are *condemned*, yet they are *positively many*; so *many*, as to shock the humanity of every man that has not lost all feeling – and this is the consequence of a precarious and uncertain administration of justice; for, were justice invariably and steadily administered, according to the laws, and to the duty of those who are to dispense them – as offences would be *few*, so would executions be *few* also.

Fifthly. What a discouragement doth this same *parcendi rabies*[25] give to the zeal and care of the inferior magistrate! when, after much trouble, and some expence, in many cases, he is to commit an offender for trial, no other end is answered, than exhibiting a mere farce at the next assizes, where the purposes of justice are to be defeated, and consequently to be laughed at by every thief in the common gaol.

---

* This sentiment is finely touched by our inimitable *Shakespeare* – Measure for Measure, Act I. Scene 4.

> Fri. *It rested in your Grace*
> *To unloose this ty'd-up justice, when you pleas'd:*
> *And it in you more dreadful would have seem'd,*
> *Than in Lord* Angelo.
> Duke. *I do fear, too dreadful:*
> *Sith 'twas my fault to give the people scope,*
> *'Twould be my tyranny to strike, and gall them,*
> *For what I bid them do: for we bid this be done,*
> *When evil deeds have their permissive pass,*
> *And not the punishment.*[23]

Sixthly. This throws also a great damp on prosecutions; for to what purpose* is it that a man shall travel many miles, perhaps almost three parts over a large county, with a number of witnesses, when, after all, it is ten to one that the example, which he seeks to be made for the sake of the public, is turned into an encouragement to other thieves, to rob him as he returns home.

Seventhly. As it is the glory of a society, that peace and good order are maintained within it, so is it the reproach and disgrace of any people, that all manner of violence and rapine are encouraged, by a partial, uncertain, and inadequate execution of the laws.

Eighthly. How shocking is it to consider, that in a trading country like this, where persons are obliged to travel at all hours, that no man can stir out a mile from his house, without an apprehension of being robbed, and perhaps murdered! for of late, we have had instances of the most savage barbarity exercised on the persons of his majesty's subjects, whose fate it has been to be met by robbers.

For the above, and for many other reasons which might be adduced, I cannot help subscribing to that saying of Machiavel, that – 'Examples of justice are more *merciful*, than the unbounded exercise of pity.'[27] [pp. 67–74]

---

*   *Quid tristes quærimoniæ,*
Si non supplicio culpa reciditur?
                    HOR.
But wherefore do we thus complain,
If justice wear her awful sword in vain?
                    FRANCIS.[26]

from William Paley, *The Principles of Moral and Political Philosophy* (London: R. Faulder, 1785), book 6, ch. 9 (pp. 526–53).

Paley (1743–1805) was the leading popularizer of religion-based utilitarianism in his time. The son of a country clergyman, Paley was a brilliant student of mathematics at Cambridge University, and also studied classics and philosophy. After a stint as a schoolteacher he became a fellow at Cambridge, where he associated with supporters of religious toleration and cautious reform. His Cambridge lectures on moral philosophy were later refashioned as *The Principles of Moral and Political Philosophy*. Paley then became a clergyman, holding several positions thanks to patronage from friends, though his well-known liberal views were thought to have prevented him being made a bishop. He was also known for his bluntness and down-to-earth manners and lack of pretension, which some thought inappropriate to the dignity of a clergyman. In conversation he often expressed views that were more reformist than those found in his books, and he supported humanitarian causes and opposed slavery. At Cambridge he was a popular teacher and effective administrator and as a clergyman he was a popular preacher and conscientious in his duties. Well remunerated from his ecclesiastical positions, he became an important popularizer of leading Enlightenment ideas, which he sought to subordinate to a religious perspective against the freethinking, religious scepticism and outright atheism of many leading Enlightenment figures. He was alarmed by the French Revolution and sympathy for it in Britain, which many saw as the consequences of Enlightenment thinking. He countered the rise of Enlightenment and Revolutionary secularism among the professional and commercial middle classes with *A View of the Evidences of Christianity* (1794) and the popularity of writers such as Tom Paine among the working and lower-middle classes with *Reasons for Contentment, Addressed to the Labouring Part of the British Public* (1792). These defences of the established order, together with the continued influence of *Principles of Moral and Political Philosophy*, resulted in new honours and offices for Paley, but also made him the object of refutations by liberals and reformists, and secular utilitarians such as Jeremy Bentham. Responding to growing middle-class interest in secularized science, including early ideas of evolution, Paley published an argument for religion based on the apparently intelligent design of the universe, with *Natural Theology* (1802).

The Principles of Moral and Political Philosophy attempts to harness Enlightenment rationalism and utilitarianism, as ideologies of economic, social and political change and modernization, to the theology, ideology and interests of the established church, state and social order. It does so in order to palliate the social and political conflicts produced by such change and to avoid the kind of violent upheavals typified soon after the book's publication by the French Revolution. In doing this, the book is meant to be a conservatively reformist, religion-based handbook of views on leading social, economic and political issues of the time and a manual for practical everyday life of the increasingly important and powerful professional and commercial middle classes – in fact, the leaders of reformist and revolutionary movements across Europe and in the New World. The six books of *Principles* treat basic definitions and principles (Book I), moral obligations (II), relative (mainly social) duties (III), duties to ourselves (IV), duties to God (V), and elements of political knowledge (VI). These topics are set forth in a straightforward language and style, unadorned by elaborate and learned references and notes, and using Enlightenment styles of reasoning and utilitarian criteria of usefulness and effectiveness. Not surprisingly, *Principles* was made a textbook at Cambridge (training ground for the middle and upper classes), was often reprinted and widely read, and was translated into several languages.

The chapter 'Of Crimes and Punishments' is from Book VI, 'Elements of Political Knowledge' and deals with matters of growing concern to the property owning classes, and increasingly the subject of reformist polemics, proposals, and parliamentary action. Paley's arguments on this topic respond to the reformist humanitarianism of writers such as William Eden and John Howard (extracts included here), and resemble those of Martin Madan (also included here), published in the same year as Paley's *Principles*. Defending Britain's existing laws, legal system, and system of punishments, this aspect of *Principles* would make the book a favourite resource for conservatives during the French Revolution debate and after, and a favourite target, explicit or implicit, of reformers from Jeremy Bentham through William Godwin to Sir Samuel Romilly (included here).

C H A P. IX.

Of Crimes and Punishments.

THE proper end of human punishment is, not the satisfaction of justice, but the prevention of crimes. By the satisfaction of justice, I mean the retribution of so much pain for so much guilt; which is the dispensation we expect at the hand of God, and which we are accustomed to consider as the order of things that perfect justice dictates and requires. In what sense, or whether with truth in any sense, justice may be said to demand the punishment of offenders, I do not now enquire; but I assert that this *demand* is not the motive or occasion of human punishment. What would it be to the magistrate that offences went altogether unpunished, if the impunity of the offenders were followed by no danger or prejudice to the commonwealth? The fear lest the escape of the criminal should encourage him, or others by his example, to repeat the same crime, or to commit different crimes, is the sole consideration which authorizes the infliction of punishment by human laws. Now that, whatever it be, which is the cause and end of the punishment, ought undoubtedly to regulate the measure of its severity. But this cause appears to be founded, not in the guilt of the offender, but in the necessity of preventing the repetition of the offence. And from hence results the reason, that crimes are not by any government, nor, in all cases, ought to be punished, in proportion to their guilt, but in proportion to the difficulty and the necessity of preventing them. Thus the stealing of goods privately out of a shop, may not, in its moral quality, be more criminal, than the stealing of them out of a house; yet, being equally necessary, and more difficult to be prevented, the law, in certain circumstances, denounces against it a severer punishment: that is, the crime must be prevented by some means or other; and consequently, whatever means appear necessary to this end, whether they be proportionable to the guilt of the criminal or not, are adopted rightly, because they are adopted upon the principle which alone justifies the infliction of punishment at all. From the same consideration it also follows, that punishment ought not to be employed, much less rendered severe, when the crime can be prevented by any other means. Punishment is an evil to which the magistrate resorts only from its being necessary to the prevention of a greater. This necessity does not exist, when the end may be attained, that is, when the public may be defended from the effects of the crime, by any other expedient. The sanguinary laws which have been made against counterfeiting or diminishing the gold coin of the kingdom might be just, until the method of detecting the fraud, by weighing the money, was introduced into general usage. Since that precaution was practised, these laws have slept: and an execution under them would be deemed, at this day, a measure of unjustifiable severity. The same principle accounts for a circumstance, which has been often censured as an absurdity in the penal laws of this, and of most modern nations, namely, that breaches of trust are either not punished at all, or punished with less rigour than other frauds – wherefore is it, some have asked, that a violation of confidence, which increases the guilt, should mitigate the penalty. This lenity, or rather forbearance of the laws is founded in the most reasonable distinction. A due and practicable circumspection in the choice of the persons, whom they trust; caution in limiting the extent of that trust; or the requiring of sufficient security for the faithful discharge of it, will commonly guard men from injuries of this description: and the law will not interpose its sanctions, to protect negligence and credulity, or to supply the place of private care and prudence. To be convinced that the law proceeds entirely upon this consideration, we have only to observe, that, where the confidence is unavoidable, where no practicable vigilance could watch the offender, as in the case of theft committed by a servant in the shop or dwelling-house of his master, or upon property to which he must necessarily have access, the sentence of the law is not less severe, and its execution commonly more certain and rigorous, than if no trust at all had intervened.

It is in pursuance of the same principle, which pervades indeed the whole system of penal jurisprudence, that the facility with which any species of crimes is perpetrated, has been generally deemed a reason for aggravating the punishment. Thus, sheep-stealing, horse stealing; the stealing of cloth from tenters, or bleaching grounds, by our laws, subject the offenders to sentence of death: not that these crimes are in their nature more heinous, than many simple felonies which are punished by imprisonment or transportation, but because the property being more exposed, requires the terror of capital punishment to protect it. This severity would be absurd and unjust, if the guilt of the offender were the immediate cause and measure of the punishment; but is a consistent and regular consequence of the supposition, that the right of punishment results from the necessity of preventing the crime: for if this be the end proposed, the severity of the punishment must be increased in proportion to the expediency and the difficulty of attaining this end; that is, in a proportion compounded of the mischief of the crime, and the ease with which it is executed. The difficulty of discovery is a circumstance to be included in the same consideration. It constitutes indeed, with respect to the crime, the facility we speak of. By how much therefore the detection of the offender is more rare and uncertain, by so much the more severe must be the punishment, when he is detected. Thus the writing of incendiary letters, though in itself a pernicious and alarming injury, calls for a more condign and exemplary punishment, by the very obscurity with which the crime is committed.

From the justice of God we are taught to look for a gradation of punishment, exactly proportioned to the guilt of the offender: when therefore, in assigning the degrees of human punishment, we introduce considerations distinct from that guilt, and a proportion so varied by external circumstances, that equal crimes frequently undergo unequal punishments, or the less crime the greater; it is natural to demand the reason why a different measure of punishment should be expected from God, and observed by man; why that rule, which befits the absolute and perfect justice of the Deity, should not be the rule which ought to be pursued and imitated by human laws. The solution of this difficulty must be sought for in those peculiar attributes of the divine nature, which distinguish the dispensations of supreme wisdom from the proceedings of human judicature. A Being whose knowledge penetrates every concealment; from the operation of whose will no art or flight can escape; and in whose hands punishment is sure; such a Being may conduct the moral government of his creation, in the best and wisest manner, by pronouncing a law that every crime should finally receive a punishment proportioned to the guilt which it contains, abstracted from any foreign consideration whatever; and may testify his veracity to the spectators of his judgments, by carrying this law into strict execution. But when the care of the public safety is entrusted to men, whose authority over their fellow creatures is limited by defects of power and knowledge; from whose utmost vigilence and sagacity the greatest offenders often lie hid; whose wisest provisions and speediest pursuit may be eluded by artifice or concealment; a different necessity, a new rule of proceeding results from the very imperfection of their faculties. In their hands the uncertainty of punishment must be compensated by the severity. The ease with which crimes are committed or concealed, must be counteracted by additional penalties and increased terrors. The very end, for which human government is established, requires that its regulations be adapted to the suppression of crimes. This end, whatever it may do in the plans of infinite wisdom, does not in the designation of temporal penalties, always coincide with the proportionate punishment of guilt.

There are two methods of administring penal justice.

The first method assigns capital punishments to few offences, and invariably inflicts it.

The second method assigns capital punishments to many kinds of offences, but inflicts it only upon a few examples of each kind.

The latter of which two methods has been long adopted in this country, where, of those who receive sentence of death, scarce one in ten is executed. And the preference of this to the former method seems to be founded in the consideration, that the selection of proper objects for capital punishment principally depends upon circumstances, which, however easy to perceive in each particular case, after the crime is committed, it is impossible to enumerate or define beforehand, or to ascertain however with that exactness, which is requisite in legal descriptions. Hence, although it be necessary to fix the boundary on one side, that is, the limit to which the punishment may be extended, by precise rules of law; and also that nothing less than the authority of the whole legislature be suffered to determine and assign these rules; yet, the mitigation of punishment, the exercise of lenity, may, without danger, be entrusted to the executive magistrate, whose discretion will operate upon those numerous, unforeseen, mutable, and indefinite circumstances, both of the crime and the criminal, which constitute or qualify the malignity of each offence. Without the power of relaxation lodged in a living authority, either some offenders would escape capital punishment, whom the public safety required to suffer; or others would undergo this punishment, where it was neither deserved nor necessary. For if judgment of death were reserved for one or two species of crimes only, which would probably be the case if that judgment was meant to be executed without exception, crimes might occur of the most dangerous example, and attended with circumstances of heinous aggravation, which did not fall within *any* description of capital offences, and consequently could not receive the punishment their own malignity and the public safety required – and what is worse, it would be known beforehand, that such crimes might be committed, without danger to the offender's life. On the other hand, if, to reach these possible cases, the whole class of offences to which they belong be subjected to pains of death, and no power of remitting this severity remain any where, the execution of the laws will become more sanguinary, than the public compassion would endure, or than is necessary to the general security.

The law of England is constructed upon a different and a better policy. By the number of statutes creating capital offences, it sweeps into the net every crime, which under any possible circumstances may merit the punishment of death: but when the execution of this sentence comes to be deliberated upon, a small proportion of each class are singled out, the general character, or the peculiar aggravations of whose crimes, render them fit examples of public justice. By this expedient few actually suffer death, whilst the dread and danger of it hang over the crimes of many. The tenderness of the law cannot be taken advantage of. The life of the subject is spared, as far as the necessity of restraint and intimidation permits, yet no one will adventure upon the commission of any enormous crime, from a knowledge that the laws have not provided for its punishment. The wisdom and humanity of this design furnish a just excuse for the multiplicity of capital offences, which the laws of England are accused of containing beyond those of other countries. The charge of cruelty is answered by observing, that these laws were never meant to be carried into indiscriminate execution; that the legislature, when it establishes its last and highest sanctions, trusts to the benignity of the crown to relax their severity, as often as circumstances appear to palliate the offence, or even as often as those circumstances of aggravation are wanting, which rendered this rigorous interposition necessary. Upon this plan, it is enough to vindicate the lenity of the laws, that some instances are to be found in each class of capital crimes, which require the restraint of capital punishment;

and that this restraint could not be applied, without subjecting the whole class to the same condemnation.

There is however one species of crimes, the making of which capital can hardly, I think, be defended, even upon the comprehensive principle just now stated; I mean, that of privately stealing from the person. As every degree of force is excluded by the description of the crime, it will be difficult to assign an example, where either the amount or circumstances of the theft place it upon a level with those dangerous attempts, to which the punishment of death should be confined. It will be still more difficult to show, that, without gross and culpable negligence on the part of the sufferer, such examples are probable, or were ever so frequent, as to make it necessary to constitute a class of capital offences, of very wide and large extent.

The prerogative of pardon is properly reserved to the chief magistrate. The power of suspending the laws is a privilege of too high a nature to be committed to many hands, or to those of any inferior officer in the state. The King also can best collect the advice by which his resolutions should be governed; and is removed at the greatest distance from the influence of private motives. But let this power be deposited where it will, the exercise of it ought to be regarded, not as the gift of a favour, to be yielded to solicitation, granted to friendship, or, least of all, to be made subservient to the conciliating or gratifying of political attachments, but as a judicial act; as a deliberation to be conducted with the same character of impartiality, the same exact and diligent attention to the proper merits and reasons and circumstances of the case, that the judge upon the bench was expected to maintain and show in the trial of the prisoner's guilt. The questions whether the prisoner be guilty, and whether, being guilty, he ought to be executed, are equally questions of public justice. The trial of the one is as much a function of magistracy as of the other. The public welfare is interested in both. The conviction of an offender should depend upon nothing but the proof of his guilt, nor the execution of the sentence upon any thing beside the quality and circumstances of his crime. It is necessary to the good order of society, and to the reputation and authority of government, that this be known and believed to be the case in each part of the proceeding. These reflections will show, that the admission of extrinsic or oblique considerations, in dispensing the power of pardon, is a crime, in the authors and advisers of such unmerited partiality, of the same nature with that of corruption in a judge.

The aggravations which ought to guide the selection of objects for condign punishment are principally these three – repetition, cruelty, combination. The two first, it is manifest, add to every reason upon which the justice or the necessity of rigorous measures can be founded; and, with respect to the last circumstance, it may be observed, that when thieves and robbers are once collected into gangs, their violence becomes more formidable, the confederates more desperate, and the difficulty of defending the public against their depredations much greater, than in the case of solitary adventurers. Which several considerations compose a distinction, that is properly adverted to, in deciding upon the fate of convicted malefactors.

In crimes however, which are perpetrated by a multitude or a gang, it is proper to separate, in the punishment, the ring-leader from his followers, the principal from his accomplices, and even the person who struck the blow, broke the lock, or first entered the house, from those who joined him in the felony; not so much on account of any distinction in the guilt of the offenders, as for the sake of casting an obstacle in the way of such confederacies, by rendering it difficult for the confederates to settle who shall begin the attack, or to find a man amongst their number willing to expose himself to greater danger than his associates. This is another instance in which the punishment, which expediency directs, does not pursue the exact proportion of the crime.

Injuries effected by terror and violence, are those which it is the first and chief concern of legal government to repress: because, their extent is unlimited; because, no private precaution can protect the subject against them; because, they endanger life and safety, as well as property; and lastly, because, they render the condition of society wretched, by a sense of personal insecurity. These reasons do not apply to frauds, which circumspection may prevent; which must wait for opportunity; which can proceed only to certain limits; and, by the apprehension of which, although the business of life be incommoded, life itself is not made miserable. The appearance of this distinction has led some humane writers to express a wish, that capital punishments were confined to crimes of violence. In estimating also the comparative malignancy of which, regard is to be had, not only to the proper or intended mischief of the crime, but to the alarm occasioned by the attack, to the probability of still worse consequences, and to the general consternation excited by it in others. Thus in affixing the punishment of burglary, or of breaking into dwelling-houses by night, we are to consider not only the peril to which the most valuable property is exposed by this crime, and which may be called the direct and meditated mischief of it, but the danger of murder, in case of resistance, or for the sake of preventing discovery, and the universal dread with which the silent and defenceless hours of rest and sleep must be disturbed, where attempts of this sort become frequent; and which dread alone, and without the mischief which is the object of it, is not only a public evil, but almost of all evils the most insupportable. These circumstances place a difference between the breaking into a dwelling-house by day, or by night; which difference obtains in the punishment of the offence by the law of Moses,[1] and is probably to be found in the judicial codes of most countries, from the earliest ages to the present.

Of frauds, or of injuries which are effected without force, the most noxious kinds are forgeries, counterfeiting or diminishing of the coin, and the stealing of letters in the course of their conveyance; inasmuch as these practices tend to deprive the public of accommodations, which not only improve the conveniencies of social life, but are essential to the prosperity, or even the existence of commerce. Of these crimes it may be said, that, although they seem to affect property alone, the mischief of their operation does not terminate there. For let it be supposed, that the remissness or lenity of the laws should, in any country, suffer offences of this sort to grow into such a frequency, as to render the use of money, the circulation of bills, or the public conveyance of letters no longer safe or practicable; what would follow, but that every species of trade and of activity must decline under these discouragements; the sources of subsistence fail, by which the inhabitants of the country are supported; the country itself, where the intercourse of civil life was so endangered and defective, be deserted; and that, beside the distress and poverty, which the loss of employment would produce to the industrious and valuable part of the community, a rapid depopulation must take place, each generation becoming less numerous than the last, till solitude and barrenness overspread the land; until a desolation similar to what obtains in many countries of Asia, which were once the most civilized and frequented parts of the world, succeed in the place of crouded cities, cultivated fields, of happy and well peopled regions. When we carry forwards therefore our views to the more distant, but not less certain consequences of these crimes, we perceive that, though no living creature be destroyed by them, yet human life is diminished; that an offence, the particular consequence of which deprives only an individual of a small portion of his property, and which even in its general tendency seems only to obstruct the enjoyment of certain public conveniences, may nevertheless, by its ultimate effects, conclude in the laying waste of human existence. This observation will enable those, who regard the divine rule of 'life for life and blood for blood'[2] as the only authorized and justifiable measure of capital punishment, to perceive a greater resemblance than they supposed, with respect to the effects and quality of the actions, between certain atrocious frauds, and these crimes which attack personal safety.

In the case of forgeries there appears a substantial difference, between the forging of bills of exchange, or of securities which are circulated, and the circulation and currency of which are found to serve and facilitate valuable purposes of commerce, and the forging of bonds, leases, mortgages, or of instruments which are not commonly transferred from one hand to another; because, in the former case credit is necessarily given to the signature, and, without that credit, the negotiation of such property could not be carried on, nor the public utility sought from it be attained; in the other case, all possibility of deceit might be precluded, by a direct communication between the parties, or by due care in the choice of their agents, with little interruption to business, and without destroying, or much incumbering, the uses for which these instruments are calculated. This distinction, I apprehend, to be not only real, but precise enough to afford a line of division between forgeries, which, as the law now stands, are almost universally capital, and punished with undistinguishing severity.

Perjury is another crime of the same class and magnitude. And, when we consider what reliance is necessarily placed upon oaths; that all judicial decisions proceed upon testimony; that consequently, there is not a right, which a man possesses, that false witnesses may not deprive him of; that reputation, property, and life itself lie open to the attempts of perjury; that it may often be committed without a possibility of contradiction or discovery; that the success and prevalency of this vice tend to introduce the most grievous and fatal injustice into the administration of human affairs, or such a distrust of testimony as must create universal confusion and embarrassment; when we reflect upon these mischiefs, we shall be brought, probably, to agree with the opinion of those, who contend that perjury, in its punishment, especially that which is attempted in solemn evidence, and in the face of a court of justice, should be placed on a level with the most flagitious frauds.

The obtaining of money by secret threats, whether we regard the difficulty with which the crime is traced out, the odious imputations to which it may lead, or the profligate conspiracies that are sometimes formed to carry it into execution, deserves to be reckoned amongst the worst species of robbery.

The frequency of capital executions in this country, owes its necessity to three causes – much liberty, great cities, and the want of a punishment, short of death, possessing a sufficient degree of terror. And if the taking away of the life of malefactors be more rare in other countries than in ours, the reason will be found in some difference in these articles. The liberties of a free people, and still more the jealousy with which these liberties are watched, and by which they are maintained, permit not those precautions and restraints, that inspection, scrutiny, and control, which are exercised with success in arbitrary governments. For example, the spirit of the laws, and of the people, will not suffer the detention or confinement of suspected persons, without proofs of their guilt which it is often impossible to obtain; nor that masters of families be obliged to record and render up a description of the strangers or inmates they entertain; nor that an account be demanded, at the pleasure of the magistrate, of each man's time, employment, and means of subsistence; nor securities to be required when these accounts appear unsatisfactory or dubious; nor men to be apprehended upon the mere suggestion of idleness or vagrancy; nor to be confined to certain districts; nor the inhabitants of each district to be made responsible for one another's behaviour; nor passports to be exacted from all persons entering or leaving the kingdom: least of all will they tolerate the appearance of an armed force, or of military law; or suffer the streets and public roads to be guarded and patrolled by soldiers; or, lastly, entrust the police with such discretionary powers, as may make sure of the guilty, however they involve the innocent. These expedients, although arbitrary and rigorous, are many of them effectual; and in proportion as they render the commission or concealment of crimes more difficult, they substract[3] from the necessity of severe punishment. Great cities multiply crimes by presenting easier opportunities and more incentives to libertinism, which in low life is commonly the introductory stage to other enormities; by collecting thieves and robbers into the same neighbourhood, which enables them to form communications and confederacies, that increase their art and courage, as well as strength and wickedness; but principally by the refuge they afford to villany, in the means of concealment, and of subsisting in secrecy, which crouded towns supply to men of every description. These temptations and facilities can only be counteracted by adding to the number of capital punishments. But a third cause, which increases the frequency of capital executions in England, is a defect of the laws in not being provided with any other punishment than that of death, sufficiently terrible to keep offenders in awe. Transportation, which is the sentence second in the order of severity, appears to me to answer the purpose of example very imperfectly; not only because exile is in reality a slight punishment to those, who have neither property, nor friends, nor reputation, nor regular means of subsistence at home; and because their situation becomes little worse by their crime, than it was before they committed it; but because the punishment, whatever it be, is unobserved and unknown. A transported convict may suffer under his sentence, but his sufferings are removed from the view of his countrymen; his misery is unseen; his condition strikes no terror into the minds of those, for whose warning and admonition it was intended. This chasm in the scale of punishment produces also two farther imperfections in the administration of penal justice: the first is, that the same punishment is extended to crimes of very different character and malignancy; the second, that punishments separated by a great interval, are assigned to crimes hardly distinguishable in their guilt and mischief.

The end of punishment is two-fold, *amendment* and *example*. In the first of these, the *reformation* of criminals, little has ever been effected, and little I fear is practicable. From every species of punishment that has hitherto been devised, from imprisonment and exile, from pain and infamy, malefactors return more hardened in their crimes, and more instructed. If there be any thing that shakes the soul of a confirmed villain, it is the expectation of approaching death. The horrors of this situation may cause such a wrench in the mental organs, as to give them a holding turn: and I think it probable, that many of those who are executed, would, if they were delivered at the point of death, retain such a remembrance of their sensations, as might preserve them, unless urged by extreme want, from relapsing into their former crimes. But this is an experiment that from its nature cannot be repeated often.

Of the *reforming* punishments which have not yet been tried, none promises so much success as that of *solitary* imprisonment, or the confinement of criminals in separate apartments. This improvement would augment the terror of the punishment; seclude the criminal from the society of his fellow prisoners, in which society the worse are sure to corrupt the better; would wean him from the knowledge of his companions, and the love of that turbulent, precarious life, in which his vices had engaged him; would raise up in him reflections on the folly of his choice, and dispose his mind to such better and continued penitence, as might produce a lasting alteration in the principles of his conduct.

As aversion to labour is the cause, from which half of the vices of low life deduce their origin and continuance, punishments ought to be contrived with a view to the conquering of this disposition. Two opposite expedients have been recommended for this purpose; the one solitary confinement, with hard labour; the other solitary confinement, with nothing to do. Both expedients seek the same end – to reconcile the idle to a life of industry. The former hopes to effect this, by making labour habitual; the latter, by making idleness irksome and insupportable: and the preference of one method to the other, depends upon the question, whether a man is more likely to betake himself, of his own accord, to work, who has been accustomed to employment, or, who has been distressed by the want of it. When jails are once provided for the *separate* confinement of prisoners, which both proposals require, the choice between them may be soon determined by experience. If labour be exacted, I would leave the whole or a portion of the profit to the prisoner's use, and I would debar him from any other provision or supply; that his subsistence, however coarse or penurious, may be proportioned to his diligence, and that he may taste the advantage of industry, together with the fatigue. I would go farther; I would measure the confinement, not by duration of time, but by quantity of work, in order both to excite industry, and to render it more voluntary. But the principal difficulty remains still; namely, how to dispose of criminals after their enlargement. By a rule of life, which is perhaps too invariably and indiscriminately adhered to, no one will receive a man or woman out of a jail, into any service or employment whatever. This is the common misfortune of public punishments, that they preclude the offender from all honest means of future, support.* It seems therefore

---

* Until this inconveniency be remedied, small offences had, perhaps, better go unpunished; I do not mean that the laws should exempt them from punishment, but that private persons should be tender in prosecuting them.

incumbent upon the state to secure a maintenance to those who are willing to work for it; and yet it is absolutely necessary to divide criminals as far asunder from one another as possible. Whether male prisoners might not, after the term of their confinement was expired, be distributed in the country, detained within certain limits, and employed upon the public roads; and females be remitted to the overseers of country parishes, to be there furnished with dwellings, and with the materials and implements of occupation; whether by these, or by what other methods, it may be possible to effect the two purposes of *employment* and *dispersion*, well merits the attention of all, who are anxious to perfect the internal regulation of their country.

Torture is applied, either to obtain confessions of guilt, or to exasperate or prolong the pains of death. No bodily punishment, however excruciating or long continued, receives the name of torture, unless it be designed to kill the criminal by a more lingering death, or to extort from him the discovery of some secret, which is supposed to lie concealed in his breast. *The question by torture* appears to be equivocal in its effects; for, as extremity of pain, and not any consciousness of remorse in the mind, produces those effects, an innocent man may sink under the torment, as soon as the guilty. The latter has as much reason for his resolution, and as much to fear from yielding, as the former. The instant and almost irresistable desire of relief may draw from one sufferer false accusations of himself or others, as it may sometimes extract the truth out of another. This ambiguity renders the use of torture, as a means of procuring information in criminal proceedings, liable to the risk of grievous and irreparable injustice. For which reason, though recommended by ancient and general example, it has been properly exploded from the mild and cautious system, of penal jurisprudence, established in this country.

Barbarous spectacles of human agony are justly found fault with, as tending to harden and deprave the public feelings, and to destroy that sympathy with which the sufferings of our fellow creatures are beheld; or, if no effect of this kind follow from them, they counteract in some measure their own design, by sinking men's abhorrence of the crime in their commiseration of the criminal. But if a mode of execution could be devised, which would augment the horror of the punishment, without offending or impairing the public sensibility by cruel or unseemly exhibitions of death, it might add something to the efficacy of the example; and by being reserved for a few atrocious crimes, might also enlarge the scale of punishment; an addition to which seems wanting; for, as the matter remains at present, you hang a malefactor for a simple robbery, and can do no more to the villain who has poisoned his father. Somewhat of the sort we have been describing was the proposal, not long since suggested, of casting murderers into a den of wild beasts, where they would perish in a manner dreadful to the imagination, yet concealed from the view.

Infamous punishments are mismanaged in this country, with respect both to the crimes and the criminals. In the first place, they ought to be confined to offences, which are held in undisputed and universal detestation. To condemn to the pillory the author or editor of a libel against the state, who has rendered himself the favourite of a party, if not of the people, by the very act for which he stands there, is to gratify the offender, and to expose the laws to mockery and insult. In the second place, the delinquents who receive this sentence, are for the most part such, as have long ceased, either to value reputation, or to fear shame; of whose happiness and of whose enjoyments character makes no part. Thus the low ministers of libertinism, the keepers of bawdy or disorderly houses, are threatened in vain with a punishment, that affects a sense which they have not; that applies solely to the imagination, to the virtue and the pride of human nature. The pillory, or any other infamous distinction might be employed rightly, and with effect, in the punishment of some offences of higher life; as of frauds and peculation in office; of collusions and connivances, by which the public treasury is defrauded; of breaches of trust; of perjury, and subornation of perjury; of the clandestine and forbidden sale of places;[4] of flagrant abuses of authority, or neglect of duty; and lastly, of corruption in the exercise of confidential, or judicial offices. In all which the more elevated was the station of the criminal, the more signal and conspicuous would be the triumph of justice, and the more efficacious the example.

The *certainty* of punishment is of more consequence than the severity. Criminals do not so much flatter themselves with the lenity of the sentence, as with the hope of escaping. They are not so apt to compare what they gain by the crime, with what they may suffer from the punishment, as to encourage themselves with the chance of concealment or flight. For which reason, a vigilant magistracy, an accurate police, a proper distribution of force and intelligence, together with due rewards for the discovery and apprehension of malefactors, and an undeviating impartiality in carrying the laws into execution, contribute more to the restraint and suppression of crimes, than any violent exacerbations of punishment. And for the same reason, of all contrivances directed to this end, those, perhaps, are most effectual, which facilitate the conviction of criminals. The offence of counterfeiting the coin, could not be checked by all the terrors and the utmost severity of law, whilst the act of coining was necessary to be established by specific proof. The statute which made the possession of the implements of coining capital, that is, which constituted that possession complete evidence of the offender's guilt, was the first thing that gave force and efficacy to the denunciations of law upon this subject. The statute of James the First, relative to the murder of bastard children, which ordains that the concealment of the birth should be deemed incontestible proof of the charge, though a harsh law, was, in like manner with the former, well calculated to put a stop to the crime.

It is upon the principle of this observation, that I apprehend much harm to have been done to the community, by the over-strained scrupulousness, or weak timidity of juries, which demands often such proof of a prisoner's guilt, as the nature and secrecy of his crime scarce possibly admit of; and which holds it the part of a *safe* conscience not to condemn any man, whilst there exists the minutest possibility of his innocence. Any story they may happen to have heard or read whether real or feigned in which courts of justice have been misled by presumptions of guilt, is enough, in their minds, to found an acquittal upon, where positive proof is wanting. I do not mean that juries should indulge conjectures, magnify suspicions into proofs, or even that they should weigh probabilities in *gold scales*; but when the preponderation of evidence is so manifest, as to persuade every private understanding of the prisoner's guilt, when it furnishes that degree of credibility, upon which men decide and act in all other doubts, and which experience hath shown that they may decide and act upon with sufficient safety; to reject such proof, from an insinuation of uncertainty that belongs to all human affairs, and a general dread, lest the charge of innocent blood should lie at their doors, is a conduct, which, however natural to a mind studious of its own quiet, is authorised by no considerations of rectitude or utility. It counteracts the care, and damps the activity of government: it holds out public encouragement to villainy, by confessing the impossibility of bringing villains to justice; and that species of encouragement, which, as hath been just now observed, the minds of such men are most apt to entertain and dwell upon.

There are two popular maxims, which seem to have a considerable influence, in producing the injudicious acquittals of which we have been complaining. One is, 'that circumstantial evidence falls short of positive proof.' This assertion, in the unqualified sense in which it is applied, is not true. A concurrence of well-authenticated circumstances composes a stronger ground of assurance, than positive testimony, unconfirmed by circumstances, usually affords. Circumstances cannot lie. The conclusion also, which results from them, though deduced by only probable inference, is commonly more to be relied upon, than the veracity of an unsupported solitary witness. The danger of being deceived is less; the actual instances of deception are fewer in the one case than the other. What is called positive proof in criminal matters, as where a man swears to the person of the prisoner, and that he actually saw him commit the crime with which he is charged, may be founded in the mistake or perjury of a single witness. Such mistakes, and such perjuries, are not without many examples. Whereas, to impose upon a court of justice a chain of *circumstantial* evidence in support of a fabricated accusation, requires such a number of false witnesses as seldom meet together; an union also of skill and wickedness, which is still more rare; and after all, this species of proof lies much more open to discussion, and is more likely, if false, to be contradicted, or to betray itself by some unforeseen inconsistency, than that direct proof, which being confined within the knowledge of a single person, which appealing to, or standing connected with no external or collateral circumstances, is incapable, by its very simplicity, of being confronted with opposite probabilities.

The other maxim which deserves a similar examination is this, 'that it is better that ten guilty persons escape, than that one innocent man should suffer.' If by saying it is *better*, be meant that it is more for the public advantage, the proposition, I think, cannot be maintained. The security of civil life, which is essential to the value and the enjoyment of every blessing it contains, and the interruption of which is followed by universal misery and confusion, is protected chiefly by the dread of punishment. The misfortune of an individual, for such may the sufferings, or even the death of an innocent person be called, when they are occasioned by no evil intention, cannot be placed in competition with this object. I do not contend that the life or safety of the meanest subject ought, in any case, to be knowingly sacrificed. No principle of judicature, no end of punishment can ever require *that*. But when certain rules of adjudication must be pursued, when certain degrees of credibility must be accepted, in order to reach the crimes with which the public are infested; courts of justice should not be deterred from the application of these rules, by *every* suspicion of danger, or by the mere possibility of confounding the innocent with the guilty. They ought rather to reflect, that he, who falls by a mistaken sentence, may be considered as falling for his country; whilst he suffers under the operation of these rules, by the general effect and tendency of which, the welfare of the community is maintained and upheld.

from Jeremy Bentham, *Panopticon; or, The Inspection-House: Containing the Idea of a New Principle of Construction Applicable to any Sort of Establishment, in which Persons of any Description Are to Be Kept under Inspection; and in Particular to Penitentiary-Houses, Prisons, Houses of Industry, Work-Houses, Poor-Houses, Manufactories, Mad-Houses, Hospitals, and Schools; with a Plan of Management Adapted to the Principle; in a Series of Letters, Written in the Year 1787, from Crecheff in White Russia, to a Friend in England* (Dublin: Thomas Byrne, 1791), pp. iii, 4–10, 21–30, 35–43, 67–9.

Bentham (1748–1832) was the son of a well-to-do London attorney whose ambition was for his son to become lord chancellor; his mother died when Jeremy was young and his father remarried. A precocious and brilliant student, Jeremy attended Oxford University and then studied law, being admitted to the bar in 1769. Meanwhile, he had attended William Blackstone's lectures on law at Oxford, and he read widely in Enlightenment philosophers, becoming a rationalist and materialist. From these thinkers he developed the utilitarian assumptions that human conduct was governed by desire for pleasure and avoidance of pain and that the aim of social, political and economic order was to ensure the greatest happiness to the greatest number. Independently wealthy, Bentham did not have to work at law and devoted his energies to a wide range of philosophical projects, many left in manuscript at his death. As a brilliant intellectual, Bentham came to the attention of political grandees, and in 1781 was invited into the entourage and house of the Earl of Shelburne. Bentham became ambitious to enter Parliament and pursue a career in politics and government. With his beloved brother Samuel, Bentham also developed a scheme to set up business in Russia, and Samuel entered the service of a Russian prince. Here Samuel developed the idea of an 'inspection-house' for social control of various kinds; Jeremy would develop this idea into his Panopticon project. Meanwhile he continued to write and publish on a variety of subjects, and his work became known to politicians in France who would assume leading roles in the Revolution soon to break out there.

With Bentham's utilitarian assumptions, crime and punishment became a central topic in his work, for which he drew on such writers as Beccaria, Eden (both of whose writings are represented in this volume), and Montesquieu. While visiting his brother in Russia in the late 1780s, Bentham wrote a series of letters developing the Panopticon project, further stimulated by learning of the government's plan to establish a penal colony in Australia, since the independence of the American colonies had closed off that place, hitherto used for the purpose. Shelburne sent Bentham's Panopticon letters to the Irish politician John Parnell, with the result that the *Panopticon* was published in Dublin in 1791. It was a kind of advertisement, for with the return of Samuel from Russia in the same year the Bentham brothers planned to develop the Panopticon project as a business venture and a way to develop political careers. The project turned out to be protracted. Members of the government were enthusiastic but then lost interest. There were obstacles to acquiring the necessary land, and Bentham promoted the Penitentiary Act of 1794 to clear the way, and the land was acquired in 1799. War with France and the consequent social, economic and political dislocation forced other priorities on the government, which dropped the project in 1803 and revived it in 1811 with Bentham still to be the keeper. Work was started in 1812 on what was to be Millbank prison, but Bentham was no longer part of the project and in 1813 the government paid him £23,000 compensation. Millbank, originally to be known as 'the Penitentiary', was designed by William Barnes and proved difficult to build because of the improper ground on which it was constructed. It was opened in 1821, having reportedly cost the then enormous sum of £500,000.

Bentham went on to become a major figure in early nineteenth-century philosophy and his ideas of government, legislation, and economy had a wide influence during the formation of modern European and American states.

The Panopticon project attracted new attention in the 1970s with the publication of the French philosopher Michel Foucault's *Surveiller et punir: naissance de la prison* (1975; translated as *Discipline and Punish: The Birth of the Prison*, 1977), when the Panopticon was seen as marking a fundamental transformation in penology from emphasis on punishing the body to emphasis on transforming the individual subjectivity. Perhaps the most important feature of *Panopticon*, however, is its insistent relocation of punishment in a capitalist framework of investment, extraction of labour (from the convicts), and profit.

Note on the text: two silent corrections have been made.

PREFACE.

MORALS *reformed—health preserved—industry invigorated—instruction dif-*
fused—public burthens lightened—Economy seated as it were upon a rock—the
Gordian knot[1] *of the Poor-Laws*[2] *not cut but untied—all by a simple idea in Archi-*
tecture! – Thus much I ventured to say on laying down the pen – and thus much
I should perhaps have said on taking it up, if at that early period I had seen the
whole of the way before me. – A new mode of obtaining power, of mind over
mind, in a quantity hitherto without example: and that, to a degree equally without example, secured by whoever chooses to have it so, against abuse. – Such is
the engine: such work that may be done with it. – How far the expectations
thus held out have been fulfilled, the Reader will decide. [p. iii]

LETTER II.

Plan for a Penitentiary Inspection-house.

BEFORE you look at the plan, take in words the general idea of it.

The building is circular.

The apartments of the prisoners occupy the circumference. You may call
them, if you please, the *cells*.

These *cells* are divided from one another, and the prisoners by that means
secluded from all communication with each other, by *partitions* in the form of
radii issuing from the circumference towards the center, and extending as many
feet as shall be thought necessary to form the largest dimension of the cell.

The apartment of the inspector occupies the center: you may call it if you
please the *Inspector's lodge*.

It will be convenient in most, if not in all cases, to have a vacant space or *area*
all round, between such center and such circumference. You may call it if you
please the *intermediate* or *annular* area.

About the width of a cell may be sufficient for a *passage* from the outside of
the building to the lodge.

Each cell has in the outward circumference, a *window*, large enough, not only
to light the cell, but, through the cell, to afford light enough to the correspondent part of the lodge.

The inner circumference of the cell is formed by an iron *grating*, so light as
not to screen any part of the cell from the Inspector's view.

Of this grating a part sufficiently large opens, in form of a *door*, to admit the
prisoner at his first entrance; and to give admission at any time to the inspector
or any of his attendants.

To cut off from each prisoner the view of every other, the partitions are carried on a few feet beyond the grating into the intermediate area; such projecting
parts I call the *protracted partitions*.

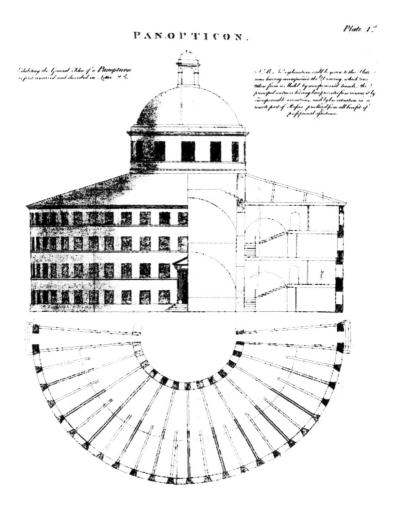

It is conceived, that the light, coming in, in this manner through the cells, and so across the intermediate area, will be sufficient for the inspector's lodge. But, for this purpose, both the windows in the cells, and those corresponding to them in the lodge, should be as large as the strength of the building, and what shall be deemed a necessary attention to economy, will permit.

To the windows of the lodge there are *blinds*, as high up as the eyes of the prisoners in their cells can, by any means they can employ, be made to reach.

To prevent *thorough light*, whereby notwithstanding the blinds, the prisoners would see from the cells whether or no any person was in the lodge, that apartment is divided into quarters, by *partitions* formed by two diameters to the circle, crossing each other at right angles. For these partitions the thinnest materials might serve: and they might be made removeable at pleasure; their height, sufficient to prevent the prisoners seeing over them from the cells. Doors to these partitions, if left open at any time, might produce the thorough light: To prevent this, divide each partition into two, at any part required, setting down the one-half, at such distance from the other, as shall be equal to the aperture of a door.

These windows of the inspector's lodge open into the intermediate area, in form of *doors*, in as many places as shall be deemed necessary to admit of his communicating readily with any of the cells.

Small *lamps*, in the outside of each window of the lodge, backed by a reflector, to throw the light into the corresponding cells, would extend to the night the security of the day.

To save the troublesome exertion of voice, that might otherwise be necessary, and to prevent one prisoner from knowing, that the inspector was occupied by another prisoner at a distance, a small *tin tube* might reach from each cell to the inspector's lodge, passing across the area, and so in, at the side of the correspondent window of the lodge. By means of this implement, the slightest whisper of the one might be heard by the other, especially if he had proper notice to apply his ear to the tube.

With regard to *instruction*, in cases where it cannot be duly given without the instructor's being close to the work, or without setting his hand to it by way of example before the learner's face, the instructor must indeed here as elsewhere, shift his station as often as there is occasion to visit different workmen: unless he calls the workmen to him, which in some of the instances to which this sort of building is applicable, such as that of imprisoned felons, could not so well be. But in all cases where directions, given verbally and at a distance, are sufficient, these tubes will be found of use. They will save, on the one hand the exertion of voice it would require, on the part of the instructor, to communicate instruction to the workmen without quitting his central station in the lodge; and, on the other, the confusion which would ensue, if different instructors, or persons in the lodge, were calling to the cells at the same time. And, in the case of hospitals, the quiet that may be insured by this little contrivance, trifling as it may seem at first sight, affords an additional advantage.

A *bell* appropriated exclusively to the purposes of *alarm*, hangs in a *belfry* with which the buildings is crowned, communicating by a rope, with the inspector's lodge.

The most economical, and perhaps the most convenient, way of *warming* the cells and area, would be by *flues* surrounding it, upon the principle of those in hot houses. A total want of every means of producing artificial heat might, in such weather as we sometimes have in England, be fatal to the lives of the prisoners: at any rate it would oftentimes be altogether incompatible with their working at any sedentary employment. The flues, however, and the fire places belonging to them, instead of being on the outside, as in hot houses, should be in the inside. By this means there would be less waste of heat, and the current of air that would rush in on all sides through the cells, to supply the draught made by the fires, would answer so far the purpose of ventilation. But of this more under the head of Hospitals.* [pp. 4-10]

---

*   There is one subject, which, though not of the most dignified kind, nor of the most pleasant kind to expatiate upon, is of too great importance to health and safe-custody to be passed over unconsidered: I mean the provision to be made for carrying off the result of necessary evacuations; a common necessary might be dangerous to security, and would be altogether incompatible with the plan of solitude. To have the filth carried off by the attendants, would be altogether as incompatible with cleanliness: since without such a degree of regularity as it would be difficult, if not ridiculous, to attempt to inforce in case of health, and altogether impossible in case of sickness, the air of each cell, and by that means the lodge itself would be liable to be kept in a state of constant contamination, in the intervals betwixt one visit and another. This being the case, I can see no other eligible means, than that of having in each cell a fixt provision made for this purpose in the construction of the building.

Betwixt every other two cells, at the end of the partition which divides them, a hollow shaft or tunnel is left in the brickwork of the exterior wall; which tunnel, if there be several stories to the building, is carried up through all of them.

Into this tunnel is inserted under each cell, the bottom of an EARTHEN PIPE (like those applied in England to the tops of chimneys) glazed in the inside. The upper end, opening into the cell, is covered by a seat of cast-iron, bedded into the brick work; with an aperture, which, neither by its size nor shape, shall be capable of admitting the body of a man. To gain the tunnel from the inside of the cell, the position of this pipe will of course be slanting. At the bottom of the tunnel, on the outside of the building an arched opening, so low as scarcely to be discernable, admits of the filth being carried away. No one, who has been at all attentive to the history of prisons, but must have observed, how often escapes have been effected or attempted through this channel.

A slight screen, which the prisoner might occasionally interpose, may, perhaps not, be thought superfluous. This, while it answers the purpose of decency, might be so adjusted as to prevent his concealing from the eye of the inspector any forbidden enterprize.

For each cell, the whole apparatus would not come to many shillings: a small consideration for a great degree of security. In this manner, without any relaxation of the discipline, the advantages of cleanliness, and its concomitant health, may be attained to as great a degree as in most private houses.

It would be regarded perhaps, as a luxury too great for an establishment of this kind, were I to venture to propose the addition of a WATER PIPE all round, with a cock to it in each cell. The clear expence would, however not be quite so great as it might seem: since by this means a considerable quantity of attendance would be saved. To each prisoner, some allowance of water must necessarily be afforded, if it were only for drink, without regard to cleanliness. To forward that allowance by hand to two or three hundred prisoners in so many different apartments, might perhaps be as much as one man could do, if constantly employed. For the raising the water by pumps to the necessary elevation, the labour of the prisoners would suffice.

As to the MATERIALS, brick, as every body knows, would be the cheapest in *****, and either brick or stone, in every other part of England. Thus much as to the shell. But in a building calculated for duration, as this would be, the expence of allowing the same materials to the FLOORS, and laying them upon ARCHES, would, I imagine, not be deemed an unsuitable one: especially when the advantage of a perfect security from fire is taken into the account.

LETTER V.

Essential points of the Plan.

IT may be of use, among all the particulars you have seen, it should be clearly understood, what circumstances are, and what are not, essential to the plan. The essence of it consists then, in the *centrality* of the inspectors situation, combined with the well known and most effectual contrivances for *seeing without being seen.* As to the *general form* of the building, the most commodious for most purposes seems to be the circular: but this is not an absolutely essential circumstance. Of all figures, however, this, you will observe, is the only one that affords a perfect view, and the same view, of an indefinite number of apartments of the same dimensions: that affords a spot from which, without any change of situation, a man may survey, in the same perfection, the whole number, and without so much as a change of posture, the half of the whole number, at the same time: that, within a boundary of a given extent, contains the greatest quantity of room: – that places the center at the lead distance from the light: – that gives the cells most width, at the part where, on account of the light, most light may, for the purposes of work, be wanted: – and that reduces to the greatest possible shortness the path taken by the inspector, in passing from each part of the field of inspection to every other.

You will please to observe, that, though perhaps, it is the most important point, that the persons to be inspected should always feel themselves as if under inspection, at least as standing a great chance of being so, yet it is not by any means the *only* one. If it were, the same advantage might be given to buildings of almost any form. What is also of importance is, that for the greatest proportion of time possible, each man should actually *be* under inspection. This, is material in *all* cases, that the inspector may have the satisfaction of knowing, that the discipline actually has the effect which it is designed to have: and it is more particularly material in such cases where the inspector, besides seeing that they conform to such standing rules as are prescribed, has more or less frequent occasion to give them such transient and incidental directions as will require to be given and enforced, at the commencement at least, of every course of industry. And, I think, it needs not much argument to prove, that the business of inspection, like every other, will be performed to a greater degree of perfection, the less trouble the performance of it requires.

Not only so, but the greater chance there is, of a given person's being at a given time actually under inspection, the more strong will be the persuasion the more *intense*, if I may so say, the *feeling*, he has of his being so. How little turn soever the greater number of persons so circumstanced may be supposed to have for calculation, some rough sort of calculation can scarcely, under such circumstances avoid forcing itself upon the rudest mind. Experiment, venturing first upon slight transgressions, and so on, in proportion to success, upon more and more considerable ones, will not fail to teach him the difference between a loose inspection and a strict one.

It is for these reasons, that I cannot help looking upon every form as less and less eligible, in proportion as it deviates from the *circular*.

A very material point is, that room be allotted to the lodge, sufficient to adapt it to the purpose of a compleat and constant habitation for the principal inspector, or head keeper, and his family. The more numerous also the family, the better; since, by this means, there will in fact be as many inspectors as the family consists of persons, though only one be paid for it. Neither the orders of the inspector himself, nor any interest which they may feel, or not feel, in the regular performance of his duty, would be requisite to find them motives adequate to the purpose. Secluded oftentimes, by their situation, from every other object, they will naturally, and in a manner unavoidably give their eyes a direction conformable to that purpose, in every momentary interval of their ordinary occupations. It will supply in their instance the place of that great and constant fund of entertainment to the sedentary and vacant in towns, the looking out of the window. The scene, though a confined, would be a very various, and therefore perhaps not altogether an unamusing one.

LETTER VI.

Advantages of the Plan.

I FLATTER myself there can now be little doubt, of the plan's possessing the fundamental advantages I have been attributing to it, I mean the *apparent omnipresence* of the inspector (if divines will allow me the expression) combined with the extreme facility of his *real presence*.

A collateral advantage it possesses, and on the score of frugality a very material one, is that which respects the *number* of the inspectors requisite. If this plan required more than another, the additional number would form an objection which, were the difference to a certain degree considerable, might rise so high as to be conclusive; so far from it, that a greater multitude than ever were yet lodged in one house might be inspected by a single person. For the trouble of inspection is diminished in no less proportion than the strictness of inspection is increased.

Another very important advantage, whatever purposes the plan may be applied to, particularly where it is applied to the severest and most coercive purposes, is, that the *under* keepers or inspectors, the servants and subordinates of every kind, will be under the same irresistible controul with respect to the *head* keeper or inspector, as the prisoners or other persons to be governed are with respect to *them*. On the common plans, what means, what possibility, has the prisoner, of appealing to the humanity of the principal for redress, against the neglect or oppression of subordinates in that rigid sphere, but the *few* opportunities which, in a crowded prison, the most conscientious keeper *can* afford – but the none at all which many a keeper *thinks* fit to give them? How different would their lot be upon this plan!

In no instance could his subordinates either perform or depart from their duty, but he must know the time and degree and manner of their doing so. It presents an answer, and that a satisfactory one, to one of the most puzzling of political questions, *quis custodiet ipsos custodes?*[3] and, as the fulfilling of his, as well as their, duty would be rendered so much easier, than it can ever have been hitherto, so might, and so should, any departure from it be punished with the more inflexible severity. It is this circumstance that renders the influence of this plan not less beneficial to what is called *Liberty* than to necessary coercion; not less powerful as a controul upon subordinate power, than as a curb to delinquency; as a shield to innocence than as a scourge to guilt.

Another advantage, still operating to the fame ends, is the great load of trouble and disgust, which it takes off the shoulders of those occasional inspectors of a higher order, such as *judges*, and other *magistrates*, who called down to this irksome task from the superior ranks of life, cannot but feel a proportionable repugnance to the discharge of it. Think how it is with them upon the present plans, and how it still must be, upon the best plans that have been hitherto devised! The cells or apartments, however constructed, must, if there be nine hundred of them, (as there were to have been upon the penitentiary house plan) be opened to the visitors, one by one. To do their business to any purpose, they must approach near to, and come almost in contact with, each inhabitant: whose situation being watched over according to no other than the loose methods of inspection at present practicable, will on that account require the more minute and troublesome investigation on the part of these occasional superintendants. By this new plan, the disgust is intirely removed; and the trouble of going into such a room as the lodge, is no more than the trouble of going into any other.

Were *Newgate* upon this plan, all Newgate might be inspected by a quarter of an hour's visit to Mr. *Akerman*.[4]

Among the other causes of that reluctance, none at present so forcible, none so unhappily well grounded, none which affords so natural an excuse, nor so strong a reason against accepting of any excuse, as the danger of *infection:* a circumstance, which carries death, in one of its most tremendous forms from the seat of guilt to the seat of justice, involving in one common catastrophe the violator and the upholder of the laws. But in a spot so constructed, and under a course of discipline so insured, how should infection ever arise? or how should it continue? against every danger of this kind, what private house of the poor, one might almost say, or even of the most opulent, can be equally secure?

Nor is the disagreeableness of the task of superintendance diminished by this plan, in a much greater degree than the efficacy of it is increased. On all others, be the superintendant's visit ever so unexpected, and his motions ever so quick, time there must always be for preparations, blinding the real state of things. Out of nine hundred cells he can visit but one at a time, and, in the mean while, the worst of the others may be arranged, and the inhabitants threatened, and tutored how to receive him. On this plan, no sooner is the superintendant announced, than the whole scene opens instantaneously to his view.

In mentioning inspectors and superintendants who are such by office, I must not overlook that system of inspection, which, however little heeded, will not be the less useful and efficacious; I mean the part which individuals may be disposed to take in the business, without intending perhaps, or even without thinking of, any other effects of their visits, than the gratification of their own particular curiosity. What the inspector's or keeper's family are with respect to *him*, that, and more, will these spontaneous visitors be to the superintendant; assistants, deputies in so far as he is faithful, witnesses and judges, should he ever be unfaithful, to his trust. So as they are but there, what the motives were that drew them thither, is perfectly immaterial; whether the relieving of their anxieties by the affecting prospect of their respective friends and relatives thus detained in durance, or merely the satisfying that general curiosity, which an establishment on various accounts so interesting to human feelings, may naturally be expected to excite.

You see, I take for granted as a matter of course, that under the necessary regulations for preventing interruption and disturbance, the doors of these establishments will be, as, without very special reasons to the contrary, the doors of all public establishments ought to be, thrown wide open to the body of the curious at large: – the great *open committee* of the tribunal of the world. And whoever objects to such publicity where it is practicable, but those whose motives for objection afford the strongest reasons for it. [pp. 21–30]

LETTER VIII.

Uses—Penitentiary-houses—Reformation.

IN my last, I endeavoured to state to you the advantages which a receptacle, upon the plan of the proposed building seemed to promise, in its application to places of *confinement*, considered merely in that view. Give me leave now to consider it as applicable to the joint purposes of *punishment, reformation*, and *pecuniary economy*.

That, in regard to persons of the description of those to whom punishments of the nature in question are destined, solitude is in its nature subservient to the purpose of reformation, seems to be as little disputed, as its tendency to operate in addition to the mass of sufferance. But, that upon this plan that purpose would be effected, at least as completely as it could be on any other, you cannot but see at the first glance, or rather you must have observed already. In the condition of *our* prisoners (for so I will call them for shortness sake) you may see the students paradox, *nunquam minus solus quam cum solus*[5] realized in a new way; to the keeper, a *multitude*, though not a *crowd; to themselves*, they are *solitary* and *sequestered* individuals.

What is more, you will see this purpose answered more compleatly by this plan, than it could possibly be on any other. What degree of solitude it was proposed to reduce them to in the once intended Penitentiary-houses, need not be considered. But for one purpose, in buildings of any mode of construction that could then and there have been in view, it would have been necessary, according to the express regulations of that plan, that the law of solitude should be dispensed with: I mean, so often as the prisoners were to receive the benefits of attendance on Divine Service. But in my brother's[6] circular Penitentiary-houses, they might receive these benefits, in every circumstance, without stirring from their cells. No thronging, nor jostling, in the way between the scene of work, and the scene destined to devotion: no quarrellings, nor confederatings, nor plottings to escape: nor yet any whips or fetters to prevent it.

LETTER IX.

Penitentiary-houses—Economy—Contract—Plan.

I AM come now to the article of *pecuniary economy;* and as this is the great rock upon which the original Penitentiary-plan, I understand has split, I cannot resist the temptation of throwing out a few hints relative to the mode of management, which I look upon as the most eligible in this view; but which could not as you will see have been established with any thing like the advantage, upon any other ground than that of my brother's inspection principle.

To come to the point at once, I would do the whole by *contract.*[7] I would farm out the profits, the no-profits, or if you please the losses, to him who, being in other respects unexceptionable, offered the best terms. Undertaking an enterprise new in its extent, in the description of the persons to be subjected to his management, and in many other circumstances, his success in it, if he does succeed, may be regarded in the light of an invention; and rewarded accordingly, just as success in other inventions is rewarded, by the profit which a monopoly secured by patent enables a man to make: and that in proportion to the success which constitutes their merit. He should have it during *good behaviour:* which you know is as much as to say, unless specific instances of misbehaviour flagrant enough to render his removal expedient be proved on him in a legal way, he shall have it for his *life.* Besides that when thus secured he can afford to give the better price for his bargain, you will presently see more material reasons, to counter-balance the seeming unthriftiness of granting him a term, which may prove so long a one. In other respects, the terms of the contract must, of course, depend upon the proportion of capital, of which the contract gave him the use. Suppos-ing the advance to amount to the whole manufacturing stock, he must of course, either pay something for his contract, or be contented with a *share* of the gross profits, instead of the whole, unless that from such profits an interest upon the capital so advanced to him should be deducted: in which case, nobody, I sup-pose would grudge him the whole neat profit after such deduction, even though the rate of interest were much below the ordinary one: the difference, between such reduced rate of interest and the ordinary one would constitute the whole of the expence which the public would be at. Suppose, to speak at random, this expence were to amount to 6, 8, or 10,000*l.*[8] a year for the 3000 convicts which it was computed, would be the standing number, to be maintained in England.* I should not imagine, that such a sum as even this latter would be much grudged. I fancy the intended expedition to Botany Bay,[9] of which I am just apprised, will be rather more expensive. Not that it appears to me that the nation would remain saddled with such an expence as this at the long run; or, indeed with any part of it. But of this hereafter.

In the next place I would give my contractor all the *powers* that his interest could prompt him to wish for, in order to enable him to make the most of his bargain; with only some slight reservations, which I will mention afterwards: for very slight ones you will find they will be, that can be needful or even serviceable in the view of preventing abuse.

But, the greater latitude he has in taking such measures, the less will he grudge the letting it be known, what the measures are which he *does* take; knowing, at the same time, that no advantage can be taken of such knowledge, by turning him out in case of his success, and putting in another to reap the fruits of his contrivance. I will then require him to *disclose*, and even to print and *publish*, his accounts: – the whole process and detail of his management: – the whole history of the prison. I will require him, I say, on pain of forfeiture or other adequate punishment, to publish these accounts, and that upon oath. I have no fear of his not publishing *some* accounts, because, if the time is elapsed and some accounts not published, a fact not liable to dispute, the punishment takes place of course: and I have not much fear that the accounts when published will not be *true:* because, having power to do every thing that is for his advantage, there is noth-ing which it is his interest to conceal; and the interest which the punishment for perjury gives him not to conceal is manifest: more especially as I make him examinable and cross-examinable *viva voce*[10] upon oath at any time.

---

* According to the Hard-Labour Bill, 2865. See the table to my View of that Bill: since then, I fear, the number has rather encreased than diminished.

It is for clearing away as much as possible, every motive of pecuniary interest, that could prompt him to throw any kind of cloak or reserve upon any of his expedients for encreasing his profits, that I would ensure them to him for *life*.

From the information thus got from him, I derive this advantage. In the cafe of his *ill* success, I see the causes of it: and not only I, but every body else that pleases, may see the causes of it: and amongst the rest, those who, in case of their taking the management out of his hands, would have an interest in being acquainted with such causes, in order to obviate or avoid them. More than that, if his ill success is owing to incapacity, and that incapacity such as, if continued, might raise my expence above the calculation, I can make him stop in time; a measure, to which he can have as little objection as myself; for it is one advantage of this plan, that whatever mischief happens must have more than eat out all *his* profits before it reaches *me*.

In the case of his good success, I see the causes of that too; and every body sees them, as before: and, amongst others, all persons who could propose to themselves to get into a situation similar to his, and who in such cafe would naturally promise themselves, in the event of their getting into his situation, a success equal to his – or rather superior; for such is the presumption and vanity natural to man.

Without such publication, who should I have to deal with, besides him? certainly in comparison, but a very few: not many more than I may have had at first; the terms, of course, disadvantageous as at first: for disadvantageous terms at first, while all is yet in darkness, they certainly must be.

After such publication, who should I have then? I should have every body: every body who, by fortune, experience, judgment, disposition, should conceive himself able and find himself inclined, to engage in such a business: and each person, seeing what advantage had been made, and how, would be willing to make his offer in proportion. What situation more favourable for making the best terms?

These best terms, then, I should make, at his death, even for his establishment: but long before that, had I others upon the carpet, I should make similar good terms for all those others. Thus I make his advantage mine, not only after it has ceased to be his, but almost as soon as it commences so to be: I thus get his success in all the rest by paying for it only in the one; and in that not more that it was necessary to pay for it.

But, *contractors*, you will say perhaps, or at least if you don't, there are enough that will, '*are a good for nothing set of people: and why should we be fleeced by them? One of them perjured himself not long ago, and we put him into the pillory. They are the same sort of gentry that are called farmers general*[11] *in France, and publicans in the gospel, where they are ranked with sinners; and nobody likes them any where.*' All this to be sure is very true – But if you put one of them into the *pillory,* you put another of them into the *post-office;* and if in the devoted city, five righteous would have screened the whole gang from the perdition called for by the enormities of ninety-five unrighteous, why should not the merits of one Palmer, be enough to make it up for the demerits of twenty Atkinsons?[12] Gentlemen in general, as I have had manifold occasion to observe, love close reasoning, and here they have it. It might be thought straying from the point, if I ventured to add, that gentlemen in the corn[13] trade, or in any other trade, have not commonly quite so many witnesses to *their bargains,* as my contractor would have to the management of *his* house. [pp. 35–43]

LETTER XIII.

Means of extracting Labour.

UNDERSTANDING thus much of his situation, my contractor, I conceive, notwithstanding the checks you have seen, will hardly think it necessary to ask me, how he is to manage, to persuade his boarders to set at work. Having them under this regimen, what better security he can wish for of their working, and that to their utmost, I can hardly imagine. At any rate he has much better security, than he can have for the industry and diligence of any ordinary journeyman at large, who is paid by the day, and not by the piece. If a man won't work, nothing has he to do, from morning to night, but to eat his bad bread and drink his water, without a soul to speak to. If he will work, his time is occupied, and he has his meat and his beer, or whatever else his earnings may afford him, and not a stroke does he strike but he gets something, which he would not have got otherwise. This encouragement is necessary to his doing his utmost; but more than this is not necessary. It is necessary, every exertion he makes should be sure of its reward: but it is not necessary, that such reward be so great, or any thing near so great, as he might have had, had he worked elsewhere. This confinement, which is his punishment, preventing his carrying the work to another market, subjects him to a monopoly; which the contractor, his master, like any other monopolist, makes of course as much of as he can. The workman lives in a poor country where wages are low; but in a poor country, a man who as paid according to his work, will exert himself at least as much as in a rich one. According to Mr. Arthur Young,[14] and the very cogent evidence he gives, he should work more: for more work that intelligent traveller finds always done in dear years than in plentiful ones: the earnings of one day affording in the latter case, a fund for the extravagance of the next. But this is not all. His master may fleece him if he pleases, at both ends. After sharing in his profits, he may again take a profit upon his expence. He would probably choose to employ both expedients together; the tax upon earnings if it stood alone, might possibly appear liable to be evaded in some degree, and be frustrated in some cases, by a confederacy between the workmen and their employers out of doors: the tax upon expenditure, by their frugality; supposing that virtue to take root in such a foil: or in some instances, perhaps, by their generosity to their friends without doors. The tax upon earnings would probably not be laid on in an open way, upon any other than the *good* hands: whose traffick must be carried on, with or without his intervention, between them and their out-of-door employers. In the trades which he thought proper to set up of himself for his *capable* hands, his *promising* hands, and his *drones*, the tax might be levied in a more covert way by the lowering of the price paid by him in comparison of the free prices given out of doors for similar work. Where he is sure of his men as well with regard to their disposition to spend as with regard to their inability to collude, the tax upon expenditure, without any tax upon profits open or covert, would be the least discouraging; it would be the least discouraging for the present, as the earnings would sound greater to their ears: and with a view to the future, as they would thereby see (I mean such of them as had any hopes of releasement) what their earnings might at that happy period, be expected to amount to, in reality as well as in name. [pp. 67–9]

from John Howard, *The State of the Prisons in England and Wales, with Preliminary Observations, and an Account of Some Foreign Prisons and Hospitals,* 4th edn (London: J. Johnson, C. Dilly, and T. Cadell, 1792), pp. 4–19, 214–16, 469–72, 483–4.

Howard (*c.* 1726–90) was probably the most famous humanitarian of the late eighteenth century, and his exertions for prison reform are commemorated by the fact that organizations devoted to this cause are still today known as John Howard Societies – with Elizabeth Fry Societies devoted to the plight of female prisoners (see the selection from the biography of her included in this volume). He was the son of a tradesman who had become modestly wealthy as partner in a London carpet and upholstery business; his mother died while he was an infant. By his own account poorly educated, he was apprenticed by his father to a firm of wholesale grocers. On their father's death in 1742 Howard and his sister became financially independent; Howard toured France and Italy. After returning to London, he married his landlady and housekeeper in 1752; she died three years later. On a voyage to Lisbon his ship was captured by a French privateer and along with the crew and other passengers he was incarcerated at Brest; the prison conditions left a lasting impression on him. After his release he devoted himself to improving his estate in England, and married again, in 1758; his second wife died in 1765 after bearing their only child, a son, who became insane as a young man and died in 1799. Always in poor health, Howard nevertheless travelled on the Continent.

On appointment as high sheriff of Bedfordshire in 1773 he turned to one of the office's major responsibilities, oversight of the county jails, and was shocked at the abuses he found. He devoted the rest of his life to investigating prison conditions in Britain and on the Continent at first hand, resulting in his two famous works, *The State of the Prisons in England and Wales* (1777), reprinted several times with additions, and *An Account of the Principal Lazarettos of Europe* (1789). He died in southern Russia while on one of his investigative trips. Howard's reputation after his death was harmed by stories that his harsh discipline had caused his son's insanity.

Most of the main features of Howard's prison reform writing are seen in the excerpts here – improved prison conditions, design and administration; alleviation of the plight of imprisoned debtors; elimination of diseases caused and spread by poor prison conditions; abolition of fees extorted from prisoners by warders, officers of the courts and other prisoners; banning of the sale of alcohol in prisons; separation of different classes of prisoners to prevent the hardened criminals from corrupting the neophytes; provision of work to sentenced prisoners; and the provision of religious counsel and instruction.

SECTION I.

GENERAL VIEW OF DISTRESS IN PRISONS.

THERE are prisons, into which whoever looks will, at first sight of the people confined, be convinced, that there is some great error in the management of them: their sallow meagre countenances declare, without words, that they are very miserable. Many who went in healthy, are in a few months changed to emaciated dejected objects. Some are seen pining under diseases, '*sick, and in prison;*'[1] expiring on the floors, in loathsome cells, of pestilential fevers, and the confluent small-pox: victims, I must not say to the cruelty, but I will say to the inattention, of Sheriffs, and gentlemen in the commission of the peace.[2]

The cause of this distress is, that many prisons are scantily supplied, and some almost totally destitute of the necessaries of life.

There are several *bridewells*[3] (to begin with them) in which prisoners have no allowance *of Food* at all. In some, the keeper farms[4] what little is allowed them: and where he engages to supply each prisoner with one or two pennyworth of bread a day, I have known this shrunk to half, sometimes less than half the quantity, cut or broken from his own loaf. FOOD.

It will perhaps be asked, does not their work maintain them? for every one knows that those offenders are committed to *hard labour*.[5] The answer to that question, though true, will hardly be believed. There are few bridewells in which any work is done, or can be done. The prisoners have neither tools, nor materials of any kind: but spend their time in sloth, profaneness[6] and debauchery, to a degree which, in some of those houses that I have seen, is extremely shocking.

Some keepers of these houses, who have represented to the magistrates the wants of their prisoners, and desired for them necessary food, have been silenced with these inconsiderate words, *Let them work or starve*. When those gentlemen know the former is impossible, do they not by that thoughtless sentence, inevitably doom poor creatures to the latter?

I have asked some keepers, since the late act for preserving the health of prisoners, why no care is taken of their sick: and have been answered, that the magistrates tell them *the act does not extend to bridewells*.*

In consequence of this, at the quarter sessions[7] you see prisoners, covered (hardly covered) with rags; almost famished; and sick of diseases, which the discharged spread where they go; and with which those who are sent to the county-gaols infect these prisons.

The same complaint, *want of food*, is to be found in many *county gaols*. In above half these, debtors have no bread; although it is granted to the highway-

---

* If the late act does not include bridewells, it is required, by an act 7th James I. Cap. IV. that 'the masters and governors of – houses of correction shall have some fit allowance – for the relieving of such as shall happen to be weak and sick in their custody.'

man, the house-breaker, and the murderer: and medical assistance, which is provided for the latter, is withheld from the former. In many of these gaols, debtors who would work are not permitted to have any tools, lest they should furnish felons with them for escape or other mischief. I have often seen these prisoners eating their water-soup (bread boiled in mere water) and heard them say, 'We are locked up and almost starved to death.'

As to the relief provided for debtors by the benevolent act, 32d of *George* II. (commonly called the lords act, because it originated in their house) I did not find in all England and Wales (except the counties of Middlesex and Surrey) *twelve debtors* who had obtained from their creditors the four-pence a day, to which they had a right by that act. The means of procuring it were out of their reach. In one of my journies I found near six hundred prisoners, whose debts were under twenty pounds[8] each: some of them did not owe above three or four pounds: and the expence of sueing for the aliment is in many places equal to the small debts; for which some of these prisoners had been confined several months.

At Carlisle[9] but one debtor of the forty-nine whom I saw there in 1774, had obtained his groats:[10] and the gaoler told me, that during the time he had held that office, which was fourteen years, no more than four or five had received it; and that they were soon discharged by their creditors neglecting to pay it. No one debtor had the aliment in York castle, Devon, Cheshire, Kent, and many other counties. The truth is, some debtors are the most pitiable objects in our gaols.

To their wanting necessary food, I must add not only the demands of gaolers, &c. for fees; but also the extortion of bailiffs.[11] These detain in their houses, (properly enough denominated *spunging-houses*[12]) at an enormous expence, prisoners who have money. I know there is a legal provision against this oppression; but the mode of obtaining redress (like that of recovering the groats) is attended with difficulty: and the abuse continues. The rapine of these extortioners needs some more effectual and easy check: no bailiff should be suffered to keep a public house;[13] the mischiefs occasioned by their so doing, are complained of in many parts of the kingdom.*

Here I beg leave to mention the hard case of prisoners confined on exchequer processes;[14] and those from the ecclesiastical courts:[15] the latter are excluded from the privilege of bail;[16] and the former, generally, from the benefit of insolvent acts.[17]

---

*   By the statute 32d George II. it is enacted, that 'No sheriff, bailiff, &c – shall convey any person arrested – to any public victualling or other drinking-house – without the consent of the person so arrested.' Now if the bailiff himself keeps a public house, this seems to preclude the debtor's choice; he must go to a public house, or directly to gaol.

Felons have in some gaols two pennyworth of bread a day; in some three half-pennyworth; in some a pennyworth; in some none: the particulars will be seen hereafter in their proper places. I often weighed the bread in different prisons, and found the penny loaf seven ounces and a half to eight ounces, the other loaves in proportion. It is probable that when this allowance was fixed by its value, near double the quantity that the money will now purchase, might be bought for it:* yet the allowance continues unaltered: and it is not uncommon to see the whole purchase, especially of the smaller sums, eaten at breakfast; which is sometimes the case when they receive their pittance but once in two days: and then on the following day they must fast.

This allowance being so far short of the cravings of nature, and in some prisons lessened by farming[18] to the gaoler, many criminals are half starved: such of them as at their commitment were in health, come out almost famished, scarce able to move, and for weeks incapable of any labour.

Many prisons have *no Water*. This defect is frequent in bridewells, and town WATER. gaols. In the felons courts[19] of some county-gaols there is no water: in some places where there is water, prisoners are always locked up within doors, and have no more than the keeper or his servants think fit to bring them: in one place they were limited to three pints a day each: a scanty provision for drink and cleanliness! And as to *Air*, which is no less necessary than either of the two preceding arti- AIR. cles, and given us by Providence quite *gratis*,[20] without any care or labour of our own; yet, as if the bounteous goodness of Heaven excited our envy, methods are contrived to rob prisoners of this *genuine cordial of life*,[21] as Dr. *Hales*[22] very properly calls it: I mean by preventing that circulation and change of the salutif-erous[23] fluid, without which animals cannot live and thrive. It is well known that air which has performed its office in the lungs, is feculent and noxious. Writers upon the subject shew, that a hogshead[24] of air will last a man only an hour: but those who do not choose to consult philosophers,[25] may judge from a notorious fact. In 1756, at *Calcutta* in *Bengal*, out of a hundred and seventy persons who were confined in a hole there one night, a hundred and fifty-four were taken out dead.[26] The few survivors ascribed the mortality to their want of fresh air; and called the place *Hell in miniature*.

Air which has been breathed, is made poisonous to a more intense degree, by the effluvia from the sick, and what else in prisons is offensive. My reader will judge of its malignity, when I assure him, that my clothes were in my *first* journies so offensive, that in a post-chaise I could not bear the windows drawn up; and was therefore obliged to travel commonly on horseback. The leaves of my

---

* In 1557, a penny loaf of wheat bread weighed twenty-six ounces. In 1782, the weight of a *twopenny* white loaf, at *London*, was eighteen ounces; at *Edinburgh*, nineteen ounces and a half; at *Dublin*, sixteen ounces; in September 1783, at *London*, one pound three ounces; and the 4th of August 1783, in *Dublin*, only eleven ounces three drachms.

memorandum-book were often so tainted, that I could not use it till after spreading it an hour or two before the fire: and even my antidote, a vial of vinegar, has, after using it in a few prisons, become intolerably disagreeable. I did not wonder that in those journies many gaolers made excuses; and did not go with me into the felons wards.

I learn from a letter to Sir *Robert Ladbroke,* printed in 1771, page 11, that 'Dr. *Hales,* Sir *John Pringle,* and others have observed, that air, corrupted and putrefied, is of such a subtile and powerful nature, as to rot and dissolve heart of oak;[27] and that the walls of buildings have been impregnated with this poisonous matter for years togeher.'*

From hence any one may judge of the probability there is against the health, and life, of prisoners crowded in close rooms, cells, and subterraneous dungeons, for fourteen or fifteen hours out of the four-and-twenty. In some of those caverns the floor is very damp: in others there is sometimes an inch or two of water: and the straw, or bedding, is laid on such floors; seldom on barrack-bedsteads. Where prisoners are not kept in under-ground cells, they are often confined to their rooms, because there is no court belonging to the prison, which is the case in many city and town gaols: or because the walls round the yard are ruinous, or too low for safety: or because the gaoler has the ground for his own use. Prison-

SEWERS.   ers confined in this manner, are generally unhealthy. Some gaols have no *Sewers* or vaults; and in those that have, if they be not properly attended to, they are, even to a visitant, offensive beyond expression: how noxious then to people constantly confined in those prisons!†

One cause why the rooms in some prisons are so close,[28] is the window-tax which the gaolers have to pay: this tempts them to stop the windows, and stifle

BEDDING.   their prisoners.‡ In many gaols, and in most bridewells, there is no allowance of *Bedding* or *straw* for prisoners to sleep on; and if by any means they get a little, it is not changed for months together, so that it is offensive and almost worn to dust. Some lie upon rags, others upon the bare floors. When I have complained

---

*   See also the *Philosophical Transactions,* Vol. XLVIII. Part I. *page* 42.

†   An act made in Ireland the 3d year of his present Majesty, for better preventing the severities, &c. has the following clause: 'Whereas many infectious disorders are daily produced by the confinement of numbers in close prisons, whereunto there is no back-yard adjoining, and the lives of his Majesty's subjects are endangered by the bringing of prisoners into public streets for air; be it enacted – that every grand jury at the assizes or quarter sessions – may be enabled, and they are hereby required and directed, to contract either by lease, or to purchase a piece of ground next adjoining the gaol, or as near as conveniently can be had thereto, and cause to be erected necessary houses, and a wall sufficient for the security of the said prisoners.'

‡   This is also the case in many work-houses and farm-houses, where the poor and the labourer are lodged in rooms that have no light, nor fresh air: which may be the cause of our peasants not having the healthy ruddy complexions one used to see so common twenty or thirty years ago. The difference has often struck me in my various journies.

of this to the keepers, their justification has been, 'The county allows no straw; the prisoners have none but at my cost.'

The evils mentioned hitherto affect the *health* and *life* of prisoners. I have now to complain of what is pernicious to their MORALS; and that is, the confin-   MORALS. ing all sorts of prisoners together: debtors and felons, men and women, the young beginner and the old offender; and with all these, in some counties, such as are guilty of misdemeanors[29] only; who should have been committed to bridewell to be corrected, by diligence and labour; but for want of food, and the means of procuring it in those prisons, are in pity sent to such county gaols as afford these offenders prison-allowance.

Few prisons separate men and women in the day-time. In some counties the gaol is also the bridewell: in others those prisons are contiguous, and the court-yard common. There the petty offender is committed for instruction to the most profligate. In some gaols you see (and who can see it without sorrow) boys of twelve or fourteen eagerly listening to the stories told by practised and experienced criminals, of their adventures, successes, stratagems, and escapes. I must here add, that in some few gaols are confined idiots and *Lunatics*.   LUNATICS. These serve for sport to idle visitants at assizes,[30] and other times of general resort. Many of the bridewells are crowded and offensive, because the rooms which were designed for prisoners are occupied by the insane.* Where these are not kept separate, they disturb and terrify other prisoners. No care is taken of them, although it is probable that by medicines, and proper regi-men, some of them might be restored to their senses, and to usefulness in life.

I am ready to think, that none who give credit to what is contained in the fore-going pages, will wonder at the havock made by the *Gaol-fever*.[31] From my own   GAOL-FEVER. observations in 1773, 1774 and 1775, I was fully convinced that many more prisoners were destroyed by it, than were put to death by all the public execu-tions in the kingdom.† This frequent effect of confinement in prison seems generally understood, and shews how full of emphatical meaning is the curse

---

*   See Irish Act, the 3d of George III. p. 478. where such persons are required to be kept sepa-rate.

†   I have in my possession a large copper-plate, first published in 1772, by Sir *Stephen Theodore Janssen*, shewing the number of malefactors executed in London for the twenty-three preceding years; and the crimes for which they suffered. I will give an abridgment of it in a table at the end of the book. In it will be seen, that the total number of executions in London for those twenty-three years, was 678; the annual average is between 29 and 30. I leave to others the discussion of the ques-tions, whether those executions were too numerous? whether all the crimes for which they were inflicted, were deserving of death? An ingenious writer, Mr. *Eden, Principles of Penal Law, page* 306, observes that 'the accumulation of sanguinary laws is the worst distemper of a state. Let it not be supposed, that the extirpation of mankind is the chief object of legislation.' – And it may be left to any one to judge, whether, including debtors and petty offenders, the number of those that died in the several London prisons of the gaol-fever, does not exceed the number of those that were executed annually during that time. I have not the number of executions in all the counties, but am well assured it falls still much shorter of the number that perished in prisons.

of a severe creditor, who pronounces his debtor's doom to *rot in gaol*. I believe I have learned the full import of this sentence, from the vast numbers who, to my certain knowledge, and some of them before my eyes, have perished by the gaol-fever.

But the mischief is not confined to prisons. Not to mention now the number of *sailors*, and of *families* in America, that have been infected by transports; – multitudes caught the distemper by going to their relatives and acquaintance in the gaols: many others from prisoners discharged; and not a few in the courts of judicature.

In *Baker's Chronicle*,[32] *page* 353, that historian mentioning the assize held in Oxford castle 1577 (called from its fatal consequence the *black assize*) informs us, that 'all who were present died within forty hours: the lord chief baron,[33] the sheriff, and about three hundred more.' Lord chancellor *Bacon*[34] ascribes this to a disease brought into court by the prisoners; and Dr. *Mead*[35] is of the same opinion.

The first of these two authors, Lord *Bacon*, observes, that 'the most pernicious infection next the plague, is the smell of a jail; when the prisoners have been long and close and nastily kept: whereof *we have had, in our time, experience twice or thrice*; when both the judges that sat upon the jail, and numbers of those who attended the business, or were present, sickened and died.'*

At the Lent assize in Taunton,[37] 1730, some prisoners who were brought thither from Ivelchester gaol, infected the court; and lord chief baron *Pengelly*;[38] Sir *James Sheppard*, sergeant;[39] *John Pigot*, Esq. sheriff, and some hundreds besides, died of the gaol-distemper. At Axminster, a little town in Devonshire, a prisoner discharged from Exeter gaol in 1755, infected his family with that disease; of which two of them died; and many others in that town afterwards. – The numbers that were carried off by the same malady in London in 1750, two judges, the lord mayor, one alderman, and many of inferior rank, are too well known to need the mentioning farther particulars.

Sir *John Pringle*[40] observes that 'jails have often been the cause of malignant fevers;' and he informs us, that in the late rebellion in Scotland,[41] above two hundred men of one regiment were infected with the jail-fever, by some deserters brought from prisons in England.†

Dr. *Lind*,[42] physician to the royal hospital at Haslar, near Portsmouth,[43] shewed me in one of the wards a number of sailors ill of the gaol-fever, brought on board their ship by a man who had been discharged from a prison in London. The ship was laid up on the occasion. That gentleman, in his *Essay on the Health of Seamen*, asserts, that 'The source of infection to our armies and fleets are undoubtedly the jails; we can often trace the importers of it directly from them.

---

*   Natural History, Exp. 914. See also *Plot*'s History of Oxfordshire, *p.* 25.[36]

†   Observations on the Diseases of the Army, *pages* 47, 296.

– It often proves fatal in impressing men on the hasty equipment[44] of a fleet.*
– The first English fleet sent last war to America, lost by it above two thousand men.' In another place he assures us, that 'the seeds of infection were carried from the guard-ships into our squadrons'[45] – and the mortality, thence occasioned, was greater than by all other diseases or means of death put together.'†

It were easy to multiply instances of this mischief; but those which have been mentioned are, I presume, sufficient to shew, even if no mercy were due to prisoners, that the gaol-distemper is a *national concern* of no smal importance.

The general prevalence and spread of wickedness in prisons, and abroad by the discharged prisoners, will now be as easily accounted for, as the propagation of disease. It is often said, 'A prison pays no debts;' I am sure it may be added, that a prison mends no morals. Sir *John Fielding*[46] observes, that 'a criminal discharged – generally by the next sessions, after the execution of his comrades, becomes the head of a gang of his own raising:' – improved, no doubt, in skill by the company he kept in gaol. And petty offenders who are committed to bridewell for a year or two, and spend that time, not in hard labour, but in idleness and wicked company, or are sent for that time to county gaols, generally grow desperate, and come out fitted for the perpetration of any villany. – Half the robberies committed in and about London, are planned in the prisons, by that dreadful assemblage of criminals, and the number of idle people who visit them. – How contrary this to the intention of our laws with regard to petty offenders; which certainly is to correct and reform them! Instead of which, their confinement doth notoriously promote and increase the very vices it was designed to suppress. Multitudes of young creatures, committed for some trifling offence, are totally ruined there. I make no scruple to affirm, that if it were the wish and aim of magistrates to effect the destruction, present and future, of young delinquents, they could not devise a more effectual method, than to confine them so long in our prisons, those seats and seminaries (as they have been very properly called) of idleness and every vice.

Shall these irregularities, the sources of misery, disease, and wickedness, be endured in a nation celebrated for good sense and humanity; and who from these principles, do treat one sort of prisoners with tenderness and generosity? I mean prisoners of war.[47] These have provision in plenty; some to spare and sell to the soldiers on guard;‡ we frequently saw their stated allowance hung up for their inspection. Some prisons have large areas for them to walk in; and at night every man had a hammock to himself. It is the farthest thing in the world from

VICIOUS
EXAMPLES.

---

*   *Page* 307.
†   *Page* 5.
‡   I am now speaking of the practice of the war before last. The daily allowance, to six prisoners was, nine pounds of bread – four pounds and a half of beef – three pints of pease, four days in a week – six quarts of beer. – On Friday they had not the beef; but a pound and a half of butter instead of it. – On board the men of war, indeed, they were upon short allowance.

my wish to deprive captives of any one of these benefits – I am only desirous of seeing the same humanity shewn to our own countrymen in distress: so that a consistent and uniform practice may prove our benevolence to be a firm and steady principle; and that those who are censorious may find no occasion for ascribing our kind usage of foreigners to a less amiable motive.

Here it will be said, prisoners of war are not felons, nor yet debtors; and government is sometimes, at the end of a war, reimbursed the expence of maintaining them. This latter I believe is fact; and the former is true without dispute: we do not look upon foreign enemies, nor they upon us,* as either debtors or felons: we cut one another to pieces in battle, but when that is over we grow cool and compassionate. I grant there is a material difference in the circumstances of foreign and domestic prisoners, but there is none in their nature. Debtors and felons, as well as hostile foreigners, are *men*, and by men they ought to be treated as men.

Those gentlemen who, when they are told of the misery which our prisoners suffer, content themselves with saying, *Let them take care to keep out*, prefaced perhaps, with an angry prayer; seem not duly sensible of the favour of Providence which distinguishes them from the sufferers: they do not remember that we are required to imitate our gracious Heavenly Parent, who is *kind to the unthankful, and to the evil*:[48] they also forget the vicissitudes of human affairs; the unexpected changes to which all men are liable: and that those whose circumstances are affluent, may in time be reduced to indigence, and become debtors and prisoners. And as to criminality, it is possible, that a man who has often shuddered at hearing the account of a murder, may on a sudden temptation commit that very crime. *Let him that thinks he standeth take heed lest he fall*,[49] and commiserate those that are fallen.

---

* I must not be understood here to mean a compliment to the French. How they then treated English prisoners of war, I knew by experience in 1756; when a Lisbon packet (the Hanover) in which I went passenger, in order to make the tour of Portugal, was taken by a French privateer. Before we reached Brest, I suffered the extremity of thirst, not having for above forty hours one drop of water; nor hardly a morsel of food. In the castle at Brest, I lay six nights upon straw: and observing how cruelly my countrymen were used there, and at Morlaix, whither I was carried next; during the two months I was at Carhaix upon parole, I corresponded with the English prisoners at Brest, Morlaix, and Dinnan: at the last of those towns were several of our ship's crew, and my servant. I had sufficient evidence of their being treated with such barbarity, that many hundreds had perished; and that thirty-six were buried in a hole at Dinnan in one day. When I came to England, still on parole, I made known to the commissioners of sick and wounded seamen, the sundry particulars: which gained their attention, and thanks. Remonstrance was made to the French court: our sailors had redress: and those that were in the three prisons mentioned above, were brought home in the first cartel-ships. – A *Lady* from Ireland, who married in France, had bequeathed in trust with the magistrates of St. Malo's, sundry charities; one of which was a penny a day to every English prisoner of war in Dinnan. This was duly paid; and saved the lives of many brave and useful men. – Perhaps, what I *suffered* on this occasion, increased my sympathy with the unhappy people, whose case is the subject of this book.

But it may be said, enough of the declamatory kind has been written, by others. Much, it is true, has been written: and I beg leave to transcribe almost verbatim a few lines from a celebrated author, which may be thought to come under that description. After representing the sufferings of prisoners, he goes on to this purpose, 'The misery suffered in gaols is not half their evil; they are filled with every sort of corruption that poverty and wickedness can generate: with all the shameless and profligate enormities that can be produced by the impudence of ignominy, the rage of want, and the malignity of despair. In a prison the check of the public eye is removed; and the power of the law is spent. There are few fears, there are no blushes. The lewd inflame the more modest; the audacious harden the timid. Every one fortifies himself as he can against his own remaining sensibility; endeavouring to practise on others the arts that are practised on himself; and to gain the applause of his worst associates by imitating their manners.'[50]

Besides the grievances already mentioned; there are several *bad customs* in gaols, and relating to them, which aggravate the distress of prisoners. I shall enumerate these distinctly, yet concisely.

SECTION II.

BAD CUSTOMS IN PRISONS.

A CRUEL custom obtains in most of our gaols, which is that of the prisoners demanding of a new comer *Garnish*,[51] footing, or (as it is called in some London gaols) chummage. 'Pay or strip,' are the fatal words. I say *fatal*, for they are so to some; who having no money, are obliged to give up part of their scanty apparel; and then if they have no bedding or straw to sleep on, contract diseases, which I have known to prove mortal.*[52]   GARNISH.

In many gaols, to the garnish paid by the new comer, those who were there before make an addition; and great part of the following night is often spent in riot and drunkenness. The gaoler or tapster finding his account in this practice, generally answers questions concerning it with reluctance. Of the garnish which I have set down to sundry prisons, I had my information from prisoners who paid it. But I am aware that the sum is sometimes varied by sets of succeeding prisoners, and the different circumstances of a new comer. In some gaols, if a felon can pay the debtors garnish (which is commonly more than that of the felons) he is

---

* 'In the year 1730, Nicholas Bennet, Joseph Robinson, John Head and George Taverner, were indicted at the Old Bailey for robbing John Berrisford of two half-guineas, two sixpences, and two half-pence, in New Prison under the pretence of garnish, which fact being plainly proved, they were all found guilty of an assault and robbery; and to deter others from the infamous and inhuman practice of taking the money, and if they had none, of stripping poor prisoners that were upon any account committed to prison, so that often-times they have perished for want of cloathing and necessaries, they received sentence of death.' *Burton's New View of London, page* 468.

entitled to partake of the garnish paid afterwards by new-come debtors. In a few places, this demand has been lately waved; in two or three, strictly prohibited by the magistrates

GAMING.

Gaming in various forms is very frequent; cards, dice, skittles, missisippi and portobello-tables,[53] billiards, fives,[54] tennis, &c. In the country the three first are most common; and especially cards. There is scarce a county gaol but is furnished with them: and one can seldom go in without seeing prisoners at play. In London, all the sorts that I have named were till lately in use. I am not an enemy to diverting exercise: yet the riot, brawling, and profaneness, that are the usual consequences of their play; the circumstances of debtors gaming away the property of their creditors, which I know they have done in some prisons to a considerable amount; accomplishing themselves in the frauds of gamblers, who, if they be not themselves prisoners, are sure to haunt where gaming is practised; hindering their fellow-prisoners from walking in the courts while they play, of which inconvenience I have heard them complain: these seem to me cogent reasons for prohibiting all kinds of gaming within the walls of a prison

IRONS.

Loading prisoners with *heavy Irons*, which make their walking, and even lying down to sleep, difficult and painful, is another custom which I cannot but condemn. In some county gaols and even *bridewells* the *women* do not escape this severity: but in London they do: and therefore it is not necessary in the country.* The practice must be mere tyranny: unless it proceed from avarice; which I rather suspect; because county gaolers do sometimes grant dispensations, and indulge their prisoners, men as well as women, with what they call 'the choice of irons,' if they will pay for it.

The author of *A Letter to Sir Robert Ladbroke*[55] on Prisons (particularly on Newgate, which was then to be rebuilt) cites in *page* 79, the opinion of Lord Coke, *Horn's Mirror of Justice*,[56] &c. against this oppression; and adds afterwards, 'The learned editor of *Hale's History of the pleas of the crown*[57] likewise declares, that fetters ought not to be used, unless there is just reason to fear an escape, as where the prisoner is unruly, or makes an attempt to that purpose; otherwise, notwithstanding the common practice of gaolers, it seems altogether unwarrantable, and contrary to the mildness and humanity of the laws of England, by which gaolers are forbid to put their prisoners to any pain or torment.'

The Gentlemen of the *Gaol-committee*, who distinguished themselves by an accurate and zealous inquiry into the abuses practised by gaolers;† in their

---

* Lord *Loughborough*, Lent assize 1782, at Thetford laid a fine of £20 on the gaoler of Norwich castle, for putting irons on a woman.

† This Committee is celebrated by *Thomson*, in his poem entitled *Winter*, 340, &c. *pr.* edit. 1738.

——— Can I forget the generous few,
Who, touch'd with human woe, redressive sought
Into the horrors of the gloomy jail?

Report[58] concerning the Fleet prison, 20th March 1728, after mentioning a petition presented to the judges by one who had been put in irons by the wardens, informs us, that the judges reprimanded the wardens, and *declared*, that 'a gaoler could not answer the ironing of a man before he was found guilty of a crime.' – To the plea which gaolers use in defence of this practice, that 'It is necessary for safe custody,' an answer may be given in the words of lord chief justice *King*[59] (afterwards lord chancellor) to the wardens of the same prison, when he forbade dungeons, which they had made use of. That judge *declared*, 'they might raise their walls higher, &c.' See the *Report* of the same Committee. To what lord *King* suggested of *raising the walls*, one might presume to add – The number of turnkeys should be increased in proportion to the number of prisoners. – If the daring character of our felons should seem, after all, to make it necessary to confine them in irons, it would be right, at least, to bring them into court without irons, unless they have escaped, or attempted it before their trial.*

The Marquis *Beccaria*, in his *Essay on Crimes and Punishments*,[60] page 75, observes that 'Imprisonment, being only the means of securing the person of the accused, untl he be tried – ought – to be attended with as little severity as possible.' – The distress occasioned by chains is increased by

Varying the *towns* where quarter-sessions and assizes[61] are held: so that prisoners have to walk in irons ten or fifteen miles to their trial: and sometimes to towns that have no prison; where numbers of both sexes are shut up together for many days and nights in one room. This occasions such *confusion and distress*, and such shrieks and outcries, as can be better conceived than described. Surely prisoners ought to be conveyed in carts; or else committed at first to the town where the sessions or assizes are to be held. And in that town a proper prison ought to be built. *Gaol-delivery*[62] is in some counties *but once a year*. What reparation can be made to a poor creature for the misery he has suffered, and the corruption of his morals, by confinement in a prison near twelve months before a trial, in which, perhaps he is at last declared by his country *not guilty*?

The judicious Marquis, whom I quoted above, asserts, that 'Privation of liberty being a punishment, ought not to be inflicted before condemnation, but for

VARYING TOWNS.

GAOL-DELIVERY.

> Unpitied, and unheard, where misery moans;
> Where sickness pines ——————
> Hail, Patriot Band! who, scorning secret scorn,
> When Justice, and when Mercy led the way,
> Dragged the detected monsters into light,
> Wrench'd from their hand Oppression's iron rod.
> ——————————————
> Much still untouch'd remains ———
> Much is the Patriot's weeding hand requir'd.

*　'It is the law of the land, and certainly ever hath been so, that a prisoner ought not at any time to be charged with fetters; unless the jailer be constrained to have recourse to them by the actual necessity of safe custody.' *Principles of Penal Law*, p. 187.

as short a time as possible.' And in cases of guilt, his doctrine is, 'The more immediately after the commission of a crime, a punishment is inflicted, the more just
and useful it will be.' This sentiment is illustrated by a variety of acute remarks
in the chapter *of the Advantage of immediate Punishment*. My mind reverts to
an admirable thought of Mr. *Eden's*; *Principles of Penal Law*,[63] page 330. 'A very
slight reflection, on the numberless unforeseen events which a day may bring
forth, will be sufficient to shew that we are all liable to the imputation of guilt;
and consequently all interested, not only in the protection of innocence, but in
the assignment to every particular offence, of the smallest punishment compat-
ible with the safety of society.'

One cause of gaol-delivery being so seldom, is *in some places* the *expence* of
entertaining the judges and their retinue. At Hull they used to have the assize
but once in seven years. Peacock a *murderer* was in prison there near three years:
before his trial the principal witness died; and the murderer was acquitted. They
now have it once in three years

CLERKS OF
ASSIZE, &C.

Although acquitted prisoners are by the late act in their favour* cleared of
gaolers fees; they are still subject to a similar demand made by *Clerks of assize* and
Clerks of the peace,† and detained in prison several days after their acquittal. At
assize, till the judges: at quarter-sessions, till the justices of peace leave the town;
in order to obtain those fees, which the gentlemen say are not cancelled by the
act. And yet the express words of it are, *Acquitted prisoners 'shall be immediately
set at large in open court.'* It is evident then, that all fees of the commitment in
respect to the prisoner, are by this act totally abolished.

Since the said act, the clerks of assize in some circuits have started a new
demand upon the gaoler, for the judge's certificate of acquitment; *viz.*[64] six shillings and eight pence[65] for the first prisoner acquitted; and a shilling for each of
the rest: or two shillings for every one. I have copies of two receipts given by the
clerk of the Western circuit to the gaolers of Exeter and Salisbury. One of them is
as follows: 'Received 1 April 1775 of Mr. Sherry gaoler one pound eight shillings
and eight pence for his certificate entitling him to his gaol fees for the county of
Devon *per* J. F**** Clerk of the Assize.' – The gaoler told me this was for twenty-
three acquitted prisoners.

I was informed at Durham, that judge *Gould,* at the assize 1775, laid a *fine*
of fifty pounds on the gaoler *for detaining* some acquitted prisoners, for the fees
of the clerk of assize. But upon the intercession of the Bishop (proprietor of the

---

*   14th *George* III.
†   See the Table of the Fees of the Clerks of Assize at the end of the book.
      The Clerk of the Peace in one county demands as follows:

| For | larceny and acquitted, | - £1 | 7 | 0 | Whipped publicly, | £1 | 3 | 4 |
| | Petty larceny, | - - - - - 1 | 8 | 4 | Bastardy, | | 0 17 | 4 |

gaol) the fine was remitted; and the prisoners set at large: the judge ordering the clerk of assize to explain to him in London the foundation of his demand.

One pretence for detaining acquitted prisoners is, that 'It is possible other indictments may be laid against them before the judge leaves the town.' I call it a *pretence*, as the grand jury[66] are often dismissed some days before that time, and because those who do satisfy the demands of the clerk of assize are immediately discharged. Another pretence is, the gaoler tells you 'he takes them back to knock off their irons.' But this may be done in court: in London they have an engine or block, by the help of which they take off the irons with ease in a minute; the machine is brought into court, and the acquitted prisoner is immediately discharged. If, according to what I proposed, prisoners were tried out of irons, this pretext would be entirely remove.

Clerks of assize, and of the peace, ought most certainly to have a consideration for their service to the public: the thing I complain of is what I am led to by my subject, that is, the demand that is made directly or indirectly upon *acquitted* prisoners.*

Some gaolers live *distant* from the prison, in houses that do not belong to the county. Non-residence is not consistent with the attention that is requisite for securing the prisoners; and preserving good order, cleanliness, &c. – Over the door of some of the houses of these keepers is wrote, 'Spirituous liquors sold here.' GAOLERS NON-RESIDENT.

Debtors *crowd* the gaols (especially those in London) with their *Wives* and *children*. There are often by this means, ten or twelve people in a middle-sized room; increasing the danger of infection, and corrupting the morals of children. This point ought (no doubt) to be treated with tenderness. Man and wife should not be totally separated; but no women, unless prisoners, should ever be permitted to continue so much as *one night* in any prison; except, perhaps, when their husbands are dangerously ill. Yet the little probability there is of an industrious woman being of much service to her family in a prison: the number of men in the same room; and of lewd women admitted under the name of wives; prove that this affair needs some regulation. WIVES AND CHILDREN.

Some gaols are *private property:* in these the keepers, protected by the proprietors, and not so subject as other gaolers to the controul of magistrates, are more GAOLS PRIVATE PROPERTY.

---

* The clerks of assize give to the judges large sums for their places. One of the present gentlemen gave for his place £2500. On many accounts these places ought not to be *bought* of the judges. If they were only *presented*, the fees might be much lower. – The demand from the gaoler for a copy of the judge's calendar is now £1:1:0: whereas his Majesty's Commissioners for inquiring into the officers and their fees, &c. in the *Home Circuit*, were of opinion that a demand not near so much was enormous, as we see in their report, dated 1st December 1735 (MS. *page* 21;)

'Paid by the gaoler of the County of *Surry* for the copy of a calendar - £ 0   7   6

And by the gaoler of each of the other countys - - - - - - - - - 0   5   0

'As to these two last Fees or articles, We are of opinion that they are unreasonable and no ways to be justified, &c.'

apt to abuse their prisoners, when a temptation offers. One of these gaols some years ago was quite out of repair, and unsafe; and the proprietor not choosing to repair it, the gaoler to confine his prisoners took a method, that was really shocking.* Some years before that, a prisoner in another of these gaols was tormented with thumbscrews.[67] The grand jury took up the case, and remonstrated to the proprietor; but in vain. I had the account from a worthy friend of mine, who was upon that very jury.†

Of the complaints, which I have hitherto made only in general terms, I shall give instances in the account of particular prisons. To that account I refer, for *evidence* and *fact*.

NUMBER OF PRISONERS.

In the spring 1776, I summed up carefully the total number of prisoners in the sundry prisons. My list was as follows:

	Debtors.	Felons, &c.	Petty Offenders.	*Total.*
1. In Middlesex, *i.e.* London and Westminster; together with three prisons in Southwark, *viz.* the King's Bench, Marshalsea, and Borough-compter, -	1274	228	194	1696
2. In the other thirty-nine counties of England, - - - - - - - - - - -	752	617	459	1828
3. In the twelve counties of Wales, - - -	67	27	—	94
4. In city and town-gaols, - - - - - -	344	122	—	466
	2437	994	653	4084

Petty offenders in the Welch county gaols, blank in the third column third line, are included in the preceding number of felons, &c. 27: most of the gaols in those counties being also the county bridewells.

Petty offenders, blank in third column fourth line, are included in the number 459 of petty offenders in the thirty-nine county gaols; and in the number 122 second column, fourth line.

All that were in the county-gaols besides *debtors*, I have reckoned in the list of *felons*, &c. although many were *petty offenders* and *fines*.[68]

In the third column, under *petty offenders* are included a few *felons* occasionally committed to bridewells.

I have found by carefully examining sundry gaols, that, upon an average, *two dependants* (by which I mean wives and children‡) may be assigned to each man in prison. My computation is confirmed by the account which we have from the benevolent society at the *Thatched-house*,[69] March 27, 1782, as follows. Since their institution in 1772,

---

*   See account of Ely gaol.
†   Durham.
‡   I do not include *parents*, many of whom I have seen sorrowfully attending at prisons, and deeply sharing in the distress arising from the confinement of their children.

```
        Discharged debtors,  -  -  -  -  -  7196
               who had wives,  -  -  -  -  -  4328
                and children,  -  -  -  -  - 13126
                                               ‾‾‾‾‾
Persons immediately benefited,  -  -  -  - -24650.
```

We have farther confirmation by the account from the *Bristol society*; who in their list published May 31, 1775, have

```
        Persons discharged,  -  -  -  -  -  -  73
             who had wives,  -  -  -  -  -  -  45
              and children,  -  -  -  -  -  - 120
                                               ‾‾‾
                   Total  -  -  -  -  -  238.
```

And I find by the account of the society for the discharge of persons imprisoned for small debts in Dublin, that a greater number of dependants are there assigned. For the number of persons discharged by the society from the institution on the 15th of May 1775, to May 1782, was

```
                          -  -  -  -  -  1134
     Dependants on them,  -  -  -  -  -  3611
                                          ‾‾‾‾
          Total relieved  -  -  -  -  -  4745.
```

Each of these totals is considerably larger than the respective products of multiplication by my rule: the first exceeds by 3062, the second by 19, and the last by 1343. – There is indeed commonly a surplus among *debtors*, but a deficiency *among felons*, &c. reduces the average of dependants to that which I stated.

If then to the total number in England and Wales, that is,4084
You add twice that number of dependants, - - - 8168

```
    The number of the distressed is,  -  -  -  -  -12252.
```

It appears from the foregoing table of prisoners, that their number has been greatly magnified by conjectural computations; but surely the real numbers, with those partaking of their distress, is an object worthy the farther attention of the legislature. [pp. 4–19]

[Newgate Prison]

The cells built in Old Newgate a few years since for condemned malefactors, are still used for the same purpose. I shall therefore give some account of them. There are upon each of the three floors five; all vaulted, near 9 feet high to the crown. Those on the ground-floor measure full 9 feet by near 6; the five on the first story are a little larger (9½ by 6) on account of the set-off in the wall; and the five uppermost, still a little larger for the same reason. In the upper part of each cell, is a window double grated, near 3 feet by 1½. The doors are 4 inches thick. The strong stone wall is lined all round each cell with planks, studded with broad-headed nails. In each cell is a barrack-bedstead. I was told by those who attended them, that criminals who had affected an air of boldness during their trial, and appeared quite unconcerned at the pronouncing sentence upon them, were struck with horror, and shed tears, when brought to these darksome solitary abodes.

The chapel is plain and neat. Below is the chaplain's seat, and three or four pews for the felons; that in the centre is for the condemned. On each side is a gallery: that for the women is towards their ward: in it is a pew for the keeper, whose presence may set a good example, and be otherwise useful. The other gallery towards the debtors ward is for them. The stairs to each gallery are on the outside of the chapel. I attended there several times, and Mr. *Villette*[70] read the prayers distinctly, and with propriety: the prisoners who were present, seemed attentive; but we were disturbed by the noise in the court. Surely they who will not go to chapel, who are by far the greater number, should be locked up in their rooms during the time of divine service, and not suffered to hinder the edification of such as are better disposed.

The *Chaplain* (or *ordinary*) besides his salary, has a house in Newgate-street, clear of land-tax; lady *Barnardiston's* legacy,[71] £6 a year; an old legacy paid by the governors of St. Bartholomew's hospital, £10 a year; and lately had two freedoms[72] yearly, which commonly sold for £25 each; and the city generally presented him once in six months with another freedom. Now he has not the freedoms, but his salary is augmented to £180, and the sheriffs pay him £3 : 12 : 0. He engages when chosen to hold no other living.[73]

Debtors have every Saturday from the chamber of London eight stone[74] of beef: *fines* four stone: and some years *felons* eight stone. Debtors have several legacies. I inquired for a list of them, and Mr. *Akerman* told me the table in *Maitland's Survey*[75] was authentic. The amount of it is £52 : 5 : 8 a year. There are other donations mentioned by *Maitland*, amounting to sixty-four stone of beef, and five dozen of brad.*

To these he adds the donation of '*Robert Dow*,[76] who left £1 : 6 : 8 yearly for ever to the sexton or bellman of St. Sepulchre's, to pronounce solemnly two exhortations to the persons condemned, the night before their execution; in these words

> You prisoners who are within
> Who for wickedness and sin,

after many mercies shewn you, are now appointed to die tomorrow in the forenoon, give ear and understand that tomorrow morning the greatest bell of St. Sepulchre's shall toll for you in form and manner of a passing bell as used to be

---

*   After the riots in 1780 the debtors were confined in Clerkenwell bridewell, and the New-Prison; but at my last visit they were in Newgate.

tolled for those that are at the point of death, to the end that all godly people may pray, &c. &c.'*

Here I cannot forbear mentioning a practice which probably had its origin from the ancient mode of torture, though now it seems only a matter of form. When prisoners capitally convicted at the *Old Bailey* are brought up to receive sentence, and the judge asks, 'What have you to say why judgment of death and execution should not be awarded against you,' the executioner slips a whipcord noose about their thumbs. – This custom ought to be abolished.

At my visit in 1779, the gaol was clean, and free from offensive scents. On the felons side, there were only three sick, in one of the upper wards. – An infirmary was building near the condemned cells. Of the 141 felons &c. there were 91 convicts and fines, who had only the prison allowance of a penny loaf a day: Mr. *Akerman* generously contributed towards their relief. In the felons court, the table of fees painted on a board was hung up.

This gaol was burnt by the rioters in 1780,[77] but is rebuilt on the same plan. The men's quadrangle is now divided into three courts. In the first court, are those who pay three shillings and six-pence a week for a bed; in the next, the poorer felons; and in the other, *now* the women. – Under the chapel, are cells for the refractory. Two rooms, adjoining to the condemned cells, are built for an infirmary, in one of which at my last visit there were sixteen sick. Of the two hundred and ninety-one prisoners in 1782, two hundred and twenty-five were men, and sixty-six women. Upwards of an hundred of them were *transports*,[78] eighty-nine *fines*, twenty-one under sentence of death, and the remainder lay for trial. Some of the condemned had been long sick and languishing in their cells.†

TABLE OF FEES.

London sc.[79]   A TABLE of FEES to be taken by the Gaoler or Keeper of New-   NEWGATE.
gate within the said City of London for any Prisoner or Prisoners committed or coming into Gaol or Chamber-Rent there or discharge from thence in any *Civil Action* settled and established the nineteenth day of December in the third year of the reign of his Majesty King *George* the Second *Annoque Domini*[80] 1729 pursuant to an Act of Parliament lately made intituled An Act for the Relief of *Debtors* with respect to the Imprisonment of their Persons.

---

*   *Maitland's History of London*, vol. I. *p.* 26. edit. 1760.
†   At the end of the book, I shall give a table of all the executions for London and Middlesex, during twelve years past.

    An execution day is too much, with us, a day of riot and idleness, and it is found by experience, that the minds of the populace are rather hardened by the spectacle, than affected in any salutary manner. Might not these evils be amended by having the report within a week after sentence, and the execution, soon after, either in the area before Newgate, or before the sessions-house?

    Since the above was written, I learn with satisfaction that the *place of execution* is altered according to the foregoing idea.

	£.	S.	D.
Every prisoner on the master's-side shall pay to the keeper for his entrance fee -	0	3	0
Every prisoner on the master's-side shall pay for chamber-room use of bed bedding and sheets to the keeper there being two in a bed and no more each *per* week - - - - - - - - - - -	-0	1	3
Every prisoner on the said master's-side who at his own desire shall have a bed to himself, shall pay to the keeper for cham-ber-room use of bed bedding and sheets *per* week - - - -	-0	2	6
Every debtor shall pay to the keeper for his discharging fee- - -	-0	6	10
And to all the turnkeys two shillings and no more - - - - -	-0	2	0

No other fee for the use of chamber bed bedding or sheets or upon the commit-ments or discharge of any prisoner on any civil action

Edwd Becher　　Rob^T Raymond
Robt Alsop　　R. Eyre
In^o Barnard　　Thos Pengelly

　　Mr. *Akerman* shewed me another table of fees, which was given him for his direction when he commenced keeper. It is as follows:

Fees to be taken by the keeper of Newgate.

	£.	S.	D.
For every debtor's discharge	0	8	10
For every felon's discharge	0	18	10
For every misdemeanour	0	14	10
Every debtor's entrance on the master's side	0	3	0
Every felon's entrance on the master's side	0	10	6
Every person admitted into the press-yard	3	3	0
For every transport's discharge	0	14	10
For every bailable warrant	3	6	8

Rix.　　*Rob. Willmott.*
Rob. Ladbroke.
Walter Bernard.
Samuel Pennant. [pp. 214–16]

CONCLUSION.[81]

It was once my intention to have published the preceding account of English prisons, without any of the introductory matter which composes the former part of this volume. But thinking, from a close attention to the subject, that it was in my power in some instances to suggest remedies to the evils of which I had been witness; and aware of the common proverbial objection 'that it is easier to find faults than to mend them;' I imagined I should be culpable in suppressing any thing which might conduce to improvement in a matter I had so much at heart.

A person of more ability, with my knowledge of facts, would have written better: but the object of my ambition was not the fame of an author. Hearing the *cry* of the MISERABLE, I devoted my time to their relief. In order to procure it, I made it my business to collect materials, the authenticity of which could not be disputed. For the warmth of some expressions where my subject obliges me to complain, and for my eagerness to remove the several grievances, my apology must be drawn from the deep *distress* of the *sufferers*, and the impression the view of it made upon me – An impression too deep to be effaced by any length of time!

What I have proposed throughout my work is liable, I am sensible, to some objections; and these will, doubtless, be heightened by the cavils of those whose interest it is to prevent the reformation of abuses on which their ease or emolument may depend. Yet I hope not to be entirely deserted in the conflict: and if this publication should be the means of exciting the attention of my countrymen to this IMPORTANT NATIONAL CONCERN – of alleviating the distresses of poor debtors and other prisoners – of procuring for them cleanly and wholesome abodes; and exterminating the gaol-fever, which has so often spread abroad its dreadful contagion – of abolishing, or at least reducing, the oppressive fees of clerks of assize, and of the peace – of preventing the sale of liquors in prisons – of checking the impositions of gaolers, and the extortions of bailiffs – of introducing a habit of industry into our bridewells; and restraining the shocking debauchery and immorality which prevail in our gaols and other prisons – if any of these beneficial consequences shall accrue, the writer will be happy in the pleasing reflection that he has not lived without doing some good to his fellow-creatures; and will think himself abundantly repaid for all the pains he has taken, the time he has spent, and the hazards he has encountered.

TABLES.

TABLE I.

GENERAL HEADS OF REGULATIONS
PROPOSED TO BE ESTABLISHED IN
PENITENTIARY HOUSES
OR
HOUSES OF CORRECTION.

SHOULD the design of erecting Houses of Correction on an enlarged and improved plan, *similar to* that in the excellent *Act* 19th *George* III. drawn up by Sir *William Blackstone* and Mr. *Eden*, be carried into execution; it will be a most important object to frame a set of regulations for their proper government. In order to facilitate the consideration of this point, I have put down under a few general heads, those circumstances which appear to me most deserving of attention; examples of which, carried into practice, may be found in different parts of my book.

I shall in the first place, however, declare my opinion, that no regulations will, in reality, be executed with due care and attention, if these houses are not erected *so near* the Metropolis or other capital towns, as to be *easily accessible* by those who may be entrusted with the inspection of them. And this appears to me a matter of so much consequence, as to overbalance *every* consideration which might be supposed to render a different situation more eligible.

SECURITY.

Situation – contrivance of the building – lodging up stairs or over arcades – clothes of two colours – turn-stiles and low gates – alarm-bell – double doors, one iron-latticed – high wall surrounding – number and disposition of turnkeys – military guard if necessary – gaoler's windows looking on the yard – collar, ring, or somewhat of that kind to be worn for discovery on escapes – times of opening and shutting up to be strictly observed – caution in admitting visiters – only to be admitted at certain times – not many at once – to be searched for tools, spirituous liquors, &c.

HEALTH.

Fresh and sweet air – open windows and apertures for a thorough draught of air – prisoners made to go out and air themselves at proper times – privies properly situated – the sewers spacious.

Cleanliness. 1. The prisoners persons – use of baths at admission and other times – to wash before meals – water in the courts and wards – towels, sinks, &c. in proper places – heads shaved – encouragements to the most cleanly.

2. Their clothes – linen clean, how often – other clothes – bedding – beds brought out and beat.

3. The house – washing and sweeping of cells – work-rooms – staircases – galleries &c. – sewers – drains – yards – plenty of water – waste water through the privies – scraping the walls – lime-whited twice a year.

DIET.

Provisions, quantity – and quality – proportioned to work – difference in summer and winter – hot provisions daily – breakfast – dinner – supper – what – manner of dividing and sharing – hours of meals – allowance in weight – inspectors of provision – house weights – liquor what – measure of – prisoners allowed to purchase, what – and when.

CLOTHING.

A prison uniform – materials – colour, &c. – linen provided – stockings – shoes, &c.

LODGING.

Separate cell for each prisoner – sexes separated – linen, and bedding – what – difference in summer and winter – upon barrack-beds – or iron – or wooden bedsteads – flues or stoves to warm the cells in winter – time allotted for sleep.

FIRING.

Fuel what kind and quantity – when and how long – fires, where to be made – stoves – flues, &c.

RELIGIOUS INSTRUCTION AND MORALS.

Chaplain, his duty – what and when – private admonitions to young offenders – catechising – chapel – manner of placing the prisoners in – persons to overlook their behaviour – reward and punishment for behaviour at – visitors dismissed at service time – prisoners reading chapters or prayers – Bibles, books provided – grace at meals – no gaming – or drinking – ministers of different persuasions allowed.

EMPLOYMENT.

Proportioned to strength – and to degree of criminality – hours of – kinds of – within doors and without doors – number working together – tasks – mere labour – or manufactures requiring ingenuity – the labour of each distinguishable from that of another – working at their own trades – clothing, &c. of the house made by prisoners – washing – baking – proportion of profit to be allowed to prisoners.

Wholesomeness of an employment – ready sale of manufacture – conveyance of raw materials and manufacture – tools required, not dangerous ones – returned at night.

REWARDS.

Shortening term of confinement – work lighter or more agreeable – order of being served at meals – better provision – degree of liberty allowed – cells more convenient – profit of work – distribution of charity – advance into a higher class – money given at discharge – clothes given at discharge – a character at discharge.

PUNISHMENTS.

Abridgment of diet – or coarser kind – hard or disagreeable work – marks of disgrace; wearing collar, &c. – stripes – term lengthened on attempts to escape – shutting up the refractory in strong rooms – solitary confinement and work.

TREATMENT OF SICK.

An infirmary – medical attendance – medicines – freer allowance of diet, wine, bark, &c. – clean linen – fresh air – nurses, number of – precautions against infection – fumigation – clothes exposed to fire – in an oven – or buried – room for convalescents – gradual return to usual diet and labour.

PROCEEDINGS ON DEATH OF PRISONERS.

Coroner – jury how composed – funeral – without the precincts – how attended – expence allowed for.

GOVERNMENT OF PRISON.

Magistrates. To visit at proper periods – without previous notice – to see and examine all prisoners separately – to fix rewards or punishments – a room for in the prison.

Inspectors. By whom appointed – their duty – time of continuance in office – how often to visit – at unexpected times – to view the whole prison, and hear prisoners complaints – to examine and weigh provisions – to enquire the conduct of prisoners and represent proper objects for favour – attendance at chapel – no salary – but some honorary distinctions.

Gaoler. His duty – inspection of – complaints against admitted – obliged to constant residence – allowed no profit in provisions, liquor, &c. – salary of – manner of choosing him – no rent or taxes to pay – no fees, or private emoluments from prisoners.

Matron. Salary of – duty.

Turnkeys, number of – by whom appointed – salary – their office.

Manufacturer. Salary of – duty.

Taskmaster. Salary of – duty.

REGULATIONS MADE KNOWN.

Tables hung up – intelligibly drawn up – of the duty of officers – of keepers – of prisoners – of hours of opening and shutting – of work – of behaviour of prisoners to keeper, &c. – of rewards and punishments – of attendance on divine service – of diet – where hung – how made known – painted on a board – printed and given to each prisoner – to be read at certain times – by chaplain – or keeper. [pp. 469–72]

TABLE IX.[82]

ABSTRACT of Sir STEPHEN THEODORE JANSSEN'S TABLE of *Criminals Condemned*;[83] *Executed*; and *Pardoned*, at the Old Bailey, LONDON, from the Year 1749 to 1771 both Inclusive.

		Condemned.	Executed.	Pardoned &c.
Peace	1749	61	44	17
	1750	84	56	28
	1751	85	63	22
	1752	52	47	5
	1753	57	41	16
	1754	50	34	16
	1755	39	21	18
Peace		—— 428	—— 306	—— 122
&	1756	30	13	17
War				
War	1757	37	26	11
	1758	32	20	12
	1759	15	6	9
	1760	14	10	4
	1761	22	17	5
	1762	25	15	10
War				
&	1763	61	32	29
Peace		—— 236	—— 139	—— 97
Peace	1764	52	31	21
	1765	41	26	15
	1766	39	20	19
	1767	49	22	27
	1768	54	27	27
	1769	71	24	47
	1770	91	49	42
	1771	60	34	26
		—— 457	—— 233	—— 224
		——	——	——
Total		1121	678	443

TABLE X.

NUMBER of CONVICTS *Executed*, for LONDON and MIDDLESEX, during the last Twelve Years.*

	Murder		Coiners		Rioters		Various Crimes.		
	Men.	Women.	Men.	Women.	Men.	Women.	Men.	Women.	
From Dec. 1771 to Dec 1772,	3	-	2	-	32	-	-	-	37
Dec. 1772 to Dec 1773,	1	1 burnt	1	-	29	-	-	-	32
Dec. 1773 to Dec 1774,	-	1	-	-	31	-	-	-	32
Dec. 1774 to Dec 1775,	1	1	3	-	40	1	-	-	46
Dec. 1775 to Dec 1776,	6	-	8	-	24	-	-	-	38
Dec. 1776 to Dec 1777,	2	-	1	-	29	-	-	-	32
Dec. 1777 to Dec 1778,	1	-	1	-	31	-	-	-	33
Dec. 1778 to Dec 1779,	-	-	2	1 burnt	19	1	-	-	23
Dec. 1779 to Dec 1780,	1	-	2	-	24	1	19	3	50
Dec. 1780 to Dec 1781,	1	-	1	-	33	5	-	-	40
Dec. 1781 to Dec 1782,	-	-	-	-	44	1	-	-	45
Dec. 1782 to Dec 1783,	-	-	6	-	-	1	52	-	59
	16	3	27	1	388	10	19	3	467

[pp. 483–4]

* This table, together with *Janssen's*, gives the total number of executions for thirty-five years past.

from William Godwin, *An Enquiry Concerning Political Justice,*
and Its Influence on General Virtue and Happiness, 2 vols
(London: G. G. and J. Robinson, 1793); vol. 2, book 7, chapters 1,
3, 6, and 8.

Godwin (1756–1836) was born in Cambridgeshire, son of a Dissenting clergyman and a shipowner's daughter, and received a progressive modern education
at Hoxton Dissenting Academy, north of London, to prepare him for the ministry. He also read widely in Enlightenment materialist philosophy and eventually
became and atheist and anarchist. Like many with similar views, he welcomed
the French Revolution as the harbinger of a comprehensive reform of society, politics and economy. Aiming to live by writing, he had published novels
and political pamphlets early in his career, but in 1793 became an intellectual
celebrity with the appearance of his long-meditated and systematic treatise on
anarchism, *An Enquiry Concerning Political Justice*.

This approached the increasingly virulent and divisive public debate on the
Revolution indirectly, in the light of universal principles of human nature, based
on the idea of justice as a rational principle regulating social relations without
need of political or other institutions – in short, philosophical anarchism. *Political Justice* argues that social and political circumstances construct the individual
in a necessary process of cause and effect, or 'necessitarianism'; corrupt and unjust
societies construct corrupt and vicious individuals, perverting humanity's innate
benevolence and powers of reason. To make virtuous individuals requires not a
reformed society and state, however, but elimination of the state and the spread
of education and enlightenment, allowing the individual's innate benevolence
and sense of justice to operate without restraint or coercion and so to practise
rational 'political justice'. Godwin's book thus put the contemporary debate on
crime and punishment in a radically new context. *Political Justice* rejects both
Christian approaches such as those of Madan and Paley included here, with
their insistence on innate human depravity and unreason, and humanitarian
approaches such as those of Howard and Eden, also included here, with their
insistence on social and institutional reform as the means to reduce crime. Godwin argues for abolition, not reform, of the legal, judicial and penal systems as

the only way to achieve true social justice, consequently eliminating crime and the need for punishment, as seen in the extracts included here.

Godwin's influence went far beyond philosophers, however. A year after *Political Justice*, he published a novel, *Things As They Are; or, The Adventures of Caleb Williams*, illustrating the central ideas of *Political Justice* in an individual case for a wider readership that would not pick up or comprehend a philosophical treatise. The novel had an impact similar to the treatise. Meanwhile, however, the deepening national and international crisis, signalled by arrest and trial of his close friends for sedition, as well as new influences such as his lover, the feminist Mary Wollstonecraft, led Godwin to reconsider the role of volition and the feelings. He set about exploring these issues over the next four decades in a revised edition of *Political Justice*, essays, five further novels, drama, literary and social histories, and other works. This aspect of his writing fed into many Romantic writers' preoccupation with individual subjectivity and social alienation, seen in such writers as the poet Byron, Gothic novelists and dramatists, and others such as the novelist Charles Whitehead, whose fictional study of criminal psychology, the *Autobiography of Jack Ketch* (1835), is included in this series.

Nevertheless, Godwin's philosophical ideas and adaptation of the novel form to serve them had an immediate and lasting influence, especially on reformist writers. Immediately, his influence was seen in the fiction of his friends Thomas Holcroft, Mary Wollstonecraft and Mary Hays, as well as others; he also influenced later generations of writers, such as the so-called 'Newgate novelists' dealing with crime and punishment and led by Edward Lytton Bulwer, whose *Paul Clifford* (1830) is included in this series.

Note on the text: I have omitted those of Godwin's footnotes that are cross-references to other passages in *Political Justice*, though the frequency of these does reinforce the sense of the text being a self-enclosed philosophical discourse.

BOOK VII.

OF CRIMES AND PUNISHMENTS.

CHAP. I.

LIMITATIONS OF THE DOCTRINE OF PUNISHMENT WHICH RESULT FROM THE PRINCIPLES OF MORALITY.

DEFINITION OF PUNISHMENT.—NATURE OF CRIME.—RETRIBUTIVE
JUSTICE NOT INDEPENDENT AND ABSOLUTE—NOT TO BE VINDI-
CATED FROM THE SYSTEM OF NATURE.—DESERT A CHIMERICAL
PROPERTY.—CONCLUSION.

THE subject of punishment is perhaps the most fundamental in the science of politics. Men associated for the sake of mutual protection and benefit. It has already appeared, that the internal affairs of such associations are of infinitely greater importance than their external. It has appeared that the action of society in conferring rewards and superintending opinion is of pernicious effect. Hence it follows that government, or the action of the society in its corporate capacity, can scarcely be of any utility, except so far as it is requisite for the suppression of force by force; for the prevention of the hostile attack of one member of the society upon the person or property of another, which prevention is usually called by the name of criminal justice, or punishment.

Before we can properly judge of the necessity or urgency of this action of government, it will be of some importance to consider the precise import of the word punishment. I may employ force to counteract the hostility that is actually committing on me. I may employ force to compel any member of the society to occupy the post that I conceive most conducive to the general advantage, either in the mode of impressing soldiers and sailors, or by obliging a military officer or a minister of state to accept or retain his appointment. I may put an innocent man to death for the common good, either because he is infected with a pestilential disease, or because some oracle has declared it essential to the public safety. None of these, though they consist in the exertion of force for some moral purpose, comes within the import of the word punishment. Punishment is generally used to signify the voluntary infliction of evil upon a vicious being, not merely because the public advantage demands it, but because there is apprehended to be a certain fitness and propriety in the nature of things, that render suffering, abstractedly from the benefit to result, the suitable concomitant of vice.

The justice of punishment therefore, in the strict import of the word, can only be a deduction from the hypothesis of free-will, and must be false, if human actions be necessary. Mind, as was sufficiently apparent when we treated of that

Definition of punishment.

Nature of crime.

subject, is an agent, in no other sense than matter is an agent. It operates and is operated upon, and the nature, the force and line of direction of the first, is exactly in proportion to the nature, force and line of direction of the second. Morality in a rational and designing mind is not essentially different from morality in an inanimate substance. A man of certain intellectual habits is fitted to be an assassin, a dagger of a certain form is fitted to be his instrument. The one or the other excites a greater degree of disapprobation, in proportion as its fitness for mischievous purposes appears to be more inherent and direct. I view a dagger on this account with more disapprobation than a knife, which is perhaps equally adapted for the purposes of the assassin; because the dagger has few or no beneficial uses to weigh against those that are hurtful, and because it has a tendency by means of association to the exciting of evil thoughts. I view the assassin with more disapprobation than the dagger, because he is more to be feared, and it is more difficult to change his vicious structure or take from him his capacity to injure. The man is propelled to act by necessary causes and irresistible motives, which, having once occurred, are likely to occur again. The dagger has no quality adapted to the contraction of habits, and, though it have committed a thousand murders, is not at all more likely (unless so far as those murders, being known, may operate as a slight associated motive with the possessor) to commit murder again. Except in the articles here specified, the two cases are exactly parallel. The assassin cannot help the murder he commits any more than the dagger.

Retributive justice not independent and absolute:

These arguments are merely calculated to set in a more perspicuous light a principle, which is admitted by many by whom the doctrine of necessity has never been examined; that the only measure of equity is utility, and whatever is not attended with any beneficial purpose, is not just. This is so evident a proposition that few reasonable and reflecting minds will be found inclined to reject it. Why do I inflict suffering on another? If neither for his own benefit nor the benefit of others, can that be right? Will resentment, the mere indignation and horror I have conceived against vice, justify me in putting a being to useless torture? 'But suppose I only put an end to his existence.' What, with no prospect of benefit either to himself or others? The reason the mind easily reconciles itself to this supposition is, that we conceive existence to be less a blessing than a curse to a being incorrigibly vicious. But in that case the supposition does not fall within the terms of the question: I am in reality conferring a benefit. It has been asked, 'If we conceive to ourselves two beings, each of them solitary, but the first virtuous and the second vicious, the first inclined to the highest acts of benevolence, if his situation were changed for the social, the second to malignity, tyranny and injustice, do we not feel that the first is entitled to felicity in preference to the second?' If there be any difficulty in the question, it is wholly caused by the extravagance of the supposition. No being can be either virtuous or vicious who has no opportunity of influencing the happiness of others. He may indeed, though now solitary, recollect or imagine a social state; but this sentiment and the propensities it generates can scarcely be vigorous, unless he have hopes of being at some future time restored to that state. The true solitaire cannot be considered as a moral being, unless the morality we contemplate be that which has relation to his own permanent advantage. But, if that be our meaning, punishment, unless for reform, is peculiarly absurd. His conduct is vicious, because it has a tendency to render him miserable: shall we inflict calamity upon him, for this reason only because he has already inflicted calamity upon himself? It is difficult for us to imagine to ourselves a solitary intellectual being, whom no future accident shall ever render social. It is difficult for us to separate even in idea virtue and vice from happiness and misery; and of consequence not to imagine that, when we bestow a benefit upon virtue, we bestow it where it will turn to account; and, when we bestow a benefit upon vice, we bestow it where it will be unproductive. For these reasons the question of a solitary being will always be extravagant and unintelligible, but will never convince.

It has sometimes been alledged that the very course of nature has annexed suffering to vice, and has thus led us to the idea of punishment. Arguments of this sort must be listened to with great caution. It was by reasonings of a similar nature that our ancestors justified the practice of religious persecution: 'Heretics and unbelievers are the objects of God's indignation; it must therefore be meritorious in us to mal-treat those whom God has cursed.' We know too little of the system of the universe, are too liable to error respecting it, and see too small a portion of the whole, to entitle us to form our moral principles upon an imitation of what we conceive to be the course of nature. *not to be vindicated from the system of nature.*

It is an extreme error to suppose that the course of nature is something arbitrarily adjusted by a designing mind. Let us once conceive a system of percipient beings to exist, and all that we know of the history of man follows from that conception as so many inevitable consequences. Mind beginning to exist must have begun from ignorance, must have received idea after idea, must have been liable to erroneous conclusions from imperfect conceptions. We say that the system of the universe has annexed happiness to virtue and pain to vice. We should speak more accurately if we said, that virtue would not be virtue nor vice be vice, if this connection could cease. The office of the principle, whether mind or whatever else, to which the universe owes its existence, is less that of fabricating than conducting; is not the creation of truth, and the connecting ideas and propositions which had no original relation to each other, but the rendering truth, the nature of which is unalterable, an active and vivifying principle. It cannot therefore be good reasoning to say, the system of nature annexes unhappiness to vice, or in other words vice brings its own punishment along with it, therefore it would be unjust in us not by a positive interference to render that punishment double. *Desert a chimerical property.*

Thus it appears, whether we enter philosophically into the principle of human actions, or merely analyse the ideas of rectitude and justice which have the universal consent of mankind, that, accurately speaking, there is no such thing as desert. It cannot be just that we should inflict suffering on any man, except so far as it tends to good. Hence it follows that the strict acceptation of the word punishment by no means accords with any sound principles of reasoning. It is right that I should inflict suffering, in every case where it can be clearly shown that such infliction will produce an overbalance of good. But this infliction bears no reference to the mere innocence or guilt of the person upon whom it is made. An innocent man is the proper subject of it, if it tend to good. A guilty man is the proper subject of it under no other point of view. To punish him upon any hypothesis for what is past and irrecoverable and for the consideration of that only, must be ranked among the wildest conceptions of untutored barbarism. Every man upon whom discipline is administered, is to be considered as to the rationale of this discipline as innocent . Xerxes[1] was not more unreasonable when he lashed the waves of the sea, than that man would be who inflicted suffering on his fellow, from a view to the past, and not from a view to the future.

Conclusion.   It is of the utmost importance that we should bear these ideas constantly in mind during our whole examination of the theory of punishment. This theory would in the past transactions of mankind have been totally different, if they had divested themselves of all emotions of anger and resentment; if they had considered the man who torments another for what he has done, as upon par with the child who beats the table; if they had figured to their imagination, and then properly estimated, the man, who should shut up in prison some atrocious criminal, and afterwards torture him at stated periods, merely in consideration of the abstract congruity of crime and punishment, without any possible benefit to others or to himself; if they had regarded infliction as that which was to be regulated solely by a dispassionate calculation of the future, without suffering the past, in itself considered, for a moment to enter into the account.

CHAP. III.

OF THE PURPOSES OF COERCION.

NATURE OF DEFENCE CONSIDERED.—COERCION FOR RESTRAINT—FOR REFORMATION.—SUPPOSED USES OF ADVERSITY—DEFECTIVE— UNNECESSARY.—COERCION FOR EXAMPLE—I. NUGATORY.—THE NECESSITY OF POLITICAL COERCION ARISES FROM THE DEFECTS OF POLITICAL INSTITUTION.—2. UNJUST.—UNFEELING CHARAC- TER OF THIS SPECIES OF COERCION.

PROCEED we to consider three principal ends that coercion proposes to itself, restraint, reformation and example. Under each of these heads the arguments on the affirmative side must be allowed to be cogent, not irresistible. Under each of them considerations will occur, that will oblige us to doubt universally of the propriety of coercion. In this examination I shall take it for granted that the persons with whom I am reasoning allow, that the ends of restraint and example may be sufficiently answered in consistency with the end of reformation, that is, without the punishment of death. To those by whom this is not allowed in the first instance, the subsequent reasonings will only apply with additional force.

The first and most innocent of all the classes of coercion is that which is employed in repelling actual force. This has but little to do with any species of political institution, but may nevertheless deserve to be first considered. In this case I am employed (suppose, for example, a drawn sword is pointed at my own breast or that of another, with threats of instant destruction) in preventing a mischief that seems about inevitably to ensue. In this case there appears to be no time for experiments. And yet even here meditation will not leave us without our difficulties. The powers of reason and truth are yet unfathomed. That truth which one man cannot communicate in less than a year, another can communicate in a fortnight. The shortest term may have an understanding commensurate to it. When Marius[2] said with a stern look and a commanding countenance to the soldier that was sent down into his dungeon to assassinate him, 'Wretch, have you the temerity to kill Marius!' and with these few words drove him to flight; it was, that he had so energetic an idea compressed in his mind, as to make its way with irresistible force to the mind of his executioner. If there were falshood and prejudice mixed with this idea, can we believe that truth is not more powerful than they? It would be well for the human species, if they were all in this respect like Marius, all accustomed to place an intrepid confidence in the single energy of intellect. Who shall say what there is that would be impossible to men with these habits? Who shall say how far the whole species might be improved, were they accustomed to despise force in others, and did they refuse to employ it for themselves?

Nature of defence considered.

But the coercion we are here considering is exceedingly different. It is employed against an individual whose violence is over. He is at present engaged in no hostility against the community or any of its members. He is quietly pursuing those occupations which are beneficial to himself, and injurious to none. Upon what pretence is this man to be the subject of violence? For restraint? Restraint from what? 'From some future injury which it is to be feared he will commit.' This is the very argument which has been employed to justify the most execrable of all tyrannies. By what reasonings have the inquisition,[3] the employment of spies and the various kinds of public censure directed against opinion been vindicated? Because there is an intimate connexion between men's opinions and their conduct: because immoral sentiments lead by a very probable consequence to immoral actions. There is not more reason, in many cases at least, to

Coercion for restraint:

apprehend that the man who has once committed robbery will commit it again, than the man who dissipates his property at the gaming-table, or who is accustomed to profess that upon any emergency he will not scruple to have recourse to this expedient. Nothing can be more obvious than that, whatever precautions may be allowable with respect to the future, justice will reluctantly class among these precautions any violence to be committed on my neighbour. Nor are they oftener unjust than they are superfluous. Why not arm myself with vigilance and energy, instead of locking up every man whom my imagination may bid me fear, that I may spend my days in undisturbed inactivity? If communities, instead of aspiring, as they have hitherto done, to embrace a vast territory, and to glut their vanity with ideas of empire, were contented with a small district with a proviso of confederation in cases of necessity, every individual would then live under the public eye and the disapprobation of his neighbours, a species of coercion, not derived from the caprice of men, but from the system of the universe, would inevitably oblige him either to reform or to emigrate. – The sum of the argument under this head is, that all coercion for the sake of restraint is punishment upon suspicion, a species of punishment, the most abhorrent to reason, and arbitrary in its application, that can be devised.

for reform-
ation.

The second object which coercion may be imagined to propose to itself is reformation. We have already seen various objections that may be offered to it in this point of view. Coercion cannot convince, cannot conciliate, but on the contrary alienates the mind of him against whom it is employed. Coercion has nothing in common with reason, and therefore can have no proper tendency to the generation of virtue. Reason is omnipotent: if my conduct be wrong, a very simple statement, flowing from a clear and comprehensive view, will make it appear to be such; nor is there any perverseness that can resist the evidence of which truth is capable.

Supposed
uses of
adversity:

But to this it may be answered, 'that this view of the subject may indeed be abstractedly true, but that it is not true relative to the present imperfection of human faculties. The grand requisite for the reformation and improvement of the human species, seems to consist in the rousing of the mind. It is for this reason that the school of adversity has so often been considered as the school of virtue. In an even course of easy and prosperous circumstances the faculties sleep. But, when great and urgent occasion is presented, it should seem that the mind rises to the level of the occasion. Difficulties awaken vigour and engender strength; and it will frequently happen that the more you check and oppress me, the more will my faculties swell, till they burst all the obstacles of oppression.'

The opinion of the excellence of adversity is built upon a very obvious mistake. If we will divest ourselves of paradox and singularity, we shall perceive that adversity is a bad thing, but that there is something else that is worse. Mind can neither exist nor be improved without the reception of ideas. It will improve more in a calamitous, than a torpid state. A man will sometimes be found wiser at the end of his career, who has been treated with severity, than with neglect. But because severity is one way of generating thought, it does not follow that it is the best.

It has already been shown that coercion absolutely considered is injustice. Can injustice be the best mode of disseminating principles of equity and reason? Oppression exercised to a certain extent is the most ruinous of all things. What is it but this, that has habituated mankind to so much ignorance and vice for so many thousand years? Can that which in its genuine and unlimited state is the worst, become by a certain modification and diluting the best of all things? All coercion sours the mind. He that suffers it, is practically persuaded of the want of a philanthropy sufficiently enlarged in those with whom he is most intimately connected. He feels that justice prevails only with great limitations, and that he cannot depend upon being treated with justice. The lesson which coercion reads to him is, 'Submit to force, and abjure reason. Be not directed by the convictions of your understanding, but by the basest part of your nature, the dread of present pain, and the pusillanimous terror of the injustice of others.' It was thus Elizabeth of England and Frederic of Prussia[4] were educated in the school of adversity. The way in which they profited by this discipline was by finding resources in their own minds, enabling them to regard unmoved the violence that was employed against them. Can this be the best possible mode of forming men to virtue? If it be, perhaps it is farther requisite that the coercion we use should be flagrantly unjust, since the improvement seems to lie not in submission, but resistance.

But it is certain that truth is adequate to awaken the mind without the aid of adversity. Truth does not consist in a certain number of unconnected propositions, but in evidence that shows their reality and their value. If I apprehend the value of any pursuit, shall I not engage in it? If I apprehend it clearly, shall I not engage in it zealously? If you would awaken my mind in the most effectual manner, tell me the truth with energy. For that purpose, thoroughly understand it yourself, impregnate your mind with its evidence, and speak from the clearness of your view, and the fulness of conviction. Were we accustomed to an education, in which truth was never neglected from indolence, or told in a way treacherous to its excellence, in which the preceptor subjected himself to the perpetual discipline of finding the way to communicate it with brevity and force, but without prejudice and acrimony, it cannot be doubted, but such an education would be much more effectual for the improvement of the mind, than all the modes of angry or benevolent coercion that can be devised.

The last object which coercion proposes is example. Had legislators confined their views to reformation and restraint, their exertions of power, though mistaken, would still have borne the stamp of humanity. But, the moment vengeance presented itself as a stimulus on the one side, or the exhibition of a terrible

[margin:] defective:

[margin:] unnecessary.

[margin:] Coercion for example:

example on the other, no barbarity was then thought too great. Ingenious cruelty was busied to find new means of torturing the victim, or of rendering the spectacle impressive and horrible.

It has long since been observed that this system of policy constantly fails of its purpose. Farther refinements in barbarity produce a certain impression so long as they are new, but this impression soon vanishes, and the whole scope of a gloomy invention is exhausted in vain.*[5] The reason of this phenomenon is that, whatever may be the force with which novelty strikes the imagination, the unchangeable principles of reason speedily recur, and assert their indestructible empire. We feel the emergencies to which we are exposed, and we feel, or we think we feel, the dictates of truth directing to their relief. Whatever ideas we form in opposition to the mandates of law, we draw, with sincerity, though it may be with some mixture of mistake, from the unalterable conditions of our existence. We compare them with the despotism which society exercises in its corporate capacity, and the more frequent is our comparison, the greater are our murmurs and indignation against the injustice to which we are exposed. But indignation is not a sentiment that conciliates; barbarity possesses none of the attributes of persuasion. It may terrify; but it cannot produce in us candour and docility. Thus ulcerated with injustice, our distresses, our temptations, and all the eloquence of feeling present themselves again and again. Is it any wonder they should prove victorious?

The necessity of political coercion arises from the defects of political institution.

With what repugnance shall we contemplate the present forms of human society, if we recollect that the evils which they thus mercilessly avenge, owe their existence to the vices of those very forms? It is a well known principle of speculative truth, that true self love and social prescribe to us exactly the same species of conduct. Why is this acknowledged in speculation and perpetually contradicted in practice? Is there any innate perverseness in man that continually hurries him to his own destruction? This is impossible; for man is thought, and, till thought began, he had no propensities either to good or evil. My propensities are the fruit of the impressions that have been made upon me, the good always preponderating, because the inherent nature of things is more powerful than any human institutions. The original sin of the worst men, is in the perverseness of these institutions, the opposition they produce between public and private good, the monopoly they create of advantages which reason directs to be left in common. What then can be more shameless than for society to make an example of those whom she has goaded to the breach of order, instead of amending her own institutions, which, by straining order into tyranny, produced the mischief? Who can tell how rapid would be our progress towards the total annihilation of civil delinquency, if we did but enter upon the business of reform in the right manner?

*   *Beccaria, Dei Delitti e delle Pene.*

Coercion for example, is liable to all the same objections as coercion for restraint or reformation, and to certain other objections peculiar to itself. It is employed against a person not now in the commission of offence, and of whom we can only suspect that he ever will offend. It supersedes argument, reason and conviction, and requires us to think such a species of conduct our duty, because such is the good pleasure of our superiors, and because, as we are taught by the example in question, they will make us rue our stubbornness if we think otherwise. In addition to this it is to be remembered that, when I am made to suffer as an example to others, I am treated myself with supercilious neglect, as if I were totally incapable of feeling and morality. If you inflict pain upon me, you are either just or unjust. If you be just, it should seem necessary that there should be something in me that makes me the fit subject of pain, either desert, which is absurd, or mischief I may be expected to perpetrate, or lastly a tendency to reformation. If any of these be the reason why the suffering I undergo is just, then example is out of the question: it may be an incidental consequence of the procedure, but it can form no part of its principle. It must surely be a very inartificial and injudicious scheme for guiding the sentiments of mankind; to fix upon an individual as a subject of torture or death, respecting whom this treatment has no direct fitness, merely that we may bid others look on, and derive instruction from his misery. This argument will derive additional force from the reasonings of the following chapter.

2. unjust.

Unfeeling character of this species of coercion.

CHAP. VI.

SCALE OF COERCION.

ITS SPHERE DESCRIBED.—ITS SEVERAL CLASSES.—DEATH WITH TORTURE.—DEATH ABSOLUTELY.—ORIGIN OF THIS POLICY—IN THE CORRUPTNESS OF POLITICAL INSTITUTIONS—IN THE INHUMANITY OF THE INSTITUTORS.—CORPORAL PUNISHMENT.—ITS ABSURDITY—ITS ATROCIOUSNESS.—PRIVATION OF FREEDOM.—DUTY OF REFORMING OUR NEIGHBOUR AN INFERIOR CONSIDERATION IN THIS CASE.—ITS PLACE DEFINED.—MODES OF RESTRAINT.—INDISCRIMINATE IMPRISONMENT.—SOLITARY IMPRISONMENT.—ITS SEVERITY.—ITS MORAL EFFECTS.— SLAVERY.—BANISHMENT.—1. SIMPLE BANISHMENT.—2. TRANSPORTATION.—3. COLONISATION.—THIS PROJECT HAS MISCARRIED FROM UNKINDNESS—FROM OFFICIOUSNESS.—ITS PERMANENT EVILS.—RECAPITULATION.

IT is time to proceed to the consideration of certain inferences that may be deduced from the theory of coercion which has now been delivered; nor can any

Its sphere described.

thing be of greater importance than these inferences will be found to the virtue, the happiness and improvement of mankind.

And, first, it evidently follows that coercion is an act of painful necessity, inconsistent with the true character and genius of mind, the practice of which is temporarily imposed upon us by the corruption and ignorance that reign among mankind. Nothing can be more absurd than to look to it as a source of improvement. It contributes to the generation of excellence, just as much as the keeper of the course contributes to the fleetness of the race. Nothing can be more unjust than to have recourse to it, but upon the most undeniable emergency. Instead of multiplying occasions of coercion, and applying it as the remedy of every moral evil, the true politician will anxiously confine it within the narrowest limits, and perpetually seek to diminish the occasions of its employment. There is but one reason by which it can in any case be apologised, and that is, where the suffering the offender to be at large shall be notoriously injurious to the public security.

Secondly, the consideration of restraint as the only justifiable ground of coercion, will furnish us with a simple and satisfactory criterion by which to measure the justice of the suffering inflicted.

The infliction of a lingering and tormenting death cannot be vindicated upon this hypothesis; for such infliction can only be dictated by sentiments of resentment on the one hand, or by the desire to exhibit a terrible example on the other.

To deprive an offender of his life in any manner will appear to be unjust, since it will always be sufficiently practicable without this to prevent him from farther offence. Privation of life, though by no means the greatest injury that can be inflicted, must always be considered as a very serious injury; since it puts a perpetual close upon the prospects of the sufferer, as to all the enjoyments, the virtues and the excellence of a human being.

In the story of those whom the merciless laws of Europe devote to destruction, we sometimes meet with persons who subsequently to their offence have succeeded to a plentiful inheritance, or who for some other reason seem to have had the fairest prospects of tranquillity and happiness opened upon them. Their story with a little accommodation may be considered as the story of every offender. If there be any man whom it may be necessary for the safety of the whole to put under restraint, this circumstance is a powerful plea to the humanity and justice of the leading members of the community in his behalf. This is the man who most stands in need of their assistance. If they treated him with kindness instead of supercilious and unfeeling neglect, if they made him understand with how much reluctance they had been induced to employ the force of the society against him, if they presented truth to his mind with calmness, perspicuity and benevolence, if they employed those precautions which an humane disposition would not fail to suggest, to keep from him the motives of corruption and

Its several classes.

Death with torture.

Death absolutely.

obstinacy, his reformation would be almost infallible. These are the prospects to which his wants and his misfortunes powerfully entitle him; and it is from these prospects that the hand of the executioner cuts him off for ever.

It is a mistake to suppose that this treatment of criminals tends to multiply crimes. On the contrary few men would enter upon a course of violence with the certainty of being obliged by a slow and patient process to amputate their errors. It is the uncertainty of punishment under the existing forms that multiplies crimes. Remove this uncertainty, and it would be as reasonable to expect that a man would wilfully break his leg, for the sake of being cured by a skilful surgeon. Whatever gentleness the intellectual physician may display, it is not to be believed that men can part with rooted habits of injustice and vice without the sensation of considerable pain.

The true reasons in consequence of which these forlorn and deserted members of the community are brought to an ignominious death, are, first, the peculiar iniquity of the civil institutions of that community, and, secondly, the supineness and apathy of their superiors. In republican and simple forms of government punishments are rare, the punishment of death is almost unknown. On the other hand the more there is in any country of inequality and oppression, the more punishments are multiplied. The more the institutions of society contradict the genuine sentiments of the human mind, the more severely is it necessary to avenge their violation. At the same time the rich and titled members of the community, proud of their fancied eminence, behold with total unconcern the destruction of the destitute and the wretched, disdaining to recollect that, if there be any intrinsic difference between them, it is the offspring of their different circumstances, and that the man whom they now so much despise, would have been as accomplished and susceptible as they, if they had only changed situations. When we behold a string of poor wretches brought out for execution, justice will present to our affrighted fancy all the hopes and possibilities which are thus brutally extinguished, the genius, the daring invention, the unshrinking firmness, the tender charities and ardent benevolence, which have occasionally under this system been sacrificed at the shrine of torpid luxury and unrelenting avarice.

The species of suffering commonly known by the appellation of corporal punishment is also proscribed by the system above established. Corporal punishment, unless so far as it is intended for example, appears in one respect in a very ludicrous point of view. It is an expeditious mode of proceeding, which has been invented in order to compress the effect of much reasoning and long confinement, that might otherwise have been necessary, into a very short compass. In another view it is not possible to express the abhorrence it ought to create. The genuine propensity of man is to venerate mind in his fellow man. With what delight do we contemplate the progress of intellect, its efforts for the discov-

Marginal notes:

Origin of this policy:

in the corruptness of political institutions:

in the inhumanity of the institutors.

Corporal punishment. Its absurdity.

Its atrociousness.

ery of truth, the harvest of virtue that springs up under the genial influence of instruction, the wisdom that is generated through the medium of unrestricted communication? How completely do violence and corporal infliction reverse the scene? From this moment all the wholesome avenues of mind are closed, and on every side we see them guarded with a train of disgraceful passions, hatred, revenge, despotism, cruelty, hypocrisy, conspiracy and cowardice. Man becomes the enemy of man; the stronger are seized with the lust of unbridled domination, and the weaker shrink with hopeless disgust from the approach of a fellow. With what feelings must an enlightened observer contemplate the furrow of a lash imprinted upon the body of a man? What heart beats not in unison with the sublime law of antiquity, 'Thou shalt not inflict stripes upon the body of a Roman?'[6] There is but one alternative in this case on the part of the sufferer. Either his mind must be subdued by the arbitrary dictates of the superior (for to him all is arbitrary that does not stand approved to the judgment of his own understanding); he will be governed by something that is not reason, and ashamed of something that is not disgrace; or else every pang he endures will excite the honest indignation of his heart and fix the clear disapprobation of his intellect, will produce contempt and alienation, against his punisher.

Duty of reforming our neighbour an inferior consideration in this case.

The justice of coercion is built upon this simple principle: Every man is bound to employ such means as shall suggest themselves for preventing evils subversive of general security, it being first ascertained, either by experience or reasoning, that all milder methods are inadequate to the exigence of the case. The conclusion from this principle is, that we are bound under certain urgent circumstances to deprive the offender of the liberty he has abused. Farther than this no circumstance can authorise us. He whose person is imprisoned (if that be the right kind of seclusion) cannot interrupt the peace of his fellows; and the infliction of farther evil, when his power to injure is removed, is the wild and unauthorised dictate of vengeance and rage, the wanton sport of unquestioned superiority.

When indeed the person of the offender has been first seized, there is a farther duty incumbent on his punisher, the duty of reforming him. But this makes no part of the direct consideration. The duty of every man to contribute to the intellectual health of his neighbour is of general application. Beside which it is proper to recollect what has been already demonstrated, that coercion of no sort is among the legitimate means of reformation. Restrain the offender as long as the safety of the community prescribes it, for this is just. Restrain him not an instant from a simple view to his own improvement, for this is contrary to reason and morality.

Its place described.

Meanwhile there is one circumstance by means of which restraint and reformation are closely connected. The person of the offender is to be restrained as long as the public safety would be endangered by his liberation. But the public safety will cease to be endangered, as soon as his propensities and dispositions have undergone a change. The connection which thus results from the nature of things, renders it necessary that, in deciding upon the species of restraint to be imposed, these two circumstances be considered jointly, how the personal liberty of the offender may be least intrenched upon, and how his reformation may be best promoted.

The most common method pursued in depriving the offender of the liberty he has abused is to erect a public jail in which offenders of every description are thrust together, and left to form among themselves what species of society they can. Various circumstances contribute to imbue them with habits of indolence and vice, and to discourage industry; and no effort is made to remove or soften these circumstances. It cannot be necessary to expatiate upon the atrociousness of this system. Jails are to a proverb seminaries of vice; and he must be an uncommon proficient in the passion and the practice of injustice, or a man of sublime virtue, who does not come out of them a much worse man than he entered.

An active observer of mankind,*[7] with the purest intentions, and who had paid a very particular attention to this subject, was struck with the mischievous tendency of the reigning system, and called the attention of the public to a scheme of solitary imprisonment. But this, though free from the defects of the established mode, is liable to very weighty objections.

It must strike every reflecting mind as uncommonly tyrannical and severe. It cannot therefore be admitted into the system of mild coercion which forms the topic of our enquiry. Man is a social animal. How far he is necessarily so will appear, if we consider the sum of advantages resulting from the social, and of which he would be deprived in the solitary state. But, independently of his original structure, he is eminently social by his habits. Will you deprive the man you imprison, of paper and books, of tools and amusements? One of the arguments in favour of solitary imprisonment is, that it is necessary the offender should be called off from his wrong habits of thinking, and obliged to enter into himself. This the advocates of solitary imprisonment probably believe will be most effectually done, the fewer be the avocations of the prisoner. But let us suppose that he is indulged in these particulars, and only deprived of society. How many men are there that can derive amusement from books? We are in this respect the creatures of habit, and it is scarcely to be expected from ordinary men that they should mould themselves to any species of employment, to which in their youth they were wholly strangers. But he that is most fond of study has his moments when study pleases no longer. The soul yearns with inexpressible longings for the society of its like. Because the public safety unwillingly commands the confinement of an offender, must he for that reason never light up his countenance with

Sidenotes: Modes of restraint.

Indiscriminate imprisonment.

Solitary imprisonment.

Its severity.

---

*   Mr. Howard.

a smile? Who can tell the sufferings of him who is condemned to uninterrupted solitude? Who can tell that this is not, to the majority of mankind, the bitterest torment that human ingenuity can inflict? No doubt a mind truly sublime would conquer this inconvenience: but the powers of such a mind do not enter into the present question.

Its moral effects.

From the examination of solitary imprisonment in itself considered, we are naturally led to enquire into its real tendency as to the article of reformation. To be virtuous it is requisite that we should consider men and their relation to each other. As a preliminary to this study is it necessary that we should be shut out from the society of men? Shall we be most effectually formed to justice, benevolence and prudence in our intercourse with each other, in a state of solitude? Will not our selfish and unsocial dispositions be perpetually increased? What temptation has he to think of benevolence or justice who has no opportunity to exercise it? The true soil in which atrocious crimes are found to germinate, is a gloomy and morose disposition. Will his heart become much either softened or expanded, who breathes the atmosphere of a dungeon? Surely it would be better in this respect to imitate the system of the universe, and, if we would teach justice and humanity, transplant those we would teach into a natural and reasonable state of society. Solitude absolutely considered may instigate us to serve ourselves, but not to serve our neighbours. Solitude, imposed under too few limitations, may be a nursery for madmen and idiots, but not for useful members of society.

Slavery.

Another idea which has suggested itself with regard to the relegation of offenders from the community they have injured, is that of reducing them to a state of slavery or hard labour. The true refutation of this system is anticipated in what has been already said. To the safety of the community it is unnecessary. As a means to the reformation of the offender it is inexpressibly ill conceived. Man is an intellectual being. There is no way to make him virtuous, but in calling out his intellectual powers. There is no way to make him virtuous, but by making him independent. He must study the laws of nature and the necessary consequence of actions, not the arbitrary caprice of his superior. Do you desire that I should work? Do not drive me to it with the whip; for, if before I thought it better to be idle, this will but increase my alienation. Persuade my understanding, and render it the subject of my choice. It can only be by the most deplorable perversion of reason, that we can be induced to believe any species of slavery, from the slavery of the school boy to that of the most unfortunate negro in our West India plantations, favourable to virtue.

Banishment.

A scheme greatly preferable to any of these, and which has been tried under various forms, is that of transportation, or banishment. This scheme under the most judicious modifications is liable to objection. It would be strange if any scheme of coercion or violence were not so. But it has been made appear still more exceptionable than it will be found in its intrinsic nature, by the crude and incoherent circumstances with which it has usually been executed.

Banishment in its simple form is evidently unjust. The citizen whose residence we deem injurious in our own country, we have no right to impose upon another.

Banishment has sometimes been joined with slavery. Such was the practice of Great Britain previously to the defection of her American colonies. This cannot stand in need of a separate refutation.

The true species of banishment is removal to a country yet unsettled. The labour by which the untutored mind is best weaned from the vicious habits of a corrupt society, is the labour, not which is prescribed by the mandate of a superior, but which is imposed by the necessity of subsistence. The first settlement of Rome by Romulus and his vagabonds[8] is a happy image of this, whether we consider it as a real history, or as the ingenious fiction of a man well acquainted with the principles of mind. Men who are freed from the injurious institutions of European government, and obliged to begin the world for themselves, are in the direct road to be virtuous.

Two circumstances have hitherto rendered abortive this reasonable project. First, that the mother country pursues this species of colony with her hatred. Our chief anxiety is in reality to render its residence odious and uncomfortable, with the vain idea of deterring offenders. Our chief anxiety ought to be to smooth their difficulties, and contribute to their happiness. We should recollect that, the colonists are men for whom we ought to feel no sentiments but those of love and compassion. If we were reasonable, we should regret the cruel exigence that obliges us to treat them in a manner unsuitable to the nature of mind; and having complied with the demand of that exigence, we should next be anxious to confer upon them every benefit in our power. But we are unreasonable. We harbour a thousand savage feelings of resentment and vengeance. We thrust them out to the remotest corner of the world. We subject them to perish by multitudes with hardship and hunger. Perhaps to the result of mature reflection banishment to the Hebrides, would appear as effectual as banishment to the Antipodes.[9]

Secondly, it is absolutely necessary upon the principles here explained that these colonists, after having been sufficiently provided in the outset, should be left to themselves. We do worse than nothing, if we pursue them into their obscure retreat with the inauspicious influence of our European institutions. It is a mark of the profoundest ignorance of the nature of man, to suppose that, if left to themselves, they would universally destroy each other. On the contrary, new situations make new minds. The worst criminals when turned adrift in a body, and reduced to feel the churlish fang of necessity, conduct themselves upon reasonable principles, and often proceed with a sagacity and public spirit that might put the proudest monarchies to the blush.

Meanwhile let us not forget the inherent vices of coercion, which present themselves from whatever point the subject is viewed. Colonization seems to be the most eligible of those expedients which have been stated, but it is attended with considerable difficulties. The community judges of a certain individual that his residence cannot be tolerated among them consistently with the general safety. In denying him his choice among other communities do they not exceed their commission? What treatment shall be awarded him, if he return from the banishment to which he was sentenced? – These difficulties are calculated to bring back the mind to the absolute injustice of coercion, and to render us inexpressibly anxious for the advent of that policy by which it shall be abolished.

Recapitulation.   To conclude. The observations of this chapter are relative to a theory, which affirmed that it might be the duty of individuals, but never of communities, to exert a certain species of political coercion; and which founded this duty upon a consideration of the benefits of public security. Under these circumstances then every individual is bound to judge for himself, and to yield his countenance to no other coercion than that which is indispensibly necessary. He will no doubt endeavour to meliorate those institutions with which he cannot persuade his countrymen to part. He will decline all concern in the execution of such, as abuse the plea of public security to the most atrocious purposes. Laws may easily be found in almost every code, which, on account of the iniquity of their provisions, are suffered to fall into disuse by general consent. Every lover of justice will uniformly in this way contribute to the repeal of all laws, that wantonly usurp upon the independence of mankind, either by the multiplicity of their restrictions, or severity of their sanctions.

CHAP. VIII.

OF LAW.

ARGUMENTS BY WHICH IT IS RECOMMENDED.—ANSWER.—LAW IS, I. ENDLESS—PARTICULARLY IN A FREE STATE.—CAUSES OF THIS DISADVANTAGE.—2. UNCERTAIN—INSTANCED IN QUESTIONS OF PROPERTY.—MODE IN WHICH IT MUST BE STUDIED.—3. PRETENDS TO FORETEL FUTURE EVENTS.—LAWS ARE A SPECIES OF PROMISES—CHECK THE FREEDOM OF OPINION—ARE DESTRUCTIVE OF THE PRINCIPLES OF REASON.—DISHONESTY OF LAWYERS.—AN HONEST LAWYER MISCHIEVOUS.—ABOLITION OF LAW VINDICATED ON THE SCORE OF WISDOM—OF CANDOUR—FROM THE NATURE OF MAN.—FUTURE HISTORY OF POLITICAL JUSTICE.—ERRORS THAT MIGHT ARISE IN THE COMMENCEMENT.—ITS GRADUAL PROGRESS.—ITS EFFECTS ON CRIMINAL LAW—ON PROPERTY.

A FARTHER article of great importance in the trial of offences, is that of the method to be pursued by us in classing them, and the consequent apportioning the degree of animadversion to the cases that may arise. This article brings us to the direct consideration of law, which is without doubt one of the most important topics upon which human intellect can be employed. It is law which has hitherto been regarded in countries calling themselves civilised, as the standard, by which to measure all offences and irregularities that fall under public animadversion. Let us fairly investigate the merits of this choice.

The comparison which has presented itself to those by whom the topic has been investigated, has hitherto been between law on one side, and the arbitrary will of a despot on the other. But, if we would fairly estimate the merits of law, we should first consider it as it is in itself, and then, if necessary, search for the most eligible principle that may be substituted in its place.

It has been recommended as 'affording information to the different members of the community respecting the principles which will be adopted in deciding upon their actions.' It has been represented as the highest degree of iniquity, 'to try men by an *ex post facto*[10] law, or indeed in any other manner than by the letter of a law, formally made, and sufficiently promulgated.' Arguments by which it is recommended..

How far it will be safe altogether to annihilate this principle we shall presently have occasion to enquire. It is obvious at first sight to remark, that it is of most importance in a country where the system of jurisprudence is most capricious and absurd. If it be deemed criminal in any society to wear clothes of a particular texture, or buttons of a particular composition, it is natural to exclaim, that it is high time the jurisprudence of that society should inform its members what are the fantastic rules by which they mean to proceed. But, if a society be contented with the rules of justice, and do not assume to itself the right of distorting or adding to those rules, there law is evidently a less necessary institution. The rules of justice would be more clearly and effectually taught by an actual intercourse with human society unrestrained by the fetters of prepossession, than they can be by catechisms and codes. One result of the institution of law is, that the institution once begun, can never be brought to a close. Edict is heaped upon edict, and volume upon volume. This will be most the case, where the government is most popular, and its proceedings have most in them of the nature of deliberation. Surely this is no slight indication that the principle is wrong, and that of consequence, the farther we proceed in the path it marks out to us, the more shall we be bewildered. No talk can be more hopeless than that of effecting a coalition between a right principle and a wrong. He that seriously and sincerely attempts it, will perhaps expose himself to more palpable ridicule, than he who, instead of professing two opposite systems, should adhere to the worst. Answer. Law is, 1. endless: particularly in free states.

There is no maxim more clear than this, Every case is a rule to itself. No action of any man was ever the same as any other action, had ever the same degree of utility or injury. It should seem to be the business of justice, to distinguish the Causes of this disadvantage.

qualities of men, and not, which has hitherto been the practice, to confound them. But what has been the result of an attempt to do this in relation to law? As new cases occur, the law is perpetually found deficient. How should it be otherwise? Lawgivers have not the faculty of unlimited prescience, and cannot define that which is infinite. The alternative that remains, is either to wrest the law to include a case which was never in the contemplation of the author, or to make a new law to provide for this particular case. Much has been done in the first of these modes. The quibbles of lawyers and the arts by which they refine and distort the sense of the law, are proverbial. But, though much is done, every thing cannot be thus done. The abuse would sometimes be too palpable. Not to say, that the very education that enables the lawyer, when he is employed for the prosecutor, to find out offences the lawgiver never meant, enables him, when he is employed for the defendant, to find out subterfuges that reduce the law to a nullity. It is therefore perpetually necessary to make new laws. These laws, in order to escape evasion, are frequently tedious, minute and circumlocutory. The volume in which justice records her prescriptions is for ever increasing, and the world would not contain the books that might be written.

2. uncertain:

The consequence of the infinitude of law is its uncertainty. This strikes directly at the principle upon which law is founded. Laws were made to put an end to ambiguity, and that each man might know what he had to depend

instanced in questions of property.

upon. How well have they answered this purpose? Let us instance in the article of property. Two men go to law for a certain estate. They would not go to law, if they had not both of them an opinion of their success. But we may suppose them partial in their own case. They would not continue to go to law, if they were not both promised success by their lawyers. Law was made that a plain man might know what he had to depend upon, and yet the most skilful practitioners differ about the event of my suit. It will sometimes happen that the most celebrated pleader in the kingdom, or the first counsel in the service of the crown, shall assure me of infallible success, five minutes before another law officer, styled the keeper of the king's conscience, by some unexpected juggle decides it against me. Would the issue have been equally uncertain, if I had had nothing to trust to but the plain, unperverted sense of a jury of my neighbours, founded in the ideas they entertained of general justice? Lawyers have absurdly maintained, that the expensiveness of law is necessary to prevent the unbounded multiplication of suits; but the true source of this multiplication is uncertainty. Men do not quarrel about that which is evident, but that which is obscure.

Mode in which it must be studied.

He that would study the laws of a country accustomed to legal security, must begin with the volumes of the statutes. He must add a strict enquiry into the common or unwritten law; and he ought to digress into the civil, the ecclesiastical and canon law. To understand the intention of the authors of a law, he must be acquainted with their characters and views, and with the various circumstances, to which it owed its rise, and by which it was modified while under deliberation. To understand the weight and interpretation that will be allowed to it in a court of justice, he must have studied the whole collection of records, decisions and precedents. Law was originally devised that ordinary men might know what they had to depend upon, and there is not at this day a lawyer existing in Great Britain, presumptuous and vain-glorious enough to pretend that he has mastered the code. Nor must it be forgotten that time and industry, even were they infinite, would not suffice. It is a labyrinth without end; it is a mass of contradictions that cannot be extricated. Study will enable the lawyer to find in it plausible, perhaps unanswerable, arguments for any side of almost any question; but it would argue the utmost folly to suppose that the study of law can lead to knowledge and certainty.

A farther consideration that will demonstrate the absurdity of law in its most general acceptation is, that it is of the nature of prophecy. Its task is to describe what will be the actions of mankind, and to dictate decisions respecting them. Its merits in this respect have already been decided under the head of promises. The language of such a procedure is, 'We are so wise, that we can draw no additional knowledge from circumstances as they occur; and we pledge ourselves that, if it be otherwise, the additional knowledge we acquire shall produce no effect upon our conduct.' It is proper to observe, that this subject of law may be considered in some respects as more properly belonging to the topic of the preceding book.[11] Law tends no less than creeds, catechisms and tests, to fix the human mind in a stagnant condition, and to substitute a principle of permanence, in the room of that unceasing perfectibility which is the only salubrious element of mind. All the arguments therefore which were employed upon that occasion may be applied to the subject now under consideration.

3. pretends to foretel future events.

Laws are a species of promises:

check the freedom of opinion:

are destructive of the principles of reason.

The fable of Procrustes[12] presents us with a faint shadow of the perpetual effort of law. In defiance of the great principle of natural philosophy, that there are not so much as two atoms of matter of the same form through the whole universe, it endeavours to reduce the actions of men, which are composed of a thousand evanescent elements, to one standard. We have already seen the tendency of this endeavour in the article of murder. It was in the contemplation of this system of jurisprudence, that the strange maxim was invented, that 'strict justice would often prove the highest injustice.'*[13] There is no more real justice in endeavouring to reduce the actions of men into classes, than there was in the scheme to which we have just alluded, of reducing all men to the same stature. If on the contrary justice be a result flowing from the contemplation of all the circumstances of each individual case, if the only criterion of justice be general

---

* *Summum jus summa injuria.*

utility, the inevitable consequence is that, the more we have of justice, the more we shall have of truth, virtue and happiness

Dishonesty of lawyers.

From all these considerations we cannot hesitate to conclude universally that law is an institution of the most pernicious tendency.

The subject will receive some additional elucidation, if we consider the perniciousness of law in its immediate relation to those who practise it. If there ought to be no such thing as law, the profession of a lawyer is no doubt entitled to our disapprobation. A lawyer can scarcely fail to be a dishonest man. This is less a subject for censure than for regret. Men are the creatures of the necessities under which they are placed. He that is habitually goaded by the incentives of vice, will not fail to be vicious. He that is perpetually conversant in quibbles, false colours and sophistry, cannot equally cultivate the generous emotions of the soul and the nice discernment of rectitude. If a single individual can be found who is but superficially tainted with the contagion, how many men on the other hand, in whom we saw the promise of the sublimest virtues, have by this trade been rendered indifferent to consistency or accessible to a bribe? Be it observed, that these remarks apply principally to men eminent or successful in their profession. He that enters into an employment carelessly and by way of amusement, is much less under its influence (though he will not escape), than he that enters into it with ardour and devotion.

An honest lawyer mischievous.

Let us however suppose, a circumstance which is perhaps altogether impossible, that a man shall be a perfectly honest lawyer. He is determined to plead no cause that he does not believe to be just, and to employ no argument that he does not apprehend to be solid. He designs, as far as his sphere extends, to strip law of its ambiguities, and to speak the manly language of reason. This man is no doubt highly respectable so far as relates to himself, but it may be questioned whether he be not a more pernicious member of society than the dishonest lawyer. The hopes of mankind in relation to their future progress, depend upon their observing the genuine effects of erroneous institutions. But this man is employed in softening and masking these effects. His conduct has a direct tendency to postpone the reign of sound policy, and to render mankind tranquil in the midst of imperfection and ignorance. It may appear indeed a paradox to affirm that virtue can be more pernicious than vice. But the true solution of this difficulty lies in the remark, that virtue, such as is here described, is impossible. We may amuse ourselves with enquiring in such instances as this whether theory could not afford us a better system of intellectual progress than the mixed system which takes place in the world. But the true answer probably is, that what we call vice is mere error of the understanding, a necessary part of the gradation that leads to good, and in a word that the course of nature and the course of a perfect theory are in all cases the same.

The true principle which ought to be substituted in the room of law, is that of reason exercising an uncontroled jurisdiction upon the circumstances of the case. To this principle no objection can arise on the score of wisdom. It is not to be supposed that there are not men now existing, whose intellectual accomplishments rise to the level of law. Law we sometimes call the wisdom of our ancestors. But this is a strange imposition. It was as frequently the dictate of their passion, of timidity, jealousy, a monopolising spirit, and a lust of power that knew no bounds. Are we not obliged perpetually to revise and remodel this misnamed wisdom of our ancestors? to correct it by a detection of their ignorance and a condemnation of their intolerance? But, if men can be found among us whose wisdom is equal to the wisdom of law, it will scarcely be maintained, that the truths they have to communicate will be the worse for having no authority, but that which they derive from the reasons that support them.

Abolition of law vindicated on the score of wisdom:

It may however be alledged that, 'if there be little difficulty in securing a current portion of wisdom, there may nevertheless be something to be feared from the passions of men. Law may be supposed to have been constructed in the tranquil serenity of the soul, a suitable monitor to check the inflamed mind with which the recent memory of ills might induce us to proceed to the exercise of coercion.' This is the most considerable argument that can be adduced in favour of the prevailing system, and therefore deserves a mature examination.

of candour:

The true answer to this objection is that nothing can be improved but in conformity to its nature. If we consult for the welfare of man, we must bear perpetually in mind the structure of man. It must be admitted that we are imperfect, ignorant, the slaves of appearances. These defects can be removed by no indirect method, but only by the introduction of knowledge. A specimen of the indirect method we have in the doctrine of spiritual infallibility. It was observed that men were liable to error, to dispute for ever without coming to a decision, to mistake in their most important interests. What was wanting, was supposed to be a criterion and a judge of controversies. What was attempted, was to endue truth with a visible form, and then repair to the oracle we had erected.

from the nature of man:

The case respecting law is exactly parallel to this. Men were aware of the deceitfulness of appearances, and they sought a talisman to guard them from imposition. Suppose I were to determine at the commencement of every day upon a certain code of principles to which I would conform the conduct of the day, and at the commencement of every year the conduct of the year. Suppose I were to determine that no circumstances should be allowed by the light they afforded to modify my conduct, lest I should become the dupe of appearance and the slave of passion. This is a just and accurate image of every system of permanence. Such systems are formed upon the idea of stopping the perpetual motion of the machine, lest it should sometimes fall into disorder.

This consideration must sufficiently persuade an impartial mind that, whatever inconveniences may arise from the passions of men, the introduction of fixed laws cannot be the genuine remedy. Let us consider what would be the operation and progressive state of these passions, provided men were trusted to the guidance of their own discretion. Such is the discipline that a reasonable state of society employs with respect to man in his individual capacity: why should it not be equally valid with respect to men acting in a collective capacity? Inexperience and zeal would prompt me to restrain my neighbour whenever he is acting wrong, and, by penalties and inconveniences designedly interposed, to cure him of his errors. But reason evinces the folly of this proceeding, and teaches me that, if he be not accustomed to depend upon the energies of intellect, he will never rise to the dignity of a rational being. As long as a man is held in the trammels of obedience, and habituated to look to some foreign guidance for the direction of his conduct, his understanding and the vigour of his mind will sleep. Do I desire to raise him to the energy of which he is capable? I must teach him to feel himself, to bow to no authority, to examine the principles he entertains, and render to his mind the reason of his conduct.

The habits which are thus salutary to the individual will be equally salutary in the transactions of communities. Men are weak at present, because they have always been told they are weak, and must not be trusted with themselves. Take them out of their shackles; bid them enquire, reason and judge; and you will soon find them very different beings. Tell them that they have passions, are occasionally hasty, intemperate and injurious, but they must be trusted with themselves. Tell them that the mountains of parchment in which they have been hitherto intrenched, are fit only to impose upon ages of superstition and ignorance; that henceforth we will have no dependence but upon their spontaneous justice; that, if their passions be gigantic, they must rise with gigantic energy to subdue them; that, if their decrees be iniquitous, the iniquity shall be all their own. The effect of this disposition of things will soon be visible; mind will rise to the level of its situation; juries and umpires will be penetrated with the magnitude of the trust reposed in them.

Future history of political justice. Errors that might arise in the commencement.

It may be no uninstructive spectacle to survey the progressive establishment of justice in the state of things which is here recommended. At first it may be a few decisions will be made uncommonly absurd or atrocious. But the authors of these decisions will be confounded with the unpopularity and disgrace in which they have involved themselves. In reality, whatever were the original source of law, it soon became cherished as a cloke for oppression. Its obscurity was of use to mislead the inquisitive eye of the sufferer. Its antiquity served to divert a considerable part of the odium from the perpetrator of the injustice to the author of the law, and still more to disarm that odium by the influence of superstitious awe. It was well known that unvarnished, barefaced oppression could not fail to be the victim of its own operations.

To this statement it may indeed be objected, 'that bodies of men have often been found callous to censure, and that the disgrace, being amicably divided among them all, is intolerable to none.' In this observation there is considerable force, but it is inapplicable to the present argument. To this species of abuse one of two things is indispensibly necessary, either numbers or secrecy. To this abuse therefore it will be a sufficient remedy, that each jurisdiction be considerably limited, and all transactions conduced in an open and explicit manner. – To proceed.

The juridical decisions that were made immediately after the abolition of law, would differ little from those during its empire. They would be the decisions of prejudice and habit. But habit, having lost the centre about which it revolved, would diminish in the regularity of its operations. Those to whom the arbitration of any question was intrusted, would frequently recollect that the whole case was committed to their deliberation, and they could not fail occasionally to examine themselves respecting the reason of those principles which had hitherto passed uncontroverted. Their understandings would grow enlarged, in proportion as they felt the importance of their trust, and the unbounded freedom of their investigation. Here then would commence an auspicious order of things, of which no understanding of man at present in existence can foretel the result, the dethronement of implicit faith and the inauguration of unclouded justice. *Its gradual progress.*

Some of the conclusions of which this state of things would be the harbinger, have been already seen in the judgment that would be made of offences against the community. Offences arguing infinite variety in the depravity from which they sprung, would no longer be confounded under some general name. Juries would grow as perspicacious in distinguishing, as they are now indiscriminate in confounding the merit of actions and characters. *Its effects on criminal law:*

Let us consider the effects of the abolition of law as it respects the article of property. As soon as the minds of men became somewhat weaned from the unfeeling uniformity of the present system, they would begin to enquire after equity. In this situation let us suppose a litigated succession brought before them, to which there were five heirs, and that the sentence of their old legislation had directed the division of this property into five equal shares. They would begin to enquire into the wants and situation of the claimants. The first we will suppose to have a fair character and be prosperous in the world: he is a respectable member of society, but farther wealth would add little either to his usefulness or his enjoyment. The second is a miserable object, perishing with want, and overwhelmed with calamity. The third, though poor, is yet tranquil; but there is a situation to which his virtue leads him to aspire, and in which he may be of uncommon service, but which he cannot with propriety accept, without a *on property.*

capital equal to two fifths of the whole succession. One of the claimants is an unmarried woman past the age of childbearing. Another is a widow, unprovided, and with a numerous family depending on her succour. The first question that would suggest itself to unprejudiced persons, having the allotment of this succession referred to their unlimited decision, would be, what justice is there in the indiscriminate partition which has hitherto prevailed? This would be one of the early suggestions that would produce a shock in the prevailing system of property. To enquire into the general issue of these suggestions is the principal object of the following book.[14]

An observation which cannot have escaped the reader in the perusal of this chapter, is, that law is merely relative to the exercise of political force, and must perish when the necessity for that force ceases, if the influence of truth do not still sooner extirpate it from the practice of mankind.

William Hodgson, *The Case of William Hodgson, Now Confined in Newgate, for the Payment of Two Hundred Pounds, After having Suffered Two Years' Imprisonment on a Charge of Sedition, Considered and Compared with the Existing Laws of the Country* (London: Daniel Isaac Eaton;[1] John Smith, [1796]).[2]

The Case of William Hodgson represents a body of middle-class prison protest literature that linked individual cases of abuse of the legal and penal systems to general political principles rooted in the philosophy of the French, Scottish, English and other Enlightenments of the eighteenth century, as informing discourses of the French Revolution and sympathetic political movements across Europe and in the New World. Parallel to this 'true victim' literature was a body of novels, plays and poems fictionalizing similar instances of oppression, such as William Godwin's *Things As They Are; or, The Adventures of Caleb Williams* (1794), Mary Wollstonecraft's *Maria; or, The Wrongs of Woman* (1798) and Mary Hays's *The Victim of Prejudice* (1799).

Hodgson (1745–1851) had studied medicine in the Netherlands and practised in London, becoming a republican and reformist through reading French Enlightenment philosophers. Like others with similar views, he welcomed the French Revolution, and he joined the London Corresponding Society, a body of working-class and middle-class men devoted to political education and reform. The government and political conservatives regarded such associations as dangerous and harassed and prosecuted leading members. Hodgson was convicted in December 1793 of toasting the French republic and comparing the king to a German hog butcher. Sentenced to two years in Newgate and a fine, he was unable to obtain his release on expiration of his confinement because he still owed the money and so was liable to detention for debt – a form of persecution practised by officials on other dissidents. In prison, Hodgson wrote a political manifesto, *The Commonwealth of Reason* (1795; republished 1820), connected by language and broad political principles to this personal account exemplifying what reformers considered to be the oppressive and corrupt existing system, symbolized by Newgate. On his release, like many erstwhile political agitators Hodgson turned to promoting the public good through information and education, as a writer and publisher. He translated Holbach's materialist *System of*

Nature (4 vols, 1795–6), edited a poetry anthology (1796), issued proposals for a work on the rights of women, compiled an edition of Aesop's fables (1800), wrote a life of Napoleon, assembled a prose anthology (1812), and wrote a French grammar (1819). Among his friends were Benjamin Franklin and the South American politician and general, Simon Bolívar.

To the People of England.

IT may sometimes happen that the fate of an insignificant individual involves that of a whole nation, and it has therefore occurred, that the people, abstracting the punishment from the man, have found it to be for their general safety to examine thoroughly the whole affair, and compare the practice of the law with the theory.

This it was in the case of the great, the virtuous, the immortal SYDNEY,[3] whose execution will remain as indelible a stain on the British annals, as does that of that best and wisest of mankind, the truth-loving SOCRATES,[4] on those of Athens. What friend to humanity but blushes for the conduct of the GRECIANS on that occasion? Or where is the FREEMAN but detests the name of the bloody JEFFERIES,[5] who passed a sentence which the Parliament of England thought it becoming their respect for justice to reverse, inasmuch as they then could, declaring the monster who pronounced the infernal decree, for ever infamous?

I do not pretend that my sentence is of this nature; all I shall say is, that as far as my simple abilities have permitted me to view it, under all its circumstances, it has to *me* the appearance of not being conformable to the laws of my country; and this conviction in my own mind, however erroneous it may prove upon the riper consideration of more enlightened men, has determined me to submit a few words to the attention of the English people. I am further urged to this measure by the reflection, that no man can faithfully discharge that duty which he owes to his fellow-creatures, whenever he withholds from them any thing in which he has rational grounds for supposing their interest to be implicated.

The people of every country have a right to claim the due execution of the law as the price of their obedience to the ruling powers; and it requires no sophistry to discover, that whenever the compact is broken on either side, the parties are, in the eye of REASON, and according to the rules of JUSTICE, liable to an infliction of punishment, suited to the injury which their conduct has done to that society of which they form only integral portions.

In ENGLAND a solemn engagement takes place between the Executive Power and the People, on every renewal of the person who fills the kingly office; which, in the understanding of English jurisprudence, never dies. This engagement is, that the man or woman who exercises the functions of the first Magistrate,[6] 'solemnly promises and swears to govern the people of this kingdom of England, and the dominions thereto belonging, according to the Statutes in Parliament agreed on, and the Laws and Customs of the same; and that he or she will, to his or her power, cause law and justice in mercy to be executed in all his or her judgments.'[7] The obedience of the people to this magistrate is implied, and the consequence is, that whoever violates the law is liable to such punishment as the law so violated has prescribed and directed to be inflicted on the delinquents, without respect of persons; which punishment, although frequently a latitude is left for its mitigation, is always fixed at the maximum: and, in order that arbitrary measures might not obtain, the law has enacted as a fundamental principle, that, in all cases, although the chief executive magistrate be the general prosecutor, in virtue of his office, and all infliction takes place in his name, no condemnation to punishment shall be considered as legal which has not previously received the sanction of a jury, composed of twelve peers of the party arraigned at the bar of national justice.

This sacred principle, I allow, has been abrogated in Revenue concerns;[8] but yet remains entire for every other purpose.

I shall for a moment digress, to shew how jealous the men of England have been of the exact fulfilment of this covenant, a violation of it, on the part of the executive power, having brought a man of the name of CHARLES STUART,[9] who filled the regal chair in the year 1649, to the scaffold, where he lost his head; and obliged another man, of the name of JAMES STUART, who also held the reins of government in the year 1688, to fly from the threatened vengeance of an injured and insulted people; after which fugitation, or as it was then termed, '*abdication*,' in imitation, I suppose, of the ancient Greeks, who, previous to their total subjugation to the arm of tyranny, had softened down every expression in such a manner, that it was difficult to understand their meaning in any thing; and the death of a man of the name of WILLIAM OF NASSAU, who was called in to supply the deficiency, and of a woman named ANNE, of the STUART line; the family of the GUELPHS, then and now exercising the functions of ELECTOR in a certain portion of German territory, called HANOVER, were sent for to perform the duties of first magistrate in the British dominions; and a man of the name of GEORGE GUELPH, was invested with that dignity in the year 1714: the office being declared by the law of this country hereditary, it has remained in this family ever since, who have all sworn the oath hereinbefore quoted.

Having proceeded thus far, I shall, for the clearer elucidation of this business, quote a part of the law of 'this kingdom of England,' as it stood on the day when I received sentence.

First, then MAGNA CHARTA[10] recites, section 24 – 'A free-man shall not be amerced[11] for a small fault, but according to the degree of the fault; and for a great crime, in proportion to the heinousness of it, saving to him his contenement;[12] and after the same manner a merchant, saving to him his merchandize.'

Section 47 – 'We will sell to no man, we will deny to no man, or defer right nor justice.'

Section 64 – 'All unjust and illegal fines, and all amerciaments[13] imposed unjustly, and contrary to the laws of the land, shall be done away.'

Secondly, the BILL OF RIGHTS,[14] recites, section 10 – 'That excessive bail ought not to be required, nor excessive fines imposed, nor cruel and unusual punishments inflicted.'

These are some of the provisions of the law of England, by which the chief magistrate has sworn to govern the people of this realm: few, I think, will deny that the present family would, in all probability, never have been placed at the head of the executive department of this country, had it not been for the violation of these provisions by the STUART family, and the punishments inflicted on that excluded race, in consequence of such transgressions; neither will many be found to contravene the position, that whatever deviates from them, is an infraction that nearly concerns the interest of every man in the country.

I shall, therefore, without ceremony, proceed to state my case, leaving it for those who may peruse it to draw their own conclusions. It is briefly this:

On 9th December, 1793, I was tried at the bar of the Old Bailey, on a charge of having given as a toast, 'THE FRENCH REPUBLIC;' and also, of having 'COMPARED THE KING TO A GERMAN HOG BUTCHER;' of these charges I was found guilty!!!!!! and sentenced '*to be confined in Newgate for Two Years', to pay a Fine of Two Hundred Pounds, and to find securities in Four Hundred Pounds for Two Years' longer;*' and, but whether meant as a second sentence or not I cannot tell, about five minutes after pronouncing the above, the *sapient* Recorder[15] of London added, with a voice that no doubt he intended should be terrific; – '*and farther, that you remain in Prison until the Fine be paid.*'

The two years I have remained in the common gaol of Newgate, conformably to the Sentence, they expired on the 8th December 1795;[16] and I am now detained for the Fine and the Bail, the former of which it is utterly impossible for me to pay, as I am not either worth the money, nor have I any likelihood of being so, at least while my habitation shall be within the stone walls and massive doors of NEWGATE.

I shall not here enter into any investigation of the matters charged against me – I shall only remark, that on my trial I admitted that the words were spoken by me – I never did nor ever shall deny them, if, in the eye of impartial JUSTICE they can be considered as an infringement of the law, I was willing to abide the consequence, and I have so done; for I am neither ashamed of the language I have held, nor do I feel the slightest contrition for having used it: I here, in the face of the whole world, avow my opinion to be, that a REPUBLIC is the best suited to the happiness of the French people. As a MAN it is my right to have an opinion on this and every other subject; and, as an ENGLISHMAN, I never shall be either afraid or ashamed to declare my opinion freely, let the consequence be what it may; but I contend, that in no possible case ought the law to be stretched or rendered subservient to the views of any man or Junto[17] of men, and that whenever it so happens that the law is exceeded, from that moment it ceases to be the cause of an individual, and becomes the cause of the community at large.

Suppose, for a moment, we enquire into the nature of the offence charged against me; what denomination does it bear? Let us ask REASON, and the LAW.

First, then, REASON says it is a DIFFERENCE OF OPINION: upon what? Why, upon the means most likely to promote that which ought to constitute the great end of human actions – the happiness of the human race, living together in society. Is there any breach of MORALITY in this? All rational men must, I think, answer in the negative. Wherefore, then, is it punished? Because administration[18] does not concur in your ideas, and thinks them dangerous. Be it so: – I submit. – But will any man come forward and say, I am not equally zealous for the felicity of my countrymen as the most strenuous defender of the minister, or even as this minister himself? Perhaps there may. To such I answer, ye are mistaken. My aim is to augment the welfare of my native land. We differ in the mode by which it is to be effected; that is all. He imagines, that it will be best atchieved by the misery and slavery of other countries: I think, that the more happiness and liberty other nations enjoy, the greater portion of these blessings will result to ourselves. And for this reason I was, and still am, decidedly of opinion, that the war with the French people,[19] on account of changing their government, is both impolitic and immoral; and calculated to embitter the cup of felicity out of which ENGLISHMEN, in common with the rest of mankind, have an indisputable right to drink.

Of those who think, that no man should be permitted to differ, with impunity from the measures of government, I would ask, What proof have ye, that the methods pursued by the minister are such as tend to render the people happy? Let us look through the nation, and ask the commercial men, if their interest has been promoted by this war? The bankrupt list will give an unequivocal answer to this question. Ask the tender orphans, thrown ruthless on the world; will they speak of the advantages they have reaped? Ask the disconsolate widows – the grey-headed fathers, robbed of the support of their tottering age – the sisters, who mourn the loss of brothers – the fond mother, whose darling son has been violently forced from her maternal arms, to fight in a cause his soul detests, and who only performs the work of blood under the terrors of a mutiny act – ask the starving poor, deprived of employ by the operation of his schemes – or ask the tradesman[20] – the mechanic[21] – the husbandman – the labourer, whose earnings are now inadequate to the purchase of the necessary comforts of life, owing to the multitudinous taxes levied to support his all-destructive plans; – will any of these say, that those opinions to which he so pertinaciously adheres, have added to their quantum of happiness? Look at them! the answer is legibly written in their squalid misery. And will any man deny that these constitute a great majority of the inhabitants of these islands? As well might he affirm, that the pensioned[22] sycophants of government bear the whole expence of the war. Where, then, is the demonstration of the superiority of his opinions? Might it not then be fair in any man to say; your means have been tried, and found sadly deficient to the end proposed: mine have this advantage; they cannot render things worse than they are: they may, perchance, improve their condition: and, having never yet been put into practice, it is not possible to determine, without presumptive arrogance, that they may not, at least, be preferable to those which have regulated your conduct; inasmuch as they will be less destructive. Yours depopulate the earth, without making those who remain happy; mine will not decrease the number of men, if they add not to their felicity.

Next, the LAW says it is a MISDEMEANOUR; that is an offence of less magnitude than SINGLE FELONY.[23] Well, then, what is the punishment for single felony? Why, sometimes, a month's imprisonment; sometimes three months'; sometimes twelve months'; sometimes three years'. But at the expiration of these terms, is there a large sum of money to pay, and securities to find against future attacks on the public? No. – Then is it not a solecism, to make the punishment of that which is by LAW declared to be the smaller offence fall heavier on the individual than that which is attached to the greater? Who will be hardy enough to say no? The swindler, the perjurer, the thief, is transported for seven years; the time expired, he is again at liberty, without any further precaution, to pursue his vicious propensities and to violate every moral duty. While the man, whose only crime is to differ with those in power on the best means of preventing these depredations, and securing the liberty and happiness of his fellow citizens, is to be punished with imprisonment for life, by the dextrous means of imposing upon him a fine which he is unable to pay, and directing him to find sureties which he cannot get! If this be MORALITY, I envy not its possessors.

I wish it to be clearly understood, that I have no intention by this address to ask any favour of the government; on the contrary, were there only the alternative left me, to rot and perish in my prison for want, or to ask indulgence or mercy at the hands of administration, I would prefer the former. – No! – never shall it be said, with truth, that I cringed and stooped, and kissed the rod of oppression; and as I consider myself oppressed by the sentence passed against me, I never can nor shall contemplate the parties concerned in it with any other sensation than that of the most sovereign contempt.

MERCY is only to be asked by criminals – FAVOURS but of those whom we consider worthy our esteem – the government, therefore, has nothing in its power to offer me, except solid and substantial JUSTICE, that I should not deem myself eternally disgraced by accepting.

The Public will, I trust, pardon this intrusion of an individual of no other consequence that as he may be found to have been the medium through which their rights have been invaded.

To give them the opportunity of comparing the administration of the law with its spirit, was the only motive for their being thus addressed by their

Fellow Countryman,

WILLIAM HODGSON.

Newgate,
Feb. 9, 1796.

P. S. I should be wanting in that gratitude which can alone distinguish a mind alive to the generous dictates of sensibility, were I to neglect this opportunity of offering, at the shrine of those noble, respectable, and virtuous characters, who have stood so philanthropically prominent in subscribing a part of the sum necessary to rescue me from perpetual incarceration, that tribute of acknowledgement which flows from a heart whereon their benevolence is deeply engraven. It shall be my task to treasure in my memory their flattering exertions, and my highest ambition to prove myself not unworthy the favours they have conferred. – Should their liberal efforts ultimately fail of success, the remembrance of their kindness cannot fail to alleviate the bitter pangs of imprisonment, as it will be my greatest pride to reflect, that some of the wisest, most celebrated, and best men of the day, came forward to ameliorate my sufferings; and my first care shall be, to teach my infant daughter to lisp forth thanks to the benefactors of her father.

from George Walker, *The Vagabond: A Novel*, 2 vols (London: G. Walker, and Lee and Hurst, 1799), vol. 1, pp. 134–51.

Walker (1772–1847), born in London, was apprenticed to a bookseller at fifteen and opened his own shop at seventeen. He turned to writing and a number of works are attributed to an author of this name, including the Gothic Romances *The Romance of the Cavern* (1792), *The Haunted Castle* (1794), *Cinthelia* (1797), and *The Three Spaniards* (1800); the 'political romances' *Theodore Cyphon* (1796) and *The Vagabond* (1799); a number of songs; *Poems on Various Subjects* (1801); the children's books *Travels of Sylvester Tramper* (1813) and *Adventures of Timothy Thoughtless* (1813) and a poem on the battle of Waterloo (1815).

The Vagabond is an 'Anti-Jacobin' novel, attacking the so-called 'English Jacobins', or supporters of the French Revolution, such as William Godwin, from whose treatise on philosophical anarchism the chapters on crime and punishment are included here. The term 'Jacobin' was used by anti-Revolutionaries to smear people like Godwin by associating them with the violent Jacobin faction of French Revolutionaries. Anti-Jacobin novelists, including Walker, represented Revolutionary sympathizers as self-serving schemers and demagogues, leading the gullible to violence and destruction, as here, where Walker has cast the action back to the time of the infamous Gordon Riots of 1780, when an anti-Catholic mob burned Newgate and other buildings and rampaged for several days. The extract illustrates the continuing importance of Newgate as a symbol in popular and political culture. The same episode would provide a central incident for Charles Dickens's historical novel, *Barnaby Rudge* (1841).

CHAPTER VI.

THE VAGABOND ACHIEVES SEVERAL NOBLE EXPLOITS—AN
UNEXPECTED MEETING IN THE CELLS OF NEWGATE—A
SLIGHT IDEA OF A REVOLUTION.

I DESCENDED amongst the mob, and grasping a pole with blue colours, and the words *No Popery* inscribed upon it, – 'Let us go,' cried I, 'my dear boys. No Popery! Lord George Gordon for ever!' A loud and repeated huzza rent the air, and the prodigious mass of people pressed after me towards Newgate. I was astonished in myself at the change of my fortune: I had but an hour before, been in danger of being stoned by the very mob, that under my commands, would have made no scruple of setting London on fire; but such is always the reward of great talents, in moments of popular commotion; it is then great men are brought forward from obscurity.

Thousands were already assembled before the august deposit of trembling victims: our reinforcement was received with the triumphant shouting of the patriotic bands, who felt the energy of liberty pulsating in every artery. The air was crimsoned with the flames of the jailor's house, and his furniture was cast into a bon fire, which sparkled in my eyes like an offering to the Goddess of Reason,[1] or like that glorious flame which consumed all bonds and engagements when equality was established by Lycurgus at Sparta.[2]

I hastened to second the attack upon this grand fortress, by leading my followers into Newgate Street, where, with sledge-hammers, crows, and iron pallisadoes,[3] we soon broke an entrance into these detestable abodes, where the poor criminals were panting for freedom. With an high ladder and in the fight of thousands, I scaled the lofty walls, exulting as I rose at the glorious prospect before us, and waving my colours as a trophy of conquest.

We soon penetrated into the wards of this almost impenetrable building, which short-sighted politicians might have supposed capable of repulsing an invading army: but the energies of the people are unresistable when determined on emancipation, and *unopposed*.

Fire balls and fire brands soon set the timbers in flames. I ran from one ward to the next, and from cell to cell, sounding the tidings of liberty, and receiving a thousand blessings from those tongues which had too often been turned to curses and execrations. Pick-pockets, cut-purses, shop-lifters, and felons of every denomination, hailed the dawn of returning freedom, and sprang forward to a glorious consummation, helping us to destroy this dreadful tomb to all who despise the laws, and claim the natural privilege of dividing property.

The flames raged and ran with rapidity among the thick oak planking, which cracked with the noise of thunder; the smoke and heat was nearly suffocating, and many in their over eagerness to clear the dungeons, fell martyrs in the glorious cause. In a cell which I had nearly overlooked, I found a miserable wretch half naked upon the ground. I had broke open his door with an iron crow, and the first object he saw was a tremendous blaze of light, which proceeded from the opposite wainscot on fire. – He had long heard the shouts of exulting thousands, and the burstings of the fire. – 'Heaven and earth,' cried he, 'is the day of judgement come? Or have I sunk alive into hell? Are you a fiend?' said he, staring wildly, and starting from me. 'Are you come to pitch me into everlasting flames?

To say truth, my figure was not a little hideous, for I was covered with all sorts of dirt, swelled in my face from the different bruises I had received, and streaked with blood from a cut in my head by the falling of a plank: but how was I astonished to perceive by the light of the fire, the great Stupeo,[4] the wonderful philosopher,[5] in chains.

'Exult,' cried I, 'you are revenged, my master, my tutor, liberty has reared her standard on these walls, and the fabric of selfish tyranny is tumbling about our ears. Haste, get these irons off, and join in the noble cause of liberty and man.'

Stupeo immediately started up, uttering incoherent expressions of joy. I hurried him from the chamber of his studies into the press yard, where his detestable fetters were knocked off, and being refreshed with a large goblet of wine from the cellars of the jailor, we went into the street to enjoy the exultation of the surrounding multitude, and the most tremendous sight that can well be conceived; a sight which awed the military into inaction, and struck the magistrates into a panic of the most pusillanimous nature: but cowardice is ever allied to terror, and I stood considering how best to exert the force now in action, that the greatest blow might be struck to the present detestable system of monopolised property.

Part of the army of patriots remained upon the walls, and dancing round the ruins to prevent every attempt at extinguishing the flames: the rest followed Stupeo and myself, who encouraged them to persevere and be free. The crowd would have destroyed Langdale's, a large distillers, in Holborn, but I represented that this was a paultry business, when we had yet to open the doors of so many jails to the liberation of our brethren; besides, we had already near four hundred felons amongst us, and the augmentation of this force was a grand point, for who could fight for freedom like those who had experienced its loss.[6]

As we proceeded, every passenger was stopped and plundered, and from every house was collected, two or three times over, considerable contributions. I would have remonstrated, but a fellow, who had been confined on a charge of murder, and whom I had liberated, swore he would rip me up alive if I attempted to prevent it; and indeed, though his argument was not in the line of reason,[7] Stupeo reconciled me to the practice.

'In revolutions and public commotions,' said he, 'no man in Athens[8] was allowed to be neutral: every man who does not fight for us, ought to be considered as against us; and if we follow the new philosophy, we should shew no mercy to those who support the system of despotism.'*

Having liberated the prisoners in Clerkenwell,[9] our forces were divided to objects of less moment. That division under our direction, proceeded to Lord Mansfield's;[10] and there liberty and rational principles received a complete triumph over all regular order. The musty records of precedents, cases and law, made a fire to warm the people they had so long enslaved: I own I wished to have preserved several works of curiosity and art, but Stupeo would not suffer a thing to be taken. – 'Let them all perish together,' said he, 'we have yet remaining too much of art to be happy; let us not stain the cause with the appearance of selfishness.'

'But why then,' said I, 'are we to plunder the poor inhabitants? Surely it were better to supply ourselves from stores like these?

'No,' answered he, 'can you not perceive that the destruction of property must be the grand aim; from those who have little we must take that little, and the hoards of affluence must be utterly destroyed: as long as one single cart-load of property remains in any country, there will be no genuine equality.'

From these ever-memorable exploits, I and Stupeo, with several select leaders, retired to an obscure public-house, to contrive and arrange the undertakings of the ensuing night. I already fancied myself as great as the immortal John the Painter.[11]

At our meeting, several foreigners of *liberal principles*[12] were present. A plan was proposed for organizing the body of the people, and urging them to throw off the yoke of dependence, and declare themselves free. A paper, titled the *Thunderer*,† was drawn up by Stupeo, which he hoped would kindle the glow of enthusiasm, and awake the people to their rights.

The prisons were condemned to destruction, that none of our brave followers might be deprived of their liberty. The New-river water[13] was to be cut off, that we might have the town effectually at command, and compel those weak and obstinate people who were afraid of joining our standard. The Museum[14] we fixed upon as a good deposit for stores after all that trumpery[15] should be burnt, which gives edge to a childish employment of time. The toll-houses on the bridge we condemned, because bridges ought to be built without subjecting individuals to expence. The East-India warehouses and the Custom-house,[16] we considered as large lumber rooms for monopolising property that belonged to every body.

The Tower and the Bank[17] were two grand objects, behind which we could entrench in defiance of the troops, which were drawing towards the town from

---

*   An article in the Jacobin Creed.
†   SEE THE POLITICAL MAGAZINE FOR 1780.

every quarter; and indeed, our plans were too extensive and grand for me to detail in minutiæ.

In the attack upon the Bank I was severely wounded in the hand by a musket bullet, for there the soldiers recovered their thirst for blood, and fired upon the innocent people, who were gloriously fighting for liberty. We determined there to conquer or die, being strongly reinforced by the Borough[18] patriots, who had burnt the toll-houses on the bridge in their rout. To place a just sense of our cause before them, an horse, loaded with the chains of Newgate, was driven through the crowd in place of colours, and every breast beat with throbs of vengeance at the sight.

A body of savages on horseback cut down several with their swords, and the infantry made use of their infernal muskets, which severely galled the unarmed patriots. It was shocking to hear the tremendous roar of exulting rage sink after every platoon, as if it was exhausted.

Poor Stupeo, who stood beside me, encouraging a band of those whom the ignorant call felons, to an attack on the infantry, with iron spikes and bottles, received a shot that laid him dead beside me. The mob, who now began to faint from the unequal contest, trampled over him and hurried me along with them. I endeavoured to rally them, and one of them dashed a link into my face, which I returned by shooting him with a pistol, for I had found a very good pair in an house we had gutted, and nothing could be more proper than turning the weapons of tyrants against themselves.

I was confounded at the fickle disposition of a mob, which can only arise from their want of instruction, and so long as what is called civil order and police exists, I very much fear the people will never unanimously rise: but, however, truth is making a rapid progress, and it must irresistibly break forth into a glorious day.[19]

The mob would have executed summary justice upon me for the murder of the link-bearer, had I not escaped through the narrow streets into Holborn, where Langdale's (the distiller) was on fire. Torrents of spirits ran in the streets, and being played upon the neighbouring houses for water, augmented the danger and the flames.

Here the military destroyed a great number of patriots, who were dancing round the fire, or tumbling the furniture out at the windows; while many others fell victims to the half-rectified[20] spirits which ran in torrents through the streets.

I saw clearly it was a lost cause, for want of a more regular organization, and I lamented that we had not made better use of the time allowed by the timidity (they called it humanity) of the government; we should then have reduced the whole city to an heap of ashes, from which liberty, like a phœnix, would have arisen in ten-fold splendor: the mass of luxury and of wealth would have been annihilated, and the partial injury individuals might have received would have been amply compensated by the new order of things which must have arisen.

It would have been, as Stupeo often said, talking of revolutions like the fermentation of anarchy, which from all the rage of lust, of revenge, of murder, of cruelty, of rapine, and unheard-of distress, sinks into a glorious and heart-soothing calm.*

Indeed, nothing could be more dreadfully great than the appearance of London on that glorious night. The large body of fire issuing from the different conflagrations of the Fleet Prison, King's Bench,[21] toll-houses on Black-Friars Bridge, Mr. Langdale's two immense warehouses full of spirits, and a vast number of small fires, together with the illuminations, which of themselves would have rendered the streets as light as day, all ascending into the air, and consolidating together, formed an atmosphere of flames, impressing the mind of the spectator with an idea as if not only the whole metropolis was burning, but all nations yielding to the final consummation of all things:[22] but how much greater must have been the sight, amidst which even the soul of a modern philosopher might tremble, would it have been to see the flames chasing the distracted people from street to street; to see the enemies of liberty perishing in heaps before the burning sword of retributive justice; to see the rage of lust despoiling those disdainful beauties, whose love heretofore was only to be won by cringing; to see trembling tyrants biting the dust, and drinking their own blood as it mingled in the kennels; to hear amidst all this uproar, the thunder of cannons, the whistling of bullets, the clashing of swords, the tumbling of houses, the groans of the wounded, the cries of the conquerors, and see, amidst the blazing and red-hot ruins, the sons of Freedom and Liberty waving the three-coloured banners, dropping with the blood of their enemies, and hailing the everlasting Rights of Man!!![23]

Ah! how dear must such a scene be to the *friends of liberty* and *universal man;* nor should the paultry consideration of two or three thousand being massacred to satiate private revenge be taken into the account of so great, so immortal a consideration.

---

*   Pain and Godwin on Revolutions and Anarchy.

from John Aldini, *An Account of the Late Improvements in Galvanism, with a Series of Curious and Interesting Experiments Performed before the Commissioners of the French National Institute, and Repeated Lately in the Anatomical Theatres of London ... To Which Is Added an Appendix, Containing the Author's Experiments on the Body of a Malefactor Executed at Newgate* (London: Cuthell and Martin; and John Murray, 1803), pp. 189–203.

Giovanni Aldini (1782–1834) was professor of physics at the University of Bologna, Italy, and nephew of Luigi Galvani, proponent of Galvanism, or the theory that electricity was the vital element in animals. Galvanists thought that electrical experiments would help reveal the nature of life, and would have practical benefits such as enabling revival of dead persons. Aldini and others demonstrated this idea through experiments, often held in public, applying electrical charges to dead animals and humans. Whatever the scientific justification for or value of these experiments, such new discoveries, often demonstrated with considerable showmanship to a paying public, were topics of considerable popular interest and entertainment at the time. England offered particular opportunities for such researches because by law the corpses of executed murderers could be turned over to anatomists for use in instruction or experiments, as both a further deterrent to crime and a public benefit. This practice was, however, deeply resented by the lower classes, whose members made up most of the criminals at any time, and who were fiercely dependent of what they saw as their rights over their own bodies – a fact Aldini refers to at the beginning of the extract here. Famously, Aldini's experiments, along with those of other 'Galvanists', interested the poet Percy and the novelist Mary Shelley, and the latter incorporated the theme into her novel, *Frankenstein; or, The Modern Prometheus* (1818). The subject of the experiments, an artisan named John Foster or Forster, was executed in 1803 for murdering his wife and daughter. The account of his trial is in the *Proceedings of the Old Bailey* and an account of his trial and execution, included here, was published in the next version of the famous *Newgate Calendar* (1810).

APPENDIX. NO. I.

An Account of the Experiments performed by J. ALDINI *on the Body of a Malefactor executed at Newgate Jan. 17th 1803.*

INTRODUCTION.

THE unenlightened part of mankind are apt to entertain a prejudice against those, however laudable their motives, who attempt to perform experiments on dead subjects; and the vulgar[1] in general even attach a sort of odium to the common practice of anatomical dissection. It is, however, an incontrovertible fact, that such researches in modern times have proved a source of the most valuable information, in regard to points highly interesting to the knowledge of the human frame, and have contributed in an eminent degree to the improvement of physiology and anatomy. Enlightened legislators have been sensible of this truth; and therefore it has been wisely ordained by the British laws, which are founded on the basis of humanity and public benefit, that the bodies of those who during life violated one of the most sacred rights of mankind, should after execution be devoted to a purpose which might make some atonement for their crime, by rendering their remains beneficial to that society which they offended.[2]

In consequence of this regulation, I lately had an opportunity of performing some new experiments, the principal object of which was to ascertain what opinion ought to be formed of Galvanism[3] as a means of excitement in cases of asphyxia and suspended animation. The power which exists in the muscular fibre of animal bodies some time after all other signs of vitality[4] have disappeared, had before been examined according to the illustrious Haller's[5] doctrine of irritability;[6] but it appeared to me that muscular action might be excited in a much more efficacious manner by the power of the Galvanic apparatus.

In performing these experiments, I had another object in view. Being favoured with the assistance and support of gentlemen eminently well skilled in the art of dissection, I proposed, when the body should be opened, to perform some new experiments which I never before attempted, and to confirm others which I had made above a year ago on the bodies of two robbers decapitated at Bologna.

To enlarge on the utility of such researches, or to point out the advantages which may result from them, is not my object at present. I shall here only observe, that as the bodies of valuable members of society are often found under similar circumstances, and with the same symptoms as those observed on executed criminals; by subjecting the latter to proper experiments, some speedier and more efficacious means than any hitherto known, of giving relief in such cases, may, perhaps, be discovered. In a commercial and maritime country like Britain, where so many persons, in consequence of their occupations at sea, on canals, rivers, and in mines, are exposed to drowning, suffocation, and other accidents, this object is of the utmost importance in a public view, and is entitled to every encouragement.

Forster,[7] on whose body these experiments were performed, was twenty-six years of age, seemed to have been of a strong, vigorous constitution, and was executed at Newgate on the 17th of January 1803. The body was exposed for a whole hour in a temperature two degrees below the freezing point of Fahrenheit's thermometer; at the end of which long interval it was conveyed to a house not far distant, and, in pursuance of the sentence, was delivered to the College of Surgeons.[8] Mr. Keate,[9] master of that respectable society, having been so kind as to place it under my direction, I readily embraced that opportunity of subjecting it to the Galvanic stimulus, which had never before been tried on persons put to death in a similar manner: and the result of my experiments I now take the liberty of submitting to the public.

Before I conclude this short introduction, I consider it as my duty to acknowledge my obligations to Mr. CARPUE,[10] lecturer on anatomy, and Mr. HUTCHINS, a medical pupil, for the assistance they afforded me in the dissection. I was also much indebted to Mr. CUTHBERTSON,[11] an eminent mathematical instrument maker, who directed and arranged the Galvanic apparatus. Encouraged by the aid of these gentlemen, and the polite attention of Mr. KEATE, I attempted a series of experiments, of which the following is a brief account.

EXPERIMENT I.

ONE arc being applied to the mouth, and another to the ear, wetted with a solution of muriate of soda (common salt), Galvanism was communicated by means of three troughs combined together, each of which contained forty plates of zinc, and as many of copper. On the first application of the arcs the jaw began to quiver, the adjoining muscles were horribly contorted, and the left eye actually opened.

EXPERIMENT II.

On applying the arc to both ears, a motion of the head was manifested, and a convulsive action of all the muscles of the face: the lips and eyelids were also evidently affected; but the action seemed much increased by making one extremity of the arc to communicate with the nostrils, the other continuing in one ear.

EXPERIMENT III.

The conductors being applied to the ear, and to the rectum, excited in the muscles contractions much stronger than in the preceding experiments. The action of those muscles furthest distant from the points of contact with the arc was so much increased as almost to give an appearance of re-animation.

EXPERIMENT IV.

In this state, wishing to try the power of ordinary stimulants, I applied volatile alkali[12] to the nostrils and to the mouth, but without the least sensible action: on applying Galvanism great action was constantly produced. I then administered the Galvanic stimulus and volatile alkali together; the convulsions appeared to be much increased by this combination, and extended from the muscles of the head, face, and neck, as far as the deltoid. The effect in this case surpassed our most sanguine expectations, and vitality might, perhaps, have been restored, if many circumstances had not rendered it impossible.

EXPERIMENT V.

I next extended the arc from one ear to the biceps flexor cubiti,[13] the fibres of which had been laid bare by dissection. This produced violent convulsions in all the muscles of the arm, and especially in the biceps and the coraco brachialis[14] even without the intervention of salt water.

EXPERIMENT VI.

An incision having been made in the wrist, among the small filaments of the nerves and cellular membrane, on bringing the arc into contact with this part, a very strong action of the muscles of the fore-arm and hand was immediately perceived. In this, as in the last experiment, the animal moisture was sufficient to conduct the Galvanic stimulus without the intervention of salt water.

EXPERIMENT VII.

The short muscles of the thumb were dissected, and submitted to the action of the Galvanic apparatus, which induced a forcible effort to clench the hand.

EXPERIMENT VIII.

The effects of Galvanism in this experiment were compared with those of other stimulants. For this purpose, the point of the scalpel was applied to the fibres, and even introduced into the substance of the biceps flexor cubiti without producing the slightest motion. The same result was obtained from the use of caustic volatile alkali[15] and concentrated sulphuric acid. The latter even corroded the muscle, without bringing it into action.

EXPERIMENT IX.

Having opened the thorax and the pericardium,[16] exposing the heart *in situ*,[17] I endeavoured to excite action in the ventricles,[18] but without success. The arc was first applied upon the surface, then in the substance of the fibres, to the carneæ columnæ,[19] to the septum ventriculorum,[20] and lastly, in the course of the nerves by the coronary arteries, even with salt water interposed, but without the slightest visible action being induced.

EXPERIMENT X.

In this experiment the arc was conveyed to the right auricle,[21] and produced a considerable contraction, without the intervention of salt water, but especially in that part called the appendix auricularis: in the left auricle scarcely any action was exhibited.

EXPERIMENT XI.

Conductors being applied from the spinal marrow to the fibres of the biceps flexor cubiti, the gluteus maximus,[22] and the gastrocnemius, separately, no considerable action in the muscles of the arm and leg was produced.

EXPERIMENT XII.

The sciatic nerve[23] being exposed between the great trochanter of the femur[24] and the tuberosity of the ischium,[25] and the arc being established from the spinal marrow to the nerve divested of its theca,[26] we observed, to our astonishment, that no contraction whatever ensued in the muscles, although salt water was used at both extremities of the arc. But the conductor being made to communicate with the fibres of the muscles and the cellular membrane, as strong an action as before was manifested.

EXPERIMENT XIII.

By making the arc to communicate with the sciatic nerve and the gastrocnemius muscle,[27] a very feeble action was produced in the latter.

EXPERIMENT XIV.

Conductors being applied from the sciatic to the peronæal nerve,[28] scarcely any motion was excited in the muscles.

EXPERIMENT XV.

The sciatic nerve being divided about the middle of the thigh, on applying the conductors from the biceps flexor cruris[29] to the gastrocnemius, there ensued a powerful contraction of both. I must here observe that the muscles continued excitable for seven hours and a half after the execution. The troughs were frequently renewed, yet towards the close they were very much exhausted. No doubt, with a stronger apparatus we might have observed muscular action much longer; for, after the experiments had been continued for three or four hours, the power of a single trough was not sufficient to excite the action of the muscles: the assistance of a more powerful apparatus was required. This shows that such a long series of experiments could not have been performed by the simple application of metallic coatings. I am of opinion that, in general, these coatings, invented in the first instance by Galvani, are passive. They serve merely to conduct the fluid pre-existent in the animal system; whereas, with the Galvanic batteries of Volta,[30] the muscles are excited to action by the influence of the apparatus itself.

FROM the above experiments there is reason to conclude:

I.

That Galvanism exerts a considerable power over the nervous and muscular systems, and operates universally on the whole of the animal œconomy.[31]

II.

That the power of Galvanism, as a stimulant, is stronger than any mechanical action whatever.

III.

That the effects of Galvanism on the human frame differ from those produced by electricity communicated with common electrical machines.

IV.

That Galvanism, whether administered by means of troughs, or piles,[32] differs in its effects from those produced by the simple metallic coatings employed by Galvani.

V.

That when the surfaces of the nerves and muscles are armed with metallic coatings, the influence of the Galvanic batteries is conveyed to a greater number of points, and acts with considerably more force in producing contractions of the muscular fibre.

VI.

That the action of Galvanism on the heart is different from that on other muscles. For, when the heart is no longer susceptible of Galvanic influence, the other muscles remain still excitable for a certain time. It is also remarkable that the action produced by Galvanism on the auricles is different from that produced on the ventricles of the heart, as is demonstrated in Experiment the tenth.

VII.

That Galvanism affords very powerful means of resuscitation in cases of suspended animation under common circumstances. The remedies already adopted in asphyxia, drowning, &c. when combined with the influence of Galvanism, will produce much greater effect than either of them separately.

TO conclude this subject, it may be acceptable to the reader to have a short but accurate account of the appearances exhibited on the dissection of the body, which was performed with the greatest care and precision by Mr. Carpue. 'The blood in the head was not extravasated,[33] but several vessels were prodigiously swelled, and the lungs entirely deprived of air; there was a great inflammation in the intestines, and the bladder was fully distended with urine. In general, upon viewing the body, it appeared that death had been immediately produced by a real suffocation.'[34]

It may be observed, if credit can be given to some loose reports, which hitherto it has not been in our power to substantiate, that after this man had been for some time suspended, means were employed with a view to put an end to his sufferings.[35]

From the preceding narrative it will be easily perceived, that our object in applying the treatment here described was not to produce re-animation, but merely to obtain a practical knowledge how far Galvanism might be employed as an auxiliary to other means in attempts to revive persons under similar circumstances.

In cases when suspended animation has been produced by natural causes, it is found that the pulsations of the heart and arteries become totally imperceptible; therefore, when it is to be restored, it is necessary to re-establish the circulation throughout the whole system. But this cannot be done without re-establishing also the muscular powers which have been suspended, and to these the application of Galvanism gives new energy.

I am far from wishing to raise any objections against the administration of the other remedies which are already known, and which have long been used. I would only recommend Galvanism as the most powerful mean[36] hitherto discovered of *assisting* and increasing the efficacy of every other stimulant.

Volatile alkali, as already observed, produced no effect whatever on the body when applied alone; but, being used conjointly with Galvanism, the power of the latter over the nervous and muscular system was greatly increased: nay, it is possible that volatile alkali, owing to its active powers alone, might convey the Galvanic fluid to the brain with greater facility, by which means its action would become much more powerful in cases of suspended animation. The well known method of injecting atmospheric air ought not to be neglected; but here, likewise, in order that the lungs may be prepared for its reception, it would be proper previously to use Galvanism, to excite the muscular action, and to assist the whole animal system to resume its vital functions. Under this view, the experiments of which I have just given an account, may be of great public utility.

It is with heartfelt gratitude that I recall to mind the politeness and lively interest shown by the members of the College of Surgeons in the prosecution of these experiments. Mr. Keate, the master, in particular proposed to make comparative experiments on animals, in order to give support to the deductions resulting from those on the human body. Mr. Blicke[37] observed that on similar occasions it would be proper to immerse the body in a warm salt bath, in order to ascertain how far it might promote the action of Galvanism on the whole surface of the body. Dr. Pearson[38] recommended oxygen gas to be substituted instead of the atmospheric air blown into the lungs. It gives me great pleasure to have an opportunity of communicating these observations to the public, in justice to the eminent characters who suggested them, and as an inducement to physiologists not to overlook the minutest circumstance which may tend to improve experiments that promise so greatly to relieve the sufferings of mankind.

from Sir Richard Phillips, *A Letter to the Livery of London, Relative to the Views of the Writer in Executing the Office of Sheriff* (London: T. Gillet, 1808), pp. 76–101.

Phillips (1767–1840) was born and educated in London and tried school-teaching and small business in Leicester before turning to bookselling, which he expanded to include printing, print-selling, a commercial lending library and a newspaper. A republican and radical reformer, as well as a vegetarian, he was eventually imprisoned for selling Tom Paine's *Rights of Man*. When a fire destroyed his business he took the insurance money and set up business in St Paul's Churchyard, London, centre of English publishing. He associated with reformists and published a wide range of books and periodicals, including the important *Monthly Magazine*. He was a pioneer of cheap and instructive literature for the lower and middle classes, and the taint of his radicalism remained with him. His business prospered, however, and in 1807 he was elected one of the sheriffs of the City of London, and knighted as a consequence in 1808. While in office he put the debtors' prisons under better management and established a relief fund for debtors, as well as writing several books on the duties of a sheriff and the prisons, including the one excerpted here. After this period his business declined but he remained active in publishing and writing about his eccentric scientific views. He retired to Brighton in 1823.

A Letter to the Livery of London addresses the 'Livery' as the governing body of the City of London, composed of the various 'livery' companies, or chartered bodies originally derived from various guilds of artisans and merchants of London. The book reports Phillips's and others' observations on law enforcement and prisons while he was sheriff of London, and was widely influential in stimulating public discussion and parliamentary action in these areas. Building on the work of earlier humanitarian reformers such as William Eden and John Howard (included here) and drawing on his long commitment to social and political reform, Phillips's *Letter* helped set the terms for legal and penal reform over the next few decades and is a classic of reform journalism and advocacy of this time and on these issues, with such books as H. Grey Bennet's *Letter to the Common Council and Livery of the City of London, on the Abuses Existing in Newgate* (1818) and Thomas Fowell Buxton's *Inquiry, whether Crime and Mis-*

ery Are Produced or Prevented, by Our Present System of Prison Discipline (1818),
also included here. The selection from Phillips's *Letter* here deals particularly
with Newgate Prison, which Phillips represents as approaching the slave ships of
the period in unnecessary horrors of over-crowding and abuse.

THE PRISONS.

I AM now about to treat of that subject which is not only of the greatest import-ance, in connection with the office of Sheriff,[1] but which is that department of the Sheriff's duty about which the feelings of my own heart were the most deeply interested when I entered into office. I had long viewed these places, particularly the crowded prisons of the metropolis, as mansions of misery, in which were often united in the same person the whole dismal catalogue of human woes. The deprivation of liberty alone is a heartrending punishment to every human being, however luxuriously he may be provided for in his prison, and however little may be the effect of that imprisonment on his dearest connexions. But in the prisons of the metropolis, there are superadded to the overwhelming idea of personal restraint, the loathsomeness of the place, the immediate contact of kindred mis-eries; want of food and every other necessary; loss of character; dread of future consequences; wives, children, and frequently aged parents, involved in one common ruin, and plunged in shame and wretchedness; the prisoner suffering at the same instant the complicated tortures of despair, remorse, and unavailing repentance! How inglorious, and how cowardly, to add to such a load of misery by unnecessary privations and reproaches! How interesting the task of lighten-ing it by attentions, by charities, by administering pity, and by infusing hope!

Such were the impressions and the feelings under which I entered into the office of Sheriff, and by which I am still influenced, after twelve months inter-course with the prisons, notwithstanding the cabals and misrepresentations of which I have found myself the object.

I feel, at the same time, as strongly as any man can do, that crimes must be punished, and that indolence and vice ought not to be suffered to put industry and virtue out of countenance. Yet to the good and virtuous the victims of crime and imprudence are nevertheless fit objects of compassion; – we may detest the crime, yet pity the criminal, and relieve the distresses of his innocent dependants. Besides, crimes vary in their degree, and criminals in moral turpitude. The prin-ciples of the laws of Draco,[2] which punished every crime alike, and which spared the life of no offender, are no longer recognized. The law, stern as it is, admits of degrees and modifications of punishment; and ought individual feelings to be less susceptible of such distinctions? Ten persons may have committed, under different circumstances, the same crime, and the law will adjudge them all to death; but our feelings will assign to them ten different degrees of criminality; and if we were inclined to punish one or two according to the letter of the law, we should be disposed to mitigate the punishment of three or four, and probably to pity, relieve, and pardon the others. This case, though put hypothetically, proves the excellency of that branch of our constitution which places in the Crown the power of dispensing with the severity of the penal laws; and it also affords a foundation to that code of charity and humanity which I am desirous to establish in favour of those who, from defect of education, from necessity, or from other circumstances, have offended against the laws. The sacred maxims, '*Judge not lest ye be judged,*' and '*Let him that is guiltless cast the first stone,*'[3] emphatically teach us the same just and liberal principle of looking towards our offending and fallen fellow-creatures with charity and compassion.

The prisons of the metropolis which are properly under the jurisdiction of the Sheriff's of London are NEWGATE, which is the *county gaol*; the POULTRY COMPTER, and the GILTSPUR-STREET COMPTER, which are *the city prisons*, each Sheriff taking cognizance of that Compter which is the nearest to his residence; and LUDGATE, which is a prison for debtors who are citizens of London.

In Newgate are generally confined from FOUR TO FIVE HUNDRED PRISONERS, male and female, consisting of county debtors, – felons convicted and unconvicted, – state prisoners, – and fines,[4] or those sentenced to a definite term of imprisonment. I learn that there have been as many as SEVEN HUNDRED AND FIFTY confined at one time in this prison, but the average of the present year has not exceeded four hundred and twenty, although at particular times there have been as many as five hundred and fifty.

When it is considered that Newgate is situated in the centre of this great metropolis, that its external dimensions are only 105 yards by 40 yards, and that not more than a fourth of this superficies can be occupied as dwellings for the prisoners, it will at once be obvious that mere personal restraint is not the greatest evil suffered by those who have the unhappiness to be detained within its walls; I understand that when the number of prisoners exceeds six hundred, fevers have generally begun to shew themselves; and in 1789, when the number amounted to nearly eight hundred, a contagious fever broke out, and carried off five or six of the prisoners per day. It is the fashion, in considering this subject, to talk only of the health of the metropolis, and no doubt this is a very serious and important object; but is it not a thousand times more shocking to lodge persons by restraint in a focus of disease, – to keep them in an atmosphere of pestilence, whence they have no power to escape?

Thank God that, during our year, we have not been visited by this calamity; and if the system of cleanliness which we have enforced be persevered in, contagion, I hope, will never be generated *while the prisoners do not exceed* 600. I verily believe, however, and I am confirmed in the opinion by medical men, that contagious disorders are very likely to shew themselves, and consequently to endanger the health of the metropolis as often *as the number shall exceed SEVEN HUNDRED*.

To convey a general idea of Newgate to those who never inspected its interior: I shall suppose my reader to be standing in the Old Bailey,[5] opposite the

Keeper's house. The corner of the building which adjoins Newgate-street and the Old Bailey, is the debtors' yard, and behind it is a narrow slip, called the condemned yard. Behind the Keeper's house, extending a little to the right and left, are three yards appropriated to the felons; and the right hand corner, next to the Sessions House,[6] is the yard for state, or superior prisoners, and behind it is a slip, called the women's yard; these two yards corresponding exactly with those at the other end of the prison.

Retaining the present separations of the different classes of the prisoners, I am not aware that much better economy can be made of the interior of this building; but it will appear that the building itself is in its size altogether inadequate to the purposes to which it is appropriated.

As all the yards are fully as crowded as they ever ought to be, and as the present separation is not so great as is necessary, no addition can be made to the prisoners in the yards the least crowded by drafts from those that are over crowded. The latter are the DEBTORS' YARD and the WOMEN-FELONS' YARD, classes of prisoners who must obviously be kept by themselves. To convey a just idea of these yards, and of the wards in which the prisoners live and lodge, the most apt comparison will be the engraved representation of a slave ship, which, a few years ago, was circulated through England with so much effect. When the prisoners lie down on their floors by night, there must necessarily, at least in the women's wards, be the same bodily contact, and the same economical disposition of heads and legs, as were represented in that drawing of the deck of a slave ship.[7]

When I entered into office, and for a considerable time afterwards, there were in the women-felons' yard, in Newgate, from one hundred to one hundred and thirty women; at the commencement of a Sessions there are generally the latter number, and there have been instances of the numbers being from one hundred and sixty to one hundred and seventy! These occupy two wards 37 feet by 13, and there is also a sick ward, and three little rooms, called the Master's side. One hundred and twenty-five women will then be divided in the following manner:

Master's side - - - - - - -	7
Sick ward* - - - - - - -	8
Small end rooms - - - - - -	10
Two wards (50 each) - - - - -	<u>100</u>
- - - - - -	125

Fifty-six and sixty have however been known to be in one of these wards.

The wards being thirteen feet wide, admit, by night, of two rows to lie down at once in a length of thirty-seven feet; that is to say, twenty-five or thirty women, as it may be, in a row, having each a breadth of eighteen inches by her

---

* Generally women with young children, or with some infirmity.

length! They have told me, that at times when the place is much crowded, all the interstices of the floor are covered, and two or three lie in breadth in the space afforded by the difference between the thirteen feet, the breadth of the room, and the length of two women. To convey an accurate idea on this subject, I have sketched, on the following page, the dimensions of the room, and have shewn how fifty women are obliged to lie in this manner on the bare boards, leaving not more than eighteen inches in breadth to each!

PLAN OF A FEMALE WARD IN NEWGATE,

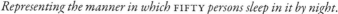

Representing the manner in which FIFTY *persons sleep in it by night.*

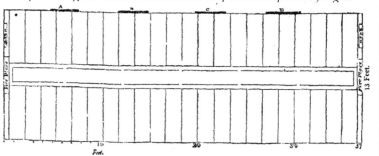

In presenting to you the condition of these unhappy women in so striking a manner, my sole object is to demonstrate, that the prison of Newgate ought to be enlarged. I am not aware that, in the present construction of the prison, any new dispositions can be made of the prisoners in general, which can give the females more room than they now have. I ought also to remark, that the yard in which they are at liberty to walk during the day, is altogether as inadequate for air and exercise, as are the wards for the purpose of sitting and sleeping!*

The deplorable condition of human creatures, huddled together in the manner described, requires neither amplification nor exaggeration to produce such an effect on the minds of my fellow citizens, as cannot fail to procure them relief. Let it, however, be remembered, that the prisoners thus treated are not robust men, inured to hardships and severities of climate: but FEMALES, many of them

---

*   At the back of these wards is an airy passage, leading to the bail-docks, which is admirably calculated to afford a free current of air to this crowded place, and additional space for exercise to these prisoners. The external wall is, however, so low, that they cannot be left in this passage without the hazard of an escape. I took much pains, at different times, to procure the use of this place for these women, and have frequently had the satisfaction to see them taking the air in it, in the presence of a turnkey. Should not the prison be enlarged, on a proper scale, I recommend it as a temporary measure to the Committee of City Estates, to consider of the means of making this passage secure; so that the door into it may be constantly left open. Perhaps also two additional wards might be extended from the south-east corner into the yard which faces the Sessions House.

of delicate habits, UNCONVICTED as well as convicted, and charged with the smaller, as well as the greater offences!

In regard to the Debtors' yard, the other crowded part of this prison, I observe, that the average number rather exceeds two hundred; the whole of whom are crowded into a corner of Newgate not fifty yards square. The number of wards in which these two hundred persons reside is sixteen, two of which are occupied by females; and to these is attached a slip of yard, separated from the mens' court by a wall. Three of the mens' wards are provided with small cabins for sleeping; but in all the open wards the prisoners are obliged to place their beds, if they have any, indiscriminately, or lie down on the floor where they can find a space. In these common wards, the situation of the debtors is little better, in point of room, than that of the women on the felons' side. For example, in the ward called the long ward, 35 feet in length and 13 feet in breadth, there are usually 30 prisoners, which affords a breadth of only 26 inches to each prisoner, allowing space for door-ways and fire-places. The horrors of such a situation, during the night, when the prisoners are all locked up in their respective wards, especially during the heat of summer, may be better conceived than described. Persons who have broken no moral law, most of them the victims of misfortune, and many of them confined for exceedingly small debts, depressed by want, and every privation, are thus thrown together, without regard to their difference of education, to their various habits of life, or to their degrees of religious or moral feeling!*

I may in this place so far digress, as to observe, that no imprisoned debtors in this country are, generally speaking, in so bad a condition as those who are arrested in the county of Middlesex, and who are unable to pay the fees of removal to the King's Bench.[8] The space allotted to them in the county gaol of Newgate is altogether unequal to so vast a number of persons. Instead of numerous small rooms, as in the King's Bench, and Fleet Prisons,[9] each for the accommodation of one or two persons, Newgate has only sixteen rooms, in each of which from ten to thirty debtors are, by night and day, obliged to live in common. The ties of domestic affection are thus necessarily severed during their confinement, as their wives and children can visit them only in these public wards, and that during the day. They are also subjected, without any sufficient reason that I am aware of, to the general coercion of the prison, and like the felons are locked up in their respective wards: whereas, in the above-named prisons, the prisoners are allowed to walk in the open yard at all hours, by day and night.† And further, there is no

---

*   It seems inconsistent with the liberal spirit of our laws to commit a debtor to a *criminal* prison, especially to one so proverbially characterised in that respect as is Newgate. If Physicians' College cannot be procured, may it not be worth the while of the County of Middlesex to build a separate prison for debtors?

†   As two watchmen are always stationed on the top of Newgate during the night, I conceive no escape could take place in consequence of conceding such an indulgence to the debtors in Newgate. But it must be the result of the *united* opinions of both the Sheriffs and the Gaoler.

provision for granting rules, either permanently or by the day. I ought, however, to state an advantage which distinguishes a *county gaol* from those prisons – that every prisoner is allowed fourteen ounces of bread per day; and in Newgate the debtors partake of certain allowances of meat, made, according to ancient custom, by the Sheriffs.*

Having, as I humbly conceive, proved that Newgate is too small to accommodate its usual number of prisoners (whether we consider the character of humanity for which this nation has always been distinguished, or the security of the Metropolis from contagious diseases), it maybe expected that I should be prepared to point out some practicable means by which it may be enlarged. Those means are fortunately in our power. Adjoining to the back part of Newgate is the spacious building of Physicians College,[10] which I have been informed is about to be disposed of. This place would, with little expense of alteration, make an excellent prison for county debtors, communicating by a door with Newgate. In that case, there would be an additional yard for the women-felons, and the proper and necessary separation might be made among the different classes of offenders, who are now mixed indiscriminately in this inadequate prison.

In the want of room is comprehended most of the evils which belong to this prison. Separation[11] cannot be effected among the different classes of the prisoners while there is only one small yard, containing but two wards, for every description of women, and while there are but two common yards for every description of men. Those only committed for trial; those actually convicted; hardened and first offenders; the profligate and the evil disposed; the innocent and the guilty ought not to be mingled indiscriminately together. While this is the practice, Newgate is necessarily little better than a public seminary of vice, and for teaching the art of thieving: I have been shocked to see boys of thirteen, fourteen, and fifteen, confined for months together in the same yard with hardened and incorrigible offenders. Those committed for first or for small offences, are constantly placed within this same sphere of moral contamination. I have attempted all that could be done with two yards; and for many months the transports[12] and respites from death have been kept in one yard, while the fines and persons committed for trial have been kept in the other. Of course, however, amidst persons of these two general descriptions, would be found every shade of depravity; and it would have afforded me the highest satisfaction to be able, if I had possessed the means, to divide the convicts into two classes, and the others into three, consisting of old offenders, of first offenders, and of boys.

Among the women, all the ordinary feelings of the sex are outraged by their indiscriminate association. The shameless victims of lust and profligacy are

---

* In the Appendix will be found, a Letter from an intelligent Debtor in Newgate, detailing the miseries of the debtors, and pointing out the means of improving the law of debtor and creditor, so that these long imprisonments might be spared.

placed in the same chamber with others, who, however they may have offended the law in particular points, still preserve their respect for decency and decorum. In immediate contact with such abandoned women, other young persons are compelled to pass their time between their commitment and the sessions,[13] when, of course, it often happens that the bill is not found against them by the Grand Jury, or they are acquitted by the Petty Jury![14] Separation, in any degree, would be useful; and I think it possible, at some expence, even in the present size of the building, to divide these females into their two distinct classes; but if the city of London should make the addition to the prison which I have previously suggested, all the degrees of separation may take place, which are necessary to the comfort and reform of these unhappy persons.

I could fill a volume with details of the objects which have claimed the attention of myself and my Colleague[15] in our visits to this prison. For many months I persevered in the plan of walking through it, generally accompanied by him, twice in every week; labouring incessantly to promote among the prisoners a spirit of cleanliness, to diminish the wretchedness of their situation, and by attentions of every kind to inspire them with a sense of gratitude to us, and of consequent contrition for their offences. Experience on this subject convinces me that kindness to persons in this forlorn and destitute condition, operates more effectually in bringing offenders to a proper sense of their faults, than any system of indiscriminate punishment. When I came into office, I was illiberally told, that those whose pardon we might obtain would return to our custody before the twelve months expired; that I should find that kindness would be thrown away upon this description of persons; and that the iron hand of the law was the only means of dealing with them. Doubtless these cautions might be just, when applied to professional thieves and hardened offenders; but such are not the majority of those who are brought to the bar of the Old Bailey. By far the greater number of these are first, or young offenders, who are often sincerely repentant for the crime they have committed, and are operated upon by every motive that can influence a human being, never to be found again in the same situation. Our laws annex a given punishment to a given crime, and do not distinguish between these classes of offenders; the tears of parents and relatives are, therefore, generally shed in vain for young persons who have committed a crime under the impulse of a momentary temptation, or with the thoughtlessness which characterizes their age. To such persons, and to others possessing similar claims to compassion, I have never hesitated to listen with an ear of sensibility; and I have never been ashamed to plead their cause to those who have had the power to relieve them, whatever might be the degree of apathy and official coldness with which I have been received.

I have already said enough to prove that no man is a more zealous friend than I am to the principles of the English constitution. The English Parliament would, however, meet every year, and pass new laws in vain, if that constitution could possibly have provided for every difficulty and malpractice that might arise. It is one of the glories of the constitution, that it provides such means for perpetually renovating itself; and that the details of our laws and institutions are not unalterable, like those of the Medes and Persians.[16] Parliament has more than once sanctioned the idea that our criminal code ought to be submitted to a general revision, and I heartily concur with it in the same opinion. The changes of manners among the people, of the value of money, and of the public policy of the government, require the radical alteration of many of our penal statutes, and the whole of them require to be systematized, and reduced to a compendious and intelligible form:* such a work, performed on liberal and humane principles, would confer more glory on the present age than all the naval and military achievements of which we have the happiness to boast. I should then hope to see the penal laws, after the manner of those of the DIVINE LEGISLATOR (who has set us the example), posted in all our churches and public buildings, and so addressed to the capacity of every class, as that no man should have reason to plead his ignorance of the consequences of any crime as an excuse for his having committed it.

I have already remarked, that, at the time we entered into office, the women's yard in Newgate was more crowded than it has since been with prisoners of every class. Among them were about fourscore under sentence of transportation, a few for life, some for fourteen years, and a considerable majority for seven years. As of course there existed among these persons as many different shades of criminality and moral turpitude, as there were persons; and as the wards were crowded in an alarming degree, and many of these persons had remained in this school of vice for nearly two years, we felt it our duty to submit all the circumstances to the Secretary of State. The official course, as may be supposed, was to relieve the crowded state of the prison, by ordering the preparation of ships to convey the whole to Botany Bay.[17] Giving way to my natural feelings, and to the solicitations which had been addressed to me by many of these poor women, I was led to enquire particularly into their cases, and the result was a recommendation, on the part of myself and colleague, of about fifty of them to pardon, or to a mitigation of punishment.

---

*   I have read somewhere, that there exist on our statute-book no less than two hundred and fifty offences which are punishable with death! Being determined to publish a small tract, under the title of 'Hints for Petty Jurymen,' similar to those which I have printed in the Appendix to Grand Jurymen, I requested an eminent, and very Learned Barrister, to make out for me a complete table of crimes and punishments, which I intended to annex to such a pamphlet: I find, however, that he considers his task as almost impracticable, and that this section of my tract is likely to be much larger than all the other sections put together.

from Andrew Knapp and William Baldwin, *Criminal Chronology; or, The New Newgate Calendar; Being Interesting Memoirs of Notorious Characters, Who Have Been Convicted of Outrages on the Laws of England, during the Seventeenth Century, and Brought Down to the Present Time, Chronologically Arranged* ..., 5 vols (London: [J. and J. Cunder;] Nutall, Fisher, and Dixon, Liverpool, 1810), vol. 4, pp. 182–9.

This entry represents the vast body of criminal biographies known under the general title 'the Newgate Calendar' and collected in a succession of editions with that or similar or different titles. Related to these biographies and in many cases the source of them is that body of criminal biography known as 'last dying words and confessions', probably going back to the beginnings of printing, at least. These were sold individually as broadsheets or chapbooks and aimed to capitalize on the crowds gathered to witness public hangings, or were hawked about the streets as a form of news. By the early eighteenth century, collections of the criminal lives, often based on trial reports, were sold in parts and bound volumes.

These included (the list is not exhaustive!) *The Tyburn Calendar; or, Malefactors Bloody Register* (1705); *A Compleat Collection of Remarkable Tryals of the Most Notorious Malefactors* (4 vols. 1718–21); Alexander Smith's *A Compleat History of the Lives and Robberies of the Most Notorious Highwaymen, Foot-Pads, Shop-Lifts and Cheats, of Both Sexes* (5th edn, 3 vols, 1719); Charles Johnson's often reprinted *A General and True History of the Lives and Adventures of the Most Famous Highwaymen, Murderers, Street-Robbers, etc.* (1734); John Osborn's *Lives of the Most Remarkable Criminals Condemned and Executed for Murder, Highway Robberies, Housebreaking, Street Robberies and other Offences* (1735); *The Bloody Register: A Select and Judicious Collection of the Most Remarkable Trials, for Murder, Treason, Rape, Sodomy, Highway Robbery, Pyracy, House-Breaking, Perjury, Forgery, and Other High Crimes and Misdemeanours; from the Year 1700, to the Year 1764 Inclusive,* (4 vols, 1764); *The Newgate Calendar; or, Malefactors' Bloody Register* (3 vols, 1774–8); William Jackson's *The New and Complete Newgate Calendar; or, Villany Displayed in All Its Branches* (6 vols, 1795), issued in parts; Andrew Knapp and William Baldwin's *The New Newgate*

Calendar; Being Interesting Memoirs of Notorious Characters, Who Have Been Convicted of Outrages on the Laws of England, During the Seventeenth Century, Brought Down to the Present Time (5 vols, 1809–13), apparently issued in 100 24-page to 32-page parts, and republished in 123 16-page parts (4 vols, 1824–8); *The Annals of Crime, and New Newgate Calendar* (1833–4), issued in 53 weekly parts; *Martin's Annals of Crime; or, New Newgate Calendar and General Record of Tragic Events: Including Ancient and Modern Modes of Torture, etc.* (1836–8), issued in at least 108 parts; George Theodore Wilkinson and others, *The Newgate Calendar Improved: being Interesting Memoirs of Notorious Characters Who Have Been Convicted of Offences against the Laws of England, during the Seventeenth Century, and Continued to the Present Time* (6 vols, 1836); and Camden Pelham, *The Chronicles of Crime; or, The New Newgate Calendar* (1841). The list continues through the nineteenth and into the twentieth century. Several 'Newgate calendars' are online as page images or in full text, though the latter have not been edited and have apparently not been proofread.

In view of the availability of the Newgate Calendars, just one 'life' is presented here, that of George Foster (or Forster), hanged on 18 January 1803 for murder of his wife and daughter. This example is included here to illustrate the genre at large and also for its connection with the issue of disposal of the hanged man's body for anatomical experiment, a longstanding practice formalized by legislation in 1752, and deeply resented by the lower classes. The experiments on Foster's body by the Italian scientist and showman Giovanni Aldini are described by the latter in *An Account of the Late Improvements in Galvanism* (1803), excerpts from which are included here. Aldini's book and Foster's body entered literature a few years later as one of the sources of Mary Shelley's Gothic-political romance, *Frankenstein; or, The Modern Prometheus* (1818).

GEORGE FOSTER,

EXECUTED AT NEWGATE, JANUARY 18, 1803, FOR THE MURDER OF HIS WIFE
AND CHILD, BY DROWNING THEM IN THE PADDINGTON CANAL; WITH A
CURIOUS ACCOUNT OF GALVANIC EXPERIMENTS ON HIS BODY.[1]

THE unfortunate George Foster, whose conviction, as stated by the Lord Chief Baron[2] in charging the jury, was most entirely upon circumstantial evidence, was put upon his trial, on the horrid charge above mentioned, at the Old Bailey, January 14, 1803.[3]

The first witness was Jane Hobart, the mother of the deceased,[4] who stated, that she lived in Old Boswell-court,[5] and that for some time back, the deceased and her infant[6] lived with her, but that she generally went on the Saturday nights to stay with the prisoner, who was her husband; that she left the witness for that purpose a little before four o'clock, on the evening of Saturday the 4th of December, taking her infant child with her; and that she never heard of her from that time until she was found drowned in the Paddington canal.[7] The prisoner had four children by her daughter – the one above alluded to, another was dead, and two were in the workhouse at Barnet.[8]

Joseph Bradfield, at whose house the prisoner lodged, in North-row, Grosvenor-square,[9] saw the deceased with him on the Saturday night of the 4th of December, and they went out together about ten o'clock on the Sunday morning. The prisoner returned by himself between eight and nine o'clock at night, which did not appear remarkable, as the deceased was not in the habit of sleeping there, except on the Saturday nights. This witness did not consider them to be on very good terms, arising, as he believed, from the deceased's wishing to live with the prisoner: she used to call at his lodgings once or twice in the week, besides the Saturdays, on which nights she always waited to get some money from him. On the Sunday following, the prisoner and another person went with the witness to see his mother at Highgate,[10] and on their return, the prisoner asked if his wife had been at his lodgings; but which on his cross-examination, he admitted might arise from his being surprised at her not coming as usual.

Margaret Bradfield, wife of the last witness, corroborated his testimony, with the addition, that on the Wednesday she saw the child which had been found in the Paddington canal, and which she was positive was the same that the deceased had taken out with her on the Sunday morning.

Eleanor Winter, who kept what was usually called the Spotted Dog, but which is now called the Wellbourne Green tavern, between two or three miles from Paddington, along the canal, swore that she perfectly recollected the prisoner's coming to her house on the morning of the 5th of December, with a woman, and a child with him: they staid at her house, where they had some beef-steaks, beer, and two glasses of brandy, till near one o'clock. – While they were there, she observed the woman to be crying, and heard her say, she had been three times there to meet a man who owed her husband some money, and that she would come no more. This witness had seen the body of the woman that was found in the canal, and she was certain of its being the same woman, who was with the prisoner at her house, on the above morning.

John Goff, waiter at the Mitre tavern, about two miles further on the canal, related, that the prisoner, with a woman and child, came to their house some time about two o'clock on Sunday the 5th of December: they had two quarterns of rum, two pints of porter, and went away about half past four. The Mitre is situated on the opposite side of the canal to the towing path;[11] and when the prisoner and the woman went away, they turned towards London on that side of the canal, though there was no path-way, and it would take them at least a quarter of an hour to get to the first swing-bridge[12] to cross over; there was a way to pass through a Mr. Fillingham's grounds, which would lead them to the Harrow-road, and which he believed to be much nearer than the side of the canal: but then persons going that way got over the hedge, and he perceived, from the kitchen window where he was standing, the prisoner and the woman go beyond that spot. They had no clock in the house, but he had no doubt as to the time, from its being very near dark when they went away. On being questioned by one of the jury, he said, that besides the place to which he alluded for passing through Mr. Fillingham's ground, there was a gate about one hundred yards further on, and to which the prisoner and woman had not got over when he lost sight of them.

Hannah Patience, the landlady of the Mitre tavern, recollected seeing the prisoner there on Sunday, Dec. 5, with a woman and child: they had been there a good while before she saw them. She served them with a quartern of rum, and they had a pint of beer after it. They left the Mitre about half past four, as far as she could judge from the closing of the evening, for they had no clock. – She also recollected Sarah Daniels coming to buy a candle to take to her master: they were then gone, and as they were going out, the woman threw her gown over the child, saying, 'This is the last time I shall come here.' – In a minute or two the prisoner came back to look for the child's shoe, which could not be found, and then followed the woman. This witness took no particular notice of them, but thought she had seen them at her house two or three times before.

Sarah Daniels, aged nine years, was examined by the court as to her knowledge of the sanctity and solemnity of an oath, and being satisfied with her answers, she was sworn, and said, that she met a man following a woman with a child, walking by the canal, as she was going from Mr. Fillingham's to the Mitre; and from the circumstance of its being near their time of drinking tea, she was sure that it could not want much of five o'clock.

Charles Weild, a shopmate of the prisoner, stated, that he met him a little after six o'clock, in Oxford street, on the evening of Sunday the 5th of December, and that they went together to the Horse Grenadier public-house, where they continued till after eight.

John Atkins, a boatman employed on the canal, said, about eight o'clock, on the morning of Monday, he found a child's body, under the bow of the boat, at the distance of a mile from the Mitre; that in consequence of some directions which he received from Sir Richard Ford,[13] he dragged the canal for three days, on the last of which, close under the window of the Mitre, he pulled up the woman's body, entangled in a loose bush. He had before then felt something heavy against the drag, at near 200 yards towards London from the house, but he could not ascertain whether that was the body or not.

Sir Richard Ford produced the examination which the prisoner signed at Bow-street Office, after being questioned as to its being the truth, and cautioned as to the consequences it might produce. The account which the prisoner then gave, was as follows:

'My wife and child came to me on Saturday se'nnight,[14] about eight o'clock in the evening, and slept at my lodgings that night. The next morning, about nine or ten o'clock, I went out with them, and walked to the New Cut[15] at Paddington: we went to the Mitre tavern, and had some rum, some porter, and some bread and cheese. Before that we had stopped at a public-house, near the first bridge, where we had some beef-steaks, and some porter; after which she desired me to walk further on by the cut; so I went with her. I left her directly I came out of the Mitre tavern, which was about three o'clock, and made the best of my way to Whetstone,[16] in order to go to Barnet, to see two of my children, who are in the workhouse there. I went by the bye lanes, and was about an hour and a half walking from the Mitre to Whetstone. When I got there, I found it so dark that I would not go on to Barnet, but came home that night. I have not seen my wife nor child since; I have not enquired after them, but I meant to have done so to-morrow evening, at Mrs. Hobart's. – I came home from Whetstone that evening between seven and eight o'clock; I saw no person in going to Whetstone, nor did I stop any where, at any public-house, or elsewhere, *except the Green Dragon, at Highgate where I had a glass of rum.** My wife had a black gown on, and a black bonnet; the child had a straw bonnet, and white bed-gown;[17] my wife was a little in liquor.[18]

(Signed) 'GEORGE FOSTER.
'Witness, Richard Ford,
December 27, 1802.'

---

* The words in Italic were interlined, and the latter part added at the prisoner's request.

'Prisoner says, before he left the Mitre Tavern, on the said Sunday his wife asked the mistress of the inn, whether she could have a bed there that night, which the prisoner afterwards repeated; that she asked half a crown[19] for one, which the prisoner and his wife thought too much, and the latter said she would go home to her mother.'

The latter part of this was positively contradicted by the landlady, not a single word about a bed having passed between her and the deceased.

W. Garner, a shopmate of the prisoner, called upon him at the Brown Bear, in Bow-street, after he was taken into custody; to whom the prisoner said, he was as innocent of the charge as the child unborn; and that if any one would come forward to say, or swear, that he was at such a place on that night, he should be cleared immediately. The witness understood him to refer to the Green Dragon, at Highgate.

James Bushwell,[20] a coach-maker, declared, that the prisoner was one of the most diligent men he had ever employed;[21] and, from his having so very good an opinion of him, on hearing he was in custody, he went himself to see if he could render him any service; that upon his making that offer, the prisoner replied, that if it was not too much trouble, he would thank him to go to the Green Dragon, at Highgate, and enquire if a man was not there on the Sunday evening, who had a glass of rum, and asked after Mrs. Young: with which he complied; but, as the rules of evidence would not admit of Mr. Bushwell's giving the answer,

Elizabeth Southall, who keeps the Green Dragon, was called, who said she perfectly recollected such a circumstance, but she could not exactly say what Sunday it was; and, besides, the man who did so inquire, had a woman with an infant in her arms with him, and to whom the man turned round and said, that is Bradfield's mother.

The prisoner made no other defence than contradicting some parts of the evidence of the waiter at the Mitre.

George Hodgson, Esq. coroner of the county,[22] and before whom an inquest on these bodies had been taken, said there was not the least mark of violence upon either the woman or the child; of course, the report of the latter's arm being broken was false.

From being acquainted with the place, he was examined particularly as to the way through Mr. Fillingham's grounds, and which he affirmed to be far the nearest way to town. He could not undertake to say what the actual distance from the Mitre to Whetstone was, but he was sure it could not be less, even through the lanes and over the fields, than seven or eight miles, and about the same distance from Whetstone to town.

Four witnesses were called to the prisoner's character, who all agreed in his being an industrious and humane man.

The Chief Baron, in summing up to the jury, said, that this was a case which almost entirely depended upon circumstances, but in some cases that might be best evidence, as it was certainly the most difficult, if not impossible, to fabricate; they, however, would deliberately judge how far they brought the charge home to the prisoner, so as not to leave a doubt on their minds before they pronounced him guilty. His lordship noticed some inconsistencies in the written paper which the prisoner had signed, observing, that in one part of the story the prisoner was contradicted by several witnesses; and that it was scarcely to be presumed that the prisoner could walk such a distance (from the Mitre to Whetstone) in so short a time. There were other traits of the story which were also extremely dubious. The learned judge then went through the whole of the evidence, remarking thereon as he proceeded; and the jury, after some consultation, pronounced a verdict of guilty.

This was no sooner done, than the recorder[23] proceeded to pass sentence upon the prisoner; which was, that he be hanged by the neck, next Monday morning, until he be dead, and that then his body be delivered to be anatomized, according to the law in that case made and provided.[24]

This unfortunate malefactor was executed pursuant to his sentence, January 18, 1803. At three minutes after eight, he appeared on the platform, before the debtor's door,[25] in the Old Bailey, and after passing a short time in prayer with Dr. Ford, the Ordinary[26] of Newgate, the cap was pulled over his eyes, when the stage falling from under him, he was launched into eternity.

When he ascended the platform, his air was dejected in the extreme, and the sorrow manifested in his countenance, depicted the inward workings of a heart conscious of the heinous crime be had committed, and the justness of his sentence.

From the time of his condemnation to the moment of his dissolution, he had scarcely taken the smallest nourishment, which operating with a tortured conscience, had so enfeebled him, that he was obliged to be supported from the prison to the gallows, being wholly incapable of ascending the staircase without assistance. Previous to his decease, he fully confessed his having perpetrated the horrible crime for which he suffered: – confessed that he had unhappily conceived a most inveterate hatred for his wife, that nothing could conquer, and determined him to rid himself and the world of a being he loathed: – acknowledged also, that he had taken her twice before to the Paddington canal, with the wicked intent of drowning her, but that his resolution had failed him, and she had returned unhurt; and even at the awful moment of his confession, and the assurance of his approaching dissolution, he seemed to regret more the loss of his infant, than the destruction of the woman he had sworn to cherish and protect. He was questioned, as far as decency would permit, if jealousy had worked him to the horrid act; but be made no reply, except saying, that 'he ought to die;' and dropped into a settled and fixed melancholy, which accompanied him to his last moments. He was a decent looking young man, and wore a brown great coat, buttoned over a red waistcoat, the same in which be was tried.

He died very easy;[27] and, after hanging the usual time, his body was cut down, and conveyed to a house not far distant, where it was subjected to the Galvanic process, by Professor Aldini,[28] under the inspection of Mr. Keate, Mr. Carpue, and several other professional gentlemen. M. Aldini, who is the nephew of the discoverer of this most interesting science, showed the eminent and superior powers of Galvanism to be far beyond any other stimulant in nature. On the first application of the process to the face, the jaw of the deceased criminal began to quiver, and the adjoining muscles were horribly contorted, and one eye was actually opened. In the subsequent part of the process, the right hand was raised and clenched, and the legs and thighs were set in motion.* Mr. Pass, the beadle[29] of the Surgeons' Company,[30] having been officially present during this experiment, was so alarmed, that he died soon after his return home of the fright. Some of the uninformed byestanders thought that the wretched man was on the eve of being restored to life. This, however, was impossible, as several of his friends who were under the scaffold, had violently pulled his legs, in order to put a more speedy termination to his sufferings. The experiment, in fact, was of a better use and tendency. Its object was to show the excitability of the human frame, when this animal[31] electricity is duly applied. In cases of drowning or suffocation, it promises to be of the utmost use, by reviving the action of the lungs, and thereby rekindling the expiring spark of vitality. In cases of apoplexy, or disorders of the head, it offers also most encouraging prospects for the benefit of mankind.

The professor, we understand, had made use of galvanism also in several cases of insanity,[32] and with complete success. It is the opinion of the first medical men, that this discovery, if rightly managed and duly prosecuted, cannot fail to be of great, and perhaps, as yet, unforeseen, utility.

---

* An experiment was made on a convict, named Patrick Redmond, who was hanged for a street-robbery, on the 24th of February, 1767, in order to bring him to life. It appears that the sufferer had hung twenty-eight minutes, when the mob rescued his body, and carried it to an appointed place, where a surgeon was in attendance to try the experiment *bronchotomy*, which is an incision in the wind-pipe, and which in less than six hours, produced the desired effect. A collection was made for the poor fellow, and interest made to obtain his pardon. For it will be remembered, that the law says, the condemned shall *hang until he is dead*; consequently men, who like Redmond, recovered, are liable to be again hanged up until they are dead. [Knapp and Baldwin's footnote]

[Daniel Defoe and another], *The Fortunes and Misfortunes of Moll Flanders, Who Was Born in Newgate, and During a Life of Continued Variety for 60 Years Was 17 Times a Whore, 5 Times a Wife, Whereof Once to Her Own Brother, 12 Years a Thief, 11 Times in Bridewell, 9 Times in New Prison, 11 Times in Wood-street Compter, 6 Times in the Poultry Compter, 14 Times in the Gatehouse, 25 Times in Newgate, 15 Times Whipt at the Cart's Tail, 4 Times Burnt in the Hand, Once Condemned for Life, and 8 Years a Transport in Virginia; at Last Grew Rich, Lived Honest, and Died a Penitent* (London: J. Pitts, n.d.[1]).[2]

Defoe's novel, originally published in 1722, was a well-known female-rogue narrative, or fictitious criminal autobiography, but like other picaresque fiction of the earlier eighteenth century, it began to fall out of favour with the middle-class reading public by the late eighteenth and early nineteenth centuries. Originally over 400 pages long, by the mid-eighteenth century it had been converted from first-person to the more usual popular third-person narrative form and cut down to eight pages; this version was reprinted several times, including the version here, published by Pitts, perhaps the most famous or infamous publisher and distributor of street literature in the early nineteenth century. By now, Defoe's crime fiction had hooked on to the popularity of true-crime literature, collected and represented by the successive editions generically known as the 'Newgate Calendar'. Though never nearly as popular as Defoe's *Robinson Crusoe*, which was a European and transatlantic bestseller, by the 1810s *Moll Flanders* had acquired a street life of its own, with chapbook editions at Newcastle, Paisley and Edinburgh, as well as London and in the United States. In the formation of a British 'national' literary canon in the early nineteenth century, Defoe's fiction remained problematic, as it dealt with criminality and sexuality to an extent disapproved of by many or most in the middle-class reading public. This chapbook version of *Moll Flanders* is included here, along with the street ballad 'Newgate Walls', as an example of the cheapest, most widely circulated forms of Newgate narrative, printed for a readership who cared nothing for authorship, literary origins, or middle-class standards of taste, morality and lawfulness.

THE subject of the following history, is one of the most surprising accounts that ever was wrote of any of the female sex. It is of the one Moll Flanders, whose unhappy parents having abandoned all honour, were committed to Newgate, in the reign of James the First, for breaking open the house of a goldsmith, in Lombard-street. They were both tried and condemned at the Old Bailey for their lives; and Thomas Flanders, the husband, hung at Tyburn,[3] but his wife pleaded her belly,[4] she was respited till after the birth of Moll, when she suffered the same fate as her husband.

This Moll Flanders was born in the year one thousand Six hundred and thirty seven, in Newgate from whence she was stole away by some gypsies, with whom[5] she lived till she was near twelve years of age, about which time she made her escape from them, in order to seek her own fortune in the world. After her escape, as before mentioned, she came again to Newgate, where she married a highwayman, with whom she lived six years. She then took up with one Mob a highwayman, who was hanged at Tyburn, but deserted him four years before he suffered, and lived with the Golden Farmer, a [man] with whom she had not lived two years, before he was committed to Newgate for a murder, and deservedly hanged for the same.

Then Moll became a hempen widow, for Hind and Mob were hanged also. She thought these misfortunes were owing to her own inconstancy, therefore resolved to enter into the state of matrimony, in which she was more criminal; for first she was married to her own brother, committing the sin of incest. She had not been married to him above a year, before he was shot dead on Hounslow Heath, in attempting to rob a gentleman in his coach. Nevertheless, she married soon after married James[6] Thompson, a turnkey of the Marshalsea prison, with whom she lived three quarters of a year, when she ran away from him, taking with her all her cloaths.[7]

Then she married William Darman, a solicitor; with him she lived a year, all which time she was not without a black eye; for being jealous, he beat her unmercifully. He sold her to a hangman under[8] a gibbet for a shilling, and they agreeing were married. She afterwards married one John Catholic, who loved her so well for her wit, that he used her in strategems to take the person he was to arrest; however, after living four years with the bailiff, he died. Thus was she eight years a wife to several husbands; though she lived easy with the last yet, by spending, he died in such bad circumstances, that she was turned out of her house, and all her goods seized.

Being thus reduced and in great want, she turned thief, robbing her ready-furnished lodgings, and going into alehouses, and stealing several tankards, and having the luck to get off, she at length commenced shoplifter; and of her proficiency in which the following circumstance will satisfy the reader: one day Moll going into a sempstress's-shop in Cheapside, said, she wanted half a dozen shifts;[9]

several were shewed her that she liked very well as to the making, but doubting the length, they went to the back part of the shop to try one on, Moll[10] seemed to measure it at the bottom, by pulling it down, and sticking two or three pins in the bottom of the sempstress's petticoat and smock, so that if she took it off it must pull up her petticoat and shift. Moll takes a good booty that lay on the counter and runs off. The sempstress followed, crying, Stop thief! and endeavoured to pull off the shift, exposing her bare buttocks to hundreds, who diverted themselves with her instead of looking after the thief; in short they hallowed her home, thinking none but a mad woman would appear in the streets as she did, and Moll in the Mean time got off. The sempstress, who had lost above thirty pounds worth of lace, was jeered by her neighbours to her death with the cry of Stop Thief! which afterwards cost her many pounds in serving warrants to make people silent.

Moll being so successful in her prejects invented another scheme; and that was to dress herself like a person of quality, and frequent the gardens and public places of diversion, where she was dexterous at picking pockets, and stealing ladies watches and tweezers from their sides.[11]

For about twenty-five years Moll followed this trade, insomuch, that she was more notorious than the German Princess and Poll Pines,[12] the first of which was executed at Tyburn, and the other got off with being burnt in the face. But as the proverb says, The pitcher never goes so often to the well, but it comes home broke at last; for Moll being apprehending attempting to rob the lodging of the old Duchess of Lenox, in Privy Garden, she was committed to Newgate, tried at the Old Bailey and condemned; but as she had not carried off any thing of value, the Dutchess requested the recorder[13] of the city to give a favourable report to his majesty, and she came off with transportation.

Moll having gone through a variety of misfortunes in England, is at last got to America, where,[14] instead of living by whoredom, married, &c. there she now is hoeing, weeding, and picking of tobacco both late and early, lies upon straw, goes in a manner naked, is an eye witness of the cruelty of the Indians to her own sex, has much work hard lodging, and slender diet, which made her wish she was in England again, repenting she spent so uncomfortable and dangerous a state both to soul and body.

However Moll was obliged to make the best of the bad market, and performed her service for eight years, when being out of her time, and quite weaned from coming over to England, continued still in Virginia, and was entertained in the house of her master and mistress, and her master dying shortly without issue, her mistress soon made her directress of her affairs, which she managed so well to the mind of her mistress, that she not long surviving her husband, left Moll a legacy, which she improved before her death, to the value of fourteen thousand pounds, living an honest and pious life, just in her dealings, hospitable to her poor neighbours, charitable to her slaves, and especially to her unfortunate country people. She released several out of their slavery, insomuch that she gained the love of the people in Virginia. At last she was seized with an asthma, or shortness of breath, and finding that her death drew nigh, she made due[15] preparation, and died a true penitent, aged threescore. She was buried in St. Mary's Church, James-Town, the chief Town in Virginia, and her death was much lamented by all who knew her. On her tomb is the following epitaph.

THE EPITAPH.

Newgate, thy dwelling was, thy beauty made thee
A goddess seem, and that alone betrayed thee.
Twelve years a whore, a wife unto my brother,
And such a thief there scarce could be another.
Unweary'd traveller, whither dost thou roam,
Lo! in this place remote to find a tomb?
Transported hence to heaven 'tis hop'd thou'rt sent,
Who wicked lived, but died a penitent.

from Sir Samuel Romilly, *Observations on the Criminal Law of England, as It Relates to Capital Punishments, and on the Mode in Which It Is Administered* (London: T. Cadell and W. Davies, 1810), pp. 3–28.

Romilly (1757–1818) was born in London to descendents of seventeenth-century French Protestant refugees. Taken into the family jewelry business, he prepared himself by private study for a law career and was called to the bar in 1783. He developed reformist ideas and read such writers as Cesare Beccaria and John Howard, and published a reply to Martin Madan (all of whose works are included here). Despite continuing doubts about the ethics of the law he developed a lucrative practice by the early 1790s. He welcomed the French Revolution and thought England had things to learn from French law reforms, but the increasing violence of the Revolution moderated his enthusiasm. He supported the anti-slavery movement and interested himself in humane treatment of animals. Enjoying some political patronage, he entered Parliament and was made solicitor general, or government lawyer, in the coalition government of 1806–7. He remained an important reformist voice in Parliament and increasingly devoted himself to criminal law reform, with mixed success. In his last years he suffered from depression and after the death of his wife he committed suicide by cutting his throat.

Believing in appeal to reason rather than emotion, he wrote in an energetically forensic style. His *Observations* on the death penalty is a classic of advocacy of humane laws within the framework of a utilitarian rationalism, drawing on the work of eighteenth-century reform writers from Beccaria through Howard to Godwin.

OBSERVATIONS, &c.

THERE is probably no other country in the world in which so many and so great a variety of human actions are punishable with loss of life as in England. These sanguinary statutes, however, are not carried into execution. For some time past the sentence of death has not been executed on more than a sixth part of all the persons on whom it has been pronounced, even taking into the calculation crimes the most atrocious and the most dangerous to society, murders, rapes, burning of houses, coining, forgeries, and attempts to commit murder. If we exclude these from our consideration, we shall find that the proportion which the number executed bears to those convicted is, perhaps, as one to twenty: and if we proceed still further, and, laying out of the account burglaries, highway robberies, horse-stealing, sheep-stealing, and returning from transportation,[1] confine our observations to those larcenies,[2] unaccompanied with any circumstance of aggravation, for which a capital punishment is appointed by law, such as stealing privately in shops, and stealing in dwelling-houses and on board ships, property of the value mentioned in the statutes, we shall find the proportion of those executed reduced very far indeed below that even of one to twenty.

This mode of administering justice is supposed by some persons to be a regular, matured, and well-digested system. They imagine, that the state of things which we see existing, is exactly that which was originally intended; that laws have been enacted which were never meant to be regularly enforced, but were to stand as objects of terror in our statute-book, and to be called into action only occasionally, and under extraordinary circumstances, at the discretion of the judges. Such being supposed to be our criminal system, it is not surprising that there should have been found ingenious men to defend and to applaud it. Nothing, however, can be more erroneous than this notion. Whether the practice which now prevails be right or wrong, whether beneficial or injurious to the community, it is certain that it is the effect not of design, but of that change which has slowly taken place in the manners and character of the nation, which are now so repugnant to the spirit of these laws, that it has become impossible to carry them into execution.

There probably never was a law made in this country which the legislature that passed it did not intend should be strictly enforced. Even the Act of Queen Elizabeth, which made it a capital offence for any person above the age of fourteen to be found associating for a month with persons calling themselves Egyptians,[3] the most barbarous statute, perhaps, that ever disgraced our criminal code, was executed down to the reign of King Charles the first, and Lord Hale[4] mentions 13 persons having in his time been executed upon it at one assizes. It is only in modern times that this relaxation of the law has taken place, and only in the course of the present reign that it has taken place to a considerable degree. If we look back to remote times, there is reason to believe that the laws were very rigidly executed. The materials, indeed, from which we can form any judgment on this subject, are extremely scanty; for in this, as in other countries, historians, occupied with recording the actions of princes, the events of wars, and the negotiations of treaties, have seldom deigned to notice those facts from which can be best collected the state of morals of the people, and the degree of happiness which a nation has at any particular period enjoyed. Sir John Fortescue, the chief justice, and afterwards the chancellor of Henry VI., in a very curious tract on absolute and limited monarchy, in which he draws a comparison between England and France, says, that at that time more persons were executed in England for robberies in one year than in all France in seven.[5] In the long and sanguinary reign of Henry VIII. it is stated by Hollinshed[6] that 72,000 persons died by the hands of the executioner, which is at the rate of 2,000 in every year. In the time of Queen Elizabeth, there appears to have been a great relaxation of the penal laws, but not on the part of the crown; and Sir Nicholas Bacon, the lord keeper, in an earnest complaint which he makes to parliament on the subject, says, 'it remains to see in whose default this is;' and he adds, 'certain it is, that her Majesty leaveth nothing undone meet for her to do for the execution of laws;'[7] and it is related, that in the course of her reign 400 persons were upon an average executed in a year.

These statements, however, it must be admitted, are extremely vague and uncertain, and it is not till about the middle of the last century that we have any accurate information which can enable us to compare the number capitally convicted with the number executed. Sir Stephen Janssen, who was chamberlain of London,[8] preserved tables of the convicts at the Old Bailey and of the executions. These tables have been published by Mr. Howard,[9] and they extend from 1749 to 1772. From them it appears, that in 1749 the whole number convicted capitally in London and Middlesex was 61, and the number executed 44, being above two-thirds. In 1750 there were convicted 84, and executed 56; exactly two-thirds. In 1751, convicted 85, executed 63; about three-fourths. In the seven years which elapsed, from 1749 to 1756 inclusive, there were convicted 428, executed 306: rather less than three-fourths. From 1756 to 1764, of 236 convicted, 139 were executed; being much more than half. From 1764 to 1772, 457 were convicted, and of these 233 were executed; a little more than half. From this period to 1802 there has not been published any accurate statement on this subject. But from 1802 to 1808 inclusive, there have been printed, under the direction of the Secretary of State for the Home Department,[10] regular tables of the number of persons convicted capitally; and of those on whom the law has been executed; and from these we find, that in London and Middlesex,[11] the numbers are as follows:

	Convicted.	Executed.	
In 1802	97	10	about 1-10th
1803	81	9	— 1-9th
1804	66	8	about 1-9th
1805	63	10	about 1-6th
1806	60	13	about 1-5th
1807	74	14	about 1-5th
1808	87	3	— 1-29th
Total	528	67	rather more than 1-8th

It appears, therefore, that at the commencement of the present reign, the number of convicts executed exceeded the number of those who were pardoned; but that at the present time, the number pardoned very far exceeds the number of those who are executed. This lenity I am very far from censuring; on the contrary, I applaud the wisdom as well as the humanity of it. If the law were unremittingly executed, the evil would be still greater, and many more offenders would escape with full impunity: much fewer persons would be found to prosecute, witnesses would more frequently withhold the truth which they are sworn to speak, and juries would oftener in violation of their oaths acquit those who were manifestly guilty. But a stronger proof can hardly be required than this comparison affords, that the present method of administering the law is not, as has been by some imagined, a system maturely formed and regularly established, but that it is a practice which has gradually prevailed, as the laws have become less adapted to the state of society in which we live.

There is no instance in which this alteration in the mode of administering the law has been more remarkable, than in those of privately stealing in a shop or stable, goods of the value of five shillings,[12] which is made punishable with death by the statute of 10 and 11 William III., and of stealing in a dwelling-house property of the value of forty shillings,[13] for which the same punishment is appointed by the statute of 12 Ann, and which statutes it is now proposed to repeal. The exact numbers cannot, from any thing that has hitherto been published, be correctly ascertained; but from Sir Stephen Janssen's tables[14] it appears, that after laying out of the calculation the numbers convicted of murder, burglary, highway robbery, forgery, coining, returning from transportation, and fraudulent bankruptcies, there remains convicted at the Old Bailey of shop-lifting and other offences of the same nature, in the period from 1749 to 1771, 240 persons, and of those no less than 109 were executed.

What has been the number of persons convicted of those offences within the last seven years does not appear; but from the tables published under the authority of the Secretary of State, we find that within that period there were committed to Newgate for trial, charged with the crime of stealing in dwelling-houses, 599 men and 414 women; and charged with the crime of shop-lifting, 506 men and 353 women; in all 1,872 persons, and of these only one was executed.

In how many instances such crimes have been committed, and the persons robbed have not proceeded so far against the offenders as even to have them committed to prison: how many of the 1,872 thus committed were discharged, because those who had suffered by their crimes would not appear to give evidence upon their trial: in how many cases the witnesses who did appear withheld the evidence that they could have given: and how numerous were the instances in which juries found a compassionate verdict, in direct contradiction to the plain facts clearly established before them, we do not know; but that these evils must all have existed to a considerable degree, no man can doubt.

Notwithstanding these facts, however, and whether this mode of administering justice be the result of design or of accident, there are many persons who conceive that it is upon the whole wise and beneficial to the community. It cannot, therefore, but be useful to examine the arguments by which it is defended. Discussions on such subjects are always productive of good. They either lead to important improvements of the law, or they afford additional reasons for being satisfied with what is already established.

It is alleged by those who approve of the present practice, that the actions which fall under the cognizance of human laws are so varied by the circumstances which attend them, that if the punishment appointed by the law were invariably inflicted for the same species of crime, it must be too severe for the offence, with the extenuating circumstances which in some instances attend it, and it must in others fall far short of the moral guilt of the crime, with its accompanying aggravations: that the only remedy for this, the only way in which it can be provided that the guilt and the punishment shall in all cases be commensurate, is to announce death as the appointed punishment, and to leave a wide discretion in the judge of relaxing that severity, and substituting a milder sentence in its place.

If this be a just view of the subject, it would render the system more perfect, if in no case specific punishments were enacted, but it were always left to the judge, after the guilt of the criminal had been ascertained, to fix the punishment which he should suffer, from the severest allowed by our law to the slightest penalty which it knows: and yet what Englishman would not be alarmed at the idea of living under a law which was thus uncertain and unknown, and of being continually exposed to the arbitrary severity of a magistrate? All men would be shocked at a law which should declare that the offences of stealing in shops or dwelling-houses, or on board ships, property of the different values mentioned in the several statutes, should in general be punished with transportation, but that the King and his judges should have the power, under circumstances of great aggravation, respecting which they should be the sole arbiters, to order that the offender should suffer death; yet such is in practice the law of England.

In some respects, however, it would be far better that this ample and awful discretion should be formally vested in the judges, than that the present practice should obtain; for it would then be executed under a degree of responsibility which does not now belong to it. If a man were found guilty of having pilfered in a dwelling-house, property worth forty shillings, or in a shop that which was of the value only of five shillings, with no one circumstance whatever of aggravation, what judge whom the constitution had intrusted with an absolute discretion, and had left answerable only to public opinion for the exercise of it, would venture for such a transgression to inflict the punishment of death: but if in such a case, the law having fixed the punishment, the judge merely suffers that law to take its course, and does not interpose to snatch the miserable victim from his fate, who has a right to complain? A discretion to fix the doom of every convict, expressly given to the judges, would in all cases be most anxiously and scrupulously exercised; but appoint the punishment by law, and give the judge the power of remitting it, the case immediately assumes a very different complexion. A man is convicted of one of those larcenies made capital by law, and is besides a person of very bad character. It is not to such a man that mercy is to be extended; and, the sentence of the law denouncing death, a remission of it must be called by the name of mercy; the man, therefore, is hanged; but in truth it is not for his crime that he suffers death, but for the badness of his reputation. Another man is suspected of a murder, of which there is not legal evidence to convict him; there is proof, however, of his having committed a larceny to the amount of forty shillings in a dwelling-house, and of that he is convicted. He, too, is not thought a fit object of clemency, and he is hanged, not for the crime of which he has been convicted, but for that of which he is only suspected. A third upon his trial for a capital larceny[15] attempts to establish his innocence by witnesses whom the jury disbelieve, and he is left for execution, because he has greatly enhanced his guilt by the subornation of perjured witnesses. In truth, he suffers death, not for felony,[16] but for subornation of perjury, although, that be not the legal punishment of this offence.

If so large a discretion as this can safely be intrusted to any magistrates, the legislature ought at least to lay down some general rules to direct or assist them in the exercise of it, that there might be, if not a perfect uniformity in the administration of justice, yet the same spirit always prevailing, and the same maxims always kept in view; and that the law, as it is executed, not being to be found in any written code, might at least be collected with some degree of certainty from an attentive observation of the actual execution of it. If this be not done, if every judge be left to follow the light of his own understanding, and to act upon the principles and the system which he has derived partly from his own observation, and his reading, and partly from his natural temper and his early impressions, the law, invariable only in theory, must in practice be continually shifting with the temper, and habits, and opinions of those by whom it is administered. No man can have frequently attended our criminal courts, and have been an attentive observer of what was passing there, without having been deeply impressed with the great anxiety which the judges feel to discharge most faithfully their important duties to the public. Their perfect impartiality, their earnest desire in every case to prevent a failure of justice, to punish guilt, and to protect innocence, and the total absence with them of all distinctions between the rich and the poor, the powerful and the unprotected, are matters upon which all men are agreed. In these particulars the judges are all actuated by one spirit, and the practice of all of them is uniform. But in seeking to attain the same object, they frequently do, and of necessity must, from the variety of opinions which must be found in different men, pursue very different courses. The same benevolence and humanity, understood in a more confined or a more enlarged sense, will determine one judge to pardon and another to punish. It has often happened, it necessarily must have happened, that the very same circumstance which is considered by one judge as matter of extenuation, is deemed by another a high aggravation of the crime. The former good character of the delinquent, his having come into a country in which he was a stranger to commit the offence, the frequency or the novelty of the crime, are all circumstances which have been upon some occasions considered by different judges in those opposite lights: and it is not merely the particular circumstances attending the crime, it is the crime itself, which different judges sometimes consider in quite different points of view.

Not a great many years ago, upon the Norfolk circuit,[17] a larceny was committed by two men in a poultry yard, but only one of them was apprehended; the other having escaped into a distant part of the country, had eluded all pursuit. At the next assizes the apprehended thief was tried and convicted; but Lord Loughborough,[18] before whom he was tried, thinking the offence a very slight one, sentenced him only to a few months imprisonment. The news of this sentence having reached the accomplice in his retreat, he immediately returned, and surrendered himself to take his trial at the next assizes. The next assizes came; but, unfortunately for the prisoner, it was a different judge who presided; and still more unfortunately, Mr. Justice Gould,[19] who happened to be the judge, though of a very mild and indulgent disposition, had observed, or thought he had observed, that men who set out with stealing fowls, generally end by committing the most atrocious crimes; and building a sort of system upon this observation, had made it a rule to punish this offence with very great severity, and he accordingly, to the great astonishment of this unhappy man, sentenced him to be transported. While one was taking his departure for Botany Bay, the term of the other's imprisonment had expired; and what must have been the notions which that little public, who witnessed and compared these two examples, formed of our system of criminal jurisprudence?

In this uncertain administration of justice, not only different judges act upon different principles, but the same judge, under the same circumstances, acts differently at different times. It has been observed, that in the exercise of this judicial discretion, judges, soon after their promotion, are generally inclined to great lenity; and that their practical principles alter, or, as it is commonly expressed, they become more severe as they become more habituated to investigate the details of human misery and human depravity.

Let us only reflect how all these fluctuations of opinion and variations in practice must operate upon that portion of mankind, who are rendered obedient to the law only by the terror of punishment. After giving full weight to all the chances of complete impunity which they can suggest to their minds, they have besides to calculate upon the probabilities which there are, after conviction, of their escaping a severe punishment; to speculate upon what judge will go the circuit, and upon the prospect of its being one of those who have been recently elevated to the bench. As it has been truly observed, that most men are apt to confide in their supposed good fortune, and to miscalculate as to the number of prizes which there are in the lottery of life, so are those dissolute and thoughtless men, whose evil dispositions penal laws are most necessary to repress, much too prone to deceive themselves in their speculations upon what I am afraid they accustom themselves to consider as the lottery of justice.

Let it at the same time be remembered, that it is universally agreed, that the certainty of punishment is much more efficacious than any severity of example for the prevention of crimes. Indeed this is so evident, that if it were possible that punishment, as the consequence of guilt, could be reduced to an absolute certainty, a very slight penalty would be sufficient to prevent almost every species of crime, except those which arise from sudden gusts of ungovernable passion. If the restoration of the property stolen, and only a few weeks, or even a few days imprisonment, were the unavoidable consequence of theft, no theft would ever be committed. No man would steal what he was sure that he could not keep; no man would, by a voluntary act, deprive himself of his liberty, though but for a few days. It is the desire of a supposed good which is the incentive to every crime: no crime, therefore, could exist, if it were infallibly certain that not good, but evil must follow, as an unavoidable consequence to the person who committed it. This absolute certainty, however, is unattainable, where facts are to be ascertained by human testimony, and questions are to be decided by human judgments. All that can be done is, by a vigilant police, by rational rules of evidence, by clear laws, and by punishments proportioned to the guilt of the offender, to approach as nearly to that certainty as human imperfection will admit.

There is another point of view in which this matter may be considered; and which will make it evident that it would be more expedient that the judges should have the power vested in them by law, of appointing the punishment of every offence after it had been established with all its circumstances in proof, and of proportioning the particular nature and degree of the punishment to those circumstances, than that, for such offences as I am speaking of, so severe a punishment should be fixed by law, with a power left in the judges according to circumstances, to relax it. In the former case it is highly probable that the discretion would in practice be exercised by none but the judges, that is, by magistrates accustomed to judicial investigations, fully aware of the importance of the duties which they are called on to discharge, and who from the eminence of their stations, are, and cannot but be sensible, that they are under a very great degree of responsibility to the public. According to the practice which now prevails, this most important discretion is constantly assumed by persons to whom the constitution has not intrusted it, and to whom it certainly cannot with the same safety be intrusted; by prosecutors, by juries, and by witnesses. Though for those thefts which are made capital by law, death is seldom in practice inflicted; yet as it is the legal appointed punishment, prosecutors, witnesses, and juries, consider death as that which, if it will not with certainty, yet possibly may be the consequence, of the several parts which they have to act in the judicial proceeding: and they act their parts accordingly, though they never can, in this indirect way, take upon themselves to prevent the execution of the law, without abandoning their duty; and in the case of jurymen and witnesses, without a violation of their oaths.[20]

There is still another view which may be taken of this subject, and which is perhaps more important than those which have been already considered. The sole object of human punishments, it is admitted, is the prevention of crimes; and to this end, they operate principally by the terror of example. In the present system, however, the benefit of example is entirely lost, for the real cause of the convict's execution is not declared in his sentence, nor is it in any other mode published to the world. A man is publickly put to death. All that is told to the spectators of this tragedy, and to that part of the public who hear or who read of it, is, that he stole a sheep, or five shillings worth of goods privately in a shop, or that he pilfered to the value of forty shillings from his employer in a dwelling-house, and they are left in total ignorance that the criminal produced upon his trial perjured witnesses to prove an alibi, or some other defence, and that it is for that aggravation of his crime that he suffers death. The example cannot operate to prevent subornation of witnesses to establish a false defence, for it is not known to any but those who were present at the trial, that such was the offender's crime; neither can it operate to prevent sheep-stealing, or privately stealing in a shop, or larceny in a dwelling-house, because it is notorious that these are offences for which, if attended with no aggravating circumstances, death is not in practice inflicted. Nothing more is learned from the execution of the sentence, than that a man has lost his life because he has done that which by a law not generally executed, is made capital, and because some unknown circumstance or other existed either in the crime itself, or in the past life of the criminal, which in the opinion of the judge who tried him, rendered him a fit subject to be singled out for punishment. Surely if this system is to be persevered in, the judge should be required in a formal sentence to declare why death is inflicted, that the sufferings and the privations of the individual might be rendered useful to society in deterring others from acting as he has done, and drawing on themselves a similar doom. The judge would undoubtedly be required to do this if the discretion which he exercises in point of fact, were expressly confided to him by law. But unfortunately, as the law stands, he is supposed not to select for capital punishment, but to determine to whom mercy shall be extended; although these objects of mercy, as compared with those who suffer, are in the proportion of six to one. Were recorded reasons to be required of the judge, it will be said, they must be his reasons for extending mercy, which is his act, not his reasons for inflicting punishment, which is the act of the law: an additional proof of the mischief which results from leaving the theory and the practice of the law so much at variance.

In truth, where the law which is executed is different from that which is to be found in the written statutes, great care should be taken to make the law which is executed known, because it is that law alone which can operate to the prevention of crimes. An unexecuted law can no more have that effect, than the law of a foreign country; and the only mode that can be adopted for making known the law which is executed, is that of stating in a written sentence the circumstances which have rendered the crime capital. Such written sentences, like the reported decisions upon the common law, would stand in the place of statutes. It must, however, be admitted, that it would be still more desirable, that instead of having recourse to such substitutes, the law should be embodied in written statutes.

Another consequence of the present system is, that it deprives juries of the most important of their functions, that of deciding upon facts on which the lives of their fellow-subjects are to depend. The circumstance of aggravation, whatever it be, for which the judge inflicts the punishment of death, in reality constitutes the crime for which he suffers. If, for example, the judges made it an invariable rule to leave for execution every man convicted of highway-robbery, who had struck or done any injury to the person of the party robbed, and to inflict only the punishment of transportation, for robbery unattended with such violence, the effect would be the same as if the crimes of mere robbery, and of robbery with violence offered to the person, so distinct in themselves, were distinguished by written laws, and were made punishable, the one with death, and the other with transportation. The effect would be the same with respect to the punishments, but by no means the same with respect to the mode of trial. Because if the law had considered them as distinct offences, it would be the province of the jury to decide whether the circumstance of aggravation, which altered the nature and description of the crime, did or did not exist; whereas in the present system, it is the judge alone on whom that important office is devolved. The fact of violence may in his opinion be established, though the jury may have withheld all credit from the witness who swore it. That fact has probably not been investigated with the same accuracy as the other parts of the case, because it is to constitute no part of the finding of the jury. It is in truth altogether immaterial to the verdict which they have to pronounce, which is merely whether the prisoner be guilty or not guilty of the robbery. The same observation may be made upon every other circumstance of aggravation which decides the fate of convicted criminals; the judge necessarily acts upon his own opinion of the evidence by which these circumstances are supported, and he sometimes proceeds upon evidence not given in open court, or under the sanction of an oath.

With all the objections, however, which there are to this mode of administering justice, it has long prevailed, and consequently it has many defenders. Among those there is none whose arguments deserve more attention than Dr. Paley,[21] not so much on account of the force or ingenuity of those arguments, as of the weight which they derive from the respectable name of the writer who uses them. Every thing that is excellent in the works of such a man, renders his errors, where he falls into error, only the more pernicious. Sanctioned by his high authority, they are received implicitly as truths by many persons who, if they met with them in a writer of inferior merit or reputation, would not fail to canvass them, and to detect their fallacy.[22]

from James Neild, *State of the Prisons in England, Scotland, and Wales* ... (London: John Nichols and Son, 1812), pp. 415–30.

Neild (1744–1814) made a fortune as a London jeweller and retired in 1792. Early in life he had already turned to penal reform and philanthropic work – hence his attention in his *State of the Prisons* to the many charities established to assist debtors, convicts and those awaiting trial in prison. He visited prisons all over Britain and reported on their deficiencies, particularly in a series of 'Prison Remarks' published in the *Gentleman's Magazine* from 1803 to 1813. After his death, however, his reputation as a humanitarian suffered from reports that he had mistreated his son. Like John Howard's more famous *State of the Prisons* (1777, expanded in successive editions), Neild laboured to accumulate facts and figures as a basis for proposing detailed and comprehensive legal and penal reform, as evidenced in the extract here.

GROUND PLAN OF NEWGATE.

NEWGATE. *London.*

Gaoler, *John Kirby;* now *John Addison Newman.* Salary, 450*l.*[1]
Fees, for Debtors and Felons, &c. as per following Tables.

TABLE I. *Debtors.*

LONDON, SC.

'A TABLE of FEES, to be taken by the Gaoler or Keeper of the Prison
of *Newgate*, within the said City of London, for any Prisoner or
Prisoners committed or coming into Gaol, or Chamber-Rent
there, or discharged from thence, in any *Civil Action*: Settled and
established the 19th day of December, 1729.

	s.	d.
Every Prisoner, on the *Master's-Side*, shall pay to the Keeper, for his Entrance Fee -	3	0
Every Prisoner, on the Master's-Side, shall pay for chamber-room, use of bed, bedding, and sheets, to the Keeper, there being two in a bed, and no more, each per week - - - - -	1	3
Every Prisoner, on the said Master's-Side, who, at his own desire, shall have a bed to himself, shall pay to the Keeper for chamber-room, use of bed, bedding, and sheets, per week - -	2	6*
Every Debtor shall pay to the Keeper, for his discharging Fee - - - - -	6	10
And to all the Turnkeys, 2*s.* and no more - - - - - - - - - - - - - - - -	2	0

No other Fee for the use of chamber, bed, bedding, or sheets; or upon the
commitment or discharge of any Prisoner on any *Civil Action.*

EDW. BECHER.	ROB. RAYMOND.
ROB. ALSOP.	R. EYRE.
JOHN BARNARD.	THO. PENGELLY.[2]

	s.	d.
The Fee to the Middlesex Sheriff's Office, for every Debtor's discharge, for one Action, is -	4	6
And for every additional Action, more - - - - - - - - - - - - - - - - - -	2	6.'

But Messrs. *BURCHELL*, the present humane Deputy Sheriff, sometimes
remit this Fee, upon the Keeper's Certificate of the Debtor's being poor, and
unable to pay it. The Warrant of such discharge is given under the Hand and Seal
of the Sheriff of Middlesex, and is called '*The Red Seal.*'† The Fee for a *London*

---

* Or, to any price, according to the quality of the Prisoner, and the nature of his or her accommodation.

† A Seal, in which are quartered the Arms of both the Gentlemen appointed by the City to be Sheriffs, who, together, make one Sheriff of Middlesex. The impress of it is always placed after the names of the Sheriff upon the Warrant of Discharge in *red wax*, and hence it obtained the name.

Debtor's Discharge from the Sheriffs, is the same as before stated in my Account of *Ludgate Prison*. See Page *363*.[3]

TABLE II. *Felons, &c.*
Hung up, in several places, on the *Criminal* Side of NEWGATE.

	£.	s.	d.
'For every Felon's discharge -	0	18	10
For every Misdemeanour -	0	14	10
For every Felon's Entrance on the Master's-Side - - - - - - - -	0	10	6
For every Person admitted into the *Press-yard* - - - - - - - - -	3	3	0
For every Transport's discharge - - - - - - - - - - - - - - - - - - -	0	14	10
For every Bailable Warrant -	3	6	8.

ROBERT WILMOTT.   ROB[t] LADBROKE.
W[M] BARNARD.   SAMUEL PENNENT.

'And to the Clerk of the Peace, or Clerk in Court
of the Session of Gaol Delivery of Newgate.

	£.	s.	d.
'For every Felon's discharge -	0	6	2
For every Petty Larceny -	0	4	10
For every Misdeameanour -	0	10	0.'

Garnish, DEBTORS; on the *Cabin-Side*, a subscription of one Guinea, for coals, candles, mops, brooms, &c. at entrance, and a gallon of ale on quitting the Prison.

On the *Master's-Side*, a subscription of thirteen shillings and four-pence, for coals, &c. and a gallon of beer at entrance.

On the *Common-Side* a subscription of eight shillings and ten-pence for coals, &c. and a gallon of beer.

Those, who, from their poverty, cannot pay this last-mentioned sum, are to wash and clean the wards.

FELONS, on the *Master's-Side*, pay about thirteen shillings Garnish, and those on the Common-Side, about eight shillings, according to the price of coals and candles; and those who, from their poverty, cannot pay the same, are required to afford a greater share of labour, in washing and cleansing the Felon-wards.

The above several sums are paid to the *Stewards* of the Wards on the *Debtors'-Side;* and to the *Gatesmen* and *Wardsmen* on the *Felons'-Side;* and laid out towards purchasing coals, wood, candles, mops, brooms, and other necessary articles.

The Stewards, Gatesmen, and Wardsmen entrusted with these respective charges, have each a double allowance of bread.

In a room, formerly the Tap, *Anne Sell*, a free Vintner, supplies the Criminal Prisoners with wine; and serves out the beer which is sent to the Prison from the Public Houses; for which she is allowed two-pence per gallon.

Chaplain, or Ordinary; The Rev. Dr. *Forde*.[4]

Duty, Prayers and Sermon every Sunday Morning, and Prayers in the Afternoon: also Prayers every Wednesday and Friday Morning; and private Prayers, on Tuesday and Saturday, to those under Sentence of Death. After the Recorder's Report, he attends those Convicts who are to suffer,[5] twice a day, and on the Morning of Execution; as does likewise a Catholic Priest, with those who are of the Romish Church.

Salary, 200*l.* and a House adjoining to the Gaol. Also 6*l. per annum*, from Lady *Barnardiston's* Legacy, and 10*l.* a year, from an old Legacy, paid by the Governors of St. Bartholomew's Hospital. Over and above which, sundry sums have been occasionally presented to the Ordinary by the Court of Aldermen.

Surgeon, Mr. *William Box*, who visits the Prison daily.

Salary, 100*l.* and Medicines, for Debtors as well as Criminals, paid for by the City.

There is no Surgeon's Book kept in Newgate. But I am informed he makes a regular Return to the Court of Aldermen, and another Return to the Court every day, during the Sessions at the Old Bailey, of the state of Health in the Gaol; together with a Certificate, that the several persons to be called on, are fit and able to take their trials, or otherwise. No Prisoner is ever brought to the Bar of the Old Bailey without such Certificate.

The Surgeon also attends the removal of Convicts, and others; who are never sent to any other place of confinement, without his Certificate of their being free from putrid or infectious fevers, and fit to be removed.

Number of Prisoners.

	Debtors.	Felons, &c.		Debtors.	Felons, &c.
1800, June 14th,	199 - -	289.	1806, May 24th,	198 - -	205.
1801, April 27th,	275 - -	375.	1807, March 16th,	175 - -	204.
1802, April 3d,	221 - -	418.	1808, March 12th,	197 - -	182.
1803, July 2d,	191 - -	519.	1809, June 16th,	252 - -	234.
1804, Feb. 10th,	204 - -	317.	1810, April 19th	184 - -	347.
1805, April 22d,	149 - -	287.	1811, Jan. 16th,	233 - -	396.*

*   Of these, 84 were under Sentence of Death; and Eight Lunaticks.

There were in Newgate, at the following periods of passing the Insolvent Bill,

	Debtors.	Discharged.	Left.		Debtors.	Discharged.	Left.
1794,	209	78	131.	1804,	180	42	138.
1797,	182	45	137.	1806,	184	63	121.
1801,	273	143	130.	1809,	238	76	162.*

Allowance, to every *Debtor* fourteen ounces of the best wheaten bread, daily.†

The Debtors on the *Poor* and *Women's-Side* have eight stone (or sixty-four pounds) of beef, divided weekly amongst them, without bone, such as clods and stickings;[6] which is paid for by the Sheriffs.

To the *poor Criminals*, ten stone of beef every Saturday; four stone every Tuesday, and four stone every Thursday; besides an allowance of mutton for the sick, and ten ounces of the best bread daily to each Criminal; Together also with a weekly allotment of rice, or potatoes, – and sometimes of coals, to the amount of about fourpence each Criminal; or (as nearly as may be) according to the then value of twenty-eight ounces of bread. The meat is paid for by the Sheriffs, and the bread, rice, &c. by the Court of Aldermen.

There are also sundry *Donations* to the poor Men and Women *Debtors*, payable at different periods; some of which are regularly paid, and others discontinued; as will appear by the following Lists.

A List of Donations to the Poor Debtors confined in Newgate.
Lady-Day quarter.

When paid.	Donors' Names.	By whom paid.	Amount.[7]		
Quarterly	Sundry Persons ‡	Leathersellers Company[8]	§ 0	4	0
Ditto	Mr. John Meridith	Skinners Company	0	5	6
Ditto	Mr. John Draper	Ditto	0	3	4
Ditto	Sir Thomas Gresham, Knt.[9]	Chamberlain of London	2	10	0
Half-Yearly	Lady Ramsay	Christ's Hospital	1	5	0
Ditto	Lady Maurice	Armourers and Braziers Company	¶ 0	15	0
Yearly	Alderman Sir John Heydon	Mercers Company	5	0	0
Ditto	Sir Roger Martin, Knt.	Ditto	2	0	0
Ditto	South Sea Annuity	Ditto	1	10	2
Ditto	Mr. John March	Ditto	0	10	0
Half-yearly	Mr. John Wooller	Merchant Taylors Company	0	10	0
Quarterly	Mr. Peter Blundell[10]	Ditto	0	10	0
Ditto	Mr. Peter Blundell	Haberdashers Company	0	10	0
Ditto	Sadlers Company	Sadlers Company	0	2	6
End of Term	Barons of the Exchequer	Exchequer Office, Temple	0	6	8
			£. 16	2	2.

*   In Middlesex alone, between six and seven thousand persons are annually arrested on mesne process, and about half of them for debts under twenty pounds. The total number, in the kingdom, may be reckoned at 80,000l. And if all do not go immediately to the Common Gaols, they are, for a time, in the custody of Bailiffs, and in lock-up houses.

†   There is a want of regularity and correctness in making the loaves of bread; many of which I have found, when weighed singly, to be deficient two ounces, and some to be over-weight. There are, likewise, persons within the prison, who sell green-grocery and meat, with measures, weights, and scales, not stamped.

‡   Taylor, Grosvenor, &c.

§   And eight dozen of bread.

¶   And five dozen of bread.

MIDSUMMER QUARTER.

When paid.	Donors' Names.	By whom paid.	Amount.		
Quarterly	Sundry Persons*	Leathersellers Company	† 0	4	0
Ditto	Mr. John Meridith	Skinners Company	0	5	6
Ditto	Mr. John Draper	Ditto	0	3	4
Ditto	Sir Thomas Gresham, Knt.	Chamberlain of London	2	10	0
Ditto	Mr. Peter Blundell	Merchant Taylors Company	0	10	0
Ditto	Mr. Peter Blundell	Haberdashers Company	0	10	0
Ditto	Sadlers Company	Sadlers Company	0	2	6
Two Terms	Barons of the Exchequer	Exchequer Office, Temple	0	13	4
			£. 4	18	8.

MICHAELMAS QUARTER.

When paid.	Donors' Names.	By whom paid.	Amount.		
Quarterly	Sundry Persons‡	Leathersellers Company	§ 0 4		0
Ditto	Mr. John Draper	Skinners Company	0 3		4
Ditto	Mr. John Meridith	Ditto	0 5		6
Ditto	Sir Thomas Gresham, knight	Chamberlain of London	2 10		0
Half-Yearly	Lady Ramsay	Christ's Hospital	1 5		0
Ditto	Lady Maurice	Armourers and Braziers Company	¶ 0 15		0
Ditto	Mr. John Wooller	Merchant Taylors Company	0 10		0
Quarterly	Mr. Peter Blundell	Ditto	0 10		0
Ditto	Mr. Peter Blundell	Haberdashers Company	0 10		0
Ditto	Sadlers Company	Sadlers Company	0 2		6
			£. 6 15		4.

CHRISTMAS QUARTER.

When paid.	Donors' Names.	By whom paid.	Amount.		
Yearly	Company of Parish Clerks	Brought to Prison, Nov. 1	1	1	0
Ditto	Receiver General of Land-Tax	Auditor's Office, Palace-Yard	2	3	4
Ditto	Sir John Kendrick[11]	Drapers Company	2	0	0
End of Term	Barons of the Exchequer	Exchequer Office, Temple	0	6	8
Yearly	Sundry Persons**	Leathersellers Company	†† 0	14	0
Quarterly	Mr. John Meridith	Skinners ditto	0	5	6
Ditto	Mr. John Draper	Ditto	0	3	4
Ditto	Sir Tho. Gresham, Knt.	Chamberlain of London	2	10	0
Yearly	Fishmongers Extra Bounty	Fishmongers Company	4	0	0
Ditto	Mr. Thomas Kneesworth	Ditto	1	0	0
Ditto	Mrs. Letitia Smith	Ditto	0	3	4
Ditto	Sir Stephen Peacock	Haberdashers Company	4	0	0
Quarterly	Mr. Peter Blundell	Ditto	0	10	0
Ditto	Mr. Peter Blundell	Merchant Taylors ditto	0	10	0
Yearly	Mr. William Parker	Ditto	2	0	0
Ditto	Mrs. Margaret Crawthorn	Cutlers Company	0	13	0

* Taylor, Grosvenor, &c.
† And eight dozen of Bread.
‡ Taylor, Grosvenor, &c.
§ And eight dozen of Bread.
¶ And five dozen of Bread.
** Taylor, Daniel, &c.
†† And eight dozen of Bread.

When paid.	Donors' Names.	By whom paid.	Amount.		
Ditto	Mrs. Margaret Hargrave	Clothworkers Company	0	5	0
Ditto	Archbishop of Canterbury	At Lambeth Palace	1	0	0
Ditto	Mr. John Gerrard	Salters Company	0	6	2
Ditto	Sir William Horne	Ditto	0	5	0
Ditto	Sir John Peachey	Grocers Company	0	5	0
Ditto	Mr. Thomas Dawson	Churchwardens of St. Ethelburga	0	9	0
Ditto	Mr. Robert Ramston	31, Orchard Street, Portman-Sq*	1	0	0
Quarterly	Sadlers Company	Sadlers Company	0	2	6
			£. 23	14	10.

Provisions, with additional Donations, and to what purpose they are applied.

Mrs. Margaret Dane, from the Ironmongers Company, 18 stone 6 lbs. of beef, and five dozen penny loaves, sent for to the Hall on the 5th of November.

The parish of St. Dunstan in the East, 20 stone of beef, and a peck of oatmeal, sent to the Prison on Christmas-eve by the Churchwardens. Legacy of Thomas Cottle; – see Ludgate, page 367.

Allhallows, Lombard-street, 17*s.* laid out in beef every two years. Brought to prison.

St. Andrew Undershaft, 17*s.* laid out in beef every two years. Brought to prison.

St. Ethelburga, 9*s.* laid out in beef every two years. Brought to prison.

Mrs. Margaret Simcott, 65 penny loaves, to be delivered every 56 days. Brought to prison.

Mrs. Fisher, executrix of Mrs. Eliz. Misson, 6*l.* yearly, in February, being the produce of 200*l.* India Annuities. Will, dated 23d May, 1770, proved at London, 9th March, 1774. – See Ludgate, page 369. This legacy is reluctantly and irregularly paid.

☞ Through the exertions of the attentive Keeper of this Gaol, a very excellent arrangement took place in 1807, for the distribution of the Prison-Charities: By which all the Prisoners are equally benefited, and the monies arising therefrom *laid out in necessaries for their use*, instead of the quarterly distribution, as heretofore, in money; which, but too frequently, was spent in liquor, by those only who happened to be in Prison at the time the said Charities became payable.

The *Debtors* are also especially relieved by the humanity of the SOCIETY, held at No. 7, *Craven-street* in the *Strand*, who monthly vote large sums towards procuring their Discharge, and paying their Fees. For the same merciful purpose, money is likewise issued by some of the *City Companies;* by a liberal Society at *Mile End;* and, for unfortunate Inhabitants of *Christ-Church Parish*, by the Common-Councilmen there.†

Twice in a year, the Debtors have, moreover, a share of *one hundred pounds;* laid out, first, by the Lord Mayor, and, secondly, by the Sheriffs, in the purchase of

---

*   Mr. Vinnicombe, 31, Orchard Street, Portman-Square.

†   See before, page 235.

provisions and coals; and distributed to all the Prisoners in *Newgate*, *Ludgate*, and the *two Compters*, according to the number of persons in each of those Prisons.

Broken victuals[12] are often sent by the Master of the London Coffee-house, by Mr. Alderman Birch in Cornhill, and by the Masters of the City of London Tavern: Of the two former of which the more distressed Debtors sometimes partake; and of the latter they have lately appointed a Collector, to attend daily, and receive them.

I should now proceed to my *Remarks*, but that the following Document seems previously to demand the present, as the most suitable place for its insertion. It is a *List*, very different indeed from those which have just preceded it: – a painful List, of what are called '*Courts of Conscience Debtors:*' of the *Debts* they had incurred: of the times of their commitment to Newgate; and of the charges accumulated against them for Costs, upon such very inconsiderable demands.*
It were easy to extend the melancholy detail; but I forbear: –

Reverence for existing law precludes the saying more, than
——'Pity it is, 'tis true!'[13]

Date of Warrants.	Defendants' Names.	Debts.		Costs.	
1797.		s.	d.	s.	d.
February 7,	John Allen	3	5	8	8
May 11,	William Gough	3	10	8	10
October 15,	Thomas Blackburn	2	0½	6	10
	Ditto	1	5	6	10
December 14,	Ann Jones	2	3	8	10
1798.					
April 12,	Charles Burnet	3	10	8	10
September 20,	Thomas Blackburn	2	6	8	10
November 9,	Elizabeth Irvine	3	9	8	8
1799.					
August 15,	Caleb Only	3	9	8	10
22,	Thomas Dobson	1	0	8	10
September 1,	John Hyder	3	10	8	8
October 1,	Susannah Evans	2	2	6	8
17,	William Owen	3	0	8	8
1800.					
March 13,	Abraham Slater	3	4	6	10
July 24,	John Jones	3	0	6	10.

* From the best accounts I could extract from the Books, there were One Thousand Three Hundred and Twelve *Debtors* committed to Newgate by the Court of Conscience, from the 1st of January 1797, to the 1st of January 1808. And the number of *Creditors*, who recovered Debt and Costs in consequence of such imprisonment, amounted to *One Hundred and Ninety-seven*. Wretched harvest, from barren soil!

REMARKS.

NEWGATE, formerly one of the gates of the City of London, was first erected in the reign of Henry the First, or of Stephen, his successor, for the conveniency of such, as had occasion to pass from the *North East part of the City to Holborn;* the passage at that period being much obstructed by the enclosing of ground for the building of *St. Paul's Cathedral:* so that the way became very circuitous and dangerous from thence *through Ludgate,* which had originally been the usual thoroughfare.

This *New-Gate,* after having, for upwards of six hundred years, been used as a Prison for Felons and other offenders, was, about 40 years ago, pulled down, and the present Gaol erected; which, having been destroyed by the Rioters in 1780, has since been rebuilt, and appropriated, as before, for the reception of persons charged with offences committed in London and Middlesex; and also for the custody of all manner of persons committed by either House of Parliament, by the Secretary of State, by the Court of King's Bench, or either of the Judges thereof: by his Majesty's Judges of Assize; by the several Commissioners of Bankrupts, Customs, Excise, &c. and by the Magistrates in and for the City of London and County of Middlesex; as also of *Debtors* arrested by the Sheriff of Middlesex: no London Debtor being ever brought hither, without being likewise charged with some offence cognizable by a Court or Magistrate having Criminal Jurisdiction, or unless sent by the Sheriffs of London, from the Compters, or Ludgate, by *Duci facias.*[14]

The Mayor and Commonalty of London, or their Deputies, may also arrest and take Felons, Thieves, &c. who are found in the Borough of Southwark, and commit them to this Gaol of Newgate.

The Prisoners in this strong-hold are divided into two general classes; viz. *Debtors,* and *Criminals;* and those of the latter description into four other classes:

I. *Capital Convicts,* under Sentence of Death.

II. *Transports,* and *Respited Convicts.*

III. Persons under Sentence of *Imprisonment,* for certain determinate periods of time; or until they shall have paid certain Fines or Amercements: And

IV. Prisoners detained for *Trial;* not so much distinguishing between the *magnitude* of the particular Crimes wherewith they stand charged, or of which they may be convicted, as between the *Habits of Life* of the individuals; many of whom are well known in Courts of Justice; and who, although at times they may be committed for crimes apparently or comparatively small, are yet of manners more likely to corrupt the morals of young offenders, than some of those Convicts who are under Sentence of Transportation, or Fine, or Imprisonment. The

Males, too, of all the above criminal classes are kept separate from the Females of their class; and so, likewise, are the Capital Convicts from other Criminals.

This Gaol of Newgate is accordingly divided into *eight separate and distinct court-yards;* of which, two on the North-West angle are appropriated for Debtors, viz.[15]

Nº. I. The Men Debtors' court, 49 feet long, by about 31 feet wide, leading to three Wards, called 'The *Cabin-Side;*' each Ward being 37 feet long by 14½ wide, and having four cabins or small rooms in each, of about 7 feet and a half square, and capable of containing twenty-four persons within the three Wards, reckoning two to each cabin: also leading to two other Wards, called the *Master's Side*, being each 23 feet long by 14½ wide, capable of containing about twenty persons; and to a day-room of the same dimensions, fitted up with benches and settles, after the manner of a tap-room in a public house; and also leading to eight other wards, called the *Common-Side*, one of which is 36 feet; six others, about 23 feet; and the one other 18 feet in length; all of these are about 15 feet wide, and together capable of containing about 90 persons.

No. 2. The Women-Debtors' court-yard, about 49 feet long by 16 feet wide, leads to two Wards; one of which is 36 feet long by 15 feet wide, and the other 18 feet long by 15 wide; and these are calculated to contain about 22 persons.

All the before-mentioned Wards are about 11 feet high. These yards are separated from each other by a stone wall 15 feet high, and both well supplied with water. The Debtors, who are enabled, all find their own beds and bedding; but the poor, as well Debtors as Criminals, are sometimes supplied with rugs by the City.

No. 3. The Capital Convicts' court-yard; which is also called the '*Press-Yard*,' on account of a press having been, of old time, kept there, for the punishment of persons who *stood mute* through obstinacy, and refused to plead to the indictments found against them. The manner was this: the culprit being laid upon his back, a board was placed over him, on which was put a succession of heavy weights, until he either pleaded Guilty or Not Guilty to the indictment, or died through the extremity of pressure. This barbarous custom, however, has been justly abolished for nearly a century; nor is it now customary (as heretofore) for the Executioner to put a whip-cord round the thumbs of condemned Prisoners, when brought up to receive Judgment of Death; nor for the Bellman of St. Sepulchre's parish to go into the passage leading to the cells, to pronounce two exhortations to such condemned persons on the solemn night before their execution; their time, it is hoped, being much better employed in prayer, and preparation for so awful an event, assisted by some *pious Christians, who frequently come from various parts of the Metropolis, and pray with them the whole of that night*, and until the *Ordinary*[16] arrives in the morning, to attend them in their last moments, having administered to them the Sacrament the day before.

This court-yard is about 83 feet long, by 20 wide at one end, and about 15 at the other end, leading to the *Condemned Room.* This is a day-room for the Capital Convicts, and is about 35 feet by 18; behind which is the cold bath, and over it the Men's Infirmary, of the same dimensions, having five sash windows, and a fire-place. It is about 11 feet high, (like the former apartments) and furnished with eleven iron bedsteads, sacking bottoms, flock bed and bolster, three blankets, two sheets, and a rug to each.

The Press-Yard also leads to the *Condemned Cells,* fifteen in number; which are all vaulted, and nearly 9 feet high, to the crown of the arch. Those upon the ground-floor measure full 9 feet by 6: those on the first story are a little larger, about 9 feet 6 inches by 6 feet, on account of a set-off in the wall; and the five uppermost are a little larger still, for the same reason. In the upper part of each of these condemned cells is a window, double grated, of 2 feet 9 inches wide, by 14 inches high. The doors are 4 inches thick; through each of which a circular aperture, of 2⅜ inches diameter, was made by Mr. *Kirby,* the late worthy Keeper of this Gaol, for the purpose of admitting a free current of air; and in each cell is a barrack bedstead on the floor, without bedding.

The strong stone-wall is lined all round each cell with planks, studded with broad-headed nails.

No. 4. The *Chapel-Yard* is about 43 feet long by 25; in which, as nearly as may be, are confined the Men Transports, and oldest offenders. It leads to five wards, of 20 feet by 15 each, and to one other ward of 15 feet square; all of them fitted up with barrack bedsteads on the floor, without bedding, and capable of containing about 60 Prisoners. This yard, also, as its name indicates, leads on to the body of the Chapel; on the stair-case to which are two rooms, each 15 feet square; and used for the confinement of those accomplices in crimes, who are usually termed '*King's Evidence*', and admitted to give testimony on the part of the Prosecution. Here, therefore, they are kept retired, and separate from the reach of the other joint offenders, who might otherwise be inclined to ill treat, or perhaps to murder them.

There are two other stair-cases to the galleries of the Chapel; one leading from a lodge on the Debtors' Side, the other from a lodge on the Felon Side of the Gaol.

No. 5. The Middle Yard, about 50 feet by 25, in which the less profligate are confined, leads on to five wards, each 38 feet long by 15; fitted up with barrack bedsteads on the floor, without bedding, and capable of containing about 120 persons. In this middle yard there is also an arcade under the Chapel, in which are three cells, for the temporary confinement of very refractory Prisoners.

No. 6. The Men Felons' Master-Side yard, which also is about 50 feet by 25, and contains the more decent and better-behaved Prisoners, leads on to a room, in which are lodged those Prisoners called '*Gatesmen;*' whose business it is to direct the friends of the others in this Gaol to the different wards in which they are confined. It leads, likewise, to seven wards; one 38 feet long, four of about 20 feet, the other two of about 15 feet, and all of them nearly 15 feet wide. These are capable of containing about 90 persons; and are supplied with barrack-beds, and bedding on the floor, furnished by the Gaoler, at 2*s.* 6*d.* per week each.

No. 7. The Women Felons' two court-yards, laid into one, adjoin each other at right angles; the one 40 feet, the other 20 feet long; and both about 10 feet wide. These lead to nine wards, three of which are about 30 feet by 15; the other six about 15 feet by 10; and all fitted up with barrack-bedsteads laid on the floor, except one large ward on the attick story, which is set apart for the *Female Infirmary.* This capacious apartment has four casement windows, and two fire-places; and, like all the other wards, is about 11 feet high. It is furnished with ten iron bedsteads, sacking bottoms, flock bed, bolster, &c. to each, exactly the same as in the Men Felons' Infirmary, already described under No. 3. The other eight wards can accommodate about 90 persons; and in this range all sorts of Female Criminals are confined, there being no other suitable means of keeping them distinct in their respective classes.

☞ The Women's wards are generally, indeed, so crowded, as *not to admit a space of twenty inches* for each to sleep, on the bare boards, and without any bedding whatever!

No. 8th, and last, is the court-yard called the *State-Side,* about 40 feet long by 30; where such Prisoners are safely associated, whose manners and conduct evince a more liberal style of education, and who therefore are lodged apart from all other districts of the Gaol. This yard leads to twelve rooms; three of them about 21 feet by 15, the next three about 18 feet by 15; three others nearly 15 square, and the rest about 11 feet square. These rooms are calculated to receive 30 persons, and furnished by the Keeper with bedsteads, bedding, &c. at seven shillings each per week.

All the several floors throughout this ample Prison have sewers, or water-closets, properly disposed. The eight courts above enumerated are well supplied with water; and dust-bins of stone are suitably distributed, to receive all the ashes and other dirt, which are taken away every week by the City Scavenger.

The two *lodges,* or first entrances to the Debtors' and Felons' Sides of Newgate, have each a small room adjoining, where one or more of the Turnkeys, like the eyes of *Argus,*[17] keep watch and ward day and night. They have, likewise, stair-cases leading to the Chapel Galleries, like those before noticed; and also to two rooms, with two cells in each, which are set apart either for the temporary confinement of refractory Debtors, or for Female Convicts unhappily ordered for execution; no Woman Convict being ever, otherwise, confined in a *cell.* The same stair-cases lead also to the apartments of the servants belonging to the Prison.

On the Debtors' Side, and beyond the lodge, is a convenient room for the Turnkeys; and near it a grating, through which the Debtors receive their beer from the neighbouring publick houses. The Felons' Side has a similar accommodation; and this mode of introducing their beverage is adopted, because no publican, as such, can be permitted to enter the interior of this Prison.*

There is, likewise, a convenient room beyond the Felons' Side lodge, to accommodate the servants of the Gaol. This, formerly, (when the Keeper had permission to sell beer,) was the tap-room; and, near to it is another apartment, heretofore called the '*Wine Room*' with a copper,[18] &c. fixed up, in order to cook the provisions humanely sent in by the Lord Mayor, the Sheriffs, and other friends. Into this apartment persons accused of Felony are now occasionally admitted; either to consult with their legal advisers, or to see such of their relatives or acquaintance, as may not be allowed to visit them in their own wards.

On the *top of the Gaol* are a watch-house, and a sentry-box; where two or more guards, with dogs and fire-arms, in addition to the Turnkeys below, watch all night.

Adjoining to the Felons' Side lodge is also the Keeper's office, where the Prison Books are kept; and his Clerk, called the *Clerk of the Papers,* attends daily, (Sundays excepted,) from ten in the morning till two in the afternoon, and from four till eight in the evening.

Here are also communications, from the Men Felons' Master Side Yard, and from that of the Female Felons, with the Sessions-House in the Old Bailey, by means of an arched passage, through which the Prisoners are led into Court to take their Trials.

This Prison, though comparatively vast, is generally crowded. Newgate will conveniently accommodate *ninety-four* Men, and *sixteen* Women Debtors; also *three hundred* Men, and *eighty* Women Criminals; making a total of 490 persons. It might be rendered capable of containing about 750 persons in the whole, allowing a space of 7 feet 6 inches by 3 feet for every Criminal, and rather more for every Debtor, according to the size and shape of the room. The greatest number of Debtors ever confined here at one time, has been 285 Men, and 40 Women: and, astonishing as it may appear, I have been informed that there have been in it nearly *nine hundred Criminals* at the same time; making, in all, upwards of *twelve hundred* Prisoners!

---

* The *Bar*, newly made, by which the quantity of liquor daily consumed is ascertained, proves to be a very good alteration, and, under proper restrictions, may prevent excess. Thus, also was prevented the frequency of Clubs, resorted to in consequence of cards sent out to persons who were not Prisoners. For instance: 'Mr. Such-a-one's Public.   Free and Easy Society, at No.   .'

'Mrs. So-and-so's Route.   A Dance at No.   .'

These took place generally twice, and sometimes three times in a week.

☞ An excellent opportunity was offered to the City, of building a *detached Prison for Debtors* on the side where Surgeon's Hall once stood: And, indeed, unless the Debtors be removed, to give room for a more effectual separation of Criminal Prisoners, I fear it will be very difficult to restrain that licentious inter-course, which every where presents itself in this peculiar region of Enormity; and which the utmost vigilance of the worthy Keeper cannot prevent, so long as an audacious spirit of prophaneness and vice shall continue to prevail in the lower classes of the people.

From the frequency of my visits to this much-interesting Gaol, I have so often witnessed the very distressful state of apparel, and filthy appearance of the poorer Females, particularly Convicts, crowded together in few rooms, like sheep in a pen, that it was matter of surprize there should be, comparatively, so small a number on the sick list, or that the Gaol-Fever did not prevail! One half of the Prisoners, especially the *Women*, are miserably poor; and, having pawned or sold their apparel, are covered, and scarcely covered, with rags. To prevent a circumstance so very offensive, every *Criminal*, at least, should be clad in some Uniform, that could not be disposed of; and their own clothes tied up in a bun-dle, laid aside during their stay, and then exchanged, upon their quitting the Prison. This, also, might be very beneficial to the more indigent *Debtors*, who, in any Prison, are with great difficulty to be kept in a state of cleanliness.

There were already two rooms set apart for the sick Felons, Male and Female: and lately a room, on the attick story, with four iron bedsteads and bedding, has been fitted up for the use of the *Debtors;* who, before, had no such accommoda-tion, and were therefore necessarily obliged to be put into the *Felons' Infirmary*. There was something shocking in the idea; and upon this subject I had a con-ference with that truly philanthropick character, Dr. *Lettsom*.[19] He accordingly accompanied me several times to Newgate; humanely visited the sick; examined every part of the Gaol; and gave it as his opinion, that an additional convales-cent-room was absolutely necessary.

The want of a sufficiently *thorough* AIR is a very great inconvenience to this Prison: and although, from its structure, the evil may in some measure be irre-mediable, yet, at the back part of the building, towards the East, there is a yard, or area, belonging to the *Royal College of Physicians*, which, if that learned and benevolent Body could be induced to part with, would be a great acquisition to Newgate. A space might thus be obtained for making a very practicable improve-ment to this important edifice. A wall, about 20 or 30 feet distant from that part of the Prison, might then be built; back windows might also be made in those Eastern Wards; and if some adjacent premises in Warwick Lane were likewise attainable, it would allow space sufficient for more ample Infirmaries, together with warm baths, and *another cold bath.* The present one is certainly very incommodious; since no person can use it, without first coming into the press-yard, amongst the *Capital Convicts.**

There are no established RULES and ORDERS hung up in this Prison for its government; the whole as it were resting with the Keeper. But I understand that the Worshipful Court of Aldermen have recently appointed a Committee, for the purpose of framing some *Rules* to be observed by the Debtors. In the mean time, several regulations have been judiciously adopted; and attended with such salutary effects, that the worthy Keeper says he has not now any complaint to make against the Debtors.

The CHAPEL is plain and neat; the Prisoners silently attentive: No noise in the court-yard; nor devotion interrupted or destroyed by opening and shutting the door during Divine Service, as too often happens in the King's Bench Prison.

Below is a pew belonging to the Chaplain; and adjoining to it a larger one for *Men Criminals;* opposite to which are three benches, enclosed with an iron railing, set apart also for men of that class, – Capital Convicts excepted, who sit in a pew about the middle of the Chapel, with a large table in it; whereon a *coffin* is placed, whenever any persons but *Murderers* are ordered for execution. Those sentenced for murder are always kept on bread and water, within their cells, where the Ordinary or other Minister attends them.

Facing the Communion Table are the reading-desk and pulpit. On the South side is a gallery for Debtors: on the North side another for Female Criminals; in which last-mentioned gallery, at the West end, and over the Chaplain's pew, is an enclosed seat for the Sheriffs.

The Chapel not being large enough to contain all the Prisoners in the Gaol, they are often left to their own option: those, however, who do not attend Divine Service on Sunday, are generally detained in their several Wards, to avoid hindering the edification of such as are sincerely and better disposed.

There seems to be a deficiency in the manner of conducting the sacred Service, from the want of a discreet and steady person, capable of leading the *Responses,* and setting and joining in the *Psalm.* This I should conceive to be a very essential business, and especially to be observed *in all Gaols;* inasmuch as the neglect of religious duties, both in principle and in manner, is generally the first fatal step towards a reprobate and dishonest course of life. Criminals in Gaols, being for the most part ignorant of their duty to their Creator, are often at a loss how to conduct themselves in Chapel, without having some person in the Lay-Clerk's

---

*   An additional cold-bath might be made under the stairs of the South Wing of the Prison, where there is a space 10 feet by 8; and about 10 feet distant from a well, now flagged over, in which the water is 9 feet deep: or it may be supplied from a cock close by, which has New-River water laid on three days in the week.

desk, to whom they may look up as a guide for their proper demeanour; For want of which, they either irreverently sit down, when they ought to stand up or kneel; or else employ themselves in scribbling on the benches, or have their eyes, and of course their thoughts, wandering from their duty. This, indeed, I am informed, is a frequent cause of complaint by the Ordinary against them; whereas it is to be hoped, that a good pattern set them from the desk before-mentioned, might in a great measure be the means of bringing many to a sense, both of the sacredness of the place, and of what they all alike owe to the GOD and Saviour of all.

The danger, in point of Health, to the Prisoners, and to the City, has at times been very imminent, from the great number of persons crowded together in a space comparatively small. The number of Prisoners here in May 1802, was *eight hundred and sixty seven;* and the average number of some years previous, had been from six to seven hundred.

The number of deaths, between the first of January and the first of May, in the year 1803, was *forty-nine;* many of whom we may reasonably suppose to have died of putrid disorders, as I have been informed that some very hale and robust men, who had been removed from the Poultry Compter[20] in a perfect state of health, but a few days before, were among the number just mentioned. Since, however, a more frequent removal of Convicts has taken place, the deaths have happened more amongst the Debtors than the Criminals; possibly, because the average number of their description has not been so much reduced (except immediately after the passing of an Insolvent Act) as that of the Felons; whose average has been reduced by nearly one half, and of whom two only appear to have died within the last two years; and of the whole Gaol-List, whether Debtors or Felons, not one died of putrid or infectious fever within the same period. Let me here also observe, that if all the Sheriff's Debtors in the vicinity of London were taken (as formerly) by *habeas corpus*,[21] before a Judge, to be charged in execution, their average number in the common Gaols would be much reduced; as there would then remain none but those upon Mesne-Process,[22] together with the Court of Conscience[23] Debtors; and a still greater security from the danger of contagion might be expected.

Heretofore, the Gaol was not sufficiently supplied with soft water, to cleanse the court-yards, and the well of the pump frequently became dry: But the City have now (1807) caused the supply of water to be daily renewed, instead of three times a week; and have also erected an Engine, by which the water can easily be forced, through leaden hose, into every part of the Prison.

The Act and Clauses are conspicuously hung up; and the Gaoler is intelligent and humane.

Prisoners discharged from hence *by Proclamation*, are liberated in a morning, and have one shilling each given them. Others are dismissed as *acquitted on Trial*, in the day-time, or in the evening, *without any money* being given. This is the more to be regretted, as I am credibly informed that an instance has occurred, of a Woman's having been discharged *penniless* on one day, and brought in again on the next!

The number of Prisoners on Mesne-Process, for want of Bail, in Newgate, on the 4th May, 1807, for Debts *under* 20*l. was forty-eight*, having 85 Children.

The number, of the same description, for Debts above 20*l.* was, at the same time *twenty-five*, having 57 Children.

And the number for Debts above 30*l.* and under 40*l.* at the same period, was *thirteen*, having 25 Children.

The number of Prisoners on Mesne-Process for want of Bail in Newgate, on the 28th June, 1809, for Debts *under* 20*l.* was 66, having 43 Wives, and 127 Children.

The number of the same description, for Debts *above* 20*l.* and under 30*l.* was at the same time forty-four, having 27 Wives and 69 Children.

And the number, for Debts above 30*l.* and under 40*l.* at the same period, thirty-two, having 21 Wives, and 63 Children.

☞ Since writing the above narrative of Newgate, I have been informed that the College of Physicians have determined to dispose of the whole of their premises in Warwick-lane. It is much therefore to be hoped, that so unlooked-for, and so excellent an opportunity, may not be lost by the City of London;[24] as thus every means will be happily afforded, to *build a separate Gaol for the Debtors;* and thereby render that for the Felons far more commodious, unoffensive, wholesome, and secure.

from Henry Grey Bennet, *A Letter to the Common Council and Livery of the City of London, on the Abuses Existing in Newgate, Showing the Necessity of an Immediate Reform in the Management of that Prison* (London: James Ridgway, 1818), pp. 40–79.

Bennet (1777–1836) was the second son of the earl of Tankerville and the daughter of a London banker. As a second son he had to seek out a profession. Educated at Eton and Cambridge, he tried the army and diplomacy before taking up the law and then politics, being elected a Member of Parliament in 1806, where he associated with the reformist Whigs around Samuel Whitbread. In Parliament he constantly harassed and irritated the government and the Prince Regent, attacking army expenditure, limitations of civil liberties, taxes, expenditure on the royal household, colonial maladministration, the abuse of the insane and of child chimney sweeps, corporal and capital punishments and especially the criminal law system. With Sir Samuel Romilly, Sir Richard Phillips and others he repeatedly agitated for parliamentary inquiry into and reform of the criminal laws and the penal system, with some success during the 1810s and early 1820s. In 1824 he withdrew from political life, however, after the death of two of his children and a year later was involved in a scandal for sexually importuning a young male servant while travelling on the Continent. Thereafter he and his wife lived in Italy.

Bennet's *Letter* is characteristic of the intense debate on crime and punishment in the years after the Napoleonic Wars, when demobilization of large numbers of soldiers and sailors and economic depression sharpened social and political conflict. Like other key documents from this period, Bennet's relies on firsthand observation and direct involvement, as seen in the extract here.

The question is here then raised. What are these unanswerable reasons, why the Prisons of London should not furnish, by their good management, an example to the rest of the kingdom? To be sure, if, in the discussion of the propriety, policy, or practicability of a measure, one party is to take for granted, that there is some insurmountable obstacle to the attainment of the object in dispute, the question is at an end, and there is no occasion to debate farther. The first point then is to ascertain the nature and amount of this impediment. Now I will venture to assert, that if I was to give a man a thousand guesses, he would never discover what this all-powerful obstacle is. It is then neither more nor less than the poverty of the City of London: their inability, from want of funds, to construct a Prison large enough to contain the criminals whom they are called upon to confine. It is no answer to those who object to the overcrowding of these Prisons to say that the confined space renders it necessary; for the reply is, Why is there that want of room? This argument of want of room, to make those arrangements which humanity and sound policy require, is not new: it has been advanced at all times when abuses were to be continued, when an indifference to the happiness and improvement of mankind was to be justified to the world, if not to our own consciences, and a bad system practically maintained, though upon acknowledged principles it was indefensible.

In the Hospitals at Paris, prior to the Revolution, want of room was also pleaded as a reason why four and sometimes six persons were placed together in the same bed: and so slow was the progress of reform, that the same evils complained of in 1657 existed in 1767. In these Hospitals, in 1784, two thousand six hundred sick patients filled the space of nine hundred and seventy toises,[1] or five thousand eight hundred and twenty feet, one person being placed above the other; so that those who lay on the uppermost shelf were visited by the means of a ladder. Thirteen inches were allowed for each patient, five inches less than the space allotted for the females in Newgate. I entertain no doubt, that many good and praiseworthy persons defended these arrangements, such is the bias always felt to support what already exists: but the reformers prevailed at last, and the old system was abandoned. Though the advice may be unpalatable to the vanity of Englishmen, I can assure them, that while we have something to learn from our neighbours in the management of Prisons, there is also valuable instruction to be gained by studying the economy of their Hospitals.

But to return to this plea of poverty: unless I had heard it advanced by persons who really were at large without a keeper, I should not have believed, that men of sound minds could have urged it. What! the City of London too poor to build a Prison! the metropolis of this great empire, the wealth of which is proverbial; which contains all that widely circulated mercantile opulence, ready to burst its own warehouses with its richly varied exuberance! That this emporium of wealth, commerce, and luxury, should pretend to be too poor to construct a fit Prison for its own criminals, cannot surely be brought forward as a serious argument. No, gentlemen, no; all this is idle mockery. The City of London is never too poor when a feast is to be given; or when millions are to be spent to further its own trade. Why then should poverty be pleaded when it is called on to perform its duties?

The Report farther states, that it would be necessary to cover ground to the amount of thirty acres, if a Prison was to be constructed upon the model of those which they examined in various counties in the kingdom. To be sure, if there is to be the same waste of space, and the same clumsy arrangement, as is the peculiar character of all the Prisons which the City of London has built, and particularly the new one in Whitecross Street,[2] I hardly see a limit to the space, or an end to the expense. But I will take the liberty of suggesting, that there would be no difficulty in building an airy, light, commodious Prison for one thousand persons, each with a separate cell or room, for a less sum than that ill-constructed edifice has cost.

The point, then, at issue between the Public and your Magistrates is this: – Shall they (I care not under what excuses of want of room or want of funds) so construct, regulate, and manage these Prisons, as not only to inflict as much bodily pain and suffering as they can, while preserving life, upon the miserable victims who are confined within their walls, but also, whether they shall keep an organised school for the propagation of every species of crime, for vitiating youth, for corruption of manners, and for changing the first aberration from moral rectitude into confirmed habits of fraud and robbery?

If there were even any serious obstacles to the destruction of the old system, the advantage of getting rid of it would amply compensate the Public for any sacrifice they might make. But in truth there are none. The City of London is bound by its charter to maintain the Prisons of the county of Middlesex. If they then really can make out a case to the satisfaction of the Public, by a fair exposure of their accounts, that they are unable so to do, there can be no doubt, that, on proper application to Parliament, relief would be afforded them.

There are two ways of doing this. First, To raise the money by a rate on the inhabitants of the City. Secondly, To compel the inhabitants of Middlesex to pay a fair proportion of the cost.

I have certainly no wish to call on the City of London to make any popular sacrifice; and I heartily concur with the indignation, which your late worthy Chief Magistrate[3] expressed, when a proposition to that effect was indecently hinted by Lord Liverpool.[4] But we are driven to no such sad dilemma: a new and fit Prison might be constructed, without trenching[5] on one of the rights of popular election; and the mere allusion to it, on the part of the Prime Minister, is a great insult to the Livery of London.[6] I contend, that the Public have a right to call upon the Magistrates of the City to maintain its Prisons after the most approved reformatory system, &c.; that *something more than an approach* to the judicious management of the best Gaols in the country is expected from them: and I must add, that disposition is alone wanted fully to effect these objects.

From the Returns laid before Parliament it appears, that no less than six thousand four hundred and thirty-nine persons were committed to the Prisons of the City of London in four years, from 1813 to 1816, inclusive. Of these, four thousand and thirteen were convicted, one thousand five hundred and forty-three acquitted, against seven hundred and forty-three no bill was found, and one hundred and twenty-seven were discharged by proclamation. It is then evident, that more than one third of all the persons committed to these Prisons were, in the eye of the law, innocent of the crimes laid to their charge. How many of these were really innocent, I can have no means of judging; but that the number of this class was great, I can have no doubt. I intreat you, then, seriously to think, how many of your innocent fellow creatures have been condemned to associate with convicted guilt, to pass in torture and misery the period between their commitment and acquittal.

But setting aside all consideration of bodily suffering, loss of character, and all the calamities which fall upon the families of the poor, the inevitable consequence of imprisonment, I beg you to calculate how many of these hundreds of persons were there for the first time of their lives; and how grievous were the effects of their promiscuous assemblage; of the loss of self respect, and the exposure of the young and unwary to the arts of the fraudulent, and the taunts and mockeries of the idle, the profane, and the desperate. 'In a Prison,' writes Dr. Johnson, 'the check of the public eye is removed, and the power of the law is spent. There are few fears; there are no blushes. Every one fortifies himself against his remaining sensibility, endeavouring to practise upon others the arts that are practised on himself, and to gain the applause of his worst associates by imitating thir[7] manners.'[8]

During the first three years of the period above referred to, forty girls and two hundred and eight boys, under fifteen years of age, were committed to Newgate; and from the 1st of January, 1816, to the same day, 1817, eighty-five girls, and four hundred and twenty-nine boys, under twenty years of age, were confined in that Prison; and thus were more than five hundred young persons exposed last year to the contamination of the Prison System of the metropolis, and by much the greater proportion of them were associated with old offenders, and hardened delinquents. I contend, that the public have a right to demand from the magistrates so to construct their Prisons, that of the children, the innocent at least, should not be made criminal by example and education. Even if safe detention and not reformation be all that the City System aims at, and that, if in 1817 those, who are the organs of law and justice in the metropolis, cannot contemplate an approach even of correcting by discipline the morals and manners of the vicious and profligate, the people of England are entitled to expect, that even the guilty shall not be corrupted and made worse by means that ought to be used for the purposes of making them better.

The main question, then, to be considered is, what is really the present reformed state of Newgate?

The Classification of Prisoners.

There are several yards and wards in Newgate, in which the male prisoners are classed after the following manner. First, Those committed for trial for felonies. Second, Convicts. Third, Misdemeanors. Fourth, Fines.[9] Fifth, Those under sentence of death. Sixth, Boys under the age of fifteen, for all offences.

You will observe, therefore, that the classification is of the most general kind. The youth accused of the smallest felony is confined with the most notorious criminal; with those charged with murder, piracy, housebreaking, and highway robbery. The application, then, of the principle of classification is scarcely worth notice, and the objections to the mixing of all sorts of offenders together, the youthful with the adult criminal, he who has committed his first offence with him whose life has been passed in the perpetration of crimes, from simple fraud to aggravated felonies, remain as strong as before, and the evil is very little lessened by the limited classification here practised: so that, when you are told that the system of classification is adopted at Newgate, you are told that which is only partially true. The tried and untried are not now mixed together, except in one ward, and that only for the present. The fines, and the accused of misdemeanors, and the felon convicts, are not now shut up in the same yard; *but persons, whose crimes are of a different character and complexion, all the steps and stages of guilt, are associated together.* The school of crimes is still kept up; and though the teachers may have their range of instruction narrowed, yet, that these preceptors are active and diligent, as far as their field of enterprise extends, though not so much mischief is done, or so much youth and comparative innocence debauched and ruined, yet those who visit Newgate oftenest, and know what goes on there best, can furnish ample evidence of the extent and consequences of this system. The reform is good the little way it goes. Why then stop short, and not *approach* somewhat nearer to carrying into practice the statutes of the 19th, 24th, and 31st Geo. III?[10] The letter and spirit of these acts direct a proper classification of prisoners, with a view of preventing the hardened from corrupting the youthful criminal. Let us then examine, if either the letter or the spirit is substantially carried into effect in Newgate. I saw there, in November last, several boys mixed with men convicts, in their yard. I interceded for one, a child in appearance and manner, and he was removed into the school, where he ought to have been placed long before; as his offence, though heavy, was his first, and his artless and simple behaviour bespoke a want of familiarity with the ways of guilt. I saw him taken out of the circle of his associates, and I considered him as a fit object for the Penitentiary, at Milbank:[11] but a few days after he was *removed to the Hulks,*[12] *there to be reformed,* and to learn those lessons of religion and morals, that regard for the property of others, and that respect for the laws of his country, which are taught in those acknowledged receptacles of purity and virtue.

I visited Newgate again on the 20th of December. It contained then but few prisoners, the sessions having lately terminated. There were only thirty-nine fines, or persons of all ages and characters, under sentence of imprisonment for a limited period. Among them were Brock, Pelham, and Power;[13] a lad sentenced to a few months imprisonment for a fraud; and a man imprisoned for five years for an attempt to commit an abominable crime:[14] four of the fines were under twenty years of age. No doubt the morals of these young persons must be much benefited by the company in which they were placed.

There were one hundred and twenty-three convicts under sentence for life, fourteen, and seven years, promiscuously together, in different wards. Of these, forty-seven were under twenty years of age, and many of them of the early ages of fifteen and sixteen. Among the untried for felonies, fourteen out of fifty-seven were under twenty years of age. Many of these wretched beings were there for their first offences; and the Saturday preceding my visit, an account being taken of the whole number then under confinement, out of two hundred and three, tried and untried, forty-seven had been in Newgate before.

Of the young convicts, by far the greater part will be sent to the Hulks to join company with the poor boy, who was hurried there last November; and from the manner in which they have been classed, the associates they have met, the lessons of the academy in which they have studied, and the arts therein taught, when their time of punishment is expired, they will, I make no doubt, be found again in Newgate, to teach other youths the lessons in which they have been themselves instructed, and to keep unbroken a single link in that chain of offences, which, beginning by a simple fraud, ripens into robbery and murder. For my own part, with all the horror that I feel at the system of capital punishments, which prevails in this country, and though the very contemplation of the possibility of the act makes me shudder, yet, when I think of the wretched forlorn state of these miserable beings, many without a friend or home, but their Gaoler and their Prison, the pains that are taken to vitiate and the indifference to reform, I am at times inclined to think the mercy of the Crown, that saves their lives, to be the greatest cruelty. I am sure, to the victims themselves, death is better than the life to which they are reserved. This however is most true, that to those, who think that, when the offenders are lodged in Prison, when the forms of the law are spent, all care of them should cease, and who practically consider all reformation hopeless, there is but one more step to take; and that is, to recur again to the ancient practice, to exhibit again rows of thirty and forty offenders on the scaffold, to place in a line ten or twenty children to be executed in the face of day, in the nineteenth century of the Christian æra: the spectacle to be performed in the capital of the freest country in Europe, amid a people whose vain boast it is, that they are more humane, more tender hearted, more sparing of human life than their neighbours. Horrible as this exhibition would be, *disgraceful* to us as Christians and civilized beings, if the interest of the wretches, whom we save to plunge them deeper in perdition, were consulted, it would be the most merciful plan. Nine-tenths of these commit offences from misery, from the seduction of others, from the neglect or want of parents. If, then, reformation of these miserable beings is not to be looked to, but their punishment alone is to be considered, experience has shown, that the milder punishment does not deter. The choice is then narrowed, and we must recur again to the disgraceful severities of our ancestors.

But I contend, that the reformatory system is alone that which ought to be pursued; and the first step to be taken in it is, in the earliest stage of guilt, so to separate and to class as to make the objects of legal detention, or criminal punishment, better for the moral discipline to which they have been subjected. It is for these reasons that I call upon you to admit of no delay, to hear of no excuse; but to insist upon your magistrates and representatives adopting some efficient plan to give to their Prisons that reformatory character, which the well-being of society demands from their hands.

In respect to the women prisoners, a great and important change for the better in the mode of confining them has taken place. They are not now the tried, and untried, mixed together; those under sentence of death are placed by themselves: but even here the convicts and fines are not separated. Girls of the tenderest years are associated with the most profligate characters. On the 20th of December last, there were ninety-seven female prisoners in Newgate, seventeen only of whom were for trial. The greatest proportion of the tried were convicts; one of them was only eleven years of age; and of the whole number eighteen were under twenty-one. The humane and excellent management of Mrs. Fry and the Society of Friends[15] has placed this part of the Prison in a state of comparative excellence. The disgusting scenes that formerly occurred there have ceased. But the system, even as it is, cannot be persevered in, and the benefits of this meagre and limited classification preserved, if more room be not given; for the numbers now are nearly equal to filling the space allotted to them, and one hundred and seventy women have been confined there at the same time. No praise of mine can add weight to the tribute of general applause which Mrs. Fry and her Committee of Friends have received from all who have witnessed their efforts.

Those who visit Newgate must be satisfied, that much good has been done; not indeed, by rules and regulations emanating from the Prison Committee of

Aldermen, but by the exertions of individuals, who have devoted their time to the reformation of the vicious and the relief of the distressed. The necessity for their labour, and the praise bestowed on their benevolence, is not flattering to the regular legitimate managers of this Prison. If the regulations were as they ought to be, and places of separate confinement provided for the different classes of offenders, according to the plans now universally approved of, Mrs. Fry would have found half her task performed. She might have stimulated the idle to industry, instructed the ignorant, reformed the profligate by precept and example, and consoled the unfortunate; and she and her friends would not have to lament that their labours are rendered comparatively of little use from the absence of those means of classification, which are essential to the success of any plan of rational reform. The want of these means was strikingly illustrated, during my visit to Newgate on the 20th of December. I found two convicts among the untried female prisoners; and, upon inquiry why they were placed there, was told they were *too bad and abandoned to be kept with their companions:* so that the punishment inflicted upon these profligate and convicted felons was to place them, not by themselves, but with those whom the law considers as innocent. Thus those, who were untried, were punished by being compelled to have, as associates, women who were even outcasts from the society of convicted felons.

Perhaps, among these seventeen untried persons, who were forced to keep company with these two women, there might have been a girl[16] circumstanced as one was in this part of the Prison last year. She was crowded into a room with an assemblage of idle, drunken prostitutes and thieves; with a woman committed for, and I believe afterwards convicted of child murder. This poor girl was an unwilling instrument of a man, who seduced her into an attempt to utter a forged note. She pleaded guilty, and her life was saved; but she was sentenced to be transported. From the kindness of Mr. Capper,[17] who is ever ready to relieve real distress, and to lessen the severities of our penal laws, operating on individual cases, she was placed in the Penitentiary at Milbank, where she has so conducted herself as to merit the praise of the managers of that excellent institution. While this young person was in Newgate (and she was but eighteen), her modest appearance and manner attracted the notice of all who visited the Prison. Among others, an American gentleman, who was told there, that I had interested myself to preserve her from the ruin with which she was menaced, wrote to me to entreat that I would not relax my endeavours to save her from the *Hell upon Earth*, as he called this Prison.

Think, then, I intreat you, what must have been the feelings of a modest girl, in such a situation; and then remember, that, while I write this, many may be in a similar condition. A single breach of the law, however trifling, may lead to detention in Prison; though the person so confined may have, with this exception, every moral feeling, as pure as those of the best of us. And these miserable beings (miserable because they are prisoners, but more to be pitied because they are confined with all that is bad, profligate, and base) must be corrupted, almost past all redemption, by the want of that proper classification which I am contending for. What then is wanted here is room for their separation; and till that is obtained, Mrs. Fry may do much to relieve present misery: her charity may be like the benevolence of her heart, boundless: she may remedy magisterial neglect: she may relieve individual wretchedness: she may lessen all the evils attendant on this mode of confinement: but the disease is past her cure. It is, however, in your hands: you can furnish a remedy; and that can alone be found in the construction of a Prison, upon a plan embracing all those reformatory advantages, the usefulness of which are now no longer matters of dispute.

The Condemned Cells.

There are fifteen condemned cells in Newgate, each nine feet long by seven wide, furnished with one barrack or bedstead; and in which, according to Mr. Newman, two persons *may* lie. These cells were originally constructed for the solitary confinement of those who were condemned to death, in the period between their sentence and its execution. From their size, it is evident they were not designed to hold more than one person; and yet two are almost constantly confined there, and very often three. In the last session, before the Report was made, forty-three persons were shut up in these cells. On the 20th December last there were twenty-seven capital convicts in them, the product of the session which was just terminated; and in all probability an equal if not a greater number will be convicted in the present January. Thus, then, these cells will be filled with their ordinary complement of three persons in each. Of the twenty-seven convicts, fifteen were under twenty years of age; and two of them infants of the tender years of thirteen and nine, who were both capitally convicted of highway robbery on the person, and by the evidence of a child of six years of age.

It must be remarked here, first, that about one in ten or twelve of the persons capitally convicted are executed: and, secondly, that sometimes three, four, and even six months elapse before their fate is determined.*

I shall say nothing of the nature of the laws that inflict the penalty of death on such a variety of offences, nor of the method adopted to get rid of their severity, which is the real cause of the delay between the sentence and its execution – the Recorder[18] being employed in trying over again all the cases that have been determined by the Judges and Juries, seeking out reasons in good character, and in

---

*   On the 31st March, 1814, Mr. Newman stated to a Committee of the House of Commons, that before the last Report one person had been in the cells since 1812. In February last there were above one hundred persons under sentence in Newgate, five of whom had received sentence in July, four in September, twenty-nine in October, twenty-nine in December, twenty-one in January, and twelve in the February sessions, which were not then closed.

the complexion of the crime, in order to be enabled to recommend the remission of the punishment to the Prince Regent.[19] This curious anomaly in the execution of our penal statutes, and this triumph of humane manners over ferocious laws, I shall abstain from commenting on; but I intreat you to pay attention to what passes in these cells in that interval between the sentence, its remission, or its execution.

I conclude we are agreed upon the utility of solitary confinement as a moral regimen, thereby leading the sinner to repentance, and preparing him to meet, with religious hope, the death to which he is condemned; or, if the sentence of the law be not carried into effect, by leading to such communion with himself as shall fix in even a wavering mind resolutions of future amendment. I conclude we agree in this view of the subject; for, if we do not, I cannot hope to carry you with me to the conclusion I seek to draw; and the observations I am about to make will appear strange and fanatical to those, who view, either with approbation or indifference, those unseemly exhibitions which daily occur in this part of the Prison of Newgate.

As long as these cells were considered as instruments of moral discipline, that arrangement was wise, which closed their doors on the solitary prisoner from two in the afternoon to nine in the morning, leaving him only five hours for the enjoyment of air, exercise, and the society of his friends and companions; but where there is no solitary confinement, and no moral discipline, this mode of imprisonment *is only so much bodily torture.*

It is well observed by one of our greatest writers on these subjects, 'that a man in solitary confinement feels not those emotions of friendship and enmity which society has created. He has no longer that variety of thoughts, which result from the conversation of his companions, and the view of external objects, or the pursuits of business or pleasure. By the deprivation of light, the number of impressions is considerably diminished; the mind of the prisoner is reduced to a state of vacuity, to an internal darkness; and, deprived of the support which his passions might afford, renders him sensible of his own weakness. In fact, this pain is not sufficiently acute to occupy the mind entirely, and to take from it the power of reflection: on the contrary, he feels more than ever the necessity of calling to his aid all the train of ideas which his situation presents to him; and the most natural is, that train of events by which, step by step, he has been led to the commission of the crime, for which he now undergoes the punishment – the crime, of which all the pleasures are past, and nothing left behind but its fatal effects. He recals to himself now his days of early innocence and happiness, which assume a new interest when contrasted with his present misery: he repents of his misconduct; and, if he have a wife, or children, or parents, his affection for them is rekindled in his heart, with regrets for the sorrow he has brought on them. Another advantage of this situation is, that it is singularly favourable for the influence of religious appeals, in the entire absence of all pleasures, either external or internal. Religious thoughts assume a new authority. Struck with his misfortunes, and the events which led to the discovery of his crime, he feels that it is a Divine Providence that has led him by secret ways, and defeated all his precautions to save himself against detention. If it be God that punishes, God only can save. A man must be cast in another mould than the rest of his fellow creatures to refuse, in such a moment as this, the aids and consolations of religion.'*

These trains of thought and action are the most important of the benefits to be obtained by the system of solitary confinement; and I do not believe, that, among the male prisoners at least, many examples can be brought, where, under that discipline, the stoutest heart has not been humbled, and the most ferocious spirit subdued. This, then, is the theory of some of the wisest men who have adorned the age and country in which they lived; and the names, if not the works of Montesquieu, Beccaria, and Bentham,[20] must be familiar to every person of good education. The practice, too, wherever adopted, whether in England or elsewhere, in Flanders, or in America, has always been attended with the best results.

What, then, is the practice in Newgate. There is the infliction of much bodily torture, in crowding two and three wretches, loaded with heavy irons, into the small space of nine feet by seven, from five in the afternoon to nine in the morning, and keeping them thus confined for months; but there is no mental punishment, there is no moral reform. In these dreary hours (and I speak from undoubted information) nine-tenths of the prisoners pass their time in discussing their chances of pardon, in projects for the future; not plans of amendment, but schemes for fresh depredation. There is no time for reflection: there is little sorrow, no repentance: the hardened encourage the timid, and all are deprived of that secret communion with their own hearts, which can exist only in a state of solitude. When indeed the fatal warrant comes down, in proportion of former confidence is present despair. The few feverish days and nights soon fleet away; and the poor wretch, bewildered more than penitent, is led to the scaffold, and is executed in the sight of thousands – pitied by all, an example to none.

But even when the day is fixed for this execution, there is no separation of those who are to suffer death from those whose fate is *undetermined*. The unhappy lad Vartie,[21] who was lately executed, complained heavily of the company in which he was associated; and justly considered the enormity of this treatment, as one of the greatest of his afflictions, and as an aggravation of his cruel fate. There are at present fifteen boys in the condemned cells under twenty years of age; two of them infants of thirteen and nine years old. The late keeper of Newgate (Mr. Newman), after the establishment of the school, was accustomed to place

---

* Theorie des Peines et des Recompenses par Jeremie Bentham, p. 124, 125.

in it children, or young persons of a better description than ordinary felons, who were sentenced to death. As these persons were never executed, the separation of them from their companions was a wise and rational measure; and I can speak from my own knowledge of the fact, that several of these wretched beings have, by these means, under Providence, been saved from final ruin. That arrangement is however at an end; for your Prison Committee of Magistrates lately thought fit to summon before them the ordinary, Mr. Cotton;[22] and, after censuring him for having presumed to interfere in any part of the Prison management, came to a resolution to place all the boys (*infants* as well as *children*), who were convicted, *ironed*, in the cells with the most hardened and guilty malefactors, there to remain, unless removed by the special order of the Prison Committee. Thus neither the sheriffs, nor the ordinary, nor the keeper, have in this respect any authority in the Prison. As might have been supposed, the object of this resolution was less to re-assume an authority which others had usurped, and to do the same thing, though by a different machinery, than to prevent the thing being done at all. Accordingly, the first result of this inhuman and irrational order has been the placing of two children, infants in mind as well as body, ironed, in the same cell with another man. The good sense and humanity of Mr. Brown, the keeper, have instructed him to place them with a well-conducted and orderly convict; but they are still exposed to the conversation of all around them during the day; and if the cells, as is often the case, had been filled with persons of the most depraved habits and character, with these the children must have passed sixteen hours out of the twenty-four.

I abstain from all comment on this transaction; but I entreat some of you to visit Newgate: see with your own eyes these miseries, and then rest, if you can, one hour without endeavouring to force the recal of this mischievous mandate.

Of all the persons who are now in the cells, few, if any, will be executed; but, by the mode in which they are confined, not one of the good effects which their melancholy situation might have led to will be obtained. The hardened criminal will confirm in his impenitence those who, under a better regimen, might have been reclaimed; and by far the greater part of these men, boys, and children, will quit the society in which your magistrates have compelled them to associate, with the loss of all that was good (be it little or much) which belonged to their character when they entered the fatal walls of this Prison; with all sense of shame obliterated; and instructed alone in the various means by which their companions have forfeited their lives to the laws of their country. Remember, I pray you, that 'though in the world there is a mixture of good and bad, in a Prison the society is composed of individuals more or less corrupted: it is even to the most corrupted a place of the greatest danger – What must it be, then, for that class of prisoners who are there for their first offence? They have yielded to the temptations of indigence: they have been drawn in by bad example: they are of that age when the heart is flexible, and not yet hardened to crime: a punishment well administered will be salutary. If instead of being reformed they become more vicious, if from small frauds they go on to robbery and murder, it is the education of the Prison that you must blame.'*

The School.

On the appointment of Mr. Cotton as ordinary of Newgate, one of his first acts was the establishment of this School. All, however, was not even here done, which was requisite, to separate the young from the old offender. The boys were taken from the society of the men, and at least some hours in the day were occupied in reading and writing, and in receiving moral and religious instruction; it is evident, therefore, though they might not become much better, that the confinement in Prison did not make them worse. At first they were placed in a very confined room, from whence they were removed into larger apartments, having the use of a yard to play about in, and enjoy the air. At present this is taken from them: they are again shut up in close rooms, being permitted only the use of a yard for a short time in the day. When I visited them, on the 20th of December, they had all the appearance of bad health. The whole arrangement was manifestly deteriorated; and it is evident to all, who take an interest in the institution, that it is no favourite, and is gradually dying away; soon, I make no doubt, to cease altogether. The boys were dirty, ragged, and wretched, and the rooms close and offensive. A small increase of numbers, in their present situation, would probably produce among them a fever.

Food.

When the Committee of the House of Commons examined the condition of Newgate in 1814, they reported, that the food was insufficient. Accordingly the Aldermen of the City felt themselves obliged to augment the allowance, and the following arrangement took place: fourteen ounces of bread to be delivered daily to each prisoner, and two pounds of meat, without bone, weekly.

The Committee appointed to visit the different Prisons in the kingdom proposed, that one pound and a half of bread be given daily, one pint of good gruel every morning for breakfast, and the meat withheld, except half a pound to be delivered every Sunday to those who conduct themselves well: but as yet this recommendation has not been adopted, with the exception of withholding the meat. In this recommendation I most cordially concur. At present the allowance of food is not sufficient; and no one can visit Newgate, and see the appearance of a prisoner, when first brought in there, if in good health, and contrast it with

---

*   Theorie des Peines et des Recompenses, p. 137.

his looks after a few months confinement, and not be convinced, that want of sufficient food is the cause of that change. When the prisoners possess money to purchase, or friends to supply them with additional food, they still continue to preserve a healthy appearance: it is only the poor and the friendless who suffer from the scantiness of the allowance.

Mr. Howard[23] remarks, that prisoners require a greater degree of food to preserve health than persons at large. Their minds being depressed so, they need more nourishment than those who are at liberty. I have no doubt of the correctness of this opinion, and any one, who takes the trouble of making the inquiry, will learn, that the artisan, the manufacturer, and the husbandman, are so reduced by scanty food, as well as by the loss of the habit of labour, as not to be able to do half the work, when discharged from Prison, which they were able to perform when first committed to it. Besides, this deficiency of proper nutriment leads to diseases, such as declines,[24] &c. &c. I am no friend to luxury in a Prison; but the torture of famine and disease is not in the sentence of the law, which inflicts imprisonment: least of all is it warrantable previous to conviction, when safe detention is all that is contemplated. One pound and a half of the best wheaten bread daily, together with the two pounds of meat weekly, is the least that a prisoner requires, of the ages of fifteen to thirty; and I have no doubt, that the allowance of food in Newgate is not equal to the sustentation of the human frame.

Bedding and Clothing.

The Visiting Committee of the City of London recommend, in their Report, that iron bedsteads should be provided, and bedding furnished; and that, for the future, all traffic in the hiring of beds should be abolished. *This recommendation has not been followed:* nothing has been done; and the practice objected to remains as before: nor is there any appearance of there being any plan in agitation to carry into effect this wholesome advice.

The male prisoners in Newgate, who cannot afford to pay for the hire of a bed, sleep on the bare boards, in the same room in which they have passed the day, the City furnishing only two rugs[25] for each person. On the 20th of November, I found thirty convicts in one room in the middle yard, eleven of them being under twenty years of age, and one only sixteen. The room is calculated to hold twenty-five; though, when the Prison is full, fifty have been stowed in it. There were then two wards entirely unoccupied; and I can imagine no other reason for thus crowding thirty persons, in one room, than that of economy. But shall the saving of a sack of coals be set against the convenience, not to say the health of the prisoners?

One might have thought, that the experience of the year, when above three hundred persons have been attacked by fever in the Prison, owing to its crowded state, would have secured the wretched prisoners from being penned in a room, like sheep in Smithfield;[26] but the Visiting Managers of your Prison think otherwise; and thus these convicts will remain, till they are removed either to the Hospital or to the Hulks. They complained heavily of what they suffered in the night from heat, closeness, and offensive smells. Besides, as the prisoners, in this mode of confining them at night, are for the greater part unable to take off their clothes, and are thus compelled to wear them unchanged, perhaps for months, the want of personal cleanliness, the necessary result of such neglect, must be very injurious to health. Those, who can afford to pay for their beds, which consist of a mattrass spread on the floor, are in constant contact with those, who, from poverty, are compelled to sleep as above described.

Mr. Howard, and all who have written on the economy of Prisons, insist on the necessity, for the due preservation of health, of the prisoners undressing themselves at night. In all of the well-managed County Prisons, a bed and bedstead, blankets, and in some places sheets, are furnished. Is it, I ask then, creditable to the City of London, that the same system should not be adopted in Newgate? I abstain from all remarks on the moral and physical evils engendered by this mode of imprisoment:[27] I leave them to your imagination. They are too revolting to be even stated. But if they cannot be thought on without disgust and pain, what must *they suffer who endure them?*

The poorer prisoners in Newgate are often in a most wretched condition: they are sometimes ragged, without shirts, or shoes, or stockings. I have never been there without seeing many, in this respect, in the most forlorn condition, and without hearing complaints, *from all quarters*, upon this subject. There is a fund, called the Sheriffs' Fund, appropriated partly for the purpose of clothing the naked prisoners. This fund is made up by the subscription of private individuals, who, in this instance, as in many others, step forward to remedy the neglect of the regular managers of this Prison. It originated during the shrievalty[28] of Sir Richard Phillips,[29] and has continued ever since. When I visited Newgate on the 20th of this month, the poverty, dirt, nakedness, and misery of many of the prisoners were most striking. There was not a ward, of the tried or untried, in which petitions were not presented to me for a supply of clothes. One lad, who had hardly any thing to cover him, and who was without a shirt, stated to me, that he bad been for months in that condition, his only shirt having been worn out since his commitment: he was besides without shoes or stockings. Another young man complained, that he was afflicted with a bad rupture; and that the surgeon would not supply him with a truss without a special order from the Sheriffs, which had been repeatedly applied for without effect. The boys in the school were ragged, dirty, and many without shoes and stockings.

The City Committee recommend the washing and cleaning of the prisoners, and the providing of a Prison Clothing for those whose dress is in a foul and dirty condition. This advice is good; and again it is a matter of regret, that it has been quite thrown away. The truth is, the whole question of clothing the prisoners is one that requires everywhere to be reconsidered. A practice prevails in some counties, of clothing all persons, who are committed to Gaol, in a Prison dress;[30] but this is, to my mind, most objectionable. It is, in fact, a species of punishment, and ought to be inflicted only on the guilty and convicted, and not on the accused: and I can hardly conceive any thing more wounding to the best feelings of the human heart, than to have superadded to the calamity of accusation and imprisonment, that of being compelled to put on the garb of a convict, and to be branded like a felon. Some few years back, a clergyman was accused of setting his house on fire, and on his commitment to Gaol (I think it was at Horsham[31]) it was proposed to clothe him with the Prison dress. He resisted, and actually kept his bed for several days, till he obtained the sanction of the magistrates to wear his own clothes.*[32] I cannot help thinking, that all accused persons should be permitted to wear their own clothes, unless they are so foul and dirty as to make the wearer of them a nuisance to his companions. In case of poverty, they should be supplied. The convicted should wear a prison dress, varying according to their guilt; and there should be one for those condemned to death, another for convicts, and a third for serious misdemeanors. The dress for the convicts ought to be furnished by the Government; and a little regulation would render the arrangement easy. They are clothed when sent to the Hulks: what would be the objection to give them the same dress on their conviction, and before their removal?

The nakedness and dirt of many of the prisoners in Newgate is discreditable to the managers of the Prison; and the miseries of confinement, to a man used to better society and cleaner habits, must be dreadfully aggravated by being kept in perpetual contact with the filth and squalid poverty of his more destitute companions.

I do not know how the Sheriffs' Fund is administered, nor have I any acquaintance with the present Sheriffs. The last Sheriffs, Messrs. Kirby and Thorpe, I often found in Newgate, relieving the distressed, and remedying, as far as they had the power, the bad system of the Prison. I beg also to be understood as imputing no

---

*   To this case may be added another: it is that of a man of *good connections and considerable property*, who became bankrupt, misconducted himself before the Commissioners, and was by them committed to Gaol; where, on being received, *his head was shaved, and a Prison dress put upon him.* At the next meeting of the Commissioners he was discharged. Of course common misdemeanors should not be compelled to wear a Prison dress. Persons convicted of political libel ought to be exempt. The treatment these offenders, as they are called, have met with, is highly discreditable to our magistracy. Mr. Gilbert Wakefield, Mr. Winterbotham, and many others, suffered the greatest indignities.

blame to the new keeper, Mr. Brown, for all the bad that is visible in this place of sorrow and misery, but not of repentance: neither he nor the Sheriffs are masters of the Prison. Mr. Brown is active and intelligent, and has done more to remedy the evils than has been performed since the period of Mr. Howard's visitation in 1787. What remains is to be performed by others. There is, however, as the preceding pages have shown, much to do; but the radical evil is the deficiency of room, a want of a proper locality, in which prisoners can be confined; and till that is obtained, the City Magistrates may make long speeches and write large books; they may censure the ordinary, or cripple the power of the Sheriffs; they may either form or not form Rules and Regulations; they may attend every day or not go round the Prison for a month; they may keep their eyes open or shut, Newgate will remain just what it is, an academy for the instruction of crime, a disgrace to the Police[33] of the Metropolis and the Nation.

Irons.

All the prisoners committed for felony, the tried and *untried,* are ironed.[34] I have no doubt, that thus confining a prisoner before trial is contrary to law, and can only be justified for the purposes of safe custody; and when a prisoner can be detained in security without irons, the imposition of them is not only illegal, but a wanton cruelty. Formerly, when there was an indiscriminate admission of strangers, and when during the day there were often nearly as many visitors as prisoners within the walls, the chances of escape were great. The wearing of irons was then a mark of distinction, and thus rendered their chances less favourable. I never thought the argument a good one; but it was admitted, and the use of irons was general. However, at present the keeper has most wisely restricted this admission of visitors; and the City Committee even go as far as to object to the imposition of irons on persons committed for the smaller offences – why then continue them at all on the accused?

If they are necessary, it must be, surely, because Newgate is an unfit place to confine prisoners, because it is secure in no way. There is no inspection either by day or night, because the prisoners are kept together in large masses, and there are no means of preventing the hardy and desperate from attempting their escape. Thus, then, the abolition of the torture of irons can alone be gained by changing the form and structure of the Prison.*

---

* In several of the best County Prisons, such as Bury, Cambridge, and Lancaster, irons are not used, either upon the accused or convicted. – *Report of the Committee of the Court of Aldermen.* The keeper of Bury St. Edmunds told me, he had the power to use fetters, but he never found them necessary. In proportion as Prisons are well constructed and managed, the use of fetters it dispensed with.

In France, where personal liberty is not much respected by the Government, no one is ironed until he is convicted. Why should a contrary practice prevail in England?

There are many other heads of inquiries, as connected with this Prison, upon which I have some remarks to make. They are of minor detail.

The employment of prisoners in any way is strongly objected to by the City Committee; and yet they are so employed; they fill the places of wardsmen,[35] and in some instances of gatesmen, &c. This system has been much abused, and requires to be nearly[36] watched. I am unwilling to state all I know upon this subject, but shall content myself with requesting you to bear in mind a principle of Prison Government, perhaps one of the most essential; it is, that the less the prisoners are employed in the management of the affairs, or in controlling the actions of each other, the better will that Prison be regulated: a contrary practice produces many evils; and the more you inquire into that of Newgate in this particular, the more you will be satisfied with the truth of the proposition.

The City Committee also advised, that the shutters for the windows should be so constructed as to admit air and light, and at the same time prevent the prisoners from looking into any other yard of the Prison. At present, no change has taken place; and while I was there last week, with the ordinary, I was in the fine yard,[37] hearing the petition of some of the persons who were confined there. The windows of one, the convict apartment, that overlooked it, were crowded, and a conversation of mockery, oaths, and indecency ensued, that strongly illustrated the value of the Committee's recommendation. Out of these windows the felon convicts can converse at pleasure with those confined for misdemeanors.

The employment of prisoners in labour is of great importance. I learn that a mill,[38] somewhat similar to that in Bedford Gaol, is about to be constructed. Whatever provides occupation, if it be but for one hour in the day, is good. A confirmed thief dreads labour more than he does the gallows. But until the Prison is enlarged, and arranged after another plan, it is not possible to provide work for the male prisoners in Newgate.

Before I conclude this Letter, which the importance of the subject has drawn out to a greater length than originally was intended, I cannot refrain from expressing my astonishment at a report which the Grand Jury[39] of Middlesex, who, in the discharge of their duty, inspected Newgate last session, have thought fit to make of the state of that Prison. It is not for me to doubt, whether the Grand Jury inspected the Prison at all; but the result of their visit satisfies me, that their praise must have been comparative only, as they surely did not mean to set forth to their fellow citizens, *that their high admiration of the excellent arrangements which exist in Newgate* had reference to any thing but the deplorable and disgraceful condition in which it was only a few months ago. They could not have noticed the want of proper classification,[40] nor the state of the condemned cells, nor the manner in which the prisoners sleep, nor the promiscuous assemblage of all kinds of misdemeanors in the fine yards, nor the bad success of most of the recommendations of the City Committee, nor the want of separation of old and young offenders in all parts of the prison; for if they had noticed these deficiencies, I am sure twenty-four Englishmen could not have passed a vote of high admiration. The slight want of matting and covering is, in fact, a want of proper rugs and bedding; and the nudity, or the deficiency of shirts, shoes, and stockings, cannot but be taken as trifling exceptions to those excellent arrangements, which are the theme of this extraordinary panegyric.

The report has surprised every one: and how twenty-four persons, who were not led about blindfolded, or who had ever seen any other Prison but their own Newgate, or who had one moment thought on the subject, or who had even read the quarto volume which the City Committee published, could have screwed up their consciences to such a pitch, is to me inconceivable. They, I trust, will forgive me, when I put in carelessness and ignorance as pleas in their favour; and having some experience of what visiting magistrates have permitted in the county of Middlesex and elsewhere, I can make allowances for the errors of a London Grand Jury.

I have, however, no doubt, that each individual of the Grand Jury, if taken round the Prison of Newgate, and shown what is daily and hourly exhibited there, would concur in all the remarks made in the preceding pages, and would regret that he had been induced to give even a momentary support to a system, which the commonest understanding must allow to be censurable. I solicit, then, from them, and from you, Gentlemen, a personal investigation of the abuses of the Prison system of Newgate. I call upon you to see with your own eyes, and hear with your own ears. Compare my statement with the report of the Grand Jury. Whether you concur with me or not in the reasoning which I have adopted is a matter of slight importance, when compared with what I feel will be the result of a minute examination of the points at issue between us. Of this I am assured, that 'if only half the misery which is felt by some shall be seen by others, it will fill them with horror;'[41] and it rests with you, Gentlemen, to correct the evil, and to terminate the horrors.

I have the honour to be,
  Gentlemen, with great respect,
   Your obedient Servant,
    H. GREY BENNET.
Upper Grosvenor Street,
December 31, 1817.

from Thomas Fowell Buxton, *An Inquiry, whether Crime and Misery Are Produced or Prevented, by Our Present System of Prison Discipline*, 3rd edn (London: John and Arthur Arch, 1818), pp. 16–27, 63–70, 88–100.

Buxton (1786–1845) was a lifelong humanitarian campaigner. As a child he spent much time with the Gurneys, a prominent Norwich family of bankers and philanthropists, and after a brilliant career as a student at Trinity College, Dublin, he married into the family. The prison reformer Elizabeth Fry was his sister-in-law. He went into the brewery business in London, and in 1816 led a fund-raising campaign to help the starving poor there. Following his sister-in-law's lead, and the example of earlier campaigners such as John Howard, he investigated prison conditions in England and especially London, and published his Inquiry to national and international acclaim. Buxton was elected to Parliament the same year and joined the prison reform group there. He took up the anti-slavery campaign and eventually became one of its leading figures, succeeding William Wilberforce.

Buxton's *Inquiry* provides detailed information as a basis for promoting reform of the criminal laws and London prisons. Like most reformers of this period, he used the utilitarian argument that reform was not only humane but would reduce crime. Buxton particularly emphasized provision of remunerative work to prisoners and allowing them part of their earnings for present use and part for receipt on release from prison, so as to accustom them to work discipline and an investment mentality.

Note on the text: two silent corrections have been made, supplying missing quotation marks.

The Borough Compter.*[1]

Our prisoners have all that prisoners ought to have; without Gentlemen think they ought to be indulged with Turkey carpets.

Parliamentary Debates.

THIS prison belongs to the city of London, and its jurisdiction extends over five parishes. – On entrance, you come to the male felons' ward and yard, in which are both the tried and the untried – those in chains and those without them – boys and men, – persons for petty offences, and for the most atrocious felonies; – for simple assault, – for being disorderly, – for small thefts, – for issuing bad notes, – for forgery and for robbery. They were employed in some kind of gaming, and they said they had nothing else to do. A respectable looking man, a smith, who had never been in prison before, told me that 'the conversation always going on, was sufficient to corrupt any body, and that he had learned things there he never dreamed of before.'

You next enter a yard nineteen feet square; this is the only airing place for male debtors and vagrants, female debtors, prostitutes, misdemeanants, and criminals, and for their children and friends. There have been as many as thirty women; we saw thirty-eight debtors, and Mr. Law, the Governor, stated, when he was examined, that there might be about twenty children.†

On my first visit, the debtors were all collected together up stairs. This was their day-room, bed-room, workshop, kitchen, and chapel. On my second visit, they spent the day and the night in the room below; at the third, both the room above, and that below, were filled. The length of each of these rooms, exclusive of a recess in which were tables and the fire-place, is twenty feet. Its breadth is three feet, six inches for a passage, and six feet for the bed. In this space twenty feet long, and six wide, on eight straw beds, with sixteen rugs, and a piece of timber for a bolster, twenty prisoners had slept side by side the preceding night: I maintained that it was physically impossible; but the prisoners explained away the difficulty, by saying, 'they slept edgeways.' Amongst these twenty, was one in a very deplorable condition; he had been taken from a sick bed, and brought there; he had his mattress to himself, for none would share it; and indeed my senses convinced me, that sleeping near him, must be sufficiently offensive.

I was struck with the appearance of one man, who seemed much dejected; he had seen better times, and was distressed to be placed in such a situation. He said he had slept next to the wall, and was literally unable to move, from the pres-

---

*   Visited: – December 16th, 1817 – and January 26th, 1818 – January 30th – February 3d; with S. Hoare, jun. Esq. Banker; and I have his authority to say, that his observations concur in every respect with my statements. – Feb. 16th – *when I read this description to the Governor, which he confirmed in every particular.*

†   Report of the Committee of the House of Commons.

sure. In the morning, the stench and heat were so oppressive, that he and every one else on waking, rushed, unclothed as they must be, into the yard; and the turnkey told me, that 'the smell on the first opening of the door, was enough to turn the stomach of a horse.'

I cannot reflect on the scene I witnessed, without grief; almost every man looked ill, and almost every one who had been here any time, said he had had a severe illness; we were all immediately struck with their squalid appearance. It may perhaps be supposed, that we were duped by our imaginations; that observing the closeness, and want of exercise to which they were subjected, and ascribing to these causes their usual effect, we concluded without sufficient examination, that the prisoners must be unhealthy. The following fact, for the accuracy of which I appeal to my respectable companions,*[2] will evince that I describe, not merely what I expected to see, but what we actually saw. I called my friends together, and requested their attention: I then addressed myself to one of the prisoners at another part of the room, to whom we had not previously spoken, and said, 'I perceive by your appearance, you have not been here long?' – 'Only nine days,' was his answer. To another, 'I fear you have been here some time?' 'Yes, Sir, three months.' To another, 'You have been here very long, I should suppose?' – 'Nearly nine months.' In fact, I pointed out five, and from their looks, predicted nearly the period of their confinement; nor was I once deceived.

I have seen many hospitals and infirmaries, but never one, to the best of my belief, in which the patients exhibited so much ill health. The following facts deserve attention: on my second visit there were thirteen persons confined on criminal charges, on whom five were under the Surgeon's[3] hands, as cases of Fever. On my first visit we observed in one of the cells, a lad in bed, and seemingly very ill with Fever; the window was closed, and the reason given was, that the air would be dangerous to him; yet the preceding night two other prisoners had slept with him in a room seven feet by nine. The three were,

JAMES McINTOSH, charged	with felony.
THOMAS WILLIAMS,[4]	with stealing a piece of Gingham.
JEREMIAH NOBLE,	with an assault.

And no alteration was intended, neither indeed was any possible.

We conceived that to place persons, for the night, in this corrupt and infected air, close by the source of that infection, was inevitably to taint them with disease. This conjecture was unhappily verified; for at my next coming, I observed in the

---

*   Mrs. Fry, St. Mildred's Court; Miss Sanderson, Old Jewry; members of the Ladies' Committee of Newgate; – Mr. Crawford, Secretary of the society for the prevention of juvenile delinquency. – Mr. Wood, a member of the Philadelphia Society for prisoners; the latter Gentleman subsequently told me, that, shocked as he had been at the general state of our prisons, nothing had struck him so deeply as the deplorable wretchedness manifest in the countenances of these prisoners.

list of those who had been seized with fever, the names of Thomas Williams, and Jeremiah Noble.*⁵ Now, mark the case of Jeremiah Noble; he is charged with an assault, and the law condemns him to a short imprisonment, preparatory to his trial. But the regulations of the city inflict on him in addition, a disease very dangerous in its nature, very suffering in its progress, and very enfeebling in its consequences. The vigor of his constitution may surmount it, but all prisoners have not vigorous constitutions: thus, the most venial offence which calls down the visitation of the law,† a debt of one shilling, or a fraud to the amount of one penny,‡ may be punished with a lingering and painful death.

Now, it is evident, that the regulations of this prison are calculated to produce, and to communicate disease. The next question is, what measures are taken to cure it? Till very lately there was no Surgeon or Apothecary provided, nor any medicine allowed. There is no infirmary; but one of the female apartments is used as such, when the prison is comparatively empty. When a debtor is ill, he is separated from the others by a blanket; but how effectual that separation must be, which takes place in a room of 20 feet in length, and in which twenty persons sleep side by side, will require no peculiar sagacity to determine. When a criminal is ill, however infectious may be his complaint, however offensive, however requiring quiet, there is generally no separation at all. I observed in the Surgeon's

---

* The following minutes are extracted from the Surgeon's book:

Dec. 10. – M'Intosh has a feverish complaint.

Dec. 14. – M'Intosh better, the other prisoners healthy.

Dec. 27. – Williams, Noble, and Rawlins, are ill.

Dec. 30. – The above are attacked with fever.

Observ. – M'Intosh is declared to be ill of a fever on the 10th, and on the 16th, I find that Williams and Noble had slept with him the preceding night. On the 27th, they also are seized with fever. – If my reader will pay attention to these dates, I think he will concur with me in the conclusion I have formed, viz. that Williams and Noble derived their disorder from sleeping with M'Intosh.

† What is the smallest debt for which you have ever known a prisoner in that prison? *Ans.* I have known them there for one shilling. – *Evidence of Mr. Law, keeper of the Borough Compter, before the Police Committee*, 1814.

‡ Some friends of mine, who are indefatigable in visiting prisons, saw in a yard at Coldbath Fields, four men and thirty boys; amongst the rest, a lad of fifteen years of age, whose open countenance induced them to inquire into his case. He was employed by a Corn Chandler, at Islington, and sent by his master with a cart and horse to London. There is in the middle of the City Road, a temporary bar, at which I have sometimes seen a collector of tolls, and sometimes not. He passed through this without paying the toll of one penny, declaring he saw no person there: he was summoned before a magistrate the next day, fined forty shillings, and in default of payment, sentenced to a month's imprisonment. My friends inquired into the character of his parents, and found them highly respectable. The father, the present, and the former master, gave the boy a very good character; and the latter, a small shop-keeper, offered ten shillings towards his release: my friends paid the fine, and the boy was liberated. Had he passed a month with the associates with whom he was placed, it will hereafter appear that it is more than possible he would have been ruined for ever. Upon his discharge, he thanked the gentlemen in the most grateful terms: adding, I will always be a good boy, and never get into prison again.

book, a multitude of judicious observations as to the unwholesomeness of the prison, amongst the rest the following:

October 7, 1817.

'The prison is clean, but from its crowded state there are seven requiring medical assistance; – if fever ensue in consequence, the greatest danger is to be apprehended, from a total want of accommodation to separate the sick.'

(Signed)   W. H. BOX.

I fear I shall hardly be credited when I assure my readers, that as yet, I have not touched upon that point in this prison which I consider the most lamentable, – the proximity between the male debtors and the female prisoners. Their doors are about seven feet asunder, on the same floor; these are open in the daytime, and the men are forbidden to go into the women's ward; – but after the turnkey left us, they confessed that they constantly went in and out; and there is no punishment for doing so.* That this is the fact, appears by the evidence of the Governor before the Police Committee. Ques.† Is it possible for the men to get into the sleeping wards of the women? Ans. I cannot say that it is impossible. Is any thing done to prevent them, if the parties consent? No.

Thus the male debtors reside, (without any partition but an open space of seven feet), close by females sent there for debt, for assaults, for misdemeanors, and for prostitution. Am I not warranted in saying, that the regulations of this prison encourage licentiousness? For what is to prevent promiscuous intercourse, and public acts of obscenity, except the directions of the jailer at a distance, or the virtue of those females who are imprisoned for the want of virtue. Females are sometimes accused of offences, of which they afterwards demonstrate their innocence. Maid-servants in respectable families, of hitherto unblemished reputation, may be, and are often, charged in error, with purloining small articles belonging to their master or mistress. Imagine an innocent girl, who had hitherto been shielded from even allusions to vice, brought to this prison, and placed at once within the view and within the range of this unbridled harlotry. Can her mind escape pollution? Can she shut her eyes and her ears to the scenes which are passing around her? Is not residence in this place, (however innocent she may have been of the imputed crime), an eternal stain upon her character? The law is justly jealous of female reputation; but here, as if forgetful of its own principles, it robs the unprotected and often innocent girl, of her fair name, exposes her virtue to temptation, and places before her eyes, vice in its worst and most degrading realities. To answer to all this, that those who come here, cannot be made worse,

---

*   In the hot nights of summer, when the prison is very full, the Governor has to choose between the evils of excluding the air by shutting the doors, or admitting the men, by opening them; that is – between disease and dissoluteness.

†   Committee on State of Jails, in London, 1814, page 61.

is to say, that female debtors are always prostitutes, and that accusation is proof. I can well conceive, that where prisoners are guilty of some petty offence alleged against them, yet that they may not be utterly depraved; a girl for the gratification of her vanity, may secrete an article of dress: she is very wrong: but, because she has descended one step in the scale of vice, it does not follow inevitably, that she has fallen to its lowest abominations. But it may be said I overstate the case; that the opening of the doors is an event of rare occurrence; and that the rules of the prison, (to the violation of which no penalty is attached – in fact, therefore, the recommendations of the jailer) may have weight enough to stifle the calls of licentious passion. Be it so. – There is at least one scene of gross and revolting indelicacy which no female can escape. There is but one yard and one privy for men and women, and every woman must pass through this yard. The turnkey on the one hand, and the more respectable of the debtors on the other, told me that it was always an occasion for coarse jests, and 'for a piece of fun.'

I pass over some other points without comment; such, for instance, as the window of the room of the female debtors and misdemeanants, being so near to the felons' yard, as to allow of conversation, which as the Governor told me, often occasions the most offensive language; so offensive, indeed, that the debtors had lately complained of it.

But I would seriously address myself to those who have the power to alter these enormities. In the courts of Aldermen and Common-council, the majority are men of property, education, and feeling. I would ask each amongst them, who has a daughter, whether he would not rather follow her to her grave, than see her placed in such a dreadful brothel. And, while the subject is before them, and before Parliament, I will fairly declare my opinion, that if invention had been racked to find out methods of corrupting female virtue, nothing more ingeniously effectual could have been discovered, than the practices of the Borough Compter. Perhaps that attention may be paid to the recommendations of a visiting magistrate, which may be withheld from an unauthorized individual as I am. I extracted the following observations from the minute book: –

'I am compelled to lament the utter impossibility of classification,[6] to prevent the union of persons charged with all offences; and, moreover, to notice the great impropriety of female felons being introduced in the day, not only to female, but to male, debtors; having but one yard for the joint recreation, and necessary purposes,'

(Signed)   JAMES WILLIAMS.

July 22, 1817.

The date of this observation is very remarkable. It is the last which appears in the visiting magistrates' book. Thus, this prison, within less than five minutes walk of London Bridge; – a prison which outrages every feeling of common humanity, which is really shocking, and melancholy, and disgraceful; – a prison, in which the period of each man's captivity may be judged by the degree of languor and sickliness visible in his countenance; – a prison, the regulations of which openly violate the law of the land, and are the direct reverse of the rules recommended by the Committee of Aldermen;* – a prison, in which I have witnessed as much of what is truly deplorable and dismal, as it ever was my misfortune to behold; in which it is difficult to determine, whether the vice it encourages is, or is not, surpassed by the measure of misery it inflicts; this prison has not, as far as appears, been visited by one single official person, capable of redressing the slightest of its atrocious evils, for a period of more than six months.

No cooking utensils are provided. The allowance of food is fourteen ounces of bread per day, and one pound of the 'clods and stickings of beef'[7] twice per week. I maintain that this is a system of starvation.

Let any person – let the magistrates especially, who appoint this as a sufficiency of diet, compare this quantum of food with their own consumption, and they will need little authority to induce them to concur with me; but I will mention the information I received from a lady, who must know the realities of the case, and who is above all suspicion of exaggeration. She told me, 'that those who have only the prison allowance gradually decline in health. Four women and four children have lately died in Newgate, whose death may be ascribed in great part, to the want of food.'

No provision of labour is appointed. At my first visit to the debtors, by the kindness of the jailer,† some were employed in making shoes and clothes, and expressed their gratitude, for the ease to their minds, and the relief to their families, which this labour afforded; one, the father of a large family, was engaged in repairing his children's shoes. But when I next went, the crowded state of the prison rendered work impossible. As I stood in the yard, instead of hearing as I have elsewhere heard, the sounds so grateful in a prison, the rap of the hammer, and the vibrations of the shuttle, our ears were assailed with loud laughter, and the most fearful curses; when we entered, we saw three separate parties at cards, one man reading a novel, and one sitting in a corner intent upon his Bible.

There is no school; no soap is allowed; and a prisoner, when he arrives, is turned in amongst the rest without any examination as to the state of his health. This may account for a remark in the apothecary's book, January 5th, 1818. – 'Some of the prisoners have contracted the itch.'[8] The case of one man struck me much: he was found in a most pitiable state in the streets, and apprehended as a vagrant; he was at first placed with the debtors, but he was so filthy, and so cov-

---

*   Report, p. 5. Printed 1815.

†   Mr. Law is a man of great humanity, which he has evinced, as I know, by many efforts to procure situations for discharged prisoners, as well as by every possible attention to the cleanliness and comfort of those who are committed to his care.

ered with vermin, (to use the expression of the turnkey, 'he was so lousy,') that his removal was solicited. I saw him lying on a straw-bed, as I believed at the point of death, without a shirt, inconceivably dirty, so weak as to be almost unable to articulate, and so offensive, as to render remaining a minute with him quite intolerable; close by his side five other untried prisoners had slept the preceding night, inhaling the stench from his mass of putrefaction, hearing his groans, breathing the steam from this corrupted lungs, and covered with myriads of lice from his rags of clothing; of these his wretched companions, three were subsequently pronounced by the verdict of a jury 'not guilty,' and of these one was Noble, whose case I have before described. The day after their discharge, I found the two who were convicted almost undressed; on asking the reason, they said their clothes were under the pump to get rid of the vermin received from the vagrant; his bed had been burnt by order of the jailer; his clothes had been cut off, and the turnkey said, one of his companions had brought him his garter, on which be counted upwards of forty lice.

The jailer told me, 'that in an experience of nine years he had never known an instance of reformation; he thought the prisoners grew worse, and he was sure, that if you took the first boy you met with in the streets, and placed him in his prison, by the end of a month, he would be as bad as the rest, and up to all the roguery of London. Half his present prisoners have been there before, and upon an average he thinks if one hundred are let out, he shall soon have from twenty to thirty back again, besides those who go to other jails.'

I will not trouble my reader with any further observations upon this prison, but he must determine for himself, whether crime and misery are produced or prevented in the Borough Compter. [pp. 16–27]

Bury Jail,

AND

House of Correction.*[9]

THIS Jail is the best constructed, of any that I have seen in England; the regulations by which it is governed are exceedingly wise and humane; and it possesses the grand requisite of a Governor, who discharges his duty with equal zeal and fidelity.

The nature of the building will be easily understood. An external wall surrounds the whole: the Governor's house is in the center; from its windows every yard is visible, and it is hardly possible, that any breach of the rules can be practised without being observed, either by himself or some one of his family. He told me that the experience of twenty years as a jailer, had taught him that the

---

*   Visited, January, 1818.

main points for prison discipline, for the security, morals, and health of the prisoners, are: –

Classification – Employment – and cleanliness.

Classification is carried to almost its greatest limit. There is a separate building and yard, for prisoners of the following descriptions: –

Males.

No. 1 and 2. Debtors.

   3. King's Evidence,[10] when there are any; and occasionally other prisoners.

   4. Convicted of misdemeanors, and small offences.

   5. Transports, and convicted of atrocious felonies.[11]

   6. Untried for atrocious offences.

   7. Untried for small offences.

Females.

   8. Debtors.

   9. For trial.

   10. Convicted of misdemeanors.*

   11. Convicted of felonies.*

There is a well merited discretion given to the Governor, to alter these rules, in the following manner: a notorious thief, who has before been imprisoned, may be apprehended for a petty offence: to place him amongst petty offenders is to subject them to corruption. He is, therefore, confined with the untried for 'atrocious offences.' On the other hand, a youth of respectable habits, evidently unhardened in guilt, may be charged with an atrocious offence; he is placed amongst the untried for small offences.

It is to be observed, that there is no separation of boys from men, or of untried women, whether their offences are small or great; but the building appropriated for King's evidence, may generally be devoted to the confinement of boys.

The prison is calculated to hold eighty-four persons, and there are eighty-four separate sleeping cells; consequently each person, when they have only that number, sleeps by himself, which the Governor thinks a regulation of great importance. But at present there are considerably more: – it is, therefore, necessary to place more than one in a room, and the Governor, in these cases, places three together; having had reason to apprehend that evil arises if two sleep in the same cell.

Health is preserved and improved by the cleanliness of person, apartments, and yards.

---

*   These are in a detached house of correction.

Prisoners, when they arrive, have their hair cut short, and this is so continued. They must wash well every morning, and do not receive their allowance till this is done. There are cold and warm baths.

Prisoners are shaved every Saturday, and put on clean linen (provided, if necessary, by the County) on the Sunday; each day-room, workroom, and cell, is swept every morning, and washed twice a-week in the summer, and once in the winter; and the passages, apartments, and cells, are white-washed after each assize. Prisoners, when they enter, are examined; if necessary, they go into the warm bath, and at night their clothes are baked; and, if they appear ragged, they are provided with plain clothes at the expense of the County.

Employment.

When an untried prisoner comes in, it is at his option whether he will work: if he is so inclined, any work to which he has been accustomed is provided, if possible; and, to encourage his labour, the whole amount of his earnings is given to him.

The earnings of the convicts are divided in the following manner: – one-fifth to the Governor, two-fifths to the County, two-fifths to the prisoner, of which he receives half, and half is reserved till his departure. Then, sufficient also is given him to carry him home, and a small sum to support him, till he can look out for work.

That part of the money, which is received in prison, may be thus expended. One of the porters goes round twice a week, and writes down those things which the prisoners wish to purchase. This list, sometimes amounting to 200 articles, is submitted to the Governor, who puts his pen through those, which he deems improper. He then orders the others, and the prisoners receive them at cost price, and have weights, scales, and measures, to satisfy them as to the quantity. All spirituous liquors are strictly forbidden.

The work consists in making clothes, shoes, list-shoes,[12] straw-hats, &c.; and grinding at a mill, of a peculiar construction, somewhat similar to a turn-spit. They walk in rows, and the machine is turned rather by their weight than their exertions. The advantage is, that no man can avoid his share of labour. This mill is worked by gangs, above and below, who are also classified, and if there are not sufficient of one description, the number is made up by drafts from another; but under the following judicious regulations: – if the number of convicts for heinous offences is not sufficient, the most atrocious in crime, or the most depraved in character, from the misdemeanants, are added; on the other hand, if the number of misdemeanants is too small, it is made up from the most orderly of the criminal ward.

Under the article health, I omitted to mention that the jail is distant about half a mile from the town, and stands in a dry and airy situation, and every precaution is taken to ventilate the rooms. This, the Governor deems very important, as he has found that the prisoners consider that comfort consists in closeness, and would, if permitted, exclude all air. He finds the prisoners grow fat and improve in health; which he ascribes to exercise, cleanliness, and the absence of stimulating liquors.

Irons[13] are never used but as a punishment.

The bedsteads are of iron; a straw palliasse, two blankets, and a rug, compose the bedding. The food is, for untried one pound and a half of bread per day, and one pound of cheese per week; with an addition of one pound of meat per week for convicts, whose work at the mill is hard, and therefore requires further nourishment. It was formerly the practice to dress their meat and to furnish them with soups, but, at the request of the Governor, this has been discontinued, as he finds it necessary for the purpose of giving a proper moral influence to the Governor, that he should be, not only above fraud, but above the suspicion of it; and this suspicion might be generated, if they do not receive their provisions in a raw state.

There is an infirmary in every ward, and bibles and prayer-books. The Governor seldom goes round, without being solicited for permission to learn to read and write.

This is effected, by giving small rewards to those in each ward, who have capacity and inclination to teach others. Almost all, therefore, who remain any length of time, learn these important accomplishments, and he always has found a great avidity in the prisoners to be instructed.

Almost every man who remains after conviction, learns some trade, which may hereafter be an aid to his family, if it does not become his regular business; for instance, all the convicts for atrocious crimes have learned to make list shoes, and straw hats. This trade they exercise in the intervals when they are not employed at the mill, and they contrive to earn for themselves, from one to about three shillings per week. The Governor thinks that prisoners ought not to be employed, merely or principally as a speculation of profit; because, the produce of such labour, from fluctuations in its value, and from the inexpertness of the workmen, may often be very inconsiderable: but he deems it a matter of vital importance, that they should be employed, from the moral effect produced. If there were no gain, if there were a loss by their labour, he would still employ them and pay them for their work, as the only method of avoiding disturbances, improving their character, and insuring their security.

He thinks that no general rules relative to solitary confinement[14] ought to be made, because of its different effect on different people. Some years ago he had two men, (as he thinks) from the same farm-yard, condemned to solitary confinement; one, a stupid sluggish fellow, slept away his time; the other, an active, energetic man, was almost driven out of his senses; so much so, as to render it necessary to relax his punishment.

His experience has led him to approve of labour, not only as contributing to the security and morals, but also to the comfort of prisoners. He lately had occasion to punish one ward, which he did by depriving them of the materials of extra labour, and not a day passed in which he did not receive solicitations for its return, and promises of amendment. He lately received, from a neighbouring workhouse, a woman who was guilty of very outrageous conduct, and absolutely refused to do any work; the Governor was requested to do his utmost for her reformation: he confined her alone without work, and while I was there, she solicited a wheel[15] in the most urgent manner, saying, employment would ease her mind, and help her to while away the time.

As for their conduct after they leave prison, he has repeatedly had persons who have before been confined, call upon him to thank him for the lessons they had learnt in prison: he knows many, who having been dissolute characters before, immediately on leaving prison went to honest labour, and are now industrious and respectable men.

Masters have thanked him for the reformation of their servants; one within this week assured him, that a boy, who, before his imprisonment, was of the most abandoned character, has since become quite an example to his other labourers.

Two young men were confined for the same offence; he lately saw a letter from one to a comrade in prison, describing his own mal-practices, with considerable exultation; but, saying, as for George, (the other) he has turned out quite a fool, he works all the week, goes to church on a Sunday, and will not speak to his old acquaintance. The father of this lad, who has thus deserted his former practices and accomplices, called in the interval of my two visits, to express his thankfulness; his words were, as for the boy, it is salvation to him, and poor as I am, it is worth more than a hundred pounds to me; I wish he had been with you five years ago.

He believes that no serious misconduct in any way could take place, without some of the prisoners giving him information; – lately, the turnkey was called up by the prisoners in the night; they said they were sure they heard some one attempting to escape. This information led to the detection of a man, who had already cut the windows of his cell.

He does not allow any gaming, or chucking halfpence: which he prevents, by requiring the ward to inform him if it takes place, and confining them all for the day, if he discovers it.

He observed, that the rules of a prison ought not to be too severe, but rigidly enforced; as simple as possible, for if they were intricate, if the concern did not move mechanically, it would soon get out of order.

He observed, also, that it was plain justice to treat an untried prisoner with as little restraint as possible.

Such are the rules of this prison, and such the results of the experience of the Governor: if the health of a prisoner, his security, and the prevention of crime, be important matters in the conduct of a jail, the following facts speak for themselves.

There is no prisoner at this time ill.

In eighteen years, but one prisoner has escaped, and he in the middle of the day, and in double irons.

In every hundred prisoners, there are not five who have been here before. At this moment, out of one hundred and thirty, there are seven such, four for atrocious offences, and three for assaults, or petty misdeeds.

He never has riots, or quarrelling, or swearing.

This jail reflects the highest credit on the magistrates of the district; and they receive, from their humane labours, the most important advantages.

I left this account with the Governor for a week, that he might correct any inaccuracies; he confirmed every thing which is here stated, but insisted on my suppressing a paragraph at the end, in which I had expressed my opinion of his conduct. [pp. 63–70]

Penitentiary, Millbank.*[16]

THIS house of correction, on which it is proposed to expend nearly 400,000l.[17] is built in a very low situation. In consequence of a defect in the foundation, two towers have already been taken down to prevent their falling, and two more are in a precarious state.

I mention these circumstances, because they have occasioned considerable expense; and this may be confounded with the inevitable charges of the Penitentiary system, and thus a prejudice may arise against it. But it is evident that the system cannot be charged with any errors in the situation which is chosen.

With respect, however, to the part now building, such precautions have been used, as to remove all apprehensions of danger.

When a prisoner is brought here, he is first placed in the reception room, and examined by the surgeon; he is then bathed, and his clothes, if unfit to be preserved, are burnt; if decent, they are sold, and entered to his credit, in the 'Prisoner's Property Book.' He then is placed in the first class, and while he remains in it, he works in the cell in which he sleeps, separate from all other prisoners. When he is advanced to the second class, he performs his work in the larger cells, in company. If he is in the first, he may be advanced to the second, when he merits this indulgence; or being in the second, he may be degraded to the first,

---

*   With S. Hoare, jun. Esq. Dec, 26, 1817; and on Feb. 21, 1818, in company with Mr. W. Allen, I read this to the Governor, with a request that any errors might be pointed out.

for misbehaviour. A regulation in the same spirit, allows a diminution of the period of his sentence, upon a favourable representation from the committee.

The hours of work are about nine, and the produce of his labour is thus divided – in every pound,

	s.	d.
The establishment has	15	0
The prisoner	2	6
The master-manufacturer	0	10
The taskmaster of the pentagon	0	10
The turnkeys of the pentagon	0	10
	20	0

The prisoner's money is placed to his credit, and reserved for his use on his departure, and a statement of his account is furnished to him.

There is a master-manufacturer, who is acquainted with the nature of such manufactures as are introduced; he directs all contracts for materials, has the custody of them, receives them from the prisoners in the shape of goods, and is responsible for all deficiencies.

There is a task-maker for every pentagon, who superintends the work of the prisoners, and instructs those who are ignorant.

A prison dress is provided, and each class is distinguished by different clothing.

The diet for men daily, is one pound and a half of bread, one pound of potatoes, a pint of hot porridge for breakfast, and the same for supper, and either 6 ounces of coarse meat, without bone, and after boiling, or a quart of excellent broth, thickened with vegetables.

A prisoner is allowed to see his friends in presence of one of the officers, by an order of the committee, upon a representation from the chaplain and governor, stating that he is entitled to the favour.

At his discharge he receives, in addition to the per centage, to which he is entitled, decent clothing, and suitable tools; or money to the amount of £3;[18] and at the expiration of a year, in some cases, if his conduct merits it, a further gratuity.

The duty of the chaplain is to read prayers and preach a sermon twice on a Sunday; to read prayers daily in the infirmaries; to obtain an intimate knowledge of the disposition and character of every prisoner; and to allot a considerable portion of his time to their religious instruction. He superintends their progress in reading and writing; and supplies them with suitable books and tracts. These various and important duties are, I have reason to think, faithfully performed.

Our first visit was to the chaplain: he gave us a very encouraging account of the effects of the system. He had observed visible amendment in many, and he thought that there was not one who had not received some degree of improvement. On the preceding (Christmas) day, he had admitted fifty to the Sacrament, all of whom he considered eligible; others he had refused.

His intercourse with the prisoners had led him to believe, that the general state of our jails is a principal cause of the increase of crime. They had given him the most frightful descriptions of the scenes they had witnessed, and the language and practices to which they had been exposed; and he had come to the conclusion, from their representations, that if a person went into the generality of our prisons uncorrupted, it was next to impossible that he should go out so.

The governor fully confirmed the account given by the Chaplain, of the amendment of the Prisoners, and mentioned the observation of a man, who had lately been discharged: he said upon his release he had called at Newgate; and though he had been confined there four years, he never knew how bad it was till now, that he had experienced the difference between it and the Penitentiary.

The Governor told me 'that the grand secret was, employment. Labour was the right hand of police; that while the prisoners were employed, they were decent in their behaviour and language; but that if they were not engaged in work, they would be in mischief; in fact, he found, by repeated experience, that when work ended, his troubles began.'

The women were all engaged in cooking, washing, ironing, and various kinds of needle-work; their earnings are about six pounds per annum; and their behaviour gave me a very favourable impression of the effects of employment, combined with religious instruction.

Those men who were at work, were shoe-makers, taillors, carpet-weavers, and carpenters, and one or two had learned to saw.

The surgeon visits the prison daily, and he made a very satisfactory report of their health, which was confirmed by their looks: he ascribes this to the regularity of their habits and diet, their personal cleanliness, and the exclusion of intoxicating liquors.

Every part of the building was remarkably clean, and free from offensive smells.

In the former edition I was compelled to lament, that I found two-thirds of the men and boys unemployed, I felt that the continuance of this defect would not only destroy this, but every future attempt to reform prisoners; and, under this impression, I made the following remarks.

I look upon the Penitentiary, at Millbank, as a grand national experiment of the effects of regular employment upon the depraved; but if employment is to be withheld, it becomes, in fact, an experiment of the effects of idleness.

It is essential, that all persons who come here ignorant of a trade, should be taught one, and that they should be kept invariably to it. They must be compelled to work, or the system must fail, and all the horrors and absurdities of the old method – commitments to hard labour, where nothing is to be done, and houses of correction, where all are corrupted – must be renewed, deriving authority and confirmation from the failure of this great and expensive attempt.

But I am far from thinking compulsion will be necessary. I asked a great many if they were willing to work, and invariably they lamented the hardship of having nothing to do, and expressed their willingness to do any thing. The Governor, in my presence, threatened one man to take away his work, and afterwards told me, the fulfilment of that threat would be the greatest punishment he could inflict.

At Ghent[19] – at Philadelphia[20] – at Bury – on the female side of Newgate – on the female side of this very Institution – all work, and consider it a privilege to be allowed to do so.

But it is contended that proper work is not procurable. At the 'Refuge for the Destitute,'[21] I saw many boys, and the average of their earnings, in making shoes, baskets, and clothes, was six shillings per week, at the end of the first year; twelve shillings at the end of the second; eighteen shillings at the end of the third. In the fifth they were capable of earning men's full wages. But I have a still stronger illustration. There never probably was a period in which labour was so difficult to be obtained, or so small in value as in 1817, and, perhaps, no part of England suffered so severely for want of work, as Spitalfields.[22] From the extent of the distress, only the most helpless were admitted into the workhouse. Men were almost entirely excluded; and its inhabitants consisted principally of widows with large families, women near confinement, idiots, children, the sickly, the infirm, and the aged,

The average number of persons in this workhouse was 470: – viz.

Persons able to work	140
House servants, Nurses who went out to attend the sick	40
Persons from age and infirmity, unable to work	200
Idiots and children	90
	470

	£.	s.	d.
The whole amount of earnings	906	14	3
Allowance to the poor on their earnings, including the house servants	218	4	0
Balance	£ 688	10	3

Considering that all these were more or less disabled, and that the benevolent managers of the poor, had not the advantage of finding a market in the wants of government; this statement proves that all that is necessary to procure a provision of work at the Penitentiary, is ingenious contrivance, and vigilant attention to the demands for manufactured commodities.

Supposing, however, it should be found that while the decrepit are capable of productive labour in Spitalfields, the young and the vigorous are incapable at Millbank; recourse must then be had to unproductive labour. It is a matter of no great concern to the state, whether a thousand pounds more or less is earned in this prison; but it is a matter of the utmost importance, whether the principle has, or has not, a fair trial.

Again then, I must entreat the managers of this institution, to direct all their energy to this point, and to consider the constant employment of every individual, as a measure of the most vital consequence. The failure, or success, of the scheme, the cause of humanity, so near to the hearts of its benevolent projectors, and so intimately connected with its successful issue, depend upon this; if prisoners are released, who have served an apprenticeship to idleness, they will go forth, not reformed, but confirmed in those habits, which inevitably lead to crime. It would be sufficiently lamentable, to see our prisons again crowded with culprits, for whose improvement so much labour, time, and money, have been expended; but this is the least of the evils. The cause will suffer. This splendid establishment will stand a perpetual answer to every argument in favour of attempting reformation. Thus early, then, I enter a protest against the efficacy of the Penitentiary system being decided by the result of this experiment, except it be fairly made.

These observations (true as I must contend they are in themselves) have ceased to be applicable to the Penitentiary at Millbank. I visited it, May 16, 1818, and found, with hardly an exception, all the prisoners employed.

I am far from pretending to have had any share in producing this alteration; it would probably have taken place if my observations had never been made; for I found in the gentleman on whom the superintendance chiefly devolves, an entire concurrence in the views I had formed of prison discipline, and a conviction as deeply rooted as my own, that reformation in jails, without constant labour, is a vain and idle expectation.

The former dearth of employment seems to have arisen from the institution being as yet in its infancy. Even this difficulty has now been surmounted; and the committee, in their report to parliament, declare 'they see no reason to doubt, that when the system of manufacture shall be fairly brought into operation, most of the male prisoners will earn a sufficient sum to defray the cost of their food and clothing.' It is not for me to anticipate what may be the results of this experiment. Long probation and experience alone can determine upon its merits; considering the short time that has elapsed, any instances of permanent and radical reformation can hardly be expected. In the absence of these, however, it is allowable to rejoice in strong symptoms of its commencement.

I happened to see a boy whom I had known in Newgate, where he was to be found before every session, and where he bore the worst character for violence and wickedness. I well recollect feeling much compassion for him, in the persuasion that judicious discipline might still reclaim him – circumstanced as he was, when in prison, placed in the center of evil and corrupting associates – when out of prison, ignorant of every method of obtaining an honest livelihood; I could consider him in no other light, than as a wretch reared for the gallows. His fate, however, has, I trust, been arrested. He has now been three months at the Penitentiary. He told me with evident pride, that he could already make a pair of shoes – that he earned from three to four shillings weekly – and for his character he referred me to his superiors. From his task-master I heard that be was quiet, attentive, and industrious; and the chaplain described him as a boy of whom he entertained much hope.

Between the conductors of this institution and myself, there may be, and I must confess there are, many points of difference. I think the building deficient in inspection, the rules deficient in encouragement for labour, the dietary too abundant, the time of recreation too short: still be it observed, these are differences merely as to the mode of carrying agreed and conceded principles into execution.

Bearing then a willing testimony to the great change which has been effected of late in point of labour, and to the continuance of those arrangements, which make this prison so remarkable for cleanliness and order, I must yet be allowed to differ with its conductors upon some points of minor importance.

1st. The edifice is too costly; it is built upon a scale which will for ever discourage imitation. This institution ought to be an example to the country, an illustration in every particular of the methods by which the reformation of criminals may be accomplished; but is there any town or any county in this kingdom which could take the Penitentiary for its model, or which would not at once relinquish a plan entailing so vast an expenditure? A considerable portion of the cost arises from the multitude of small workrooms into which each pentagon is divided. It is supposed that prisoners work better in small than in large communities. Now if this opinion should prove to be erroneous, it is evident that dispensing with the partitions would cause a considerable reduction of expense, as well as a great addition of room; in short, the building would cost much less, and contain many more persons. At Ghent, this is done: the prisoners work in very large companies, and it is impossible to desire greater assiduity or silence. The rule is very simple; if a man will not work hard, he is debarred from working altogether; if he will not perform his task in silence, he is placed in solitude.

2ndly, One hour seems too little for the prisoners to be in the air. Some outdoor work, something in the way of hard labour ought to be provided; otherwise the prisoners at the expiration of four or five years will have become so tender, and so susceptible of cold, as to be unfit for any but sedentary employments.

3rdly, The interest which a prisoner has in the produce of his labour is too remote. The full term of his imprisonment must expire, and then he is allowed to participate; but in the long and tedious interval there is nothing to cheer or invigorate his industry.

In making rules, it is manifestly prudent to consider the character of those who are to be governed by them. What then is the character of the inhabitants of the Penitentiary? Are they persons who are disposed to calculate on distant advantages, who are framed with that reasonable texture of mind which can resist the allurements of idleness, in the prospect of recompense hereafter? Are they not rather the creatures of present impulse, persons who have already sacrificed every thing to immediate gratification, and are imprisoned because they have so done? Would our jails be crowded as they are, if men, before the commission of crimes, weighed the pleasures against the consequences, and upon this comparison made their election? Evidently not. Criminals are, generally, men of strong passions and little reflection. The present is uppermost with them, and to affect their minds, you must hold out the temptation of speedy enjoyment. Habits of indolence are deep and inveterate, their influence acts at every moment; you wish to eradicate these habits. The motive you employ then must be one of great cogency and power, and of instant application. A prisoner, unaccustomed for a long time to labour, sits down to his work: you see his task proceeds heavily: then try to reason away his sloth. Tell him that if he works hard that day, he will be sixpence the richer at the end of five years: – Will that affect him? Will the delight arising from so distant a prospect disengage his mind from its indolent propensities? Can we indeed doubt what will be the issue of so unequal a conflict? Or, on the other hand, tell him that if he works hard that day, he will receive so much that night, to be sent to his family, or to be expended in procuring enjoyments for himself. Then you offer a motive which he can clearly estimate, and it is probable that the immediate gratifications of industry will be greater than those of idleness.

In advancing these opinions, I feel the more confident because the mode of acting pursued by a great proportion of mankind, furnishes a melancholy attestation of their truth. How many men are there who clearly perceive, that the illicit gratifications of sense can only be secured at the expense of eternal happiness, and yet how many will grasp at the enjoyments of the present hour, though purchased at so desperate a price.

For the purpose of giving a stimulus to a prisoner's exertions, he must share the profits of his own labour. Upon this point we are agreed, – when – is the only question. A part, I admit, must be retained till he leaves prison; for these small savings, by enabling him to return home, to purchase tools, to support himself till he finds work, will prevent the necessity of his resorting to his evil practices for subsistence. A part ought as certainly, I contend, to be given him for his immediate use. A willingness to work is the principle you want to implant, and by making labour directly productive of comfort or convenience, you do much towards rendering it agreeable. The three best jails which I have seen, are those at Ghent, at Bury, and at Ilchester;[23] and in all of these a certain portion of his earnings is allotted to the prisoner, part of which is reserved till his departure, and a part is given for present expenditure. Very soon after I had seen the Penitentiary, the governor of Bury jail called upon me: he told me that on the preceding day he had left his prison at five o'clock in the morning; and at that early hour he had counted thirty-four spinning wheels in full activity. The prisoners had petitioned for permission to take their machinery into their night cells, that they might commence their labour before the regular hours. Their work had become not a matter of compulsion, but of indulgence – a reward for good conduct. After he had seen the Millbank Penitentiary, I asked him what would be the consequence, if the regulations there used, were adopted by him. The consequence would be, he replied, that every wheel would be stopped. I would not be considered as supposing that the prisoners will altogether refuse to work at Millbank. They will work during the stated hours, but the present incentive being wanting, the labour will, I apprehend, be languid and desultory.

If these objections appear to be valid, the remedy is easy. The dietary is manifestly too good. I would recommend a considerable reduction, still leaving a sufficiency, – for instance, let the allowance of meat be discontinued. This will occasion a saving to the establishment. Let this amount, and perhaps a part of the sum funded for his future use, be given weekly as an encouragement to industry. If he wishes for meat or any other indulgence, let him purchase it. Let superior food be the direct consequence of superior exertion. I must repeat that I am much deceived, if a man will not work more cheerfully and more industriously, if he finds the product of his morning's labour in his dinner and in his supper, than if he waits five years for it. [pp. 88–100]

Anon., *Newgate Walls* (*c*.1820s).

This is an anonymous ballad of the kind hawked about the streets and markets of London and other towns for several centuries. 'Newgate Walls' appears on the same sheet with the songs 'The Knight of the Golden Crest', 'The Lass of Teviot Side' and 'The Minstrel Boy'. The original is in the British Library, London (shelfmark C.116f.1.(3)).

NEWGATE WALLS.

IT was on one summer's morning fair,
  The sun shone bright the sky looked clear,
The sun shone bright on Newgate walls,
  Away away our turnkey calls

From the start we did set out,[1]
  Down Ludgate hill without fear or doubt
As Blackfriars we did pass by,
  There's no mail coach with us could come nigh

At Greenwich town we made no long stay,
  But down the River we bore away,
With aching hearts at Sheerness we lay,[2]
  Waiting to sail to Botany bay.[3]

We had scarcely set one foot on land,
  Before a shovel was put in our hand,
A shovel and a wheelbarrow too,
  Which caused our poor hearts to rue.

They asked us from whence we came,
  We told them from Horsemonger Lane[4]
Then serve your king and country true,
  And we'll behave like a friend to you.

Now my seven years[5] is gone and past,
  And I'll return to my favourite lass
Fill up your glasses you sons of glee
  And drink success to sweet liberty.

Anon., *The Life of Richard Turpin, a Most Notorious Highwayman: Comprising a Particular Account of All His Adventures, Until His Trial and Execution at York*, 3rd edn (London: J. Langham; J. Mackenzie, [*c.* 1820]).[1]

Richard or Dick Turpin (1706–39) is one of the most famous English criminals of the past three centuries, rivaled only by Jack Sheppard, with others, such as Claude Duval and Tom King, coming behind. Turpin was hanged at York on 7 April 1739 for horse-stealing, rather than for highway robbery, the crime for which he became famous. Shortly after his execution a chapbook appeared at York and London detailing his life, crimes and trial. Turpin was also a familiar figure from the 'Newgate Calendar', or collections of criminal biographies published under various titles from the early eighteenth century at least – although Turpin was never imprisoned in Newgate. It was around 1800, however, that Turpin's popularity began to take off, with chapbooks published by Ann Lemoine (1801, 1807, 1808) – substantially the same text as the one here – followed by others from the leading publishers of the new form of fashionable sixpenny street literature: Fairburn, Dean and Munday, Hodgson, and Catnach of London; Walker of Otley; Kendrew of York; Richardson of Derby; and others. It was, however, W. Harrison Ainsworth's Newgate novel of 1834, *Rookwood: A Romance*, that gave Turpin his modern and still familiar face of the gentleman highwayman. But this figure had already been shaped four years earlier from the Turpin material, with an admixture of Tom King and other highwaymen, by Edward Lytton Bulwer, as the eponymous hero of his novel *Paul Clifford* (1830), included in this series. Assisted further by stage melodramas depicting his exploits, then a series of dime novels, followed by a magazine and comic books, Turpin went on to become the most familiar criminal in modern English-speaking culture, and the most familiar outlaw after Robin Hood.

This edition is included here, along with the street ballad 'Newgate Walls', the chapbook version of Defoe's novel *Moll Flanders*, the life of the murderer John Foster from the *Newgate Calendar*, and a later true crime chapbook of the murder of Henry Ducker, to illustrate the cheap popular literature of crime and punishment in the early nineteenth century, which spoke to the lower classes' perceptions of crime and punishment, and from which were fashioned the middle-class three-volume Newgate novels such as *Paul Clifford*, *Jack Sheppard*, and *Rookwood*.

Note on the text: four silent corrections of typographical errors have been made.

THE transactions of this most notorious offender made a greater noise in the world, at the time they happened, than those of almost any other malefactor whose life is recorded in the penal collection[2] of this country; and as they were the cause of much alarm in the places where they were acted, a particular account of him cannot be unwelcome to the reader.

Richard Turpin was born at Hempstead, in Essex, where his father followed the occupation of a butcher with a fair reputation; and, after being his usual time at school, he was apprenticed to a butcher in Whitechapel,[3] but did not serve out his time, for his master discharged him from his house for the brutality and egregious impropriety of his conduct, which was not in the least diminished by his parents' improper indulgence in supplying him with money, which enabled him to cut a dash round the town among the blades[4] of the road and turf,[5] whose company he affected to keep.

His friends thinking that marriage, and a settlement in life, would bring him over from his irregular courses, persuaded him to marry, which he did with one Hester Palmer, a young woman of a decent family, at East Ham, in Essex; but he had not long been married before he fell into his old ways again, and soon became acquainted with a gang of thieves, whose depredations terrified the whole county of Essex, and neighbourhood of London. His share of the spoil was not sufficient, it appears, to support him in his extravagance, for he joined sheep-steeling to footpad[6] robbery; and was at last obliged to fly from his place of residence for a stealing young heifer, which he killed and cut up for sale.

Soon after this, he stole two oxen from one farmer Giles, of Plaistow and drove them to a butcher's slaughtering-house near Waltham Abbey. Giles's servants came to this place in pursuit of the cattle, where finding two carcases cut up, that answered the description of their master's property in size, and shrewdly suspecting Turpin, who did not deny being the owner of the goods, they made a strict search after the skins, and having found them, they had not the smallest doubt of his having stolen the identical beasts which they were in search of. No doubt remaining who was the robber, a warrant was procured for his apprehension; but he soon had scent that the runners[7] were in pursuit of him, and got off in time, before they could secure him. He made his escape out of the window of the house where he was, just at the moment they were entering the door.

Finding his situation at Waltham Abbey rather perilous, he retreated into the Hundreds[8] of Essex, where he found greater security; but as he could not live long without a fresh supply of money, he hit upon a new scheme to support himself, and that was, to rob the smuggler he happened to meet with on the road; but he took care not to attack a gang, only such solitary travellers as fell in his way, and then he did it with a colour of justice; for he constantly pretended to have a deputation from the customs, and so took their property in the king's name. He got tired of this kind of business after a while; and the retirement to which he was condemned, in this pursuit, not suiting the volatility of his disposition, he went in search of the gang with whom he had before connected himself, the principal part of whose depredations were committed upon Epping Forrest,[9] and the adjacent part; but this business soon becoming an object of magisterial inquiry,[10] he again returned to the solitude of the country with some more of the gang, and they became notorious deer-stealers; and Turpin being a good shot, he sent many a good buck up to his connexions in London.

But this business, like the former, not succeeding to their expectations, they determined to commence housebreakers; and in this they were much encouraged by joining with Gregory's gang,[11] as it was then called, a company of desperadoes[12] that made the Essex and adjacent roads very dangerous to travel. In these marauding expeditions they made many desperate and successful attempts; one in particular at the house of Mr. Strype, an old man, who kept a chandler's shop at Watford, where they got a good booty; for they robbed the house of all the money and other valuables in it, but did not offer the professor any personal abuse; and this moderation was entirely owing to Turpin, who did not permit his comrades to proceed to violence, that his own character might not be charged with unnecessary cruelty.

In one night's time this gang robbed Chinkford[13] and Barking churches of all the moveables left in the vestries; but the plate[14] at both places being placed in the respective churchwardens' possession, they got but an indifferent booty. Turpin eluded, with some of his companions, the search that was made after them; but three were taken, one of whom turned evidence,[15] and the other two were transported.

Notwithstanding his character was pretty well blazoned about, two months after this affair happened he had the audacity to venture as far as Suson, in Essex, whither his wife had retired, and here he lived unnoticed for six months; but when his concealment was discovered, he made a quiet retreat by night, and nothing was heard of him until the robbery of Farmer Lawrence, when he joined with others called the Essex gang,[16] the principals of whom were Ned Rust, George Gregory, Fielder, Rose, and Wheeler. This Gregory was an old offender, and had robbed in conjunction with Dick Swift, both scholars of Jonathan Wild,[17] who had but lately been hanged. These followed deer-stealing in the day time; but beginning to be too well known by the keepers, and not finding money come in so fast as they expected, they formed themselves into a body, by Turpin's directions, and went round the country at night, and whatever house they knew had any value in it they marked. Their method was, one to knock at the door, and, as soon as it was opened, the rest rushed in and plundered; and such was their impudence and connexions, that they were not satisfied always with the money, plate, watches, or rings they found, but even took away the household goods, if they suited them.

Somehow or other, Turpin became acquainted with the circumstances of an old woman who lived at Loughton,[18] that always kept a great quantity of ready cash by her; whereupon he and the gang agreed to rob her; and when they came to the door, Wheeler knocked at it, and Turpin and the rest forcing their way into the house, blindfolded the eyes of the old woman and her maid, and tied the legs of her son, a well-grown lad, to the bedstead, and proceeded to rob the house; but not at first finding the wished-for booty, they all set about a consultation what to do to get at it; for they were certain she must have a considerable sum concealed somewhere or other about the house. Turpin began to examine her where her money and effects were hid, telling her at the same time, that he knew she had money, and it was in vain to deny it, for have it they would. The old gentlewoman being very loath to part with her money, persisted in it that she had none, and would not declare any thing more of the matter; upon which some of the gang were inclinable to believe her, and were sorry for their disappointment, but Turpin as strenuously insisted she had money, as she said that she had none, and at last, with horrid oaths and imprecations, swore he would put her on the fire. She continued obstinate for all that, imagining that he meant only to threaten her; and so very fond was she of her darling gold, that she even suffered herself to be served as he had declared, and endured it for some time, till the anguish at last forced her to make a discovery, which when she had done, they took her off the grate, and robbed her of all they could find. Some persons talk of a much larger sum, but it is certain they stole upwards of four hundred pounds,[19] and decamped safely with the booty.

The next place they robbed was a farmer's at Ripple Side, near Barking,[20] where the people of the house not coming to the door as soon as they wanted them, they broke it open. They first of all, according to their old scheme, gagged, tied, and blind-folded all they found in the place capable of opposing them; and then robbed the house of about 700l.[21] which delighted Turpin so much, that he exclaimed, 'Aye, this is the thing! That's your sort for the rag, (a cant term for money) if it would but last!' and they safely retired with their prize, which amounted to above 80l. a man. This robbery was committed in the beginning of the year 1730. This success so much flushed Turpin and his associates, that several others joined them, insomuch, that they became a formidable crew, and many times, when together, defied the legal authority of the magistrates; and their adroitness was such, that they escaped detection for many months.

Some little time after they determined to attack the house of Mr. Mason, the keeper of Epping Forest, who was pitched upon to feel the effects of their resentment for his former vigilance in disturbing their poaching incursions into his district. But Turpin was not concerned in this affair; for he happened at that time to be at London, where drinking too freely, he forgot his appointment; but the job was done without him by Rust, Rose, and Fielder, who previously bound themselves together by oath not to leave a whole thing in the house. Fielder got over the wall, and broke in backward, when letting in his companions, they proceeded to their business. Mr. Mason was at home sitting up by the fire in his bed-room, with his father, an aged gentleman. After using their usual means of tying their hands and feet, they asked the old man if he knew them; but answering he did not, they carried him into the kitchen, and put him under the dresser. Mr. Mason had a sack forced over his head, and tied round his waist; and in the flurry his little girl got out of bed, and, without any clothes on, hid herself in the hog-sty. Turpin's absence from this expedition was a very unfortunate circumstance to the forest-keeper's family, for they proceeded to greater lengths in their mischief than he would have permitted them had he been present, as he was always satisfied with the plunder, without adding cruelty to oppression. They now went up stairs, and broke every article of furniture in the house. The china and glass made a dreadful ringing; the chairs were piled upon the fire; looking-glasses, drawers, and tables, were beat to pieces with bed-posts; while the beds and carpets were cut to pieces without remorse. This wanton havoc produced them but little, besides the brutal satisfaction of revenge; and they would have retired without a single guinea,[22] had it not been that, in the general wreck of every thing, a china punch-bowl was broke, that stood a little out of the way, upon an upper shelf, and out of it dropped 122 guineas, which they picked up and retired with, after they had done as much mischief as they possibly could, and got safe off, no doubt, very well satisfied with the severe retaliation they had made. They then took the road to London; and coming through Whitechapel met Turpin, with whom they went to the Bunhouse, in the Rope-fields, where they shared their booty with him, which proves the old adage, 'there is honour among thieves,' though he had not taken any active part in the execution of the villany.

The booties they had successively made themselves masters of, had not in the least abated their ardour in the pursuit of more; for, like the miser, the spend-thrift felon is never satisfied, but the more he gets, the more he lavishes; and though he does not secure any thing for a rainy day, takes every opportunity to get more; or, as some of the fraternity have been heard to say, they often rob for nothing else but 'to keep their hands in.'

The next robbery of note they committed was about seven or eight o'clock in the evening. Rust, Turpin, Fielder, Walker, and three others, came to the house of Mr. Saunders, a wealthy farmer at Charlton, in Kent, and knocked at the door, enquired if Mr. Saunders was at home. Being answered he was, and the door opened, they all rushed in, went directly to the parlour, where Mr. Saunders, his wife, and some friends were at cards; but desired them not to be frightened, for they would not hurt their persons, if they sat still and made no disturbance. The first thing they laid hands on was a silver snuff-box, which lay upon the table before them; and having secured the rest of the company, obliged Mr. Saunders to go about the house with them, and open his closets, boxes, and escritoire,[23] whence they took upwards of one hundred pounds in money, and all the plate in the house, a velvet hood, mantle, and other things. Whilst this was doing, the servant maid got loose, ran up stairs, barred herself in one of the rooms, and called out of the window for assistance, in hopes of alarming the neighbourhood; but one of the rogues ran up stairs after her, and with a poker broke open the door, brought her down again, bound her, and all the rest of the family; then they rifled the house of divers other things of value; and finding in their search some bottles of wine, a bottle of brandy, and some mince pies, they all sat down, drank a bottle of wine, eat a mince pie, and obliged the company to drink a glass of brandy each. Mrs. Saunders fainting away with the fright, they got her a glass of water and putting some liquor into it, gave it to her, and were very careful to recover her. They staid a considerable time in the house after feasting, and packing up their booty; and when they departed, they declared that if any of the family gave the least alarm within two hours, or even advertised the marks of the plate they had taken, they would remember them for it, for they would return and murder them at a future time. This robbery was concerted at the George, at Woolwich,[24] whence they proceeded to put their design in execution; and when they had effected it, they crossed the water, and brought their goods to an empty house in Ratcliff Highway, provided for them by one of Dick Swift's acquaintances, where they deposited their plunder, and divided the produce.

They next proceeded into Surry,[25] where Turpin, Rust, Swift, Fielder, and Walker, robbed Mr. Sheldon's house, a lone building near Croydon Church, where they arrived about seven o'clock in the evening. They began their operations here by securing the coachman in the stable attending the horses, whom they bound hand and foot, and afterwards locked him safe in. His master being in an out-house[26] and hearing some strange voices in the yard, was proceeding that way to know the cause, when he was met by Turpin and Walker, who seizing him, compelled him to show them the way into the house, which, when they had got into, they secured the door, and confined the rest of the family in one room, over which, within and without, they set a guard. Mr. Sheldon's servant man unluckily coming to the door from abroad was first knocked down and then dragged into the passage, and tied while they ransacked the house. But they were very much disappointed; for they found but little plate and no cash. From Mr. Sheldon's person they took eleven guineas; two of which Turpin returned him, begging pardon for what they had done, and wished him a good night.

Notwithstanding the situation in which they had left the people here, they had the temerity and assurance to go to the Half-moon tavern at Croydon, where they each regaled themselves with a glass of spirits, and changed one of the guineas they had so recently taken from Mr. Sheldon. In their way out one of them let fall a diamond pin of great value in the passage, which was found by the servant girl, and returned to the owner. This business being completed, they came to the Black-horse, in the Broadway, Westminister, near which Rust and Rose lodged, with one Fletcher, and the notorious Nan Turner, of Golden Lane memory, who secreted herself here from the pursuit of justice, for the murder of a fellow lodger of her own sort. Here they concerted another robbery, of which Rose and Fielder were for that time the captains.

These robberies had hitherto been carried on entirely on foot, with only the occasional assistance of a hackney coach; but now they aspired to appear on horseback, for which purpose they hired horses at the Old Leaping-bar, in High Holborn,[27] whence they set out about two o'clock in the afternoon, and arrived at the Queen's Head, near Stanmore,[28] at five, where they staid to regale themselves. It was by this means that Wood, the master of the house, had so good an opportunity of observing the horses, as to remember the same again when he saw them afterwards in King Street, Bloomsbury,[29] where they were taken. About five o'clock they went from Wood's, the Queen's Head, to Stanmore, and staid there from six, until about seven o'clock, and then all went away together for Mr. Lawrence's,[30] which was about a mile from thence, where they arrived about half an hour after seven. Mr. Lawrence had just before been paying off some workmen, who were discharged, and gone from the house.

On their arrival at Mr. Lawrence's, they alighted from their horses at the outer gate; and Fielder getting over the hatch into the sheep yard, met with Mr. Lawrence's boy putting up[31] some sheep. They seized and presented a pistol to him, Fielder saying he would shoot him if he offered[32] to cry out; and then took the boy's garters,[33] and tied his hands, inquiring what servants Mr. Lawrence kept, and who was in the house, which they obliged him to tell them. They told him they would not hurt him, but that he must go to the door with them; and when they knocked at it, if any body within should ask who it was, that the boy was to answer, and bid them open the door to let him in, and they would give him some money. Accordingly, they led the boy to the door, but he was so terrified that he had no power to speak; whereupon Gregory knocked at the door, upon which they all rushed in with pistols in their hands, crying out, D—n[34] your blood, how long have you lived here? And immediately seizing Mr. Lawrence and his man, threw a cloth over their faces and then took the boy, and led him into the next room, with his hands tied, demanding of him what firearms Mr. Lawrence had in the house; and being told there was none but an old gun, they went and fetched that, and broke it to pieces; then took Mr. Lawrence's man, bound his hands, led him into the room where the boy was, and made him sit down there; and also bound Mr. Lawrence. Turpin cut down his breeches, and they fell to rifling his pockets, out of which they took one guinea, one Portugal piece of thirty-six shillings, about fifteen shillings in silver, and his keys. They said that money was not enough, that they must have more, and drove Mr. Lawrence up stairs, where coming to a closet, although they had taken the key from Mr. Lawrence before, and had it in their custody, yet they broke open the door, and took out from thence two guineas, ten shillings in silver, a silver cup, thirteen silver spoons, two gold rings, and what they could find; and in their search meeting with a bottle of elder wine, they obliged the servants to drink twice of it. Dorothy Street, the maid servant, being in the back house churning, and hearing a noise, suspected they were thieves who were got into the house; and, in order to save herself, she put out the candle; but they rushed in upon her, tied her hands, and then brought her into the room where the other servants were: they then rifled the house of all they could get, linen, table-cloths, napkins, shirts, and the sheets from off the beds; and trod the beds under feet, to discover if any money was concealed therein. Suspecting there was more money in the house, they brought Mr. Lawrence down again, and threatened to cut his throat; and Rose put a knife to it, as if he intended to do it, to make him confess what money was in the house. One of them took a chopping-bill,[35] and threatened to cut off his leg. They then broke his head with their pistols, and dragged him about by the hair of his head. Another of them took a kettle of water off the fire, and flung it upon him; but it did no other harm than wetting him, by reason the maid had just before taken out the greatest part of the boiling water, and filled it again, with cold. After this they dragged him about again, swearing they would 'do for him' if he did not immediately inform them where the rest of his money was hid. They then proceeded to make a farther search; and Gregory, who acted as chief in this affair, swore to the maid, that if she would tell or show him where the money was hid, he would give her something charming fine to wear; to which she replied, she could not inform him of any. This did not in the least satisfy him, for he forced her up stair, where he acted with great violence:[36] and, after bolting the door, swore he would shoot her, if she offered to cry out, telling her it would be better for her master's family if she did so; or he would go to her master's son's house, which was next adjoining, and strip it of every thing; for he said he knew the master was from home. Not being able to get any thing out of her, he tied her fast to the bed-posts, and left her; not forgetting to threaten her with his immediate return if she offered to make the least disturbance.

He then returned to the boy, and inquired whether his master's son would return that night; and being informed he would, he said that he would also go there and see the house. Upon this two of them took the boy out to the place; but, on further consideration, they did not attempt any thing there that night. Upon their return they rummaged every thing in the house; in a chest which belonged to Mr. Lawrence's youngest son, they turned out 20l.[37] and packed up the linen, and withdrew threatening to return again in half an hour, and kill every one they should find loose. So saying, they locked them all in the parlour, took the keys of the back and front door, and threw them down the privy, which was in the area.[38]

Some of the goods were lost by the way; for they were in such haste to get off, that they looked back for nothing; and some were afterwards found in Field Lane, and others in Chick Lane and Saffron Hill, where the gang mostly resided, and where some were taken. Turpin by this robbery got but little; for out of 271*l.*[39] they got in the whole, he distributed among them all but three guineas and six shillings and sixpence.

Such frequent robberies, and the particulars of this atrocious one, being represented to the king, a proclamation was issued for the apprehension of the offenders, and a pardon and 50l. was offered to any of the party who would impeach his accomplices. This, however, had no effect; for they continued their depredations with more systematical ingenuity, and at such distances that none could be aware of their approach. The success they met with elated their spirits, and encouraged them to bid defiance to the executive laws of the country.

In the mouth of danger, and in the midst of alarm, which their audacities had occasioned, Turpin and his gang were as careless as they were heedless. The White Hart, at the upper end of Drury Lane, was their constant place of rendez-vous. Here they planned their nightly visits, and here they divided their spoil, and spent the property they unlawfully acquired. The gang all this time con-sisted of a great number, from the bold adventurer on horseback, to the pitiful stripper of children's clothes.

From thence issued a select band to rob Mr. Francis, a farmer, near Mary-le-bone,[40] where they arrived about dusk; and while they were making their observations on the premises, one of them perceiving somebody in the cow-house, they went in, and finding a man there, they seized and bound him, swearing they would shoot him if he made any attempt to loosen himself, or cry out. They then proceeded to the stable, where was another of the farmer's servants, whom they served in the same manner. Scarce had they performed this, before Mr. Francis, who had been abroad, and coming home, they met at the gate as he was going up to his door. Three of the gang laying their hands upon his shoulder, prevented him from going any further; and the farmer not at first apprehending them to be thieves, but frolicsome fellows, only said to them, 'Methinks you are mighty funny, gemmen.' On which, showing their pistols, they told him no harm should come to him if he would but give one of them an order to his daughter for one hundred pounds in cash; which Mr. Francis refusing to do, alleging his incapa-bility, not having half so much money by him, they forced him by the arm into the stable to his man, where they bound him also, and left him under the care of Rust and Bush, who stood over them with loaded pistols, whilst the rest went to the house. Upon their knocking at the door, Miss Francis opened it, supposing it to be some of the men, when Wheeler and four others rushed in, and they secured her also. Turpin coming in with the last, prevented them from being too violent with the young lady; only threatening if she made any resistance she would be worse used. The maid servant hearing this, cried out, Lord, Mrs. Sarah, what have you done? On which one of them struck the maid, and the other Mr. Francis's daughter, and swore they would murder them if they did not hold their peace. Mrs. Francis hearing the disturbance, and being apprehensive of some danger, cried out, Lord, what's the matter? On which Fielder stepped up to her, and cried, D—n you, – you old bitch, I'll stop your mouth presently! And immediately broke her head with the handle of his whip, and then tied her down in a chair, bleeding as she was.

The maid and daughter were bound in the kitchen, and Gregory was set to watch them, who stood guard over them with a pistol in his hand, to prevent their crying out for assistance, or endeavouring to get their liberty, whilst the other four were rifling the house. In it they found, besides other things, a silver punch ladle, a silver strainer, a silver cup, a pair of silver spurs, a coral set with silver, a mourning ring with a cipher,[41] a gold ring enameled with a blue stone in the middle, and a diamond on each side, and two angels holding a crown; a gold ring set with a stone, and four diamonds; two gold rings with posies;[42] a wig, six handkerchiefs, four shirts, a velvet hat, two pistols, a piece of gold with a hole in it, thirty-seven guineas, and ten pounds in silver, which they took away with them; as also shirts, stockings, and divers other sorts of goods. They spent about an hour and a half in plundering and rifling the house, while Gregory stood sentry over old Mrs. Francis, her daughter, and maid; and Rust and Bush over Mr. Francis and the two men servants in the stable. When they had packed up their booty, they laid severe injunctions upon every one in the house not to stir, under penalty of direct death, and quietly rode off with all they had got.

When they came to divide plunder, Turpin prevented them from cheating one another, which some seemed inclined to do; and gave to each of them 9l. 2s. 6d. The guineas were secreted by him who laid hands on them from the rest of his companions, which, when Turpin afterwards found out, he made him pay severely for; for he informed against him to the officers of justice, which occasioned his being taken up, and he was soon afterward hanged at Tyburn.[43]

They formed the design to rob the house of Justice Asher, near Leigh, in Essex, upon the information of the woman who kept company with Rose, and with that intention met at a public house near Leigh, and in the evening went to put their design in execution; but not rightly knowing their way into the house, they got to the side of a lane near it, waiting for an opportunity, and with that tied their horses against some furze bushes, and concealing themselves under them, intended to have surprised somebody passing that way, and to have obliged them to have shown them the way to the door; but whilst they were thus lying perdue[44] there, they heard several persons riding along together, which happened to be some of the neighbouring farmers, who had been at the justice's, and overhearing their discourse, supposed the justice had other company still remaining at his house, and did not think it advisable to attempt it at that time; they therefore adjourned their design, which so far proved of advantage to them, that it prevented their being taken, which otherwise they could hardly have avoided, by reason that having been observed in the neighbourhood, they were suspected to be smugglers; and information having been given to the custom-house and other officers thereabout, a party of dragoons were sent out in search after them, whom they met; but not having anything with them, they were suffered to pass; whereas if they had committed the robbery they intended, and had been stopped by the soldiers, the goods, upon search, would have been found upon them; and though they might have been only stopped on suspicion of being smugglers, they would thereby have been discovered to be housebreakers, and committed accordingly.

These transactions alarmed the whole country, nobody thinking themselves safe; upon which Mr. Thomson, one of the King's forest-keepers, went to the Duke of Newcastle's office, [45] and obtained his Majesty's promise of a reward of one hundred pounds for whoever should apprehend any of them. This made them rather more shy than they were before; but, however, they could not conceal themselves entirely, and they still frequented their old haunts; when some of the justice's men hearing that a number of them usually met at an alehouse in an alley in Westminster, they went thither, where, finding Turpin, Fielder, Rose, and Wheeler, after a short conflict with cutlasses, the three last were secured, but not till one Bob Berry, a cork-cutter, had his arm dangerously cut across a little below the elbow. During the scuffle, Turpin made his escape out of a window, and getting a horse, rode away immediately. Wheeler turned evidence,[46] and two of the others were hanged in chains.

This affair broke up the gang. Turpin being now left to himself, had more prudence than to follow the house robbing immediately after, particularly as he was so well known; and having some money in his pockets, he took a resolution to be concerned with no other gang, but to act entirely on his own bottom. With this view, he set off toward Cambridge, which he judged would be the best place, as he was not known in that part of the country.

Near Alton he met with an odd encounter, which got him the best companion he ever had, as he often declared. King,[47] the highwayman, as he was returning from this place to London, being well dressed and mounted, Turpin seeing him have the appearance of a substantial gentleman, rode up to him, and thinking him a fair mark, bid him stand and deliver, and therewith producing the things, (i.e. pistols,) King fell a laughing at him, and said, 'What, dog rob dog! Come, come, brother Turpin, if you don't know me, I know you, and should be glad of your company.' After a mutual communication of circumstances to each other, they agreed to keep company, and divide good or ill fortune, as the trumps[48] might turn up. In fact, King was true to him to the last, which was for more than three years, when King met with his fate by a ball on the road.

They met with various fortunes; but being both too well known to remain long in a place, and as no house that knew them would receive them in it, they formed the resolution of making themselves a cave, covered with bavins[49] and earth, and for that purpose pitched upon a convenient place, enclosed with a thicket, situated on the Waltham side of Epping, near the sign of the King's Oak. Here they excavated, and covered with the thicket wood and quickset,[50] a place large enough to receive them and their horses; and while they lay quite concealed themselves, could, through several holes, discover the passengers as they went along the road; and as they thought proper, would issue out, and rob them in such a bold and daring style, that they were more admired than blamed. The very higglers[51] on the road did not always escape their requisitions, but they were mostly repaid again; whilst those who went armed lost their pieces, were wounded and robbed of all they carried about them. Turpin's wife was their messenger, went to market for victuals for them, supplied them with linen, and frequently remained there a whole week together.

In this place Turpin live, ate, drank, and lay, for the space of six years, during the first three of which he was enlivened by the drollery of his companion, Tom King, who was a fellow of infinite humour in telling stories, and of unshaken resolution in attack or defence.

These forest partners used frequently to issue from their cell like the thieves from the cave in Gil Blas,[52] and take a ride out in quest of plunder. King and he once riding towards Bungay, in Suffolk, met two young market women, who had just received a considerable sum of money for corn. King proposed to rob them, but Turpin dissuaded him from it, alleging for a reason, that they were two pretty inoffensive girls, and he would not be concerned in it. King swore he would rob them and accordingly did, against Turpin's consent, which occasioned a dispute between them.

One day, as they were spying from their cave, they discovered a gentleman riding by, that King knew very well to be a rich merchant near Gresham College, Broad Street, who was going thither from his estate near Fair-Mead-Bottom. This gentleman was in his chariot, and had two of his children with him. His name was Bradele. King first attacked him on the Loughton road; but he being a man of great spirit, offered to make resistance, thinking there had been but one; upon which King called Turpin by the nick-name of Jack, and bid him hold the horses' heads. They proceeded first to take his money, which he readily parted with, but demurred a good while upon parting with his watch, which he said was a family piece, being the dying bequest of his father. The altercation though short, being accompanied with menaces and threats, frightened the children in the coach, the biggest of whom, a boy, persuaded his father to let him have it. An old mourning ring was the next object of their requisition, which, though of a very trivial value, King was insisting to take away, when Turpin interposed, and said, they were more of gentlemen than to deprive any one of their friends' respect which they wore about them, and bid King upon this desist from his demand. This concession on the part of the robbers induced the gentleman to ask a further favour, which was, that they would permit him to purchase his watch back again? Upon which, King said to Turpin, 'Jack, he seems to be a good honest fellow, shall we let him have the watch?' 'Aye', said Turpin, 'do just as you will.' Bradele inquiring what would be the price, King said six guineas, adding, 'We never sell one for more, if it be worth six and thirty;' upon which Mr. Bradele promised not to discover them, and said he would leave the money at the Sword-blade Coffee-house in Birchin Lane; when Turpin cried out, 'Aye, but King, insist upon no questions being asked.'

It would be an endless task to relate every particular robbery they committed while in connection together in this fastness of the forest; for it is generally known, at that time there was no regular police established by government, as is now; and the improved state of the roads together, make it impossible for such daring disturbers of the peace to reign any great length of time in one place.

The mail[53] having been robbed upon Stamford Hill,[54] the bag and most of the letters were found scattered near that part of the forest which was suspected to be the abode of Turpin and his accomplice; for several circumstances had occurred to make it a probable event that he might be found thereabouts; besides, the Woodford stage-coach-man, who knew him perfectly well, as well as his colleague King, had often been heard to say, that if any person would give him arms and a hundred pounds, dead or alive, he would give some account of Turpin; but his time was not yet arrived, although he had so long been the terror and talk of the country round London, as well as at remoter distance.

Turpin and King next stopped a person of very decent appearance, near Hackney, and demanded his money: but the gentleman, bursting into tears, said he was in circumstances of distress, and possessed only eighteen pence; on which, instead of robbing him, they made him a present of half-a-crown:[55] a proof that sentiments of humanity may not be utterly banished even from the bosom of a thief. On their return to town they robbed a man of fourteen shillings, and then went to their old place of retreat.

On the day after this transaction they went to the Red Lion alehouse, in Aldersgate Street, where, having drank all day, and being unable to pay the reckoning, they called for more liquor, and then quitted the house, saying they would soon return. Going immediately toward Islington, they met a gentleman, to whom they said, they wanted a small sum to pay their reckoning. On this the gentleman called out thieves! and made all possible resistance; notwithstanding which, they robbed him of a gold watch, which they carried to town and pawned; and then going to the alehouse, defrayed the expenses of the day.

Soon after, they rode to Finchley Common, where meeting only with empty carriages, they were returning to London, when they met the Barnet coach, near Islington, and robbed the company of about fifteen shillings. On the following day they collected 6*l*. 12*s*. and 6*d*. and 4*l*. 5*s*. 9*d*. from another of the Barnet coaches, and nine shillings from the Highgate stage, on their return to town: and this was the whole of the booty they obtained that day.

Turpin having lost his horse, he stole one out of a close.[56] This was a black one; and some people being at work in a field within sight, he threw a handful of silver among them, and made off; but the same evening he changed his black one for a chestnut mare, which he found in a field, and upon her made the best of his way to the forest.

He next stopped a country gentleman, who clapping spurs to his horse, Turpin followed him, and firing a pistol after him, which lodged two balls in his horse's buttocks, the gentleman was obliged to surrender. He robbed him of fifty shillings, asking him if that was all, and the gentleman saying he had no more, Turpin searched him, and found two guineas more in his pocket-book, out of which he returned him five shillings, but at the same time told the gentleman, it was more than he deserved, because of his intention to have *cheated* him.

Turpin had gone on for a long while in a most notorious and defying way, and the reward for apprehending him had induced many to attempt it. Amongst the rest was the ranger Thomson's man. This fellow must needs go in company with a higgler. Turpin was unarmed, standing alone, and not knowing the man, took him for one poaching for hares, and told him he would get no hares near that thicket. 'No,' says the fellow, 'but I have got a Turpin,' and presenting his gun at him, commanded him to surrender. Turpin stood talking with him, and receding back to his cave, laid hold of his carbine, and shot him dead, at which the higgler made off. The man's death obliged Turpin to make off precipitately; so he went farther into the country in search of King; and sent his wife a letter to meet him at a public-house in Hertford, who accordingly went, with two of Squire H—s's servants. She waited for him about half an hour, and when he came to the house, he asked for her by a fictitious name, left on purpose. He soon found she was there, and going to her through the kitchen, he saw a butcher to whom he owed five pounds; the butcher taking him aside, 'come Dick,' says he, 'it would be of great service,' Turpin replied, his wife was in the next room, and she had money. And he would get some of her, and pay him presently. The butcher apprised two or three who were present who it was, and that he would get his five pounds first, and then take him; but Turpin, instead of going to his wife, jumped out of the next window, took horse, and went away immediately, without seeing her, while the butcher waited some time in expectation of receiving his five pounds.

Affairs wore a serious aspect for a while, and Turpin was forced to be very cautious in his approaches to the metropolis, yet he ventured sometimes too near, as the sequel will show. King and Turpin being driven about, they joined with one Potter, a daring roadsman, who had a good horse. In his company they stopped several gentlemen on horseback and in post-chaises, from whom they levied considerable sums. Turpin, the better to disguise himself, now wore sometimes a miller's frock, quite white; at other times he had a black one on like a waggoner. In this disguise, but upon a good horse, he ventured over the forest towards London, when, within about three hundred yards of the Green Man, he overtook one Mr. Major, the owner of *White Stockings*, the race horse; and although they were so near the houses, Turpin ventured to rob him. He took from him his whip, and finding he had a better horse than his, made him dismount, change, and stay till he had changed saddles likewise, and then rode towards London. Mr. Major got to the Green Man, and acquainted Mr. Bayes with it, who immediately said 'I dare swear it is Turpin has done it, or one of that crew, and I'll endeavour to get intelligence of your horse. This that they have left you is stole, and I would have you advertise it.' This was accordingly done, and the horse proved to have been stolen from Plaistow Marshes; and the saddle, which he had kept, was stole from one Arrowsmith.

This robbery was committed Saturday night, and on the Monday following, Mr. Bayes received intelligence that such a horse as Mr. Major had lost was left at the Red Lion Inn, in Whitechapel. He accordingly went thither and found it to be the same, and then resolved to wait till somebody came to fetch it. Nobody came at the time it was left for; but about eleven o'clock at night King's brother (as it afterwards proved) came for the horse; upon which they seized him immediately, and taking him into the house, he said he bought it, and could produce proof of it. But Mr. Bayes looking on the whip in his hand, found the button half broke off, and the name Major upon it, which seemed a confirmation of the thing. They charged a constable with him; but he seemed frightened, and they declaring that they did not believe but the horse was for somebody else, and if he would but tell them he should be released, he told them there was a lusty man in a white duffel coat, waiting for it in Red Lion Street; Mr. Bayes immediately went out, and finding him as directed, perceived it was King, and coming round upon him, attacked him. King immediately drew a pistol, which he clapped at Mr. Bayes's breast, but it luckily flashed in the pan: upon which King struggled to get out his other, that had twisted round the pocket, but could not. Turpin, who was waiting but at a small distance on horseback, came up, when King cried out, 'Damn ye, shoot him, Dick, or we shall be taken;' at which instant Turpin let fly one of his pistols, and the other directly afterward. Both shots missed Bayes, but severely wounded King in two places, who cried out 'Why, Dick, you have killed me, or nearly so.' Turpin hearing this, and finding his case to be desperate indeed, rode away as fast as possible. Some accounts say that King died a week after; but with more certainty it may be asserted, that he was the masked highwayman that was shot near Enfield by the King's German messenger, in attempting to rob him in a post-chaise. This happened but a short time afterward, King and Turpin never met after this; but King called him a coward and one wanting resolution.

Bayes soon after this got intelligence that Turpin might be found at a noted house near Hackney Marsh, and that when he rode out he always had three brace of pistols about him, and a carbine slung. Upon enquiry this was found to be true, which made Mr. Bayes desist in the pursuit.

Turpin for a while showed great signs of uneasiness, often using something like the following expressions to his landlord: – 'Why, Sam, what shall I do? Damn that fellow Dick Bayes, I'll be the death of him, I will. Where shall I go? For I have lost the best companion I ever had in my life: I have shot poor King in endeavouring to rescue him from the shark's paws.' He retained this resolution to the last; but he never had an opportunity of putting his revenge in practice.

Some time after he returned to the forest again, and attempted to rob Captain Thomson and his lady in an open chaise, but the captain firing a carbine at him which missed, Turpin fired a pistol after the Captain, which went through the chaise, between him and his lady, without any other damage than tearing the left sleeve of his coat. The Captain driving hard, and being just in sight of a town, Turpin thought it not proper to pursue him farther.

After this he still kept about the forest, till he was harassed almost to death, for he did not dare go near his old place of safety, the cave, which was ransacked as soon as discovered after his shooting the keeper's man; and when they found his habitation out, it contained two shirts in a cloth bag, five pair of stockings, various shoes and boots, some few utensils to cook with, a quantity of shot, flints, and powder, the remains of a bottle of wine, and some ham and pieces of bacon; so that, being driven from place to place he skulked about the outskirts of the woods, and was once very near taken, when Mr. Ives, the King's huntsman, took out two dry-footed[57] hounds to find him; but perceiving them at a distance, before they had got scent of him, he got up a tree, and saw them go underneath him, without noticing his retreat; upon which he at last took the resolution of going down into Yorkshire.

The public heard very little of Turpin for near two years after this. The first notice of him was from the minister of Long Sutton, in Lincolnshire, who was a magistrate of the place. There he was taken into custody, but he escaped from the constable as he was conducting him back from examination, and hastened to Welton in Yorkshire, where he assumed his wife's maiden name (Palmer,) and took upon himself to appear like a gentleman.

He then took a large house at Brough, near Market-Cave, in Yorkshire, from whence to Welton he carried on an extensive trade in horses, selling and exchanging; and at the time of the races, he is said to have realized about one thousand pounds, which enabled him now to keep the first company stirring in those parts. On one of these occasional visits to Brough, he fell in with the celebrated Dickey Dickinson, the humorous governor of Scarborough Spa, to whom he sold a horse, which four years afterwards was claimed by Squire Moore as his property, he having lost it off the marshes in Lincolnshire.

He went again to Long Sutton, in Lincolnshire, where the people, he thought, would not know him; and as he abounded in money, he proposed to himself to commence a dealer in horses. In his way thither he met a man on horseback, with a large box before him; and, and upon enquiry he found him to be a mountebank,[58] travelling the country for the public good and his own. After a short introduction, Turpin proposed to keep him company, which was no sooner mentioned than agreed upon; and at the first stop they made, Turpin undertook the part of distributing the bills,[59] which in a few hours brought a number of persons round him. The next being Market day, and seeing a number of good horses at the inn where he put up at, he made free with one, leaving his own in the same stall. His partner's satchel, or leather sack, hanging conveniently by the fire-side, he turned out all the doctor's compositions, and filled it from the box of a jew pedlar, with which he decamped, without being then perceived. He disposed of his horse at Long Sutton for ready money to a young farmer? and found another credulous enough to let him have one upon security of the hardware and goods of which he robbed the jew.

Soon after this, he met a young woman in a neat dress, sitting under a tree that grew on the road side; and being in a melancholy posture, he was very importunate to know the occasion of her being in that situation. The young woman, after returning him thanks for his civility, assured him she was only resting herself from her fatigue, being going on foot to her father's house, which was not far distant. Upon hearing this, Turpin dismounted and requested her to take his place, and sit upon the saddle, which she declined. However, at the next inn, he borrowed a pillion, and got up before her, and in that manner they reached the village where the young woman's father dwelt. He called upon her next day, and was well entertained by the family; and putting himself forward as a horse dealer, traveling upon business, he procured himself the credit of two good draught horses, which he soon sold, but forgot to pay for them at the time promised. His temerity could now only be equalled by his impudence. His depredations were now the talk of the whole kingdom. His activity and success were equal; and although a reward of two hundred pounds[60] was offered by his Majesty, with a free pardon to any of his accomplices, it failed of bringing him up; and the newspapers continually reported fresh feats of his felonies. This proclamation and reward appeared in the Gazette[61] of June 14, 1737, as may be seen in the London Magazine for that year, vol. 6th, page 335.[62]

He could never thoroughly leave off visiting his old haunts; for the afore-mentioned Magazine mentions a robbery committed by him singly, upon a gentleman in his own chaise at Holloway,[63] from whom he took a considerable sum. The gentleman observed to him, when he attacked him first, that he had reigned long enough, and ought to leave off thieving; to which he replied, 'Pray, Sir, don't you seem to mind it; my time is not now; nor you the man to take me; but tip me the cole[64] or I'll --' he then rode off, and passed two gentlemen's servants with led horses, showing his pistols. Turpin had been frequently known to levy contributions as near London as the back of Islington,[65] and in a few hours after to rob in a distant country.

It is very remarkable that, for such a course of time, as from the date of the King's reward of two hundred pounds for his apprehension, he should still go on with his depredations with the most audacious impunity, insomuch that it affected the national character in the eyes of foreigners, who could not help remarking, that the native bravery of the English was supine in bringing such a daring offender to justice. In fact, his feats of equestrian agility were so surprising, and his identity so uncertain, that to these circumstances alone may be ascribed his long evasion from the iron hand of the law.

He had been at Suson, and drank very free at the Cock there. Early in the morning he set off, and robbed a gentleman of fifty guineas[66] and a valuable watch, in the environs of London. Apprehensive of being known and pursued, he spurred his horse on and took the northern road, and, astonishing to relate, reached York the same evening, and was noticed playing at bowls in the bowling-green with several gentlemen there, which circumstance saved him from the hands of justice for that time. The gentleman he robbed knew him to be Turpin, and caused him to be pursued and taken at York: he afterwards swore to him and the horse he rode on, which was the identical one he arrived upon in that city; but on being in the stable, and his rider at play, and all in the space of four-and-twenty hours, his alibi was admitted; for the magistrates at York could not believe it possible for one horse to cover the ground, being upwards of one hundred and ninety miles, in so short a space. He is reported, upon this occasion, to have used his horse to raw beef upon the bit in his mouth. Some go so far as to say he always rode with fowls' guts tied round it. Be this so or not, it was a race that equaled, if not surpassed, the first achievements of turf velocity.[67]

Notwithstanding the dreadful scenes of robbery (and sometimes cruelty) in which Turpin was engaged, he gave several proofs of his possessing a heart capable of feeling for the distress of a fellow-creature, and a spirit of generosity. He once met a country dealer coming up to market on the Essex road, whom he commanded to stop, and deliver him his money. The poor man told him he had but fifteen shillings and sixpence, which he said was his all, and if it was taken from him he should be reduced to absolute want. Turpin, whose finances were quite exhausted, answered, there was no time to be lost; his money he must have; but at the same time desired him to be in a certain part of Newgate Street on a particular hour the next day, with his hat in his hand; and if a person walked by and dropped anything into his hat, to take no notice, but go immediately about his business. The man accordingly took his station at the time appointed, and had not been there more than half an hour, before he felt something fall into his hat, and upon opening the small packet, to his great joy, he found it to contain ten guineas.

Another time he robbed a poor woman returning from Ferry-bridge, where she had been to sell some commodities: and soon after hearing that she was distressed by her landlord for rent, he contrived to relieve her in the following singular manner. He found out her abode, and threw into her window, through the glass, a leather bag, containing gold and silver to the amount of six pounds, perhaps the produce of some recent robbery.

For the two last years of his life he seems to have confined his residence to the county of York, where he appears to have been so little known, that his company was chiefly with the best yeomen of the country. He often accompanied the neighbouring gentlemen in their parties of hunting and shooting; and one evening, on a return from an expedition of the latter kind, he saw one of his landlord's cocks in the street, which he shot at and killed. One Hall his neighbour seeing him shoot the cock, said to him, 'Mr. Palmer, you have done wrong in shooting your landlord's cock;' whereupon Palmer said if he would stay whilst he charged his piece, he would shoot him too. Mr. Hall hearing him say so, went and told the landlord what Palmer had done and said. Thereupon the landlord immediately went with Mr. Hall to Mr. Crowle, and got his warrant for apprehending him; by virtue of which warrant he was next day taken up, and carried to the general quarter sessions, then at Beverly, where he was examined by George Crowle, Hugh Bethel, and Marmaduke Constable, Esqrs. three of his Majesty's justices of peace for the East Riding of Yorkshire; and they demanded sureties for his good behaviour, and he refusing to find such, was by them committed to the house of correction.

Irritated by this insolent and very foolish behaviour, Mr. Hall moved every gentleman of his acquaintance against him; and though in itself but a trivial circumstance, it led to more serious circumstances, and to his fatal catastrophe in the end, as the reader will observe.

The gentleman having taken several informations from persons of Brough and Welton, about Palmer's frequently going into Lincolnshire, and usually returning with plenty of money, and several horses which he sold or exchanged in Yorkshire, had just reason to suspect that he was either a highwayman or a horse-stealer; and being desirous of doing his country justice, and fearful to oppress the innocent, the next day they went to the said John Palmer, and examined him again, touching where he had lived, and to what business he was brought up; who then said, he had about two years before lived at Long Sutton, in Lincolnshire, and was by trade a butcher; that his father then lived at Long Sutton, and his sister kept his father's house there; but he having contracted many debts, for sheep that proved rotten,[68] so t hat he was not able to pay for them, he was therefore obliged to abscond, and came and lived in Yorkshire. The Justices upon this confession, thought it the best way to send into Lincolnshire, to inquire into the truth of this matter; and Mr. Robert Appleton, clerk of the peace for the riding, then wrote a letter to Long Sutton, signifying the whole affair; which letter was sent by a special messenger, and given to one Mr. Delamere, a justice of the peace, who lived there; and Mr. Appleton received a letter from him in answer thereto, with this account, that the said John Palmer had lived there about three quarters of a year, and had before that been once apprehended, and made his escape, and that they had a strong suspicion he was guilty of horse-stealing.

Another information gave notice, that he had traveled through various parts of the north of England in different disguises, during which he had sold several horses, mares, and foals, which had been claimed by different owners, and for which there were several informations lodged against him for horse-stealing. Upon this, the magistrates thought it prudent to remove him from Beverly house of correction to York Castle, where the report of his being detained brought many persons from all parts of the country: and in less than two months, two persons from Lincolnshire came and claimed a mare and foal, and likewise a horse, which he had stolen in that county.

Captain Dawson, of Ferrarby, was one among the claimants. His horse was that on which Turpin, alias Palmer, rode on when he came to Beverly, and which he had stole from off Hickington Fen in Lincolnshire.

After he had been in prison five months, he wrote the following letter to his brother in Essex.

DEAR BROTHER,   *York, Feb.* 1739

I am sorry to inform you, that I am now under confinement in York Castle, for horse-stealing. If I could procure an evidence from London to give me a character, that would go a great way toward my good, and might procure in the end my enlargement and acquittal. It is true I have been here a long while, but never wrote before. Few people know me. For Heaven's sake, dear brother, do not neglect me: you will know what I mean when I say

I am yours,
        JOHN PALMER.

His brother refused to take the letter, and it was returned unopened to the post office in Essex, because the brother would not pay for it. The letter being accidentally seen by a Mr. Smith, the Schoolmaster of the town, he recognized the hand-writing to be Turpin's, for he had taught him to write at his father's. This coming to the knowledge of the magistrates, they subpœned[69] Mr. Smith, by whom it was discovered, that the John Palmer was Richard Turpin. Upon the trial this schoolmaster and another gentleman proved his identity.

On the rumour that the noted Turpin was a prisoner in York Castle, persons flocked from all parts of the county to take a view of him, and debates run very high whether he was the real person or not. Among others who visited him, was a young fellow who pretended to be well acquainted with the famous Turpin, having rode several miles with him a hunting. After having regarded him a considerable time with looks of great attention, he told the keeper he would bet him half-a-guinea he was not Turpin, the horse-stealer; on which the prisoner, whispering the turnkey, said, 'Lay him, Jack, and I'll go you halves.'

When he was on his trial, his case seemed much to affect he hearers. He had two trials, upon both of which he was convicted upon the fullest evidence. During his abode in the castle, the turnkeys are said to have made more than an hundred pounds by showing him, and selling him and his acquaintances and visitors liquors.

He wrote to his father upon being convicted, to use his interest to get him off for transportation; but his fate was at hand; his notoriety caused application to be ineffectual. To his letter the father returned the following answer: –

DEAR CHILD,

I received your letter this instant with a great deal of grief. According to your request, I have writ to your brother John, and Madam Peck, to make what intercession can be made to Colonel Watson, in order to obtain transportation for your misfortune; which had I 100*l.* I would freely part with to do you good. In the mean time my prayers are for you; and for God's sake give your whole mind to beg of God to pardon your many transgressions, which the thief upon the cross received pardon for at the last hour, though a very great offender. The Lord be your comfort, and receive you into his everlasting kingdom.

     I am your distressed,
       Your loving father,
        JOHN TURPIN
Hempstead,
March 29, 1739

THE TRIAL

Of JOHN PALMER, *alias* PAUMER, alias RICHARD TURPIN, *at the Assizes holden at the* Castle *of* York, *in and for the said county, the* 22d Day of March, *1738-9, before the Hon.* Sir William Chapple,[70]

Knt, *Judge of the Assize, and one of His Majesty's Justices of the Court of King's Bench, for stealing a* Black Gelding, *the Property of* Thomas Creasey.

Court. (Call Thomas Creasey.) – Sir, was you in possession of a gelding in August last?

A.   Yes I was.

Q.   About what time did you miss it?

A.   The 18th day of August last I missed this gelding.

Q.   Where did you find him, and what colour was he;

A.   I found him at the Blue Bell, in Beverly.

Q.   How came you to hear he was there?

A.   Richard Grasby was the person who told me it was my gelding.

Q.   Did you describe the gelding to him.

A.   Yes, and then he told me it was the same.

Q.   Upon that what did you do?

A.   I went to the landlord of the house at Beverley and described him to him.

Q.   Do you remember what description you gave him of the gelding?

A.   Yes, the description was a black gelding with a little star on the forehead.

Q.   What did he (the landlord) do then?

A.   I went with him and he showed me the horse.

Q.   What month was it?

A.   The month of August last.

Q.   Did you take any means to recover your property;

A.   I hired men and horses, and rode forty miles round about us, to hear of it, and got it cried in all the market towns about us.

Court to James Smith.

Do you know the prisoner Palmer, at the bar; Look at him, and tell what you know of him.

A.   Yes. I knew him at Hempstead in Essex, where he was born, and where his father kept the Bell. I knew him ever since he was a child.

Q.   What is his name?

A.   Richard Turpin. I knew his relations, father and mother; and he married one of my maids.

Q.   What! Was you with him frequently?

A.   Yes.

Q.   When did you see him last?

A.   It is about five years since I saw him.

Q.   Have you any particular marks to show this is the man?

A.   This is the very man.

Q.   Did you teach him at school?

A.   Yes, I did; but he was only learning to make letters, and, I believe, he was three quarters of a year with me.

Q.   Do you think this is he?

A.   Yes, this is the man.

Q.   As you lived there, why did you come down here to this place?

A.   Happening to be at the Post Office, where I saw a letter directed to Turpin's brother-in-law, who, as I was informed, would rather lose the letter than pay the postage; upon that account taking particular notice thereof, I thought, at first, I remembered the superscription, and concluded it to be the hand writing of the prisoner Turpin; whereupon I carried the letter before a magistrate who broke the same open, (the letter was subscribed John Palmer) and I found it sent from York castle. I had several of Dick Turpin's bills, and knew his hand.

Q.   Are you sure this is his letter? (a letter produced in court.)

A.   Yes, I am sure that is his letter.

Q.   Was that the cause of your coming down?

A.   I was sent for by the justices to come down.

Q.   How happened you to take notice of this letter?

A.   Seeing the York stamp.

Q.   From these circumstances did you come down here;

A.   Yes, indeed I did come upon this account.

Q.   When you came to the castle, did you challenge him or know him?

A.   Yes, I did, upon the first view of him, and pointed him out from among all the rest of the prisoners.

Q.   How long is it since you saw him last?

A.   I think about five years.

Q.   Do you know anything more of him?

A.   I think he might be about eleven or twelve years old when I went to the excise; and he worked with his father, who was a butcher.

Q.   Was he ever set up in the butchering trade?

A.   Yes; I know he was.

Q.   How long might he live in that way?

A.   I cannot tell. He lived at —* in Essex, and left it about six years; and he after kept a public house.

Q.   Did you afterwards see him?

A.   I saw him afterwards, six miles from thence.

Q.   What became of him then?

A.   I do not know more; only the last time I saw him I sold him a grey mare, about five years ago, before my brother died.

---

*   There was such a noise it the Court, that a gentleman who took down the trial could not distinctly hear the name of the place.

Q.   Do you know more of him?

A.   This I know of him, and I have been many times in his company, and frequently with him.

Court. Palmer, you are allowed the liberty to ask Mr. Smith any questions.

Prisoner. I never knew him.

When Mr. Smith first came to York, in February last, he was examined at the castle by several of his Majesty's Justices of the Peace for the County, and gave him the same account as above.

Mr. Edward Saward, of Hempstead, in Essex, called.

Court. Do you know this Richard Turpin?

A.   Yes, I do know him; he was born and brought up at the Bell; his father kept a public house.

Q.   How long have you known him?

A.   I have known him these twenty-two years, *upon my soul* (here the Counsel reproved Saward, and said to him Friend, you have sworn once already, you need not swear again.) I knew him ever since he was a boy and lived at the Bell.

Q.   How long did he live there?

A.   I cannot exactly tell; he lived with his father, and I was very great with him.

Q.   Did you know him after he had set up for himself?

A.   Yes, I knew him perfectly well then, and I have bought a great many good joints of meat from him *upon my soul*.

Upon this the justice reprimanded him, and advised him not to speak so rashly, but to consider he was upon oath, and that he should speak seriously.

Q.   Did you know him since he left Hempstead?

A.   I was with him at his house at Hempstead.

Q.   Did you see him there?

A.   I saw him frequently; I can't tell how often.

Q.   How many years since he left Hempstead?

A.   He came backward and forward.

Q.   How long is it since you saw him last?

A.   About five or six years ago.

Q.   Can you say this assuredly or firmly?

A.   Yes, I never saw him since.

Q.   Had he settled dwelling?

A.   Not that I know of.

Q.   Now look at the Prisoner; is this Richard Turpin?

A.   Yes, yes, Dick Turpin, the son of John Turpin, who keeps the Bell at Hempstead.

Turpin denied he knew this Edward Saward, but seemed at last to own Mr. Smith.

Counsel to Mr. Smith.] Mr. Smith, when you spoke to him in the castle, did you know him?

A.   Yes, I did; and he did confess he knew me; and said unto me two or three times, Let us bring our eyes with drink. And I drank with him, which is this Richard Turpin.

Upon this the prisoner seemed to be much affected and showed a great deal of anxiety.

Court to the Prisoner.

Have you any thing more to say ?

Prisoner. I have sent a subpoena for a man and his wife; they were present when I bought them.

Q.   What is his name?

A.   I cannot tell; therefore I desire some longer time, that these witnesses may be examined. I also sent a special messenger with a letter.

Mr. Griffith the goaler, being called, said the messenger is come back.

Court. What say you to that?

Prisoner was silent.

Thomas Creasey was again called in and cross-examined.

Q.   Are you sure the gelding he showed you was yours.

A.   Yes, I am.

Q.   But are you very sure that was your gelding?

A.   Yes, yes; indeed I am.

Did you show him to any person?

A.   Yes, I did; I showed him to Carey Gill, the constable at Welton.

Court to Carey Gill the Constable.] What do you know concerning the prisoner?

A.   He was take up by me for SHOOTING A COCK, upon which I carried him to Beverly sessions.

Q.   Which way did you carry him? Or how did he go?

A.   He rode upon a horse which he called his own.

Did you see the horse?

A.   Yes. It was the same horse he came from Welton upon.

Court to Thomas Creasey.] How did you get your horse again?

A.   I got him from the justice by his order.

Q.   How many miles was it from home you got this horse?

A. It was about fifty miles from the waterside to Welton.

Was it the same horse you heard described?

A. Yes, it was.

Q. What marks had he?

A. He was a black gelding, with a little star on his forehead, and carried a good tail.

Court to James Smith.] How long is it since you have know the prisoner at the bar? Look at him again.

Smith. I have known him from his infancy these twenty-two years; and he is the very Richard Turpin which I have know at Hempstead, and the very son of John Turpin in that town.

Court to Prisoner.] Have you any more to say?

Prisoner. I bought this horse at Whitehead.

The Jury brought in their verdict, and found him Guilty.

When the Judge was asked what reason he had to give why sentence of death should not be pronounced against him?

Prisoner. It is very hard upon me, my Lord, because I was not prepared for my defence.

Court. Why was you not? You knew the time of the assizes as well as any person here.

Prisoner. Several persons who came to see me, assured me, that I should be removed to Essex to be tried there; for which reason I thought it needless to prepare witnesses for my defence.

Court. Whoever told you so were highly to blame; and as your country has found you guilty of a crime worthy of death, it is my office to pronounce sentence against you.

The morning before Turpin's execution, he gave 3*l*. 19*s*. amongst five men, who were to follow the cart as mourners, with hatbands and gloves, and gave gloves and hatbands to several persons more. He also left a gold ring, and two pair of shoes and clogs, to a married woman at Brough, that he was acquainted with, though he at the same time acknowledge he had a wife and child of his own.

He was carried in a cart to the place of execution, on Saturday, April 7th, 1739, with John Stead, condemned also for horse-stealing. He behaved himself with amazing assurance, and bowed to the spectators as he passed. It was remarkable that as he mounted the ladder, his right leg trembled, on which he stamped it down with an air, and with undaunted courage looked round about him; and after speaking near half an hour to the topsman,[71] threw himself off the ladder,[72] and expired in about five minutes.[73]

His corpse was brought back from the gallows about three in the afternoon, and lodged at the Blue Boar, in Castlegate, till ten in the next morning, when it was buried in a neat coffin in St. George's Church Yard, without Fisher-gate Postern, with this inscription R.T. 28* The grave was dug very deep; and the persons whom he appointed his mourners, as above mentioned, took all possible care to secure the body; notwithstanding which, on Tuesday morning, about three o'clock, some persons were discovered moving off with it, having taken it up. The mob having got scent where it was carried to, and suspecting it was to be anatomized,[74] went to a garden in which it was deposited, and brought away the body through the streets of the city, in a sort of triumph, almost naked, being only laid on a board, and covered with straw, and carried on four men's shoulders, and buried it in the same grave, having first filled the coffin with slacked[75] lime.

---

*   He confessed to the hangman that he was thirty three year of age.

from [John Bigge], *Report of the Commissioner of Inquiry into the State of the Colony of New South Wales* (1822), pp. 1–5, 20, 61, 63, 68–70, 74–7, 105–6, 125, 140.

John Thomas Bigge (1780–1843), author of this and two further reports on the judicial establishment and the state of agriculture in New South Wales, was a son of the high sheriff of Northumberland, England. He was educated at Oxford and trained for the bar. In, 1813, after several years of successful practice, he was appointed chief justice of Trinidad and in 1819, commissioner of inquiry into the colony at New South Wales, Australia. The commission sprang from concern in the British government that penal transportation was ceasing to be a deterrent to criminals because of the reported leniency and humanitarianism of the colony's governor, Lachlan Macquarrie, but Bigge was privately authorized by lord Bathurst, secretary of state for the colonies, to investigate every aspect of the colonial administration and the conduct of its officers. Bigge was seen to associate with some of Macquarrie's local critics, and he gathered testimony in an often informal way that invited accusations against Macquarrie and others. Bigge, himself a member of the English upper-class and administrative elite, disapproved of Macquarrie's encouragement of freed convicts, or 'emancipists', most of whom came from lower-class backgrounds. Relations between Bigge and Macquarrie deteriorated. Opinion now is that Bigge's *Report* ignored the colony's unique and difficult history and hence the work that Macquarrie and others had done in transforming an often unruly and corrupt penal colony into a reasonably well-regulated and steadily developing part of the British empire. After Bigge returned to England in 1821 he was appointed to similar commissions of inquiry into the colonies of Mauritius, Cape of Good Hope and Ceylon, and produced another series of reports. Later, ill health prevented him from accepting appointment to report on clerical establishments in England.

Bigge's *Report* has nine sections (two sections are numbered VI): 'I. Condition and Treatment of Convicts during the passage to New South Wales' (pp. 1–13); 'II. Debarkation and Muster of the Convicts, Male and Female' (pp. 13–20); 'III. Nature of the Employment of Convicts when retained in the service of Government' (pp. 21–52); 'IV. Superintendence of Convicts in the service of Government' (pp. 52–60); 'V. Subsistence and Clothing of the Convicts retained by Government; and Employment of Female Convicts' (pp. 60–74); 'VI. Nature of the Labour of Convicts in the Service of Settlers' (pp. 74–98); 'VI. Control of Convicts in the Service of Settlers' (pp. 98–118); 'VII. Nature and extent of Remissions of Punishment, and their effects upon the Convicts' (pp. 118–55); 'VIII. Nature of the future Establishments for Convicts in New South Wales' (pp. 155–75); 'Appendix' (tables and documents, pp. 176–86). The *Report* has been discussed mainly in regard to its related themes of the treatment and control of convicts, their punishment and reformation and colonial administration in New South Wales. In fact, the underlying preoccupation of the *Report* is with effective extraction of labour from the convicts for the establishment of a colony reproducing the social and economic relations, values, and hierarchies of Britain.

Note on the text: present editor's omission indicated by three points of ellipsis in square brackets; two silent corrections have been made.

MY LORD,[1]

BEFORE I proceed to lay before your Lordship a statement of the manner in which the Convicts are employed and managed in the settlements of New South Wales[2] and Van Dieman's Land,[3] I have thought it expedient to preface such a statement with a few observations upon the transportation and treatment of them during the passage, as it is now conducted; upon the manner in which their disembarkation is effected; and the general circumstances that attend their introduction to the scenes of their future servitude and punishment.

[*from* I. Condition and Treatment of Convicts during the passage to New South Wales.]

THE transportation of convicts, as far as it regards their health, appears to have undergone very considerable improvement since the mortality that occurred in the ships General Hewit, Surrey, and Three Bees,[4] in the year 1814.

The investigation that took place at Sydney, at that period, into the conduct of the masters of those vessels, and the report made to Governor Macquarrie[5] by Mr. Redfern[6] the assistant-surgeon on the colonial establishment, have furnished to His Majesty's government ample and very accurate means of providing against the recurrence of similar calamities.

The recommendations that were made by Mr. Redfern, under the several heads of clothing, diet, air, and medical assistance, appear, in as far as they have been adopted, to have been amply justified, by the diminished mortality in the voyages performed by convict ships from England to New South Wales; and of those that have not yet been adopted, there appears only to be one that is of material importance.

It has been truly observed by this gentleman, that in the voyages that are commenced in the later periods of the European winters, or the commencement of spring, and which terminate with the same seasons in New South Wales and in Van Dieman's Land, or the latitudes in which the latter part of the voyages are most frequently made, the convicts are exposed to great and sudden vicissitudes of climate; the greatest and most prejudicial being found to be that which occurs in the first removal of the convicts from the hulks to the transports in cold seasons, and when dressed in much lighter clothing than that to which they have been previously accustomed. The change of climate, likewise, that occurs after passing the Cape of Good Hope, in the 40th degree of south latitude, from the months of May and June to the months of September and October, requires greater warmth of clothing than that which can be afforded by the present allowance; and by indisposing the convicts to be as much upon deck as before, is the cause of obstructing the ventilation of the prison.

As a remedy for this evil, Mr. Redfern has suggested, that for convicts who are exposed to it, there should be provided woollen, instead of duck trowsers, together with flannel drawers and waistcoats.

Upon this recommendation, I would observe, and to meet the objection that Mr. Redfern has anticipated of the greater danger of contagion, and of the want of cleanliness from the use of woollen, rather than of linen clothing, that cloth or woollen trowsers and shirts are constantly worn by sailors in warm climates, and that with a view to secure the principal objects of additional warmth and cleanliness, two pair of flannel drawers to each convict, to be worn with the duck trowsers, might be advantageously substituted for the additional woollen trowsers that he has proposed.

It seems to be generally admitted, that the allowance of food provided by the present scheme of victualling, is amply sufficient during the voyage; and the only evil, against which it is necessary now to provide, is the abstraction of any portion of the quantity allowed, or the substitution, that is not unfrequently attempted, of the good provisions found by government, for those of inferior quality, with which the transport ships, either through the avarice of their owners, or the fraud of their agents, are sometimes supplied.

An important check upon this abuse has been afforded by that article of the instructions to the surgeon superintendent, by which he is directed to attend the opening of every cask of provisions, and to note it in his journal. It would appear, however, from the evidence of the principal superintendent of convicts, William Hutchinson,[7] that complaints are most frequent from them, respecting the short issues of provisions during the voyage, and that the captains of the transport ships, on approaching the port of destination, are in the habit of making compromises with the convicts, in money, to the amount of the quantity kept back. This appears to have taken place on board the Daphne[8] convict ship, and was considered by the magistrates, to whom the complaint of the convicts was referred, as sufficient ground for dismissing it.

The practice also observed by the captains of convict ships, and permitted by the commissariat officers, of receiving back, from the remains of provisions and stores delivered at Sydney, the allowance of eighths for issuing them, seems to have admitted great opportunity, as well as temptation, for a fraudulent abduction of the government provisions.

This practice has now been checked by a particular instruction from the Navy Board, by which the captains of transport ships are expressly prohibited from making or receiving such deduction; and the allowance of eighths is only made when they pass their accounts to the satisfaction of the Victualling Board in London. As a further check, however, upon any fraudulent change in the issue of provisions that may escape the attention of the surgeon superintendent, it will be found useful to establish a regulation, that one person from each of the messes, into which the convicts are distributed, should be required to attend in rotation at the delivery and weighing of the provisions. In some of the transports this duty has been confined to one and the same individual of the mess throughout the whole voyage; but as it is obvious that the chances of successful corruption or imposition are less when tried with many than with few, the daily change in the delegation of individuals from the mess is much to be preferred to the other mode, and is not found to be attended with any inconvenience.

The complaints, however, of the convicts are not entirely confined to a subtraction of the proper allowance of their provisions. It frequently happens that various articles of store, or of wearing apparel furnished by their friends on leaving England, are put on board the ships for the convicts, and according to the evidence of William Hutchinson, the superintendent, they have not been always punctually delivered; and in some cases they have been damaged, or their contents purloined and appropriated by the sailors.

The communication that necessarily takes place between the convicts and the sailors during the passage, and the disposition that is common to both to dissipate their resources for the sake of some temporary enjoyment, to indulge their passion for gambling, or excite it in others, will render the decision of their complaints very difficult to the magistrates at Sydney.

It is not desirable, generally, that the convicts should arrive in New South Wales with money or the means of procuring it; and it is still less desirable that their possession of it should be known, except to the surgeon superintendent, the captain and mate of the ship. But in order to prevent the feeling of disappointment or exasperation that the loss of their property must occasion, and to diminish the temptations to gamble for it during the voyage, it would be advisable that a list of all packages allowed to be put on board for the convicts should be made out and attested by the captain and mate of each vessel previous to sailing; that they should be kept in a separate and secure place during the passage; and that the captain and mate should be held responsible for their delivery on the arrival of the ship at Sydney. This arrangement would doubtless exclude access to the packages during the voyage, and interfere perhaps with the object of sending them on board; but to this it is a sufficient answer, that the possession of property leads only to thefts, and consequently to augmented punishment; and that the encumbrance of packages in the prison deck, if left in the possession of the convicts themselves, would be a great obstruction to ventilation and cleanliness.

The instructions furnished by the Navy Board to the surgeon superintendent, do not specify the frequent admission of the convicts on deck, as an important means of preserving their health; but as the instructions furnished to the master require him to comply with the applications of the surgeon for that as well as other purposes beneficial to the convicts, it was, doubtless, intended to leave a discretion to be exercised by the surgeons, as well in regulating the frequency of their access to the deck, as to their numbers at one and the same time. The exercise of this discretion depends of course upon the state of the weather and the capacity of the deck, but it likewise depends upon the experience of the surgeon superintendent, and the degree of confidence that this experience may lead him to place in the character of the convicts. It accordingly happens, that those surgeons and masters to whom this particular service is new, will not allow more than one half of the prisoners to remain on deck at one time, and will not take off their irons till an advanced period of the voyage: others, on the contrary, allow as many of them as please to come upon deck, and encourage them to remain there as long as they do not interfere with the operations of the ship, and frequently take off their irons, or a part of them, in a fortnight after leaving England.

The advantages arising from allowing the convicts a free access to the deck, in giving effectual ventilation to the prisons, and in preserving their health, are justly and strongly described by Mr. Redfern in his report to Governor Macquarrie; and these advantages, and the feelings that accompany the enjoyment of them, are so important in preserving discipline as well as health during the voyage, that they ought not to be risked from an unwarrantable distrust of the convicts, or from an apprehension of any combined attempt to obtain possession of the ship. As the release from the incumbrance of irons is always an indulgence to the convicts, so is the return to the use of them a salutary punishment that may supersede the necessity of having recourse to flogging.

The fear of combinations amongst the convicts to take the ship, is proved by experience of later years to be groundless; and it may be safely affirmed, that if the instructions of the Navy Board are carried into due effect by the surgeon superintendent and the master, and if the convicts obtain the full allowance of provisions made to them by government, as well as reasonable access to the deck, they possess neither fidelity to each other, nor courage sufficient to make any simultaneous effort that may not be disconcerted by timely information, and punished before an act of aggression is committed. A short acquaintance with the characters of the convicts, promises of recommendation to the governor on their arrival in New South Wales, and an ordinary degree of skill in the business of preventive police, will at all times afford means of procuring information; and with a view to afford those of more complete protection against any open violence during the day, when the convicts are on deck, it is expedient that the ships that are taken up for this service, should, if possible, be provided with poops,[9] upon which the military guard may at all times be posted. They are thus more completely separated from the convicts in the hours of duty or of exercise; and they are sufficiently elevated above the deck to observe their motions, and if necessary, to control them.

Although, in the transportation of female convicts to New South Wales, the preservation of their health has been more easily and generally accomplished than that of the males, yet no scheme of superintendence has yet been devised by which their intercourse with the crew can be entirely prevented. From the evidence of Mr. Cordeaux, Mr. Gyles, and Mr. Walker,[10] who were passengers on board the convict ship Friendship,[11] prostitution appears to have prevailed in a great degree, and the captain and surgeon at last connived at excesses that they had not the means to resist, or any hope of suppressing. The account given by Mr. Gyles, of the proceedings of the voyage, differs very materially from the testimony of Mr. Cordeaux and Mr. Walker; and the accounts of all are still more pointedly contradicted by the evidence of the superintendent Hutchinson, who states that the female convicts from the ship Friendship declared, on their arrival at Port Jackson,[12] that they were perfectly satisfied with the conduct of the captain, a declaration that is further confirmed by the result of Mr. Secretary Campbell's muster of them, at the conclusion of which it is stated 'that no complaints were made.' The characters likewise given by Mr. Gyles of several of the female convicts, differ as materially from those that were given by the master and surgeon superintendent of the Friendship on their arrival at Port Jackson.

Mr. Gyles has asserted that no precautions were adopted by the captain or surgeon to prevent an improper intercourse between the crew and the convicts; and it certainly appears, by the evidence of Mr. Cordeaux, that the very simple and obvious one of depositing the keys of the prison in a place of security during the night, was not resorted to till after a complaint was made at St. Helena,[13] by the surgeon, to Admiral Plampin.[14] In consequence of this neglect, a very general intercourse took place between the crew and the female convicts; and after it had been once permitted, the captain and the surgeon, though not without a sense of the advantages that they expected to derive from a strict performance of their duty, had lost that authority over their subordinate officers, that might have enabled them to have enforced some restraint upon the crew; their attempts to restore it were ineffectual, and, in making them, they were opposed by the vicious inclinations of the women themselves.

The conduct of the captain has been censured by Mr. Gyles for inhumanity, especially in the infliction of punishment; but it does not appear that in any instance it exceeded the compulsory, but injudicious, use of a wooden collar. The want of cleanliness that has been stated by the same person, in his letter to Mr. Marsden,[15] as the effect of negligence on the part of the captain and surgeon, is imputed by Mr. Cordeaux to the perverse dispositions of the women, and the reluctance of the captain to have recourse to force, by which alone he thinks their dispositions could have been controlled.

The circumstances that took place on board the female convict ship Janus,[16] are detailed in the minutes of evidence that were taken by myself upon the investigation, ordered by Governor Macquarrie, of the complaint of two female convicts that had been assigned to Mr. Bayley.[17] It is to be remarked, that the advanced state of pregnancy in which these women were found to be previous to the departure of the captain and mate of the ship from Port Jackson, occasioned their complaints to be preferred through Mr. Bayley, their master, to the governor, although, at the muster that took place on board the ship, no complaint of any kind is recorded by Mr. Secretary Campbell to have been made to him, nor was any complaint addressed to any other quarter. From the evidence, however, it appears, that all the evils that unrestrained intercourse between the crew of the ship, and a number of licentious women could produce, existed to their full extent in the voyage of the Janus from England, during the stay of the vessel at Rio de Janeiro, and until its arrival at New South Wales. The death of the surgeon superintendent, on the passage from Rio de Janeiro to Port Jackson, has necessarily deprived the inquiry of satisfactory proofs of the attempts made by him to check the profligacy of the officers and crew; but it appears that the attempts of the captain were neither sincere nor effectual. With the knowledge, indeed, that the sailors could not fail to obtain of his participation, as well as the mate's, in the same intercourse in which they had so freely indulged, it was not to be expected that their admonitions, if sincere, could have been effectual. The captain has denied that his intercourse with Mary Long was of an improper or immoral kind; but the testimony of the Rev. Mr. Conolly and Mr. Therry[18] both agree in the frequency and long duration of the visits of this woman to the captain's cabin; and it is also to be observed, that he has not denied the allegation made by her upon oath, of his being the father of the child with which she was pregnant when the inquiry took place.

Of the degree of resistance that may be expected to be made, to all attempts to impose restraint upon the crews of female convict ships, during their passage from England to New South Wales, the journal of Dr. Reed,[19] surgeon superintendent of the ship Morley,[20] may afford some means of forming a judgment. All the influence both in the captain, surgeon and passengers, that could be derived from good example, and all the advantages of a most patient and courageous resistance to the vicious inclinations of the crew, were not sufficient to prevent them from obtaining access to some of the women who had yielded to their persuasions. It is necessary however to observe, that in the fitting of female convict ships for transportation, a greater degree of attention seems to have been paid to the comfort of the prisoners, than is consistent with the prevention of intercourse between them and the sailors. There seems to be no reason for not giving the same degree of strength to the stauncheons that surround the fore and after hatchways, that has been found so effectual in those of male convict ships; and with this precaution, there is less to be apprehended from the destruction or temporary removal of the wooden gratings that cover the hatchway, or the padlocks by which they are fastened. The most assailable points of the prison are the two small fore-hatchways that give light and air to the hospital; and here it is necessary that the iron gratings should be of the strongest description, for the descent from them to the hospital is easy, and the attempts to break through them are, in a great measure, removed, from the observation of the officers of the deck.

The apartment for the free women and children should always be placed between the sailors birth and the prison, and the partition should be made of exactly the same thickness and strength as that which separates the same apartments in the male convict ships.

In taking a review of the circumstances that have attended the transportation of male and female convicts from England and Ireland to New South Wales, and the gradual improvement that has taken place in the system during the last six years, it appears certain that the voyage may be performed with perfect security to the health and persons of the convicts. For attaining these objects nothing more seems necessary than a strict adherence to the instructions issued by the Navy Board to the surgeons superintendent, at the commencement and during the progress of the voyage, and a determination manifested by the proper authorities in New South Wales to listen to and investigate any complaints that may be made known to them on its termination. [pp. 1–5]

[*from* II. Debarkation and Muster of the Convicts, Male and Female.]

THE application for distribution of the female convicts is regulated by different principles.[21] Great difficulty is found in preventing boats from hovering round the ships; but no person is permitted to go on board without a pass from the superintendent. This privilege is granted only to inquire for servants; and the applications having been previously made to the superintendent, the women are sent to their respective places of destination as soon as the muster is completed.

The governor has not been in the habit of inspecting the female convicts on their arrival, but a list of them and the persons to whom they are assigned is constantly sent to him. Each person who receives a female convict signs an indenture in which he obliges himself, under a penalty of 20*l.*[22] to retain her in his service for the space of three years, providing sufficient subsistence, clothing, washing and lodging, and not to part with her either directly or indirectly during the term, without the approbation or authority of a magistrate, or in case of misconduct proved and determined before him. Married female convicts are assigned without such indenture to their husbands, whether free or convict; and, in many cases, both receive tickets of leave,[23] as affording greater facilities of support.

The females likewise who bring property with them, or are recommended by the captains or surgeons superintendent of the ships, receive tickets of leave on their arrival. The consequences of this indulgence are described by the principal superintendent to give encouragement to improper intercourse between the officers of the ships and the women, and to lead to their cohabitation with individuals in Sydney that, not unfrequently, terminates in marriage.

Those who are accompanied by children, are rarely taken by settlers, and are sent to the factory at Paramatta.[24] Indeed of late it would appear by the evidence of the superintendent Hutchinson, that a greater number of female convicts of every description have arrived, than were required by the settlers of New South Wales; and consequently those who were not sent to Van Dieman's Land, were consigned to the factory at Paramatta.

In their passage thither from Sydney, which, according to the evidence of Mr. Oakes,[25] lasts from the morning till the evening, if the wind be fair, and during the night if it be adverse, great irregularities take place; and the women frequently arrive at Paramatta in a state of intoxication, after being plundered of such property as they may have brought from the ships with them, during the time they stop at a public house on the shore of the Paramatta river. They are accompanied by a constable in each boat, who, in case of negligence, would be liable to be broke; but this precaution does not prevent the existence of the irregularities that it is meant to check. [p. 20]

[*from* V. Subsistence and Clothing of the Convicts retained by Government; and Employment of Female Convicts.]

On the arrival of every convict in New South Wales, a suit of clothing is given to him, consisting of a coarse woollen jacket, and waistcoat of yellow or grey cloth, a pair of duck trowsers, a pair of worsted stockings, a pair of shoes, two cotton or linen shirts, a neckhandkerchief, and a woollen cap or hat. A singular exception was made to this issue during my residence in Van Dieman's Land, in consequence of the scarcity of government clothing. The convicts that had been sent out in the Prince Regent transport from Ireland, had been remarkable for the care they had taken of their clothing; and as it consisted of the grey cloth of that country, it was found to be stronger and more durable than any other. Upon the debarkation of these convicts, their spare clothing was taken away and sent to George Town,[26] where it certainly was more urgently required; but the effect that this surrender produced upon their dispositions was very unfavourable, in their reluctance to labour, and their wilful destruction of the clothes they had procured. A similar deprivation of their new slop-clothing[27] took place on the arrival of the Dromedary[28] store ship, and the debarkation of the greatest number of the convicts at Hobart Town.[29]

The issue of clothing to the government convicts ought regularly to be made to them every six months. It consists of a woollen jacket or frock, and trowsers of the colonial manufacture, a pair of shoes, and a linen shirt, made up in the lumber yard at Sydney. The convicts that are exposed to harder labour in the quarries, and the carters and bullock drivers, each receive a pair of shoes every three months. The summer clothing to the convicts in the barracks, consists of a canvas smock frock, one linen or cotton shirt, two pair of trowsers, (one of which ought to be reserved for use on Sundays) one pair of shoes, and one cap. Until the end of the year 1820, these supplies were furnished from the old canvas and sheeting that were found in the commissariat stores, and that had remained there for several years. The convicts out of barrack have had no regular slop-clothing issued to them for two years; but their allowance, differs in no respect from that of the convicts in the barrack.

The chief engineer is of opinion that some loss is occasioned in the issue of clothing to the convicts when made up, and that it would be better to issue it as it is wanted, and according to the size of the wearer, than to adhere to the present practice of a general issue to the convicts of every ship on their arrival, which, when made at one and the same time, is followed by absolute loss, or a disposal of it for money, which the convicts lay out in the purchase of spirits. A regulation of that kind would certainly be useful; but according to the present scale of employment of the government convicts, it would require a much more accurate account of the issues of clothing than is now kept in the convict barrack at Sydney; and it would also occasion a more entire separation of the tradesmen employed in making it up from the other mechanics in the lumber yard, than that which its present limits would allow.

The largest portion of the clothing for the convicts, that has, for the last few years, been sent with them for distribution on arrival, consisted of a coarse yellow cloth; it is not so strong as the grey cloth worn by the convicts, and brought with them from Ireland; but it possesses the advantage of being conspicuous, which the other does not, and of exhibiting more distinctly the marks that may be put upon it. It is observed by the chief engineer, that the issue of coarse woollen stockings to the convicts is an expense that might well be spared; and this observation is confirmed by the general practice of the labouring classes of the colony of New South Wales, who rarely or ever make use of them. The expense also of issuing waistcoats to the convicts destined for New South Wales is unnecessary, as they rarely make use of them, and they only afford the means of procuring spirituous liquors. The difference between the climate of Van Dieman's Land and New South Wales will not admit of the reduction of those articles from the dress of the convicts transported thither. [p. 61]

The weekly rations issued to the convicts employed by government have undergone many variations since the arrival of Governor Macquarrie in New South Wales. On the 21st of January of the year 1810, an order was made for

11½ lbs. of wheat, 7 lbs. of beef, or 4 lbs. of pork, 6 oz. of sugar, or 1 lb. of wheat, or 2 lbs. of maize. In the month of March of that year, an alteration was made in the quantity of wheat to settlers, free persons and prisoners, and 6 lbs. of wheat and 13 lbs. of maize were issued. In the month of January 1814, the same ration was reduced, to 6 lbs, of bread, 1½ lb. of sugar, and 1 lb. of rice. In July of that year it was increased to 7 lbs. of bread, 1½ lb. of sugar, and half a pound of rice; and in the month of September this ration of bread was ordered to be composed of one-third of Indian corn meal. In the month of March 1815 the ration issued to the troops consisted of 13 lbs. of wheat; and to every other class it consisted of 10 lbs. of wheat and 6 lbs, of maize; and in the month of August of the same year, the first of these rations was reduced to 11½ lbs. of wheat, with 6 oz. of sugar; and to the other classes comprising convicts, 8½ lbs, of wheat, 6 lbs. of Indian corn, and 6 oz. of sugar. The same scale of rations, with similar and occasional deductions, continued to be issued until the 16th August 1817, when in consequence of a scarcity of wheat, a general reduction of the rations took place, and 6 lbs. of wheat, 1½ lb. of sugar, and 1 lb. of rice were issued to all classes, but an augmentation was made in the quantity of meat from 7 lbs. to 8 ½ lbs. On the 20th September of the same year, a further reduction of the wheat ration took place from 6 lbs, to 3 lbs.; with an addition of 6 oz. of sugar and 1 lb. of rice. And on the 27th December 1817, the usual full ration of 11½ lbs. of wheat, 7 lbs. of beef or 4 lbs. of salt pork, with 6 oz. of sugar, was resumed. [p. 63]

Yielding to the recommendations made to him by the captains and surgeons of the female convict ships, Governor Macquarie has given tickets of leave to some of the females on their arrival; and influenced also by a wish to economize the public expenditure, he has given the same indulgence to those who were represented to him as having money, by which they have established themselves in the town of Sydney, and at once been placed on a level with the emancipated and free convicts of their own sex. In this state, which cannot be considered as a state of punishment, and which tends to produce a belief that opulence can redeem the consequences of crime, these women form connections with the convicts whom they have formerly known in England, or support themselves by any casual demand for their labour. Those also who have children, and have any means of supporting themselves, are furnished with tickets of leave. The government is thus relieved from the expense of their maintenance, and they are themselves benefitted by being saved from the consequences of consignment to the factory at Paramatta.

The principal superintendent Hutchinson, in the original distribution of the female convicts, is sole judge of the propriety or impropriety of the applications that are made for them. His orders are to refuse them on the application of single men, unless their character should be such as to preclude the suspicion of unworthy and immoral motives. The exercise of this delicate and important duty is thus committed to a person, who is himself not exempt from the charge of immoral habits and connections, and not sufficiently raised above the rank of ordinary applicants to resist improper applications with firmness. His knowledge of the inhabitants of Sydney enables him to form an opinion of the motives that guide their applications for female convicts; but of the condition of those who reside in the country, he is entirely ignorant. Refusals to such applications are, however, but rarely made; and no complaints of that nature were addressed to me. I am likewise bound to state, that after entertaining much suspicion myself of the manner in which this part of the duty of the principal superintendent was performed, and after some inquiry respecting it, I was not able to obtain any satisfactory proof of corrupt motives in the distribution that had been made by him of the female convicts. It is admitted by him, that their cohabitation was the frequent consequence of the indulgence afforded to them on their arrival; and that it was not an offence of which he conceived himself bound to take cognizance. The removal of the female convicts from Sydney to Paramatta has been already mentioned. On their arrival there, they are allowed to remain in a wooden building that is near the factory; and if they have succeeded in bringing their bedding from the ships, they are permitted to deposit it there, or in the room in which the female prisoners are confined for punishment. The first of these apartments is in the upper floor of a house that was built for the reception of pregnant females. It contains another apartment, on the ground floor, that is occupied by the men employed in the factory. It is not surrounded by any wall or paling; and the upper room or garret has only one window, and an easy communication with the room below. No accommodation is afforded for cooking provisions in this building; nor does there exist either inducement to the female convicts to remain in it, or the means of preventing their escape. The greater portion, therefore, betake themselves to the lodgings in the town of Paramatta, where they cohabit with the male convicts in the employ of government, or with any persons who will receive them. Their employment in the factory consists of picking, spinning and carding wool. They are tasked to perform a certain quantity in the day, and when their task is finished, which is generally at one o'clock, they are allowed to return to their lodgings. Their weekly ration consists of four pounds ten ounces of flour, and the same quantity of meat, or two pounds of pork; and the same ration is issued to the females who are confined for punishment. The children who accompany their mothers to Paramatta are maintained by government, and receive one half of the ration last described. As there is a general objection amongst the settlers, to receive into their families female convicts who are accompanied by children, it is their lot to remain longer in Paramatta, and at the factory, than others. The factory itself consists of one long room that is immediately above the gaol, having two windows in front that look into the gaol yard, one in the end of the building, and two windows looking into a yard that is immediately behind. The dimensions of the room are 60 feet by 20; and at one end are store-rooms, where the wool, yarn and cloth are kept. There is one fire-place, at which all the provisions are cooked. The women have no other beds than those they can make from the wool in its dirty state; and they sleep upon it at night, and in the midst of their spinning wheels and work. No attempt has been made to preserve cleanliness in this room, as the boards had shrunk so much, that when they were washed, the water fell through them into the prison rooms below. The walls of the room and the roof bore equal marks of neglect; and the drains in the yard were in the highest degree offensive.

Colloquial intercourse always took place between the female convicts and the male convicts confined in the prison, except during the hours of labour; for in the windows there was nothing more than three wooden bars, and inside shutters. A range of wooden buildings had been erected on one side of the yard below, connected with the gaol and factory by a wall of ten feet. In this range, and in a small building attached to one of the side walls, were placed the looms, where the cloth was wove by male convicts assigned for the purpose. At a little distance from the factory, and beyond this wall, was the superintendent's house and garden, containing four small and inconvenient rooms. Mr. Oakes, the superintendent, had for some time ceased to inhabit them himself, and had converted one of them into a stable; but he had continued for his own use the cultivation of a small garden and a paddock immediately adjoining. The care of the factory, therefore, except during the hours of labour, was committed to a constable, who was still a convict, who had continued in that office for 15 years, and received no larger allowance as a reward for his fidelity than a ration and a half. The security for the performance of his duty, depends upon the risk of detection; the same presumptive check that is supposed to provide for the official integrity of many other establishments in New South Wales, aided by the further probability of disclosures, to which the intoxication of the women would lead, if they were permitted by the constable to go out of the factory, when confined there. Considered as a place of punishment for offences committed by female convicts in New South Wales, the factory at Paramatta acted merely as a temporary restraint from indiscriminate intercourse or unchecked dissipation. The labour of the females, confined for punishment, was not greater than those that were retained there for employment; and their diet was in nowise inferior. The only punishment that it inflicted was that of moral and physical degradation, beyond the low state of existence from which many of them had previously been taken; and reducing those who had been in better situations, nearly to the same level. The women who had become most profligate and hardened by habit, were associated in their daily tasks with those who had very lately arrived, to whom the customs and practices of the colony were yet unknown, and who might have escaped the consequences of such pernicious lessons, if a little care and a small portion of expense had been spared in providing them with a separate apartment during the hours of labour. As a place of employment, the factory at Paramatta was not only very defective, but very prejudicial. The insufficient accommodation that it afforded to those females who might be well disposed, presented an early incitement, if not an excuse, for their resorting to indiscriminate prostitution; and on the evening of their arrival at Paramatta, those who were not deploring their state of abandonment and distress were traversing the streets, in search of the guilty means of future support. The state in which the place itself was kept, and the state of disgusting filth in which I found it, both on an early visit after my arrival, and on one preceding my departure; the disordered, unruly and licentious appearance of the women; manifested the little degree of control in which the female convicts were kept, and the little attention that was paid to any thing beyond the mere performance of a certain portion of labour. Mr. Oakes, the superintendent, has justified himself by the abandoned habits of the women, and the want of means to make their punishment effectual. It must be acknowledged, that in such a building as the factory, his task was a hopeless one: it might have been made more effectual by his more constant and contiguous residence, but he was charged with the duties of chief constable in the town of Paramatta, and carried on the business of a baker. No instance was represented to me of his improper connivance in the misconduct of the women; and the magistrates of Paramatta, to one of whom he had given serious cause of offence, bore testimony to the activity and perseverance that he displayed in the performance of his duty, as superintendent of the factory.

The evil consequences arising to the colony from the indiscriminate association, and the unrestrained prostitution of so many licentious women, have been seriously felt by the inhabitants at large. With the temptations that their residence in Paramatta afforded, and the slight degree of punishment that confinement in the factory inflicted, no female convict, when assigned to a respectable family, could be taught the value of such a situation, or could be made to feel the necessity of obedience. [pp. 68–70]

[*from* VI. Nature of the Labour of Convicts in the Service of Settlers.]

THE nature of the labour performed by convicts, assigned to the settlers in New South Wales, has undergone some alteration since the earlier years of its establishment.

In the month of January 1804, an order was issued by Governor King,[30] requiring all persons who applied for convicts to sign an indenture, by which they covenanted to clothe and maintain them according to the same rate of allowance that was afforded by government to the convicts in its employ, for the space of 12 calendar months, under penalty of paying 1 *s.* for every day of the term that was unexpired, unless they could give a satisfactory reason for their discharge. In return for this allowance, the convicts were compelled to perform a certain portion of labour for their masters, that had been regulated and set forth in an order issued by Governor Hunter[31] in the years 1798 and 1799; and it was repeated in the subsequent order of Governor King. The work required from a convict was, to labour for ten hours, throughout, the year, for five days in the week, and six hours on Saturdays. As it was found that they were frequently enabled to perform their allotted task in a less time, they were allowed to apply such portion, as they could save from their government hours, to their own benefit, reservation being made to the master of a preferential right to the services of his convict servant, if he could afford or thought fit to employ and pay for them. The rate of payment for this extra, labour, as well as for the labour of freemen, was fixed by Governor King at the same time, and continued at the same rate until the month of December, 1816.

The quantity of labour that a settler was entitled to exact from the convict servant, in the regulated hours, is set forth in a schedule annexed to the order of Governor King, and is acted upon at the present moment; subject to such modifications as the magistrates may think fit to make, in consequence of stress of weather, state of the land, or the strength of the convict labourer.

It is stated by Mr. Oxley, that in the earliest periods the labour of the whole day was exacted from the convicts; and this rule was not relaxed until a scarcity of provisions having occurred, their labour ceased at three o'clock on each day, to enable them to work at gardens in the town of Sydney. Since that period, this dispensation grew into a general custom; and wages were assigned to the convicts for such labour as they might perform for their master after three o'clock on each day. The mischievous consequences that were found to arise, from the inability of the poorer classes of settlers to pay for the extra labour of their convicts, or even to pay the wages of their regulated labour, appear to have been severely felt in the colony, in the year 1814, by the unauthorized dispersion of the convicts in search of employment in distant districts, and in the means of secreting stolen property that was afforded to them, by the permission of their masters, to feed pigs and poultry on their farms in lieu of wages.

For the prevention of these evils, the settlers who did not require the entire services of the men assigned to them, or who could not afford to pay for them, were required to return them forthwith to the principal superintendent of Sydney, or to the magistrates of the different districts. The amount of the wages that a settler was compellable, under this order, to pay to his convict labourer, varied with the fluctuating value of the paper money, in which all payments were made, until the month of December 1816. At that period, the amount of the annual wages, payable to every male convict employed by a settler, was fixed at 10*l.* sterling; and if the regular allowance of clothing was found by the master, he was entitled to deduct from this amount the sum of 3*l*.

To every female convict, the annual amount of wages was fixed at 7*l*. and the deduction for clothing was fixed at 1*l*. 10*s*. This adjustment of prices was referred by Governor Macquarrie to the magistrates of the colony, and agreed upon by them at the same period; in which was ordered, that all payments in colonial currency should cease, and thenceforth be calculated in sterling.

Such are the conditions upon which the convicts in New South Wales are at present assigned to settlers; and although they have ceased for some time to be secured by any written stipulation, yet they are considered to be established by custom, and to form a guide for the decisions of the magistrates in all disputes that occur between the settlers and their convict servants.

It was never permitted, at any period in the colony, to a master to inflict corporal punishment upon his convict labourer; and reference to a magistrate was always and is now enjoined for the purpose of substantiating the mutual complaints that arise between them. These complaints are found, in most cases, to proceed from the reluctance or inability of the convict to perform his task; from his attempts to plunder his master's property, or that of the convicts about him; or from the manner in which his wages are paid by his master. A very large proportion of the convicts assigned to the settlers, having, in the later periods of the colony, consisted of the lowest classes of labourers from the manufacturing districts of Great Britain, or from the populous towns, much difficulty has been experienced in training them to agricultural labour on their arrival, and this difficulty has increased as the system of agriculture in the colony has improved. Hence have arisen the perpetual changes of the convict labourers from the service of one settler to another, and the expense to the crown in maintaining those that are returned as useless and unprofitable.

This evil has been necessarily accompanied by a violation of Governor King's order, that every settler should retain a convict assigned to him for the space of one twelvemonth; and the inconvenience was afterwards so strongly felt, that Governor Macquarrie, on the 30th September 1815, directed that no settler or other person should send back to the government gangs any servants assigned to them, unless for the commission of some fault or crime, or unless they should be found unfit for manual labour from sickness or other infirmity. It is stated by Mr. Rouse, the superintendent of convicts at Paramatta, that this order was violated in one month after its promulgation, and that it was found impracticable to adhere to it.

The great inconvenience and interruption that complaints against these servants occasion to the settlers, and the risk to which they are exposed in leaving their property to seek redress, from the magistrates, is severely felt by all the inhabitants of the colony; some of them, especially those who had themselves been convicts, feel a degree of commendable reluctance in making a complaint against a convict labourer for mere incapacity, and would rather submit to the unrequited expense of his maintenance than be the cause of the infliction of unmerited punishment. This feeling is in some degree attributable to a sympathy with that condition which was once their own, and is not corrected until they acquire property, and a disposition to improve and augment it. Others, influenced by less humane considerations, or by a dislike of the trouble of complaining, allow the convict to seek employment where he can find it, or leave him in the towns, where he is apprehended. He is in these cases sent to gaol; where he receives an allowance of one pound of bread per day, until he is taken by another settler; and if he should be sent to Sydney or Paramatta, he is placed in one of the government gangs. By this means his incapacity for agricultural labour is not removed, and his dispositions and habits of indolence are in most cases confirmed.

The effect of the labour required from the convicts, assigned to the settlers, varies with their character and condition. In the service of the more opulent, who can afford to pay for a greater quantity of labour than is required by the government orders, the convict will generally perform, and will earn more than his annual wages after an experience of one year. He is thus confined during the day to his master's farm, and prevented from rambling in pursuit of plunder; and the fatigue of the day's labour disposes him to tranquillity and to rest at night. He finds that, by increased exertion, he possesses the means of improving both his present and future condition; and he every day becomes more skilful in that species of labour, by which he may hereafter seek to establish himself in the possession of property, and make it available for his support.

The employment of convicts in the service of the lower classes of settlers, who cannot afford to pay them any thing beyond their rations, or to stimulate or reward their industry by paying for their extra labour, is, on the contrary, very pernicious. The convict is thus allowed to leave his home in pursuit of labour that he cannot find there, and he is out of the reach even of the imperfect control of his necessitous master. Governor Macquarrie has endeavoured to restrain this practice by several orders; and in some of the districts, chiefly occupied by the lower class of settlers, the magistrates have lately found it necessary to enforce their execution, both by exacting the fine imposed by those orders, and by removing the convict labourers from the control of those settlers who could not furnish them with employment. It may also be generally observed, that whenever the demand for the produce of agricultural labour in New South Wales is diminished, either to the richer or the poorer classes of settlers, the effect will be the same; neither of them will then continue to employ or maintain convicts, much less to stimulate their industry in the production of a commodity that is unsaleable: whereas, under the operation and encouragement of a steady market, the settler can both afford to give his convict servants such a liberal allowance of food as will make them satisfied with their condition and willing to remain in it, and can give that stimulus to their exertions that supersedes the necessity of coercion, and leaves the convict neither time nor strength to undertake enterprizes of a criminal nature.

It is the want of this stimulus to the labour of the convict, or the fear of producing greater mischief by applying it, that was noticed as the great defect in the system of government labour in the towns; and it is precisely in these points that the labour of convicts assigned to respectable and opulent settlers in the country, has appeared to me to be so much to be preferred, and so well calculated to answer the colonial as well as the penal objects of the establishment of New South Wales. It has unfortunately happened, that the attention of the colonial government has hitherto been fixed upon the production of two objects, for which its own consumption formed at once both the demand and the limit; and the perpetual variations that have occurred in that demand, together with certain other difficulties in supplying it, have rather had the effect of deterring than of stimulating the efforts of respectable settlers in the cultivation of grain, and the largest supplies have been furnished by the lower classes.

The payment of wages for the regulated labour of the convicts, or for their earnings by extra labour, is generally made to them in articles of consumption, such as tea, sugar, and tobacco; and on the larger estates an account is kept by the owner or his overseer of the quantities of work performed, and of articles issued in payment.

By the last order of Governor Macquarrie, and by the decisions of the magistrates, the convicts are considered to be entitled to demand their wages in money; but the difficulty that they find in purchasing the different articles that they require, and the evil consequences of the unrestrained purchase of spirits, have given rise to the custom of paying the largest proportion of wages in New South Wales in articles of consumption, such as tea, sugar, and tobacco, and which are better known under the general designation of 'property.' The prices of these articles vary from 40 to 70 per cent, above the wholesale ready money prices, and from 25 to 35 per cent. above the retail prices of Sydney; these variations depending upon local circumstances, and being liable, when disputed, to the final adjustment of the magistrates. [pp. 74–7]

[*from* VI.[32] Control of Convicts in the Service of Settlers.]

Instances very frequently occur of the marriage of convicts with emancipated convict women, and with young women who are born in the colony, to which the latter are as much prompted by their early dispositions to marriage, as by the associations into which they are led, from the admission of the convict labourers to the houses and tables of the lower classes of emancipated convict settlers, to whom they are assigned. The marriage of the native born youths with female convicts are very rare; a circumstance that is attributable to the general disinclination to early marriage that is observable amongst them, and partly to the abandoned and dissolute habits of the female convicts, but chiefly to a sense of pride in the native-born youths, approaching to contempt for the vices and depravity of the convicts, even when manifested in the persons of their own parents. [...]

As no information is transmitted in the hulk lists, of the single or married state of the convicts, and when there are so many motives in New South Wales for concealing it, it is very difficult, almost impossible, to ascertain it.

Two affecting consequences of a second marriage, contracted in New South Wales during the life-time of a first and absent husband, are mentioned by Mr. Marsden in his evidence; and he states such marriages to have been of frequent occurrence. These consequences maybe greatly obviated, by requiring the gaolers of the different prisons in England to communicate the information that they may receive respecting the single or married condition of the convicts sent to the hulks; and by adding these particulars, corrected by subsequent inquiry there, to the communications transmitted in the hulk lists. A much better chance will then exist of obtaining a true statement, when the advantages attending the marriage state in New South Wales are unknown or unperceived, than when they form, as they certainly do in that colony, a very strong temptation to imposture.[33]

This disposition is further prompted by an idea that was represented to me to have prevailed amongst the convicts, that capital conviction followed by sentence of death, afterwards commuted to transportation for life, operated as a dissolution of the marriage contract; and it may therefore be an additional reason for disappointing, by early inquiry, any undue expectations to which such an idea must give rise.

The power of assigning female convicts from the factory to individuals, has been intrusted to the acting magistrates at Paramatta, Mr. Marsden and Mr. Hannibal M‹Arthur.[34] The conduct of these females in service, is the subject of frequent complaint to the magistrates, and in that case they are returned to the factory.

The connections that they form in service, and in the families of the settlers, end either in marriage or in their return to Paramatta, where the offspring of their illicit intercourse is maintained at the expense of the crown, in return for their own labour. As long as the great disproportion continues to exist between the male and female population in New South Wales, the temptations to illicit intercourse in both, and all the crimes that are committed for the purpose of supporting it, must be expected to prevail. Female convict servants will continue to be seduced from the houses of their masters, and will find asylums in the houses of single men, under the pretence of service; and the still greater evil will continue, of the seduction of the native-born young women by the male convicts, and their marriage with them. It is not therefore without serious apprehension, that the most intelligent persons in the colony have contemplated any reduction in the number of female convicts to be transported thither in future; and have been led to consider, that any additional facilities given by government to the return of those whose terms of service have expired, independent of such as they may acquire by their own good conduct in the colony, would occasion an additional expense to government, and operate as an encouragement to profitable prostitution: particular exceptions no doubt will occur, where it may be advisable to afford these facilities to married women, who have left families in England; but to these, even in the present state of the colony, there exist such ample opportunities, by good conduct in service, of realizing the means of return, that if their absence from their native country, and their punishment, be prolonged, it may without injustice be attributed to themselves. [pp. 105–6]

[*from* VII. Nature and extent of Remissions of Punishment, and their effects upon the Convicts.]

The system of granting tickets of leave to convicts on their arrival, who are able to support themselves by their labour, or by the means that they have brought with them, operates as an encouragement to industry; but, at the same time, it too quickly and too abruptly elevates them from a condition of punishment to a condition of comparative enjoyment; there are many instances at Sydney of the successful exertion of these people as retail traders; but their industry feeds their vanity as well as their vices, and they speedily lose that sense of humility and contrition which is essential to a state of punishment and reform.

Another evil arising from it is, the state of apparent equality in which it places them with that part of the population that came free to the colony; and with those who, having been sent as convicts at a period when similar indulgences were not so freely granted, feel surprise and some degree of mortification, when they see them bestowed upon persons who, in their opinion, have done nothing to deserve them. [p. 125]

By the last muster taken by the magistrates of New South Wales, in the month of October 1820, and by the muster taken in Van Dieman's Land, there were 3,617 male and female convicts whose terms of sentence had expired; 182 whose sentences had been absolutely, and 1,170 whose sentences had been conditionally, remitted; making a total number of 1,352 remitted convicts, out of a population that amounted to 29,407 souls.

As I felt it to be a matter of importance to ascertain the quantity of land held by this description of persons in New South Wales; and as the form in which Governor Macquarrie determined that the muster of 1820 should be taken by the magistrates, did not afford the means of ascertaining this point, I requested the magistrates, in a circular letter that I addressed to them previous to the muster, to take an account of the quantity of land held by persons in each district, whose sentences had either expired or had been remitted. These returns were transmitted to me; and I find that out of 389,288 acres of land, granted and held in New South Wales, 22,238 acres were either granted to or held by the class of remitted convicts; and 48,906 by convicts whose sentences have expired.

They constitute the middle and lower order of settlers in the colony, and having in general begun with very limited means, they have been obliged to depend solely upon the return of the produce of their land. It is through their means, therefore, that the greatest quantity of grain has been produced for the consumption of the colony; and it is also through their want of means, and their want of capital and skill, that the productive powers of the soil, that is not generally a fertile one, have been exhausted by repeated cropping. Many of the original grantees are now either reduced to a state of dependence upon their creditors, or are seeking for opportunities of redeeming themselves, by removal to some new and more productive tracts. There are, however, exceptions to these cases, and they consist of the emancipated convicts, who, during servitude, were enabled to accumulate property, and acquired a knowledge of agricultural occupations, and who obtained grants of some portion of the rich lands in the valley and plain, that are fertilized by the inundations of the rivers Nepean and Hawkesbury. [p. 140] from Edward Gibbon Wakefield, *Facts Relating to the Punishment of Death in the Metropolis* (London: James Ridgway, 1831), pp. 16–28, 82–101.

Wakefield (1796–1862) was born into a London Quaker family and partly raised by his grandmother, Priscilla Wakefield (1751–1832), writer of science books for children and a book on the condition of women. Edward was rebellious and after being expelled from several schools he was shipped off to Italy at seventeen to be secretary to the British envoy at Turin. Back in London, he persuaded a seventeen-year-old heiress to elope with him. He returned to diplomatic service in Italy for a while, but after return to England his wife died bearing their second child. Now ambitious to become an MP, and needing money to do so, Wakefield abducted a fifteen-year-old heiress and persuaded her to marry him, but he was arrested and jailed in Newgate, and the marriage was annulled.

Newgate experience transformed Wakefield into a social campaigner, culminating in publication of his *Facts Relating to the Punishment of Death*, one of the landmarks of prison and law reform advocacy. Promoting emigration as part of the solution to crime, Wakefield published a fictional account of a settler's experience in Australia and formed the National Colonisation Society, to replace convict transportation with a systematic government-sponsored emigration program. Wakefield broadened his platform for national social reform to include increasing wages and ensuring cheap food. Disappointed in his projects for settlements in Australia and New Zealand, he joined Lord Durham, governor-general of the Canadian colonies, and may have helped Durham write his reform-oriented *Report* on government of Canada. Wakefield returned three times to Canada, where he promoted land schemes and a canal, was elected to the assembly of Lower Canada (present-day Québec), and acted as unofficial advisor to successive governors. He then turned his attention again to New Zealand, and would eventually die there.

In the Introduction to *Facts*, Wakefield stated his purpose as being 'to lay before the public some information illustrative of the effects of Capital Punishment, as administered in London and Middlesex' (p. v), drawn from various reports to Parliament and from his own observation while incarcerated in Newgate from 1827 to 1830. The book is desultory in form, in fact a collection of essays on various topics, such as crime prevention policy, juvenile crime, receivers of stolen goods, defects in the system of judge and jury, transportation, and of course various aspects of the death penalty. The excerpts included here deal with juvenile crime, at this time a national obsession, and with the circumstances and psychology of those condemned to death.

NURSERIES OF CRIME.

NEWGATE itself, as I shall have occasion to show hereafter, is the greatest *Nursery* of capital crime. London abounds with smaller nurseries of petty offences by persons of every age, from infancy to manhood. I had the opportunity of strictly examining more than a hundred thieves, between eight and fourteen years, as to the immediate cause of their becoming thieves; and in nineteen cases out of twenty it appeared, that the boy had not committed his first crime spontaneously, but had been persuaded to commence the career of thieving by persons whose business it is to practise this kind of seduction.

The most numerous class of such seducers consists of experienced thieves, both men and boys, who look out for boys not criminal, to whom they represent the life of a thief as abounding in pleasure. The object of these representations is to obtain instruments, with which experienced thieves may commit robberies with less danger to themselves – participators, whose ignorance of the trade subjects them to be put forward into the most dangerous situations, and to be cheated in the division of the spoil. But words are not the only means of seduction employed in such cases: food is given to the hungry, and all kinds of stimulating enjoyments are presented to others, who do not want the means of subsistence. I state what I know to be a fact, in saying, that a practised thief often spends as much as £10[1] in the course of a few days for the purpose of corrupting a youth, by taking him to playhouses and other shows, and allowing him to eat and drink extravagantly at pastry-cooks, fruit-shops, and public-houses. The inevitable consequence of such indulgences is the victim's discontent with his previous mode of life; and when this feeling predominates, he is considered ripe for receiving without alarm the suggestions of his seducer. Very often a still more effectual means of seduction is applied, viz.[2] the precocious excitement and gratification of the sexual passion, by the aid of women in league with the thieves, and to whom is commonly entrusted the task of suggesting to the intoxicated youth, that robbery is the only means, and a safe means, of continuing to enjoy a life of riotous debauchery. This method of seduction succeeds, I believe, *invariably*. For the information of those who may think the statement overcharged, I add, that a large proportion of the boys above twelve years of age, and some even younger, committed to Newgate, have been connected with women; a fact of which there is constant proof, since these boys are every day visited by their mistresses, under the name of 'sisters;' and the greater part of their conversation in the prison, which is sometimes, and might be always, overheard, turns upon their amours. In very many cases women are wholly maintained by young thieves, whom they will dress in a frill and a pinafore to appear at the bar of the Old Bailey. But such boys as these, however young, are of the class of seducers, being already practised thieves. Where women are employed as seducers, they are but the instruments of practised thieves – of those whom the law designates as 'notorious thieves,' and with whom, notwithstanding, the Police seldom interfere, unless they be taken in the act of robbery. From this statement it will be seen, that one of the most effectual means of *preventing* robberies would be an active, watchful, and constant interference with the measures pursued by thieves for increasing the number of their own body.

Another class of seducers consists of both men and women, but principally of old women, the keepers of fruit-stalls and small cake-shops, which stalls and shops they keep but as a cloak to their real trade, – that of persuading children to become thieves, and receiving goods stolen by children. The methods of seduction pursued by these people are for the most part similar to those adopted by the class mentioned above; but they are distinguished from the thieves by some peculiarities. Residing always in the same spot, and apparently engaged in an honest calling, they have superior opportunities of practising on children, who, until known to them, were perfectly well disposed. Several instances came to my knowledge of boys, the sons of decent trades-people,[3] carefully educated, apprenticed to some trade, and with every prospect of leading an industrious and honest life, who were seduced by persons of the class in question. The course of seduction is about as follows.

The child buys fruit and cakes at the stall or shop, of which the keeper takes pains to form a familiar acquaintance with him, by conversation, artful it must be called in this case, but such as is used by all good teachers in order to gain a pupil's confidence. He passes the shop one day without money, and is invited to help himself upon trust. If he yield to the first temptation, it is all over with him. Considering his previous acquaintance with the tempter, it is almost a matter of course that he yields. Once in debt, he continues to indulge himself without restraint, and is soon involved far beyond his means of repayment. Where is the Police to save him? No act of robbery has been committed, and the Police therefore is absent. Probably his parents or master have impressed on him that it is wrong to run in debt. He is already criminal in his own eyes. Instead of confessing his difficulty to his friends, he thinks of them with fear. All his sensations are watched by the wretch, who now begins to talk slightingly of harsh parents and task-masters, and insinuates her own superior affection. By degrees, more or less slow according to the degree of her art and the excitability of the boy's temperament, she gets a complete mastery of his mind. At length she guides him to the first step in crime, by complaining of want of money, perhaps threatening to apply to his parents, and suggesting that he may easily repay her by taking some trifling article from his master's shop. The first robbery committed, the chances are a thousand to one that the thief will sooner or later be transported[4] or hanged. He goes on robbing his master or perhaps his parents: the woman disposes of the stolen property, giving him only a moderate share of the money obtained: she introduces him to other boys, who are following the same career: he soon learns to prefer idleness and luxuries to labour and plain food; and, after a while, becoming an expert thief, deserts his original seducer, with whom he is no longer willing to share the fruits of his plunder, connects himself with a gang, probably takes a mistress, and is a confirmed robber on the high road to Botany Bay or the gallows.

This is a history, not a fable. Let the present or the late schoolmaster of New-gate be examined, and he will confirm every word of it; adding, that no quarter of London is without seducers of this class, who follow their horrid trade, (for it is a regular trade,) taking but little precaution to escape the notice of the Police, and *quite without serious interruption*. I would rest the accuracy of my statement on such an experiment as this: Let twenty boys, selected by the Newgate School-master, be from time to time discharged from prison, and every one of them shall straight proceed to one of these pest-houses, shall leave it with money in his pocket, and, if watched, shall be seen to pursue the sort of career which I have described. The selection should be made so that every quarter of the metropolis might be tried, from Whitechapel to Hyde Park Corner, and from Pentonville to Kennington.[5] If one of the boys, being properly selected and so discharged, did not prove the existence, and the undisturbed existence, too, of one of these nurseries or forcing-houses[6] of crime, my statement should be considered an exaggeration. I know the fact to be, that the greater number of the smallest boys discharged from Newgate for want of prosecution or evidence, or after undergo-ing a sentence of whipping, do instantly proceed to places of this description, as to their home; and at one time I knew the names and addresses of more than twenty persons who lived by this villainous trade.

Where is the Police? I have asked myself the question a thousand times. Not the actual Police Officers but the Law of Police[7] is to blame. To say that a law might not be framed, which, if duly executed, would root out these pests of soci-ety, appears nonsensical, even though we admit that it is better ten guilty should escape than one innocent person be punished. In this case there need be no very severe punishment. *Disturbance* is the point to aim at. Is it better that scores of innocent children should be every year seduced into the crime, than that occasionally an innocent old woman should be put to inconvenience? Besides, the offences of *prompting to robbery* and *harbouring of thieves* might be defined pretty clearly, and the question of guilt left to the judge and jury. Satisfactory evi-dence of the offence would be more easily procured in those cases of multiplied crime than in many capital cases where the crime is single. But such a law would be of little avail, without measures for giving to those charged with its execution the strongest motive for a diligent performance of their duty. At present, the Police of prevention, if we have one at all, is without any such motive.

Another class of nurseries of crime, not indeed to be found in every quarter of London, but confined to certain districts, such as St. Giles's,[8] the low parts of Westminster, and both sides of Whitechapel, are lodging-houses, kept generally by receivers of stolen goods, and resorted to by none but thieves or those who are on the point of becoming thieves. Houses of this description often contain fifty beds. Into some of these, boys only are admitted; the purpose of such exclusiveness being, on the part of the boys, to preserve their independence, that is, to escape the controul of persons stronger than themselves, – (they are equal and often superior to grown thieves in skill, presence of mind, and knowledge of their business,) – and on the part of the lodging-house keepers, to prevent the men from robbing the boys, so that they, the lodging-house keepers, may reap as much as possible of the boys plunder. Women, however, are not excluded. It would be more correct to say that girls of all ages above ten (for it is seldom that the female companion of thieves lives to be a woman,) are admitted, not on their own account as independent lodgers, but as the acknowledged mistresses of the boys who introduce them. The scenes of profligacy that occur in these dens are indescribable, and would be incredible if described. Passing them over with no other remark, it must be stated, that one of these dens becomes the *new home* of a boy who is on the point of turning thief. Here, if he have any remains of honesty or wholesome fear, all impressions of that kind are quickly and for ever effaced. Here, too, receivers of stolen goods are admitted, who upbraid the boys if they have been unsuccessful, and show them handfuls of gold, as an inducement to greater daring the next day. At one time, early in 1830, there were half-a-dozen boys in the school-yard of Newgate, who had lodged together in one of these houses, and during their confinement a man, who had not been suspected before, was convicted of receiving stolen goods. This man happened to be placed in the yard next to that of the school; and I heard many conversations between him and the boys, and afterwards, when he had left the prison, frequently questioned the boys about him. Altogether I learned, that for several years past he had been in the constant habit of visiting a coffee-shop attached to a boy-thieves' lodging-house near Houndsditch,[9] always carrying with him a quantity of gold, which he used to show to the boys, not merely urging them to earn some of it, by bringing to him stolen goods at a more secret place, but suggesting to them all sorts of robberies, the plan of which it was part of his business to concoct, whilst apparently occupied with some honest calling. He was, as I understood, not unlikely to be pardoned, in consequence of the interference on his behalf of a nobleman with whom his brother lived as servant. My attention was first directed to him by seeing him give money to the boys; and I soon found that these presents were bribes for their silence. He passed for a religious man with the Keeper and Chaplain, always attended chapel with an air of great devotion, and generally snatched up a Bible when any officer of the prison was likely to observe him. His sentence was, I think, seven years' transportation; so that, as transports of seven years are generally kept in the hulks for not more than three or four years, he will probably be turned loose and resume his business some time in 1834. [pp. 16–28]

THE CELLS OF NEWGATE AND CONVICTS UNDER SENTENCE OF DEATH.

THE last act for the regulation of prisons[10] was framed, I have been told, for the purpose of introducing a system of strict classification of offenders in Newgate, as well as in other prisons. If so, the legislature must have been extremely ignorant concerning the true character of the jail of Newgate, which is not a house of correction, or penitentiary, but merely a prison of detention, – a sort of metropolitan watchhouse, for the secure custody of persons about to be tried or executed. The exceptions to the general rule are few and unfrequent, consisting of persons sentenced, or ordered to be imprisoned, by the High Court of Admiralty, the Commissioners of Bankrupt, the Court of King's Bench, and the two Houses of Parliament.[11] The great mass of prisoners in Newgate, therefore, are persons awaiting trial, and presumed by the law to be innocent. To classify them strictly, – for instance, to separate those charged with murder from those charged with petty larceny, – would be to establish a murderers' ward, to increase the prejudice against the persons confined in it, and to act in direct opposition to the legal presumption of innocence. The Court of Aldermen, under whose superintendence Newgate is placed, make no such distinctions; and, indeed, were they inclined to make them, in obedience to repeated and urgent recommendations to that effect, from the late Secretary of State for the Home Department,[12] the extent and form of the prison would still interfere with the plan, or rather render it impracticable. Some classification, however, does take place. The women are entirely separated from the men; boys under fourteen years of age, and not known as old offenders, are kept by themselves in what is called the School; prisoners under sentence of transportation (who, if the Secretary of State did his duty, would be removed instantly after sentence, but who often remain for weeks, crowding the prison and greatly increasing the difficulties of its administration,) are also kept by themselves; and lastly, convicts under sentence of death are confined in the press-yard[13] and cells, where they are cut off from communication with every other part of the prison.

The greatest number of persons confined in the cells of Newgate during any part of the three years in question was fifty-nine; but the average may be stated at about twenty. The average period of detention in the cells – that is, between sentence at the Old Bailey and the decision of the King in Council[14] – is about six weeks.

The cells consist of a number of chambers, placed in three rows one above the other, in a stone building which fronts one side of the press-yard, at the northeast corner of the prison, adjoining the residence of the Ordinary or Chaplain, which is the first house on the south side of Newgate Street, as you go towards Cheapside. Each cell is eight feet long by six wide, and generally contains three, sometimes four, prisoners. The only furniture of the cells consists of a rope mat and a common stable rug[15] for each prisoner, with an iron candlestick for the use of the party. The walls, floors, and roofs of the cells are of stone. The only communication of the cells with the outward air is by a hole through the front wall, which is three feet thick; and this hole is all but stopped by two frames of close iron bars, crossed. The time during which the prisoners are strictly confined to their cells, is from dusk till daylight during winter, and from dusk till eight o'clock next day in summer. In winter, and in the neighbourhood of St. Paul's, dusk begins at three o'clock in the afternoon, and daylight at nine in the morning, leaving to convicts under sentence of death six hours of the twenty-four for washing, eating, exercise, intercourse with their friends, the chapel service, which they attend every day, and, lastly, exertions to propitiate the King in Council, on whose opinion of their cases depends the question of life or death. At the southern extremity of the cells are two large rooms for the use of the prisoners during the day. The continuous outer wall of the cells and of these rooms, being about twenty yards long, forms one side of the press-yard; the other side is a blank stone wall, of the same height, the distance between them being but a few yards; and the two ends of this narrow gloomy place are formed by blank stone walls, armed, like the others, with spikes and *chevaux de frize*.[16] The mode of entrance to the cells is by a narrow dark staircase, and by similar passages running at the back of each row of cells, into which the strong door of each cell opens. The only entrance to the press-yard is through narrow and devious passages, defended by several doors of great strength, and during the day by watchful turnkeys, and, finally, by a door way in the southern wall of the press-yard, where a gate of iron bars confines the prisoners, whilst it permits them to communicate with their friends across a short passage terminated by another gate of bars; a turnkey being placed between those two gates to see and hear all that passes. The wall, which forms the northern extremity of the press-yard, abuts upon Newgate Street, and, whatever its thickness, that space alone divides the convict under sentence of death from the busy or thoughtless crowd without, whose voices and even steps he may sometimes hear.

The only capital convicts not removed to the cells instantly after trial, are murderers, women, and very young boys.

During the few hours that remain to the murderer after sentence, he is confined in a solitary cell, set apart for that purpose. If visited at all, it is only by a clergyman, and that by stealth, as it were, since it is understood that the offices of religion are denied to the murderer. In the same unostentatious way he is taken to the scaffold, and is put to death without any religious ceremonies or other formal observances, – a mode of treatment widely different, it will be seen, from that pursued towards most other persons under sentence of death.

Women under sentence of death, if for murder, are confined in solitary cells during the few hours that they have to live, and are executed, like the men, without ceremony, – if for any crime less than murder, they remain on the women's side of the prison, and do not undergo any extraordinary confinement or restriction, except being carefully watched, to prevent suicide.

Boys under fourteen years of age, who are sentenced to death, generally remain in the school, and are treated like all other prisoners of their own age. These form an exception to the ordinary practice as to convicts under sentence of death. They and the officers of the prison know, that they will not be executed; and the sentence passed on them, being a mere formal lie, they are not placed, as one may say, betwixt life and death, and do not require any unusual precautions for their safe custody.

The only object of the more strict mode of confinement pursued with the mass of convicts under sentence of death, is to defeat attempts at escape and suicide. Such attempts are always made, or, at least, contemplated, by a portion of the convicts sentenced to death at each Old Bailey Sessions. Attempts at escape, generally by hardened offenders who are convicted of some grave offence; and attempts at suicide, by persons of a better station, who have been convicted of such crimes as arson or forgery, and on whom the expected disgrace of a public execution produces, according to the nature of their minds, either a phrensy of fear – when they may be considered insane, – or a deliberate resolve to choose what they consider the lesser evil. Attempts at escape are made or contemplated at all times indifferently, from the moment after sentence up to the very morning of execution; but attempts at suicide are seldom made until after an unfavourable decision by the Council, when, in some cases, a long period of agonizing suspense has destroyed the convict's mind; or, in others, the near approach of death by the executioner utterly deprives him of hope.

One case of an attempt either at suicide or escape, which of the two was never precisely ascertained, I ought to mention, as illustrative of the effects of the punishment of death; – John Williams,[17] an active young fellow, twenty-three years old, was convicted of 'stealing in a dwelling-house,' and his sentence not being reversed, was, on the 13th Dec. 1827, ordered to be executed on the 19th. On the morning of execution, he managed to elude the watchfulness of the turnkeys, and to climb up the pipe of a cistern in the press-yard, as some supposed with the intention of drowning himself in the cistern, but more probably with the wild hope of escaping. Be this as it may, he fell into the pavement of the yard, and seriously injured his legs. Though every one knew that he would be hanged presently, he was attended by a surgeon, who dressed his wounds with the same care as if surgical skill could have preserved the use of those limbs for years. He was carried from the press-yard to the scaffold, and in the struggle of death, blood flowed from his wounds, which became visible to the crowd. This shocking scene was known and commented upon by a great part of the population of London. What were its effects on the minds of those who make our laws, I cannot guess; but I know that it produced on two classes of people in London feelings highly prejudicial to the object of all punishment – the repression of crime. Respectable shopkeepers in the neighbourhood of the scene of execution were heard to say, that worse than a murder had been committed, and that they should like to see the Home Secretary treated in the same way; and I am acquainted with one person, who was robbed to a large amount in the following year, but who was deterred from endeavouring to detect the thieves, merely by the impression left on his mind by this circumstance. Within Newgate, amongst the mass of prisoners awaiting their trials, a sentiment of ferocious anger and desperate recklessness was created, such as, if frequently aroused and generally prevalent, would be the cause of innumerable and horrid crimes.

It should be remembered, here, that a batch of convicts is sentenced to death every six weeks in London, and that one or more, out of nearly all these bodies of prisoners, attempt escape or suicide. In almost every case, the newspapers publish some of the circumstances; and by one means or other all the prisoners in Newgate, and a great number of criminals in and about the metropolis, are sure to become acquainted with them. Every case produces more or less of the effects which I have described. A good effect, one of them may be called, by those who think that public executions tend to repress crime. It must be acknowledged, that these frequent attempts at escape and suicide have the effect of keeping all the horrors of the punishment of death, (that it has horrors no one will deny,) constantly before the public eye; but whether or not the effect in question be a good one, depends upon whether or not public executions deter from crime. I shall notice that point by-and-bye. Meanwhile, it must be plain that, whatever the evil effect of the punishment of death in arraying the public against the law, and in hardening the minds of criminals, part of such effect is produced by the frequent attempts at suicide which take place amongst persons under sentence of death.

That such attempts hardly ever succeed, is owing to the more severe mode of confinement adopted as to this class of prisoners, and, I do but justice to the keeper of Newgate in adding, to his incessant watchfulness. Mr. Wontner,[18] I am sure, would admit, that the most anxious part of his duty is the prevention of escapes and suicides.

It must not be supposed, however, that the keeper of Newgate, or his servants, treat prisoners under sentence of death with peculiar harshness. On the contrary, a stranger to the scene would be astonished to observe the peculiar tenderness, I was going to add respect, which persons under sentence of death obtain from all the officers of the prison. Before sentence, a prisoner has only to observe the regulations of the jail in order to remain neglected and unnoticed. Once ordered to the cells, friends of all classes suddenly rise up; his fellow prisoners, the turnkeys, the chaplain, the keepers, and the sheriffs, all seem interested in his fate; and he can make no reasonable request that is not at once granted by whomsoever he may address. This rule has some, but very few, exceptions; such as where a hardened offender behaves with great levity and brutality, as if he cared nought for his life, and thought every one anxious to promote his death. Speaking generally, prisoners under sentence of death are, I repeat, treated with peculiar tenderness; and the only distinction made amongst those who behave with common decency is, that persons convicted of forgery excite an extraordinary degree of interest in all who approach them. By observing this distinction, I was led to suppose, that the interest which is felt for every capital convict, except murderers, must be created by a sense of repugnance to the punishment about to be inflicted upon him; for there can be no doubt, that those who object to the punishment of death generally, are especially opposed to its infliction for the crime of forgery.

The absence of distinction as to all other cases must be accounted for as follows: – During the early part of my confinement in Newgate,[19] I used frequently to ask questions of the keeper and chaplain as to the probable fate of certain convicts, whose appearance in chapel had attracted my notice; and for some time I was astonished, by always receiving for answer, in words to this effect – 'it is impossible to say – the Council decides – we know some to be more guilty than others and more deserving of the severest punishment, but it so often happens that those escape whom we think most guilty, and those suffer whom we believe to be least guilty, that we can never give an opinion on the subject.' I afterwards discovered that persons under sentence of death in Newgate are engaged in a lottery, of which the blanks[20] are death, and that an attempt to foretell the result in any case would be mere guesswork. This point will be more fully explained hereafter. I mention it now, only for the purpose of showing the state of mind, in which all convicts under sentence of death must remain between the sentence and the decision of the Council, and of thereby explaining why, allowing for the distinction of forgery cases, the sympathy of the officers of the prison for the inhabitants of the cells is indiscriminate.

Because the public are not aware of the kindness shown generally to persons under sentence of death, they may imagine that it is concealed from the criminals of the metropolis. Just the reverse is the case, if the other prisoners in Newgate are prevented from observing what passes in the cells, the friends and relations of those, who are there confined, spread abroad a knowledge of every word and act of compassion. That they do so, and especially amongst the criminal classes, is proved by this – that the other prisoners in Newgate, who cannot observe what passes in the cells, are always quickly informed thereof by the persons who come to visit them, and who, of course, acquire their knowledge from the visitors of the cell prisoners. At any rate, the other prisoners are at all times fully impressed with the idea, that a prisoner in the cells is an object of pity, sympathy and interest. One example of this feeling may be properly cited.

A boy named Rogers,[21] who had been confined in the school-yard before trial, was sentenced to death, and, contrary to the usual practice with boys of his age, was, immediately after sentence, removed from the school to the cells. I saw him arrive in the school to fetch his clothes, coming from the bar, where sentence of death had just then been passed on him. He told the schoolmaster with great glee, that he was ordered to the cells; and when the other boys crowded round him to learn why he was to be removed, he answered their questions in a triumphant tone, and showed, by his whole manner as well, that he enjoyed the importance conferred on him, by being placed amongst those of whom no one can say which of them will, or will not, be executed. To guard against misapprehension, I must state that this prisoner had no fear on his own account: he knew very well that his extreme youth would save him from the punishment to which he had been sentenced. His satisfaction at being sent to the cells is mentioned, therefore, only for the purpose of illustrating the general feeling of prisoners not in danger, as to the importance acquired by those, who are in extreme danger of suffering the last punishment.

It would be sufficiently injurious, if the importance which criminals derive from being sentenced to death were thoroughly concealed from all other criminals. Even in that case a very hurtful confusion of ideas as to the object of punishment must occur amongst the convicts themselves and whatever portion of the public, not criminal, should become acquainted with their conditions and feelings in this respect. But who shall define any limit to the evils, which arise from a universal feeling amongst the criminal classes, that to be condemned to the greatest punishment is to be taken out of the class of criminals, and to obtain, instead of the dislike usually awarded to known criminals, greater tenderness and respect than are often bestowed upon strangers of unquestioned virtue? If any one would thoroughly comprehend the description which I am endeavouring to give of the treatment of convicts under sentence of death, let him spend an hour in the cells of Newgate on the day after the sentences of death have been passed at the Old Bailey, and he will there see a number of the worst criminals (not murderers) attended by the keeper of the prison, the chaplain, and perhaps the sheriffs, and receiving from all these words of condolence, offers of service, professions of interest, delivered in a tone and manner so friendly and sympathising, that were he to fall upon the same scene without any previous knowledge of its true character, he might suppose that he witnessed the sad and affectionate intercourse of parents with their children in distress. There may be readers who will blame these officers of justice, for so commiserating the state of men in the course of suffering a merited punishment for the good of society. I pretend not to defend them otherwise than by saying, that they cannot help what they do. A late sheriff, who, before the trial of a man for uttering[22] forged notes, had spoken rather harshly of the prisoner's crime, when informed of the same prisoner's danger, could not help letting tears run down his face, nor hinder his voice from faultering, and his whole frame from being agitated, whilst he expressed his anxious wish to *do every thing in his power* for saving the convict's life. The gentleman in question was Mr. Wilde,[23] of whose humanity I shall have to speak again by and by. Now, it should be known, that in the eyes of 99 out of 100 of the criminals of the metropolis, the sheriff, with his fine coach, full dress, and gold chain, is a personage of great importance; whence the reader will understand that his compassion is all the more esteemed by the criminal, and admired by others of the same class. I have frequently seen the more ignorant sort of convicts highly elated by a long conversation with the sheriff, during which he had but assured them that he feared their situation was desperate; and in these cases, which occurred in the Infirmary, whither the prisoners addressed had been removed on account of illness, other prisoners, awaiting trial, seemed – I cannot speak of their innermost thoughts, but they seemed – to envy the capital convicts the distinction of being commiserated by a person in authority. What I have said of the sheriffs is equally true of the keeper, who is next in authority, and whom the prisoners respect accordingly; of the chaplain, and of others who visit the prison from motives of religion, humanity, or curiosity. *Every one* who comes in contact with a man whose death by the hangman is probable, treats him, not as a criminal, but, as an unfortunate. In the treatment of other prisoners, even before trial when they are presumed to be innocent, I never observed any thing like commiseration from persons in authority over them. At the best they are treated with neglect, except for their safe custody; and all convicts not capital are treated as criminals. The same men, once capitally convicted, are treated as brothers or children in distress. Why is the capital convict – he whose crime is most grave and is proven – so favourably distinguished? Because the punishment of death shocks every mind to which it is vividly presented, and overturns the most settled notions of right and wrong. [pp. 82–101]

from Thomas Wontner, *Old Bailey Experience: Criminal Jurisprudence and the Actual Working of Our Penal Code of Laws; also, An Essay on Prison Discipline, to Which Is Added a History of the Crimes Committed by the Offenders in the Present Day* (London: James Fraser, 1833), pp. 37–58, 294–303, 307–14, 328–30.

The author of *Old Bailey Experience* seems to be that Thomas Wontner (1813–73) who was born at Kingston-on-Thames, south-west of London, son of John Wontner[1] and Mary Hoff. John Wontner (1784–1833) was a successful London clockmaker who became keeper, or governor, of Newgate Prison in 1822 and eventually marshal of His Majesty's Gaols. Thomas Wontner practised law as a solicitor, apparently counselling prisoners in Newgate in the period before publication of *Old Bailey Experience*; he later founded a law firm that served as solicitors to the Metropolitan Police, the Treasury (government finance department), and Home Office. Wontner also published a pamphlet, *Abolition of Pauperism* (1835), and *The Forensic Victimologist: Humorous and Lachrymous Tales of the Law, Illustrative of British Jurisprudence in Theory and Practice* (1838).

Old Bailey Experience is one of those books that is based on firsthand observation and it addresses the nineteenth-century debate on crime and punishment from that perspective. Like late eighteenth-century commentators such as Martin Madan and William Paley, selections of whose work are included in this volume, Wontner argues that leniency, inefficiency and inconsistency in application of the criminal laws defeat their purpose – to reduce crime and reform criminals. In tune with the trend of the penology debate at this time, he dismisses theory for an approach based on experience and observation. One of his main concerns is with juvenile offenders. Like most middle-class observers and commentators, Wontner's book is often sharply observed. He tried to understand the mentality of offenders, but in the end could only see it as a defective or perverse form of his own middle-class consciousness rather than a social psychology of calculated defiance of and resistance to economic and social structures that marginalized and exploited the lower classes. Like certain other books on crime and punishment, such as William Eden's *Principles of Penal Law* (1771; extracts included in the present volume), Wontner's book was probably at least partly an advertisement for the young man's professional abilities; like Eden's book, Wontner's seems to have been successful in this respect.

Note on the text: […] indicates the present editor's omission.

CHAPTER II.

General Remarks on the Prisoners confined in Newgate before and after Trial, and the Effects of Punishment in deterring Men from Crime.

THE object of the penal law is the prevention of crime. The guilty are to be punished, that society may be deterred from delinquency. Have our laws had this result? This is a subject which has for a long time engaged the attention of both the legislator and philanthropist. Many chimerical theories have been advanced, which, when examined, have been found in no way applicable to the purpose for which they were intended. No plan hitherto adopted has made crime even stationary; it having progressed one-fourth in the last seven years.

To treat on any subject successfully, and to grapple with it fairly, it is necessary that those who write on the subject should be practically acquainted with all its bearings. They should have mixed with the parties, that they may become possessed of all the latent springs which influence their conduct. In laws relating to trade, when any alterations are contemplated, a committee of the legislative body is formed, and evidence procured from among those most likely to be affected by the measure, and who are generally best acquainted with the subject. This is esteemed the surest source of correct information, as doubtless it is. Allowances, however, must be made for natural prejudices and bias to particular interests. So, in inquiries respecting the increase of crime, the best information is to be had from the offenders themselves. Obstacles certainly occur peculiar to such an investigation, in the characters of the parties to be examined, and the interest the examinants would think they had in misleading the examiners. To this are to be added their faithlessness and general depravity; and as few long accustomed to crime ever seriously reform, so as to take a sincere interest in the better regulation of society, little can be expected from them by any casual compunctions of conscience. Moreover, few traffickers in crime possess either education or ability to benefit the world by communicating their experience. In any case, such beings, long accustomed to trample on all principles, would be incompetent to assist us much in tracing the influences which draw so many into the trade of plunder, and by what spell it is they continue their vicious courses in the very teeth of the law, and at the foot of the gallows. Nearly three years experience in Newgate, and at the court where they are tried, have enabled me to arrive at certain conclusions. The circumstances under which I obtained these opportunities for observation is not necessary for me to state; suffice it to say, I was brought immediately into contact with the inmates of the prison, and that I had opportunities of seeing the prisoners in their unguarded moments – freed from all caution, and without their having had any motive for practising deception. During the period of my attendance I was employed in giving them advice, and was confidentially intrusted with their secrets for the purpose of defending them when in danger of punishment. I was, moreover, engaged as their amanuensis, both before and after their convictions, by which means I have become possessed of their true feelings, together with their standing and grade as professed thieves.

During the first eight months of my observations at Newgate, my surprise was much excited by the regular manner in which the prison became occupied, over and over again, after each sessional clearance, by the self-same persons. It perplexed me much to account for the apparent uniformity of crime in the metropolis, the committals being on an average about fifty per week, accompanied by an unvarying increase of one-eighteenth in each session of six weeks. On a more intimate knowledge of the character of these men, I thought I soon discovered the cause. If all the crimes committed were of such a nature as might be supposed to arise incidentally out of the very character of man and the construction of society, in which some were exposed to great temptation, possessing but a small share of virtue, whilst others, blessed with a stronger portion of power to overcome the temptation, were but little subjected to it, no hope, in a population like that of London, could be entertained of ever remedying the evil: but it is otherwise, there being comparatively but very few cases of casual dereliction from honesty when the temptations and population are considered. All there is to do, therefore, is to get rid of a certain party, or set of men. There is a distinct body of thieves, whose life and business it is to follow up a determined warfare against the constituted authorities, by living in idleness and on plunder. The problem of their increase was solved when I saw so many of their known party let off every season with some slight punishment, by which means they were soon again at their trade; taking care, however, to send into Newgate thirty or forty young hands each before they would themselves be again caught. It is the practice of all the old and knowing thieves, who have the reputation of being clever at business, to draw in young ones, and make them do all that part of the work incurring risk. I knew one man of whom it was said upwards of a hundred had been 'put away by him' – a term they have, when one is supposed to have been the cause of another's apprehension by leading him into crime. The term 'desperate,' as usually applied to these men, must not be taken in its common acceptation – bold, daring, absence of fear, and careless of personal danger. They are all, without exception, pusillanimous and rank cowards. The desperation they possess is that of a determined and inveterate gambler; they are ever employed in calculating the chances for and against them, in every unlawful adventure they think of embarking in; if they can but make the chances in their favour, (that is, of escaping,) they will unhesitatingly engage in any scheme or attempt at robbery. If, however, the commission of it be attended with the least possible risk of personal danger on the spot, they will always forego the adventure; and they have their exact odds in favour of every species of crime. The higher the game, they say, the less the risk. The high and safe game, however, requires a capital, as in the more honourable walks of life, to make an appearance – to move about with facility, and, in what they denominate style. It is astonishing with what pleasure some of them will speak of the prospects they have of soon leaving off the dangerous walk of business they have followed, and embarking in that which brings more profit and less risk – each saying, 'If I get off easy this time, I shall alter my game; I know I am a good workman, and ought to have been better employed.' The character of one is the character of the whole class; their manners and notions are all of one pattern and mould, which is accounted for by their general acquaintance with each other, and their habits of association. They have a peculiar look of the eye, which may be known by any one much accustomed to see them; and the developement of their features is strongly marked with the animal propensities. So very similar are their ideas and converse, that in a few minutes' conversation with any one of the party, I could always distinguish them, however artfully they might disguise themselves, and attempt to mislead me. They may be known almost by their very gait in the streets from other persons. Some of the boys have an approximation to the face of a monkey, so strikingly are they distinguished by this peculiarity. They form a distinct class of men by themselves, very carefully admitting noviciates into their secrets; he, however, who has graduated under one of their own approved body is unhesitatingly admitted into full confidence. He must, notwithstanding, prove himself acquainted with all the cramp[2] terms peculiar to their craft, or he will still be considered 'green,' and not fit to be trusted. There is not one of the select who is not able to relate the whole history of any other individual in their body – how he first began, who first taught him, what he has done and suffered, &c. &c. They form one club, to whom all the *fences* are known, (receivers of stolen goods,) who will never purchase of a new hand without a proper introduction, for fear of '*a plant*' (being betrayed). An initiate is, in consequence, constrained to trust his spoils to some old offender, until he can himself become better acquainted, and gain confidence with the buyer.

In a recent work on Newgate,[3] there is mention made of a man who was in the habit of going to a house in Wingfield Street, Whitechapel, and showing the boys large sums of money, and asking them to bring him goods to buy; from which it is understood he enticed them to commit crime. This man was in Newgate, under a sentence of fourteen years' transportation; and being known to some boys then in confinement, they mentioned to me that they had seen him with money, and that they thought him rich, saying how anxious he always was to purchase goods of them. But then the boys were known to him. It is a mistake to suppose he or any of his craft would go out to entice unknown persons to crime. The risk here is too great, and the parties too wary. Mr. Wakefield, to whom I told this anecdote, has misunderstood the matter. I mention this, conceiving there is a false notion regarding the temptations the receivers of stolen goods are supposed to hold out to crime. It is said, if there were no receivers, there would be no thieves; and the authorities have been advised to aim more at the buyer than the thief – *cui prodest scelus, is fecit.*[4] That the receiver is as bad as the thief, must be admitted; but if it be resolved to a question of policy, I say, remove the thieves if you can, who will for ever, while they remain at liberty, make others, and annoy society. If, by any possibility, all the buyers of stolen goods could be annihilated, in twenty-four hours their places would be filled up by others embarking in the trade. The profits are too large, and the chances of detection too remote, until the thieves are removed, ever to blot them, as a class, out of society. Every regular thief, let out upon the town, draws into crime, in the course of one year, a dozen more, which continues the species; and this will ever be the case until the system at the Old Bailey[5] be altered, where there really appears to be much more anxiety to take out of society casual offenders than the born and bred thief, whose whole life has been devoted to plunder. I have said they reckon all their chances: 1st, of their not being detected in the offence; 2dly, of their being acquitted; and 3dly, of coming off with what they call a small *fine* (short imprisonment). The only punishment they dread is transportation;[6] they hold all others in contempt; and I believe even that of death would lose its terrors, did it not lead to the greatest of all their dreads, viz.[7] transportation for life. Death, indeed, has no terrors for any one, until met with at close quarters. Tell the thief of death, and he will answer, 'Never mind, I can die but once!' Name transportation, and they turn pale. This cannot be too strongly enforced on the presiding judges at the Old Bailey. Full three-fourths of the prisoners, every session, are determined offenders, all of whom are regardless of imprisonment for a short period. Their spirits enable them to surmount such trifles, when the prospect of again returning to liberty and enjoyment is not very remote. 'Go along, time!' they cry; 'only three months and a *teazing*. Never mind! that's over in ten minutes; (meaning the flogging;) I would take one for each month, if the *old fellow* (the judge) would let me off the imprisonment.' If for crime *well-defined* transportation were sure to follow, there would soon be less business to do at the Old Bailey. A uniform plan of transportation for all known thieves would soon remove the whole fraternity of them out of society. It is of no use to pass this sentence on all brought to the bar for a whole day together, right or wrong, and then relax for a day or two, and pass minor sentences: it is the known thief who should be selected, and transported, being the only punishment he dreads. [...]

By a reference to the Old Bailey session calendar, it will be seen that about three thousand prisoners are annually committed to Newgate, making little short of four hundred each session, of which there are eight in a year. Out of the gross number, about three hundred and fifty are discharged by proclamation. Of these nothing can be said, as they must be considered innocent of the crimes with which they were charged, there not being *primâ facie*[8] evidence to send them on their trials. There remain two thousand five hundred and fifty who are tried, with the progressive increase of four-sevenths annually. Some persons have supposed this accumulation of offenders bears a regular proportion to the progress of population. As well may they assert that the demand for thieves in society regulates the supply, as in other markets of merchandise. The cause is in the mal-administration of the laws – the sending out so many old offenders every session to teach and draw in the more juvenile and less experienced hands – with the uncertainty of punishment, by the inequality of sentences for crimes of a like nature – to which may be added the many instances of mistaken, or rather *mis-directed* leniency, compared with others of enormous severity for trifling offences; all which tend to induce the London thieves to entertain a contempt for that tribunal. An opinion prevails throughout the whole body, that justice is not done there. I do not mean to say they complain of the sentences being too severe generally; for that would be natural enough on their parts, and not worth notice. They believe every thing done at that court a matter of chance; that *in the same day, and for a like crime*, one man will be sentenced to *transportation for life*, while another may be let off for *a month's imprisonment*, and yet both equally bad characters.

It only needs that punishment should be sure to follow the conviction for crime, and that the judgments should be uniform and settled, to strike terror into the whole body of London criminals. Out of the two thousand five hundred and fifty annually tried, nearly one-fourth are acquitted, leaving little short of two thousand for sentence in each year. Of these the average transported are eight hundred: deduct two hundred for cases of an incidental nature, *i.e.* crimes not committed by regular offenders, and there remain one thousand professed thieves who are again turned loose in a short period on the town, all of whom appear in due course again at the court of the Old Bailey, or at some other, many times in the revolution of one year. Here lies the mischief. An old thief will be sure to enlist others to perpetuate the race. There is no disguising the fact: the whole blame is with the court whose duty it is to take cognizance of these characters. Whilst the present system in pursued, of allowing so many old offenders to escape with trifling punishments, the evils will he increased, and the business of the court go on augmenting, by its own errors. The thief is now encouraged to speculate on his chances – in his own phraseology, 'his good luck.' Every escape makes him more reckless. I knew one man who was allowed a course of seventeen imprisonments and other punishments, before his career was stopped by transportation; a sentence which does, however, sooner or later overtake them, and which would be better both for themselves and the country were it passed the first time they were in the hands of the court as known thieves. Observing only a certain, and nearly an equal, number transported each session, they have imbibed a notion, that the Recorder cannot exceed it, and that he selects those to whom he takes a dislike at the bar, not for the magnitude of their offences, but from caprice or chance. It is under this impression they are afraid of speaking when in court, lest they should give offence, and excite petulance in the judge, which would, in their opinion, inevitably include them in the devoted batch of transports, of which their horror is inconceivable: first, because many have already undergone the punishment; and secondly, all who have not are fully aware of the privations to which it subjects them. Their anxious inquiry regarding every particular relating to the treatment, is a strong manifestation of their uneasiness on this subject. Yet Mr. Wontner and Mr. Wakefield (says the *Quarterly* reviewer) think neither transportation nor the hulks[9] have any terrors for them. How they come to this opinion, I cannot imagine. If they draw their inference from the noise and apparent mirth of the prisoners when they leave Newgate for the hulks, I think their premises false.

The transports are taken from Newgate in parties of twenty-five, which is called a draft. When the turnkeys lock up the wards of the prison at the close of the day, they call over the names of the convicts under orders for removal, at the same time informing them at what hour of the night or morning they will be called for, and to what place and ship they are destined. This notice, which frequently is not more than three or four hours, is all that is given them; a regulation rendered necessary to obviate the bustle and confusion heretofore experienced, by their friends and relatives thronging the gates of the prison, accompanied by valedictory exclamations at the departure of the van in which they are conveyed. Before this order arrives, most of them have endured many months' confinement, and having exhausted the liberality, or funds (perhaps both) of their friends, have been constrained to subsist on the gaol allowance. This, together with the sameness of a prison life, brings on a weariness of mind, which renders any change agreeable to their now broken spirits; the prospect of a removal occasions a temporary excitement, which, to those unaccustomed to reason on the matter, may appear like gaiety, and carelessness of the future. The noise and apparent recklessness, however, on these occasions, are produced more by those prisoners who are to remain behind, availing themselves of the opportunity to beguile a few hours of tedious existence by a noisy and forced merriment, which they know the officers on duty will impute to the men under orders for the ship. This is confirmed by the inmates of the place being, on all other nights of the year, peaceable after they are locked up in their respective wards. Those who suppose there is any real mirth or indifference among them at any time, have taken but a superficial view of these wretched men. Heaviness and sickness of heart are always with them; they will at times make an effort to feel at ease, but all their hilarity is fictitious and assumed – they have the common feelings of our nature, and of which they can never divest themselves. Those who possess an unusual buoyancy of spirits, and gloss over their feelings with their companions,

I have ever observed, on the whole, to feel the most internal agony. I have seen some thousands under this sentence, and never conversed with one who did not appear to consider the punishment, if it exceeded seven years, *equal to death*. May, the accomplice of Bishop and Williams,[10] told me, the day after his respite, if they meant to transport him, he did not thank them for his life. The following is another striking instance of the view they have of this punishment. A man named Shaw,[11] who suffered[12] for housebreaking about two years since, awoke during the night previous to his execution, and said, 'Lee!' (speaking to the man in the cell with him,) 'I have often said, I would be rather hanged than transported; but now it comes so close as this, I begin to think otherwise.' Shortly afterwards he turned round to the same man and said, 'I was wrong in what I said just now; I am still of my former opinion: hanging is the best of the two;' and he remained in the same mind all the night. The first question an untried prisoner asks of those to whom he is about to intrust his defence is, 'Do you think I shall be transported? Save me from that, and I don't mind any thing else.' One thing, however, is clear: no punishment hitherto has lessened the number of offenders; nor will any ever be efficient, until the penalties awarded by the law unerringly follow conviction, especially with the common robbers. There requires an immediate alteration of the mode of removing convicts to their stations. The expense of land carriage is enormous as now managed, and quite unnecessary, as it would be much more conveniently performed, by a vessel constructed for the purpose being brought up the Thames to Blackfriars Bridge. The present system is continued only on the principle of its being a city job, and throws money into the hands of those whose emoluments are already sufficiently great.

Turn over the pages of the Old Bailey session papers for years past, and you cannot but be struck with the anomalies which are there apparent, with respect to crimes and the sentences which have followed. The impression a perusal of these papers made on my mind, was as if all the business had been done by lottery; and my observation during twenty-two sessions on the occurring cases has tended to convince me, that a distribution of justice from that wheel of chance could not present a more incongruous and confused record of convictions and punishments. In no case (always excepting the capitals) can any person, however acute and experienced, form the slightest opinion of what the judgment of the court will be. Of this the London thieves are fully aware. I never could succeed in persuading one before his trial, that he was deprived of all chance of escape. They will answer, 'Look what a court it is! how many worse than me *do* scramble through; and who knows but I may be lucky.' What men know they must endure, they fear; what they think they can escape, they despise: their calculation of three-fourths escaping is very near the truth. Hope, the spring of action, induces each to say to himself, 'Why may I not be the lucky one?' THE CHANCE THUS GIVEN OF ACQUITTAL IS THE MAIN CAUSE OF CRIME. I do not mean to say three-fourths come off free; they are subjected to some kind of punishment, (excepting a few cases of judgment respited:) the others feel, no doubt, what they undergo, but it is only as a soldier in the fight considers a scratch – otherwise coming off with a whole skin, being ready for action again. Another evil arises out of this irregularity of judgments. All punishments are rendered severe and useful in proportion as the offender feels he deserves it, and is conscious of having only his *quantum meritus*.[13] This the convict can now never feel; seeing his companion in crime let off for a few months' imprisonment, he (his companion) having been guilty of an offence equal to his own, and for which he (the convict) is transported for life. Those connected with the court, in the conversations I have had with them, say, 'Circumstances of character occasion the apparent anomalies;' being unable, or perhaps unwilling, to give a better. That a good character does not avail the prisoner, or direct the court in its judgments, may be seen by a mere inspection of the printed trials, and is better known to all who have watched the proceedings of this court for any time. Hundreds of cases might be cited to illustrate this fact. I remember the case of two butchers, whose briefs I wrote, which occurred last year. One was an old, the other a young man, both having been in the employ of the prosecutor. They were charged with stealing a breast of mutton from their master: both were found guilty.[14] The old man had persons to speak as to his character for honesty for forty years last past (his former masters;) the young one had not a solitary witness to say a word for him. The former was sentenced to fourteen years' transportation; the latter to six months in the house of correction. When the prosecutor heard of the circumstance, he got up a petition to the secretary of state for the remission of the sentence, in which he stated that on the trial he himself had given the old man a good character, and not the other. Instances of this kind occur out of number to confirm the rogues in their preconceived notions of the uncertainty of punishment, and that 'the greatest crimes come off the best.' This is an aphorism among the thieves. I have seen some of them, after being sentenced by the court, dance for hours, calling out continuously, 'Did I not tell you all, the biggest rogues get off the best?' The scene in the several yards of Newgate on the sentence-days, after the judgments have been passed, defies any description on paper. Some will be seen jumping and skipping about for hours, frenzied with joy at the very unexpectedly mild sentence passed on them; others are cursing and swearing, calling down imprecations on the Recorder, for having, as they say, so unfairly measured out justice; all agreeing there is no proportion in the punishments to the crimes. It may be said, it is of little import what these men think, so they are punished. But is it of no importance under what impression the others are discharged? If the discharged feel (as assuredly they do) that punishment is a matter of chance, they return to their habits as the hazard-player goes again to the dice, in hopes of coming off a winner, and reimbursing himself for former losses. There is another evil comes out of these unequal sentences. The discontent it produces on the minds of those who fall under the more heavy judgments, which militates against their reformation: instead of reflecting on their situation as brought on by themselves, they take refuge in complaint and invective, declaring they are 'sacrificed,' – in their own language, 'murdered men.' I have often said, 'Why complain? You knew the consequence of detection.' 'Yes,' would be the reply; 'but look at the case of Tom — and Bill —. Not that I am sorry they have got off; but is it not a shame to give me a *lifer*, and they only a month each?' Such answers are always given when any attempt is made to reconcile them to their fate. They carry this feeling with them to the hulks, where they amuse each other with all the tales of hardship within their knowledge; meditating revenge, by which they mean becoming more desperate in crime, and making reprisals on the public, when they shall be again at large. They become imbued with a notion the judge has more to answer for than themselves. Opinions of this nature are very common among them, and prevent the discipline to which they are submitted having its proper effect. Minds in the state of theirs seize on any supposed injury to brood over and stifle their own reproaches. Of this *dernier ressort*[15] they would be deprived, if equal sentences were passed on all for like offences, being known offenders. They are now all ill-used men, by comparison with others who have been more fortunate. The present system holds out so many chances for the offender to escape, that it acts as an inducement to continue his practices, and to all loose characters, not yet accomplished in the art of plunder, to become so. Again, by the discharge of so many known thieves every session, so many masters are sent into the town to draw in and teach others, by which a regular supply is brought up to fill the ranks of those who full in the conflict.

There is no known crime, operating to the injury of society, for the punishment of which a statute has not been provided, and the penalties in which generally have not been considered too severe. If, then, it be not for lack of Draconian[16] enactments that crime increases, the error must lie in the administration of them. An examination into the constitution of the court of the Old Bailey, and the manner the business is there performed, will, I think, prove this to be the case. The monstrous acts of carelessness, and consequent injustice, emanating from the Old Bailey court, are incredible to persons who have been accustomed to consider it, like others, pure and unvitiated by patronage and influence. No one unacquainted with the business of the place can possibly have a conception of the number of persons who influence the judges in a multiplicity of cases every session, – always excepting the capitals, because the law relating to them, be it good or bad, is clear and defined. A sentence of death always follows the conviction, after which the prisoner's fate is in the hands of the king and council. The Old Bailey court is under the jurisdiction of the lord mayor and the court of aldermen, one of whom must be on the bench to complete a court. This body elects the judges, consisting of the Recorder and Common Serjeant, who have an assistant judge, now Serjeant Arabin,[17] all of whom are in daily intercourse with the other city authorities. Throughout the year, meetings out of number take place on city business, besides dinner and convivial parties, at which the aldermen and other gentlemen of city influence are constantly in the habit of meeting these judges, on the familiar terms of intimates; consequently, through these channels, any representation may be made to a judge before trial, either for or against the prisoner. Tales may be poured into his ears, day after day, in various ways, so that the judge himself shall not see the motive, until a prejudice be effected, which renders him unfit for his office. It may be asked, what motive any of these gentlemen can have in prejudicing the case of a prisoner? I answer, none personally; but when it is considered they have all been in trade, and have numerous connexions, either commercial or otherwise, in all the grades immediately below their own, and looking at all the ramifications by which society is linked together, especially in this metropolis, it is easy to conceive that through such channels claims will be made on them not always to be resisted, and from them to the judge. That they do interfere I know, as do all others any way connected with the court or prison. It is not a postulate, but a demonstrable fact; not an occurrence now and then, but an everyday affair. All who know any thing of the internal machinery of Newgate and the Old Bailey, know the truth of this statement; and that there are other undue influences exercised of a more pernicious nature, of which I shall speak presently. One case out of many known to me I will relate. A linendraper's shopman was committed for robbing his master's till, marked money having been found upon him. A few days after his committal he was recognized by one of the turnkeys, who had formerly been servant to his father, an officer in the marines. The man took an interest in the young linendraper's fate, and four days previous to his trial told him, in my presence, that he had managed his business, but could not get him off for less than three months' imprisonment. He was subsequently sentenced for precisely that term. In this instance we begin with the lowest instrument, a turnkey! yet it went up, step by step, until it reached the judge, who acquiesced in a sentence previously arranged by another having a very different duty to perform. In the same ward with this young man were others whose offences did not exceed his, yet they were sentenced to seven and fourteen years' transportation. That it is highly proper the judge should be allowed a discretion in every case, must be admitted: but is this discretion to allow others *out of court* to do their business? I should have said, the prisoner in the last case cited had no person to give him a character. The turnkey's conduct I applauded, as it proceeded from gratitude to the family. He is not to blame; and I should not have mentioned the circumstance, but to show how certain it is that the court suffers itself to be led by others.

In every session there is a small class of prisoners very opposite from the regular thief, consisting of clerks, and others in a similar walk of life, many of whom have probably for the first time offended against the law, by embezzlement, or otherwise robbing their employers. In these cases the sentences run in extremes; the fullest penalty of the law being exacted in some, while others are fined a shilling and discharged, or, having their judgments respited, are allowed to go at large, in the hope they will sin no more. Here, if any rule of action could be recognized, and character had its weight in court, all would be fair; but unfortunately it is not so, – some, having the best of characters up to the moment of the commission of the offence, are sentenced to the severest punishments at the bar, – others, without any such advantage (at least in open court,) escape entirely free. IN ALL SUCH CASES IT IS INFLUENCE WITH THE JUDGES WHICH PRODUCES ITS DISPARITY. It has often happened, when I have applied to make a prisoner's brief, that a letter would be put in my hand; on reading which, I learnt some friend, or father's friend, or friend's friend in the second or third degree, had seen a certain alderman, who had made a promise to interfere. Probably I should be asked if he (the prisoner) might rely on the success of the interest; in which case I invariably told them they might be sure of his (the alderman) having the ability, if he could be brought to exercise it. I was never mistaken: when the promise was made, the party always got off, and the instances within my own knowledge are not a few. This influence is often used in a more unjust manner. When a confidential clerk or warehouseman in charged with embezzlement, it not unfrequently happens the prosecutor has a motive for being anxious to secure the entire riddance of the prisoner, by having him sent out of the country, he (the prisoner) being in possession of secrets which it might not be so well to have divulged. To accomplish this, hyperbolical reports of the man's extravagance are circulated – his having kept one or more mistresses, &c. &c. – that he has been doing this for a long period, by robbing his master. All this, poured into the proper city channels, never fails to reach the judge who tries him, and produces the object sought, viz. transportation for fourteen years. Few will be disposed to complain of the instances of mercy; but it is the mode of doing it with which I find fault, and which makes it an abuse of justice. The pure stream is polluted – a door is open by which the worst of mischiefs enter. This can only be reformed by the appointment of judges out of city influence. There is no prejudication with the regular judges of the country. In their hands the course of justice goes on in one pure and uninterrupted stream. The lives and liberties of nearly three thousand human beings come under the cognizance of the Old Bailey court every year. Does it not appear extraordinary that the management of a business of such national importance should be in the hands of judges who are not one remove from the middle classes of the community, and who, it is well known, mix every day with their fellow-citizens, so as to hear every current tale connected with the very cases in which they are a few hours afterwards called on to adjudicate – often coming into immediate contact with the prosecutors, who, for reasons before stated, have occasionally an interest in prejudicing the judge? Calumny is often added to oppression, if but for the sake of justifying it. The dinners during sessions are very bad things, and assist much in working mischief. There the city judges, lord mayor, aldermen, sheriffs, and many others, sit down together every day during sessions, talking over all the affairs and occurrences of the day, as they may chance to be brought on the tapis.[18] There any wish may be expressed to a judge regarding a prisoner, and story told without the accused having the opportunity to rebut it – any enormity softened down to a venial offence, or any peccadillo swelled to a most atrocious crime. All who know any thing of the city corporate body are aware that they are not only divided into political parties, but also those of sectarianism, and that there is a puritanical party, who are so extremely tenacious of any member of their sect coming to harm, that under their protection getting into Newgate is of no consequence. Hence the fine of one shilling and discharge of the cheesemonger's clerk who had thirty-two cases of embezzlement against him, and to which he pleaded guilty, being so advised, which is usual when a prisoner has a friend to protect him, as it avoids a trial, and he passes through the ordeal unobserved. This man told me his sentence BEFORE HE WENT UP TO THE COURT, and borrowed a shilling of a person to prepare himself for it. Letters were inserted in the 'Weekly Dispatch' from the firm this man had robbed, inquiring who advised the late Common Serjeant to pass so *just* a sentence, which enabled the man to join an opposition house to the prosecutor's within a few days, to their great prejudice. A promise was given that an inquiry should be made; it has, however, passed away, like all promises of this nature. Another extraordinary feature in this case is, that some other person had promised to protect the prisoner from transportation, and the prosecutors had been led to expect a sentence of two years imprisonment in Newgate, (so they expressed themselves in their letter to the editor of the 'Weekly Dispatch,') with which they were satisfied. The prisoner, however, subsequently found another friend to interfere for him, who was less ceremonious in matters of justice, and the payment of a shilling was deemed a sufficient expiation for the crime of embezzling thirty-two separate and distinct sums of money. I have known many offenders get off with a nominal punishment, by having letters written to the judge, at the Old Bailey, from some person of known consequence. These are generally procured through some relation, who having access to the parties, excite their feelings on behalf of the prisoner. These letters are generally couched in the following strain. 'That they know (or have been well assured) that the prisoner has hitherto borne a good character; that they would themselves have attended and said as much in court, but that peculiar engagements precluded the possibility of their doing so; they, however, felt it a duty to communicate what they knew of the parties, and hope the court will allow the prisoner an opportunity of redeeming his good character, by passing a light sentence on him.' Such letters, if coming from what, in common *parlance*, is called a great man, are always influential over the minds of the judges. I shall avoid comment on this practice; I only state the fact, knowing it to be so, through the prisoners themselves, who, in many instances have apprised me beforehand that they must decline incurring any expense for a defence, having such friends to write to the judge, &c. &c.

The judges say they never suffer any thing extrajudicial to influence them. How do they know that? No one knows himself, and there is no security but by removing the possibility of his coming within the sphere of such pollution to his office. Let him be placed on a pinnacle of more importance, out of the reach of these gossips. If it were possible, a judge ought to descend from the upper world to the seat of justice, untainted and unprejudiced by any knowledge of the matter at issue. In all other courts of law this desideratum is obtained, as nearly as human arrangement can approximate to such an object. If it be thought proper, in a question involving a consideration of a few pounds, that a superior law officer of the crown should preside, of how much more importance is that of life and death, of liberty and character; a question comprehending the interests of so many – the fixing a stamp of infamy on the father of a family, and in which a wife, children, and relations, are all concerned! It is true that, during the first days of each session, one or more of the fifteen judges attend to try the capital cases; but they do not always go through the whole of these, leaving some for the Recorder. It is remarkable how the auditors and prisoners are penetrated with the manner and patience of these judges, as contradistinguished from the hurried way in which the trials are usually conducted in these courts. The effect it has on the prisoners is astonishing, notwithstanding the awful sentences which invariably follow in these cases, viz. death. They are generally satisfied they have had a fair trial; and it is a remarkable fact, that none who are tried by the city judges ever think justice has been done them. However guilty they may be, they expect a chance on their trial, and decent treatment while they are undergoing it. The most brutal are sensible of the difference so apparent when they appear before what they call 'a real judge.' I have seen them come from the court, after such treatment, positively pleased, although found guilty, saying, 'I am guilty fair enough: the judge would have let me said any thing, he is such a nice old man.' I have observed the demeanour of these men subsequently to be always better than those who could never get rid of the notion they had not had a fair chance on their trials. [pp. 37–58]

CHAPTER VI.

PRISON DISCIPLINE AND SECONDARY PUNISHMENT.

Section VII.

On Juvenile Offenders.

IT is impossible for those who are strangers to these beings to form any idea what contempt the prisoners generally have of corporeal punishment, both men and boys. I have frequently heard the aldermen and sheriffs, when in their visits to the prison and making inquiry into the nature of the several cases, threaten the boys with a severe flogging, and paint the punishment in the most horrible colours their imagination could invent. But this, so far from alarming them, had just the opposite effect, as it relieved their minds from the terrors of transportation. They forthwith resumed their wonted spirits, becoming impertinent and troublesome, saying they had been told their sentence – 'only a *teazing* and *turned up*,' (discharged;) never ceasing to boast of their supposed good fortune, and of taunting their fellow-prisoners with the want of it. This is the truth regarding the whole, not an occasional instance of some hardened and daring offender; even in their sleep they will talk of their good fortune in escaping with *only a flogging*. There is no mistake in it; the punishment is worse than useless. I am certain, if they could have shortened their durance for a week, they would offer to take two whippings instead of one, any morning, and come back to their breakfasts in good spirits. I really never knew a boy go unwillingly to be flogged, (and I have not seen a few,) as it was always, in Newgate, the prelude to his enlargement. The nights preceding the days of punishment were always spent in the most cheerful manner, for the same reason. Men, immediately after their punishment, would pass their fellow-prisoners, saying, 'Don't you wish you were as lucky?' A committing magistrate frequently, when sending a boy to Newgate, intimates to the prosecutor (who may be rather an unwilling one) that the prisoner will probably have only a whipping. This never fails to make the party saucy and troublesome all the time of his imprisonment, thinking he is sure of no further punishment. I have ever observed the boys have become bold, daring, and hardened, in proportion as they have undergone the most corporeal punishment, and probably it is so with men. I knew one boy who endured seven whippings, five private and two public.[19] He was only fourteen years of age. If a boy has once fallen into the hands of a practised thief, nothing but taking him out of society for a long period can afford any hope of his amendment; and this will fail, unless measures be used to rouse the better feelings of his nature: what is called discipline and severity will never accomplish the object; not even rewards for good conduct, under a system of heavy punishment for the reverse, can avail any thing: they will still remain the same insensible beings, hard and frozen up. The more you coerce, the further is the retrocession from the point aimed at. I wish those who have the management of boys of the description here spoken of, would reflect that, in the majority of cases, there has either been no parent, or those of such habits and temper as would have rendered orphanship a blessing; and that, in all probability, most of them under their care never had a kind or affectionate sentiment imparted to or drawn out of them, by any human being they could look to as a friend; and that they have in a manner been driven to take up arms against society, meeting, from their earliest recollections, with nothing but an enemy in man. Thoughts of this nature ever induced me to adopt a kind mode of treatment; and I have found it to succeed in a wonderful manner, even when others have said that no sense of feeling was left. I am not without a hope but that I have done some good in this way. The effect on one boy was remarkable. He had been abandoned by his parents from his infancy, and had always lived in crime. When I heard his history I became interested for him, and talked to him very much of the course he was pursuing; I reached his feelings, and the effect was wonderful. He, however, went into Newgate three times afterwards, always regretting his inability to follow my advice. Notwithstanding all his crimes, I could not but believe he was sincere in his wishes to become honest. I at length discovered he had an uncle at Birmingham, to whom I wrote: he was a poor man, but was willing to aid my views. I got the officers of the parish to which he belonged to pay for the travelling expenses to his relation, where he now is, quite reformed, and doing well in the service of a farmer. His uncle has sent me a letter of thanks, saying, the boy's only wish was to see me once more, to acknowledge his gratitude for having saved him. As it may appear extraordinary the boy should be so often in Newgate, I feel it necessary to state, the first time he was flogged, once acquitted, and twice no bill found against him.

I have said, the prisoners generally disregard minor punishments: with the younger ones it sometimes appears to act as a positive inducement to continue in their career. The boy who for his age has undergone the most punishment is the greatest man; such is their notion of consequence, which an endurance of many whippings gives them, that it is the main topic of conversation with each other. On this subject they will enlarge in the most extravagant manner, making out their offences and adventures as wonderful as their ingenuity can invent; often concluding with, 'Well, when I have another *teazing*, I shall be as good a man as Harry —.' This feeling[20] is got from the men in whose hands they have been made instruments of crime, and who relate to them tales of heroism, telling them they will be great only as they endure punishment after the Spartan fashion. They at the same time afford these deluded creatures every facility of gratifying their passions, having first promoted an early and premature sense of them. Human nature is bad enough when the passions are attended by reason, and both are developed in due course of growth towards manhood. Ought we then to be surprised at the lamentable results, when the passions are set at liberty without the guide of reason, as in the case of these poor boys? The seducers of youth find an able auxiliary in the minor theatres, where they are generally sought. The men know, if a boy has a passion for these low exhibitions, that he is a sure prize. This the boys acknowledge; and full one half have confessed to me, that the low theatres have been the cause of their entering into crime, and in very many instances the offences for which they stood committed were occasioned by their want of money to gratify this passion. When they know they are about to be discharged, the first pleasure they anticipate is going to the theatre the same evening. Although turned out without hat or shoes, and in rags, they make sure of getting the money for this purpose; and I have no doubt many go from the prison-door to stealing for no other object, – such is their infatuation for these places. The truth of this I have ascertained from several who have been detected and re-committed. I remember an instance of one who was flogged on a Friday morning, and brought in again on Saturday (the next day.) He acknowledged to me having stolen a packet of halfpence, containing five shillings, within an hour after he left the prison, for no other purpose but to see some petty exhibition, of which a companion had told him. This boy's father was a hackney coachman, and did all becoming a parent to reclaim his son; he was not yet fourteen years of age, and had been twice before in Newgate; once for manslaughter, on which he was acquitted: he admitted, however, being the cause of the death of the party, an aged woman. The second time, he was tried for robbing a man of seventeen sovereigns; for this he was whipped and discharged. For the last (the packet of halfpence) he was transported for fourteen years.

Although an advocate for the fullest liberty of the press, I regret to add, that if means could be taken to suppress the low publications, of which there are now so many sold, many boys would be saved from destruction who are now lost entirely by the influence these works have on their vitiated tastes, viz. the fictitious lives of robbers, pirates, and loose women. There is scarcely one in print that these boys have not by rote; their infatuation for them is unbounded, and the consequent perversion of their minds very fatal, in every instance when this passion seizes them. Although naturally restless in their habits, they will sit for six or eight hours together, relating and hearing tales of criminal heroes. A boy expert at telling these stories will exact and obtain half the allowance of food from the others, to gratify them in this passion. How far this taste is brought on by their mode of tuition is not unworthy a consideration: full five-sixths of them are from the national schools, where they are taught to read entirely from the Scriptures, and never see any other works of interest. It is highly probable, if books of general history were put into their hands, and their tastes directed to substantial food for the mind, by which they might acquire a desire for the knowledge of facts instead of fiction, they might be excited to a better kind of reading, and much of the mischief avoided. I would not be understood, that the Scriptures are not of the first importance, but I object to their being almost the only book put into their hands when learning the first elements of reading. Little works of morality, with natural and general history, are decidedly the most proper for their years, and best calculated to excite a taste for knowledge in general; reserving two days in the week for the New Testament with the junior classes, and an extra day for the Old with the more advanced in reading. With the assistance of the Rev. Mr. Cotton and Mrs. Fry,[21] I succeeded in obtaining a stock of these books; and I am satisfied, from my experience with nearly five hundred boys, that no other is so well calculated to engage their attention.

On the subject of boys engaged in crime, many volumes might be written, illustrative of their habits and character, showing by what means they are brought into it, their peculiar situation in life, and cruel treatment under petty offences, many of whom are driven by circumstances into the commission of crime. It has always distressed me to hear of any sentence exceeding seven years being passed on a youth under fourteen years of age, as he can scarcely be considered morally responsible for his own actions at this period of his existence; but as they are made instruments in the hands of others to commit depredations, and thus rendered not only dangerous to society but to themselves, when considered as men, it is of the first importance they should be secured, until their minority be expired, taking care in the interim to give such instruction as the nature of the case will admit of. But to subject *them when men* to the severest of all punishments, viz. slavery for life, for an action *committed when boys*, I cannot but think both cruel and unjust in the extreme. The Roman law of the twelve tables,[22] ordained that an open theft should be whipped with rods, and condemned to slavery, if he had attained the age of puberty; or only whipped if he was not of ripe age. We are, probably, the first and only nation on the face of the earth who, in the adult, punish the crimes done in infancy. The Old Bailey court, however, in proportion to the numbers, as often sentence boys as men to transportation for fourteen years and life. For one prisoner I felt very much, who was sent for the latter term; he was under thirteen years of age, and not a known offender; his crime was stealing his companion's hat, while they were looking at a puppet-show. The unfortunate boy says, 'he knocked it off in fun,' and that some other person must have found it. He was not taken up until the following day, and the hat was never produced. The policeman who took him into custody resided next door to the prisoner's mother, and was heard to say, 'the boy had thrown stones at him, and that he would give him a *lift*.'[23] I know not what he said on the trial, but such was his heavy sentence. The mother was a widow, and he was her only son. I shall never forget her distress and agony of feeling when she heard his fate. Nothing can be more absurd than the practice of passing sentence of death on boys under fourteen years of age for petty offences. I have known five in one session in this awful situation; one for stealing a comb almost valueless, two for a child's sixpenny story-book, another for a man's stock, and the fifth for pawning his mother's shawl. In four of these cases the boys put their hands through a broken pane of glass in a shop-window, and stole the articles for which they were sentenced to death, and subsequently transported for life. This act, in legal technicality, is house-breaking. The law presumes they break the glass, and it is probable in most instances they do so. In two of the cases here named, however, the prosecutrix's daughter told me there was only a piece of brown paper to supply the place of that which once had been glass. In the latter case, the unfortunate mother caused her son to be apprehended, in the hopes of persuading the magistrate to recommend him to the Refuge for the Destitute, or some other charitable institution.[24] She, however, in the course of her examination, said she was from home, and that the house was locked up at the time of the shawl being taken, which was afterwards found at a pawnbroker's. This made it housebreaking; and, in spite of all the mother's efforts, he was condemned to death. He is now in the Penitentiary.[25] The judges who award the punishments at the Old Bailey appear to me as if they were under the influence of sudden impulses of severity, there being at no time any regular system to be recognized in their proceedings. This the prisoners know, and speculate on, particularly the boys. There is not at this moment a question of any comparative magnitude before the public, equal to that of how we shall treat and deal with juvenile vagrants and offenders. Those who now come under the law are treated in every respect as men, and held as responsible for their actions, although they have been cast upon the waters of life, not only without rudder or pilot, but without a bark to float them, so that they are struggling for life the moment they come into it; being like the small inhabitants of the ocean, the same instant which animates them, also informs them of the danger of being devoured by those of their own species who have had a pre-existence. The majority of those who have not yet fallen under the law, are rapidly imbibing the opinions and principles (as all do) of those about them in childhood, and are being prepared to swell the criminal calendar of the country. Habit, which by a kind appointment of nature, was intended for our good, is, by the neglect of those in power, converted into a mischief. All, taking man in the aggregate, are born with equal talent, why, therefore, under a prudent and virtuous governorship, should not one cast of thinking be imparted to all whom we have the power of educating? We see the effect of the turn of mind in families when one system of education is adopted for all the children; and so it would be in nations, were an universal and well-digested plan enforced on those who are deprived of the protection and advice of a natural parent.

May 15th, 1833, a boy of twelve years of age was sentenced to seven years transportation for stealing two penny rolls; it was said he was a bad character, but if we are to transport all the bad characters at twelve years of age, that is, all who are the sons of low, vulgar, and uneducated parents in this metropolis, there will soon be a great demand for tonnage amongst our shipping interest. And if we are not to transport all for like offences, being the same characters, why one? The Recorder*[26] in his wisdom will reply, it is good now and then to make examples, as a terror to others; – always harping upon *terror*. If he had said it was to prevent penny rolls being stolen, I should say his course will succeed though it is not a just one. For as long as this boy's case is remembered by the fraternity, they will naturally put the question to themselves, whether it is not the height of folly to sneak for twopenny plunder in a town like this, where there is such abundance of property, when, if they steal hundreds of pounds, the sentence will be no more heavy, but probably less. Should the boy be retained on board the hulks, and discharged when he is nineteen years of age, will he be improved, and with what notions of law and justice will he come into the world, always remembering that twopence valued in baked flour had caused him seven years' incarceration, many whippings, hard fare, and toilsome labour, besides fixing on him, at the most important period of his existence, the stamp of felon – the state of adolescence being ever referred to, when a man makes his first essay for a start in life? Suppose him to embark again in his old calling, employing boys to aid him, as he himself had been employed; the first principle he inculcates is, 'go for heavy stakes,' we need not then rob so often, and shall run less risk; remember my case, seven years for twopence. This is, in fact, the grand argument used to young and timid by the old rogues to induce them to become more bold and daring.

Every motive which can urge men to reflect and act are involved in this question, whether considered generally as regards the nation, or particularly as relates to individuals. It comprehends national character, national and political stability, national prowess and wealth, and national happiness. It includes not only the moral conduct of the nation, but of each individual, as the mere knowledge of the corrupt and untaught state of human nature affords excuses for others to commit indiscretions, who are by birth and education taught better. Youthful delinquency concerns every one as regards his own private property, and that of his posterity. Each parent is interested for his children, in the moral condition of the people, even as viewed in the highways, and the family of every householder, from the duke to the lowest-rate trader is affected by the moral condition of the menials they are constrained to employ, and who nearly all emerge from a state of poverty to occupy these stations. All the cardinal virtues call loudly on man to assist by his advice, pocket, and exertions, to further the views of those who are anxious to deal with this subject on broad and useful principles. Religion, humanity, charity, and justice, demand some legislative measure. [pp. 294–303]

---

* Whilst this work was in the press this gentleman resigned his office in consequence of Job Cox, who was under sentence of death, being reported for execution contrary to the order of the council.

Section VIII.

On the Effects of Theatrical Exhibitions on Untaught Boys.

MANY well-intentioned persons have denounced all theatrical representations as prejudicial to the morals of the public; the mischievous effects, however, arise only from private and minor theatres;[27] few can conceive or depict the demoralizing consequences of young persons being allowed to congregate in these places, many of which are unlicensed, and carried on in violation of the law. It has ever been admitted that the stage has a strong moral controlling influence over a large body of the people, and does much in forming the character and manners of those whose avocations prevent them from mixing more with the world, than associating with their own classes, constraining them, in seeking for other models of character and rules of real life, to fly to the stage. It therefore becomes an important and imperative duty of those who take on themselves the destinies of a powerful and populous people, to regulate theatrical representations, under which it may be estimated that the tastes (and even the turn of thinking) of one moiety of the town populations are formed. These exhibitions are established ostensibly only as places of amusement; but if you wish readily to form a correct opinion of a people, study their games and amusements, from the rustic at a wake or fair to the exclusives at Almack's, or the *elite* at the Italian Opera House.[28] The stage considered with reference to the large theatres,[29] does more than the pulpit in promoting virtue, and in repressing the vicious habits of society. They aim at the improvement of the world through its amusements. They endeavour to show, that honesty and virtue in man, and chastity in woman, are the only paths to happiness, through the agency of real and ideal characters; the stage exalts mankind in sentiment, instructing them to cherish and cultivate their kindlier feelings: if a robber, a villain, or a frail female be introduced into their representations, a moral lesson is always imparted in the denouement. 'To hold as 'twere the mirror up to nature: to show virtue her own form, scorn her own image, and the very age and body of the times its form and pressure;'[30] as they were wont to write on the proscenium, *veluti in speculum*.[31] I wish as much could be said for those theatres which rank immediately below the two principal ones; but I believe no man of real observation will presume to say much in their praise. There is indeed a great outcry made by some on their behalf, but it is only among those whose tastes are vitiated, and with whom grimace and buffoonery is more agreeable than good sense – where are represented *outré*[32] imitations of characters which never had existence in real life, *compositum miraculi câusa*,[33] which are garnished with gross ribaldry. This is a dish of amusement but too frequently offered, and applauded by our young cits,[34] who waste the meridian of their youth in picking up from these sources scraps of low wit, sayings, and vile puns, blended with much foolery. One half their nights are spent in again retailing them out to those with whom they herd, to provoke a laugh, in some back-room of a public-house, over noggins of ale and goes of brandy, enveloped in tobacco smoke. Under a conservative moral government, this would be reformed altogether; it has, however, nothing *per se*,[35] it may be said, to do with crime, but be it remembered, that the more fool you allow a man to make himself, the less chance he has of obtaining or retaining a position in society, whereby he may get his bread, and preserve his honesty; especially as such habits ever in the end lead to the confirmation of a confirmed inebriate. If the performances at the second-rate theatres are injurious to the morals of the *soi-disant*[36] gentleman and actor, who for the most part may be supposed to have had some kind of education, what must representations of the vilest nature effect on the totally ignorant and uneducated! Such are nightly, in every quarter of the town, being exhibited, where may be seen crowds of children of both sexes, under twelve years of age, sitting in pairs, playing off all the vulgar familiarities of grown up, but low and lewd persons. Here the highwayman, the brigand, the pirate, and even the murderer, are shown under circumstances of the most favourable view; their crimes being either wholly excused, or very much palliated, and a taste engendered among youth for every species of adventure connected with desperate undertakings. Ignorant and uneducated children of both sexes, if constitutionally of a temperament above par, immediately on witnessing these representations, take fire, and imaginatively become heroes and heroines; they set up half the night, imitating to the best of their ability the scenes which they have beheld on the stage; and from that moment all moral restraint on their desires are lost. That it should be so is natural: although untaught and low-born, they nevertheless latently possess all the feelings of those more auspiciously placed in life, which being precociously and suddenly excited, in the absence of a matured and controlling judgment, burst forth with a violence overwhelming in its effect. The mind having never undergone a proper tempering, by progressive reading, and consequent regular development of its powers, is taken by storm, and surprised, when they feel as if they had sustained an internal mental explosion – a mine of desires are sprung, of which they heretofore had no comprehension. All the little materials for thinking which they may have collected in their circumscribed experience, is spread to the winds like the ashes in a volcano. They then become bent on exploits of some kind, and on the unbridled indulgences of those passions, which at this critical period of their lives are awakened: in this feverish state, there is no one near them competent to reason down their intemperate sensations, and they fall an easy victim into the service of any one who is willing to receive them for initiation into crime. If those in authority think this fruitful source of crime overdrawn, or that the instances by which, through this source (low theatres) criminals are made, are few, I can only invite them to accompany me on an examination of the unfortunate boys now in custody, on board the

Euryalus convict ship, at Chatham,[37] or in the Penitentiary,[38] when I doubt not of making it sufficiently evident and clear to them, that the pernicious conse-quences to society, arising from theatrical representations, far exceeds any account which can be written of them in a work not entirely devoted to that especial purpose. The afterpiece of 'Black-eyed Susan'[39] owes all its attraction, with the vulgar, (and they have been its chief admirers,) to the incident in it of William stabbing his officer, his subsequent trial, and the solemn preparations for his execution before the audience. Whether the organ of destructiveness is predominant in our natures, I will not undertake to determine, but I am acquainted with some extraordinary natural, or rather unnatural, effects, the wit-nessing of executions have produced, and have noticed the influence on the juvenile part of the audience at a theatre, which in a low exhibition generally forms the majority. I have invariably found them to show more signs of interest, and even internal delight, when one or more deaths are annexed to the catas-trophe of the plot of a performance. The excitement evinced both by males and females, is extraordinary, and there cannot remain a doubt but that the sensa-tions at the time are of a pleasurable kind. These observations I have had confirmed by overhearing a party of boys who were committed for trial: in their conversations they minutely detailed to each other their sensations at different periods of their lives, some of which occurred under very peculiar circumstances. Two of them very circumstantially described the effect of witnessing an execu-tion at the Old Bailey. It appeared that they had not both been present at the same execution, yet their feelings were precisely similar, and the same day on which they were each spectators, led to the same results in each case. By the sym-bolism of the nerves we are informed that a consent of all the different parts of the body are kept up; but how the sensations of pleasure can be imparted when the mind is labouring under a feeling of horror at beholding the violent death of a fellow-creature, must be left for the solution of the phycologist[40] – he who has a knowledge of all science, human and divine. The same effects transpire under the punishment of flogging – *that is, priapism;*[41] the fact is in itself curious, and is here stated for a two-fold purpose; one, as it in some measure explains how the horror supposed to be produced by witnessing an execution is counteracted in young minds, and rendered nugatory as example, by the super-excitement of the other feelings of nature; and, secondly, as it points out the impropriety of accus-toming young persons to scenes of horror and high excitement, whether acted in real life, or on the stage. I should have much interesting matter to add on this subject, for the consideration of those who are fond of the study of human nature, but it must be perceived that there is an embarrassment attending any writer who may pursue this subject further: my object in alluding to the mystery, is to call the attention of government to the consideration of juveniles, and to recommend that a more efficient *surveillance* should be instituted over all theatrical exhibitions, and particularly that they should increase the penalties against those who open unlicensed places of amusement; a practice which is now very prevalent in every low neighbourhood. It was only on the 19th of last February, (1833,) that sixty-five persons were apprehended in the vicinity of Clarence market, Regent's Park; this capture took place in consequence of an intimation given by myself to the police. Had not an inhabitant of the parish interfered, it is probable the proprietors would have kept open the premises for months, as many others are doing, whilst I now write, to the utter ruin of all the children in the neighbourhood where the establishment is opened. The admittance to the place to which I allude was sixpence; at many it is as low as one penny, obtaining a new audience every hour. These things must not be allowed to be continued; nothing, however, but a board of public morals, armed with discretionary powers, to use the police as may be found necessary on any emergency, will meet the evil. If a proper example were made of a few of these panderers to the vitiated tastes of the juvenile and untaught members of this overgrown metropolis, the proprietors of these polluting exhibitions would in a short time be driven from their ground. They must, however, be made to feel the full weight of the law, and be taught that it cannot be violated with impunity. But so long as the profits of their calling exceed the penalties, what hope can reasonably be entertained of exterminating them from society in which their practices are so mischievous. I am, however, aware that many difficulties present themselves to the legislature in any attempt they may be disposed to make in circumscribing what are falsely called the recreations and amusements of the poorer classes. There is, however, one regulation which I think might be adopted without meeting with objection or opposition from any man, namely, that the proprietors of all theatres, other places of amusement, and public-houses, tea gardens, &c. &c. (i. e. of every place of entertainment,) should be prohibited, under pain of fine, &c. from admitting any boy or girl, under the apparent ages of fifteen years, unless in company with, and under the protection of, an adult. Although this measure would not entirely meet the evil, yet, it would throw so many obstacles in the way of young persons catering for themselves in matters of amusement, as to lessen the number of instances of corruption, and constrain youth to seek their pleasures through the concurrence only of their parents and guardians. Many licensed victuallers too pander to the appetites of youth, and betray them into crime; those who have back rooms in private parts of the town allow mere children to meet and dance the night through, providing them with music, lights, &c. for the sake of their custom, and other advantages they contrive to pick out of them, not unfrequently buying their stolen property; but cheating them in every way. I have myself known of thirty of these placed at one time, where females, but mere children to view, from twenty to fifty in number, might every night be seen, tawdrily decked out, with baldrick[42] and tiara, dancing with all the airs of a *Bona*

Roba,[43] with their fancy men. Sometimes, too, they mask it, by exchanging the whole, or part of each others dresses, or casmisating[44] themselves – an amusement always reserved for gala nights. These assemblies are flashly[45] designated cock and hen, chicken hops, or the freaks of the swell kids; uncoruncated Gynecocrasy[46] is the prevailing form of government among them, and the female's every vanity is gratified, through the males, at the public expense. Libidinous desires are early excited, and crime becomes (if not before known) contemporaneous with them. If heavy fines, and other penalties, were visited on those, whether licensed victuallers or any other persons, who harboured boys and girls, the progress of this growing evil might be arrested; but a mere law being placed in the statute books will not affect it: a board of morals, having the command of their own officers, especially informed on all these subjects, can only effectually put down these, and other nuisances to the public, which affect the morals of the people. [pp. 307–14]

CHAPTER VII.

CRIMES.

'How few sometimes may know when thousands err!'[47]
'But for the miracle,
I mean our preservation, few in millions
Can speak like us.'[48]

THE multiplicity of penal enactments in this country must, in the very nature of things, defeat those ends the attainment of which ought to be the object of all law, namely, *the prevention of crime*. Our criminal code exhibits too much the appearance of a heterogeneous mass, concocted too often on the spur of the occasion, (as Lord Bacon[49] expresses it,) and frequently without that degree of accuracy which is the result of able and minute discussion, or a due attention to the revision of the existing laws, or considering how far their provisions bear upon new and accumulated statutes introduced into parliament, often without either consideration or knowledge, and without those precautions which are always necessary when laws are to be made which may affect the property, the liberty, and perhaps even the lives of thousands.

To enter into the number and nature of the laws here, would occupy too much space; some notion of their sanguinary character may, however, be formed, when it is stated that, thirty years ago, there were upwards of *one hundred and sixty* different offences which subjected the parties who were found guilty of them to death, without benefit of clergy.[50] Although in the present day, notwithstanding the severity of the laws, the different modes of committing crime are almost endless, the principal actors in criminality may be classed under the following heads: –

Housebreakers	*Vulgus*—	Craksman, pannymen.
Highwaymen and footpads		Grand-tobymen and spicemen.
Coiners		Bit-makers.
Utterers of base metal		Smashers.
Pickpockets		Buzzmen, clyfakers, conveyancers.
Stealers of goods and money from shops, areas, &c. &c.		Sneaks.
Shoplifters		Shop-bouncers.
Snatchers of reticules, watches, &c. &c. from the person		Grabbers.
Horse and cattle stealers		Prad-chewers.
Women and men who waylay inebriate persons for the purpose of robbery		Ramps.
Receivers of stolen goods		Fences.
Forgers		Fakers.
Embezzlers		Bilkers.
Swindlers of every description, among which are		Macers, duffers, and ring-droppers.
Stealing from carts and carriages of all kinds		Dragsmen.
To which may be added, all kinds of plundering on the river and its banks, on board shipping, barges, &c.		Light-horsemen, heavy horsemen, game watermen, do. lightermen, scuffle-hunters, copemcn, &c.

The whole of these are carried on by confederacies of small parties, and at other times by gangs, when their operations become more extensive. The forger and the highwayman are exceptions; the latter offence is generally committed by one or more, in a fit of need and in a state of desperation, without any system or plan for carrying on the practice; and it may be affirmed that, in almost every case of this nature, the criminal never committed a like offence before. There have been some few instances of five or six individuals associating for the purpose of committing forgeries, but the cases are rare. [pp. 328–30]

from [William Crawford and Whitworth Russell], *Reports of the Inspectors Appointed under the Provisions of the Act 5 & 6 Will. IV. c. 38, to Visit the Different Prisons of Great Britain (I. Home District). Ordered, by the House of Commons, to be Printed, 22 March 1836.* pp. 47–8, 50–3, 56–7, 67–9.

As government became more organized and systematic in the formation of the early nineteenth-century state, the British Parliament aimed to keep itself informed of the condition of the prisons by appointing inspectors and receiving their annual reports, naming particular areas for investigation from time to time. In 1835 Parliament passed the Prison Act, establishing a prison inspectorate for the entire country. Part 1 of the 1836 report for the Home (i. e., England) department was an account of the inspectors' visit to Newgate; part 2 summarized the testimony of prison officers; part 3, from which the extracts here are taken, the testimony of prisoners; part 4, extracts from reports of the House of Commons and House of Lords and others over a period of years since 1814; and part 5, 'Inference', or conclusions to be drawn from the investigations. A special section dealt at some length with the issue of 'Juvenile Depredators', concluding that the extent of the 'problem' was over-stated, but serious enough, and making recommendations on the subject. A further section dealt with 'Criminal Lunatics'. Appendixes provided a plan for restructuring the space in Newgate, statistics and lists of various kinds, extracts from the chaplain's journals, extracts from the surgeon's (physician's) journal, and extracts from the earlier reports mentioned in part four.

Like many individual and parliamentary investigators before them, the authors of the 1836 report deplored conditions they observed in Newgate: inadequate record-keeping by prison officers; routine ignoring by officers and prisoners of regulations set down by law; little provision for prisoners to work; the availability of food and alcoholic drinks beyond that permitted by regulations; continued extortion of fees from prisoners; some prisoners with inadequate clothing; inadequate and filthy bedding, fighting among prisoners and physical abuse of each other, drunkenness, destroying prison property, commercial exploitation of the prisoners by prisoners appointed as warders, poor sanitary conditions and medical provision, opportunity for prisoners of different ages and sexes to communicate and meet, the persistence of gambling, presence of 'improper' reading materials such as 'indecent' books and Sunday newspapers and the ignoring of the Bible and religious books provided by philanthropic organizations. The inspectors seemed particularly alarmed by indications of various kinds of sexual impropriety: the admission of prostitutes to the prison as visitors, if not for sexual commerce then to socialize with and bring food and other things to male prisoners; the access of men convicted or accused of homosexual offences to each other, other men, and boys; and the fact that at least one female prisoner 'X. Y.') was being favoured by the governor because of her youth and attractiveness.

Although the Home Department Report of 1836 contains a great deal of information and purports to be a rational analysis of it, the document's conclusions and recommendations are in fact driven by the agenda of its authors, Crawford and Russell. Crawford (1788–1847) was prepared for a career in commerce but converted to Evangelicalism, focusing his energies on prison reform and especially the issue of juvenile offenders. In 1833 he was sent to the United States by the government to study the rival penal systems there, and became a supporter of the 'Philadelphia' system of separate confinement and work. He had long been associated with the Quaker prison reformers, most famous of whom was Elizabeth Fry. Russell was the former chaplain of Millbank Penitentiary, opened in 1821 and based on a plan of the utilitarian Jeremy Bentham, also emphasizing separate confinement and work. Together Crawford and Russell would be unrelenting advocates of the 'separate' system of grouping prisoners in appropriately designed prisons; confining prisoners in individual cells to eliminate mutual corruption and encourage reflection, repentance and reform; enforcing work and education; and facilitating transportation, or (forcible) 'emigration', of convicts to the colonies. Having obtained the support of prime minister Lord John Russell, over the next decade Russell and Crawford, with the engineer Joshua Jebb (1793–1863), set about restructuring Britain's prisons, criminal legislation, and penal system to this program, leaving an architectural and administrative legacy that persists today.

Note on the text: one silent correction has been made.

WE now proceed to lay before your Lordship the Third Part of our Report: – Statements received from various prisoners, who either are at present, or have been recently confined in Newgate.

In putting forward, as evidence, the statements of prisoners, we beg to state the sole ground on which we have felt ourselves justified in accepting the testimony of such characters. Where the declaration of any prisoner was not sustained by collateral testimony, we have invariably rejected it; but whenever the testimony of the prisoner has been supported by the unvarying statements of others, between whom and himself there could not by possibility have been any intercourse or concert; when his testimony has been corroborated by the attestations of officers of the prison, as well as by the very nature of the case; when, further, the prisoner's testimony has been borne out by facts of which we ourselves were witnesses in the course of our numerous visits to the gaol, by day and by night; then we felt that this accumulation of evidence gave to the declaration of the first witness, though otherwise of doubtful credit, the force and weight of demonstrative certainty: and of this unquestionable character is the evidence we now adduce. [pp. 47–8]

C. D—. Is about 21 years of age. Was in Newgate about a month, a fortnight before trial, and a fortnight after. Was in the Receiving Ward the first two nights; paid 1 *d.* to the wardsman, for ward dues, the first night. Was so uncomfortable, that the next night he paid the wardsman 6 *d.* for a bed. The wardsman, who was a prisoner under sentence of seven years' transportation, had this privilege allowed him: he was complete master of that ward, and would not allow prisoners to make coffee for themselves; they must buy it of him if they wanted it, at 3 *d.* a basin-full. The wardsman used to get in a quantity of tobacco, and sell it out in pennyworths. All was quiet and still in that ward: prisoners seldom remain there more than one night. Was then examined by the Surgeon,[1] and removed to No. 21 ward, on the Master's Side: that is a more respectable yard than the Middle Yard. On entering that ward, he had to pay the wardsman 1 *s.* for ward dues: if refused, he would make them uncomfortable; and not allow them the use of a thing; nor even let them come near the fire, if he could prevent it. By paying the wardsman his fees, prisoners are allowed to make their own tea and coffee. If you have a flock bed[2] of the wardsman, instead of lying on the mats, he charges 2 *s.* 6 *d.* a week: prisoner and another joined together for a bed: it was more than he could afford to have a bed to himself. The wardsman made a collection every night amongst the men in the ward for candles; some nights he would collect 3 *d.* some nights more. He also used to sell to his fellow-prisoners tobacco and pipes, sugar and butter, and sometimes bacon and cheese, which his wife brought him in on the Sunday while the others were at chapel. He also sold beer to any prisoner who wanted more than the allowance, and which he took at the time the beer was brought to the Yard gate, three times a day, from one o'clock to three. The wardsman would take in two pails full and a large stone bottle full of beer, and lock it up in a cupboard, which he had for his use. This beer he would sell out to the prisoners in his own ward after they were locked up at night, at a profit. Gambling was going on continually every day; pitch and toss, shoving halfpence on the table, &c. No card-playing in the ward where he was; but in — ward, in the same yard, card-playing went on frequently: has seen the prisoners there playing at cards, and also at dominoes; and has seen quarrels and fighting through it, and the cards burnt. Has seen from 10 *s.* to 1 *l.*³ worth of silver on the card-table at one time. Prisoners could get almost as much beer as they liked: has seen one man take two pots of beer for himself at dinner-time, besides what he would want in the evening. It was seldom the wardsman had enough to supply all that wanted. After locking-up time, some would be gambling at one of the tables; others would be sitting around the fire singing and smoking, and talking all kinds of beastly talk, and of their crimes, and their different acts of cleverness in committing them, and putting one another up to it. The singing consisted of noisy, beastly songs. This would be going on sometimes until nearly twelve o'clock at night; but the lights were put out generally at ten o'clock. It was not safe to have money or a silk handkerchief, or anything else of value in one's pocket. Prisoner lost a silk handkerchief and two new pocket-combs, whilst walking round the yard; he got the combs returned to him, by offering 1 *s.* reward, but never knew who took them. They call picking pockets their *work*, and the more cleverly any one can do it, the more he is thought of. —, who is also a prisoner, is allowed by the Governor the privilege of writing briefs and petitions for his fellow-prisoners. For a brief of two sheets he charges 5 *s.* Prisoner was allowed to go from his own ward (the keys of which the turnkey used to leave with —) to — room, after locking-up time, to assist him in writing, for which he was allowed by — 1 *s.* for every brief and petition he wrote; also a good supper, and as much ale as he liked to drink. — used to be so much intoxicated nearly every night, as to be unable to write himself; was generally quite stupid with drinking every night, and would sometimes lie down on the bed two or three hours to recover himself. He would always have the money from the prisoners before he delivered them the brief or petition. — was also allowed the privilege of selling writing paper to the prisoners. The wardsman was allowed a double prison allowance, besides a quantity of stale prison bread, which he would get at times. This bread he would sell at 3 ½ *d.* or 4 *d.* the two-pound loaf, to the other prisoners. The prisoners got in what they wanted mostly through their friends, except porter and bread. If what their friends brought did not serve until they came again, they would purchase of the wardsman. A bible and prayer-book were allowed in the ward, but chiefly made game of; there was no chance of making use of it profitably. Prisoner was once going to write a brief for a poor prisoner, who could not afford to employ —, for which he was to be paid a trifle, but — threatened to report him to Mr. Cope, the Governor, as it was a privilege allowed him. All untried prisoners in this ward, except the wardsman, who was under sentence of two or three months' imprisonment; about twenty-two slept in one room on mats, &c. The Governor only came into the ward once during the three weeks prisoner was there. He came then in consequence of the prisoners having set fire to the bedding. They were pitching halfpence on the mats to prevent noise; some of them got larking, and upset the candles, by which accident about three of the beds caught fire. There happened to be three pails of water and a pail of cold skilly (gruel) locked up with them, with which they extinguished the flames. It was the next morning that the Governor came. He inquired how it was done. The prisoners said it was an accident. The wardsman told him that one of the prisoners was washing on one of the stools, and upset the candle. He told them to be careful in future. — came every morning about 10 o'clock. He walked through the wards and looked behind the mats, to see that there were no holes in the wall. There was no regular inspection kept up by the turnkeys; they only appeared to come when they had anything to say to the wardsman. After trial, was removed, with other prisoners, to the North Side. All tried prisoners there under sentence of transportation. The wardsman there was a transport for life. The riot, confusion, and swearing there, were worse than in the former yard. A shilling for ward dues was there demanded by the wardsman, though but seldom obtained. He had no beds to let, nor anything to sell but a few tobacco pipes; he had no convenience for taking in beer to sell; he had a double prison allowance, part of which he sometimes sold to his fellow-prisoners; he made a collection every night for candles, but got very little. There was a more respectable ward in that yard, where the ward dues were too high for most. The wardsman's name in that ward was —, a prisoner under sentence of seven years' transportation. Prisoners could have almost as much beer as they could drink in that ward, by purchasing it. They would frequently join together and take in two pails full when it was brought in, which was only once a day there. The wardsman handed the beer from the beer-man to the prisoners. Smoking, drinking, and gambling, went on there as in the other yard. There was no restraint: the officer only just went round, night and morning, to count the prisoners, and lock and unlock them; the rest was left to the wardsman. The prison allowance is brought to the yard gate, where the wardsman receives and distributes it amongst the prisoners in the wards. Has seen card-playing in — ward, but no money posted down. There were about thirty in the ward where prisoner was; all slept in one room. Each prisoner was allowed a mat and two rugs: some would sleep two together; some three, some four, and some singly. After locking up, till about 11 o'clock, smoking, drinking, singing, and all sorts of filthy conversation were going on; also tossing for money. Has seen some lose and win as much as 4 *s.* or 5 *s.* in an hour. They would toss on a mat to prevent noise. As he expected to be removed to the hulk[4] every day, he paid no ward dues, except 1 *d.* now and then for candles. — was allowed the privilege of writing petitions for prisoners, and selling writing paper. All the prisoners, tried and untried, went to chapel every morning at 10 o'clock for prayers, which are read by the Chaplain. All the morning service and lessons are read, and sometimes a short sermon out of the Book of Homilies. There are two services on the Sunday, a sermon in the morning, and prayers in the afternoon. He never saw the Chaplain in his ward or yard while he was there. He might have gone to the condemned cells. They went to chapel every morning, and twice on Sundays. Some of the prisoners went to chapel in a very ragged state; some without coats, shoes, or stockings. When the weather was cold, some would make shoes of the rugs; has seen some with rugs tied round their legs. The Surgeon never came, except to examine prisoners coming in or going out. If a prisoner was taken ill he could send for him; but he was generally a long time coming. Prisoners used to practice pocket picking. Was in that yard about a fortnight. Friends can bring prisoners what cooked victuals, tobacco, or money, they like, when they visit them. The prisoners used to contribute and have a Sunday paper regularly, generally the Weekly Dispatch,[5] on Sunday mornings. It would sometimes be lent to the other wards that could not afford to purchase one. — was employed to write briefs for the female prisoners, as well as for the male, and was allowed to go to the Women's Side to take down their statements. Prostitutes were admitted to see male prisoners; they used to bring money, clean linen, &c. for their men. He knew them to be prostitutes by their language, which he overheard when they visited. If female visitors were admitted as friends only, the interview was held in the visiting room, where they were kept about a yard and a half apart by gratings; but there was no restraint on their conversation. He has no doubt whatever of their profession, because he used to hear them telling their men how sorry they were they had not been able to bring more money, but that they had had bad nights. Several of the lowest prisoners in Middle Yard used to keep the lowest description of prostitutes, who were admitted to come and see them; they were, in fact, the girls with whom these prisoners used to live when at liberty, and whom they used to support by thieving. He used to hear the prisoners of the Middle Yard calling to those on the Master's Side, telling them who had been to see them; and by the flash names and language they used, he had no doubt that they were talking of prostitutes. There was a man of the name of —, under sentence of transportation for life; he kept a girl of the name of —, who came to see him two or three times a week, dressed very fine, and used to supply — with money and clean linen. The Governor admitted her on those days which were not visiting days. These visits of — to — took place both before and after trial. The relation of — and — was notorious through the prison, as the whole affair regarding their offence appeared in the

Weekly Dispatch of the 5th or 12th of April, and the prisoners used to joke him about it. There was also a man of the name of —, whose girl used to come, that was transported for 14 years for passing base coin. The turnkeys admitted her as his wife, but used to tell the prisoners she was not. — used to boast that he had left a quantity of bad half sovereigns[6] with his girl, which he expected she would pass. She brought him a handsome great coat, dress coat, trousers and waistcoat, in which he went up to be tried. — would laugh and say, 'She must have gulled some of the flats[7] finely' to have got him those things. Male prisoners occasionally are permitted to go round to see the female prisoners. There was a married man of the name of —, who was allowed to go round and see —, a servant girl with whom he had cohabited. They were both in Newgate for the same offence, stealing a watch from — mistress. She cleared him on their trial, out of consideration for — family. She behaved better to him than he did to her. — was very unkind to her. — drew up their brief, by which means he became acquainted with this fact. He does not know whether the Governor sanctioned this visit; it took place on a Sunday. [pp. 50–3]

L. M—, about 47 years of age. Was in Newgate from the latter part of January 1835, until the 10th of June. When first committed, was in the Receiving Ward one night. The wardsman's name was —, a prisoner under sentence of transportation. Does not recollect paying any thing on entering. He had the wardsman's bed, and some refreshment from him, some coffee, knuckle of ham, and he believes some beer. He and a young man who went in with him paid the wardsman 4 *s.* for the two, for tea, bed, and breakfast; which he thought very cheap. The time he was there was so short, that he had but little opportunity of seeing what was going on: there were several wards in that yard in which were a great many of the worst characters. He had to pass through that yard several times afterwards, for trial, for sentence, &c. when he could see a little what was going on there. They attempted to pick his and others' pockets, while merely passing through the yard on their way to the Court. Next morning early was examined by the Surgeon, and removed into Chapel Yard, No. 10 Ward, which is the most respectable Ward in that yard, being kept so by being more expensive than the others; but although they were considered the better class of prisoners, yet their language was most reprehensible, and proved that the most of them were only more respectable in dress. Each prisoner paid 2 *s.* 6 *d.* per week to the wardsman for a bed, crockery ware, &c.; had to pay 2 *s.* 6 *d.* at first, which was considered a week's pay in advance. None in that Ward lived entirely on the prison allowance, but mostly on what they received from their friends. They had tea, coffee, cooked meat, tobacco, snuff, and other articles, brought in by their friends, as much as they liked. The beer-man brought in beer every day, about the middle of the day: a pint of porter was the supposed allowance for each prisoner to have in a day, but they were not confined to that quantity; he might have had a gallon a day, if he liked: is sure that several in that ward drank a gallon of porter a day. The wardsman's name was —: he did not sell much to the others at a profit. When prisoners first came into the ward, the wardsman supplied them with meals, until such times as they could get their provisions; thinks he charged 6 *d.* for a breakfast, &c. He also used to sell his spare bread, of which he had a great deal, to the poorer prisoners of that and the next Yard. He did not take in beer to sell to the other prisoners; but Wardsmen of other Wards in that Yard did so: occasionally himself, and others in his Ward, bought beer of them. They also sold tobacco, and sometimes a little butter, to the other prisoners; but the Wardsman in his Ward did not sell such articles. The latter part of the time that prisoner was in that Ward, a footing[8] of a gallon of beer was required of every new comer. There were other fines for bad manners, &c.; this money was all laid out in beer, which was taken in a pail, and divided fairly amongst the prisoners in the Ward; it would sometimes be three or four gallons. The money which was lost at cards and draughts,[9] which was not very considerable, being only a penny a rubber,[10] was spent in beer also; sometimes they would toss for beer, and two or three times they had a lottery, a few prizes and many blanks; those who drew the prizes were exempt from paying: this money was spent in beer also, for the evening. The draughts were in the Ward when prisoner was first placed there, and no particular notice was taken of them, as they seldom played until towards the evening, mostly after locking-up time. The cards were only in the Ward about two months; they were brought in by a prisoner's wife. The cards and draughts were taken away by the Governor a week or two before prisoner left Newgate, on his being informed what was going on there by a prisoner who had left that Ward, and had been removed to the Infirmary. There were about twelve in the Ward where he was; they were locked up about dusk, which, when he first went in, was about four o'clock; after which some would play at cards, some at draughts, and some few would read until supper time, which was eight o'clock. After supper, they used to draw round the fire, and drink the beer, smoke their pipes, sing songs, and tell any stories they liked. There was much swearing and bad language, the very worst that could be used, from the first thing in the morning until the last at night. Ten o'clock was the hour for going to bed, when the lights were ordered to be put out; but some would sit up later, until eleven or twelve o'clock occasionally, but were very quiet at that late hour. He was in that ward about a week before trial, and between four and five months after. —, (imprisoned for shooting at —,) was in that ward: he was supported principally by the other prisoners: he was the only person that prisoner saw intoxicated, though some others used to drink an immense quantity of beer. A less quantity took effect on —, from his having been longer in confinement. Prisoners who had money or friends to supply them, could live very well both before and after trial. Some would get in whole joints of meat cooked. No spirits allowed; never saw any in the ward but once, and then no great quantity. After trial prisoners could see their friends once a week; before trial, three times. Prostitutes were admitted to see the prisoners and bring them things. Prisoner judges that they were prostitutes by their manner and dress. Prisoner has seen three or four visiting some prisoners, and has known others to be denied that privilege. Recollects a case where a young man was visited by a young woman of loose character with whom he had cohabited, and who was recognised by another prisoner who had also had intercourse with her. While they were together, the young man's mother came, and was refused admittance.

There were several in that ward for forgery. No housebreakers or pickpockets. Conversation generally was of an indecent nature, or about crime, and swearing. There was a young man named —, an attorney's clerk, brought to that ward; he had absconded with about 300 *l.* of his master's property. He was very quiet when he first came, but prisoner saw a great change in him for the worse before he left; went out perfectly hardened, cursing and swearing in the most outrageous manner. Newgate must have the same effect, he thinks, on all who are not well fortified in their minds against every kind of corruption and wickedness.

They were occasionally visited by the Ladies, who read and expounded the scriptures, and distributed tracts, which would soon be destroyed after the ladies were gone. All the prisoners went to chapel for prayers every morning at ten o'clock, for about twenty minutes, and twice on the Sunday. Could not complain much of the behaviour there, as the eyes of the officers were on them more in chapel; but when they came out, the same bad language, gambling, &c. went on. In the Ward where prisoner was, they took in a daily paper and a Sunday paper, regularly, which were paid for by subscription; those that read it contributed towards paying for it. The following day it was generally sold to another Ward at something less than half price. They used to lend the Dispatch to the principal turnkey on the Monday; it could be handed from their ward window into the officer's apartment, or sent by his son, who was almost always within call for the purpose of running on errands for the prisoners, for which they would pay him a penny or twopence a time. The Governor was in the habit of visiting the Ward every Sunday, and about once or twice a week besides. When he had to make any communication to a prisoner, he was always attended by a turnkey. The Chaplain came only on a Sunday after morning service. The Surgeon came only when prisoners were going out, unless sent for. The principal turnkeys came to lock and unlock, and generally once a day besides, to look round the wards, and see if any attempts had been made to break out. On one occasion the turnkeys remained in the yard nearly the whole day, he supposes in consequence of some report; but this was not continued more than two or three days. The assistant turnkey brings the keys of the Ward up into the Ward, and leaves them with the

Wardsman, or any other prisoner if he is not at hand, about a quarter of an hour before locking-up time. [pp. 56–7]

2 *R. S.* Aged about 41 years. Was committed to Newgate on the 18th of March 1835. The first night she was in the Receiving Ward had no half-pence to give the wardswoman; it was customary to give her 2 *d.* for the loan of her tea-things. There were five in the ward that night; all was very quiet there. They slept on mats, and had blankets and rugs for covering. The wardswoman went to Mrs. —'s shop and bought some tea and sugar for prisoner, and she made her own tea, and had some of the prison bread. The next morning she was examined by the Surgeon and removed to the Untried Side, No. 5 ward. There were three wards open in that yard. The ward called the Servants' Ward was the most respectable; but the Matron said there was no room for prisoner in that ward. In the ward where she was placed, the number at first was about twelve or fourteen, but it increased before trial to thirty or more. All slept on the floor on mats; at last they were obliged to sleep three on two mats, and each three had three blankets and two rugs for covering. In the day most of them were out in the yard occasionally, where there was the most shocking language, swearing, and telling every thing they had done, whom they had robbed, and where they had been; she never witnessed such scenes before, and hopes she never shall again; it was dreadful! Would rather die in the Penitentiary than go through such scenes again. They were locked up about six or seven o'clock, she thinks by Mrs. —, the Matron. Those who were poor, and could afford nothing but the prison allowance, went to bed early; others who had money, and friends to bring them things, would have supper, and sit up until 10 or 11 o'clock. After locking-up they would frequently quarrel, and very often fight; throw their shoes, and whatever they could get, at each other; and the most dreadful oaths, and the worst language, too bad to be repeated, were made use of almost every night. The Matron was frequently up in the night, by their quarrelling and fighting. One night she expected to have been killed through a quarrel between two of the women; one threw a pannikin (what the prisoners eat their soup and gruel out of) at the other, and it fell on prisoner's bed. The wardswoman, —, was a prisoner under sentence of transportation; she appeared to be a decent woman; some of the others did not like to be kept under by the wardswoman; and that occasioned some of the quarrelling; they said she was nothing better than themselves. Prisoner paid the wardswoman 6 *d.* for the use of her tea-things. The beer-man, she believes, came in once a day; the wardswoman took the beer that the prisoners wanted in a pail, which she took up to her room, and those who wanted it at night she used to let them have it; prisoner never had but two half pints of beer whilst in that ward; she had but little money, and could not afford it; a great many others in that ward had no beer. Has heard them say that each prisoner was allowed to purchase a pint of

beer a day; but as a great many in that ward had none, others who could afford it might have more than the allowance if the wardswoman had it to spare. The wardswoman took all the beer for the prisoners. Saw no one tipsy in that ward or yard: never saw a newspaper in that ward: no men prisoners were employed in that yard whilst she was there, that she saw, except one coming into the ward with coals once a week. Saw no communication between him and the women prisoners; never saw any communication between the men and women prisoners in Chapel; they could not see each other, the screen cut off all the view, and next the screen the Matron and one of the men officers sat. Some of the girls would go on with nonsense, and be noisy sometimes in Chapel, but the Matron used to check them for it. Never heard of men prisoners writing briefs for the women; prisoners could see their friends three times a week before trial. Her daughter visited her once a week generally, and brought her any little thing she wanted, such as tea and sugar, and, once or twice, a little cooked meat. The ladies came once or twice a week, and sometimes oftener, and would talk to them, and pray with them, and give them tracts, &c. The prisoners appeared generally attentive while the ladies were there, but as soon as they were gone they used to go on with their old games. After trial she was removed to No. 8 Ward, on the Tried Side. There were three wards open in that yard. The Ward she was in was called the Ladies' Ward. It was a remarkably clean and strict Ward. The Wardswoman, —, a prisoner under sentence of transportation, was very strict; suffered no bad language, nor any communication between the prisoners of other Wards and those in her Ward, if she could help it: but in the Yard all could mix together. The Tried Side was better than the Untried Side, but there was much bad language used there. One Ward particularly was very bad, where there used to be quarrelling and fighting at night; the Matron was obliged to be called there sometimes at night. In the Ward where prisoner was there were eight; all were very quiet and peaceable. She paid the Wardswoman 6 *d.* for the use of tea-things. Each prisoner was allowed to purchase a pint of beer a day there; some would fetch it themselves, and for some the Wardswoman would bring it; none in that Ward drank more than a pint a day, and some drank none. The gateswoman at Mrs. —'s gate, —, who used to take in the letters and parcels for the prisoners, got very drunk one night, and made a great disturbance. She lost her place in consequence. She was a prisoner under sentence of transportation. That was the only time prisoner ever heard a piece of work through the drunkenness of any prisoner. Other prisoners used to say that all the Wardswomen used to drink a great deal, but prisoner never saw any of them tipsy. There was no communication with the men prisoners in that yard, more than in the other. The one that came to the Ward with coals once a week was the only one she saw. Went to Mrs. —'s shop for things sometimes; never saw any men prisoners there. At the time there was a soldier tried there for murder, they in that ward clubbed together one

Sunday, and had a newspaper to have an account of his trial. The Wardswoman got it for them; that was the only newspaper she saw whilst in that yard. What that Wardswoman did with it afterwards she does not know. Prisoners' friends could visit them only once a week there; they could bring them anything, as before trial, only every thing that passed in was examined by the gateswoman that got drunk; never saw any spirits whilst in Newgate. The Ladies visited that Side oftener than the other; they used to read and pray with the prisoners in the Wards; and every Friday the prisoners went to the Committee Room, where the Ladies used to talk to them, and read the Scriptures and pray with them: most of them were very attentive at the time, but after they were gone, many of the young girls were just as wild and giddy as before. The Governor came to the Ward where she was, about once a week, and sometimes twice; would just look round and ask if there were any complaints, and go off again. Has seen him in the Yard on the Untried Side frequently, but not in the Yard on the Tried Side, except just to go through to the Wards. The Matron visited the Ward every day; would just come in and look round, and talk to the Wardswoman about the Ward and go off again. The matron on the Tried Side was Mrs. —. Never saw the Surgeon in the Wards, or in the Yards. She saw him twice whilst in Newgate; when she first came in, and the morning before she left; both times near Mrs. Brown's gate. Never saw the Chaplain in the Wards; once saw him go through the Yard, when she inquired who he was. Does not exactly know who locked and unlocked the prisoners, but thinks it was —, the gateswoman; has heard the Wardswoman say that she could not go out to the Governor's apartments, which she used to clean every morning, until — unlocked. There were some Bibles and other religious books in her Ward, and a monitor appointed, that used to read every night to them. Before trial she had no work, but after trial the Matron supplied those with needle-work that could do it; and the Ladies supplied others with knitting. [pp. 67–9] from *Memoir of the Life of Elizabeth Fry, with Extracts from Her Journal and Letters*, ed. Katherine Fry and Rachel Elizabeth Cresswell, 2 vols (London: Charles Gilpin; John Hatchard and Son, 1847), vol. 1, ch. 9.

Elizabeth Fry (1780–1845) was a member of the large and well-to-do Quaker family of Gurneys of Norwich. As a child she was nervous and a slow learner, and experienced a spiritual conversion in 1798; her strong religious feeling would bolster her life of social activism, often verging on feminism, as seen in the passages cited here. In 1800 she married Joseph Fry of a Quaker mercantile family and bore eleven children. She was active in a variety of charities for the poor, campaigned for vaccination against smallpox, and in 1813 found her most famous calling after visiting the women's side of Newgate Prison. The conditions there appalled her and she set about improving them with the help of women associates, usually supported by their men family members. She developed an increasingly formal organization and won official approval for her work, marked by the formation in 1817 of the Ladies Association for the Reformation of the Female Prisoners in Newgate. Described and promoted by Fry and others over the next few decades, the Ladies' plan of reformation was widely hailed and taken at face value, though there is evidence that many of the beneficiaries of their attention calculated it was in their interest to go along with the Ladies' schemes (see for example the testimony of Newgate prisoners in the passages in this volume from the 1836 Reports of the Inspectors of Prisons). Nevertheless, the direct action of Fry and her associates set an example to many other humanitarians and reformers, and to this day the many societies around the world for assisting imprisoned women are named after Elizabeth Fry.

This biography – or hagiography – of Fry celebrates her while quietly disclosing the emotional and psychological tensions she suffered for engaging in social work and activism of kinds usually closed to women and often disapproved of as unfeminine, but yet exploited by numbers of nineteenth-century women as a way to enter the public sphere.

Note on the text: the present editor's omission is indicated by [...]; spellings such as 'your's' for 'yours' and 'her's' for 'hers' were accepted variants at the time the book was published.

CHAPTER IX.

1817, 1818. Extract from Crabbe's Poems—Letter to her sister—General state of Prisons—School in Newgate—Case of Elizabeth Fricker—Newgate Association—Description from Buxton—Sophia de C—'s Journal—Vote of thanks from the City—Letters from Robert Barclay, Esq., &c.—Letters to her daughters—Notice in newspapers—Marriage of her brother, Joseph John Gurney—Extracts from letters—Winter in London—Examinations before House of Commons.

> One, I beheld! a wife, a mother, go
> To gloomy scenes of wickedness and woe;
> She sought her way through all things vile and base
> And made a prison a religious place:
> Fighting her way – the way that angels fight
> With powers of darkness – to let in the light:
> Tell me, my heart, hast thou such victory won,
> As this, a sinner of thy sex, hast done,
> And calls herself a sinner! what art thou?
> And where thy praise and exaltation now?
> Yet, she is tender, delicate and nice,
> And shrinks, from all depravity and vice;
> Shrinks from the ruffian gaze, the savage gloom,
> That reign where guilt and misery find a home;
> Guilt chained, and misery purchased, and with them
> All we abhor, abominate, condemn –
> The look of scorn, the scowl, th' insulting leer,
> Of shame, all fixed on her who ventures here,
> Yet all she braved; she kept her stedfast eye
> On the dear cause, and brushed the baseness by. –
> So would a mother press her darling child
> Close to her breast, with tainted rags defiled.[1]

When death has set his seal on the past, and stamped his sacred impress on the motives and actions of the departed Christian, we find a solemn pleasure in contemplating his deeds; but when those deeds are recorded by one, who has himself put off mortality, our interest becomes deepened, and we can but dwell upon the marvellous consideration of their present state of being – their thoughts – their feelings – now that, the veil of the flesh removed, they see no longer as in a glass darkly, but face to face.[2]

These lines were written by Mr. Crabbe in allusion to Mrs. Fry; his acquaintance with her was slight, but his deep reading of the human heart enabled him to appreciate her undertakings, and the personal sacrifices at which they were made.

Mildred's Court, Second Month 24*th*. – I have lately been much occupied in forming a school in Newgate, for the children of the poor prisoners, as well as the young criminals, which has brought much peace and satisfaction with it; but my mind has also been deeply affected in attending a poor woman who was executed this morning. I visited her twice; this event has brought me into much feeling, attended by some distressingly nervous sensations in the night, so that this has been a time of deep humiliation to me; thus witnessing the effect and consequences of sin. This poor creature murdered her baby; and how inexpressibly awful to have her life taken away! The whole affair has been truly afflicting to me; to see what poor mortals may be driven to, through sin and transgression, and how hard the heart becomes, even to the most tender affections. How should we watch and pray, that we fall not by little and little, and become hardened, and commit greater sins. I had to pray for these poor sinners this morning, and also for the preservation of our household from the evil there is in the world.

Extract from a letter to her sister, Rachel Gurney: –

Mildred's Court, *Third Month* 10*th* and 11*th*.

My heart, and mind, and time, are very much engaged in various ways. Newgate is a principal object, and I think until I make some attempt at amendment in the plans for the women, I shall not feel easy; but if such efforts should prove unsuccessful, I think that I should then have tried to do my part and be easy. My own Monthly Meeting, though absent from it, is rather a weight, and Gracechurch Street I am also much interested about. I have gone besides to only one London Meeting, all the time that I have been here. The poor occupy me little more than at the door – as I cannot go after them, with my other engagements; the hanging at Newgate does not overcome me as it did at first, and I have only attended one woman since the first. I see and feel the necessity of caution in this respect, and mean to be on my guard about it, and run no undue risk with myself.

I have felt in thy taking care of my dearest girls, that thou art helping me to get on with some of these important objects, that I could not well have attended to, if I had had all my dear flock round me.

The disgraceful state in which many of the prisons of the British empire were found, thirty years ago, excites our astonishment: and we naturally seek to account for the continuance of so crying an evil.

That the sceptical philosophy which prevailed towards the end of the last century, was unfavourable to questions of moral and religious reform, we cannot doubt. Whether the startling events of the French Revolution – the tremendous wars that followed it – the rise and fall of empires – had so engrossed the attention and drained the resources of the English nation, that improvement at home was neglected; or, whether looking to a still deeper source, it may be attributed to that tendency to degenerate, inherent in all human institutions; whatever the cause may have been; the fact is indisputable. Howard[3] and his humane exertions appear to have been forgotten; and Acts of Parliament to have become almost a dead letter: some, if not all the provisions of those acts, being in the vast majority of gaols, openly violated. For Counties as well as Boroughs, an old gatehouse, or the ancient feudal castle, with its dungeons, its damp, close, and narrow cells, and its windows overlooking the street, often formed the common prison of offenders of either sex, and of all grades of crime. The danger of escape was provided against, by heavy irons and fetters. Dirt and disease abounded; and even where the building contained wards and yards, the women were imperfectly separated from the men, whilst idleness, gambling, drinking, and swearing, were habitual amongst them. These evils were magnified by the crowded state of the prisons; for crime had enormously increased; and convictions had more than doubled within the ten preceding years. Of the prisons for the counties, those of Bury, Ilchester, Gloucester, and a few others, formed honourable exceptions to the general rule; and in the Metropolis, the Penitentiary at Millbank, which had been recently erected.[4]

The moral contamination produced by the disorderly state of prisons, was beginning to be perceived, and the necessity for stricter discipline and better regulations to be acknowledged.

In the United States of America, and in a few instances on the continent of Europe, the experiment had been tried; and with such success, as to establish the principle, that classification, employment and instruction tended to the reformation of the criminal, and to the decrease of crime. A deputation of the Gaol Committee of the Corporation of London was appointed, in 1815, to visit several gaols in England, especially that of Gloucester, with a view to the amelioration of those under their own jurisdiction. From this resulted some improvements in Newgate. The women from that time occupied the whole of the quadrangle, now called the 'women's side;' including what were formerly the state apartments; mats were provided for them to sleep on. Double gratings, with a space between, were placed to prevent close communication with their visitors, who were of both sexes, and many of them as vile and desperate as themselves: but to overcome the difficulty thus presented, in receiving the contributions of those whose curiosity brought them to the spot; wooden spoons fastened to long sticks were contrived by the prisoners, and thrust across the intervening space. Notwithstanding these improvements, they remained in an unchecked condition of idleness, riot, and vice of every description. They were of the lowest sort – the very scum both of the town and country – filthy in their persons, disgusting in their habits, and ignorant, not only of religious truth, but of the most familiar duties of common life.

At the suggestion of her brother-in-law, the late Samuel Hoare,[5] Esq., Mrs. Fry had, in the interval between 1813 and 1816, accompanied him in a visit to the women in Cold Bath Fields House of Correction, whose neglected state had much impressed him. Mr. Hoare, with another of her brothers-in-law, the late Sir T. F. Buxton, and some of her personal friends, were at this time occupied in forming a society for the reformation of the juvenile depredators, who infested London, in gangs. This object led them into different prisons, where their attention was soon attracted to the subject of prison discipline. Although not originating in this cause, it may be presumed, that the conversation and influence of these gentlemen would tend to keep alive, in the mind of Mrs. Fry, the interest awakened in 1813, for the female prisoners in Newgate. As in that instance, so at this time, her journal fails to convey any explicit information respecting her visits there. We are indebted to other sources, for the fact, that they were recommenced about Christmas, 1816.

On her second visit, she was, at her own request, left alone amongst the women for some hours; and on that occasion, she read to them the parable of the Lord of the vineyard, in the 20th chapter of St. Matthew; and made a few observations on the eleventh hour, and on Christ having come to save sinners, even those who might be said to have wasted the greater part of their lives, estranged from Him. Some asked who Christ was; others feared that their day of salvation was passed.

The children, who were almost naked, were pining for want of proper food, air, and exercise. Mrs. Fry, on this occasion, particularly addressed herself to the mothers, and pointed out to them the grievous consequences to their children, of living in such a scene of depravity; she proposed to establish a school for them, to which they acceded with tears of joy. She desired them to consider the plan, for without their steady co-operation she would not undertake it; leaving it to them, to select a governess from amongst themselves. On her next visit, they had chosen as schoolmistress, a young woman, named Mary Connor;[6] who proved eminently qualified for her task. She had been recently committed for stealing a watch; and became one of the first-fruits of Christian labour in that place: she was assiduous in her duties, and was never known to infringe one of the rules. A free pardon was granted her about fifteen months afterwards; but this proved an unavailing gift, for a cough, which had attacked her a short time previously, ended in consumption. She displayed, during her illness, much patience and quietness of spirit; having, as she humbly believed, obtained everlasting pardon and peace, through the merits of her Lord and Saviour. She died in this hope, 'full of immortality.'

Mrs. Fry's views were received with cordial approbation, by the Sheriffs of London, the Ordinary,[7] and the Governor of Newgate; although they looked upon it as an almost hopeless experiment. An unoccupied cell was, by their permission, appropriated for the school-room. On the day following this arrangement, Mrs. Fry, accompanied by her friend, Mary Sanderson, and with the poor prisoner, Mary Connor, as mistress, opened the school, for the children and young persons under twenty-five years of age. But from the small size of the room, they had the pain of being obliged to refuse admission to many of the women, who earnestly entreated to be allowed to share in their instructions. Mary Sanderson then visited a prison for the first time, and her feelings were thus described by herself to Sir T. F. Buxton.

'The railing was crowded with half-naked women, struggling together for the front situations, with the most boisterous violence; and begging with the utmost vociferation. She felt as if she were going into a den of wild beasts, and she well recollects quite shuddering when the door closed upon her, and she was locked in with such a herd of novel and desperate companions.'

Something similar must have been the effect on that faithful co-adjutor in this work, Elizabeth Pryor, at rather a later period, upon seeing the women, squalid in attire and ferocious in countenance, seated about the yard. From the prison door a female issued, 'yelling like a wild beast;' (these were Mrs. Pryor's own words:) she rushed round the area with her arm extended, tearing everything of the nature of a cap from the heads of the other women. The sequel too is important; for this very woman, through the grace and mercy of God, became humanized, under the instruction of the ladies. After having obtained her liberty, she married; and for years came occasionally to see Mrs. Pryor, who considered her a well-conducted person; her appearance being always most respectable.

A few other ladies gradually united themselves to those already engaged in the work, and the little school, in the cell of Newgate, continued for many weeks their daily occupation.

'It was in our visits to the school, where some of us attended almost every day, that we were witnesses to the dreadful proceedings that went forward on the female side of the prison; the begging, swearing, gaming, fighting, singing, dancing, dressing up in men's clothes; the scenes are too bad to be described, so that we did not think it suitable to admit young persons with us.'[8]

The ladies thought some of the existing evils could be remedied by proper regulations; but in the commencement of the undertaking, the reformation of the women, sunk as they were in every species of depravity, was scarcely thought of, much less anticipated. By degrees, however, the heroic little band became convinced that good might be effected even amongst these: for intercourse with the prisoners had inspired them with confidence. The poor women were earnest in their entreaties, not to be excluded from the benefits, which they began to perceive would result to themselves, from improved habits. But whilst thus encouraged on the one side, every sort of discouragement presented itself on the other. The officers of the prison, as well as the private friends of these ladies, treated the idea of introducing industry and order into Newgate, as visionary. Even some of those interested in the attempt, apprehended that it would fail, from the character of those for whose good it was intended; also from its unfavourable locality, in the midst of a great metropolis; and from the difficulty of obtaining a sufficiency of labourers for such a work. It was also urged that even if employment could be procured, the necessary materials for work would be destroyed or stolen. In recalling this period, one of those engaged in it thus writes: 'But amidst these discouraging views, our benevolent friend evinced that her heart was fixed; and trusting in the Lord, she commenced her work of faith, and labour of love.'

Mildred's Court, Third Month 7th. – My mind and time have been much taken up with Newgate and its concerns. I have been encouraged about our school, but I find my weak nature and proneness to be so much affected by the opinions of man, brings me into some peculiar trials and temptations: in the first place, our Newgate visiting could no longer be kept secret, which I endeavoured that it should be, and therefore I am exposed to praise that I do not the least deserve; also to some unpleasant humiliations – for in trying to obtain helpers, I must be subject to their various opinions; and also, being obliged to confer at times with strangers, and men in authority, is to me a very unpleasant necessity. I have suffered much about the hanging of the criminals, having had to visit another poor woman, before her death; this again tried me a good deal, but I was permitted to be much more upheld, and not so distressed as the time before. May I, in this important concern, be enabled to keep my eye singly unto the Lord, that what I do may be done heartily unto Him, and not in any degree unto man. May I be preserved humble, faithful, and persevering in it, as far as it is right to persevere. And if consistent with the Divine will, may the blessing of the Most High attend it, that it may be made instrumental in drawing some out of evil, and leading and establishing them in the way everlasting, where they may find rest and peace.

The woman here alluded to, was Elizabeth Fricker;[9] she was executed for robbing, or being accessary to robbing, in a dwelling-house. The following memorandum was written by Mrs. Fry, March 4th, 1817, the day preceding the execution.

I have just returned from a most melancholy visit to Newgate, where I have been at the request of Elizabeth Fricker, previous to her execution to-morrow morning, at eight o'clock. I found her much hurried, distressed, and tormented in mind. Her hands cold, and covered with something like the perspiration preceding death, and in an universal tremor. The women who were with her, said she had been so outrageous before our going, that they thought a man must be sent for to manage her. However, after a serious time with her, her troubled soul became calmed. But is it for man thus to take the prerogative of the Almighty into his own hands? Is it not his place rather to endeavour to reform such; or restrain them from the commission of further evil? At least to afford poor erring fellow-mortals, whatever may be their offences, an opportunity of proving their repentance by amendment of life. Besides this poor young woman, there are also six men to be hanged, one of whom has a wife near her confinement, also condemned, and seven young children. Since the awful report came down, he has become quite mad, from horror of mind. A strait waistcoat could not keep him within bounds: he had just bitten the turnkey; I saw the man come out with his hand bleeding, as I passed the cell. I hear that another, who had been tolerably educated and brought up, was doing all he could to harden himself, through unbelief, trying to convince himself that religious truths were idle tales. In this endeavour he appeared to have been too successful with several of his fellow-sufferers. He sent to beg for a bottle of wine, no doubt in the hope of drowning his misery, and the fears that would arise, by a degree of intoxication. I inquired no further, I had seen and heard enough.

In a published letter, by the Honourable H. G. Bennett,[10] addressed to the Common Council and Livery of London, on the abuses existing in Newgate, he says, in allusion to Fricker's case: –

'A man by the name of Kelly, who was executed some weeks back for robbing a house, counteracted by his conversation, and by the jest he made of all religious feelings, the labour of Dr. Cotton[11] to produce repentance and remorse among the prisoners in the cells; and he died as he lived, hardened and unrepenting. He sent to me the day before his execution; and when I saw him, he maintained the innocence of the woman convicted with him, asserting, that not Fricker, but a boy concealed, opened the door, and let him into the house. When I pressed him to tell me the name of the parties concerned, whereby to save the woman's life, he declined complying without a promise of pardon; I urged as strongly as I could, the crime of suffering an innocent woman to be executed to screen criminal accomplices; but it was all to no effect, and he suffered, maintaining to the last the same story. With him was executed, a boy of nineteen or twenty years of age, whose fears and remorse Kelly was constantly ridiculing.'

Mildred's Court, Third Month 11*th*. – My mind too much tossed by a variety of interests and duties – husband, children, household, accounts, Meetings, the Church, near relations, friends, and Newgate; – most of these things press a good deal upon me; I hope I am not undertaking too much, but it is a little like being in the whirlwind, and in the storm; may I not be hurt in it, but enabled quietly to perform that which ought to be done; and may it all be done so heartily unto the Lord, and through the assistance of His grace; that if consistent with His Holy Will, His blessing may attend it, and if ever any good be done, that the glory of the whole work may be given where it is alone due.

19th. – I yesterday applied to our Monthly Meeting for liberty to join William Forster,[12] in paying a religious visit to the families of Gracechurch Street; I think I had reason to be encouraged, from the solemn covering over us, and also the unity expressed by Friends. I thought it a great mercy and favour to have the unity of all; but I desire not to place undue dependence even on this, though it is sweet, and I esteem it a great blessing to have it. My dear sister Elizabeth was particularly favoured in what she said. If permitted to enter this service, may the Lord be with us in it, and bless us. I have not at present felt much burdened by the prospect; I consider it an honour, favour, and blessing to be engaged in the service of our great Master, even if humiliations, trials and crosses attend it.

20th. – Thou Lord, who knowest my heart and my wants, be pleased to help me under them; also permit Thy poor child to ask Thee yet to look down upon her husband, children, brothers and sisters, for good, upon all those most near and dear to her, and particularly those who are in trial.

Fourth Month 12th. – I have found in my late attention to Newgate, a peace and prosperity in the undertaking, that I seldom, if ever, remember to have done before. A way has very remarkably been opened for us, beyond all expectations, to bring into order the poor prisoners; those who are in power are so very willing to help us, in short the time appears come to work amongst them. Already, from being like wild beasts, they appear harmless and kind. I am ready to say, in the fulness of my heart, surely 'it is the Lord's doing, and marvellous in our eyes;'[13] so many are the providential openings of various kinds. Oh! if good should result, may the praise and glory of the whole, be entirely given where it is due by us, and by all, in deep humiliation and prostration of spirit.

In the month of April, 1817, the wife of a clergyman, and eleven members of the Society of Friends, formed themselves into 'An Association for the Improvement of the Female Prisoners in Newgate.' The object they had in view is stated to have been, 'To provide for the clothing, the instruction, and the employment of the women; to introduce them to a knowledge of the Holy Scriptures, and to form in them, as much as possible, those habits of order, sobriety and industry, which may render them docile and peaceable whilst in prison, and respectable when they leave it.' On comparing these intentions with the existing state of things, it is easy to believe that the scheme was viewed by those in authority as highly desirable, but almost impracticable. Still to their honour be it spoken, they promised and gave their warmest co-operation.

The concurrence of the sheriffs and city magistrates was asked and obtained. But the doubt still remained, how far the women would submit to the restraints, which it would be needful to impose upon them, in order to effect this change.

To ascertain this, the sheriffs met the ladies one Sunday afternoon at Newgate: the women were assembled, and in their presence, as well as that of the ordinary and governor, they were asked by Mrs. Fry, whether they were willing to abide by the rules, which it would be indispensable to establish amongst them, for the accomplishment of the object so much desired by them all. The women, fully and unanimously, assured her of their determination to obey them strictly. The sheriffs also addressed them, giving the plan the countenance of their approbation; and then turning to Mrs. Fry and her companions, one of them said, 'Well, ladies, you see your materials.'

How they used these 'materials,' and the blessing permitted to attend their exertions, is demonstrated by a letter received in 1820, from one of the prisoners then present.

'To Mrs. Fry.
'Parramatta, New South Wales, *July* 10*th*, 1820.

'Honoured Madam,

'The duty I owe to you, likewise to the benevolent Society to which you have the honour to belong, compels me to take up my pen to return you my most sincere thanks for the heavenly instruction I derived from you and the dear friends, during my confinement in Newgate.

'In the month of April, 1817, how deep did that blessed prayer of your's sink into my heart; and as you said, so have I found it, that when no eyes see, and no ears hear,[14] that God both sees and hears, and then it was that the arrow of conviction entered my hard heart, and in Newgate, it was that poor Harriet S—,[15] like the prodigal son,[16] came to herself, and took with her words, and sought the Lord; and truly can I say with David, "Before I was afflicted I went astray, but now have I learned Thy ways, O Lord!"[17] and although affliction cometh not forth of the dust,[18] yet how prone have I been to forget God my Maker, who can give songs in the night;[19] and happy is that soul that when affliction comes, can say with Eli, "It is the Lord,"[20] or with David, "I was dumb and I opened not my mouth, because Thou didst it,"[21] and Job, when stripped of every comfort, "Blessed be the Lord who took away, as well as gave"[22] – and may the Lord grant every one that is afflicted, such an humble spirit as theirs. Believe me, my dear madam, I bless the day that brought me inside of Newgate walls; for then it was that the rays of Divine truth shone into my dark mind; and may the Holy Spirit shine more and more upon my dark understanding, that I may be enabled so to walk, as one whose heart is set to seek a city whose builder and maker is God. Believe me, my dear madam, although I am a poor captive in a distant land,[23] I would not give up having communion with God one single day for my liberty; for what is the liberty of the body, compared with the liberty of the soul? and soon will that time come, when death will release me from all the earthly fetters that hold me now, for I trust to be with Christ, who bought me with His precious blood. And now, my dear madam, these few sincere sentiments of mine I wish you to make known to the world, that the world may see that your labour in Newgate has not been in vain in the Lord. Please to give my love to all the dear friends, and Dr. Cotton, Mr. Baker, Simpson and all, the keeper of Newgate, and all the afflicted prisoners; and although we may never meet on earth again, I hope we shall all meet in the realms of bliss, never to part again. Please give my love to Mrs. Stennett and Mrs. Guy.

     'And believe me to remain,
       'Your humble servant,
         'HARRIETT S—.'

The remainder of the history will be better told in the words of Sir T. F. Buxton. It is true that his description of the early labours of the ladies (Newgate Association) has been repeatedly before the public: but there will probably be some into whose hands this book may fall, who may not have perused it, and others, from whose memory it may have passed. We do not hesitate, therefore, to make use of details so graphic, narrated as they are by one whose exertions to benefit these 'outcasts of the people,'[24] were only excelled by her's, of whom he wrote.[25]

'Having succeeded so far, the next business was to provide employment. It struck one of the ladies, that Botany Bay might be supplied with stockings, and indeed all articles of clothing, of the prisoners' manufacture. She therefore, called upon Messrs. Richard Dixon and Co., of Fenchurch Street, and candidly told them, that she was desirous of depriving them of this branch of their trade, and stating her views, begged their advice. They said at once, that they should not in any way obstruct such laudable designs, and that no further trouble need be taken to provide work, for they would engage to do it. Nothing now remained but to prepare the room; and this difficulty was obviated, by the sheriffs sending their carpenters. The former laundry speedily underwent the necessary alterations, was cleaned and white-washed, and in a very few days, the Ladies' Committee assembled in it all the tried female prisoners. One of the ladies, Mrs. Fry, began, by describing to them the comforts to be derived from industry and sobriety, the pleasure and profit of doing right; and contrasted the happiness and peace of those who are dedicated to a course of virtue and religion, with that experienced in their former life, and its present consequences; and describing their awful guilt in the sight of God, appealed to themselves, whether its wages, even here, were not utter misery and ruin. She then dwelt upon the motives which had brought the ladies into Newgate; they had left their homes and their families, to mingle amongst those from whom all others fled; animated by an ardent and affectionate desire to rescue their fellow-creatures from evil, and to impart to them that knowledge, which they, from their education and circumstances, had been so happy as to receive.

'She then told them, that the ladies did not come with any absolute and authoritative pretensions; that it was not intended they should command, and the prisoners obey; but that it was to be understood, all were to act in concert; that not a rule should be made, or a monitor appointed, without their full and unanimous concurrence; that for this purpose, each of the rules should be read and put to the vote; and she invited those who might feel any disinclination to any particular, freely to state their opinion. The following were then read: –

Rules.

'1. That a matron be appointed for the general superintendence of the women.

'2. That the women be engaged in needlework, knitting, or any other suitable employment.

'3. That there be no begging, swearing, gaming, card-playing, quarrelling, or immoral conversation. That all novels, plays, and other improper books, be excluded; and that all bad words be avoided; and any default in these particulars be reported to the matron.

'4. That there be a yard-keeper, chosen from among the women: to inform them when their friends come; to see that they leave their work with a monitor, when they go to the grating, and that they do not spend any time there, except with their friends. If any woman be found disobedient, in these respects, the yard-keeper is to report the case to the Matron.

'5. That the women be divided into classes, of not more than twelve; and that a monitor be appointed to each class.

'6. That monitors be chosen from among the most orderly of the women that can read, to superintend the work and conduct of the others.

'7. That the monitors not only overlook the women in their own classes, but if they observe any others disobeying the rules, that they inform the monitor of the class to which such persons may belong, who is immediately to report to the matron, and the deviations to be set down on a slate.

'8. That any monitor breaking the rules shall be dismissed from her office, and the most suitable in the class selected to take her place.

'9. That the monitors be particularly careful to see that the women come with clean hands and face to their work, and that they are quiet during their employment.

'10. That at the ringing of the bell, at nine o'clock in the morning, the women collect in the work-room to hear a portion of Scripture read by one of the visitors, or the matron; and that the monitors afterwards conduct the classes from thence to their respective wards in an orderly manner.

'11. That the women be again collected for reading, at six o'clock in the evening, when the work shall be given in charge to the matron by the monitors.

'12. That the matron keep an exact account of the work done by the women, and of their conduct.

'And as each was proposed, every hand was held up in token of their approbation. In the same manner, and with the same formalities, each of the monitors was proposed, and all were unanimously approved. When this business was concluded, one of the visitors read aloud the twenty-first chapter of St. Matthew, the parable of the barren fig tree,[26] seeming applicable to the state of the audience; after a period of silence, according to the custom of the Society of Friends, the monitors, with their classes, withdrew to their respective wards in the most orderly manner. During the first month, the ladies were anxious that the attempt should be secret, that it might meet with no interruption; at the end of that time, as the experiment had been tried, and had exceeded even their expectations, it was deemed expedient to apply to the Corporation of London. It was considered that the school would be more permanent, if it were made a part of the prison system of the City, than if it merely depended on individuals. In consequence, a short letter, descriptive of the progress already made, was written to the sheriffs.

'The next day, an answer was received, proposing a meeting with the ladies at Newgate.

'In compliance with this appointment, the Lord Mayor, the Sheriffs, and several of the Aldermen attended. The prisoners were assembled together; and it being requested that no alteration in their usual practice might take place, one of the ladies read a chapter in the Bible, and then the females proceeded to their various avocations. Their attention, during the time of reading, their orderly and sober deportment, their decent dress, the absence of everything like tumult, noise or contention; the obedience and respect shown by them, and the cheerfulness visible in their countenance and manners, conspired to excite the astonishment and admiration of their visitors. Many of these knew Newgate, had visited it a few months before, and had not forgotten the painful impressions made by a scene, exhibiting, perhaps, the very utmost limits of misery and guilt.

'The magistrates, to evince their sense of the importance of the alterations which had been effected, immediately adopted the whole plan as a part of the system of Newgate, empowered the ladies to punish the refractory by short confinement, undertook part of the expense of the matron, and loaded the ladies with thanks and benedictions. About six months after the establishment of the school for the children, and the manufactory for the tried side; the committee received a most urgent petition from the untried, entreating that the same might be done among them, and promising strict obedience. In consequence, the ladies made the same arrangements, proposed the same rules, and admitted in the same manner as on the other side, the prisoners to participate in their formations. The experiment has here answered, but not to the same extent. They have had difficulty in procuring a sufficiency of work, the prisoners are not so disposed to work, flattering themselves with the prospect of speedy release; besides, they are necessarily engaged, in some degree, in preparation for their trial. The result of the observations of the ladies, has been, that where the prisoners, from whatever cause, did no work, they derived little, if any, moral advantage; where they did some work, they received some benefit, and where they were fully engaged, they were really and essentially improved.'

A gentleman well known to Mrs. Fry, who was desirous of seeing and judging for himself of the effects of this singular experiment, visited Newgate just one fortnight after the adoption of the new rules. We give his own words.

'I went and requested permission to see Mrs. Fry, which was shortly obtained, and I was conducted by a turnkey to the entrance of the women's wards. On my approach, no loud or dissonant sounds or angry voices indicated that I was about to enter a place, which I was credibly assured, had long had for one of its titles, that of "Hell above ground." The court-yard into which I was admitted, instead of being peopled with beings scarcely human, blaspheming, fighting, tearing each other's hair, or gaming with a filthy pack of cards, for the very clothes they wore, which often did not suffice even for decency, presented a scene where stillness and propriety reigned. I was conducted by a decently-dressed person, the newly appointed yards-woman, to the door of a ward, where, at the head of a long table sat a lady belonging to the Society of Friends. She was reading aloud to about sixteen women prisoners, who were engaged in needlework around it. Each wore a clean looking blue apron and bib; with a ticket having a number on it suspended from her neck by a red tape. They all rose on my entrance, curtsied respectfully, and then at a signal given resumed their seats and employments. Instead of a scowl, leer, or ill suppressed laugh, I observed upon their countenances an air of self-respect and gravity, a sort of consciousness of their improved character, and the altered position in which they were placed. I afterwards visited the other wards, which were the counterparts of the first.'

Encouraged by many concurring circumstances, the newly formed Ladies' Committee, now for the first time introduced a matron into Newgate. The prisoners were divided into classes, and placed under her superintendence. She was eventually paid in part, by the Corporation; and received in addition twenty pounds a-year from the funds of the Ladies' Association. They furnished the rooms appropriated to her, and she was regarded as their servant. The yards woman was also appointed and paid by them.

Previous to the appointment of the matron, and until she was thoroughly established in her office, some of the ladies spent the whole day in the prison amongst the women; taking a little provision for themselves in a basket, or remaining without any; and for a long time afterwards, one or two of them, never failed to spend some hours daily in this important field of labour.

From the manuscript journal of one of their number, Sophia de C—, we are permitted to present to the reader some extracts descriptive of this period: –

'*Fifth Month* 1*st*, 1817. – After nearly a sleepless night, spent in anticipation of the scenes of the morrow, I called on Dorcas Coventry, who had promised to introduce me to inspect the important labours which the Ladies of the Prison Committee had engaged in, for the reformation of the women in Newgate, for some time past. We proceeded to the felon's door, the steps of which were covered with their friends, who were waiting for admission, laden with the various provisions, and other articles which they required, either as gifts, or to be purchased, as the prisoners might be able to afford. We entered with this crowd of persons, into an anti-room, the walls of which, were covered with the different chains and fetters, suspended in readiness for the culprits: a block and a hammer were placed in the centre of it, on which the chains were rivetted. The room was guarded with blunderbusses, mounted on moveable carriages. I trembled, and was sick, and my heart sunk within me, when a prisoner was brought forward to have his chain lightened, because he had an inflammation on the ankle. I spoke to him for he looked dejected, and by no means ferocious. The turnkey soon opened the first gate of entrance, through which we were permitted to pass without being searched, in consequence of orders issued by the sheriffs. The crowd awaited until the men had been searched by the turnkeys; and the women, by a woman stationed for that purpose in a little room by the door of entrance. These searchers are allowed, if they suspect spirits, or ropes, or instruments of escape to be concealed about the person, to strip them to ascertain the fact. A melancholy detection took place a few days ago. A poor woman had a rope found upon her, concealed for the purpose of liberating her husband, sentenced to death for highway robbery, which sentence was to be put into execution in a few days. She was of course taken before a magistrate and ordered into Newgate to wait her trial. She was a young and pretty little Irish woman, with an infant in her arms. After passing the first door into a passage, we arrived at the place where the prisoners' friends communicate with them: it may justly be termed a sort of iron cage; a considerable space remains between the gratings, too wide to admit of their shaking hands. They pass into this from the airing yard, which occupies the centre of the quadrangle, round which the building runs, and into which no persons but the visiting ladies, or the persons they introduce, attended by a turnkey, are permitted to enter. This door is kept by a principal turnkey, and was opened to our attendant by his ringing a bell. A little lodge, in which an under turnkey sleeps, is also considered necessary to render the entrance secure. This yard was clean, and up and down it, paraded an emaciated woman, who gave notice to the women of the arrival of their friends. Most of the prisoners were collected in a room newly appropriated for the purpose to hear a portion of the Sacred Scriptures read to them, either by the matron, or by one of the Ladies' Committee; which last is far preferable. They assemble when the bell rings, as near nine o'clock as possible, following their monitors or wards-women, to the forms which are placed in order to receive them. I think I can never forget the impression made upon my feelings at this sight. Women from every part of Great Britain; of every age and condition, below the lower middle rank; were assembled in mute silence, except when the interrupted breathing of their sucking infants informed us of the unhealthy state of these innocent partakers in their parents' punishment. The matron read; I could not refrain from tears; the women wept also; several were under the sentence of death. Swain,[27] for forging, who had just received her respite, sat next me; and on my left hand, sat Lawrence, alias Woodman,[28] surrounded by her four children, and only waiting the birth of another, which she hourly expects, to pay the forfeit of her life; as her husband had done for the same crime, a short time before.

'Such various, such acute, and such new feelings passed through my mind, that I could hardly support the reflection, that what I saw was only to be compared to an atom in the abyss of vice, and consequently, misery of this vast metropolis. The hope of doing the least lasting good, seemed to vanish; and to leave me in fearful apathy. The prisoners left the room in order. Each monitor took charge of the work of her class on retiring. We proceeded to other wards, some containing coiners, forgers, and thieves; and almost all these vices, were ingrafted on the most deplorable root of sinful dissipation. Many of the women are married; their families are in some instances permitted to be with them, if very young; their husbands, the partners of their crimes, are often found to be on the men's side of the prison, or on their way to Botany Bay.

'Some of these poor women are really beautiful, and healthy, and even modest-looking; their figures fine, and their countenances not disfigured by the expression of sin. The greatest number appeared to me Irish, a very few Scotch, the former are always ignorant, and preserve the peculiarities of their national character, even in this abode of sorrow and captivity; for to them privation and hardship are well known, and their Roman Catholic profession places their responsibility to God, in the keeping of their priests, so that life is deprived of its heaviest burden, and they expect to be finally happy, if they attend even in that place, to the private ceremonies which their form of worship enjoins. I felt much more interested during my momentary glance, for some of these poor creatures, than for others. I was warned by my friend not to place too much dependence on expression of countenance, or on what they might say, as deception is the ruling temptation while here, and without much care, would produce mischief and injustice. They appear to be aware of the value of character, to know what is right, but to forsake it in action, finding this feeling yet alive, if properly purified and directed, it may become a foundation on which a degree of reformation can be built. In appealing to this sentiment in their breasts, and cultivating their own knowledge of it, many of the causes of former misbehaviour are crushed. Thus they conduct themselves more calmly, and decently to each other, they are more orderly, more quiet, refrain from bad language, chew tobacco more cautiously, surrender the use of the fire-place, permit doors and windows to be opened and shut, to air or warm the prison, reprove their children with less violence, borrow and lend useful articles to each other kindly, put on their attire with modesty, and abstain from slanderous and reproachful words.

'It is to be hoped that by and by, a deeper and purer sense of the truths of religion, may be found the cause of a real reformation. None amongst them was so shocking as an old woman,[29] a clipper of the coin of the realm, whose daughter was by her side, with her infant in her arms, which had been born in Bridewell;[30] the grandfather was already transported, with several branches of his family as being coiners. The old woman's face was full of depravity. We next crossed the airing-yard, where many prisoners were industriously engaged at slop-work,[31] for which they are paid, and after receiving what they require, the rest is kept for them by the Committee, who have a receipt book, where their earnings and their expenditure may be seen for any time, by the day or week. On entering the untried wards, we found the women very different from those we had just left, they were quarrelling, and very disorderly, neither knowing their future fate, nor any thing like subordination amongst one another. It resembles the state of the women on the tried side, previous to the formation of the Visitors' Committee; not a hand was employed except in mischief. One bold creature was ushered in for committing highway robbery.[32] Many convicts were arriving just remanded, from the Sessions House; and their dark associates received them with applause, such is the unhallowed fellowship of sin. We left this revolting scene, and proceeded to the school room, situated on the untried side of the prison, for want of room on the tried. The quiet decency of this apartment was quite a relief, about twenty young women rose on our entrance, and stood with their eyes cast to the ground.

'A young woman of respectable appearance, named Mary Connor, had offered herself as mistress, for keeping the young children in order; who were separated from their parents' wards, and placed in this room. I gave those who wished it, permission to read to me, several could both read and write, some could say their letters, and others were in total ignorance, they wept as I asked them questions, and I read to them the parable of the prodigal son, as being peculiarly applicable to their present situation, they then resumed their needlework. We next proceeded to the sick ward, (it was in good order,) and took a list of the additional clothes wanted there, and read a chapter from the New Testament, we then bade adieu to this dismal abode.

'*2nd.* – Rose early and visited Newgate, (accompanied by Elizabeth Pryor,) where most of the Committee met to receive the Lord Mayor, the Sheriffs, several Aldermen, among whom were Sir William Curtis,[33] Atkins, and some of the Gaol Committee, who had visited Elizabeth Fry the preceding day, in order to learn what had been done, what remained to be improved, and to lend the assistance they deemed needful in this important work. The wisdom and integrity of her purpose was made apparent to them, and the plans gradually expanded before each of them; nothing was precipitated, caution marked every step, and even the irritable state of City politics does not interfere with this attempt at improvement. The women were assembled as usual, looking particularly clean, and Elizabeth Fry had commenced reading a Psalm, when the whole of this party entered this already crowded room. Her reading was thus interrupted for a short time. She looked calmly on the approaching gentlemen, who, soon perceiving the solemnity of her occupation, stood still amidst the multitude; whilst Elizabeth Fry resumed her office, and the women their quietude; and in an impressive tone told them, she never permitted any trifling circumstance to interrupt the very solemn and important engagement of reading the Holy Scriptures; but in this instance it appeared unavoidable, from the unexpected entrance of so many persons, besides which, when opportunity offers, we should pay respect to those in authority over us, those who administer justice: she thus, with a Christian prudence, peculiar to herself, controlled the whole assembly, and subdued the feelings of the prisoners, many of whom were but too well acquainted with the faces of the magistrates, who were themselves touched and astonished at being thus introduced to a state of decorum so new within those walls; and could not help acknowledging, how admirably this mode of treatment was adapted to overcome the evil spirit which had so long triumphed there. The usual silence ensued after the reading, then the women withdrew. We could not help feeling particularly glad that the gentlemen were present at this reading; the prisoners crowded round the Lord Mayor and Sheriffs, to beg little favours. We had a long conference with these gentlemen relative to this prison and its objects, and to the wisest regulations for Prison Discipline, and the causes of crime; indeed we could not have received more kind or devoted attention to what was suggested. Elizabeth Fry's manner seemed to awaken new trains of reflection, and to place the individual value of these poor creatures before them in a fresh point of view. They talked of building a school-room, but as it would encroach on the area of the yard, the scheme was unanimously abandoned. Regulations for cooking, washing and dining were promised; but everything at present that involves expense to the city is relinquished. Economy, not parsimony was the theme of the lord Mayor; private benevolence has up to this time, supplied every extra expense, besides what is termed the Sheriffs' Gift. The Sheriffs came to our Committee-room, – they ordered a cell to be given up to the Committee for the temporary confinement of delinquents; it was to be made appear as formidable as possible, and we hope never to require it.

'12*th*. – The soldiers who guarded the interior of Newgate, were, at our request dismissed: they overlooked the women's yard and rendered them very disorderly.

'23*rd*. – I found poor Woodman lying-in, in the common ward, where she had been suddenly taken ill; herself and little girl were each doing very well. She was awaiting her execution, at the end of the month. What can be said of such sights as these.

'24*th*. – I read to Woodman, who is not in the state of mind we could wish for her, indeed, so unnatural is her situation, that one can hardly tell how or in what manner to meet her case. She seems afraid to love her baby, and the very health which is being restored to her, produces irritation of mind.'

That the scene described by Sophia de C—, was satisfactory to the City authorities, is proved by a document which Mrs. Fry and her colleagues had the gratification of receiving a few days afterwards. But before introducing copies of these papers; it is due not only to the gentlemen whose names are appended to them; but to other members of the Corporation; to recall the cordial manner in which they accepted the services of the ladies, and acknowledged the extent and importance of the improvements effected. They had themselves experienced insurmountable difficulties in the attempt to control, or to introduce order amongst the women in Newgate: and despairing of success, appear to have relinquished the task as hopeless. When therefore this new system and its unlooked for success was exhibited before them, they did not start aside mistrustful of the agency, or the novelty of the proceedings; but without hesitation gave the weight of their influence and authority to uphold those efforts, which without their support, would probably have been of short duration, and of comparatively unimportant results.[34] [...]

From a paper found among Mrs. Fry's other writings, we are enabled to give the heads of the suggestions alluded to in the minute of the Gaol Committee.

1st. Newgate, in great want of room. Women to be under the care of women, matron, turnkeys, and inspecting committee.

2nd. As little communication with their friends as possible. Only at stated times except in any very particular cases.

3rd. They must depend on their friends for neither food nor clothing; but have sufficiency allowed them of both.

4th. That employment should be a part of their punishment, and be provided for them by Government. The earnings of work to be partly laid by, partly laid out in small extra indulgences, and if enough, part go towards their support.

5th. To work and have their meals together, but sleep separate at night, being classed, with monitors at the head of each class.

Religious instruction.

The kind attention we have had paid us.

Great disadvantages arise from dependence upon the uncertainty and fluctuations of the Sheriffs' fund. Neither soap nor clothing being allowed without its aid; and the occasional help of Grand Juries, or other charitable people.

The different arrangements of the ladies, together with the purchase of clothing for the prisoners, entailed considerable expenses; which soon proved beyond their private resources; a subscription was therefore opened to meet them; to which the sheriffs added the sum of eighty pounds. Mrs. Fry, at an after period, related to one of her coadjutors, that at this time she applied to some of her own relations, for assistance in this object, for she perceived the work before her to be great, and the opening for usefulness beyond her expectation: but that to follow it up, she required the command of more money, than she could conscientiously ask from her husband. Her application was most cordially responded to by them; especially by her cousin, Hudson Gurney, Esq., and her uncle, Robert Barclay,[35] Esq.; they gave her help, and encouraged her to persevere in her important objects, desiring her to apply freely to them whenever their assistance was required.

The following extracts are from letters of Mr. Barclay's.

Bury Hill, *November* 25*th*, 1817.

'Dear Niece,

'I received by this day's post, thy interesting communication of yesterday, touching the present state of Newgate; as to the excellent plan of reform of the female convicts under the care of thyself and the committee, and I freely authorize thee to send to my sons, D. and G. B—, for twenty-five to fifty pounds, as in thy own opinion the case may now require.

'Robert Barclay.'

'Bury Hill, *December* 27*th*, 1818.

"I wish thee to consider, that all my circle sympathise with thee in thy very arduous and successful pursuits of a public as well as private nature; and in any case that wants thy support in a pecuniary line, do depend on my will and ability to give thee assistance by writing me a report of thy wishes.

'Robert Barclay.'

But far beyond any other assistance was that she received from her own brothers; who not only entered warmly into her objects of interest, but were unfailing in the generous support they afforded them. From that time, until her labours of love were ended upon earth, not one year elapsed in which they did not most liberally contribute, as occasion required to her various purposes of benevolence, leaving the division to her own judgment. Thus did He, who had called her to this work, open the hearts of persons in various circumstances, each to contribute of that which he had, some in personal exertion, and cheerful consecration of time and strength; some the countenance of their authority and official dignity, while others poured in the needful supply of silver and gold.

Plashet, Sixth Month 5th. – The Yearly Meeting over; our prisons going on; our concerns in Gracechurch Street nearly finished, but some lowness and discouragement have been my portion lately, fearing from so many objects of duty, I should become perplexed; and also others fear for me, that I should in consequence neglect my home duties. May this not be the case. Oh! may I be directed what to do, and what to leave undone, and then I may humbly trust, that a blessing will be with me in my various engagements. Cast me not off from Thy presence, O Lord! and take not Thy Holy Spirit from me; and in Thine own time, and when consistent with Thy Holy Will, restore unto me the joys of Thy salvation, and uphold me by Thy free Spirit; that in all things, I may be found doing or suffering, according to Thy will. At home and abroad, enable me also, O Lord! to feel tenderly and charitably towards all my beloved fellow-mortals, that I may have no soreness, nor improper feeling towards any; thinking no evil, bearing all things, hoping all things, enduring all things,[36] that I may walk in all humility and godly fear, before all men, and in Thy sight. Amen.

16th. – I found the prison going on in a very encouraging manner, so much quietness and order, quite like a different place to what it used to be. We may humbly trust from the fruit produced, that the blessing of the Most High has given the increase to the scattered seed.

Anon., *Full Particulars of the Examination and Committal to Newgate of Annette Myers, for the Wilful Murder of Henry Ducker, a Private in the Coldstream Guards, with a Copy of a Letter Written by the Prisoner to Deceased; and also Other Startling Information*[1] (London: Birt [1848]).

Full Particulars, author unknown, is included here to represent the large number of accounts of trials published in cheap editions in the eighteenth and nineteenth centuries. These combined news, sensational narrative and often fascinating details of personal lives. Such materials were presented within a generic framework or formula that included racy narrative of the crimes, verbatim or purportedly verbatim testimony from trials, a pious and fatalistic moral and usually a verse summarizing the main elements of the crime story with a moralizing twist. Collections of such narratives were made from time to time across these centuries, known generically as the 'Newgate Calendar'. The successors to this form of popular literature included the cheap true crime magazines and supermarket tabloids still published today, as well as true crime documentaries and adaptations. *Full Particulars* has additional interest in being an account of a crime of passion or jealousy committed by a woman who was also a foreigner.

The publisher, Birt, specialized in this and similar lines of goods. Thomas Birt was proprietor of Birt's Wholesale and Retail Song and Ballad Warehouse at 10 Great St Andrew Street at Seven Dials, London, just off Charing Cross Road and near the infamous 'rookery' or criminal neighbourhood of St Giles. The firm occupied this and other addresses in Great St Andrew Street at various times from the 1820s to the 1840s, printing and selling large numbers of ballad sheets or broadsides of the kind published since the beginning of printing, at least, on cheap paper with crude illustrations, and hawked about the streets and at markets and fairs by the indigent and homeless to make a few pennies. An example of such a sheet is the ballad 'Newgate Walls' included in the present volume. Those published by Birt include 'Smiling Nan', 'Old England Shall Weather the Storm', 'The Bold Dragoon', 'The Lamenting Maid', 'The Brigand's Ritornella' and 'The Nightingale'. Companion to these ballad sheets were accounts of true crime and executions, often including a ballad on the subject. Birt seems to have gone in for particularly sensational crimes. Examples include *Particulars of the Trials and Executions of James Butler, for Arson; Edward Martelli, and Henry Jubilee Conway, for Forgery, Who Were Executed This Morning at the Old Bailey* (c.1820s); *Execution of Mr. Fauntleroy* (1824); *Particulars of the Trials and Execution of John Jardine, for Attempting to Poison His Wife, and Wm Page, for Horse Stealing: Who Were Executed at Horsemonger-Lane, This Morning* (c.1828); *Most Horrible Murder, Rivalling in Cold-blooded Atrocity that of Mr. Weare* (1828); *Confession of the Barbarous Murder Committed by John Holloway on the Body of His Wife: and Cutting off Her Head, Arms, &Legs* (1831); and *Particulars of the Execution of Thomas Williams, Who Was Executed at the Old Bailey This Morning for a Rape on Margaret Pugh, only Nine Years of Age* (1835). Less common in Birt's repertoire, and appearing in the 1840s, were fuller version of these single-sheet publications, in chapbook form, as with *Full Particulars* of the murder of Ducker. Examples include *A Warning Voice from a Penitent Convict: The Life, Hardships, and Dreadful Sufferings of Charles Adolphus King* (1840). Birt occasionally published other kinds of material on politics and current events, in broadsheet form, such as *A Copy of the Intended Petition to Parliament* (c. 1830), *The Downfall of the Tories* (1837), and *Prince Albert in England* (1841).

Note on the text: three silent corrections have been made.

On Saturday morning, February 5th, Annette Myers[2] was placed at the bar at Bow-street police-court,[3] before Mr. Henry,[4] to undergo an examination on the charge of shooting Henry Ducker, a private in the Coldstream Guards.

The particulars of this tragical occurrence, disclose another instance of the shameful depravity and corrupt habits of that body of men to which the deceased belonged. Henry Ducker[5] was a young man, only 21 years of age, and of handsome appearance. He is described by his comrades as having been 'a good sort of fellow,' but 'rather racketty,'[6] and was known to have intercourse with six or seven women, chiefly servant-girls, from all of whom he was in the habit of extorting money, raised by whatever means, upon the strength of his supposed attachment evinced towards them. This is stated by a soldier in the same regiment, and is confirmed by the nature of the correspondence which had taken place between the deceased and the prisoner. Ducker had been in the regiment about three years, previous to which he was in the service of Captain Codrington,[7] and it is supposed that he is a married man, although we could learn no positive information upon this subject. Certain it is that, if married, he must have ceased to communicate with his wife for some time past.

The prisoner is of small stature, small features, and not so good-looking as represented. She was dressed in a neat blue velvet bonnet, puce Orleans dress, sable boa, &c., and wearing her hair in long ringlets, of decidedly French cultivation. Her age is said to be 26, and she was described in the charge-sheet as residing at 40, Albion-street, Hyde-park-garden. She is understood to be a native of Belgium. Her demeanour at the bar, when before the magistrate, was that of a person of strong determination, wholly abandoned to her fate in the consciousness that she had been justified in the dreadful act which she had committed. She appeared occasionally faint and overcome, but these were rather the results of fatigue than any feeling of contrition, no manifestation of which once escaped her.

The prisoner in answer to the questions put to her by Mr. Henry, said, in a faint voice, that she was a foreigner, having been brought up in Brussels, but understood the English language perfectly well.

The examination was then proceeded with.

Sarah Lexton sworn. – I am a servant out of place, and live at 29, West-street, Pimlico. I was in Birdcage-walk, St. James's-park, on Friday afternoon, February 4th, near Storey's-gate, at about 20 minutes to 5 o'clock, when I saw the prisoner fire a pistol at a soldier. She was about two yards behind him, and raising her hand aimed it at the back of his head. They were both walking towards Buckingham-palace. I did not particularly notice them before the occurrence, nor had I seen the pistol in her hand. The soldier fell forwards, and she threw the pistol down by his side. The soldier did not utter a word. The prisoner said nothing either, but walked in the direction of the Palace. I was too frightened to follow her, but she was soon overtaken and stopped.

Henry Killington, coachmaker, 4, Earl-street, Kensington, was also near the spot at the same time, and heard the report of the pistol. On turning round he saw the pistol in the prisoner's hand. She threw it at the feet of the soldier when he was lying prostrate on the ground. He heard her say to one of the constables, 'I did it,' or words to that effect.

The prisoner (addressing the gaoler). – When the pistol went off it dropped of itself, I did not throw it down at his feet.

John Garwood, a private in the 5th company of the 2d battalion of the Coldstream Guards, stated that the deceased was a comrade in the same regiment. We both went to parade together on Friday afternoon, February 4th, and the deceased was walking a few yards behind me when I heard the report of a pistol, and saw what the previous witnesses have described. I went towards the deceased, and while on the ground he tried to extend his arms, and made an effort to speak to me, but was unable. I had seen the prisoner near the barrack-gate when I came out of it, shortly before. I saw her with the deceased on Wednesday night. They were talking together inside the barracks. I did not notice their conversation; but I fancied they were not on good terms, as she seemed in very bad spirits. I saw them together in Birdcage-walk about a month ago. They appeared on very good terms then. I have no personal knowledge of their having ever quarrelled.

Joseph Mills, another private in the same battalion, also saw the deceased fall, after hearing the report of the pistol. He did not know the prisoner.

Two police-constables, Christopher Richards, A 187, and Thomas Paul, A 80, who were on duty in the enclosure, and were attracted by the report of the pistol, also saw the deceased soldier fall, and deposed to have taken the prisoner into custody as she was walking away towards the Palace. She exclaimed, 'I did it,' and when at the station said, 'I have intended to do it for a long time.' She asked, 'Is he dead?' and was told that he was. She made no reply to this.

James Beattie examined – I am a gunmaker living in 205, Regent-street. On Thursday evening, the 3rd of February, at ten minutes to eight, the prisoner called at my shop, and said she wanted to purchase a pistol to shoot a Newfoundland dog that had bitten several of her friends. I said I had not an odd pistol in the window, and they were, besides, too expensive for her purpose; but I thought I had an old one in the back shop that would do for her. She asked the price of it, and I replied 10s. I told her she had better let one of my men go and kill the dog. She replied that she lived too far off, at Hackney, and that her brother was going to shoot it. She also stated that 'it seemed a curious thing, no doubt, for a lady to purchase a pistol, but her brother was too lame to come out, and that was the reason.' She then asked me to load it for her, and I did so. I loaded it with powder and a leaden bullet, putting in wadding both before and after the ball. I then put it in brown paper, and tied up the lock so as to prevent accident; after which I placed it in a bag, and told her to be very careful with it. She paid the 10s., and then went away. There was nothing in her manner to excite the slightest suspicion. She was perfectly calm, and, before going out of the shop, looked up at the dial and asked if it was the right time.

Sergeant W. Love, of the Coldstream Guards, produced some letters found upon the deceased, when brought upon a stretcher to the guard-room of the Wellington Barracks. They were signed 'Annette Myers.' Witness did not know the handwriting.

His Worship said the letters could not be received, unless proof could be given of the handwriting; but the officer might take care of them, in case they should be required at the trial.

Inspector Beckerson, of the A division, deposed to have taken the charge at the station. The prisoner said, 'I did it,' and, producing three letters, asked him to read the large one. She also gave him the pistol-bag produced. The pistol was brought to the station by one of the other officers.

The letter alluded to was as follows: –

'Monday Evening.

'My dear Henry; – I take my pen in my hand to write these few lines to tell you my mind. I must say there is something the matter with you, as Sunday afternoon you did not as much as offer me your arm, but walked as if we did not know much of one another. People must have thought so to see us. It was an unkind thing for you to tell me you would go and see that young woman, and you could get some money from her, as I would not give you some. But I do not like such ways; and you say if she had not got any money, she would lend her things to get some. More fool she. No young man would wish me to do such things except it was for some good motive. But I think if any young man wishes a young woman well, and his meaning is good to her, he will not wish anything of that kind from her. Henry, for you or any other young man, I would not do such a thing, and if you are not ashamed of it, I am.

'Look back since Christmas how much you had from me; and so if that is all the love you have for me, I do not care for such love. I know you care more for that young woman than you do for me, because she can give you more money than I can; she gets it easier than I can, and she does not get it in service. You know very well that no other man but you had my company since you wished for my company; but you can please yourself. Go and see her, or any other young woman that can give you more than I have. But please to give me what you have of mine – that is, two books and the pencil that you have of mine; but I wish to see you once more to part friendly.

'You had the face to tell me one day that I could not do without you or other men. I have done before, and I can do now; but I am sure you cannot do without a woman.

'Henry, do not be afraid to face me once more, for the last time, and write to me here. I hope she will be more kind to you than I have been.

'One day you had the face to tell me that I had done nothing to what some had. I done all that lay in my power, and I am not going to do what they do to get you some money. I did not let you do what you like with me because I thought of getting some money, it was because I kindly love you. And what did you say to me in the Park last evening? Henry, I little thought then I should have to write such a letter to you as this.

'Henry, our case will be a warning to others. You will see what kind love means soon, Henry; but do not be afraid, I am not going to do anything to you. All I wish from you is to see you once more. When I asked you on Sunday if I should see you next Sunday, you said, "It all depends;" but you did not say what; but I can think what. If you like to come next Sunday, at half-past 6 o'clock, I shall be able to go out then. We can make it the last time to see one another; please to let know, as I may tell mistress in time that I want to go out then; and if you have not got a penny, as you say, you can send, as you say you can, without paying for it. I hope I have said enough for you to think what your meanings is towards me. No more. God bless you. Do not forget what I told you. I will still remain yours till we part next Sunday, or before, if you like to come down.

'I am yours affectionately,
    'ANNETTE MYERS.'

Mr. Joseph Skelton, the assistant-surgeon to the battalion, deposed to having examined the deceased. There was a wound under the back part of the head and another at the left eye, caused apparently by the passage of a bullet, and sufficient to occasion immediate death. There had not been a post mortem examination made yet.

This being the whole of the evidence, the prisoner was asked if she wished to say anything in her defence. She made no reply.

The witnesses were then bound over in the usual form, and the prisoner was fully committed to Newgate for trial[8] for the wilful murder of Henry Ducker.

It is said that the prisoner had forsaken another soldier in the regiment for the addresses of the deceased, but this did not appear during the examination.

COPY OF VERSES.

Good people all you pass this way,
One moment give attention pray,
One pitying tear in tribute pay
　　To your Annette Myers,
　　　　Who now does dwell
　　　　In Newgate's cell,
Though once was virtuous, kind, and good,
Stands charged with a deed of blood,
And sending unprepared before her God,
　　The man whom she loved dear.

Annette Myers is my name,
Once fair and spotless was my fame,
I have brought myself to grief and shame,
　　Althrough this sad affair.
　　　　I in happiness did dwell
　　　　I a service I lik'd well,
Till Ducker cross'd my path one day.
So noble he appear'd and gay
That he stole the virgin heart away,
　　From poor Annette Myers.

I loved my bonny soldier lad,
And in loving him my heart was glad,
Till made acquaintance that he had
　　Another in my room;
　　　　Then frenzy fill'd my brain,
　　　　With thoughts[9] I dare not name.
By jealousy haunted night and day,
I was determined for to slay,
The man who stole the peace away
　　From poor Annette Myers.

My wounded honour to repair,
With anxious steps my way did steer
To Regent Street as does appear,
　　And the fatal weapon bought
　　　　Then sought the spot,
　　　　In Bird-cage Walk,
Until my Henry did appear.
With fevered brow I waited there,
Determined not his life to spare,
　　Unhappy Annette Myers.

As Henry from the barracks came,
Dark revenge had filled my brain,
With steady hand I took my aim,
　　His life for to destroy;
　　　　My aim was true,
　　　　The ball if flew –
My Henry fell upon the ground,
His life had fled without a groan,
And the crimson blood flow'd from the wound,
　　Caused by Annette Myers.

When I poor Ducker thus had slain,
My bosom it was filled with pain,
To think my conscience it was stain'd
　　With such a deed of blood.
　　　　My sufferings dread
　　　　Has turned my head.
　　Ducker had not me betrayed,
He'd not been hurried to his grave,
And God's anger had not been raised,
　　On poor Annette Myers.

You females all a warning take,
By poor Annette's wretched fate,
Who now her trial does await,
　　In Newgate's dreary cell.
　　　　Be warned by me,
　　　　Shun jealousy –
To virtues ways oh! be not blind,
Think of the name you leave behind,
And always bear the fate in mind,
　　Of poor Annette Myers.

from George Laval Chesterton, *Revelations of Prison Life; with an Enquiry into Prison Discipline and Secondary Punishments*, 2 vols (London: Hurst and Blackett, 1856), vol. 1, pp. 69–87, 131–43, 175–88

Chesterton had a varied career as a soldier, serving in the Spanish Peninsular War against Napoleon, in America during the War of 1812–14 against the United States, and in Venezuela as a captain and judge-advocate in a British brigade of volunteers with the forces of Simon Bolívar. He was living on half-pay and studying to become a clergyman when, in 1829, he was appointed governor of Coldbath or Cold Bath Fields prison, a 'bridewell' or house of correction, in London.

Coldbath Fields was so named from a cold-water spring located in the Clerkenwell quarter. The prison stood where the Mount Pleasant mail sorting office now stands and was built in the seventeenth century as the house of correction for the county of Middlesex. It was rebuilt in 1794 to a design by the prison reformer John Howard to house men, women and children on short sentences; it was extended in 1850 and limited to male offenders over seventeen; it had a reputation for having a harsh and repressive regime, including use of the hated treadmill; it closed in 1885.

Chesterton was an advocate of the so-called 'separate system' of prison management, favoured by the government inspectors of prisons, William Crawford and Whitworth Russell: see the excerpts from their *Reports of the Inspectors* (1836) in this volume.

In addition to *Revelations*, Chesterton published pieces in magazines ('A Prison Anecdote', *Household Words*, 15 February 1851, pp. 496–8); *A Narrative of Proceedings in Venezuela, in South America, in the Years 1819 and 1820* (London: John and Arthur Arch, 1820); and *Peace, War, and Adventure: An Autobiographical Memoir* (London: Longman, Brown, Green, and Longmans, 1853).

Note on the text: editor's additions in square brackets.

CHAPTER VI.

REMARKABLE TRAITS OF FEMALE CHARACTER—
AN IMPORTANT DISCOVERY.

On the occasion of my first visit to the female side of the prison,[1] the scene which I witnessed was calculated to create a good impression. I had been expected, and, consequently, there was a studied arrangement, and a decorum which seemed to indicate a judicious system of control. I was ushered into a yard occupied by 'the long fines:' *i.e.*, those prisoners who had to fulfil lengthened sentences. The measurement of this division of the prison was about 60 feet long by 20 broad, and a curve in the order of muster, enabled some sixty females of various ages – but the majority decidedly young – to be ranged in single file. As I entered, they all curtsied in the most respectful manner, and with a nice precision, and I became favourably impressed with the scene before me. The principal part were clothed in the prison dress,[2] consisting of a body and skirt of coarse blue cloth, a common blue plaid neckerchief, and a plain white cap, tied under the chin. The perfect silence of the group, the stedfast countenances, respectful salutation, and affected meekness of the entire body, were calculated to lull me into the belief that there stood arrayed before me the very concentration of gentleness and tractability. Nothing, however, could be more fallacious than such a supposition, nor was I allowed to remain many days under so pleasing a delusion. Upon this occasion I cast my eyes, for the first time, upon a selection of the choicest specimens of turbulence, pugnacity, and hardihood, that the *canaille*[3] of London could claim as its own.

It would be a needless consideration, and an utter waste of delicacy, to affect to disguise their names, or to designate them by initials. Their salient reputations stood confessed, and rendered all such punctilio[4] superfluous. I will venture, therefore, upon a slight description of the more remarkable amongst this strange company.

First, there was 'Bet Ward,' a young woman of real Amazonian[5] form and stature, and of distinguished beauty. She was one of a stamp rarely exceeded in whatever constituted strength and symmetry. The spoilt child of a weak mother (who still doated on her), she had been consigned to ruin by false indulgence. Equally irascible and fearless, she was the terror of the female officials; but as she possessed a somewhat generous disposition, she was not wont to carry her violence to a very dangerous extent. B. W. was the first to assail me with vituperative language, and to indicate that she might be disposed to pay but little respect to the person of the governor. I therefore observed a cautious distance whenever I perceived her ire to become ascendant. A few years sufficed to see this once fine young woman enter the prison the mere wreck of what she originally had been. With withered features, and failing power, she exhibited the sure inroads of a licentious life, coupled with habitual drunkenness – its usual concomitant. The pride and fire of her eye were gone, and deep dejection occupied their place. From that time forth, I saw her no more, and doubt not she fell an early sacrifice to a life of vice.

'Mary Barry'[6] was also a young woman of great muscular strength, but possessing none of the rare beauty of Bet Ward. She was equal to any audacious enterprise, and would confront the male officers (who were sent to the aid of authority, on occasions of an *emeute*[7]) with the rage and fierceness of a tigress. In a memorable encounter it took six men to overpower her, and one of the number had cause to remember her resistance for many after days, so severely was he bruised. It is strange that a singular admixture should be noticeable in dispositions so apparently untameable, but these wayward creatures had become thus impulsive by the unchecked sway of temper in early life. I once administered to Mary Barry a gentle reproof for some casual fault; and, being in a docile mood, she hung down her head and coloured deeply. Such a casual trait denoted some latent gentleness, which, in one so vitiated, it would have required too much pains and devotion, in the most persevering Samaritan,[8] to have fanned into mature fruitfulness. A subsequent sentence of transportation severed Mary Barry from my further observation.

There was a remarkable woman in this ward also, whose real name was Sullivan, but who was known by the appellation of 'Slasher.' She was Irish – resided, when free, in St. Giles's,[9] and cohabited with a pugilist. Slasher also was tall and of powerful build, and had acquired her sobriquet from the aptitude she displayed in the 'art of self-defence.' A pitched battle was no unusual interlude in her course, when excited by drink; and, upon such occasions, her attitude and tactics were said to be of the most approved order. In prison, and debarred from spirituous liquor, she was the very type of peacefulness. This poor creature sank prematurely under the mortal blight of drunkenness – bequeathing to our frequent care a younger sister,[10] who resembled the elder in all respects but in her pugilistic celebrity.

Behold another Irish female athlete, in the person of 'Mary Moriarty,'[11] whose sturdy shape and physical prowess had made her most formidable to the watchmen and street-keepers of St. Giles's and its purlieus. Drunkenness and violence frequently confined her to the prison, where she had long been my dread and torment ere I became cognizant of her redeeming qualities. If ever she chanced to be casually reproved, she would abandon herself to a boundless paroxysm of rage. She cared not whom she assailed, nor what she demolished; and it behoved everyone, who valued his features or his garments, discreetly to stand aloof. She never could be consigned to durance[12] before she had fought desperately, and exhausted every imaginary phase of attack upon a host of male turnkeys.

So excessive was her fury, that it was impossible to witness her savage efforts at resistance without feelings of horror and disgust; and until she was manacled, and thus rendered powerless, it would have been madness to attempt any other expostulation than that implied by force.

One day, however, when she had been fast bound, and exhaustion had tended to subdue her reckless spirit, I approached and addressed her in terms of kindly remonstrance, expressing at the same time the pain with which I contemplated the necessity of measures thus severe against a woman. A sigh and a tear soon evinced the efficacy of my appeal; and, seizing the favourable moment, I ordered her to be at once unbound; and a perfect understanding seemed suddenly to spring up between us. From that time forth my expostulatory voice would soothe and dispel her rising anger, and render her perfectly tractable; and many were the occasions on which my gentle warning sufficed to dissipate the clouds gathering on her brows portending a tempestuous outburst of wrath.

This unhappy girl was warm-hearted and generous to a fault, but of an excitable temperament, which, uncontrolled, or misdirected by weak and vicious parents, had made her the victim of ungovernable impulses. I once sent an officer to make some enquiry in the very heart of St. Giles's (at that time a most dangerous spot to invade[13]), and when he was surrounded by a crowd of ruffians, who threatened him with violence, Mary Moriarty (then, happily, free) flew to his rescue, and, by the joint agency of threats, strength, and the influence she exercised over that low mob, she protected him from harm, and successfully covered his retreat. This she had done for my sake, and I am persuaded she would have risked her very life for my personal protection – simply from a grateful sense of my goodwill towards her. She, like all such unhappy outcasts, died prematurely under the scourge of the vile debauchery which pollutes such dens of infamy as St. Giles, and other similar localities.

Amongst the same heterogeneous group was a widow, about thirty-five years of age, who had assumed the name of Eliza Ellams. She was of respectable parentage, and of decent education; but had discarded all respectability by her uncontrollable habits of intemperance. At times she would express deep contrition for her faults, and profess a desire to reform. In one of these penitential moods, she prevailed upon the chaplain to interpose with her father in her behalf; and, by this interposition, his condition, and her real circumstances, became known to us. This disclosure presented one of my earliest insights into the all-absorbing, and scarcely-credible influence of the passion for ardent spirits; and after-experience taught me the utter hopelessness of reform (especially in the female character), when once that accursed craving had assumed a chronic form. No earthly consideration would seem equal to arrest the mastery of that unappeasable vice. In its vortex, every moral and social obligation becomes alike engulfed. The comforts of home, the advantages of station, or the sanctity of kindred – even of maternal ties – prove insufficient barriers against the inroads of that fatal thirst. It drowns all reflection, and plunges its willing votary into any excess of crime and dishonour for its own insatiate gratification. The father of Eliza Ellams proved to have been a joint-owner and master of a merchant vessel. He had realized an ample competency, and occupied a genteel residence near the Commercial-road, where he was educating his grand-daughter (this wretched woman's child), who was then about seventeen years of age, and was receiving the instruction suited to a young lady. The chaplain made a flattering report of her appearance and intelligence; and, moreover, he found her grandfather disposed (however hopeless he deemed the attempt) to make all practicable efforts to reclaim his daughter.

Such were the home abandoned, and the sacred ties rent asunder, by the terrible addiction to drink, which transformed Eliza Ellams into the lowest order of street-walker, a tattered, shoeless wanderer; and induced her to herd with the most polluted miscreants the metropolis could furnish. St. Giles's was her place of resort, and there, at length, she was picked up literally from the kennel,[14] into which she had fallen in a state of drunken insensibility; and in that shocking condition, which proved irremediable, she died.

If more were required to paint the dreadful reality of that appalling passion, I could adduce a yet more frightful instance of the callousness it engenders. It absorbs every other feeling of the heart, and stands alone an awful, cankering curse.

Persons such as Eliza Ellams would be the frequent inmates of all the metropolitan prisons, in turn; and, in this round of incarceration, those who were able (and they were but few) would write letters to their chosen friends who might be located in other prisons. This peculiar class of people were remarkable for three things. First, the stedfast, never-failing denial of guilt, notwithstanding the plainest evidence to disprove their assertions. Secondly, the complacent estimate they appeared to form of their own status, notwithstanding the damning testimony against them of nine-tenths of society in general, and their own sex in particular. And, thirdly, the farcical *empressement*[15] they threw into their attachment towards some chosen prison associate, misnamed friend.

In illustration of the third proposition, Ellams had formed a sort of romantic friendship with one Julia King,[16] who was, at that period, not the least distinguished of my flock. Julia was about 22 years of age, of short but slender form, and could boast, even in prison, of a rosy complexion to set off features of no mean order. She had become prematurely a widow, by the sacrifice of her husband's life upon the gallows, for a burglary, accompanied with violence; and Julia had made no inconsiderable advance in the path of virtue, by becoming merely a practitioner in the higher walk of uttering base coin – viz.,[17] by the circulation of counterfeit gold.

It was really amusing to con the effusions that passed between these enthusiastic correspondents. Julia wrote a small cramped hand, and little could be said in praise of her orthography, while Ellams both wrote and spelt in a creditable manner. 'My very dearest little Julia,' and 'my dearest friend,' were the relative commencements of their epistles; and thence were banded[18] from one to the other, professions of lasting attachment, and a vast amount of the sentimentality culled from low novels. While Julia King remained under my care, Ellams never omitted a P.S. with her 'respectful duty to the governor.'

The last person, amongst this singular combination of characters, whom I shall here attempt to pourtray shall be 'Ann Fisher,'[19] a young woman of short stature, and most repulsive features. She combined all the bad qualities of her criminal associates, without exhibiting one of their redeeming characteristics. She was a compound of wrath, insolence, and violence, and seemed to glory in defiance to all authority, and, if possible, to enjoy the punishment which her bad conduct entailed upon her. One day she walked deliberately up to the matron, in my presence, and dealt her a violent blow in the face, and then, squaring up to me in a fistic attitude, compelled me to think of self-defence. My prompt disposition to repel attack had the effect of arresting her aggression.

Upon one occasion, Ann Fisher suddenly approached a male officer, and spat full in his face; when the man, irritated by so foul an insult, gave her so effectual an open-handed box on the ear, as to make her stagger and fall. No one in his heart could condemn so well-merited a retaliation, which had the happy tendency of making the spiteful vixen less pugnacious thereafter. Strange to say, this creature, when subsequently under a sentence of transportation (which it caused me devout pleasure to learn was her fate), writing from her temporary abode to a 'dear friend' under my guardianship, desired her 'duty to the governor.'

Besides the characters whom I have thus sketched, there were others whose distinctive qualities rendered them unruly inmates, but the major part were gentle, and even timid, and would shed tears and exhibit intense alarm whenever the fighting propensities of our select specimens hurried them into extremities.

The illustrations I have afforded have been taken from the division allotted to 'long fines;'[20] but if my first impression of that class were favourable, owing to the temporary order which prevailed, I was, on the contrary, as much shocked and disheartened when I paid my first visit to the 'short fines.' These consisted principally of the 'disorderly women,'[21] committed under the Vagrant Act[22] (a very comprehensive statute) for terms varying from seven days to three months, which latter formed the maximum. All convictions under that act combined hard labour with imprisonment, and, at that time, and indeed long after, the treadwheel, under that sentence, became the portion of young and hearty females.

My introduction to the 'disorderly yard' impressed me with the suitability of its denomination. There had just been a dispute, which indeed was still raging, and my ears were assailed with the most unladylike language. There could not have been less than eighty girls and young women congregated in this yard, all attired in their own dresses, most of which combined the tawdry finery which distinguishes this class of persons, and which they deem so attractive in their peculiar calling.

No one who may visit a well-ordered prison of the present day, and witness the regularity, the marked decorum, and the appropriate sedateness of the female prisoners, would be led to conjecture the very opposite features of such a receptacle which my earliest experience disclosed. It was not then the hour of labour, and, consequently, the whole throng was confusedly intermingled; some were troubled, but many had become active partisans of either of the contending disputants. No sooner was I announced as the new governor, than I was surrounded by a clamorous crowd, who pressed forward to invoke my clemency; and upon this memorable occasion my hands were seized with tender *empressement*, and I was addressed as 'my love,' 'my darling,' 'my dear creature;' and all the conventional endearments of the *pavé*[23] were showered upon me. I had to struggle for enlargement, and beat a hasty retreat, quite confounded by my initiation into 'prison discipline.'

Within a short period of the exercise of my new authority, private intelligence conveyed to me the startling fact, that a well-planned system had long enabled favoured portions of the male and female prisoners daily to meet together in one of the roofs of the building, and I was furnished with a clue to the discovery of the whole contrivance, and the exact hour of the rendezvous. This clandestine arrangement was, consequently, one afternoon suddenly disturbed by my unlooked-for presence, supported by a few officials, who dared not disobey the direction to accompany me. The full extent of this iniquity stood thus divulged. The men fled with precipitate haste; but Mary Barry, and a woman, named Christmas,[24] were caught in the very act of descending from a trap-door, which opened to the roof; and the consternation occasioned by this discovery, became perfectly electric.

A close examination of the means adopted to ensure this unlawful meeting disclosed a very simple solution. The female wards, as I have already described, were merely portions of the main building imperfectly fenced off from the males' department. The roof in question, ran longitudinally over both compartments. It was accessible by an iron grating on the males' side, which had once been soldered down, but was now removable at pleasure; and, on the other side, by the trap-door I have named, which had to be reached by standing on an iron balustrade, and then climbing two or three feet up a perpendicular iron supporter, whence the trap-door was easily upraised.

Here, then, was revealed another infamous source of profit to this immaculate prison staff, of both sexes. It at once threw a light upon a delicate investigation of a few preceding years, when, in order to cloak a monstrous dereliction of duty, and to screen the real delinquents, a story was trumped up, which nearly ruined the character of a most respectable man, then clerk to the prison. The whole relation, as it affected him, was a tissue of improbabilities; but, notwithstanding, Mr. Hassell, the clerk in question, continued, to the termination of his service, to be an object of suspicion in the minds of many persons.

The prompt dismissal of the turnkey of the females' ward was the consequence of this discovery, and that event threw the matron, and the whole of her staff, into a state of the utmost alarm. I was addressed in terms of supplication, and endless were the protestations of willing submission to all such new regulations as I might deem expedient. The male turnkey's defence prevailed with the magistrates, and his dismissal was, for the time, averted.

A tolerably clear conception may now be formed of the crime and corruption which then pervaded the prison of Cold Bath Fields. It was a very hot-bed of vice, and I should not be guilty of undue exaggeration, if I were to declare my conviction, that few were the degrees, in the ample scale of human wickedness, which had not witnessed their attainment within those walls. [pp. 69–87]

CHAPTER IX.

A TALENTED PRISONER—HIS SKETCH OF THIEVES AND THEIR HABITS.

WITHIN a year of my appointment, I witnessed the trial and conviction of a young surgeon for arson.[25] The offence had been committed with the view to defraud an insurance company. He was then about twenty-two years of age, of slender form, pale face, with small and intelligent features, and sandy hair: he had also a club-foot. Nothing could be more meek and subdued than that young man's demeanour and address, and no physiognomist would ever have divined that an unusual amount of fraud lurked beneath that deceptive exterior.

The gentleness of his bearing, and the pallor of his countenance, seemed to plead with his judges in his behalf, and thus, escaping the customary doom, for such an offence, of transportation, he received the sentence of eighteen month's imprisonment and hard labour. Submitting, as he did, with exemplary quietude and patience to his new condition, in due turn, he was selected for superior employment.

At that time, prisoners were eligible for the post of instructors of the ignorant, and, in the strictest interpretation, *unlettered* beings, whom want or neglect had cast into the prison, and W—s was appointed schoolmaster to a host of thievish urchins. His education and quiet disposition quite fitted him for such an office. As unlimited intercommunication was lawful, W. had the opportunity not only freely to question his pupils, but also to glean from numerous roguish adults, ample particulars of their craft.

He duly informed me of the facts he had collated, and proposed, under my sanction, to write a compendious history of thievery, with a glossary of the terms employed by its votaries. I of course assented, and a most interesting paper was the result. It was presented to me, and I not only perused it with profitable attention, but I subsequently lent it to Mr. Chadwick,[26] whose high intelligence, and statistical indefatigability are so well known. That gentleman will doubtless yet remember that instructive treatise, since he asked my permission to lend it to a very distinguished peer, by whom it was unhappily lost, or mislaid amongst the endless variety of papers which passed through his lordship's study.

I still, however, retain from the same pen a much slighter dissertation upon thieves and their habits, which tends to illustrate the practice of that class in those days, and, in most particulars, is applicable to the present period. It is worthy of perusal, and is as follows.

'Thieves, gonophs, or crossmen, in London, are divided into several mobs or gangs, named from the district which they inhabit, distinct from each other; but the parties forming the several mobs are well known to each other – not so much of late years by any particular marks on their person, as by their constant intercourse with each other, by their frequenting the same houses, and by their suffering in the same prisons. In practising their art (or, as they express it, "when at work"), they do not indiscriminately practise all the branches of their profession. Some are more expert than others at pocket-picking; these are termed *buzmen* or *nuxmen*. This is the branch the swell mob[27] chiefly practise. Most young thieves commence their career by taking handkerchiefs, and are called *fogle-hunters* – a silk handkerchief being named a fogle – (most of 3rd Boys, 6th and 7th yards, of this class). The swell mob select some of these *kids* (boys), more expert and respectable in their appearance than their fellows, to assist them in their *skin* and *sneezer* (purse and snuff-box) buzzing depredations. Some thieves are expert at snatching anything from the person, and this branch is termed *flimping*. A lady's reticule, a gentleman's watch, or a child's necklace, in a press (or, as they term it, *a push*), is readily taken by the flimper, who, behind others, watches his opportunity to snatch it away. This is most frequently practised at theatres, on entering or retiring. Some, more daring, join in a party of four to six – meet a gentleman whom they may have seen to have money about him, or who has a watch (*yack* or *thimble*), and, by jostling and hustling him about, take away everything from him. This is done more commonly in retired places – sometimes, in public streets, and, more astounding, occasionally in the midst of the day, in the exposed streets of this metropolis: so cleverly do the parties concerned meet at the same moment around their victim, rob him, and as speedily move off in various directions to meet at some appointed place, leaving the object of plunder in a state of perfect wonder and astonishment, if not of momentary stupor. This is named *ramping*. Others, more determined, practise housebreaking: these are termed *cracksmen*. Some, to gain entrance, make use of false keys (*screws*), and these are named *screwsmen*. Most cracksmen are men who have been transported (*lagged* or *served*), and are termed tried men. They are to be considered desperate characters – men who would not scruple to take life, when their own or associates' (*pals'*) safety demands the sacrifice. Some crack a pane in a shop front, and, by passing the wet thumb along, they can direct the crack as they please; the piece of glass thus separated is to be removed in various ways – which effected, they remove jewels or silk goods, to an amazing amount. This is named *starring*. Others practise going into areas,[28] or outhouses,[29] under the pretence of begging or selling trifling articles, and take valuables, as plate,[30] &c., which may lay in their way. This thief is called a *sneaksman*. A species of this description of thieving is done by boys, who go into shops on their hands and feet, get round the counter, take the till, and then sneak out in the same manner – their safety depending on no customer coming in meantime. This is termed *lob-sneaking*. The names given to the plunderers of society appear to be of endless variety – vagrants, divided into *cadgers* and *high-flyers; showful-pitchers; smashers* or *shawnsmen*, utterers of counterfeit coin, dog-fanciers, or dog-stealers; fences, or buyers of stolen articles; Jew bouncers, those who obtain money by means of false notes-of-hand, &c., &c. – each of which, in its place, would require pages to describe.

'In their habits and manner of life, men living on the "*cross*" (by dishonesty) vary much amongst themselves. A grand distinction is to be drawn, in this respect, between the swell mob and common thieves; the former being, for the most part, men of the world, of some education – not appearing at all flash (thief-like), but, on the contrary, acting the part of gentlemen in society. Unknown as thieves, to any except their own immediate companions, they frequent those public-houses, the landlords of which they know to be what they term "right" (*i.e.* a thief's friend), who would screen them from justice, in case of necessity, by all the means in his power. The houses of this sort vary according to circumstances; those at present used, are as follows.'

Here six public-houses are named, which, at this distant period, may have acquired respectability; and, therefore, their signs are withheld.

'The apartment they make use of is generally on the first floor, and is on occasion held sacred by even the landlord himself – it is here they plan their various schemes – here they meet the evening before a levee,[31] address, or other public procession takes place, to arrange what parties are to work together, and where to meet the ensuing morning – here they assemble in the evening after the levee, to share their spoils – to joke and tell how neatly the *skins* (purses) were drawn from the *kicks* (trowsers pockets) the *thimbles* (watches), from the *gurrells* (fobs), the *ridge* (gold) or *wedge* (silver) *sneezers* (snuff-boxes) from the *fans* (waistcoat pockets), the *dummys* (pocket-books) from the *pits* (breast pockets) or *slashes* (outside coat pockets), and how the old *bloak* (old man) was *propped* (squeezed), and his skin drawn from his fan where he had been seen just before to deposit it for better security. In this apartment they agree to a marauding excursion through the country, visiting all the fairs, races, &c., on the way, appointing for their purposes, who is to act the part of countryman with the smock-frock, breeches, boots, and spurs – who the servant, and who the gentleman, and here over their bottle they tell of deeds of darkness, some of which in the cracking line (house-breaking), would cause the blood of an honest man to run cold.

'The booty they obtain is amazing, but it is as soon squandered by their profligate and generally debauched manner of living. Their life when engaged at their profession being a scene of constant anxiety, all their leisure hours are spent over the bottle and pipe. In the addresses which took place to the late Queen,[32] pocket-picking was practised to a great extent; they considered themselves unfortunate if they did not realize twenty or thirty pounds each man per night. In their business they are liable to equal fluctuations with men living in the *square* world (honest tradesmen). It is remarked that they are particularly dissatisfied, and discontented when baulked of an expected purse, more especially if they have seen its value; under such circumstances they will sit for hours in a meditating mood, without exchanging a word with their companions, who well knowing their feelings, do not interrupt them, until by the action of some intoxicating liquor their spirits revive. Some of the swell mob combine the qualifications of cracksmen and buzmen, but this is rare; they make a great deal of money at the gaming booths at the different fairs and races which they frequent, by different manœuvring games where the chances are three and four to one in their favour. When in town, and at a loss for cash, they make sure of a trifle by attending the theatre, where in the push on going in or coming out, they are certain of getting a watch or a purse at a comparative trifling risk. They frequent all public performances where a great concourse of people are assembled, as prize fights, &c.

'As a body, their system is so complete in itself, that they can obtain information on any subject at any time. They are well aware, it is confidently asserted, in many cases, of the parties who, and the time when, they have to draw sums of money from the banking houses, as also of the time when dividends have to be drawn, indeed 'tis said, their information is so sufficient on this head, that a party will go on 'change,[33] and without previous personal acquaintance, pick out his man – dog him – nor does he leave him till, in many instances, he succeeds in robbing him, sometimes under such circumstances, to an alarming amount.

'Their homes are generally in the suburbs of town; when married they, for the most part, keep cases (houses of accommodation). Some are unmarried; and these, to remove suspicion, take a small house, and keep a *joiner*, or *sheelah* (mistress), who gives out in the neighbourhood that her husband is a traveller[34] of some description or other. Others reside with those of their fraternity who occupy entire houses. The conduct of this class of thieves towards each other is in every respect strictly honourable; their attachments firm, and confidence implicit.

'Cracksmen and screwsmen come next in order to the swell mob, as to respectability of character in their profession, and, lastly, common thieves, who differ in every respect from the above, being men of no connection, many nurtured in the art from their mother's womb. They place no reliance on each other, unless obliged to do so. The thefts they commit are petty, and consequently frequent, and they must be considered as of the lowest grade in society. The houses they frequent are very low, and vary much as —'

Here three houses are named.

The writer of the paper was one of those perverse beings who, untaught by experience, still clung to the hope of thriving by chicanery. Six years subsequently to his discharge from his first sentence, he again became my prisoner. In this instance he had been guilty of an offence which none but a man of ability could commit. He had passed an examination before the College of Surgeons, for a consideration, in the name of another, for whom he was about, unlawfully, and most mischievously, to obtain a diploma.

The party represented was likewise committed, but for a longer period. He was a simple-minded, kind-hearted Irishman, who, by some means, had acquired the diploma of an M.D in the sister kingdom, and was said to be a good classical scholar.

W. had for some time been engaged as a 'grinder,' or person who 'crammed' medical students to enable them merely to pass an examination. I was anxious to know if his long incarceration of eighteen months had rendered his person so familiar to thieves as to have subjected him to the mortification of recognition, by persons whom it must necessarily have been of importance to avoid. I found, however, from his statement, that only *once* during the intervening period of six years, had he been recognized, and then in Wych Street he had heard, *en passant*,[35] a boy say to another, 'there goes our schoolmaster.' Here, we have a notable proof of the salutary metamorphosis effected by the change from the prison attire to the ordinary social costume. At the end of six months I lost sight of W., and as I saw him no more, I hope he applied his capabilities to worthier and safer objects. [pp. 131–43]

[Female Prisoners]

The most vicious portion of the female prisoners; – generally some seven or eight in number, out of an average of 250 female convicts – would present an everlasting source of turbulence and rioting. They constituted a singular exam-

ple of what may be produced by very early self-indulgence and neglect. They
were creatures inaccessible, for the most part, either to reason or kindness. Any
momentary effusion of tenderness would be stifled, in order to maintain the
vain-glorious boast of 'pluck.' The merest approach to reproof would kindle a
burst of rage; thence would follow such a volley of oaths, such terms of defiance,
and (as necessity compelled their forcible removal) such boundless pugnacity
and fierce resistance, that the spectator would wonder whether the contest could
be with devils or with women. These human pests would endure lengthened and
painful punishments, live unrepiningly upon bread and water in solitude, and
disdainfully reject the easy terms of release – viz., the promise to be well conducted.

Bridget Summers, aged 18 years, who used to enter the prison, alternately, as
a disorderly girl from the streets, and as a refractory pauper from a workhouse,
persisted so long in her 'plucky' determination, answering daily remonstrance,
and even entreaties, with contumely and frightful execrations, that, at length we
were constrained to remove her from the punishment cell by force, to obviate
serious consequences. In that instance she maintained her character with her
unfeminine companions for 'pluck,' but she profited by the lesson of her own
voluntary suffering, and thenceforth observed a discreet line of conduct in any
of the prisons – for she was an *habituée*[36] of most in turn.

A retrospect upon these unique samples of vicious character recalls the strange
anomalies which marked their course of action. With reference to Bridget Summers, after the foregoing incident, as I was walking at mid-day, in company with
two ladies, through Covent Garden,[37] I suddenly met this girl with an apparently
decent working woman. She noticed me with a face full of smiles, when, informing the ladies that she was one of my unruly clients, I stopped to speak to her. She
displayed towards me the utmost gentleness and good will, thanked me civilly
for my inquiries respecting her condition, told me she was doing well 'at shelling
in the market,' and, curtseying, took a gracious leave of me.

Her friend and general companion, Harriet Knight, a girl about the same
age, and of the identical stamp, was a very remarkable specimen of the *genus
fæmina*.[38] She had been fully as contumacious as Summers, and had voluntarily
courted nearly an equal amount of punishment, until admonished by endurance
she began to practice quietude. I was compelled to instruct the superintendents
never to speak to her unless required to do so by urgent necessity, and in case of
unusual excitement to leave her to me. I failed to succeed myself; nor did I witness the least success on the part of any other person (not even one out of the
select number of ladies, who charitably visited female prisoners) to assuage the
sour disposition of that literally spiteful girl. She was a matchless cynic; snarl-
ing and angry retort, even when she was kindly addressed, seemed with her an
instinct. Experience taught me that the only safe course to pursue towards Har-

riet Knight was to let her alone, and neither to speak to nor notice her at all. She would then sometimes go through her term with sullen taciturnity, and receive her discharge with a look of ineffable scorn and contempt.

The newspapers of that day abounded with the pugilistic exploits of a woman, who had rendered herself notorious under the name of 'Lady Barrymore.' Her real name was Mary Ann Pearce;[39] and she was one of those persons who when drunk are frantic, and was a most formidable object, either to apprehend or, indeed, safely to place at the bar of the police office.

When sober and in prison, 'Lady Barrymore' was not addicted to overt resistance; but, under the system of free license to speak, she was always counselling mischief to others. She was a woman of unusually high stature, and had, doubtless, been, when young, and under the protection of the Lord Barrymore[40] of that time, a very fine woman. She had then had a carriage kept for her, but was ultimately discarded, and, bit by bit, became a drunken street walker.

To the ignorant women, who surrounded her, she made a boast of her former finery and sumptuous style, and was amongst them a sort of dictatress upon rank and fashion. She exercised, consequently, no small influence, which was always turned to the detriment of my authority, for I found her to be a zealous fomenter of broils and resistance. At length, by a mere accident, I discovered a ready means to master her mischievous disposition. Whenever there was aught amiss in her ward, she had been ever prompt to interfere, and, when reproved, delighted to remind me, and all who listened, of her former greatness. 'I am no common person, like most in this prison. I once kept my own servants, and rode in my own carriage!' Irritated by this constant absurd reiteration, I one day said to her – 'I am afraid you are something worse than a common person, for the law has sent you here as a common prostitute;' and I desired an officer to go forthwith to the office, and bring me her commitment, that I might read the precise terms for her edification, and that of her imprisoned associates.

The blow to her pride was instantaneous. She became pale, and seemed about to swoon with horror. She gasped for breath, and, in the utmost horror, exclaimed – 'For God's sake, don't, sir! – oh, for God's sake, don't!'

Thenceforth, the merest hint sufficed to silence her, and, under the dread of losing caste, in my presence, she became a pattern of meekness.

One of the outrageous women, who at this epoch so tormented us was a creature named 'Fowler,'[41] who had won the infamous distinction of being considered the most foul-spoken woman of all who infested the prisons of the metropolis. She had been a housemaid in the family of a literary countess; but, having descended to vicious courses, her numerous bad qualities soon made her pre-eminent in abandonment. The trait of character which secures a freshness in my memory for this degraded being, is in itself somewhat amusing.

It was her custom to load me with ceaseless vituperation, and upon all such occasions, while she disparaged me to the utmost, she never failed to contrast the superior excellence of Mr. Nodder – a very worthy man, who was then governor of Tothill Fields Prison[42] – and whose duty it was frequently to receive charge of Fowler. 'Ah!' she would shriek out, with ill-stifled rage, 'you're a pretty tyrant of a governor; you're not like Mr. Nodder. Mr. Nodder is a *gentleman!*' &c., &c. I took but little heed of this uncivil contrast, but it would sometimes perplex my mind to imagine what line of conduct Mr. Nodder could possibly adopt with this fierce virago, so to win her favourable opinion.

One day, I chanced to call upon Mr. Nodder, who asked me, with seeming curiosity, how I could manage to conciliate 'that horrible wretch, Fowler,' since she always lauded me to the echo, declared me to be a 'gentleman,' while he was denounced as quite the reverse. To our mutual amusement, we found that these most extraordinary tactics were resorted to in either prison, as a sort of calming ebullition to Miss Fowler's implacable fury when under confinement.

Persons of this description, who always proved violent and untameable, were happily only few when compared with those of gentle disposition. Indeed, as I have before remarked, whenever these distressing outbursts occurred, the agitation and alarm, the sobs and tears that convulsed an overwhelming majority of these poor creatures showed, that even a life of wild licentiousness, could not, with all its demoralizing tendencies, divest most women of their inborn gentleness of heart. For the honour of human nature, this fact should never be forgotten. So many kind and amiable traits would shine forth, so much docility, cordial good-will, and grateful demonstration would adorn very many of these outcast daughters of affliction, that apart from their unhappy position you might almost be led to esteem them.

The monsters in female shape were the exceptions, but to their hateful qualities language fails to render complete justice. I have witnessed scenes of such terrific violence, arising from the reckless brutality of one or two desperate women, that the matron, all the female attendants, and every female prisoner, except the one or two infuriated combatants, have exhibited paroxysms of grief and terror, and shed such copious tears, that it became a touching spectacle for any man to witness their agony.

At the period of unrestrained communication amongst prisoners, a girl named Duthoid, aged about twenty years, of comely face and well-proportioned frame, maintained so resolute a fight with all the male officers who could possibly be detached to subdue her, that nothing within those walls could ever compare with that combat. Her strength proved to be enormous, and her spirit indomitable, but while she and other such termagants did their utmost to inflict injury, the men, on the contrary, were always enjoined to overcome the rebel women without dealing out hurtful blows. The poor fellows were sometimes sorely punished, but their forbearance in every such encounter was really most laudable. The agitation that prevailed within that ward was most impressive. Many of the prisoners fainted, and the red and swollen eyes of all, throughout that day, attested their excessive emotion.

The girl, Duthoid, who had caused this memorable sensation, was then under a sentence of one year's imprisonment. She had to endure a considerable amount of solitary confinement to atone for her very grave misconduct, and she became ashamed of her unwomanly excess. From that time forth, to the end of her term, she observed exemplary conduct; and the chief female turnkey, who, subsequently to the outrage, conceived in consequence of her penitence an interest in her, assured me she was 'a good-hearted girl.' This is another amongst innumerable examples of the results of a mother's early neglect to restrain an unruly temper.

There were not wanting occasions in which the rejection of authority displayed itself in the most amusing form, and one, in particular, surpassed most others in the rare comicality of its details.

We were compelled from want of space to place many prisoners in one sleeping-room. About the period of which I am now treating, we were tormented by the flippant impertinence of a very young girl named Lacy, who was not more than seventeen years of age, of very slender form, and possessing a thin, sallow countenance. Having very early embraced a vicious career, she was thoroughly versed in all the wickedness of her craft, and was moreover, a girl of exceeding bad temper.

On a summer evening, fourteen 'disorderly' girls were consigned to one room, and amongst that number was Lacy, to whom the retiring turnkey had given some offence before she locked the door. When this knot of vicious young husseys had been left to themselves, Lacy's rage boiled over, and she incited the rest to join her in overt violence to revenge the affront she had received. The general destruction of the windows promptly ensued, whilst shouts and menaces added to the uproar.

I was very soon apprized of the mutiny, and summoned Mr. Sims and the night-guard of male turnkeys to hasten to the spot, and there to single out the delinquents. It is, perhaps, needless to say that no female superintendent would have dared – alone and unsupported – to confront her charge, whilst thus excited. In relating what ensued, I must beg pardon of the over-scrupulous, if I am compelled, as a truthful historian, to call things by their common names, since I know not otherwise how to convey a notion of the scene.

As we approached the room, which stood at the extremity of a long passage, our ears were assailed by the angry shrieks and vociferations of the young furies, who, divested of their upper garments, stood simply in their *chemises de nuit*.[43] In the compulsory interference of the men with the women's department, all practical decorum was strictly observed; in this instance, however, there was no alternative but – as the female attendant opened the door – to rush in and bring forth the ringleaders, unless a voluntary surrender should obviate the employment of hostile measures.

I stood at the end of the passage while Sims advanced, and, as a demand to yield and to come out as they were called proved unavailing, the door was opened. The first object that caught the eye was the frail form of Lacy, who, as the prime inciter, led the van. With an indispensable utensil brandished as a weapon in the right hand, while she encouragingly waved the other, she exclaimed, in a loud voice – 'Now, if you're girls, follow me!' Thus saying, she rushed boldly on Sims, only to be instantly overpowered and secured. As usual in cases of overt resistance, the rest became alarmed, burst into tears, and calmly submitted.

In order to overcome the scepticism of many readers who might be led to doubt whether a young girl of seventeen years of age, and a prisoner, could possess the hardihood thus to act, I tender my solemn assurance that there is not one iota of exaggeration in the narrative I have just given. The whole occurrence was fraught with ludicrous accompaniments, and caused as much after-merriment.

Lacy subsequently married some low vagabond, named Goswell, and in that name she became notorious in the Bridewell[44] of Westminster, as an untameable vixen, whose excesses of violence and utter disregard of all decency made her a serious nuisance to the governor, and more especially to the matron, and all females who exercised authority there. [pp. 175–88]

EXPLANATORY NOTES

[Batty Langley], *An Accurate Description of Newgate*

1. Henry *I* ... *King* Stephen: lived 1068/9–1135 and *c.* 1092–1154, respectively; at first, part of the gatehouse of Newgate, an entrance to London through its city walls, was used as a lock-up for offenders, but a prison was made part of the gate when rebuilt in 1188 at the order of Henry II.
2. *Sir* Richard Whittington: (*c.* 1350–1423) semi-legendary figure who rose from mercer's apprentice to become a wealthy merchant and financier and Lord Mayor of London. By the early seventeenth century ballads and tales attributed his success to luck as well as diligence: his master sent a cargo to north Africa and offered Whittington the chance to invest in it; owning only a cat, he sent that. It turned out the north African king's court was infested with rats, which the cat slew, whereupon it was purchased by the king for an enormous sum, making Whittington rich. Whittington's executors obtained a license to renovate Newgate prison in 1422.
3. *Tuscan Order*: in contrast to the Doric, Ionic, Corinthian and Composite orders, the simplest of the systems of architectural design and decoration, characterized by unfluted columns, plain entablatures, unadorned column capitals and bases and short columns widely spaced
4. *Master's Side*: accommodation for those imprisoned for debt.
5. *Common Felons*: those who have committed crimes considered serious, defined variously at different times.
6. *Prov*: the Bible, book of Proverbs.
7. *Customary Dues*: fees paid according to custom rather than legislation or regulation.
8. *Pretender*: James Francis Stuart (1688–1766), known as the Old Pretender, led an unsuccessful invasion of Scotland in 1715 to reclaim the British throne forcibly abdicated by his father James II in 1688; his son, Charles Edward Stuart (1720–88), known as the Young Pretender, made a similar attempt in 1745.
9. *Pillory'd*: subjected to the legal punishment of being confined for a specified time by head and hands in a public pillory or stocks.
10. *Bilbows*: from bilbo, an iron bar for shackling prisoners, fixed to the floor.
11. *Barracks*: wooden frames for simple accommodation.
12. *Transportation*: punishment by exile for seven or fourteen years or life, at this time to the American colonies.

13. Augean *Stable*: in ancient legend, infamously filthy stables of king Augeas, which the strongman Hercules was tasked to clean and did so by diverting two rivers through them.
14. *Pressed to Death*: a punishment applied to persons who refused to plead to a criminal charge, last applied twelve years after Langley's book was published.
15. *Conveniency*: defecating and urinating.
16. 18d: 18 pence, about £9 in today's money, using the retail price index.
17. *Arch of the* Gothick *Order*: a pointed arch.
18. *Blessed Sacrament*: wafer and wine symbolizing the body and blood of Christ as sacrifice for humanity's sins, administered by the priest and consumed by the worshipper in the ritual of Holy Communion.
19. *Hempen String*: noose for hanging.
20. Tyburn: site of present day Marble Arch, at the intersection of Oxford Street and Hyde Park Lane, London; location of the gallows until 1783, to which condemned convicts were drawn in a cart from Newgate prison for public execution. Such events drew crowds and sometimes resulted in public disorder.
21. *Ceremony*: Langley's footnote identifies the donor of this ceremony as Robert Dows, or Dowe (*c.* 1523–1612), freeman of the Merchant Taylors' Company (or guild) of the City of London, engaged in trade with Russia and Spain; his philanthropy included building almshouses for the poor and funding religious instruction (including the ceremony described here) for convicts.
22. *Sale ... each*: The informal practice was made a legal requirement in 1752, when bodies of murderers were required to be hung in chains or turned over for dissection in one of the anatomy schools, as a further deterrent to the crime; this was deeply unpopular, at times leading to public disturbances after an execution.
23. viz: *videlicet*: namely (Latin).
24. *to*: probably 'to be' is meant.
25. *repreived*: more usually 'reprieved'.
26. Smithfield: main meat market in central London.
27. Fœlix ... cautum: or *Felix, quem faciunt aliena pericula cautum*, often quoted Latin proverb (attributed to first-century AD Roman philosopher Seneca) meaning, 'Fortunate the one made cautious by others' perils'.
28. *Common-Debtors*: those imprisoned for inability to pay debts.
29. Purney: Thomas Purney (1695–*c.* 1730) attended Merchant Tailors School, London and Cambridge University, graduating in 1715–6. He then attempted a career as a poet, probably as a means to obtain patronage, publishing a book of pastorals, a critical book on pastoral poetry and an anti-Jacobite poem. He also advertised a long poem on the Black Prince which was not published. He then turned to the profession of clergyman, being ordained in 1719, and was appointed Ordinary of Newgate, a post which paid relatively little (the *New Dictionary of National Biography* states his salary as £35 a year) but which enabled the holder to publish the very popular accounts of the 'last dying words' of those condemned to be hanged – Purney's predecessor left an estate of £5000 amassed from this trade. Purney failed in attempts to reduce the disorder common at Newgate chapel's services. His death may have been caused by typhus contracted at Newgate.
30. *Tythes, Easter-Offerings*: tithes; one tenth of a person's income or produce, supposed to be given to support the church and clergy; Easter offering; contribution made to the clergy on receiving a token of being prepared to take Easter Holy Communion.
31. *Cloth*: the clergy.

32. *State Prisoners*: those arrested or convicted of crimes against the state, such as treason.
33. *Quality*: social rank or status.
34. Preston *Gentlemen*: supporters of the Old Pretender defeated at the battle of Preston during the Jacobite uprising of 1715.

Cesare Beccaria, *An Essay on Crimes and Punishments*

1. Montesquieu: Charles Louis de Secondat Montesqiueu (1689–1755), French nobleman and lawyer, author of widely read books such as *Lettres persanes* (1721) and especially the influential *De l'Esprit des lois* (*The Spirit of the Laws*, 1748).
2. *sensibility*: both bodily and moral sensitivity.
3. Leze-majesty: a footnote translates this legal-French phrase as 'high-treason'.
4. *Lacedemonian or a Persian*: respectively, an inhabitant of ancient Sparta in Greece, known for abstemiousness, martial valour, moral uprightness and fierce independence, and inhabitant of the ancient Persian empire, known for luxuriousness, despotic government and subservience.
5. *Titus, an Antoninus or a Trajan*: respectively Titus Flavius Vespasianus (AD 39–81), Roman general who suppressed the Jewish revolt and later became emperor; Marcus Aurelius Antoninus (AD 121–180), Roman general, emperor and philosopher, who defended the empire against attacks from the east; and Marcus Ulpius Nerva Traianus (AD 53–117), Roman emperor who expanded the empire along the Danube river and in the east.

William Eden, *Principles of Penal Law*

1. *heading*: The title page has an epigraph from the Roman writer Cicero, *De legibus* (*Of Laws*), I.xlii: 'Est enim unum jus, quo devincta est hominum societas, et quod lex constituit una: quæ lex est recta ratio imperandi atque prohibendi: quam si quis legum Lator ignoret, is est injustus': For there is one justice, by which society binds men, and this law constitutes as one; this law is right reason commanding and forbidding; that legislator who neglects this law is unjust.
2. *Vengeance ... man*: echoing the sentiment of the Bible, Romans 12:19: 'avenge not yourselves, but rather give place unto wrath; for it is written, Vengeance is mine; I will repay, saith the Lord.'
3. *Plato*: Eden's footnote refers to Cicero, *De legibus* (*Of Laws*), citing the Greek philosopher Plato (*c.* 429–347 BC).
4. *Meti ... sunt*: Roman historian Livy (Titus Livius), *Ab urbe condita* (*The History of Rome*), book 1, ch. 28: 'Mettius Fufettius, Tullus said, if you could have kept your word and respected the treaties, I would have instructed you so in your lifetime; now, since your character is ruined, teach humanity by your punishment to hold sacred what you have violated.'
5. Qui ... videtur: Eden cites the *Digests* or *Pandects*, a summary of Roman law formulated at the order of the emperor Justinian (AD *c.* 482–565): 'Who steals by force is seen to be a worse thief.'
6. *death*: Eden's footnote in this case, as in many others through the text, refers to a particular act of parliament, in the standard form giving year of monarch's reign in which the legislation was passed, abbreviated form of the monarch's regal name (Eliz[abeth],

Geo[rge], Ed[ward], Hen[ry]. Car[olus, or Charles], W[illiam] and so on) and number (e. g., I, II, III), and number of the act (in this case, c. 4).

7. *benefit of clergy*: an ancient exemption from punishment for members of the clergy, and later for anyone who could prove literacy; it fell into disuse in the eighteenth century and was abolished in 1827; Eden's footnote indicates the source for his reference as William Hawkins, *A Treatise of the Pleas of the Crown* (1716–21), I.97.

8. *committed*: Eden's footnote includes a passage from Charles Louis de Secondat Montesquieu, *De l'Esprit des lois* (*The Spirit of the Laws*, 1748), which may be translated: 'Liberty triumphs when each punishment is based on the nature of the crime: arbitrariness ceases, punishment derives not from the lawgiver's whim but from the nature of the thing, and man does no violence to man.'

9. *writer*: Eden's footnote and the following one refer to the most widely used English legal manual, William Blackstone's *Commentaries on the Laws of England* (1765–9), IV.241 and IV.16.

10. ea sunt ... præcaventur: Eden's footnote identifies the source as the Roman writer Cicero, *Oratio pro Sexto Roscio*, ch. 40, which may be translated: 'crimes that are hardest to guard against are those to be punished most severely'.

11. *law*: Eden's footnote quotes Cicero again, his speech *In Verrem*, II.i.39, translated: 'This is a common evil, common anxiety, common danger. There are no more insidious intrigues than those concealed under pretense of duty, or the name of some obligation. For you can easily avoid an open adversary, by guarding against him. This secret, internal, and domestic evil is not only real, but even overwhelms you before you can anticipate or investigate it.'

12. *confidence*: Eden's footnote cites the French *code pénal* with two quotations, the first of which may be translated, 'Domestic theft will be punished by death', and the second, 'When someone commits domestic theft from his Lord, it is a hanging offence, for it is a kind of treason.'

13. credidisset: Eden here quotes two passages also from Cicero, *Pro Roscio Amerino*, section 116 (somewhat compressed) and 112: 'To whose Succour then can he fly, after having been injur'd by the very Succour to which he trusted? We can be upon our Guard to Strangers ... but who can guard against a Partner? For the very distrusting him does Injury to our particular Engagements'; and 'For no man gives a Commission to another, unless he thinks him his Friend; nor trusts any Man whom he does not believe to be honest. He must, therefore, be a most consummate Villain who shall at once dissolve the Ties of Friendship, and deceive the Man, who but for his trusting him would not have been injur'd'; *The Orations of Cicero*, trans. William Guthrie, 3 vols (London: T. Waller, 1743), III.82, 85.

14. Une loi rigoureuse produit des crimes: A severe law produces crimes (French).

15. soumet: Eden's footnote identifies the source as Charles Louis de Secondat Montesquieu, *De l'Esprit des lois* (*The Spirit of the Laws*, 1748); the quotation may be translated: If punishments inflicted in almost all oriental countries strike humanity with horror, it is because the despot who orders them sees himself as above the law. It is not thus in republics; laws there are always mild because those who make them submit to them.

16. *statute*: Eden's footnote cites a Swedish law in Latin: The shameless woman who, having cohabited out of wedlock, carries a child, and before giving birth does not reveal it, seeking a hiding place to bear it secretly, and then conceals it, is to be struck with an axe, and burned on the scaffold, without regard to the pretext of stillbirth or premature birth.

17. *treasons*: Eden's footnote refers to the fate of Lady Alice Lisle (*c.*1614–85) and Elizabeth Gaunt (died 1685), as narrated in David Hume's *History of Great Britain* (1754–62) and Gilbert Burnet's *History of His Own Time* (1724–34).

18. work: Eden's footnote refers to one of the works of the law writer Sir Michael Foster (1689–1763).

19. clergyable: entitled to benefit of clergy, formerly the privilege of the clergy to be tried by ecclesiastical rather than secular courts, then a privilege extended to the clergy of exemption or mitigation of usual punishments, then extended to any person who could prove literacy, in effect providing for more lenient sentences for first-time offenders; it fell into disuse by the late eighteenth century and was abolished in 1827.

20. within clergy: within the terms extending benefit of clergy.

21. *magis ... rationem*: They know more of their times than they do of right reason.

22. *Egyptians*: or Gypsies, so-called because they were thought to have originated in Egypt; Eden's footnote also refers to a declaration of Louis XIV of France, 'against Bohemians, and those who afford them refuge'.

23. *Mezentius*: in ancient Roman legend, an Etruscan king exiled for his extreme cruelty.

24. *approvers*: those who give evidence against others.

25. *offenders*: Eden uses these terms: approvers: those incriminating others; statutes of labourers: legislation restricting work conditions and wages; purveyance: enforced requisition.

26. legis: Eden's footnote identifies the source as Francis Bacon, *De dignitate et augmentis scientiarum* (1623), an expansion and translation into Latin of his *The Advancement of Learning* (1605); the passage may be translated, 'the acuteness of the ingenious is worth more than the authority of law'.

27. *weep*: Shakespeare, *Measure for Measure*, II.ii.115–23.

28. *Suffetius*: Eden's footnote identifies the source as the Roman Historian Livy (Titus Livius), *Ab urbe condita* (*History of Rome*), I.xxviii; the passage may be translated: 'Whereupon, two chariots pulled by four horses were brought up, Mettius was tied between them, and they were driven in opposite directions, taking his mangled body with them, the limbs hanging by the sinews. People all turned from this horrific sight; it was the first and last use by the Romans of a precedent so disregardful of humanity; otherwise, we can boast that other peoples have not adopted milder punishments.'

29. *furca*: a fork-shaped restraint.

30. *death*: Eden's footnote refers to and quotes from the Roman historian Suetonius's life of the emperor Caligula, ch. 27, in *The Twelve Caesars*; the passage may be translated: 'Caligula had the supervisor of his gladiator and animal exhibitions whipped before him with chains several days in succession, and only had him killed when offended by the stink of his putrefied brains.'

31. supplicium more majorum: customary or usual punishment (Latin). Eden's footnote refers to and quotes from (somewhat compressing the original) Suetonius's life of the emperor Nero, ch. 49, in *The Twelve Caesars*; the passage may be translated: 'Nero seized the letter and reading that the senate had condemned him as a public enemy, asked what the nature of the customary punishment was. And when he learned that the naked criminal was held in the furca and beaten to death with rods, terrified, he drove a dagger into his throat.'

32. *beheading*: Eden's footnote refers to the Greek history of Rome by Cassius Dio (AD 150–235)

33. servile supplicium: punishment for slaves (Latin).

34. *Constantine*: Gaius Flavius Valerius Aurelius Constantinus (AD 272–337), Roman emperor, who proclaimed Christianity the state religion in AD 313.
35. verbera ... suspendito: somewhat altered from the original Latin, 'infelici arbori reste suspendito; verberato vel intra pomerium vel extra pomerium': 'hang him by a rope on the accursed tree, scourge him either within or outside the pomerium (the sacred boundary of Rome)'. Eden's footnote identifies the source as Livy's *History of Rome*, I.i (in fact I.xxvi) and also cites Valerius Maximus, first-century AD compiler of a collection of historical anecdotes in nine books.
36. *Parricides*: Eden's footnote cites two lines from the eighth satire of the Roman poet Juvenal, which may be translated: for whose punishment should be prepared not one ape, nor one serpent, nor one sack (ll. 213–14); Eden also cites Justinian's *Digest* or *Pandects* of Roman laws, the city of Pompeii's laws on patricide, and Cicero's speech *pro Sextus Roscio*.
37. *Seneca*: Eden's Latin quotation compresses a passage in Seneca the Younger's *Epistles*, 14, roughly translated by the preceding passage in English.
38. Serræ-dissectio: Eden's footnote refers to Suetonius's life of Caligula, *The Twelve Caesars*, ch. 27.
39. bestias: combats of wild animals and condemned men.
40. præclara ... Bestiarii: from Cicero, *pro Sestio*, LXIV: 'A true aedileship! one lion, two hundred men who fight beasts'. (The aedile was a Roman civic official responsible, among other things, for putting on public entertainments such as gladiatorial contests and wild animal shows.)
41. *Decemvirs*: a commission of 'ten men' given various tasks in Roman government, such as writing laws, overseeing important public rites and so on.
42. *money*: Eden's footnote refers to the Greek orator Demosthenes, citing *Demosthenes contra Aristocratem oratio* (1530) and Samuel Petit, *Leges Atticae* (*Laws of Attica*), Paris, 1635).
43. *Man*: quotation differs slightly from the account in *A complete Collection of State –Trials, and Proceedings for High Treason, and Other Crimes and Misdemeanours*, 2nd edn, 6 vols (London: J. Walthoe, sr., and others, 1730), II.409.
44. *lingering sufferance*: Shakespeare, *Measure for Measure*, II.iv.166, spoken by Angelo to Isabella in threatening to have her brother tortured to death unless she yield to his lust.
45. perpetuo ... 'Ita feri, ut se mori sentiat': the Roman historian Suetonius's, life of Caligula, in *The Twelve Caesars*, 30: [Caligula] constantly gave this well-known order, 'Strike so that he feels he is dying'.
46. *afterwards*: conflation of lines spoken by Pompey in Shakespeare, *Measure for Measure*, IV.iii.23–32.
47. *as a man ... to come*: adapting Shakespeare, *Measure for Measure*, IV.ii.140–3, said by the Provost of Barnardine.
48. *Cicero*: quotation compressed from Cicero's oration *pro A. Caecina*, section 100: 'Exile is not a punishment but a refuge and haven from punishment. Hence there is nothing found in our law, as there is in other states, mention of crime punished by banishment. But as men aimed to avoid prison, execution, or disgrace, which are set down by the laws, they fled to exile as if to sanctuary; whereas if they chose to undergo the rigour of the law in the city, they would no more lose their civil rights than their life. Choosing to do otherwise, their rights are not taken from them but rather abandoned and cast aside by them.'

49. *Transportation*: Eden's footnote cites William Rastall, *A Collection of All the Statutes from the Beginning of the Magna Charta unto this Present Yere of Our Lorde God 1574* (London: Richard Tottell, 1574); and John Kelyng, *A Report of Divers Cases in Pleas of the Crown, Adjudged and Determined in the Reign of the Late King Charles II, with Directions for Justices of the Peace and Others* (London: I. Cleave, 1708)

50. perdere patriam, quam vitam: to lose his native land rather than his life (Latin).

51. *sanctuary*: Eden's footnote cites a manual on the customary laws of Normandy, *Le Grant coustumier du pays et duché de Normendie* (1515), and the *Mirror*, probably Peter Hughes, *Georgicum; or, A Supplement to The Mirror of Justices* (London, 1716), referring to Andrew Horne, *La Somme appellé Mirroir des Justices, vel speculum Iusticiariorum* (1642).

52. *Ja. I*: James I.

53. *Russia*: Eden's footnote refers to *Voyages en Sibérie*, probably Abbé Chappe d'Autreroche, *Voyage en Sibérie, fait par ordre du roi en 1761* (Paris: Dubure père, 1768), translated into English in 1770; or Johann Georg Gmelin, *Voyage en Sibérie: contenant la description des moeurs et usages des peuples de ce pays ...* (Paris: Desaire, 1767). The passage in the footnote may be translated: 'Exile in Siberia carries with it a kind of disapproval: it makes a man so unhappy that, though he lives amidst those like himself, everyone avoids him. and no one dares have any connection with him; but this is less because of his supposed crime than because of fear of the despot.'

54. Duri ... oppetere: The passage collates two passages from the Roman writer Cicero, *Epistularum ad familiares* (*Letters to Friends*), IV.ix, to Marcellus: 'It is hard not to long for one's native land'; and *De officiis*, I.xcvii: 'Parents are dear; children are dear; relations and friends are dear: But our native country alone involves all these ties of affection. What honest man would hesitate to meet death for his country's good?' (Cicero, *The Treatise of Cicero, De officiis*, trans. William M'Cartney, Edinburgh, 1798, p. 44)

55. *Sparta*: ancient Greek city-state famous for its simple life and martial character, verging on barbarity.

56. consumitur: Eden's footnote identifies the source as Justinian's *Digests* or *Pandects*, a summary of Roman law, L.xiii.5: 'Reputation is unimpaired worth confirmed by law and custom, which is destroyed or diminished by legal authority because of some offence of ours.'

57. *present Empress of Russia*: Catherine II (1729–96), known as 'the Great', considered a model of the enlightened despot.

58. *du Halde*: J. B. du Halde, *Description géographique, historique, chronologique, politique, et physique de l'empire de la Chine* (1735).

59. *Lord Anson's voyage*: George Anson, *A Voyage to the South Seas* (1745).

60. mort: These two passages may be translated: 'Those who, having been condemned for theft, or branded for any crime whatever, being repeat criminals, may not be sentenced to any less punishment than, for men, being sent to the galleys for a term or for life, and, for women, being branded again with a W, if a repeat thief, or with a simple V if the first brand has been incurred for another crime. And those who are condemned to the galleys for a term or for life for any crime whatever, will be branded, before being taken there, with the three letters G. A. L. so that, in case of repeat offence warranting corporal punishment, they will be punished by death.'

61. inscripti or stigmatici: marked.

62. literati: literally, 'lettered' (Latin), which can also mean literate, having literary cultivation; Eden's footnote refers to Lodovico Ricchieri (Lodovicus Caelius Rhodoginus),

Sicuti antiquarum lectionem (1516), with a quotation, 'No Samians more lettered' (branded); and to a quotation from *Casina* (II.vi.49), a play by the Roman writer Plautus, 'If this letter marked me'.

63.   quod ... duxit: from Petronius's Latin novel, *The Satiricon*, ch. 103: Eumolpus covered the foreheads of Encolpus and Gytonis with large letters and with a liberal hand freely spread the sign of fugitives over the whole face.

64.   *crime*: Eden's footnote refers to Sir Edward Coke, *Institutes of the Lawes of England* (1628–44), also known as *Commentary upon Littleton* (i.e., Sir Thomas Littleton, *Tenures*, London: R. Pynson, 1490).

65.   *reason*: Eden's footnote refers to William Nelson and Geoffrey Gilbert, *The Law of Evidence* (London: Elizabeth Nutt and R. Gosling, 1717).

66.   crimen falsi: crime of deceit (Latin).

67.   Ictus ... irrogat: Eden's footnote identifies the source as the *Digests* or *Pandects* of the Roman emperor Justinian, III.iii.22: 'The club's blow does not cause disgrace, but the reason that it is deserved does, if it is such as to bring disgrace on the convicted.'

68.   *enacting*: Eden's footnote refers to the famous *Lives* of ancient Greeks and Romans, by Plutarch (AD 46–127).

69.   *Regi*: Eden's footnote refers to D. Wilkins, *Leges anglo-saxonicae ecclesiasticae & civiles* (London: R. Gosling, 1721); H. Knighton, 'Chronica de eventibus Angliae à tempore Regis Edgari usque mortem Regis Ricardi Secundi', in R.Twysden, (ed.) *Historiae anglicanae scriptores X* (London: Bee, 1652); F. Godwin and M. Godwin, *Annales of England* (London: I. Smethwicke, 1630).

70.   *Severus*: Lucius Septimius Severus (AD 146–211), Roman general and emperor.

71.   *hand*: Eden's footnote refers to T. Fuller, *The Soveraigns Prerogative and the Subjects Priviledge* (London: H. Marsh, 1658); and D. Barrington, *Observations upon the Statutes, Chiefly the More Ancient, from the Magna Carta* (London: S. Baker, and W. Sandby, 1766).

72.   *clergable*: or clergyable: entitled to benefit of clergy.

73.   *Coke*: Eden's footnote refers to Sir Edward Coke's classic compilation and commentary, *Institutes of the Lawes of England* (1628–44); Sir William Staunford, *Les Plees du coron* (1557), or to *An Exposicion of the Kings Prerogative* (1567)

74.   Geo. III: Eden's footnote refers to the court leet, a court of record held periodically by the head of a local administrative area, and attended by the residents, and to the sheriff's tourn or turn, a circuit traveled twice a year by the sheriff, at various points on which he would hold a court leet.

75.   *deceased*: Eden's footnote refers to and quotes the provision of Roman code for public display of executed criminals, 'So that the sight of the murderers should both deter others and be a consolation to the kindred [of the victims]'.

76.   corvos: Eden's footnote identifies the source at the Roman poet Horace (Quintus Horatius Flaccus, *Epistles*, I.xvi.46–8: 'If a slave tells me, "I neither stole nor ran away," I say, you have your reward: you do not feel the whip. [He says,] I killed no man; I reply, "Nor have you fed the crows while hanging on the cross."'

77.   *defiled*: Eden's footnote cites the Bible, Deuteronomy, 21:23.

78.   licet: Eden's footnote refers to the preface to the Roman writer Aulus Cornelius Celsus (25 BC–AD 50), *De medicina*; the passage appears to be a paraphrase rather than a direct quotation, and may be translated, 'Whereby, because of the unreasonableness of the times, it is not permitted to dissect living men.' In fact, Celsus describes dissection of the living as cruel and unnecessary.

79. *writer*: Eden's footnote refers again to Barrington, *Observations upon the Statutes, Chiefly the More Ancient, from the Magna Carta* (London, 1766).

William Dodd, *Thoughts in Prison*

1. *Inquisition*: reference to the ecclesiastical tribunal of the Roman Catholic Church, charged with detecting, converting – if necessary, with torture – or executing heretics. English Protestants saw the Inquisition as characteristic of foreign despotic governments; Dodd suggests that the English prison is comparable to the Inquisition.
2. *balances*: The female personification of Justice is typically depicted as blindfolded and holding a set of scales, or balances.
3. *EXEMPLARY Punishment*: public hangings.
4. *Tent*: take notice of.
5. *madding*: frenzied.
6. *what ... Fellows*: It was notorious that pickpockets worked among the crowds assembled to see a public hanging, at a time when pickpocketing could receive the death sentence.
7. *honest Creditor ... worldlings all unknown*: It was a commonplace of the time that genteel and noble customers often kept tradespeople waiting long periods to be paid, perhaps forcing them to choose between crime or bankruptcy.
8. *Den*: prison.
9. *chains*: Dodd's footnote refers to Bedlam, a London hospital and asylum for the insane.

J. Leroux, *Thoughts on the Present State of the Prisons of This Country*

1. *tap rooms*: rooms where beer could be purchased by prisoners.
2. *excess*: here meaning excessive drinking, and perhaps other vices.
3. *keepers*: warders or guards.
4. *farm*: contract to supply, keeping the profits.
5. *gaming*: gambling.
6. *harpies*: in ancient legend, a ferocious animal with female face and bird's wings and talons, administering divine vengeance.
7. *bail*: fee or security for temporary release on undertaking to reappear at a specified time and place.
8. *Palladian windows*: large windows with central section and two narrower flanking sections, in the neoclassical style of the architect Palladio (1508–80), newly fashionable in the late eighteenth century.
9. *Water closets*: toilets.
10. *political*: of good policy, good management.
11. *their being secluded ... work of reformation*: an early statement of the view that isolation of prisoners would encourage self-reflection and the subjective transformation prerequisite to reformation in behaviour, whereas socializing among prisoners reinforced outlawed social behaviour, or crime.
12. *durance*: confinement; a word associated with chivalric literary romances.
13. *viz*: *videlicet*; namely (Latin).
14. *safe custody*: Leroux's footnote refers to John Howard's recently published survey, *The State of the Prisons in England and Wales* (1777).

[Martin Madan], *Thoughts on Executive Justice*

1. *heading*: The title-page has an epigraph from the Latin poet Horace (Quintus Horatius Flaccus, 65–8 BC), *Epistles*, I.xvi.40–2: 'Vir bonus est quis?/ Qui consulta Patrum, qui leges juraque servat, / Quo multæ magnæque secantur Judice lites': 'Who then is good? He who observes the decrees of the senate, who observes the laws and rules of justice, by whose arbitration many and important disputes are decided ...' (Christopher Smart, *The Works of Horace, Translated Literally into English Prose*, 1783, p. 317).

2. *houses*: Madan's footnote uses the French expression *par des rossignols Anglois*: by English nightingales, as a French expression for thieves.

3. King Alfred: ninth-century ruler and law-giver of the Anglo-Saxon kingdom of Wessex.

4. Oderunt ... pœnæ: Evil men avoid sin through fear of punishment (Latin), the second half of a Latin saying cited by writers from St Thomas Aquinas on, the first half of which (Oderunt peccare boni virtutis amore: The good hate sin out of love for virtue) is from Horace, *Epistles*, I.xvi.52

5. Making night hideous: Shakespeare, *Hamlet*, I.iv.54, spoken by Hamlet on seeing his father's ghost.

6. *Old-Bailey ... Assize-Calendar*: calendar or list of prisoners for trial at assizes held in county towns or at the Old Bailey, the major criminal court in central London, so called from the street in which it was situated.

7. We have ... decorum: Shakespeare, *Measure for Measure*, I.iii.19–31.

8. common *and* statute *laws*: laws embodied, respectively, in custom or in statute.

9. crown law: law relating to crimes.

10. Conquest: the Norman Conquest of England by William the Conquerer in 1066.

11. *respect*: Madan's footnote makes the following references: 'what *Cæsar* said his wife *ought to be* – Not only chaste – but unsuspected': from an anecdote in the Greek writer Plutarch's 'Life' of Julius Caesar, in which scandal linked Caesar's second wife Pompeia with a known womanizer; 'what Lord *Chesterfield* so pathetically styles, "poor human nature"': Philip Dormer Stanhope, Earl of Chesterfield, *Letters* to his son (1774), letter 95; 'as *Voltaire* says of a certain *Abbé* "*par l'excès de leurs bonnes intentions*"': Voltaire, *Discours en vers sur l'homme*, Septième discours, referring to the Abbé de Saint-Pierre, 'Il s'est rendu un peu ridicule en France par l'excès de ses bonnes intentions' ('He made himself somewhat ridiculous in France by his excessive good intentions'), *Épitres, satires, contes, odes, et pièces fugitives* ('Londres', 1771), p. 250 n.

12. oyer and terminer: to hear and determine (legal French), a commission authorizing a judge to hold courts.

13. gaol-delivery: clearing a jail by bringing its prisoners to trial and either convicting or releasing them.

14. *sit down in peace and safety*: perhaps echoing the Bible, Psalms 4:8: 'I will both lay me down in peace, and sleep: for thou, Lord, only makest me dwell in safety.'

15. *none to make them afraid*: also echoing the Bible, in several passages, e. g., Leviticus 26:6, Ezekiel 34:28.

16. grand jury: jury of inquiry, accusation, or presentment comprising from twelve to twenty-three persons (at this time, men), as distinct from the *petty jury*, or jury of trial.

17. Ut pœna ... perveniat: Punishment is inflicted on a few so as to cause dread in all; a Latin legal maxim quoted by English writers on jurisprudence from Sir Edward Coke to William Blackstone, derived from the Latin writer Cicero, *Pro A. Cluentio Habito*, 'ut metus videlicet ad omnes, poena ad paucos perveniret' (ch. 46).

18. minister of GOD for good: echoing the Bible, Romans 13:4.
19. He bears ... in vain: echoing the Bible, Romans 13:4.
20. ministry: In using this word to describe the secular work of the judge, Madan implies a parallel between such work and the spiritual ministry of the clergyman.
21. *generation to generation*: echoing several passages in the Bible, e. g., Exodus 17:6, Isaiah 34:10, and others.
22. *Blessed ... hear*: the Bible, 1 Samuel 15:13–14.
23. *accessaries*: Madan's footnote cites a passage in Shakespeare, *Measure for Measure*, I.iii.31–9.
24. Savior ... rabies: a phrase from the Latin author Claudian, *In Rufinum*, I.236–37: pardoning savagery crueller than the sword.
25. parcendi rabies: pardoning savagery (Latin).
26. Quid tristes ... *vain*: Madan's footnote cites the Latin poet Horace, *Odes*, III.xxiv.33–4, as translated by Philip Francis.
27. *Examples ... pity*: from Niccolo Machiavelli, *The Prince* (*Il Principe*, 1515), a book on how to govern, ch. 17, 'Concerning Cruelty and Clemency, and Whether It Is Better to Be Loved than Feared'.

William Paley, *The Principles of Moral and Political Philosophy*

1. *law of Moses*: the commandments or laws contained in the first five books (or Pentateuch) of the Bible, believed to be the word of God communicated to Moses.
2. *life ... blood*: echoing the Bible, Exodus 21:23.
3. *substract*: a variant of 'subtract'.
4. *places*: public offices.

Jeremy Bentham, *Panopticon*

1. Gordian knot: in ancient legend an intricate knot on an oxcart, sometimes represented as a chariot, in the city of Gordium; according to an oracle, whoever could untie the knot would become the ruler of the world; Alexander the Great, on his conquering path through west Asia, tried to untie the knot but eventually simply severed it with his sword, claiming the oracle's designation.
2. Poor-Laws: laws that established the structure, financing and conditions for providing relief to the indigent; these received much attention and reform in the late eighteenth and early nineteenth century, especially in relation to the question of whether providing such relief was a disincentive to the poor to find work.
3. quis custodiet ipsos custodes?: who will guard the guards? (Latin).
4. Akerman: Richard Akerman, keeper or governor of Newgate Prison at this time, appointed in 1754.
5. nunquam minus solus quam cum solus: never less alone than when alone (Latin).
6. *brother's*: Samuel Bentham (1757–1831), who devised the idea of an inspection-house while in Russia.
7. contract: Bentham planned to undertake the scheme himself, in company with his brother Samuel, as a way to provide Samuel with a business enterprise.
8. 10,000l: worth over £900,000 in 2006, using the retail price index.
9. *expedition to Botany Bay*: in 1787 a fleet of ships left Britain with a cargo of convicts to establish a colony at Botany Bay, Australia, arriving in 1788; Bentham would later con-

trast his Panopticon scheme with that of the penal colony in terms of extraction of labour from convicts.

10. viva voce: face-to-face, literally 'live voice' (Latin).
11. farmers general: in France, widely-despised financiers who paid the government for a contract to collect taxes, making their profit from the difference between what they paid for the contract and what they collected from taxpayers.
12. *Palmer ... Atkinsons*: John Palmer (1767–1836), richest British merchant in India, known as the 'prince of merchants'; Richard Atkinson (1738–85), merchant and a director of the East India Company, did well from government contracts, advised the government on affairs of the East India Company and died with a fortune of £300,000.
13. corn: grain in general.
14. Arthur Young: (1741–1820), son of a clergyman; turned from commerce to farming, at which he was unsuccessful, and took to traveling and writing up his observations in terms of application of capital and technology to increase productivity and profits.

John Howard, *The State of the Prisons in England and Wales*

1. 'sick, and in prison': echoing several passages in the Bible, Matthew 25:36.
2. *Sheriffs ... commission of the peace*: Sheriffs: municipal or county officers, appointed or elected, responsible for executing the laws; commission of the peace: justices of the peace, having a range of responsibilities including acting as local magistrates for petty offences.
3. bridewells: houses of correction for those convicted of lesser offences.
4. farms: contracts to someone else for a fee, leaving the contractor to extract a profit, usually at the expense of the inmates of the prison.
5. hard labour: a punishment meant as both deterrent from crime and training in work discipline, taking various forms at different times, such as beating hemp, working a manual water pump, picking oakum, or walking a large treadmill.
6. *profaneness*: swearing.
7. *quarter sessions*: trials held quarterly, or every three months.
8. *twenty pounds*: worth about £1,850 in 2006, using the retail price index.
9. *Carlisle*: county town of Cumberland, north-west England.
10. *groats*: food allowance, literally crushed grain.
11. *bailiffs*: officers empowered to execute certain legal orders.
12. spunging-houses: sponging-houses; kept by a bailiff for detention of debtors, who paid for their keep; sponging: extorting.
13. *public house*: tavern providing lodging, food, and drink.
14. *exchequer processes*: orders for seizure of goods or arrest for such matters as non-payment of excise duty or non-payment of tithes; inability to pay could result in lengthy imprisonment; widely unpopular and at times resisted by mob action.
15. *ecclesiastical courts*: courts with jurisdiction over matters spiritual, concerning religious ritual, the church, and clergy.
16. *bail*: fee or surety for temporary release from confinement while awaiting trial.
17. *insolvent acts*: legislation concerning bankruptcy; once declared bankrupt, a debtor could be released.
18. *farming*: contracting with someone to provide the service, for a profit.
19. *felons courts*: courtyards accommodating those convicted of serious offences.
20. gratis: free (French).
21. cordial of life: life-restoring and preserving substance.

22.   *Dr.* Hales: Stephen Hales (1677–1761), scientist and inventor of a mechanical ventilator for drawing fresh air into confined spaces.

23.   *salutiferous*: health-bearing.

24.   *hogshead*: liquid measure of fifty-two and a half imperial gallons (286.4 litres)

25.   *philosophers*: researchers, scientists.

26.   *taken out dead*: the infamous 'black hole of Calcutta', a small cell in which British prisoners were confined by Indian troops in 1756

27.   *heart of oak*: timber from the centre of the oak tree, and so particularly dense and hard.

28.   *close*: stifling.

29.   *misdemeanors*: lesser crimes.

30.   *assizes*: court sessions, at this time held at regular intervals and regarded as a form of public entertainment, occasioning social gatherings of various kinds.

31.   Gaol-fever: virulent typhus, or fever accompanied by weakness.

32.   Baker's Chronicle: Sir Richard Baker (*c.* 1568–1645), who spent the last years of his life imprisoned for debt, author of the widely respected *Chronicle of the Kings of England* (1643).

33.   *lord chief baron*: head of the court of exchequer.

34.   Bacon: Francis Bacon (1561–1626), lawyer, important philosopher, and politician, appointed Lord Chancellor, or chief law official of the kingdom, in 1618.

35.   Mead: Richard Mead (1673–1754), physician and art collector, author of works on poisons, on the influence of weather and air on health, and on contagious diseases.

36.   *died*: quotation from Francis Bacon, *Sylva Sylvarum; or, A Natural History* (London, 1626), Century X, no. 914.

37.   *Taunton*: county town of Somerset, south-west England.

38.   Pengelly: Sir Thomas Pengelly (1675–1730).

39.   *sergeant*: officer responsible for summoning people before the court.

40.   Pringle: military physician and epidemiologist (1707–82), born in Scotland, studied at Leiden, appointed physician-general to the army in 1744, president of the Royal Society in 1772, practised medicine in London, wrote an essay on jail-fever in Newgate.

41.   *late rebellion in Scotland*: the Jacobite uprising of 1745, the end of which Pringle witnessed.

42.   Lind: James Lind (1716–94), like Pringle, a Scot; naval physician, head of the Haslar hospital from 1758 to 1783.

43.   *Portsmouth*: important port and naval centre in south-west England.

44.   *equipment*: fitting out (for service).

45.   *guard-ships ... squadrons*: guard-ship: warship protecting a harbour and accommodating seamen until they could be assigned to other vessels, or warship protecting a squadron; squadron: a division of a fleet commanded by a flag officer.

46.   *Fielding*: (1721–80), controversial magistrate who attempted to reform policing in London; blinded by an incompetent physician; knighted 1761; half-brother of the playwright and novelist Henry Fielding.

47.   *prisoners of war*: during the American Revolutionary War.

48.   *kind ... evil*: the Bible, Luke 6:35.

49.   *Let ... fall*: the Bible, 1 Corinthians 10:12.

50.   'The misery... manners': Samuel Johnson, *The Idler*, 38 (6 January 1759); often quoted.

51.   Garnish: money taken from a new prisoner by those already there.

52. *prove mortal*: Howard's footnote refers to the trial at the Old Bailey on 28 August 1730 of four men, themselves prisoners, who attacked a recently admitted prisoner in Newgate and took his money; the accused were convicted and sentenced to death.
53. *skittles, missisippi and portobello-tables*: skittles: a form of bowling with nine pins; missisippi: game in which points are scored by pushing a ball off cushions mounted on the sides of a table-top through arches placed on the table; portobello-tables: game resembling billiards.
54. *fives*: form of handball played in a three-sided court.
55. A Letter to Sir Robert Ladbroke: by Samuel Denne (1730–99), historian and antiquary.
56. *Lord* Coke, Horn's Mirror of Justice: Sir Edward Coke (1552–1634), lawyer, politician and voluminous writer on the law; Andrew Horn (*c.* 1275–1328), compiler of a large manuscript archive of legal statutes, and collector of manuscripts, including a *Mirror of Justices*.
57. Hale's History of the pleas of the crown: Sir Matthew Hale (1609–76), *History of the Pleas of the Crown* (1736), the main authority on English criminal law until the nineteenth century, written in Latin and published after Hale's death.
58. *Report*: *A Report from the Committee Appointed to Enquire into the State of the Gaols of This Kingdom Relating to the Marshalsea Prison and Farther Relating to the Fleet Prison; With the Resolution of the House of Commons Thereupon* (London: Robert Knaplock, Jacob Tonson, John Pemberton, and Richard Williamson, 1729).
59. *King*: Peter King (1669–1734).
60. *Essay on Crimes and Punishments*: Cesare, Marquis of Beccaria, *Dei Delitti e delle pene* (1764), widely translated and influential, opposing the death penalty and promoting penal reform.
61. *quarter-sessions and assizes*: quarter-sessions: courts held quarterly, or every three months, by justices of the peace; assizes: trials.
62. Gaol-delivery: clearing a jail of prisoners by bringing them to trial to be condemned or acquitted.
63. Principles of Penal Law: William Eden (1744–1814), Baron Auckland, *The Principles of Penal Law* (1771), advocating reforms including reducing the number of capital offences.
64. viz: videlicet: that is (Latin).
65. *six shillings and eight pence*: worth about £31 in 2006, using the retail price index.
66. *grand jury*: jury of inquiry, accusation, or presentment comprising twelve to twenty-three members, who among other assigned responsibilities, examine indictments as to suitability to be submitted to a petty or trial jury.
67. *thumbscrews*: implement of torture by squeezing the thumb.
68. fines: those convicted and sentenced.
69. *benevolent society at the* Thatched-house: like the Bristol society, a charity for the relief of debtors.
70. Villette: the official chaplain of Newgate.
71. *lady* Barnardiston's *legacy*: Katherine (Banks), lady Barnardiston (died 1633), puritan philanthropist.
72. *freedoms*: freedom: right to the privileges enjoyed by 'freemen' of the City of London.
73. *living*: position in the church to which an income or property is attached.
74. *stone*: fourteen pounds in weight.

75. Maitland's Survey: William Maitland, *The History and Survey of London, from Its Foundation to the Present Time* (1756).
76. Robert Dow: or Dowe (*c.* 1523–1612), merchant and philanthropist.
77. *rioters in 1780*: the 'Gordon Riots' in which a mob protesting the Roman Catholic Relief Act rampaged through London for several days in June 1780, setting fire to Newgate prison, among other things.
78. transports: those condemned to transportation or exile to a penal colony.
79. sc: scilicet: that is to say (Latin).
80. *Annoque Domini*: and the year of our lord, i.e., AD.
81. *CONCLUSION*: pp. 469–72.
82. *TABLE IX*: pp. 482–3.
83. Criminals Condemned: Janssen (1705–77), financier, master of the Stationers' Company, Alderman, and Lord Mayor of London.

William Godwin, *An Enquiry Concerning Political Justice*

1. *Xerxes*: king of Persia from 486 to 465 BC, whose attempt to invade Greece was forestalled when a storm destroyed his fleet, whereupon he had the sea whipped as a punishment.
2. *Marius*: Gaius Marius (*c.* 157–86 BC), Roman general and politician; the incident Godwin refers to is supposed to have occurred after Marius's defeat by Sulla.
3. *inquisition*: an ecclesiastical court created by the Roman Catholic church around 1232 to weed out religious heretics, and more famously the Spanish Inquisition authorized by Pope Sixtus IV in 1478 ostensibly for a similar purpose but used by the Spanish rulers Ferdinand and Isabella to consolidate their power after their capture of Moorish southern Spain.
4. *Elizabeth of England and Frederic of Prussia*: Elizabeth I (1533–1603; reigned 1558–1603), who presided over a period of English cultural flowering and military, naval, diplomatic, and mercantile success, survived the political uncertainty of the reign of her younger brother Edward and the reign of her older, Roman Catholic sister Mary, during which she was imprisoned as a political threat. Frederick II (1712–86), king of Prussia, known as Frederick the Great, survived a harsh upbringing and brutal father to make Prussia a major military power in Europe.
5. *vain*: Godwin's footnote refers to Cesare Beccaria, *Dei Delitti e delle pene* (1764, translated into English 1767), a major source for Godwin and other advocates of legal and penal reform, such as John Howard; see the selection from Beccaria in this volume.
6. *Thou ... Roman*: By law, citizens of ancient Rome could not be punished by flogging.
7. *mankind*: Godwin's footnote refers to John Howard (1726–90), author of the pioneering legal and penal reform investigation, *State of the Prisons of England and Wales* (1777, revised and augmented), selections from which are included in this volume.
8. *vagabonds*: In ancient legend, Romulus and his twin brother Remus founded the city of Rome, but Godwin gives a critical twist to the legend by representing them as mere wanderers.
9. *Hebrides ... Antipodes*: respectively, a group of islands off the north-west coast of Scotland, and a place on the opposite side of the globe from Europe, specifically Australia and New Zealand.
10. ex post facto: with retrospective force (Latin).
11. *topic of the preceding book*: 'Book VI: Of Opinion Considered as a Subject of Political Institution'.

12. *Procrustes*: in Greek legend, a brigand who forced his victims to fit his bed by stretching their limbs or else lopping them off, hence a metaphorical figure for making all cases fit one standard.
13. *strict ... injustice*: Godwin's footnote gives the Latin maxim, 'Summum jus summa injuria', often cited, as in Blaise Pascal, *Pensées* (1670), number 878.
14. *following book*: 'Book VIII: Of Property'.

William Hodgson, *The Case of William Hodgson, Now Confined in Newgate*

1. *Eaton*: (baptized 1753, died 1814), reformist writer and publisher, member of the London Corresponding Society, prosecuted for seditious libel but released when juries refused to convict him; repressive government legislation in 1795 forced him into hiding, though he continued to publish; fled to the United States in 1797 but returned 1801 and continued his activities.
2. *title*: The pamphlet was sold at the relatively low price of three pence to promote wide circulation.
3. *SYDNEY*: Algernon Sydney (1623–83), English republican implicated in a plot to overthrow the monarchy and executed; an icon of English republicanism.
4. *SOCRATES*: fifth-century BC Greek philosopher forced by the Athenian state to commit suicide for spreading seditious ideas.
5. *JEFFERIES*: George, Baron Jeffreys (1645–89), judge infamous for his proclivity for handing out the death sentence, especially in support of the monarchy against dissidents and rebels.
6. *first Magistrate*: monarch.
7. *solemnly ... judgments*: the oath sworn by a monarch at his or her coronation.
8. *Revenue concerns*: cases before the Court of Exchequer, where juries were not used; republicans such as Hodgson promoted juries as a major defence against arbitrary rule and an instrument of constitutional government.
9. *CHARLES STUART*: Following the example of French Revolutionaries, republicans such as Hodgson refused to use regal and dynastic names and called monarchs by names they would have if stripped of royalty, as in this paragraph: Charles Stuart was Charles II, William of Nassau was William III, Anne Stuart was Queen Anne and George Guelph was George I.
10. *MAGNA CHARTA*: or Great Charter, a document imposed on King John by a group of nobles in 1215, limiting royal powers, and thereafter glorified as a foundational document of English liberties and the development of constitutional government.
11. *amerced*: punished by an arbitrary fine.
12. *contenement*: freehold, property holding.
13. *amerciaments*: fines; penalty determined by the inflictor.
14. *BILL OF RIGHTS*: a bill passed by Parliament in 1689 asserting certain citizens' rights and settling the succession of the crown; it was seen by reformers as another major step toward constitutional government.
15. *Recorder*: magistrate with a particular jurisdiction, here the Recorder of the City of London.
16. *1795*: Here two-and-one-third lines of black are inserted, perhaps indicating a censored passage or typographically symbolizing inexpressible feelings.

17. *Junto*: a self-selected committee, faction or cabal, especially of powerful men, with a particular, usually political, purpose (from Spanish).
18. *administration*: the government.
19. *war with the French people*: War broke out between Britain and France in early 1793.
20. *tradesman*: small businessman.
21. *mechanic*: artisan, skilled labourer.
22. *pensioned*: receiving unearned emoluments.
23. *MISDEMEANOUR … SINGLE FELONY*: misdemeanour: lesser crime; felony: more serious crime.

George Walker, *The Vagabond: A Novel*

1. *Goddess of Reason*: proclaimed by reformists and revolutionaries to supplant established religions which were seen as supporters of monarchic despotism.
2. *Lycurgus at Sparta*: legendary sage and lawgiver of seventh-century BC Greek city-state of Sparta, famous in Western cultural and especially republican tradition for its supposedly simple and virtuous but in fact slave-based and militaristic way of life.
3. *pallisadoes*: fences of wooden stakes (Spanish).
4. *Stupeo*: literally 'I astonish' (Latin).
5. *philosopher*: for reformists, more like the French Revolutionary *philosophe* in being a public intellectual and social critic.
6. *loss*: the third edition (1799) adds: 'Or who would level property like those who had nothing to lose, and all to gain.'
7. *reason*: supposedly glorified by reformists and revolutionaries as the means to solve all human problems.
8. *Athens*: ancient Greek city-state famous for its democratic assembly (of men) and high intellectual and cultural achievements, though these were based on a slave economy and ruthless exploitation of colonies and 'allies'.
9. *Clerkenwell*: prison in the district then at the north-east of London; Clerkenwell had a long association with political dissidence.
10. *Lord Mansfield's*: William Murray, lord Mansfield (1705–93), famous judge and government minister, whose house in Bloomsbury was burned in the Gordon Riots; the rioters sought to destroy public and judicial records.
11. John the Painter: pseudonym of James Aitken (1752–77), Scottish petty criminal and emigrant to the American colonies who returned to England to conduct an arson campaign in dockyards during the American Revolution until he was captured, convicted and executed.
12. liberal principles: the third edition adds a footnote: 'The cant word for no principles but those of profligacy, irreligion, &c.'
13. *New-river water*: manmade waterway from the River Lee to Clerkenwell, opened in 1613 to supply London with drinking water.
14. *Museum*: the British Museum, opened in 1759, and housing collections of artworks and antiquities as well as a large library.
15. *trumpery*: trash; impostures; reformists and revolutionaries were commonly represented as vandals with no respect for high culture or the past.
16. *East-India warehouses and the Custom-house*: warehouse serving the trade to the East Indies and the central building for collection of customs duties for the port of London.

17. *Tower and the Bank*: the Tower of London, a landmark fortification and state prison on the banks of the Thames; the Bank of England, main state financial institution.
18. *Borough*: Southwark, across the Thames from the City of London.
19. *truth ... day*: The statement is meant to burlesque the optimism of reformists and revolutionaries.
20. *half-rectified*: rectified: refined by repeated distillation, especially alcoholic spirits containing eleven per cent water by volume; here referring to the distilleries ransacked by the Gordon Rioters.
21. *Fleet Prison, King's Bench*: infamously filthy and overcrowded prisons housing mostly debtors.
22. *final consummation of all things*: satirical application of reference to the end of time and establishment of a divine kingdom as described in the Bible, book of Revelation, as revolutionaries often envisioned the achievement of a perfect society.
23. *Rights of Man*: slogan of reformists and title of Thomas Paine's bestselling reformist political tract (1791).

John Aldini, *An Account of the Late Improvements in Galvanism*

1. *vulgar*: lower classes, common people.
2. *offended*: There was widespread public resentment at the practise of turning the bodies of executed murderers over to anatomy schools for dissection, as instituted by a law of 1752 designed to make the punishment for murder more horrific, thereby strengthening the deterrent.
3. *Galvanism*: the production of electricity by chemical action, developed by the Italian physician Luigi Galvani (1737–98) for medical use.
4. *vitality*: life.
5. *Haller's*: Albrecht von Haller (1708–77), Swiss physiologist.
6. *irritability*: capable of being externally stimulated to vital action, such as muscular contraction.
7. *Forster*: George Forster, more usually Foster, hanged for drowning his wife and daughter; see the account of his trial, execution and Aldini's experiments from *Criminal Chronology; or, The New Newgate Calendar*, in this volume.
8. *College of Surgeons*: the Royal College of Surgeons – at this time 'surgeon' meant 'medical practitioner' – was formed by royal charter in 1800 from the Company of Surgeons, a London physicians guild formed in 1745; in 1797 the Company moved from the Old Bailey to Lincoln's Inn Fields.
9. *Keate*: Thomas Keate (1745–1821), former surgeon-general of the army and master of the Royal College of Surgeons in 1802, 1809 and 1818.
10. *CARPUE*: Joseph Carpue (1764–1846), Roman Catholic and supporter of political reform, he was the proprietor of a private anatomy school and also carried out experiments on corpses for artist friends, thereby becoming associated by the public with body-snatchers, who stole dead bodies and sold them to commercial anatomy schools.
11. *CUTHBERTSON*: John Cuthbertson (1743–1821), prominent instrument maker who specialized in electrical apparatus.
12. *volatile alkali*: ammonia.
13. *biceps flexor cubiti*: muscle enabling movement of the forearm.
14. *coraco brachialis*: an upper arm muscle.
15. *caustic volatile alkali*: ammonium hydroxide, or solution of ammonia in water.

16. *pericardium*: cavity containing the heart.
17. in situ: in place (Latin).
18. *ventricles*: chambers by which the heart circulates blood to the body.
19. *carneæ columnæ*: fleshy columns within the heart instrumental in its functioning.
20. *septum ventriculorum*: partition of the ventricles.
21. *auricle*: upper heart chamber.
22. *gluteus maximus*: largest of the three buttock muscles.
23. *sciatic nerve*: hip nerve.
24. *great trochanter of the femur*: protuberance on the upper thighbone for the attachment of muscles.
25. *tuberosity of the ischium*: bulging of the hipbone.
26. *theca*: sheath.
27. *gastrocnemius muscle*: large muscle of the calf of the leg.
28. *peronæal nerve*: nerve on the outer side of the leg.
29. *biceps flexor cruris*: hamstring muscle.
30. *Volta*: Alessandro Volta (1745–1827), Italian aristocrat, physicist and developer of the electric battery, after whom the volt system of measuring electricity was named.
31. *animal æconomy*: organized physical structure, body.
32. *piles*: batteries.
33. *extravasated*: forced out of the blood vessels.
34. *suffocation*: Hanging by a noose was meant to cause swift death by breaking the neck as the person dropped through the floor of the gallows. But difficulty in calculating the length of drop, or rope in the noose, appropriate to the weight of the victim, could all too often either cause the victim's head to be torn off or fail to break the neck, leaving the victim to die agonizingly by slow strangulation.
35. *means were employed ... sufferings*: According to the account of Foster's execution from *Criminal Chronology; or, The New Newgate Calendar* (1810), included in this volume, his friends anticipated that the drop from the gallows would fail to break his neck and, stationing themselves below, pulled on his legs to accelerate strangulation and end his suffering.
36. *mean*: perhaps a misprint for 'means'.
37. *Blicke*: Sir Charles Blicke (1745–1815), undistinguished physician appointed master of the Royal College of Surgeons and knighted in 1803.
38. *Pearson*: John Pearson (1758–1826), a physician with scientific interests.

Richard Phillips, *A Letter to the Livery of London*

1. *Sheriff*: There were two sheriffs elected annually by the City of London; they also acted as sheriffs of the county of Middlesex; one of their main duties was to inspect the prisons and report on conditions there.
2. *Draco*: seventh-century BC Athenian law scribe associated with a harsh code of laws, hence 'draconian'.
3. Judge not ... first stone: echoing well-known quotations from the Bible, respectively Mathew 7:1 and John 8:7
4. *county debtors ... felons convicted and unconvicted ... state prisoners ... and fines*: respectively, those from the county of Middlesex unable to pay debts, those guilty of serious crimes, those convicted or awaiting trial for serious crimes such as treason (broadly defined) and those unable to pay fines.

5. *Old Bailey*: street in which the court of the same name was located, connected by a passageway to Newgate Prison.
6. *Sessions House*: court house.
7. *slave ship*: referring to an engraved plan of the slave deck of the slave ship 'Brookes', published in 1789 by the Abolitionist Society, showing how slaves had to lie closely packed, head to foot.
8. *King's Bench*: another prison, located south of the Thames in Southwark, used to confine debtors and those convicted of libel and other misdemeanours; prisoners paid for their keep, as well as other fees, and the prison made a profit.
9. *Fleet prison*: another prison for debtors, located off Farringdon Road.
10. *Physicians College*: a building housing the Royal College of Physicians, a body chartered to license, oversee and improve certain categories of medical practitioners.
11. *Separation*: Keeping different classes of prisoners apart was seen by reformers as essential to preventing prisoners abusing or corrupting each other and to management, control and even rehabilitation of the criminals.
12. *transports*: those condemned to transportation to a penal colony, i.e., Australia
13. *sessions*: periods when the courts were hearing cases.
14. *Grand ... Jury*: Grand Jury: jury of inquiry, accusation or presentation of matter to be dealt with legally, comprising twelve to twenty-three members; Petty Jury: jury of trial of civil or criminal proceedings, returning a verdict.
15. *Colleague*: the other elected sheriff.
16. *Medes and Persians*: ancient peoples of what is now Iran.
17. *Botany Bay*: penal colony in New South Wales, Australia.

Andrew Knapp and William Baldwin, 'George Foster', from *Criminal Chronology; or, The New Newgate Calendar*

1. *GALVANIC EXPERIMENTS ON HIS BODY*: See the work by John (Giovanni) Aldini in this volume; galvanism is electricity produced by chemical action, as developed by Italian scientist Luigi Galvani (1737–98), and creating widespread public interest throughout Europe around 1800.
2. *Lord Chief Baron*: Sir Archibald Macdonald (1747–1826), politician and lawyer, was appointed Lord Chief Baron of the Exchequer, or head magistrate in the court of the state treasury or finance department, in 1793 and was also commissioned to hear criminal cases from time to time. Of socially conservative views, he nevertheless advocated limiting the number of capital offences and seeking certainty in conviction rather than pursuing severe punishments.
3. *January 14, 1803*: According to the Old Bailey records, the trial began on 12 January; for a transcript of the record, see *The Proceedings of the Old Bailey* ref: t18030112-86 (http://www.oldbaileyonline.org/).
4. *deceased*: also named Jane.
5. Old Boswell-court: off the Strand in the City of Westminster.
6. *infant*: according to the Old Bailey Proceedings, about one year old and named Louisa; Jane Hobart testified that she took Foster's wife and child out of the poorhouse to live with her, and that Foster wanted his wife to put the child in the workhouse with the other two children.
7. *Paddington canal*: opened in 1801.

8. *workhouse at Barnet*: workhouse: institution accommodating and employing the indigent; Barnet: village north-west of London.

9. *North-row, Grosvenor-square*: between Grosvenor Square and Oxford Street.

10. *Highgate*: village north of London.

11. *towing path*: path along one side of a canal used by people or animals towing canal barges.

12. *swing-bridge*: bridge that may be swung aside to let canal boats pass.

13. *Sir Richard Ford*: (1758–1806), energetic and efficient chief magistrate at Bow Street, central police office of London, directing the policing of the city; knighted in 1801 for his services; like many working in close proximity with jail prisoners, he died of a fever.

14. *se'nnight*: 'sevennight', a week.

15. *Cut*: canal.

16. *Whetstone*: village north-west of London.

17. *bed-gown*: nightgown.

18. *in liquor*: drunk.

19. *half a crown*: two shillings and six pence, or £8.40 in 2005, using the retail price index.

20. *Bushwell*: Bushnell, according to the Old Bailey Proceedings; at another trial in 1813 he states his coach-making business to be at 29 Oxford Street.

21. *employed*: according to the Old Bailey Proceedings, earning about twenty-four shillings a week in summer and twenty-one in winter – a relatively good wage for a labourer at that time.

22. *coroner of the county*: official responsible for conducting inquiries (inquests) into deaths by accident or violence; the inquest returned a verdict of accidental death. At the Old Bailey trial, Coroner Hodgson testified that the path taken by the defendant with his wife and child was very slippery – 'like soap' – making it easy to fall into the canal.

23. *recorder*: magistrate with jurisdiction in criminal matters for a region, in this case London.

24. *law in that case made and provided*: By a law of 1752 the body of a hanged murderer was to be hung in chains or delivered for dissection at one of the anatomy schools, in order to increase the horror of the punishment and act as a deterrent; the practice was deeply resented by the lower classes.

25. *before the debtor's door*: outside Newgate Prison, and the usual location for erecting the gallows for public executions at this time.

26. *Ordinary*: official chaplain.

27. *died very easy*: This assertion is contradicted a few lines later by the information that several of Foster's friends stationed beneath the gallows had to pull on his legs to hasten his death through strangulation by the noose, from which he was still hanging, when it became evident to them that the drop had not broken his neck and caused almost instantaneous death, as hanging was supposed to do, but often did not. Aldini's account of Foster's dissection also indicates death by strangulation.

28. *Aldini*: For Aldini's experiments on Foster's body, see his account in this volume. Giovanni Aldini (1762–1834) was an Italian physicist and showman who traveled across Europe giving highly theatrical public demonstrations of galvanism, or the application of electricity to the dead bodies of humans and animals, causing often spectacular contortions in the tissues, and leading some to speculate that galvanism could revive the dead or create life in dead tissue. Mary Shelley drew on Aldini's work for her fictional portrayal of a scientist who creates a living being from assembled human body parts, in *Frankenstein* (1818).

29. *beadle*: usher, attendant.
30. *Surgeons' Company*: a London guild of physicians formed in 1745 from an earlier organization, and reformed by royal charter as the Royal College of Surgeons in 1800.
31. *animal*: animating, life-instilling.
32. *cases of insanity*: In the twentieth century, electric shock treatment was applied to several forms of mental illness, but fell into disrepute in the 1970s through overuse.

[Daniel Defoe and another], *The Fortunes and Misfortunes of Moll Flanders*

1. *n.d.*: published some time between 1802 and 1829, when Pitts was at 14 Great Saint Andrew Street, the address given on the title page.
2. *title*: Eight pages, printed on thin grey paper, and typical of Pitts's productions, this has many press errors; these have been left uncorrected except in a few cases for sense, indicated in endnotes here; two reversed letters have been silently corrected.
3. *Tyburn*: location, at present day Marble Arch, London, where public hangings took place until 1783, when they were moved to the Old Bailey, just outside Newgate Prison.
4. *belly*: A woman under death sentence would have it deferred, and in practice commuted to transportation to a penal colony, if she could 'plead her belly', or prove she was pregnant.
5. *with whom*: original text: whom
6. *after married James*: in original: 'Jter ames' and a space indicating dropped type.
7. *cloaths*: inserted: woodcut of a lady at a spinet.
8. *under*: inserted: large woodcut of a man and woman in seventeenth-century dress.
9. *shifts*: under-smock.
10. *Moll*: inserted: large woodcut of a woman, a child in a basket, and two men, in a room, in eighteenth-century style dress.
11. *sides*: inserted: woodcut of a man outside a house.
12. *German Princess and Poll Pines*: Mary Carleton (1642–73) posed as a German Princess, among other identities, to embezzle money, was transported for theft but returned to England and was eventually arrested for stealing and executed for returning from transportation before expiry of the sentence. Poll Pines, probably Mary or Moll Pines (Poll and Moll were familiar forms of Mary), tried at the Old Bailey 20 July 1698 for theft, burglary and receiving stolen goods; Moll Pines, 'a most notorious Shop-lift, who hath been Condemn'd for her Life', is mentioned as having 'led a most lewd Life for many Years' with the thief Arthur Chambers, in Alexander Smith's *History of the Lives of the Most Noted Highway-men, Foot-pads, House-breakers, Shop-lifts and Cheats* (2nd edn, London, 1714, I.163).
13. *recorder*: magistrate with jurisdiction for a particular area, in this case London.
14. *where*: inserted: large woodblock showing panel with picture of punchbowl, beside which stand two Indians smoking.
15. *due*: original text: ue

Samuel Romilly, *Observations on the Criminal Law of England, as It Relates to Capital Punishments*

1. *transportation*: Some convicts were sentenced to transportation to a penal colony, at this time Australia, with a ban on returning to Britain for seven or fourteen years or life.

2. *larcenies*: thefts, distinguished by the law into several categories with corresponding punishments, some of which could bring the death penalty.

3. Egyptians: Gypsies, so-called from their supposed origin in Egypt.

4. *Hale*: Sir Matthew Hale (1609–75), lord chief justice of England and legal writer, author of posthumously published *Pleas of the Crown* (1678) and *History of the Common Laws of England* (1713).

5. *Fortescue … seven*: Fortescue (*c.* 1397–1479) wrote his *Difference between an Absolute and Limited Monarchy* around 1471.

6. *Hollinshed*: Raphael Hollinshed (*c.* 1525–*c.* 1580), historian and author of *Chronicles of England, Scotland, and Ireland* (1577).

7. *Bacon … laws*: Sir Nicholas Bacon (1510–79) advisor and lord keeper of the great seal to Queen Elizabeth I; Romilly has a footnote citing Sir Simonds D'Ewes (1602–50), *A Compleat Journal of the Votes, Speeches, and Debates, both of the House of Lords and House of Commons, throughout the whole Reign of Queen Elizabeth* (1693), p. 234.

8. *chamberlain of London*: official who received rents and revenues of London.

9. *Howard*: John Howard (*c.* 1726–90), prison reformer, referring to his great work, *The State of the Prisons in England and Wales* (1777), amplified in successive editions, selections included here.

10. *Secretary of State for the Home Department*: the member of the Cabinet or government council responsible for law and order.

11. *London and Middlesex*: referring to the self-governing City of London and the adjacent county of Middlesex, in which the western parts of Greater London were located.

12. *five shillings*: approximately £17 in today's money, using the retail price index.

13. *forty shillings*: approximately £135 in today's money, using the retail price index.

14. *Janssen*: Sir Stephen Janssen (died 1777), Lord Mayor of London and author of a pamphlet on smuggling and another on rebuilding Newgate Prison (1767); the reference here is to his folio sheet of tables showing the number of sessions or court sittings at the Old Bailey courts, the number of persons executed from each Sessions, and the numbers from each Sessions pardoned, transported, or died in Newgate, from 1749 to 1771.

15. *capital larceny*: theft which brings capital punishment, or the death penalty.

16. *felony*: a class of crime considered in law to be more serious than a misdemeanour.

17. *circuit*: itinerary followed by judges holding trials in various towns in a particular region.

18. *Lord Loughborough*: Alexander Wedderburn (1733–1805), lord Rosslyn; he was a Scottish lawyer who clashed with the Scottish court and left to practice law in England, becoming attorney general, chief justice of common pleas, and attorney general.

19. *Gould*: probably Sir Henry Gould (1710–94).

20. *oaths*: Here Romilly appends a two-and-a-half-page endnote on various cases in which juries used stratagems to avoid convicting someone of a capital offense.

21. *Dr. Paley*: William Paley (1743–1805), a clergyman who defended capital punishment in *The Principles of Moral and Political Philosophy* (1785), book 6, ch. 9, 'Of Crimes and Punishments', included here.

22. *fallacy*: Romilly goes on to refute Paley's arguments.

James Neild, *State of the Prisons in England, Scotland, and Wales*

1. 450l.: £450, worth about £21,000 in 2006, using the purchasing power index, much more using the average earnings index.

2. *Pengelly*: the signatories include distinguished men of the early eighteenth century: Robert Raymond (1673–1733), first baron Raymond, judge; Eyre: Sir Robert Eyre (1666–1735), judge, chief baron of the court of Exchequer; Barnard: Sir John Barnard (*c.* 1685–1764), politician, active in City of London affairs; Pengelly: Sir Thomas Pengelly (1675–1730), leading practitioner of common law in his time, and judge, though his career suffered from lack of political patronage.

3. *Page* 363: as with others of this kind, a reference to Neild's text.

4. *Forde*: the Rev. Brownlow Ford.

5. *suffer*: be hanged.

6. *clods and stickings*: coarse cuts and pieces of meat damaged by the butcher's knife.

7. *Amount*: In present-day purchasing power, £1 would be worth about £46, a shilling about £2.30, and a penny about £0.20.

8. *Company*: Many of the administrators of these charities were livery companies, originally guilds, representing and regulating particular trades, as recognized by and participating in the government of the City of London.

9. *Gresham, Knt*: Sir Thomas Gresham (*c.* 1518–79), mercer, merchant and founder of Gresham College.

10. Blundell: (*c.* 1520–1601), clothier and philanthropist.

11. Kendrick: (*c.* 1574–1624), merchant in the cloth trade and philanthropist.

12. Broken victuals: leftover food.

13. *Pity it is, 'tis true*: echoing Shakespeare, Hamlet, II.ii.97–8, spoken by Polonius.

14. Duci facias: by sheriff's order (Latin).

15. *viz*: *videlicet*: that is (Latin).

16. Ordinary: official chaplain of Newgate.

17. Argus: in ancient legend, a person with a hundred eyes, i.e, a very vigilant person.

18. *copper*: copper or iron vessel for cooking.

19. *Lettsom*: John Coakley Lettsom (1744–1815), son of a Quaker plantation owner in the Virgin Islands, West Indies; he freed the slaves when he inherited the estate, and began practising medicine; he published several books on medical and scientific subjects, founded the Medical Society, and engaged in wide-ranging philanthropy; he was a friend of Neild.

20. *Poultry Compter*: another London jail, in a part of Cheapside known as the Poultry, for debtors and those convicted of misdemeanours such as religious offences, drunkenness, homosexuality and prostitution; infamous for its bad conditions, it was removed in 1815.

21. habeas corpus: you (should) have the body (legal Latin), opening words of an order to release a person unlawfully confined or more broadly to have a confined person either charged or released.

22. *Mesne-Process*: mean or medium process (legal French): a process that intervenes between the beginning and the end of a lawsuit.

23. *Court of Conscience*: court for the recovery of small debts.

24. *opportunity ... London*: The opportunity was in fact lost.

Henry Grey Bennet, *A Letter to the Common Council and Livery of the City of London, on the Abuses Existing in Newgate*

1. *toises*: a *toise* was French measure equal to just over 6 feet, or 1.949 metres.
2. *Whitecross Street*: built in 1815 to enable Newgate to house felons only.
3. *Chief Magistrate*: Matthew Wood (1768–1843), reform sympathizer and Lord Mayor of the City of London in 1815–16 and 1816–17, during a period of serious political unrest when he opposed harshly repressive measures proposed by the national government.
4. *Lord Liverpool*: Robert Banks Jenkinson, Lord Liverpool (1770–1828), Prime Minister 1812–27.
5. *trenching*: encroaching or infringing.
6. *Livery of London*: The City of London was governed by officers elected by the Livery Companies, or guilds.
7. *thir*: perhaps a misprint for 'their'.
8. *'In a prison ... manners'*: somewhat misquoted from Samuel Johnson, *The Idler* 38 (6 January 1759).
9. *Fines*: those sentenced to confinement.
10. *19th, 24th, and 31st Geo. III*: respectively the Criminal Law Act (1774) and/or the Transportation Act (1779), the Removal of Prisoners Act (1783) and/or the Houses of Correction Act (1784), and the Gaols Act (1791).
11. *Penitentiary, at Milbank*: a large prison opened at Millbank on the Thames in south-west London, where the Tate Britain Gallery is now situated; it was built on the spoked wheel or 'panopticon' pattern proposed by the philosopher Jeremy Bentham, designed to encourage subjective reform of the convicts; it was disused for convicts in 1886 and demolished in 1890.
12. Hulks: dismasted ships anchored in the Thames river for housing prisoners.
13. *Brock, Pelham, and Power*: Thomas Brock, John Pelham and Michael Power, tried and convicted on 18 September 1816 for coining and condemned to death; they made counterfeit shillings from brass.
14. *abominable crime*: On 18 September 1816 Robert Yandell was tried and convicted for sodomy and William Tiffin was indicted for murder.
15. *Mrs. Fry and the Society of Friends*: Elizabeth Fry (1780–1845), member of the Quakers or Society of Friends and active social worker, who instituted a programme of philanthropic activities among female jail prisoners at Newgate from 1813, with apparently good reformative effect.
16. *girl*: possibly Elizabeth Stubbs, convicted for deception-forgery and sentenced to fourteen years transportation on 18 September 1816.
17. *Capper*: John Capper, superintendent of the hulks where prisoners awaiting transportation were held; he attempted for a time to improve the atrocious conditions onboard them.
18. *Recorder*: magistrate with a particular jurisdiction; the recorder of London reported convictions, with recommendations for executive action, to the King (in this case the Prince Regent, or acting king) in Council, and thus was in effect the mediator and moderator of sentences passed by the courts.
19. *Prince Regent*: George, Prince of Wales, appointed Regent in 1811, in effect ruling for his father, George III, who was judged to be insane.
20. *Montesquieu, Beccaria, and Bentham*: Charles Secondat, Baron de Montesquieu (1689–1755), political philosopher whose works were admired by reformers; Cesare, Marquis

of Beccaria (1738–1794), Italian author of *Dei Delitti e delle pene* (1764; *Essay on Crimes and Punishments*), widely influential book on penal reform; Jeremy Bentham (1748/9–1832), English utilitarian philosopher and advocate of a wide range of reforms, including prison design and administration.

21. *Vartie*: John Vartie, aged 19, classically educated, clerk in a bank at Gravesend, committed forgery to obtain money to study Hebrew in France; he was convicted on 17 September 1817 of deception-forgery; jury and prosecutors strongly recommended mercy; he was executed 11 December 1817.

22. *the ordinary, Mr. Cotton*: the Rev. Horace Cotton (1773/4–1846), official chaplain of Newgate; he collected books on angling.

23. *Howard*: John Howard (*c.* 1726–90), advocate of prison reform and author of the widely influential *State of the Prisons in England and Wales* (1777 and subsequent editions), excerpts included in this volume.

24. *declines*: diseases causing progressive weakness, such as consumption.

25. *rugs*: rough woollen coverings.

26. *Smithfield*: the main meat market in central London.

27. *imprisoment*: probably 'imprisonment' is meant.

28. *shrievalty*: period of holding the office of sheriff.

29. *Phillips*: Sir Richard Phillips (1767–1840) bookseller and reform sympathizer who instituted prison reforms during his time as one of the Sheriffs of London in 1807–8; excepts from his influential pamphlet on prison reform (1808) and his manual on *The Powers and Duties of Juries* (1811) are included in this volume.

30. *dress*: uniform.

31. *Horsham*: a Sussex market town, south and west of London.

32. *clothes*: Bennet's footnote refers to Gilbert Wakefield (1756–1801), religious controversialist imprisoned for his political writing in the late 1790s, and William Winterbotham (1763–1829), Baptist minister imprisoned in Newgate in the late 1790s for political sermons.

33. *Police*: regulation, management.

34. *ironed*: placed in iron fetters.

35. *wardsmen*: prisoners appointed to supervise their respective wards.

36. *nearly*: closely.

37. *fine yard*: yard for those sentenced.

38. *mill*: treadmill; this was a controversial innovation.

39. *Grand Jury*: in London and Middlesex, a jury of seventeen men who considered indictments for crimes and decided which should be forwarded to trial, and also (as here) investigated such other matters as assigned to them.

40. *classification*: separating prisoners into different classes, as tried and untried, and type of crime.

41. *'if only … with horror'*: not identified.

Thomas Fowell Buxton, *An Inquiry, whether Crime and Misery Are Produced or Prevented, by Our Present System of Prison Discipline*

1. *Borough Compter*: prison in Mill Lane, Bermondsey, Southwark, a district known as the Borough, used as a prison from the mid-sixteenth century to 1855; it held debtors and those convicted of misdemeanours and felonies. Buxton's footnote mentions visiting the

prison with Samuel Hoare (1783–1847), banker and Quaker, his brother-in-law and another member, by marriage, of the Gurney family.

2. *companions*: Buxton's footnote mentions some of the leading lights of transatlantic prison reform: Elizabeth Fry (1780–1845); see extracts from the biography of her, in this volume; William Crawford (1788–1847), founder in 1815 of the Society for Investigating the Causes of the Alarming Increase in Juvenile Delinquency in the Metropolis, and in the same year founder member of the Society for the Improvement of Prison Discipline and Reformation of Juvenile Offenders; and Samuel Wood, member of the Philadelphia Society for Alleviating the Miseries of Public Prisons, promoters of the 'Pennsylvania system' of prison regime, stressing work and solitary confinement for reflection and penitence; Wood became the first warden of the model East Pennsylvania 'penitentiary'.

3. *Surgeon's*: physician's.

4. *Williams*: On 29 October 1817 Thomas Williams, aged thirty-six, was sentenced at the Old Bailey to seven years transportation for stealing twenty-nine yards of cotton worth 30 shillings (worth about £83 in 2006 using the retail price index) from outside a shop in Ratcliffe Highway.

5. *Noble*: Buxton's footnote also mentions prisoner Rawlins: perhaps a Richard Rawlins, aged 45, who was sentenced at the Old Bailey on 1 April 1818 to six months confinement and whipping for theft on 14 March of some tools valued at ten shillings and ten pence from a pawnshop.

6. *classification*: separating prisoners into different categories with separate accommodation.

7. *clods and stickings of beef*: odd cuts and pieces damaged by the butcher's knife.

8. *itch*: skin disease caused by mites.

9. *Bury Jail*: at Bury St Edmunds, Suffolk.

10. *King's Evidence*: those testifying against other prisoners, separately accommodated for their own protection.

11. *atrocious felonies*: sexual, particularly homosexual offences, may be meant.

12. *list-shoes*: cloth shoes.

13. *Irons*: iron fetters.

14. *solitary confinement*: widely promoted as a means of keeping prisoners from corrupting each other and of forcing prisoners to reflect on their deeds and so repent and reform.

15. *wheel*: spinning wheel, for making thread or yarn.

16. *Penitentiary, Millbank*: located in Pimlico, south-west of the City of London, on a site now partly occupied by the Tate Britain Gallery. Begun in 1812 and opened in 1821, Millbank was designed to the 'panopticon' system of the utilitarian Jeremy Bentham by which prisoners were kept separated and housed in ranges of cells radiating from a central block from which they could be kept under surveillance. The object of this structure was to encourage prisoners to reflect on their deeds and thus proceed to repentance and reform. Those sentenced to transportation were housed here before their departure. Millbank housed convicts until 1886 and was demolished in 1890. Buxton's footnote mentions his companions on visiting Millbank. One was Samuel Hoare, who also visited the Borough Compter with Buxton (see note above); the other was William Allen (1770–1843). Son of a London silk manufacturer, he was a Quaker, scientist, anti-slavery campaigner and promoter of schools for the poor; he was one of the partners with Jeremy Bentham and Robert Owen in the New Lanark model factory and village; a few months after visiting Millbank with Buxton, Allen went to Russia to try to persuade Czar Alexander to join the anti-slavery alliance.

17. *400,000l*: £400,000, worth over £22,000,000 in 2006, using the retail price index.
18. *£3*: worth about £165 in 2006, using the retail price index.
19. *Ghent*: town in Belgium; its new prison, completed 1775, anticipated the structures and regimes sought by reformers in England and the United States, including setting prisoners to work, separation of prisoners at night and classification and separation of prisoners according to class of crime and perceived moral condition.
20. *Philadelphia*: in Pennsylvania, United States, and at this time a centre of the American Society of Friends, or Quakers; their approach to prisons differed considerably from that in effect elsewhere in the United States, stressing work and solitary confinement, to encourage reflection and repentance, rather than physical punishment.
21. Refuge for the Destitute: founded by Quaker philanthropist Peter Bedford (1780–1864) in 1806 to receive indigent and abandoned children, those released from prisons and the hulks, homeless women, and others for various reasons unable to obtain work, which was furnished to them at the Refuge.
22. *Spitalfields*: in the east of the City of London, historically a centre for silk weaving; Buxton led a fundraising campaign to feed the poor in Spitalfields.
23. *Ilchester*: town in Somerset, south-west England.

Anon., 'Newgate Walls'

1. *set out*: The song first traces the route from Newgate prison through the City of London to Greenwich where the prisoners, who have been sentenced to seven years transportation, were embarked for their voyage.
2. *Sheerness we lay*: Vessels bound for the Atlantic would lie up at Sheerness in the Thames estuary to await a favourable wind for proceeding down the English Channel.
3. *Botany bay*: in New South Wales, Australia, near which the convict colony was located.
4. *Horsemonger Lane*: location of a prison built between 1791 and 1799 in Southwark on the south side of the Thames river opposite the City of London. It was the Surrey county jail, accommodating about 300 prisoners, both criminals and debtors; public executions took place on the roof of the prison gatehouse. The prison was demolished in 1881.
5. *seven years*: Sentences of transportation were for seven or fourteen years or life; returning to England before expiry or commuting of the sentence or pardon was punishable by death.

Anon., *The Life of Richard Turpin*

1. *title*: Price Sixpence.
2. *penal collection*: for example, *The Newgate Calendar*.
3. *Whitechapel*: district in the east end of the City of London.
4. *blades*: gallants, lads.
5. *road and turf*: underworld.
6. *footpad*: highway robbery on foot.
7. *runners*: police officers charged with apprehending criminal suspects.
8. *Hundreds*: divisions of a county.
9. *Epping Forrest*: an ancient forest in Essex, north-east of London; as a royal forest, only the king could hunt there and others who did so were considered guilty of treason.
10. *magisterial inquiry*: investigation by magistrates.

11. *Gregory's gang*: a gang of deer-stealers and robbers with over a dozen members operating from Epping Forest, led by Samuel, Jasper and Jeremy Gregory; they came to specialize in violently attacking and robbing homes.
12. *desperadoes*: reckless outlaws (Spanish).
13. *Chinkford*: Chingford, village in Essex.
14. *plate*: silverware of various kinds.
15. *turned evidence*: informed on his associates in return for a lesser sentence or pardon.
16. *Essex gang*: that is, the Gregory gang.
17. *Jonathan Wild*: Arrested for debt, Wild (1683–1725) became a keeper of his fellow prisoners, lived with a succession of women after his release, became a receiver of stolen goods and middleman in returning stolen items for a fee, then a police informant and professional apprehender of criminals, as something of a celebrity. His standing fell with his involvement in capturing the popular criminal Jack Sheppard and, with his usefulness to the authorities declining, they turned on him. Sentenced to hang, he was almost pelted to death on his way from Newgate prison to the gallows at Tyburn on 24 May 1725, and executed quickly in order to forestall a riot and lynching. In popular culture he came to symbolize the corrupt state of the laws and justice system.
18. *Loughton*: in south-west Essex.
19. *four hundred pounds*: if 1730, worth about £50,000 in 2005; if 1820, about £24,000, using the retail price index.
20. *Barking*: village in Essex, near London.
21. *700l*: £700, if 1730, worth about £91,000 in 2005; if 1820, £42,000, using the retail price index.
22. *guinea*: one pound and one shilling.
23. *escritoire*: writing desk (French).
24. *Woolwich*: village and naval arsenal east of London on the south bank of the Thames river.
25. *Surry*: Surrey, county south and west of London.
26. *out-house*: subsidiary building.
27. *High Holborn*: thoroughfare to the west end of the City of London.
28. *Stanmore*: village to the north and west of London.
29. *Bloomsbury*: district in the west end of London.
30. *Lawrence's*: Joseph Lawrence, the elder.
31. *putting up*: penning.
32. *offered*: attempted.
33. *garters*: for knee-stockings, common male dress at that time.
34. *D—n*: Damn.
35. *chopping-bill*: farming implement with a long concave-shaped blade.
36. *violence*: According to Samuel Gregory's trial for this crime at the Old Bailey, 22 May 1735, he raped her.
37. *20l*: £20.
38. *area*: sunken space between a building and the street.
39. *271l*: if 1730, worth about £35,000 in 2005; if 1820, about £16,000, using the retail price index.
40. *Mary-le-bone*: village north and west of the City of London.
41. *cipher*: monogram of intertwined initials.
42. *posies*: brief mottoes.

43. *Tyburn*: site of present day Marble Arch, London, where public hangings took place until 1783.
44. *perdue*: literally, lost (French), i.e, hidden in ambush.
45. *Duke of Newcastle's office*: Thomas Holles-Pelham, Duke of Newcastle (1693–1768), prominent politician, at this time lord chamberlain, a post in the royal household.
46. *evidence*: John Wheeler was witness on 22 May 1735 at the trial of Samuel Gregory for the attack on Joseph Lawrence's house in 1734.
47. *King*: Tom King (died 1737), known as the 'gentleman' highwayman for his polite manners while robbing people; this gentlemanly quality later transferred to Turpin, and was appropriated by Bulwer Lytton for his fictional version of Turpin in the novel *Paul Clifford* (1830) in the present series.
48. *trumps*: winning cards, good fortune.
49. *bavins*: brushwood.
50. *quickset*: hedge shrub such as whitethorn.
51. *higglers*: traveling dealers in small goods such as poultry and dairy produce.
52. *Gil Blas*: widely read picaresque novel (1715–35) by Alain-René Lesage.
53. *mail*: coach carrying the mail.
54. *Stamford Hill*: north of London.
55. *half-a-crown*: two shillings and six pence, worth about £16 if in 1730, half that if 1820, using the retail price index.
56. *close*: enclosure.
57. *dry-footed*: able to pass easily over difficult ground.
58. *mountebank*: a traveling showman selling spurious remedies at market fairs and other gatherings.
59. *bills*: handbills advertising the mountebank's show.
60. *two hundred pounds*: worth about £12,000 in 2005, using the retail price index.
61. *the Gazette*: publication listing government appointments, bankrupts and official notices.
62. *page 335*: in the *London Magazine and Monthly Chronologer*, 6 (June 1737); the text of the notice reads: 'His Majesty was pleas'd to promise his most gracious Pardon to any of the Accomplices of *Richard Turpin*, who shall discover him, so that he may be apprehended and convicted of the Murder, or any of the Robberies he has committed: As likewise a Reward of 200 *l.* to any Person or Persons who shall discover the said Criminal, so that he may be apprehended and convicted as aforesaid, over and above all other Rewards to which they may be entitled.'
63. *Holloway*: a village north-east of London.
64. *cole*: money.
65. *Islington*: village north-east of and near to London.
66. *guineas*: guinea: one pound and one shilling.
67. *turf velocity*: This famous exploit seems to have led immediately after Turpin's death to several racehorses being named after him; see John Cheny, *An Historical List of All Horse-matches Run ... in England ... in 1738* (London, 1738) and subsequent editions.
68. *rotten*: diseased.
69. *subpœned*; served with a writ to appear as a witness in a court, from 'sub pœna', 'under penalty' (Latin), the first words of the writ.
70. *Chapple*: (1676/7–1745), lawyer and MP from Dorset whose career benefited thanks to his loyal support of the government of Sir Robert Walpole; knighted in 1729 and appointed a judge of King's Bench in 1737.

71. *topsman*: hangman; in fact, Thomas Hadfield, Turpin's former associate in the Gregory gang, who had been pardoned on agreeing to become a hangman.
72. *threw himself off the ladder*: Because Turpin did so, some regarded his death as suicide rather than execution, hence nobler.
73. *five minutes*: Hanging was meant to break the neck, causing almost instant death, but this failed to occur in many or most cases, and the condemned person died slowly of strangulation, as appears here.
74. *anatomized*: Corpses of the executed were commonly sold to anatomy schools for dissection classes, and legislation in 1752 made this an addition to the death penalty, though this practice was deeply unpopular with the common people, as evidenced here.
75. *slacked*: or slaked: hydrated.

[John Bigge], *Report of the Commissioner of Inquiry into the State of the Colony of New South Wales*

1. *LORD*: Henry, third Earl of Bathurst (1762–1834), held several government offices before appointment as secretary of state for the colonies in Lord Liverpool's government, from 1812 to 1827. In 1817 he became concerned that transportation of convicts to the colony of New South Wales, Australia was ceasing to be a deterrent to crime and force for reformation of criminals, and that the colony was too expensive to run, and dispatched John Bigge on a commission of inquiry.
2. *New South Wales*: founded in 1788 as a British penal colony, including the present state of New South Wales and surrounding territory, what are now Tasmania and New Zealand and Lord Howe Island and Norfolk Island.
3. *Van Dieman's Land*: or Van Diemen's Land, so named by Dutch explorer Abel Tasman after the governor of the Dutch East Indies; it was made a British penal colony in 1803, receiving about 75,000 convicts before penal transportation was abolished in 1853; Van Diemen's Land was made a colony separate from New South Wales in 1825; to bury the association with convict colonization, the island was renamed Tasmania in 1856, though the last penal settlement, at Port Arthur, was not closed until 1877.
4. *General Hewit, Surrey, and Three Bees*: The *General Hewart* (also known as *Hewit* and *Hewitt*) was a 973-ton three-deck ship built in Calcutta in 1812. The *Three Bees* was 459 tons built at Bridgewater in 1813. The *Surrey* (or *Surry*) was a 443-ton square-rigger, 117.5 feet long by 29.5 feet across, built in 1811 at Harwich; it made eleven convict voyages to New South Wales, more than any other ship in this service. The first convict fleets got most of their human cargo to New South Wales alive, if often barely so, but by the 1790s poor conditions and overcrowding were causing mortality rates as high as fifteen per cent on the voyage, and sentence of transportation was regarded by some convicts as a sentence worse than hanging. Government action improved conditions onboard ships from 1802, so that by 1814 the levels of mortality that occurred on these three ships – about eleven per cent of the convicts aboard – were regarded as a serious matter.
5. *Macquarrie*: Lachlan Macquarrie (1762–1824), born in the Inner Hebrides off the coast of Scotland, had a long career as an army officer in North America, India and Egypt before appointment as governor of the British colony of New South Wales in 1809 following the local revolt against governor William Bligh. Macquarrie re-established order and regular chain of command and embarked on infrastructure and commercial development and a programme of public works. He aimed to transform New South Wales

from a penal colony to a part of the British Empire by encouraging those convicts who had served their term or earned early release to become effective farmers and tradespeople, though his policy of appointing such 'emancipists' to administrative and judicial posts was criticized, as in this *Report*. Macquarrie had already asked to be relieved when the commission of inquiry arrived, and the criticisms in the *Report* and attacks by other administrators and colonists led to his resignation and return to Britain in 1821.

6. *Redfern*: William Redfern (*c.* 1774–1833) was born in Canada and trained in England as a naval surgeon; implicated in a naval mutiny he was condemned to death, commuted to transportation on account of his youth, and sent to New South Wales in 1801 with other mutineers. He was pardoned in 1803 on account of his medical services and was given various professional responsibilities in the colony, including investigating the high mortality among convicts on the ships referred to here. Prejudice against former convicts prevented him being appointed to a senior position, despite the support of governor Macquarrie. He was sent to England in 1821 to appeal a court decision blocking former convicts from certain property rights. After the success of the mission, he returned to New South Wales and developed his extensive properties. He died in Scotland, where he had taken his son to be educated.

7. *William Hutchinson*: (1772–1846) convicted of theft at the Old Bailey, London, and sentenced to death, commuted to transportation and arrived in New South Wales in 1799. Again convicted of theft he was sent to Norfolk Island penal colony where by hard work he acquired property and was appointed superintendent of convicts. On his return to Sydney, Governor Macquarrie appointed him to various offices of trust, including those referred to here, despite resistance to the practice by local people, the British government, and John Bigge, author of this *Report*. Hutchinson later acquired extensive property and business interests and promoted educational and cultural institutions, extension of civil rights and colonial self-government.

8. *Daphne*: transporting only male Irish convicts.

9. *poops*: a poop is a raised structure on the aft, or rear of a ship.

10. *Cordeaux ... Gyles ... Walker*: William Cordeaux (1792–1839) served in the British army commissariat before being appointed to the commissariat department in New South Wales, arriving in 1818 as a passenger on the female convict ship *Friendship* and becoming involved in the inquiry referred to here. He was later accused of misusing his offices in New South Wales; in 1825 he was appointed a land commissioner, responsible for apportioning lands, for the colony. John Gyles (died 1827) and his wife were sent to Tahiti to evangelize the native people and develop a sugar industry, arriving first at New South Wales, as described here; the mission to Tahiti failed and Gyles returned to New South Wales where he established sugar manufacture; he returned to London in 1820, and later went to Sierra Leone, where he died. Thomas Walker (1791–1861) was the son of a Yorkshire lawyer and, like Cordeaux, served in the British army commissariat before appointment to the commissary general of New South Wales. He served at various places in the colony before settling in Van Diemen's Land, later named Tasmania, in 1832.

11. *Friendship*: at least the second convict ship of this name, possibly the one launched in the Thames river in 1793.

12. *Port Jackson*: the harbour of Sydney, Australia.

13. *St. Helena*: island in the south Atlantic, an important re-supply station for ships going from Europe to South Africa, India, and Australia.

14. *Admiral Plampin*: Robert Plampin (1762–1834), British naval officer in the American Revolutionary War and the Napoleonic Wars, later serving as commander-in-chief on the island of St Helena during the beginning of Napoleon's imprisonment there.

15. *Marsden*: the Rev. Samuel Marsden (1765–1838), born in Yorkshire, son of a black-smith; he became a lay preacher and was sent to Cambridge University by an Evangelical society and then to New South Wales as assistant to the colony's chaplain, arriving there in 1794. He took up sheep-farming and was appointed a magistrate. He acted as chaplain of the Parramatta factory for women convicts, attempted to evangelize the aborigines, and travelled to New Zealand to evangelize the Maori people. Like Bigge, author of this *Report*, he was opposed to Governor Macquarrie's policy of employing freed convicts, or 'emancipists', in public offices.

16. *Janus*: originally a whaling ship, a convict transport carrying female Irish convicts from Cork, arriving in New South Wales 3 May 1820.

17. *Bayley*: Nicholas Bayly (1770–1823) was born in Wales and emigrated as an army officer to New South Wales, where he was repeatedly in or making trouble; he helped depose governor William Bligh. After first supporting Governor Macquarrie he eventually joined the latter's enemies.

18. *Conolly ... Therry*: Philip Conolly (1786–1839) and John Joseph Therry (1790–1864), Irish Roman Catholic priests sent by the government to New South Wales to serve the large numbers of Irish convicts there. In 1821 Conolly moved to Van Diemen's Land, later named Tasmania; Therry remained on the mainland and became a hardworking and trusted member of the colony, though constantly battling official and unofficial prejudice against Catholics.

19. *Reed*: David Reid (1777–1840), born in Aberdeen, Scotland, became a naval surgeon, or physician, and served at the battle of Trafalgar; later he voyaged to New South Wales several times as surgeon-superintendent of convict ships and settled there in 1822 on a land grant.

20. *Morley*: convict ship recorded as carrying Irish transports to New South Wales several times between 1817 and 1829.

21. *different principles*: i.e., than the principles governing distribution of male convicts as labourers to free settlers.

22. *20l*: £20 worth about £1,300 in 2006, using the retail price index.

23. tickets of leave: official licence to be at large, granted to certain convicts in the colony before expiry of their sentence; Governor Macquarrie used the licence to encourage convicts to become productive citizens of the colony, but the practice was controversial, offending the sense of some people, including the author of this *Report*, that class distinctions were being threatened.

24. *Paramatta*: or Parramatta, now a suburb of Sydney, Australia; site of a settlement of convicts established in 1788; a wool processing factory to employ female convicts was established there in 1804; Governor Macquarrie built a new factory there, opened in 1821.

25. *Oakes*: Francis Oakes (1770–1844), born in Warwickshire, England, worked as a shoe-maker, served as a Congregationalist missionary in Tahiti before settling in 1798 in New South Wales, where he became a police constable, shopkeeper, and a number of other things, and was regarded as not entirely trustworthy. From 1814 to 1822 he was superintendent of the Parramatta factory for female convicts.

26. *George Town*: on the island of Tasmania, third oldest settlement in Australia, founded in 1803.

27. *slop-clothing*: cheap readymade clothes.
28. *Dromedary*: the ship that carried Lachlan Macquarrie and his wife to his appointment as governor of New South Wales in 1809.
29. *Hobart Town*: founded 1803 as a penal colony, moved to its present location in 1804.
30. *Governor King*: Philip Gidley King (1758–1808), of middle-class origins in Cornwall, served as a naval officer; after the end of the American Revolutionary War he was sent in 1788 to establish a penal colony at Norfolk Island; while there, he lived with a female convict, Ann Inett, who bore him two sons. Later, on one of his business trips to England, he married Anna Josepha Coombe. He was made governor of New South Wales in 1802 and tried to reduce corruption and increase order by establishing regulations for wages, prices, weights and measures, business activities, control of alcoholic spirits, commercial monopolies, and grants of lands and tools to farmers; he established a newspaper, reduced the numbers of those dependent on government support, built fortifications, and expanded exploration and settlement to New Zealand. He was succeeded by William Bligh.
31. *Governor Hunter*: John Hunter (1737–1821), born at Leith, Scotland, studied music and prepared for the ministry but became a seaman, rising through the ranks to captain a ship in the 'First Fleet', sent to settle Botany Bay, Australia, in 1788. A few years later, in 1795, Hunter returned to assume the post of governor but, unable to resolve the conflicts between civilian settlers and the military, he was recalled in 1799, and held various naval posts, being promoted to rear admiral in 1807.
32. *VI*: There are two sections numbered 'VI'.
33. *imposture*: See an incident of this kind in Thomas Gaspey's account of colony life in his novel *George Godfrey* (1828), vol. 3, chs 2–13, included in this series.
34. Hannibal McArthur: or Macarthur (1788–1861), nephew of the formidable settler entrepreneur and politician, John Macarthur; visited Australia from 1805 to 1808 and settled there in 1812; he was made a magistrate in 1814.

Edward Gibbon Wakefield, *Facts Relating to the Punishment of Death in the Metropolis*

1. *£10*: about £670 in 2005, using the retail price index.
2. *viz: videlicet*: namely (Latin).
3. *trades-people*: people in small business.
4. *transported*: exiled to a penal colony, at this time Botany Bay, Australia, for a period of seven or fourteen years or life.
5. *Whitechapel ... Kennington*: at this time the east, west, north, and south extremities of greater London.
6. *forcing-houses*: sheds where the growth of plants is accelerated by artificial heat.
7. *Police*: policy for maintaining public order.
8. *St. Giles's*: the infamous 'rookery', or district around what is now New Oxford Street, populated by Irish immigrants, the indigent and criminals.
9. *Houndsditch*: district in the east end of the City of London.
10. *last act for the regulation of prisons*: The Gaols Act of 1823 provided, among other things, for payment of jailers and banning use of irons; lack of a system of inspection vitiated the intended improvements.

11. *High Court ... Parliament*: The High Court of Admiralty exercised jurisdiction over maritime matters; Commissioners of Bankrupts (abolished 1831) oversaw administration of the affairs of those declared bankrupt; the Court of King's Bench had theoretical jurisdiction over all criminal matters and some other matters, but in practice dealt with important cases and delegated others to local courts; it was distinct from the Court of Common Pleas and the Exchequer Court.

12. *late Secretary ... Department*: Sir Robert Peel (1788–1850), who undertook a comprehensive reorganization and reform of law and order as Home Secretary from 1822 to 1827 and 1828 to 1830.

13. *press-yard*: courtyard where formerly those who refused to plead were pressed with heavy weights to force a plea from them or to kill them.

14. *decision of the King in Council*: as to fulfilment or mitigation of sentence or pardon, especially for the death sentence.

15. *rug*: rough woollen covering.

16. chevaux de frize: lines of spikes (French), originally designed to fend off cavalry attacks in battle.

17. *John Williams*: tried and convicted 25 October 1827.

18. *Wontner*: John Wontner (1784–1833), keeper of Newgate prison, and father of Thomas Wontner, author of *Old Bailey Experience* (1833), included in this volume.

19. *confinement in Newgate*: Wakefield was jailed in 1827 for abducting a fifteen-year-old girl, an heiress, and duping her into marriage.

20. *blanks*: losing tickets.

21. *Rogers*: Samuel Rogers, aged fourteen, on 12 July 1827 convicted with James Taylor, aged 16, for stealing in a dwelling-house.

22. *uttering*: passing.

23. *Wilde*: possibly Edward Archer Wilde (1786–1871), solicitor and sheriff of Middlesex.

Thomas Wontner, *Old Bailey Experience*

1. *Wontner*: biographical information on Wontner and his family from 'thePeerage.com': http://www.thepeerage.com/p15371.htm#i153708 (visited 3 March 2007).

2. *cramp*: difficult to understand or decipher.

3. *recent work on Newgate*: Wontner inserts a footnote identifying the source as the second edition of Edward Gibbon Wakefield's *Facts Relating to the Punishment of Death in the Metropolis* (London: E. Wilson, 1832); extracts from the first edition (1831) are included in the present volume.

4. cui prodest ... fecit: Whoever benefited from the murder, committed it; from the Roman writer Seneca's tragedy *Medea*, 500–1.

5. *Old Bailey*: the main criminal court in central London.

6. *transportation*: to the penal colony in Australia, for a term of seven or fourteen years, or life.

7. *viz*: *videlicet*: that is (Latin).

8. primâ facie: obvious, not requiring investigation (Latin).

9. *hulks*: decommissioned and dismasted ships anchored in the Thames river as floating prisons.

10. *May ... Bishop and Williams*: James May, John Bishop, Thomas Williams, perpetrators of one of the more sensational crimes of this time, were convicted of murder in 1831, having sold their victims' bodies to dissection schools.

11. *Shaw*: Several men named Shaw were convicted of housebreaking in the years prior to publication of Wontner's book, but perhaps Wontner means John Shaw, aged twenty-four, sentenced to death on 9 April 1829 for housebreaking.

12. *suffered*: was hanged.

13. quantum meritus: fair price, deserts (Latin).

14. *guilty*: possibly William Green and Thomas Wilkins, butchers, convicted at the Old Bailey on 17 February 1831 of stealing some mutton from their employer.

15. dernier resort: last resort (French).

16. *Draconian*: harsh, severe, after Draco, who established a severe code of laws while archon of Athens in 61 BC.

17. *Serjeant Arabin*: a judge famous for his witticisms.

18. *tapis*: carpet (French).

19. *private … public*: 'Private' floggings were administered inside the prison, with only officials present; possibly Wontner refers to Joseph Roberts, sentenced on 9 April 1829 at age fourteen to be whipped and discharged for simple grand larceny, and again 20 October 1831 for the same offence.

20. *feeling*: 'feel-' in the original text.

21. *Rev. Mr. Cotton and Mrs. Fry*: Cotton: ordinary, or official chaplain, of Newgate Prison; Elizabeth Fry (1780–1845), campaigner for alleviation of the condition of female prisoners in Newgate: see extracts from the biography of her included in this volume.

22. *twelve tables*: the earliest Roman law code, written down in the mid-fifth century BC.

23. *lift*: perhaps the case of Samuel Cushion, aged fourteen, sentenced on 16 May 1833 at the Old Bailey to seven years transportation for stealing a hat.

24. *institution*: probably Henry Dixon, aged thirteen, sentenced to death at the Old Bailey on 8 September 1831 for theft of his mother's shawl, value seven shillings, and a towel, value four pence; the jury recommended mercy on account of his youth.

25. *Penitentiary*: Millbank Penitentiary, built according to the 'Panopticon' plan of Jeremy Bentham and opened in 1821 on the site of what is now the Tate Britain Gallery.

26. *Recorder*: Wontner's footnote refers to Job Cox, a letter-carrier aged thirty-two, sentenced to death at the Old Bailey on 16 May 1833 for stealing from the mail.

27. *private and minor theatres*: Only theatres with a royal patent or licence could put on 'legitimate' drama, or classic and new plays, but by the 1820s demand for cheap theatrical entertainment led to evasion of the restrictions by the opening of private theatres and theatres putting on musical dramas and similar entertainments.

28. *Almack's … Italian Opera House*: Almack's: an exclusive London club in King Street, St James's, opened in 1785, accepting both men and women members and directed by a committee of titled ladies, and hosting balls, gambling, and other diversions; Italian Opera House: at this time a large theatre in the Haymarket, London, specializing in ballet and Italian opera; in 1847 the Theatre Royal Covent Garden became the Royal Italian Opera, today's Royal Opera House, Covent Garden.

29. *large theatres*: Drury Lane and Covent Garden theatres.

30. *pressure*: echoing Shakespeare, *Hamlet*, II.ii.21–4, Hamlet's reflections on the theatre.

31. veluti in speculum: as in a mirror (Latin), from Francis Bacon's scientific treatise, *Novum organum* (1620), preface.

32. outré: outlandish, exaggerated (French).

33. compositum miraculi câusa: story to excite wonder; from the Roman historian Cornelius Tacitus, *Anales (Annals)*, XI.27.2.

34. *cits*: citizens, a condescending term for inhabitants of the City of London.

35. per se: in itself (Latin).
36. soi-disant: self-styled (French).
37. *Euryalus convict ship, at Chatham*: The *Euryalus* had been a thirty-six gun warship of 946 tons, launched in 1803; it served as Nelson's courier ship at the battle of Trafalgar. From 1825 to 1843 it was a convict hulk exclusively for juvenile boys, anchored at Chatham in the Medway river; at times it accommodated over 400 boys, but usually less than 200, who were put to making clothing and other tasks, and on reaching age fifteen most were transported to Australia.
38. *Penitentiary*: Millbank Penitentiary; see above.
39. *'Black-eyed Susan'*: a popular play (1829) by Douglas Jerrold.
40. *phycologist*: student of seaweeds and algae; but perhaps an error for 'psychologist'.
41. priapism: sexual arousal.
42. *baldrick*: necklace.
43. Bona Roba: literally, 'good dress' or 'good stuff' (Italian): a wench or wanton woman.
44. *casmisating*: perhaps a nonce word invented by Wontner from French for 'chemise', 'shirt' or 'blouse', or a Spanish word 'casmisa', 'shirt'.
45. *flashly*: in 'flash' or underworld slang.
46. *uncoruncated Gynecocrasy*: female rule.
47. *err*: John Milton, *Paradise Lost*, VI.148.
48. *like us*: Shakespeare, *The Tempest*, II.i.6–8.
49. *Lord Bacon*: Francis Bacon, Lord Verulam, lawyer, politician, and philosopher; 'spur of a particular occasion', from 'Letters Relating to the Author's Writings', 'To the Lord Treasurer Burghley', in *The Philosophical Works of Francis Bacon* (1733), III.414.
50. *benefit of clergy*: in early times the right of the clergy to be tried in ecclesiastical rather than secular court; subsequently a power of the court to impose a less severe sentence on a literate person, and then a means of extending leniency to first-time offenders; in disuse by the late eighteenth century and abolished in 1827.

[William Crawford and Whitworth Russell], *Reports of the [Prison] Inspectors*

1. *Surgeon*: physician.
2. *flock bed*: bed made with coarse stuffing of torn rags or tufts of cotton or wool.
3. *1l*: £1, worth about £72 in purchasing power in 2006.
4. *hulk*: decommissioned ship used as a prison ship.
5. *Weekly Dispatch*: a popular newspaper (1801–1928) published by R. Bell.
6. *half sovereigns*: coins worth two shillings and sixpence each.
7. *gulled ... flats*: deceived ... fools.
8. *footing*: fee on first admission to the place.
9. draughts: a board game also known as checkers.
10. *rubber*: set of three games.

Memoir of the Life of Elizabeth Fry, ed. Katherine Fry and Rachel Elizabeth Cresswell

1. *defiled*: The original editors insert a footnote identifying the source as George Crabbe, 'The Maid's Story', *Tales of the Hall*, (1819, ll. 643–64).

2. *see ... face*: echoing the Bible, 1 Corinthians 13:12.
3. *Howard*: prison reformer John Howard (1728–90), selections from whose pioneering investigations of prison conditions are included here.
4. *erected*: The prison was begun in 1812 and completed in 1821.
5. Samuel Hoare: (1783–1847), banker and Quaker, brother-in-law of Sir Thomas Fowell Buxton (1786–1845), another prominent prison reformer, mentioned below, extracts from whose work are included in this volume.
6. *Mary Connor*: Apparently a streetwalker, she was aged thirty when convicted at the Old Bailey on 18 September 1816 for stealing a watch from William Church, whom she had picked up in Piccadilly and agreed to have sexual intercourse with for sixpence (equivalent in purchasing power to about £1.35 today, or about £18 using the average earnings index); Connor had also been indicted at the Old Bailey on 13 September 1815 for stealing a watch from a drunk she and another woman had picked up in the street and taken to the Coach and Horses tavern in Greek Street, Soho (there is still a pub of that name there); on this occasion she was found not guilty.
7. *Ordinary*: official chaplain of Newgate Prison.
8. *with us*: The original editors insert a footnote: 'Mrs. Fry's evidence before the House of Commons.'
9. *Elizabeth Fricker*: Aged thirty, convicted at the Old Bailey on 30 October 1816 along with William Kelley, James Hitchin, and Peter Kelly for burglary and receiving stolen goods. Fricker stole silverware worth about £400 from the house of Ann Ashworth in Berners St, Marylebone, London, where Fricker was a servant; before she was hired, she had been living with Kelley in dire poverty. At the trial, Kelley tried to take the blame on himself alone. Fricker and Kelley were sentenced to death, Hitchin acquitted, and Peter Kelly sentenced to fourteen years transportation.
10. *Bennett*: Henry Grey Bennet (1777–1836), politician and humanitarian campaigner; see extract from his work on prison reform, included in this volume, with biographical headnote.
11. *Dr. Cotton*: the Rev. H. S., chaplain of Newgate prison 1823–36.
12. *Forster*: William Forster (1784–1854), Quaker minister and philanthropist.
13. *it is ... our eyes*: echoing the Bible, Psalms, 111:23
14. *when no eyes see, and no ears hear*: paraphrasing the idea of several passages in the Bible, e.g., Mark, 8:18, 'Having eyes, see ye not? and having ears, hear ye not?'
15. *Harriet S—*: probably Harriet Skelton, aged thirty-five when convicted at the Old Bailey on 18 February 1818 of coining, having forged a £5 bank note; the sentence of death would seem to have been commuted to transportation to the penal colony in Australia.
16. *prodigal son*: in the Bible, Luke, 15:1–32, Christ's parable of the son who left home and wasted his inheritance in riotous living, unlike his brother, but on returning home was nevertheless welcomed by his father; the story illustrates the godliness of forgiving and loving the sinner.
17. *Before ... O Lord*: echoing the Bible, Psalms, 119:67: Before I was afflicted I went astray; but now have I kept thy word.
18. *affliction cometh not forth of the dust*: the Bible, Job, 5:6.
19. *songs in the night*: echoing the Bible, Job, 35:10: 'But none saith, Where is my God, my maker, who giveth songs in the night?'
20. *It is the Lord*: several passages in the Bible: 1 Samuel, 3:18; 1 Samuel, 12:6; John, 21:7.
21. *I was dumb ... Thou didst it*: the Bible, Psalms, 39:9.

22. *Blessed be the Lord ... as well as gave*: echoing the Bible, Job, 1:21: 'the Lord gave, and the Lord hath taken away; blessed be the name of the Lord', Job expressing his submission to God's will.

23. *captive in a distant land*: recalling the captivity of the Jews in Babylon, before their restoration to their homeland, recounted in the Bible, book of Jeremiah.

24. *outcasts of the people*: echoing several passages in the Bible expressing sympathy for outcasts and the godliness of caring for them, e. g., Isaiah, 16:3; Psalms, 147:2.

25. *he wrote*: The original editors insert a footnote: 'An Enquiry whether crime and misery are produced or prevented by our present system of Prison Discipline. Third Edition, 1818, page 109.'

26. *barren fig tree*: in the Bible, Luke 13:6–9, a parable told by Christ, in which a man wants to cut down a fig tree because it bears no fruit, but his servant counsels caring for it for another season to see if it will bear, and if not to cut it down then; the parable signifies that one should not give up too soon on hope of redeeming a sinner.

27. *Swain*: Mary Swain, aged twenty-six, was convicted at the Old Bailey on 19 February 1817 and sentenced to death for having forged a transfer of annuity interest.

28. *Lawrence*: Ann Woodman, also known as Mrs Lawrence, aged twenty-eight, was convicted at the Old Bailey on 30 October 1816 of coining, having passed forged bank notes to John Charles, who cooperated with the police in setting a trap for her.

29. *old woman*: perhaps Elizabeth Mahoffey, aged forty-three, or Mary Mitchell, aged fifty, when indicted together for coining at the Old Bailey on 10 July 1816, with James Mahoffey and Mary Mitchell the younger, having manufactured false sixpences out of brass; Mitchell the younger was acquitted, the others found guilty.

30. *Bridewell*: the London house of correction.

31. *slop-work*: make rough clothing.

32. *bold creature ... highway robbery*: probably Mary Lowe, aged twenty-two, convicted of highway robbery at the Old Bailey on 19 February 1817, with James Davis and Samuel Hill; they assaulted William Hembrey in King Street, Drury Lane, and stole his watch and other articles.

33. *Sir William Curtis*: (1752–1829), son of a manufacturer of ship's biscuit; later banker and London alderman and MP, known for his plebeian accent, flamboyance, and down-to-earth manners.

34. *results*: Here are inserted copies of resolutions of thanks by the Gaol Committee of the Aldermen of the City of London.

35. *Hudson Gurney ... Robert Barclay*: Gurney (1775–1864), member of the extended Quaker banking and philanthropic family of that name; Barclay, member of a prominent Quaker family of London brewers and related to Hudson Gurney by marriage.

36. *bearing all things, hoping all things, enduring all things*: echoing the Bible, 1 Corinthians, 13:7: referring to charity, or brotherly love, that 'beareth all things, hopeth all things, endureth all things'.

Anon., *Full Particulars of the Examination and Committal to Newgate of Annette Myers, for the Wilful Murder of Henry Ducker*

1. Full ... information: copy from British Library, London, shelfmark 1076.1.8.(3); publication date inserted in ink in this copy; the following chapbook in the volume is the centuries-old story of a (royal) mistress, *Fair Rosamond*.

2. *Annette Myers*: According to other documents, she was a domestic servant in an upper-class family, the illegitimate daughter of a Frenchwoman and an English baronet; M. J. Wiener, 'Homicide and "Englishness": Criminal Justice and National Identity in Victorian England', *National Identities*, 6:3 (2004), pp. 203–13 (p. 210).
3. *Bow-street police-court*: A magistrates' court was located in Bow Street, in the midst of areas of high criminal activity in London, from about 1739; the court closed in July 2006, to be converted to a boutique hotel.
4. *Henry*: Sir Thomas Henry (1807–76), born in Dublin, practised law on the northern circuit in England, magistrate at Lambeth Street police court, Whitechapel, then at Bow Street from 1846, where he became chief magistrate in 1864 and was knighted in the same year; he specialized in the law of extradition and advised the government on matters relating to public entertainments and public order.
5. *Ducker*: 'Tucker' in fact, according to documents reported in Wiener, 'Homicide and "Englishness"', p. 210.
6. *racketty*: dissipated.
7. *Codrington*: Sir William John Codrington (1804–84), officer in the Coldstream Guards, served in Canada and, after this pamphlet was published, in the Crimean War, where he led the light brigade at the battle of the Alma; commended for his actions, he went on to have a distinguished military and civil career.
8. *trial*: Myers was convicted and sentenced to death, but reprieved and condemned to transportation to Australia; she was released on license after a few years (Wiener, 'Homicide and "Englishness"', p. 210).
9. *thoughts*: The word is illegible in the original text.

G. L. Chesterton, *Revelations of Prison Life*

1. *prison*: Cold Bath or Coldbath Fields.
2. *dress*: uniform.
3. canaille: mob (French).
4. *punctilio*: attention to small points (for example, of etiquette), from Italian and Spanish.
5. *Amazonian*: framed like one of the Amazons, female warriors of ancient legend.
6. *Mary Barry*: On 21 February 1828 a Mary Barry was convicted of stealing; on 10 September 1829 a Margaret Barry was convicted of stealing from a man who had engaged her as a prostitute, and she was sentenced to transportation for seven years.
7. emeute: or *émeute*: uprising (French).
8. *Samaritan*: in the Bible, Luke 10:30–5, Christ tells the parable of the member of the Samaritan tribe who stopped to aid a man from a different tribe who had been robbed and beaten, after members of the man's own tribe had passed by with indifference.
9. *St. Giles's*: district of London around what is now New Oxford Street, infamous as a 'rookery' or den of the poor and criminal classes.
10. *younger sister*: possibly Mary Sullivan, convicted on 16 September 1824 of stealing at age fourteen, and subsequently on 7 April 1825 and 6 April 1826.
11. *Mary Moriarty*: possibly Mary Moriarty who was indicted 14 September 1826 for robbing a man who had engaged her as a prostitute in St Giles for five shillings; she claimed he hit her and demanded his money back; she was acquitted.
12. *durance*: confinement.
13. *invade*: St Giles was in effect a no-go area for the authorities.

14. *kennel*: street gutter.
15. empressement: excessive cordiality (French).
16. Julia King: possibly Eliza King, since Chesterton describes her as having turned to passing counterfeit gold, and an Eliza King was convicted at the Old Bailey on 16 February 1832 of trying to pass a gilt shilling as a sovereign on two different occasions.
17. *viz*: *videlicet*: namely (Latin).
18. *banded*: bandied, passed back and forth.
19. *Ann Fisher*: An Ann Fisher, aged seventeen, was convicted on 12 May 1831 of having forged an order for shoes, a shift, and a petticoat in the name of an assistant overseer of the St Giles workhouse, in which she was incarcerated; she was sentenced to fourteen years transportation.
20. *long fines*: those sentenced to longer periods of incarceration.
21. *disorderly women*: arrested as prostitutes.
22. *Vagrant Act*: or Vagrancy Act (1824), designed to deal with the large numbers of indigent and unemployed, including disbanded soldiers and economic migrants from country to city, following the end of the Napoleonic Wars in 1815; it outlawed sleeping out, begging and other practices, and gave police powers to arrest a wide range of 'street people'; the Act also provided a means for repressing prostitution; some provisions of the Act are still in force.
23. pavé: paved path or road, street (French).
24. *Christmas*: At the Old Bailey on 11 January 1827 a Mary Ann Hill Christmas was found not guilty of theft; on 3 January 1833 an Elizabeth Christmas was found not guilty of pickpocketing.
25. *arson*: On 26 October 1826, Charles Thomas White, aged twenty-three, a bookseller, was sentenced to death at the Old Bailey for setting fire to a house in St Giles parish in an attempt to defraud the British Fire Assurance company.
26. *Chadwick*: Sir Edwin Chadwick (1800–90), civil servant who contributed to many government inquiries and administrative reforms in such areas as poor relief, factories and working hours, crime and policing, state record-keeping, public health and sanitary conditions, railway development, and others; he retired in 1854.
27. *swell mob*: those who posed as a superior order of underworld characters.
28. *areas*: open basement area between a house and the street.
29. *outhouses*: subsidiary buildings such as sheds.
30. *plate*: silverware.
31. *levee*: a morning reception, often semi-public in nature, held by a person of importance.
32. *Queen*: Caroline (1768–1821), alienated wife of George IV, whose attempt to divorce her led to widespread public outcry with mass political demonstrations featuring expressions of loyalty to her, embodied in the 'addresses' mentioned here.
33. *on 'change*: at the stock market.
34. *traveller*: in particular a commercial traveller, or person whose business requires travel.
35. en passant: in passing (French).
36. habituée: frequent visitor (French).
37. *Covent Garden*: the main fruit, vegetable, and flower market in central London, and the region around it, location of many theatres and places of public entertainment, as well as brothels.
38. genus fœmina: female kind (Latin).
39. *Mary Ann Pearce*: On 27 October 1825 a woman aged twenty-eight of this name was convicted at the Old Bailey of housebreaking (petty theft) and confined for three

months; a woman of the same name was indicted for similar offences on three other occasions between 1820 and 1829. A chapbook purporting to be an account of her amorous adventures was published in 1835 as *Details of a Demirep! or, Life and Adventures of the Celebrated Lady Barrymore, alias, Mary Ann Pierce, Fanny Norton, Jenny Go-Lightly, Crack-the-Chrystal, and Peg of the Clink.*

40. *Lord Barrymore*: probably Henry Barry, eighth Earl of Barrymore (1770–1823), since the earldom became extinct at his death.
41. *Fowler*: possibly Ann Fowler, convicted of stealing on 8 December 1825 and 16 February 1826.
42. *Tothill Fields Prison*: or Westminster House of Correction, formerly located where Westminster (Roman Catholic) Cathedral now stands; it was opened in 1834 to replace the Tothill Fields bridewell.
43. chemises de nuit: nightshirts (French).
44. *Bridewell*: house of correction.

For Product Safety Concerns and Information please contact our EU representative GPSR@taylorandfrancis.com Taylor & Francis Verlag GmbH, Kaufingerstraße 24, 80331 München, Germany

Batch number: 08153782

Printed by Printforce, the Netherlands